ARROW AND THE ASCENT OF MODERN ECONOMIC THEORY

Also by George R. Feiwel

*ARROW AND THE FOUNDATIONS OF THE THEORY OF ECONOMIC POLICY (*companion volume*) (*editor*)
*ISSUES IN CONTEMPORARY MICROECONOMICS AND WELFARE (*editor*)
*ISSUES IN CONTEMPORARY MACROECONOMICS AND DISTRIBUTION (*editor*)
SAMUELSON AND NEOCLASSICAL ECONOMICS (*editor*)
THE INTELLECTUAL CAPITAL OF MICHAL KALECKI
GROWTH AND REFORMS IN CENTRALLY PLANNED ECONOMIES
THE SOVIET QUEST FOR ECONOMIC EFFICIENCY
INDUSTRIALIZATION AND PLANNING UNDER POLISH SOCIALISM (*2 volumes*)
NEW ECONOMIC PATTERNS IN CZECHOSLOVAKIA
THE ECONOMICS OF A SOCIALIST ENTERPRISE

In preparation

*JOAN ROBINSON AND MODERN ECONOMIC THEORY (*editor*)
*IMPERFECT COMPETITION REVISITED: JOAN ROBINSON AND BEYOND (*editor*)

*Also published by Macmillan

Kenneth J. Arrow

Arrow and the Ascent of Modern Economic Theory

Edited by
George R. Feiwel
Alumni Distinguished Service Professor and Professor of Economics, University of Tennessee

MACMILLAN
PRESS

First published 1987

Published by
THE MACMILLAN PRESS LTD
Houndmills, Basingstoke, Hampshire RG21 2XS
and London
Companies and representatives
throughout the world

Printed in Hong Kong

British Library Cataloguing in Publication Data
Arrow and the ascent of modern economic theory
1. Arrow, Kenneth J. 2. Economics
I. Feiwel, George R.
330.1 HB119.A75
ISBN 0–333–36878–9
ISBN 0–333–42410–7 (two-volume set)

The tasks of economic theory include but are certainly not confined to the abstract development of very broad principles. Indeed, even to one whose interests are largely theoretical, specific problems have frequently suggested new general principles. Thus, my work contains both successive developments of large themes and much that is opportunistic and specific.

KENNETH J. ARROW

Contents

Notes on the Contributors

Kenneth J. Arrow, our protagonist, is Joan Kenney Professor of Economics and Professor of Operations Research, Stanford University. He was formerly James Bryant Conant University Professor of Economics, Harvard University. He has been President of the Econometric Society, the American Economic Association, the Institute of Management Sciences, the Western Economic Association, the International Society for Inventory Research, and is currently President of the International Economic Association. He has received the John Bates Clark medal of the American Economic Association and the Nobel Memorial Prize in Economic Science. A recipient of numerous honorary degrees, most recently from the University of Cambridge, he is a Fellow and past Vice-President of the American Academy of Arts and Sciences, a Member of the National Academy of Sciences, and a Corresponding Member of the British Academy. His many contributions include *Social Choice and Individual Values, Essays in the Theory of Risk Bearing, The Limits of Organization, General Competitive Analysis* (with F. H. Hahn), and six volumes of *Collected Papers of Kenneth J. Arrow*. He has also contributed to *Issues in Contemporary Microeconomics and Welfare* and *Issues in Contemporary Macroeconomics and Distribution.*

Robert J. Aumann is Professor of Mathematics, Hebrew University of Jerusalem. He was a Fellow of the Institute for Advanced Studies, Hebrew University of Jerusalem and Visiting Professor, Cowles Foundation and Department of Statistics, Yale University; Center for Operations Research and Econometrics, Université Catholique de Louvain; Department of Economics, Stanford University; Mathematical Sciences Research Institute (Berkeley); and Ford Visiting Research Professor of Economics, University of California (Berkeley). He is a Fellow of the Econometric Society, a Foreign Honorary Member of the American Academy of Arts and Sciences and was awarded the Harvey Prize in Science and Technology. He is a leading and prolific contributor to the theory of games, the author of *Values of Non-Atomic Games* (with L. S. Shapley) and a contributor to *Issues in Contemporary Microeconomics and Welfare.*

Christopher Bliss is Nuffield Reader in International Economics and

Fellow of Nuffield College, Oxford. He was Professor of Economics, University of Essex, and University Lecturer, Faculty of Economics and Politics and Fellow of Christ's College, Cambridge. From 1967 to 1971 he was managing editor of the *Review of Economic Studies* and since 1978 has been a Fellow of the Econometric Society. He has published a number of articles on capital theory, international trade, and macroeconomics. He is also the author of *Capital Theory and the Distribution of Income* and the co-editor of *Economic Growth and Resources* (with W. Boserup).

Margaret Bray is University Lecturer, Faculty of Economics and Politics and Fellow, Churchill College, Cambridge, and was previously Assistant Professor of Economics, Graduate School of Business, Stanford University. In 1978 she was awarded the George-Webb Medley Thesis Prize at Oxford University. She is a member of the editorial board of the *Review of Economics Studies* and has been appointed assistant editor from April 1986. She has written several papers on expectations and her research interests center on economic theory, the economics of uncertainty and information, forecast feedback, and corporate finance.

Horace 'Woody' Brock is President, Strategic Economic Decisions, Inc., Menlo Park, California, a firm that specializes in the economics of uncertainty. In connection with his analyses of the world gold and copper markets, he developed the Arrow-Bayes theory of price forecasting discussed in Chapter 18 of this volume. He is a graduate of Harvard and Princeton and his PhD thesis drew upon the theory of *n*-person games with non-transferable utility to investigate questions in welfare economics and ethics. Upon graduating, he became a senior member of the International Management and Economics Division, Stanford Research Institute, where his work focused on national energy policy, in particular on forecasting energy prices under conditions of uncertainty. His current research activity centers on the US credit market and its linkage to international capital markets. He has written a number of articles for professional journals and contributed to the *New York Times* and the *International Herald Tribune*.

Partha Dasgupta is Professor of Economics, University of Cambridge and Fellow, St. John's College, Cambridge. He was Professor of Economics, London School of Economics and Political Science, and Visiting Professor at Carnegie-Mellon, Stanford, and Jawaharlal

Nehru University, and Ford Visiting Professor at the Institute of Economic Growth, Delhi. He is a Fellow of the Econometric Society and a Member of its Council. A former associate editor of the *Journal of Development Economics*, he is currently associate editor of the *Journal of Social Choice and Welfare*. His numerous papers range over the fields of capital and optimum growth theory; taxation and trade; theory of economic development and development planning; welfare, population, and justice; natural resources; industrial structure and technical change; incentive compatibility and planning mechanisms and theory of economic equilibrium. He is also the author of *The Control of Resources*; the co-author of *Guidelines for Project Evaluation* (with S. A. Marglin and A. K. Sen) and *Economic Theory and Exhaustible Resources* (with G. M. Heal); and co-editor of several books.

Paul A. David is William Robertson Coe Professor of American Economic History, Stanford University. He was a Fullbright Scholar at the University of Cambridge, a Visiting Professor at Harvard University, Pitt Professor of American History and Institutions at the University of Cambridge, Visiting Professorial Fellow at Churchill College, Cambridge, and Visiting Fellow, All Souls College, Oxford. He was also a Guggenheim Fellow and a Fellow of the Center for Advanced Study in the Behavioral Sciences. A Fellow of the Econometric Society and of the American Academy of Arts and Sciences, he is an associate editor of *Explorations in Economic History* and of *Historical Methods*. His distinctive approach to economic history is by methods of modern economics and he has written numerous articles on topics such as the history of technological change, accumulation, economic consequences of slavery, the impact of tariff policies on industrial growth, and trends and fluctuations in wages and cost of living. His books include *Technical Choice, Innovation and Economic Growth*, *Reckoning with Slavery* (with H. Gutman, R. Sutch, P. Temin and G. Wright), and *Households and Nations in Economic Growth* (ed. with M. W. Reder).

Gerard Debreu, a mathematical economist par excellence, is Professor of Economics and Mathematics, University of California (Berkeley). He was a Research Associate at the Cowles Commission and later Associate Professor of Economics, Cowles Foundation for Research in Economics, Yale University. A recipient of several honorary degrees, he was a Visiting Professor at the Center for Operations

Research and Econometrics, Université Catholique de Louvain, Erskine Fellow and Visiting Professor, University of Canterbury (New Zealand), Overseas Fellow, Churchill College, Cambridge. A former Fellow of the Center for Advanced Study in the Behavioral Sciences and Guggenheim Fellow, he is a Fellow of the American Academy of Arts and Sciences and a Member of the National Academy of Sciences, a Distinguished Fellow of the American Economic Association, and a Chevalier de la Légion d'Honneur. In 1983 he was awarded the Nobel Memorial Prize in Economic Science. He was an organizer of the 1985–6 complexity theory and mathematical theory programme of the Mathematical Sciences Research Institute (Berkeley). His many landmark contributions to general equilibrium theory (g.e.t.) include the classic *Theory of Value* and *Mathematical Economics: Twenty Papers of Gerard Debreu.*

George R. Feiwel is Alumni Distinguished Service Professor and Professor of Economics, University of Tennessee. He has been on several occasions Visiting Professor, Harvard University and University of California (Berkeley), Visiting Professor, University of Stockholm, and on several occasions has been Senior Faculty Visitor, University of Cambridge. A Guggenheim Fellow, he is the author of more than ten books, including *The Economics of a Socialist Enterprise, The Soviet Quest for Economic Efficiency, Industrialization Policy and Planning under Polish Socialism*, 2 vols, *The Intellectual Capital of Michal Kalecki*, and *Growth and Reforms in Centrally Planned Economies.* He is also a contributor to, and editor of, *Samuelson and Neoclassical Economics, Issues in Contemporary Microeconomics and Welfare* and *Issues in Contemporary Macroeconomics and Distribution.*

Benjamin M. Friedman is Professor of Economics, Harvard University, and Director of Financial Markets and Monetary Economics Research, the National Bureau of Economic Research. He is also an Academic Consultant to the Board of Governors of the Federal Reserve System, a member of the Brookings Panel on Economic Activity and of the Council on Foreign Relations. He is associate editor of the *Journal of Monetary Economics* and director of the *Harvard Magazine.* He was a Marshall Scholar, King's College, Cambridge. He has published numerous articles on monetary economics, macroeconomics, and economic policy. Some of his more recent publications range over such topics as the effects of government deficits on US capital formation, the role of money and credit targets in the conduct of US monetary policy, the implications of private pension funds for corporate financial decisions, and the relative importance of factors affecting market interest rates. He is the author of *Economic Stabilization Policy* and *Monetary Policy in the United States*, and contributor to, and editor of, *New Challenges to the Role of Profit, The Changing Role of Debt and Equity in U.S. Capital Formation* and *Corporate Capital Structures in the United States* (forthcoming). He is also a contributor to *Issues in Contemporary Macroeconomics and Distribution*.

John C. Harsanyi is Flood Research Professor of Business Administration and Professor of Economics, University of California (Berkeley). He was formerly a Senior Fellow, Australian National University, and Professor of Economics, Wayne State University. Although he received a DPhil degree at the University of Budapest, he was a graduate student of Arrow, and in 1959 received his PhD from Stanford. He was a Fellow of the Center for Advanced Study in the Behavioral Sciences, and a Visiting Professor at the Universities of Bielefeld, Bonn, Paris, and Sydney. He is a Fellow of the Econometric Society and of the American Academy of Arts and Sciences and associate editor of *Mathematics of Operations Research*. He has contributed significantly to game theory, decision theory, mathematical economics, the use of rational-choice models in political sciences and sociology, utilitarian ethics, and the philosophy of science. He is also the author of *Essays in Ethics, Social Behavior, and Scientific Explanation, Rational Behavior and Bargaining Equilibrium in Games and Social Situations* and *Papers in Game Theory*.

Leonid Hurwicz is Regents' Professor of Economics, University of Minnesota. He is a Distinguished Fellow of the American Economic Association, a Fellow of the American Academy of Arts and Sciences, a Member of the National Academy of Sciences, a Member of the Academy of Independent Scholars, and past President of the Econometric Society. He has been Fellow of the Center for Advanced Study in the Behavioral Sciences and Visiting Professor, the Cowles Commission (University of Chicago), Stanford University, Harvard University (where he was also Frank W. Tausig Visiting Research Professor), University of California (Berkeley), Tokyo University, and from 1984 to 1985 was Sherman Fairchild Distinguished Scholar,

California Institute of Technology. In 1980 he was awarded an Honorary Doctor of Science Degree from Northwestern University. He has made notable contributions to g.e.t., design of mechanisms for resource allocation, and general economic theory and statistics. Among his numerous publications is *Studies in Resource Allocation Processes* (with K. J. Arrow). He has also contributed to *Issues in Contemporary Microeconomics and Welfare.*

Lawrence R. Klein is Benjamin Franklin Professor of Economics, University of Pennsylvania. He was formerly at the Universities of Chicago and Michigan, and the Oxford Institute of Statistics. He is Chairman of the Professional Board, Wharton Econometric Forecasting Associates, Inc.; principal investigator, Project LINK; and a Member of the National Academy of Sciences. A recipient of several honorary degrees, he is past president of the American Economic Association, the Econometric Society, and the Eastern Economic Association. In 1976 he served as co-ordinator of Jimmy Carter's Economic Task Force. He was awarded the John Bates Clark medal of the American Economic Association and the Nobel Memorial Prize in Economic Science. His numerous contributions include *The Keynesian Revolution, An Econometric Model of the United States, 1929–1952, Essay on the Theory of Economic Prediction*, and *An Introduction to Econometric Forecasting and Forecasting Models*. He has also contributed to *Issues in Contemporary Macroeconomics and Distribution.*

David M. Kreps is Paul E. Holden Professor of Decision Sciences, Graduate School of Business, Stanford University. He was Visiting Professor of Economics, Harvard University; Research Officer in the Department of Applied Economics, University of Cambridge; and Fellow Commoner of Churchill College, Cambridge. A Sloan Foundation Fellow from 1983 to 1985, he is a Fellow of the Econometric Society and co-editor of *Econometrica*. He has published extensively in the areas of choice under uncertainty, the aggregation of decisions in various economic organizations, theory of financial markets, imperfect markets with stress on dynamic games and sequential decision problems. He is also a contributor (with A. M. Spence) to *Issues in Contemporary Microeconomics and Welfare.*

Robert E. Kuenne is Professor of Economics and Director of the General Economic Systems Project, Princeton University. His numerous publications range over the fields of g.e.t., oligopoly theory, military systems analysis, operations research, and energy economics. They include *The Theory of General Economic Equilibrium, The Attack Submarine: A Study in Strategy, The Polaris Missile Strike: A General Economic Systems Analysis, Microeconomic Theory of the Market Mechanism: A General Equilibrium Approach*, and *Monopolistic Competition Theory: Studies in Impact* (editor). He has also contributed to *Issues in Contemporary Microeconomics and Welfare*.

Andreu Mas-Colell is Professor of Economics, Harvard University. Formerly Professor of Economics and Mathematics, University of California (Berkeley), he was a Sloan Fellow; a Visiting Scholar, University of Bonn; Visiting Professor, Universitat Autonoma de Barcelona and Mathematical Sciences Research Institute (Berkeley); and associate editor of the *Journal of Economic Theory* and of the *SIAM Journal of Applied Mathematics*. He is a Fellow of the Econometric Society and a Member of its Council, an associate editor of *Econometrica*, and the editor of the *Journal of Mathematical Economics*. He has written some 50 research papers on subjects ranging from abstract social problems to pricing policy for public firms. But in the main he has focused on g.e.t. where he has concentrated on extensions of the model to new areas and on treatment via calculus techniques. He is also the author of *The Theory of General Economic Equilibrium: A Differentiable Approach*.

Takashi Negishi is Professor of Economics, University of Tokyo. He was a Research Associate in the Applied Mathematics and Statistics Laboratories, Stanford University; Visiting Professor, University of New South Wales; Hill Foundation Visiting Professor, University of Minnesota; Canada Council Visiting Professor, University of British Columbia; and Visiting Lecturer, London School of Economics and Political Science. A Fellow of the Econometric Society, he has won the Nikkei Prize for Best Books in Economics in 1973 and the Matsunaga Science Foundation Prize for the Social Sciences in 1977. He is currently President of the Japanese Association of Economics and Econometrics and associate editor of the *International Economic Review, Econometrica*, and the *Journal of International Economics*. His many publications range over the fields of g.e.t., international trade, imperfect competition, welfare economics, and monetary theory. They include *General Equilibrium Theory and International Trade, Microeconomic Foundations of Keynesian Macroeconomics*, and *Economic Theories of a Non-Walrasian Tradition.* He has also contributed to *Issues in Contemporary Macroeconomics and Distribution.*

John W. Pratt is Professor of Business Administration, Harvard University. A Visiting Research Professor at Kyoto University and a Guggenheim Fellow, he is also a Fellow of the Econometric Society, the American Statistical Association, the Institute of Mathematical Statistics, and the American Association for the Advancement of Science, and in 1979 was elected Ordinary Member of the International Statistical Institute. A former editor of the *Journal of the American Statistical Association*, he is currently associate editor of the *Journal of Business and Economic Statistics* and of *Operations Research.* Mathematical statistics, risk aversion, uncertainty, externalities, and information are the fields to which he has primarily contributed. His numerous publications include *Introduction to Statistical Decision Theory* (with H. Raiffa and R. Schlaifer), *Social Experimentation: A Method of Planning and Evaluating Social Intervention* (with H. W. Riecken *et al.*), *Concepts of Nonparametric Theory* (with J. D. Gibbons), *Statistical and Mathematical Aspects of Pollution Problems* (editor), and *Principals and Agents: The Structure of Business* (editor with R. J. Zeckhauser).

Melvin W. Reder formerly Professor of Economics, Stanford University and Distinguished Professor of Economics, City University of New York, is Isidore Brown and Gladys J. Brown Professor of Urban and Labor Economics, University of Chicago. He was a Guggenheim Fellow, a Ford Faculty Fellow, a Fellow of the Center for Advanced Study in the Behavioral Sciences, and Visiting Professor, London School of Economics and Political Science. He is a leading contributor to the field of labour economics and has also written extensively on health economics, macroeconomics, imperfect competition, and welfare economics, including *Studies in the Theory of Welfare Economics, Labor in a Growing Economy*, and *Nations and Households in Economic Growth* (editor with P. A. David).

John Roberts is Jonathan B. Lovelace Professor of Economics, Graduate School of Business, Stanford University. Formerly Professor of Managerial Economics and Decision Sciences, J. L. Kellogg Graduate School of Management, Northwestern University, he was a Visiting Faculty Research Fellow, Center for Operations Research and Econometrics, Université Catholique de Louvain, a Canada Council Fellow, and a Woodrow Wilson Fellow. In 1982 he was elected Fellow of the Econometric Society and is currently associate editor of the *Journal of Economic Theory*. His many research papers concentrate in the areas of imperfect competition and information, incentives and planning, regulation, and public goods.

V. Vance Roley is Associate Professor of Finance, University of Washington. A former Assistant Vice-President and Economist of the Federal Reserve Bank of Kansas City and from 1979 to 1980 Senior Staff Economist at the Council of Economic Advisors, he is a Research Associate of the National Bureau of Economic Research. A frequent co-author of B. M. Friedman, Roley's association with him began when he was a graduate student at Harvard and research assistant to Friedman. Roley is the author of *A Structural Model of the U.S. Government Securities Market* and many articles in monetary theory and policy and financial markets.

Hugo Sonnenschein, formerly Professor of Economics at the Universities of Minnesota and Massachusetts, and Northwestern University, is Professor of Economics Princeton University. He has been Visiting Professor at a number of universities, including Stanford, Tel-Aviv, the Hebrew University at Jerusalem, Marseilles, Paris, Strasbourg, and the University of the Andes (Colombia). A Fellow of the Guggenheim Foundation, Ford Foundation, and the Social Science Research Council, he was editor of *Econometrica* from 1977 to 1984. He is a Fellow of the American Academy of Arts and Sciences and of the Econometric Society. He is the author of about 50 papers and is best known for his work on the foundations of perfect competition, demand theory, monopolistic competition, and social choice.

Robert M. Townsend, formerly at Carnegie-Mellon University, is Professor of Economics University of Chicago. A former Woodrow Wilson Fellow and Visiting Scholar at the Federal Reserve Bank of Minneapolis, he is associate editor of the *Journal of Monetary Economics* and serves on the editorial board of *Information Economics and Policy*. He is the author of more than 20 papers in decision-making under uncertainty and private information, the theory of contracts and economic organization, and monetary macroeconomics. He has also contributed (with M. Harris) to *Issues in Contemporary Microeconomics and Welfare*.

Henry Y. Wan Jr. is Professor of Economics, Cornell University and has taught at the National Taiwan University and the Universities of New South Wales, Washington, and California (Davis). In 1981 he (together with G. Leitmann) won the Louis E. Levy medal of the Franklin Institute. He is the author of *Economic Growth* and nearly 50 articles in such diverse fields as macroeconomics, international economics, theories of economic growth and dynamic general equilibrium, theory and application of differential games, economic planning, development economics, and dynamic optimization. He is also a contributor to *Issues in Contemporary Macroeconomics and Distribution.*

Robert B. Wilson is Atholl McBean professor of Decision Sciences, Graduate School of Business, Stanford University. he has taught at the University of California (Los Angeles) and was Visiting Professor, Université Catholique de Louvain. A Ford Foundation Faculty Research Fellow and Guggenheim Fellow, he was also a Fellow of the Center for Advanced Study in the Behavioral Sciences. He is a Fellow of the Econometric Society and of the American Academy of Arts and Sciences and an associate editor of *Econometrica.* He has published about 60 papers in g.e.t., game theory, uncertainty, and information. In particular, his research studies the role of information in markets and organizations and its effect on strategic behaviour, and the design of efficient institutions. He has also contributed to *Issues in Contemporary Microeconomics and Welfare.*

Richard Zeckhauser is Professor of Political Economy, the John F. Kennedy School of Government, Harvard University, where he is also Chairman of the Research Committee and Research Associate at the Business and Government Center and the Energy and Environmental Policy Center. A Charter Fellow of the Association for Public Policy and Management, he is also a Research Associate, National Bureau of Economic Research. He has written nearly 100 articles in the fields of public economics, uncertainty, information, and health economics. His publications include *A Primer for Policy Analysis* (with E. Stokey), *Demographic Dimensions of the New Republic* (with P. McClelland), *What Role for Government?* (editor) and *Principals and Agents: The Structure of Business* (editor with J. Pratt).

Preface

These two volumes are about the ascent, vicissitudes, and lacunae in the science and art of modern economics, and about Kenneth Arrow, his architectonic contributions to, and impact on, the theoretical and applied economics and moral and political philosophy of our age. They are about 'music in economics', about one of its truly creative composers, inspiring conductors, virtuoso instrumentalists and constructive critics. They are about Kenneth Arrow and some other makers of modern economic theory, both when they are right and when they are wrong, about their finished and unfinished symphonies; and about their glorious harmonies, strident dissonances, and false notes. (It is self-evident that it is easier to criticize than to create. Maughan reminds us that when one looks at a Mondrian painting one is tempted to comment how easy it seems; one could do it oneself, all one needs is a tube of red paint, a tube of black, and a ruler; he then challenges, 'try'!)

These volumes are about the new era of accretion of economic knowledge and about the axiomatization of economic theory in many fields. They are in large measure about the flowering of general equilibrium theory (g.e.t.), its rich accomplishments, unresolved central issues, and major 'scandals'; and about the quest, perils, feats, and failures in overcoming them. They are about the recent strides forward, and they offer a glimpse of the future.

'Prediction is always difficult, especially of the future', to borrow a statement attributed by Arrow to John von Neumann. When many years from now scholars come to reckon and reassess Arrow's contributions and influence, they may approach the subject from a different perspective and shift their focus of emphasis. Nonetheless the picture that emerges from these pages firmly places Arrow among the master economists of all time. He contributed to changing the course of modern economics (and to some extent of political and moral philosophy) by a number of distinct intellectual innovations. However, the sum total of his impact far exceeds his specific contributions, extending as it does to the mode of analysis, way of thinking, formulation of problems, and to continually opening up new directions of research. Arrow shares in the extension, transformation, reformulation, refining, and generalization of received theory. But more importantly he is largely instrumental in influencing, reorienting, reshaping, and conceptually enriching the economics of our age. Not only is the economics of the second half of the twentieth century to such a large measure associated with Arrow's name (either directly or indirectly, through a chain of derived work), but he is the fountainhead of the new discipline of social choice.

INTRODUCTION TO THE TWO VOLUMES

Within the (un)usual constraints under which any such study labours, we have tried to provide a comprehensive composite analysis of Arrow's approach and contributions to, and his impact on, modern economics seen from various vantage points, angles and perspectives and communicated in various forms. But no matter how hard one tries, how blessed one is with high-quality collaborators, and how advantageous the division of labour, an effort of such ambitious scope is perforce incomplete and imperfect.

The scope of Arrow's work is so wide and his influence so far-reaching, that even without presuming to cover the vast territory in all its multifaceted richness, it soon became evident, in planning this project, that we would have to resort to two volumes in order to convey the dimensions of the Arrovian phenomenon. Various chapters in these volumes attempt to provide the essence of Arrow's contributions and his approach and way of thinking. Others are mirrors of the prodigious impact he has on the moving boundaries of economics and other social sciences. Still others offer alternative approaches to issues that form an integral part of Arrow's concerns.

An important feature of these two volumes is the historical record and insights provided in the interview chapters – the commentaries and reflections of our protagonist and basically three groups of individuals: the makers of modern g.e.t., the younger generation of leading g.e. theorists and outstanding economists from other fields, and Arrow's colleagues who contribute to a composite picture of the man and scholar.

A note of warning and 'bounded' apology: one of the drawbacks of the interview format is that the scope, direction, and emphasis of the coverage in part reflect the interests of the interviewer. One of the advantages of this format is its informality. It affords a privileged insight into the make-up of the interviewee, one that is rarely available in his written word, particularly if he is a strong 'devotee of the axiomatic method'. It affords a glimpse (and in some cases much more) of how his mind works. Remarkably it removes or reduces many inhibitions or conventions that bind scholars in more formal discourse. Since there is much more to a scholar than the production of 'robust results', it is hoped that these interview chapters will provide the reader with insights into economic philosophy and into the sociology of the making of economics and will provide the young scholar with some inspiration.

A special effort has been made to preserve the informality of the interviews. We have refrained from editing (subject to the required minor corrections) to preserve the flavour, style, and spontaneity of the dialogues. Still the reader is alas short-changed, for we cannot convey here the 'irreproducibles', such as the enthusiasm and dedication to the subject, the tone of voice, the intense concentration, the mode of reaction, the warmth, smile and sometime disquietude of our interviewees.

The reader will appreciate that in a study of an economist whose vision of the world is the general dependence of everything on everything else, the division of the material into two volumes is not without its perils. In a very essential sense there is a profound congruence in Arrow's work in g.e.t., statistical decision theory, and the theory of social choice. All three may be thought of as key component parts of system design. *Grosso modo* the developments in g.e.t. and beyond constitute the vast territory of *Arrow and the Ascent of Modern Economic Theory* – an inseparable basis for *Arrow and the Foundations of the Theory of Economic Policy* which takes us into the realms of social choice theory, welfare and distribution, resource utilization, and organization. It also takes us on an exploration of the man and scholar, his values, motivations, and perceptions – all so inextricably intertwined with policy prescriptions and instruments.

Arrow and the Ascent of Modern Economic Theory

The introductory chapter (1) to this volume sets the stage by placing Arrow's contributions in the prism of the potentials and limits of economic analysis. We attempt to guide the reader through and to analyze the vast territory of Arrow's contributions from his first significant accomplishment in the social sciences (thus, not counting his 'On the Use of Winds in Flight Planning') – the pathbreaking creation of social choice theory – through the making of modern g.e.t., to his contributions in applied g.e.t. More specifically, the prologue to this chapter provides a brief characterization of Arrow's scholarly achievements and his impact on the development of economics since the early 1950s. We then proceed to review 'new' welfare economics, and Arrow's extension of the fundamental theorems of welfare economics, and we draw the relationship between the social welfare function and social choice theory. In the next section we examine why it is only with the standard Arrow–Debreu model that g.e.t. came of age, and we examine the Arrow–Hurwicz contributions to stability of general competitive equilibrium models. The discussion then proceeds to the interrelationship between existence and efficiency and some of the more recent extensions of g.e.t. The ensuing two sections concentrate on Arrow's fundamental contributions to uncertainty and information. The first highlights his contribution to the theory of individual choice under uncertainty, measures of risk aversion, and his ingenious construction of contingent securities as a theoretical device for risk sharing. The second focuses on his perception of the role of information as a key to many unresolved problems in economics, on information as a commodity, on uneven distribution of information (derived from his study of the economics of medical care), on the economics of discrimination, and on Arrow's contribution to the centralization–decentralization debate. We then take the reader through Arrow's various contributions to production, capital, and demand theories, more specifically focusing on issues such as the optimal accumulation of capital and inventories, the process of learning, and innovations. Aside from information and uncertainty, an important common theme of these somewhat diffuse contributions is the recursiveness of optimization, captured in general mathematical form as dynamic programming or control theory. After a summing up that involves some methodological discourse, we digress in an appendix that attempts to place Arrow and modern economics within the context of the dynamics of economic thought, discusses some criteria of evaluation of progress in economics, contrasts the Walrasian and Marshallian approaches, and provides some glimpses of Arrow as a historian of economic thought.

Part I is an important historical record: an oral history by the makers of modern g.e.t. A word about its cast. In the preface to the second volume (on g.e.) of his collected papers, Arrow calls attention to Debreu, Hurwicz, and McKenzie as the 'major contributors' to modern g.e.t. The reader will have no difficulty in detecting the major 'flaw' in Arrow's listing – namely, the omission of his own name from this distinguished group of scholars who have been invited to share with us their recollections of and reflections on the creative genesis of their ideas and their perspectives on the development of the science and art of economics. We are grateful to the participants and share with Professor McKenzie his regrets at being unable to take part.

Although the specific questions were tailored to fit the interests and expertise of particular interviewees, the basic line pursued here was aimed at eliciting the master-economists' perceptions of how developments in modern economic theory have enriched our understanding of economic processes, the real meaning of progress in analytical techniques, the policy implications, some of the challenges to the mainstream and their specific contributions, and the direction in which economics is going. Whatever else needs to be said about the contents of this oral history, what emerges clearly is that the developments were not merely exercises in technical virtuosity (pyrotechnics), but provided fundamentally new economic insights; that the motivation, accomplishments, and concerns of the 'makers' were widely at variance with some common misperceptions; and that modern economic theorists are not smug, they are vigilantly aware of the remaining gaps, and in a world of exaggerated claims, they continually point to the limits of analysis and try to extend the boundaries of the potentials.

In Chapter 2 Arrow answers a very broad spectrum of questions ranging from the creative genesis of his major contributions, through observations on developments in g.e.t. and on the evolution of economics in general, to the topics on which he is now concentrating, revealing in the process fascinating glimpses of his personality – a topic that in *stricto sensu* we pursue with Arrow in Chapter 23 of the companion volume. At the outset Arrow recalls how he came across the ideas of social choice and existence, how the joint paper with Debreu evolved, and characteristically he provides arguments on both sides of the question of centrality of the existence theorem. He discusses his contributions with Hurwicz on stability and then proceeds to more general and more specific questions of g.e.t., ranging from the advantages of g.e. thinking, through disequilibrium economics; dynamics and historical time; and relationship with game theory, the need to extend g.e.t. to new contexts, in particular to imperfect competition, incomplete markets, and asymmetric information. Arrow also recalls the creative genesis of his contributions to uncertainty, production, and growth, and some of his applied work (particularly the economics of medical care). In fact he does not view theory as feeding on itself, but rather as generated by applied problems. He speaks of his growing caution and modesty with regard to the possibilities of synthesizing g.e.t., statistical methods, and social choice criteria into a form of economic planning. He offers us an insight into his own ordering of his contributions and some of his disappointments. He then proceeds to some general questions, including the essence of the difference between economics and the natural sciences, realism of assumptions, a classification of the most important contributions in the last 50 years, partial equilibrium thinking, new classical macroeconomics, bounded rationality, and the large and small questions in economics. Arrow deplores modern economists' lack of interest in the important question of income distribution and in studying comparative economic systems. He believes that the most important economic contribution of the nineteenth century was the vision of the general economic interdependence, and that our twentieth-century vision has been altered significantly by the concept of scarcity of information – an idea whose consequences are not yet fully understood. Essentially imperfect competition and imperfect information, which are closely related, are grounds for rather serious departures from neoclassical economics. His current interests centre on communication and information gathering in private and collective spheres which he intuitively believes have deep implications for macroeconomics.

Gerard Debreu's work has been an inspiration and model of ascetic elegance and rigorous thinking for the younger generation of theorists. As the irrepressible Frank Hahn noted in a review of *Theory of Value: An Axiomatic Approach*, Debreu deals only with definitive results; he does not speculate or share with the reader the wider implications of his work nor does he reveal his thought processes. We are fortunate, indeed, that in Chapter 3, Debreu allows us fascinating glimpses into hitherto hidden realms. It is an externality of this study and 'bounded' pleasure to show that Frank is 'strong' on analysis, but 'short' on prediction.

Chapter 3 opens with Debreu's discussion of the centrality of the existence theorem and its essential meaning, not as a statement about the real world, but about the validity of the g.e. model; of the progressive weakening of the assumptions needed to prove existence; and of the intereaction between g.e.t. applied problems, and policy. He recalls the creative genesis of his work on the proof of existence and how, after their initial independent, essentially similar, discoveries, he and Arrow joined forces in what has come to be known as the canonical Arrow–Debreu model. Debreu muses on the advantages and disadvantages of being in a minority position such as that of mathematical economics in the early 1950s. He speaks of the extensions of the g.e. model and of the progress in the last 35 years which has been far beyond his expectations. He stresses that he tends to see theorizing in economics as being essentially mathematical in nature, but this does not mean that higher mathematics is essential to do good economic theory. In fact, there is a lurking danger of doing bad economic theory by using tools that are more sophisticated than needed. Debreu also reminds us that economists must always remain aware of the limits of what they can achieve. He does not believe that a general theory that will encompass the whole of economics will ever be available. He emphasizes that the most important things in economics are not specific topics or theorems but methods; that is, he believes that 50 years from now economic theory will have changed considerably, but the use of mathematical models, rigour, generality, and simplicity are here to stay. Debreu is currently interested in two broad avenues of research:

1. Further progress on the idea that one must make assumptions about the distribution of the characteristics of economic agents in order to explain the properties of aggregate demand, and
2. complexity theory which, he believes, may influence the economic theory of information.

In the postwar period Leonid Hurwicz is identified as a leading system designer in the great tradition of Aristotle, More, J. S. Mill, and Lange. He is not only an erudite, technically sophisticated, and proverbially precise scholar whose first-hand insights illuminate the topics of Chapter 4, but he is also a warm and humourous raconteur who adds the human touch to otherwise perhaps dry subjects.

The major theme of Chapter 4 is the stability of equilibrium, a crucial subject on which Arrow and Hurwicz so fruitfully collaborated in many papers that later constituted a substantial part of their *Studies in Resource Allocation Processes*. Hurwicz recalls that their joint work brought them into contact with two strands of thought:

1. The work on stability primarily by Samuelson and Hicks, and
2. system design by Lange and Lerner.

He reflects on their formulation of the notion of global stability rather than the stability of a particular equilibrium point, on the complementarity of the work of Gale and Scarf on instability, and on the relationship of stability theory to business cycle theory. He also offers some fascinating insights into the creative genesis and development of the significant work on decentralized systems and incentives that he has done subsequently. He points out that the concept of g.e. that he uses in system design may or may not refer to a perfectly competitive mechanism, and in his sense there is no conflict between game theory and g.e.t. Hurwicz both defends neoclassical theory from its critics and speaks of the need to go beyond.

Part II focuses on the Arrovian vision and impact on the mathematical method in economics and on applications of g.e.t. It opens with Chapter 5 where Bliss discusses the Schumpeterian concept of vision and distinguishes two aspects, namely, vision of facts and vision of meaning. After pointing to the difficulties of employing these concepts in analyzing the work of a living scholar, Bliss applies them to Arrow's work. He argues that Arrow views the economic problem as essentially a question of democratic economic planning. However, in its application this view is circumscribed by Arrow's understanding of the inescapable difficulties that stand in the way of formulating a clear and valid objective (the social welfare function) for economic planning and by his strong conviction that real-life markets are very imperfect transmitters of information when compared with those that the planning problem requires.

In Chapter 6, 'Mr. Game Theory', Robert Aumann, discusses economics and the mathematical method. He speaks of the methodological differences between game theory and g.e.t., of the influence of game theory on Arrow and on modern economics in general, and of mathematical economics and game theory as art forms. He also touches on rationality, co-operation, and the selfish motive and vividly illustrates the dualism within Arrow in this connection. Aumann compares economics to other sciences where falsifiability should not be used as a touchstone. Finally, he discusses some new developments in mathematics that may prove useful in economics.

Mas-Colell offers in Chapter 7 a perspective on development of g.e.t. from the vantage point of a leading mathematical economist one generation removed from Arrow–Debreu. Among the many issues he raises are the extensions of g.e.t. into new areas, the dramatic change in techniques of analysis, namely, the renaissance of differentiability and its implications for recent and future developments. Here emerges a fascinating and perplexing picture of the dynamics and dialectics of the development of economic science and the sociology of knowledge.

Mas-Colell also offers telling glimpses of the possible future path of development and the extent to which avant-garde mathematics shapes or conditions the development of economic theory.

Another leading second-generation mathematical economist, Sonnenschein, speaks of the 'Arrow era'. In Chapter 8 he stresses Arrow's conceptual contributions, but also reflects on the appeal of the Arrow–Debreu methods to scholars of a rigorous or formal bent of mind, and on the appropriateness of these methods to the investigations to which they have been applied. He singles out the Arrow–Hurwicz view that an allocation mechanism is very much an object of choice. He points to the diversity and pervasiveness of Arrow's influence on modern economics, from Lucasian business cycle theory to medical economics. Sonnenschein also reflects on the creative genesis of his initial argument suggesting that aggregate demand functions are not restricted by the conditions that the individual demand function arise from utility maximization. The characterization theorems have in some ways blown away myths and changed theorizing. He also speaks on more general questions, namely, the importance of the existence theorem, the subsequent extensions of g.e.t., and the stronger rationality and computability attributed to economic agents in game theory. And finally he addresses himself to much broader issues such as the differences between economics and the natural sciences, the realism of assumptions, criticism of mathematical economics, and large versus small questions.

Arrow's contemporary and colleague at the Cowles Commission, the distinguished master builder of macroeconometric models, Lawrence R. Klein (a phenomenon in his own right) vividly recalls in Chapter 9 the intensive work at Cowles in the late 1940s on macroeconometric model-building, and the insistence that everything done in that connection be firmly based on economic theory. Macroeconomics at Cowles was an integrated branch, closely tied into the whole programme. Marschak insisted that a bridge be built between micro and macroeconomics. The star-studded team soon fell apart as the early model did not perform satisfactorily. However, the later stages in the development of the macroeconometric models that Klein describes for us were fundamentally set on the basis of that early experience. He points to the usefulness of the existence proof for macroeconometric model building, to the great accomplishments of Arrow and Debreu in clarifying the meaning of the price system, and to the applicability of the Arrow–Hurwicz contributions on stability to problems that preoccupied macroeconomic model builders. Klein contrasts his approach to the aggregation problem (from micro to macro) derived from his experience at Cowles, with Samuelson who says that one should take the macroeconomy as it is and not to try to derive it as an analogue of optimizing. Klein emphasizes the strong imprint left on him by the Walrasian 'Cowles-way' of thinking about the economy in terms of an interrelated system.

Part III, on the theory of resource allocation, provides in the first chapter a historical introspection from the pen of a participant in the development of modern g.e.t. and in the ensuing chapters some attempts at solving pressing open questions. It opens with Negishi's discussion of the non-existence of equilibrium (Chapter 10). He notes Arrow's remarkable contribution to the proof of existence of an equilibrium for a competitive economy. The necessity of proving existence becomes clearer in the face of the case where no equilibrium exists even though indifference curves, production functions, and the like, are fairly well behaved. Negishi points to W. T. Thornton's *On Labour* (1869) as containing the first examples of the non-existence of equilibrium. He considers these examples quite remarkable in the sense that they spring from the discontinuity of demand curves, since other unsuccessful attempts to show non-existence of equilibrium failed because of their assumption of continuity. However, these examples, as well as that of Wald, are unsuccessful attempts at showing the non-existence of equilibrium, if we consider not the Walrasian *tâtonnement* with recontract, but the non-*tâtonnement* without recontract. From such a non-*tâtonnement* point of view, a truly important example of the non-existence of equilibrium is the one provided by Arrow; that is the case where a Pareto optimal allocation cannot be viewed as a competitive equilibrium.

Building on the canonical Arrow–Debreu model, in chapter 11 Wilson takes a first step in the construction of a Nash equilibrium for a simple model of a bid–ask market. The main result he establishes is that a generalization of the sequential equilibrium constructed by Peter Cramton for bilateral bargaining satisfies at least the necessary conditions for an equilibrium of the multilateral trading model. Such an equilibrium could be interpreted as an endogenous process of matching buyers and sellers, in which their impatience for trade derives from pressure from other traders who are competing for the opportunity to transact; in turn, as in the work of Ariel Rubinstein and in related work on auctions, their relative impatience determines the terms of trade. A key feature is that delay in offering or accepting a serious bid or ask is a trader's main signal about his private information. The proposed equilibrium provides predictions about the proportions of gains from trade that would be realized and about the series of prices that would be observed.

The g.e. analysis of imperfect competition is an area in which Arrow's contributions have been central. It is also an area whose development he considers crucial. However, despite the subject's fundamental importance, it has recently received little attention. In Chapter 12 Roberts focuses on the example of an economy in which firms set prices for all the goods in which they are interested (except the numeraire), recognizing how consumers' optimizing resource-supply and product–demand decisions are influenced by these choices and by the rationing that will occur if their choices do not balance. He obtains an explicit solution for the imperfectly competitive general Nash equilibrium. This equilibrium exhibits properties that are quite different from what one would intuitively expect on the basis of partial equilibrium analysis. Roberts suggests interesting extensions in the future.

In the following chapter (13) Pratt and Zeckhauser pick a theme illuminated both by Arrow's social choice theory and his contributions to the proof of existence, and to major issues of welfare economics. It is a theme also related to market performance in the presence of such market imperfections as externalities and asymmetric information. In broad terms Pratt and Zeckhauser are concerned with problems involving externalities, uncertainty, private information, and differing objectives among players, making team theory inapplicable, dictatorship and other 'pinning' mechanisms inadequately informed, and *laissez-faire* also inefficient. Efficiency may still be achievable if appropriate financial incentives can be created to induce agents to take actions that are optimal for the group. The incentives they consider are transfer payments that may take the form of penalties, subsidies, compensation, taxes, and the like. Their central question is: Under what circumstances can a group, using incentive-based decentralization, achieve as high an expected value as a team? They observe that in a surprisingly general class of circumstances, a group of self-interested agents, observing private information and sending signals that may not be verifiable, relying solely on incentive payments to guide their actions, can do as well as a fully co-operating team with identical communication possibilities. The payments, which can be required to balance across agents, are designed to provide each agent a monetary incentive equal to the expected externality conveyed to the group by his actions, including the signals he sends. For such incentives to be implementable, it is sufficient that each element of each agent's information either become public, be signalled by him, or be independent of the information of others; and his non-public information cannot affect another agent's value. The result obtained by Pratt and Zeckhauser applies to multistage situations. They illustrate the mechanism with a pollution-control example.

Discrimination entails the efficiency and equity of an entire economic system. In Chapter 14 Wan studies job discrimination caused by asymmetric information. His findings complement the Arrow–Phelps theory of statistical discrimination. His approach can be traced to the concept of moral hazard that Arrow propagated in economics. According to the statistical discrimination theory, uninformed firms judge the worker's human capital by race or sex, and those who suffer such bias will cumulate less human capital, thus completing the vicious circle. It is a model with an evil system, but without any evil people. In contrast, Wan assumes that workers enjoy private information regarding their effort in a random production model. Effort makes more of a difference in some jobs than in others. Profit-seeking firms offer incentive-compatible contracts including 'no-shirking' bribes. The size of the latter may differ from job to job. Firms may thus allot better jobs to their favourite workers. Only legal sanctions can assure equal treatment for equally qualified workers.

The starting point of Chapter 15 is Arrow's persistent concern with establishing the consistency of models that imply full utilization of resources with those that permit underutilization (for example, Keynesian models). Reder claims that underutilization of resources does not always imply involuntary unemployment of labour. He argues that the degree of resource utilization varies with transaction costs and indicates the extent of failure to realize potential gains in productive efficiency through further specialization in order to avoid transaction costs. Under interesting though restrictive assumptions, Reder shows that transaction costs can be raised or lowered by exogenous variations in the level of effective demand. Hence exogenous increases in effective demand increase the degree of resource utilization. Chapter 15 is concerned with models in which all but one market clear in each period with zero transaction (defined as equal to search) costs. The 'other' market also clears, but requires use of search time to do so. If the other market is the labour market, there will be search unemployment in equilibrium with the level of employment varying with the level of effective demand. But if the other market is the market for goods, there will be no unemployment although output and the degree of resource utilization will nevertheless vary with the level of effective demand. Thus, in principle, underutilization of resources reflects deficiency of aggregate demand but does not imply failure of the labour market to clear. In the real world, of course, unemployment is intimately related to the level of effective demand, but Reder considers Keynes's attempt to identify less than full resource utilization with the peculiarities of the labour market as misguided for it created an unnecessary theoretical problem.

In the final chapter (16) of Part III Dasgupta and David take an information theoretic approach to the economics of science, extending Arrow's pioneering analysis of the allocation of resources for industrial research and invention. They address the question: Is there a valid economic distinction between scientific and technological research, and if there is, what implications may this have for public policy? A brief review points to deficiencies in several of the criteria proposed for distinguishing 'scientific' from 'technological' research, such as the degree of generality, abstractness, or practicality of the knowledge sought, or the source of the financial support. They suggest that a primary differentiation arises between science and technology conceived as *social* constructions, and is manifested in the greater urgency shown by the 'scientific' community towards the disclosure of newly acquired information. Scientists, *qua* scientists, may be thought to be devoted to the growth of the stock of knowledge as a public consumption good, whereas the technological community is concerned with the flow of rents that private parties derive from discoveries and inventions. From this perspective, Dasgupta and David reconsider the role of priority as a basis for allocating rewards among scientists, its compatibility with the norm of disclosure, and the ambiguous status of patent systems. Certain ineluctable conflicts between the goals of the two research communities point to the persisting economic need for public subsidies to sustain the scientific attitude.

Decision-making under uncertainty is the large theme of Part IV. In the opening chapter (17) Harsanyi deals with the Arrovian question of attitudes towards risk. He asks: In what sense do people's von Neumann–Morgenstern (vNM) utility functions express their attitudes towards gambling? He distinguishes intrinsic attitudes towards gambling as determined by taste or distaste for the process of gambling itself; from *instrumental* attitudes towards gambling – that is, willingness or unwillingness to gamble for the sake of the prizes –

as determined by the relative importance assigned to these prizes and to the stakes at risk. Harsanyi argues that axioms of the vNM utility theory completely restrict the vNM utility functions to representing instrumental attitudes towards risk taking and prevent them from representing intrinsic attitudes towards gambling. It has often been claimed that vNM utility functions are morally irrelevant and, therefore, have no place in welfare economics and in ethics – a theme also discussed by Hammond in Chapter 4 of the companion volume. This would be true only if these utility functions measured intrinsic attitudes towards gambling. But, in fact, they measure instrumental attitudes towards gambling and, therefore, measure the relative importance assigned to various goods and services, information that is of obvious moral significance. Accordingly, Harsanyi argues, vNM utility functions have a perfectly legitimate role in welfare economics and in ethics.

In Chapter 18 Brock proposes a new theory of price forecasting. He discusses the normative implications of Bayesian decision theory for 'rational' price forecasting and then the normative theory of price forecasting. This theory is based on Arrow's characterization of general equilibrium under uncertainty via contingent commodities and contingent prices. Central to the theory is the concept of a forecasting model in 'stochastic structural form' – a probabilistic generalization of structural form microeconomic models. The model determines endogenously a probability distribution on price. The prices are called Arrow–Bayes prices. Brock then contrasts the Arrow–Bayes model with familiar econometric forecasting models, in particular Bayesian structural models that he criticizes for their linearity as well as the epistemology of their underlying information sets, in particular their inability to capture the true variance ('riskiness') of prices in a forecasting context. Brock studies the estimation of Arrow–Bayes forecasting models by means of an 'expert-system' of the kind postulated in the new field of artificial intelligence. In conclusion, he discusses some insights gained from implementing the Arrow–Bayes models which have been helpful in explaining the observed volatility of the prices of copper and of the US dollar.

The following chapter (19) generalises some of the insights by Arrow and Green and is part of a large literature on the economics of uncertainty that owes much to Arrow's work in the field. In particular, Bray and Kreps study models in which agents are unable to form rational expectations as usually understood, because they are ignorant of certain parameter values. The authors make the very demanding assumption that, this ignorance apart, agents fully understand the workings of the model, including the usually non-stationary dynamics induced by learning and forecast feedback, and learn about the model in an optimal Bayesian fashion, using a correctly specified likelihood function which amounts to assuming a more general rational expectations equilibrium than usual. They show that this assumption and the martingale convergence theorem imply that beliefs converge with probability one and will not converge to an incorrect conclusion. In a market model, where the underlying structure of the economy is stationary, trades are continuous in beliefs and the rational expectations equilibrium is unique, this result implies convergence to rational expectations equilibrium in the usual sense.

Continuing along the theme of Arrow's contributions to decision-making under uncertainty which have provided a foundation that is now standard in monetary and financial economics, Friedman and Roley provide three conclusions related to the three sections of Chapter 20: First, asset demands, with the familiar properties of wealth homogeneity and linearity in expected returns follow as close approximations from expected utility maximizing behaviour under the assumptions of constant relative risk aversion and joint normally distributed asset returns. Secondly, although such asset demands exhibit a symmetric coefficient matrix with respect to the relevant vector of expected asset returns, symmetry is not a general property and the available empirical evidence warrants rejecting it for both institutional and individual investors in the US. Finally, in a manner analogous to the finite maximum exhibited by quadratic utility, a broad class of mean–variance utility functions also exhibits a form of wealth satiation that necessarily restricts its range of applicability.

In Chapter 21 Kuenne draws upon Arrow's seminal work in the theory of risk bearing to analyze the oligopolistic firm's bidding decision in a government tender. He abandons the comfortable assumptions of competitive bidding and probes into the interfirm expectations using subjective probability, one of Arrow's early advocacies. He uses a Weibull distribution to approximate the shapes of firms' density functions for winning, and investigates the existence of an oligopoly bidding rent or surplus in firms' bids. He examines the expected behaviour of bid prices and oligopoly rents when shifts in firms' expectations of winning occur and government furnished information is provided. He also obtains expressions for the expected value of information to the firm when privately acquired.

It is fitting to conclude this part with a chapter (22) where

Townsend argues that the Arrow–Debreu model, extended to include Arrow's celebrated construct of contingent securities, is rich in empirical implications both directly on its own, and indirectly, by having stimulated contributions that seek to explain otherwise anomalous observations.

The foregoing is much enhanced by Arrow's reflections on those chapters that do not specifically assess his work, presented in Part V as a conclusion to this volume.

Arrow and the Foundations of the Theory of Economic Policy

The introduction to this volume consists effectively of two chapters: the first (1A) focuses on Arrow's development as an individual and scholar, his values and overriding social and economic concerns, and the second (1B) examines his unique creation of the theory of social choice. It is hoped that Chapter 1A complements and sheds further light on Arrow's more technical contributions explored in *Arrow and the Ascent of Modern Economic Theory*, at least for those readers who believe that biography matters. More specifically, Chapter 1A traces Arrow's family background and early socio-political outlook. It takes us through his undergraduate and graduate education and the formative influences of the environment at the Cowles Commission and Rand Corporation. An attempt is then made at brushing in bold strokes the vivid characteristics of the man and scholar, followed by an exposition of his view of the human interaction as tension between personal and social values and their confrontation with limited opportunities. We then proceed to examine Arrow's perception of design and redesign of organization as a supplement to, or improvement of, the existing system. The two final sections of this chapter deal with the Arrovian concept of freedom, equality and democracy and his abiding interest in and concern for distributive justice.

It is only appropriate to follow an exposition of Arrow's writings on the concept and desirability of distributive justice by a chapter on the means that can be used to achieve this end. And it is only fitting that Chapter 1B is written by Peter Hammond as an assessment of Arrow's work in social choice and of some recent developments. Hammond perceives Arrow's question to be: is there some acceptable middle ground between the Condorcet paradoxes and the ethical repugnance of an extreme dictatorship? He asks: What Arrow social welfare functions satisfy the Pareto condition and independence of irrelevant alternatives and are also non-dictatorial? Arrow's disquieting answer is: None. Numerous escape routes from Arrow's theorem have been devised and Hammond stresses relaxation of Arrow's independence condition to one that he calls the independence of irrelevant utilities, appropriate for Sen's powerful notion of the social welfare functional. But this route is not entirely satisfactory either. It leads to fundamental questions regarding the very nature of the 'alternatives' to be considered in the independence of irrelevant alternatives condition – questions quite new to social choice theory. In Hammond's words: 'Arrow has led us to an enormous mountain and helped us to great heights. Every time we think we are reaching the summit, however, yet higher and higher peaks appear in sight over the ridge immediately before us'. It is our good fortune to have such a knowledgeable guide as Hammond on such a remarkable adventure.

Part I deals with social choice and utilitarianism and with attempts at breaking through the confines of the Impossibility Theorem. In the opening chapter (2), Gibbard provides a fundamental discussion of utility used in social choice theory. This chapter is related to Arrow's critique of utilitarianism which, according to Gibbard, has brought to moral theory the full force of the ordinalist revolution in economics. Gibbard interprets Arrow as holding out hopes for an ordinal utilitarianism, without settling firmly in favour of a particular version. As Arrow shows, under some specific conditions, even the minimal content of the Pareto principle yields strong results. It is this minimal content of ordinal utilitarianism that Gibbard explores in this chapter. He argues that preference orderings are no substitute for happiness in moral theory; happiness has a moral significance that preference orderings lack if they are understood in a sense that satisfies the austere canons of operationalism. However, if preference orderings are understood epistemologically more liberally, quantitative notions of an individual's good should be admissible by the same standards. Gibbard then contends that there is no good reason to encumber utilitarian theory with ordinalistic restrictions.

Chapter 3 by 'one of the greatest economic theorists of all time' (to use Arrow's words), Paul Samuelson, was sparked by Arrow's 1985 Tanner Lectures at Harvard. Samuelson points out that deduced ethical rules of any plausibility are usually explicit or implicit symmetry arguments, for example, the Vickrey-Samuelson-Lerner defense of egalitarianism when each of a group of egoists joins in a unanimous vote for equality under the supposition that all are subject to asymmetric probability distribution for high or low incomes – a demonstration that can be freed of the 'expected-utility dogma'. Further, he shows that (1) by contrast, the 1955 Harsanyi proof (that an interpersonal social welfare function must be Bentham-like, strongly separable and additive) rests squarely on the 'expected-utility dogma'; (2) Rawls's minimax or 'difference' principle is gratuitous in the sense of being able to command a unanimous vote against itself by normal people with less than infinite risk aversion; and (3) Varian's definitions of fair allocation are capable of deviating from optimal feasible configurations and involve implicit symmetry commitments. Samuelson stresses that where asymmetries obtain in the real world (as between sexes or species), notions of sympathy (where one may have to envisage being either a man or a woman or a cockroach and a human) are invoked as the straw out of which the bricks of definite ethical mandates are to be deduced by contrived symmetry syllogisms. He uses an example of rockbottom simplicity, involving a handful of states of the world and a few atomic egoists, to exposit a rich and restrictive calculus of *revealed ethical preference*. This provides him, *inter alia*, a reason to doubt the attractiveness of the familiar axiom of Independence of Irrelevant Alternatives.

In Chapter 4 Hammond takes up the challenge of Arrow's social choice paradox, suggesting that it may not be insoluble. His approach involves using cardinalization of both individual and social welfare measures based on behaviour in risk-taking situations. He argues that this approach can be justified by analyzing sequential decisions in decision trees. The major part of this chapter proceeds through several logical steps to derive a form of utilitarianism closely akin to Vickrey and, more especially Harsanyi, while the latter part considers how the contradictory postulates of Arrow's Impossibility Theorem can be modified to accommodate this form of utilitarianism. Hammond concludes that Arrow's social choice theory can be reconciled with an 'ideal' version of Harsanyi's 'fundamental' utilitarianism, but at three significant costs:

1. the independence of irrelevant alternatives must be weakened, say, to independence of ethically irrelevant mixed consequences;
2. the fundamental individual norm must be dictated in the event of unresolvable differences of opinion over what it should be; and
3. consumer sovereignty must be abandoned if attitudes to risk and tastes for gambling are not to be the arbiters of trade-offs between total and equality.

In the next chapter (5) Kemp and Ng interpret Arrow's controversial independence-of-irrelevant-alternatives condition as equivalent to three subconditions: individualism, independence, and ordinalism. Individualism requires that social ordering depend only on individual preferences. Independence requires that the social ordering of any subject of alternatives depend only on information pertaining to these alternatives. This is compelling due to the mutually exclusive nature of social alternatives. Ordinalism rules out information on the intensities of preferences. They also interpret the Bergson-Samuelson tradition of writing social welfare as a function of individual ordinal utilities as implying all three subconditions. Since the other conditions of Arrow's Impossibility Theorem (weak Pareto principle, freedom of individual orderings, and non-dictatorship) are also accepted by the Bergson-Samuelson tradition, the latter, according to Kemp and Ng, is subject to Arrow's theorem and the Little-Samuelson rejection of Arrow's theorem as irrelevant to welfare economics becomes itself irrelevant with the impossibility propositions of Kemp, Ng, and Parks, within the framework of a fixed set of individual preferences. Kemp and Ng consider the admission of interpersonal comparable cardinal utilities (rejecting ordinalism) as the only reasonable way to have a consistent social welfare function and show that the recent attempts by Samuelson and Mayston to defend ordinalism are unsuccessful.

There is a manifest relationship between the ideas presented by Suppes in Chapter 6 and Arrow's fundamental work on social choice. More specifically, Suppes sets himself the task of presenting an explicit axiomatic theory of freedom maximization. The judgements of freedom required in the theory are concerned with comparisons of different sets of decisions. One set is preferred in the sense of freedom to another if it seems to offer greater freedom of choice. Suppes argues that it is a mistake to always look for a utility function either of individuals or societies. In many situations we want to retain freedom of choice in a direct sense. The theory he develops here is for the individual, but he also provides extensions to methods of aggregation. Because the axioms lead to strong measurement of freedom preferences, namely, a ratio scale, multiplicative aggregation rules related to the Nash social welfare function can be used.

This is followed by Chapter 7 where Suzumura and Suga show how the abstract social choice theory may be construed as a useful and practical framework for examining the role played by moral principles in resolving social conflicts. They shed further light on the philosophical and distributive implications of the paradox of social choice. For brevity's sake they confine their attention to a Pareto libertarian paradox à la Sen and Gibbard, and concentrate on the role played in this context by the so-called 'Golden Rule' of the Gospel: 'Do unto others as ye would that others do unto you'. They formulate two alternative interpretations of this rule in the social choice framework each of which is successful in resolving the two-person example of the paradox in question. These alternative interpretations are, however, divergent: the first version fails to provide generally a resolution for this class of paradoxes, whereas the second, when generalized, leads to a general possibility theorem. The point of this exercise lies not in the (in)appropriateness of the Suzumura-Suga interpretations of the Golden Rule, but in the claim that the general workability of a moral principle in resolving social conflicts may be formally established by constructing choice with unlimited applicability.

This part concludes with Chapter 8 where Myrdal – the grand old critic of mainstream economics – perceives welfare theory, with its foundations in utilitarian moral philosophy and steeped in hedonistic association psychology, as developed by the first generation neoclassical economists at a time when both these foundations ceased to be fully accepted by professional philosophers and psychologists. He dates the apparent isolation of economics from other social sciences from about that time and challenges modern economists for forgetting that welfare theory is founded on obsolete moral philosophy and psychology, for remaining insular, out of touch with developments in other social sciences, and for not conducting realistic psychological and sociological research about economic behaviour. Myrdal also argues for recognizing the value frame of research in order to clear the scientific investigations as much as possible from distorting biases and for the development of a psychology and sociology of social sciences and scientists.

It is a distinct privilege to open Part II on welfare and distribution with Chapter 9 where Tinbergen revisits the optimum order in an attempt to clear up the ideological rhetoric that surrounds the far from pure forms of capitalism and socialism in the world today. An important feature of his approach is that for him the set of institutions is the fundamental unknown of the optimal social order and that more than one solution can exist – an approach that is so characteristic of Arrow's work as well. While the search for an optimal mix of centralization and decentralization and growth rates continues, here Tinbergen sets himself the task of providing a theoretical frame as a basis for quantitative empirical research. He is concerned with the variables to be used for analyzing the operation of national and the much less developed supranational institutions (such as production units, schools, health care centres, markets, and public agencies) and the roles they play in optimizing the population's welfare. The variables determining human welfare imply the quantities of (material and non-material) goods and services consumed. Tinbergen distinguishes between private and collective goods and discusses productive effort and abilities on which human welfare depends. He derives the optimal social order from the maximization of the social welfare function under a number of restrictions (for example, production functions and budget constraints). Tinbergen favours measurability of social welfare along Pigovian lines and advocates a specific way of performing the measurement.

In Chapter 10 Salop and Stiglitz pick up two central themes of Arrow's work: information and welfare. The analysis of welfare economics in the presence of imperfect information is a subtle and difficult matter. It is clear that the standard proofs do not apply directly; it is also clear that economies with imperfect information will in general not perform as well as economies with perfect information. The authors construct a simple model that allows them to address the question of whether an improvement in information improves welfare. They specifically take into account not only the direct effect of the better information, but the indirect effect; since information affects demand curves, market structure will change with a change in information. They show that though increased information may lower welfare, as a result of increased market power, 'normally' an increase in information improves welfare for two reasons: the direct effect plus the indirect effect from effective competition. Moreover, if obtaining information is costly, increased product diversity may lower welfare.

Chapter 11 deals with g.e. in the context of indivisible goods, hence where several standard g.e. hypotheses are not satisfied. Maskin shows, however, that the classic Arrow-Debreu techniques can be suitably modified to overcome this difficulty. More specifically, he is concerned with the existence of fair allocations with indivisible goods; that is, an allocation of goods across consumers is fair if no consumer prefers another's consumption bundle to his own and it is Pareto efficient. When preferences and goods are well-behaved, one can establish the existence of a fair allocation in a pure exchange economy by simply observing that a competitive allocation is fair when agents have the same initial endowments. Naturally the same method of proof can be tried when goods are indivisible. To give agents equal endowments, it may be necessary to assign them fractional shares of some goods which in itself causes no conceptual difficulty but which, unfortunately, may not generate a competitive equilibrium. Indeed, a fair allocation itself may not exist unless a certain amount of a perfectly divisible good is also available. In Theorems 2 and 3 Maskin shows that, given enough of the divisible good, an equal-endowment competitive equilibrium (possibly including a system of taxes and subsidies) exists and hence so does a fair allocation. The proof relies on the standard Arrow-Debreu technique of choosing prices that maximize the value of aggregate excess demand and finding a fixed point of the cross product of this correspondence and excess demand.

In Chapter 12 Atkinson and Bourguignon pursue the subject of distributive justice – a subject that has been at the heart of many of Arrow's contributions, and one in which he maintains a constant interest. The treatment of differences in needs in assessing economic equity arouses very different reactions: Some people regard such differences as grounds for rejecting any analysis of income inequality; others simply apply equivalence scales to reduce the analysis to a single variable (income per equivalent adult). Neither is fully satisfactory and in this chapter the authors seek to follow an intermediate path. They derive criteria that can be used to make comparisons of distributions of income where there are differences in needs. They explore how these criteria, and the extent of the ranking that they permit, depend on social judgements about needs. The resulting procedure is easily implemented and is analogous to the construction of Lorenz curves.

Also on the subject of income distribution, Chapter 13 focuses on the social welfare function. Chipman assumes individual preferences to be homothetic, and represented by continuous, concave, and strictly quasi-concave utility functions that are positively homogeneous of degree 1. He also assumes the social welfare function to be an increasing, concave, and continuously differentiable function of the individual utilities. Then a necessary and sufficient condition that the optimal proportionate distribution of income among individuals be fixed, independently of prices, aggregate income, and individual preferences (subject to the above restrictions), is that the social welfare function be an increasing, continuously differentiable function of a weighted geometric mean of the individual utilities, with exponents equal to the distributive shares.

Fairness is the theme of Chapter 14 which is so much in the spirit of Arrow's long-standing concern with issues relating to social justice and with those relating to pure economic efficiency. Baumol and Fischer examine the fairness properties of Pareto-optimal differentiation between peak and off-peak period prices. They show that in the classical model of this issue in which higher peak pricing is adopted merely to induce demand to shift towards off-peak periods, thereby saving on resources needed to construct capacity, the outcome is likely to be incrementally unfair in the sense that while off-peak users are likely to benefit, peak users must be harmed in a wide variety of circumstances. However, they also point to and explore several systematic exceptions. They then turn to the more interesting case where high-peak period use creates disutility for the users, and show that here efficiency may well require higher prices in periods of lower use and that this can yield benefits to all affected parties.

In Chapter 15 Tinbergen deals with empirical specifications of individual welfare functions – a task that is related to Arrow's path-breaking theoretical work on social choice. Aware of the 'multivariate' structure of welfare, Tinbergen concentrates, however, on the economic treatment and considers two groups of welfare determinants: those related to consumption and those related to productive effort. While he does not dwell on the details of consumption, he is concerned with the characteristics of productive effort (ability and schooling).

There is much to Keynes's argument that economic theory does not provide a body of settled conclusions immediately applicable to policy; rather it is a mode of reasoning that helps the possessor to draw the correct conclusions. Part III encompasses contributions to themes that have pervaded Arrow's economic thought and writings, but that have not been at the heart of his theoretical innovations. They include his concern for unemployment, cyclical fluctuations, resource utilization, and specific policy recommendations. In the opening chapter (16) Nikaido models and works out the dynamics of growth cycles of a capitalist economy. He does so on the basis of two views:

1. The recognition that actual unemployment is to a considerable extent involuntary, so that monetary magnitudes retain some of their traditional importance for the analysis of short-term economic fluctuations – a view that Arrow also holds – contrasted with the view that only real magnitudes matter, a view that is

defendable only if the labour market (and all other markets) are assumed to clear at all times, and
2. the negation of the modern dichotomy of treating separately fluctuations as short-term phenomena and growth as evolution of supply capacity in the long run, free of fluctuations.

Actual growth occurs through fluctuations, while growth gives rise to fluctuations. Growth and fluctuations are so interrelated that they are mutually causes and effect. In Nikaido's model output is determined by effective demand originating in intended investment within the supply capacity, depending on the existing capital and labour. The intended investment is governed by the capital-labour ratio and the excess of the profit rate over the interest rate equilibrating the money market. The saving thus determined results in actual investment from which ensues capital accumulation. The supplies of labour and money grow steadily at given constant rates. These are modelled to a dynamic process in which growth and fluctuations are interrelated and their entanglement generates the evolution of the system. The process generates an undamped cyclical growth.

Chapter 17 contributes to the discussion of the scientific viability of the life-cycle hypothesis, contrasts it with the intergenerational equilibrium theory of family behaviour, and offers a clarification of the theoretical foundations of the social security controversy. Kurz reports on the results of a statistical test in which both the life-cycle theory and the effects of social security and private pensions on family savings were evaluated. The analysis is based on a new and most comprehensive data file compiled from a random sample of families in the US taken in September 1979 by the President's Commission on Social Security. This chapter discusses two broad tests of the strict life-cycle hypothesis: the prediction that a rise in social security wealth depresses private savings and the predicted 'hump' savings and implied age-asset profile. Kurz concludes that Feldstein's original analysis of the effect of social security on personal savings has not been borne out by subsequent research. Also studies of the age-wealth profile yield results that contradict the life-cycle hypothesis due to its neglect of the questions of intergenerational transfers and of the mystique of accumulation of wealth and power flowing therefrom. Kurz believes that neither the life-cycle nor the intergenerational hypotheses can provide a uniform view of behaviour of the entire population. The diversity of behaviour has to be recognized in formulating an appropriate theory of savings.

In Chapter 18 Allais attempts to clarify the concept of the money supply and to analyze the process by which the credit mechanism creates money and purchasing power, considering time as well as demand deposits and the link between the creation of money, growth, and income distribution. He provides an analysis of the banking system taking account of the maturity breakdown of assets and liabilities. He then shows that, like the notion of desired cash balances, the cash balances held (that is, the money supply) is a psychological notion whose usually considered magnitudes are only approximate indicators. This analysis is based on the notion of rates of substitutability. He relates the creation of purchasing power by the credit mechanism to the proposition that the purchasing power created is represented by the discounted present value of the interest corresponding to the currency created. Allais also analyses the conditions implied by a reform that would remove the major flaws of the existing credit system. The main text of this chapter is illustrated in special notes by some comments on the world economy and the US economy in 1984, in relation to the potential instability of the whole national and international banking system.

Part IV provides alternative outlooks and commentaries on subjects that are very closely interwoven with Arrow's concept of the organization. More specifically, the central arguments of Arrow's *Limits of Organization* are set out in Chapter 19. Whitaker considers these and related aspects of Arrow's work in the context of intellectual developments in economics of the past 20 years. He suggests that Arrow's view of organizations as evolutionary and adaptive, due to constraints on the receipt and processing of information, offers an alternative paradigm that unfortunately has not been followed up by economists.

In Chapter 20 Williamson emphasizes how influential Arrow's contributions to the study of complex economic organizations have been on the development of the new institutional economics. He shows that Arrow's interests in the institutional attributes of market and non-market modes of organization are of long standing, enduring, and reflect an awareness of the limits of such mainstream approaches as the conception of the firm as a production function, the extension of g.e.t. to deal with uncertainty, and the applied price theory orientation. More specifically, he traces Arrow's stance that institutions matter to his 1963 paper on medical care and his 1959 paper (with W. M. Capron) on the operation of shortages in the market for scientists and engineers. He stresses Arrow's impact through his contributions to information and incentive compatibility and his writings on externalities, market failures, and transaction costs. Williamson points to Arrow's acceptance of bounded rationality and opportunism (or moral hazard) in his treatment of economic organization. Obviously one of the loose ends in the study of complex economic organization is the highly complicated task of design of a control system for government. It is in the area of desirability of government intervention where markets fail that Williamson takes issue with Arrow. And another loose end that Williamson mentions is Arrow's observation about the importance of trust in economic organization.

Precisely that topic is picked up by Leibenstein in Chapter 21. He focuses on the economic consequences of the absence of trust, particularly in employment relations. He uses a version of the Prisoner's Dilemma to show that self-interest based on mutual distrust can lead two parties to choose a combination of actions that makes both worse off than a set of alternative combinations. Costs arising from distrust include loss of exchanges forgone (hiring of people), post-exchange difficulties due to misplaced trust (refunds, seeking payment for damages, litigation), and costs of substitutes for trust (insurance, monitoring, sanctions, rewards, litigation). He points to mutual *limited* trust and intra-firm conventions as a partial solution to the lack of complete trust. For a firm with some market power and a group of employees with some effort discretion there is a tendency for both to move towards minimum wages and minimum effort, a Prisoner's Dilemma problem. But limited trust based on social conventions may impose a preferable solution that may still be suboptimal. Peer-group sanctions may establish an effort convention that reduces free riding. Wage and working condition conventions may help account for wage stickiness and disturbances due to inflation.

Robin Matthews wears many hats: he has contributed to and is involved in many subjects, earthy and theoretical. A man of many talents, his special background affords us yet another perspective. Eclectic in the best Marshallian and Keynesian tradition and 'branded' for life as a student and colleague both of Hicks and Robertson and of Kahn, Kaldor, and Joan Robinson, and as a sometime 'partner in crime' of Hahn, Robin delivers his many insights in an impeccable Queen's English whose intonations and music we cannot, alas, reproduce. In Chapter 22 he shares with us his reflections on the functions of economic theory and the relationship between our awareness of what are central theoretical issues and the exigencies of specific historical periods. He speaks of the advantages of interdisciplinary research and of the dangers of economic imperialism. Switching to the more pragmatic, Matthews reflects on the conservative upsurge in economic policy, with particular reference to the UK, on the vicissitudes of the welfare state, and on the pros and cons of egalitarian income distribution. He comments on the limits of neoclassical growth theory, on Schumpeter's perceptions of the economic process, on business cycle theory, and on new classical macroeconomics.

An attempt at a composite picture of Arrow is made in Part V. The complex man and scholar is seen through his own eyes and those of his various colleagues. In Chapter 23 Arrow shares with us some recollections of his early years: his early interest in statistics, Hotelling's indelible impression on him and the congruence of their ideas, his attraction to economics, and his impressions of Wald, Burns, J. M. Clark, and Albert Hart. He speaks of his disquietude about his apparent inability to find a challenging PhD thesis topic. He recalls his initial contact with the Cowles Commission group, in particular how impressed he was by Marschak's personality and approach, the atmosphere of verbal violence fostered at Cowles by Marschak, and his own resistance to the research programme in econometric model building and readier acceptance of the switch to activity analysis. He recalls the excitement of the formative years at Rand, the big splash of game theory, and the importance for g.e.t. of the mathematical techniques discussed at Rand. He speaks of his research colleagues at Cowles most of whom have contributed vastly to modern economics and achieved due renown. Arrow recalls his early years at Stanford and his stint at Harvard. He confides his propensity to get involved in 'worthy' causes and his need to feel useful. He discusses his perception of altruism and trust in our society and concludes with a fascinating analysis of the conservative trend and the inevitable cyclicity of political moods.

This is followed by a succession of impressions. In the first chapter (24), Aumann muses about the extraordinary depth and breadth of Arrow; about his true modesty, his friendliness, and his involvement in the world about him. In Chapter 25 Hurwicz paints a vivid and generous portrait of Arrow, the collaborator, and reflects on the missionary-type service Arrow performs in the applied work he does. In the next vignette (Chapter 26) Anderson provides us with some fascination insights into the reception of Arrow's thesis on social choice at Columbia, and on the relationship between Arrow's work and the development of statistics in the last 30 years or so. Raiffa reflects in Chapter 27 on the profound impact that Arrow's work has had on his own pursuits. In the following snapshot (Chapter 28) Green offers a general appreciation of Arrow's accomplishments and points to the beneficial impact of his work in applied economics which as a result has become far more open to the theoretical approach. And another silhouette is provided by Fuchs (Chapter 29) who naturally stresses Arrow's unique contribution to the economics of medical care. In the next chapter (30) Intriligator attempts a general assessment of Arrow's impact on the development of economics by means of a tabulation of his works most frequently cited in 1966–83, though admittedly that measure is not without its drawbacks. In Chapter 31 Lipset presents an intriguing and insightful portrait of the man and scholar, his motivations and underlying tensions. The following two chapters (32 and 33) illuminate Arrow's life-long attachment to Stanford University and his extraordinary services as a university citizen – an important facet of his life. In Chapter 34 we attempt a summary on a rather whimsical note.

Again, a fitting conclusion to this volume is Part VI where Arrow reflects on those chapters that do not deal directly with his work or personality.

ACKNOWLEDGEMENTS

The advantages of division of labour is a commonplace in economics, generally traced to Adam Smith, but actually of much more ancient vintage going back at least as far as Plato. Never have I been so fully aware of how it enhances output and improves its quality as in the process of design, gestation, and fruition of this study. Mere words cannot convey how grateful I am to my 'partners in crime', not only for their contributions in a tangible sense, but for their moral support; the atmosphere of enthusiasm, creativity, and professionalism that was created; and the psychic income derived from working with them.

So many of the contributors went beyond the product with which their name is identified in the table of contents; they offered constant encouragement, good advice, and comments on some papers including the introductions that singling them out as I must is indeed an ingrate task. Mel Reder's involvement with this project is very special.

When I invited him to contribute I knew him only by repute and of his role in the 'formative' stages of the Stanford economics department. He knew even less about me. Unaware that I had refrained from informing Arrow of this study, Mel consulted him and *fortunately* let the cat out of the bag. When, with great delicacy, Mel told me what transpired, I was emboldened to approach Kenneth and ask for his co-operation. In this way Mel has contributed greatly to the over-all quality and design of the project (not to speak of his counsel and support throughout the process of gestation).

Peter Hammond is a truly extraordinary supporter among the many who have sustained this project. He was involved in many aspects throughout the process of design, gestation and fruition and brought to it his special dedication, dispassionate advice, and good nature. Moreover the project gained a true friend in Mrudula Hammond. I am indebted to Gerard Debreu not only for his co-operation in helping us to understand better the mathematical economics of our age that he in such a large measure shaped, but for his impeccable courtesy and friendliness that make working with him a pleasure. Very special thanks are also due to Lawrie Klein for sitting down to an interview late at night after a very long day at an exhausting meeting and for his long-standing encouragement and good advice. Leo Hurwicz is a fount of knowledge and wisdom on which I drew once again. I am indebted to him for the intensive sessions at the California Institute of Technology of which these interviews are only a partial reflection. I also owe much gratitude for special encouragement, wise counsel, intensive discussions and/or extensive comments on the introductions to Tony Atkinson, Bob Aumann, Will Baumol, Woody Brock, John Chipman, Paul David, John Harsanyi, Murray Kemp, Donald Kennedy, David Kreps, Bob Kuenne, Andreu Mas-Colell, Eric Maskin, Robin Matthews, Takashi Negishi, Kwang Ng, Hugo Sonnenschein, Kotaro Suzumura, Jan Tinbergen, and Richard Zeckhauser.

At various stages of this project the discussions I had with M. Abramovitz, R. Dorfman, J. T. Dunlop, E. Glustoff, B. G. Hickman, H. S. Houthakker, D. Jorgenson, L. J. Lau, J. Margolis, F. Modigliani, J. R. Moore, M. Morishima, J. Rawls, N. Rosenberg, T. Scitovsky, E. Sheshinski, H. A. Simon, A. M. Spence, L. Summers and M. Weitzman were very helpful and their good advice and encouragement are deeply appreciated. I hope it will not be taken amiss if I thank collectively the many participants of the IMSSS summer economic seminars at Stanford for fruitful discussions over a number of years. Such anonymity, however, cannot apply to the dynamic M. Kurz or to the perennial enfant-terrible-in-residence, F. H. Hahn.

It is with much gratitude that I acknowledge the very beneficial and stimulating interchanges with G. Dantzig, S. Karlin, G. Kramer, and D. Landes who have provided fascinating insights into the many dimensions of Kenneth Arrow. I am also deeply grateful to Anita Summers for her willingness to answer many questions about her brother's formative years. I am a bankrupt when it comes to acknowledging earlier discussions and influences. But in this case I would be seriously remiss not to mention my indebtedness to two extraordinary and very different economists who alas are no longer with us – Jasha Marschak and Joan Robinson.

Parts of this study were written in Kenneth Galbraith's hospitable homes in Cambridge and Newfane. While unfortunately my style was not improved by transference, I greatly profited from his vision of the world, wisdom, insights, and extraordinary kindness.

I appreciate the many services rendered by a number of individuals in various institutions and the discussions with students in several seminars. Alas, I have to thank them collectively. In view of the special burden I imposed on the reference library of the University of Tennessee, I am pleased to single out its Head, Robert Bassett. Kenneth Arrow's office and particularly his dedicated secretary Rosemary Ciernick were very helpful, as was Lillian Zabahon, during my many visits to Stanford. I am also grateful to John Pratt for exceptional assistance (transcending the contributor's intellectual input) at the very last moments of completion of this study. I also wish to thank Michael Aronson of Harvard University Press and Alvin Klevonick, the Director of the Cowles Foundation for Research in Economics for their co-operation. I appreciate Keith Povey's editorial help and am grateful to Tim Farmiloe of Macmillan for his keen interest and sound advice.

It is customary to absolve all those acknowledged from all remaining flaws; I do this with relish. One person, however, shares responsibility for much that is right and wrong with this study; it is my wife Ida who actively participated at every stage. Since she performs unremunerated labour, I offer her the following concluding words of John Stuart Mill's 1867 inaugural address at St Andrews University:

> I do not attempt to instigate you by the prospect of direct rewards, either earthly or heavenly; the less we think about being rewarded

> in either way, the better for us. But there is one reward which will not fail you, and which may be called disinterested, because it is not a consequence, but is inherent in the very fact of deserving it; the deeper and more varied interest you will feel in life: which will give it tenfold its value, and a value which will last to the end. All merely personal objects grow less valuable as we advance in life: this not only endures but increases.

It is in this spirit that these two volumes were written: what an extraordinary intellectual and spiritual experience it has been; how remarkable the process of learning by doing; and how rewarding to share it with such a highly motivated, intellectually powerful, stimulating, and appreciative group of scholars.

It goes without saying that our greatest debt of gratitude is to Kenneth Arrow for providing the intellectual capital of this study. But we are beholden to him for much, much more: I am at a loss for words to express how grateful we are to you, Kenneth, for generously granting us a privileged insight into one of the great minds in economics of all time, sharing your thoughts and feelings, revealing clues to your motivations, and above all for the way you have done this: for your great warmth and elegance and for your high standards of personal and professional behaviour. With great affection and friendship, these two volumes are dedicated to you, Kenneth.

GEORGE R. FEIWEL

1 The Potentials and Limits of Economic Analysis: The Contributions of Kenneth J. Arrow

George R. Feiwel

1 PROLOGUE

> The study of economics does not seem to require any specialised gifts of an unusually high order. Is it not, intellectually regarded, a very easy subject compared with the higher branches of philosophy and pure science? Yet good, or even competent economists are the rarest of birds. An easy subject, at which, very few excel! The paradox finds its explanation, perhaps, in that the master-economist must possess a rare *combination* of gifts. He must reach a high standard in several different directions and must combine talents not often found together. He must be mathematician, historian, statesman, philosopher – in some degree. He must understand symbols and speak in words. He must contemplate the particular in terms of the general, and touch abstract and concrete in the same flight of thought. He must study the present in the light of the past for the purposes of the future. No part of man's nature or his institutions must lie entirely outside his regard. He must be purposeful and disinterested in a simultaneous mood; as aloof and incorruptible as an artist, yet sometimes as near the earth as a politician (Keynes, 1951, pp. 140–41).

It is not difficult to detect in these revealing lines a self-portrait of their author. Keynes used them, however, as a spring board for his analysis of Marshall's 'double nature'. Surely many economists (including perhaps our protagonist) would balk at the incongruity of a comparison between Arrow and Marshall. We are, of course, referring to the 'Vision' or *Weltanschauung* of the economists and not to their methods or products.[1] Moreover, it is probably futile to compare the intellectual make-up of economists primarily, but not only, because of differences in historical setting as well as cultural, educational, genetic, and psychological influences. However different they are, neither Marshall nor Arrow (and for that matter, not even Keynes) can be credited with all of Keynes's 'ideal many-sidedness', though each possesses the quality albeit in different configurations.

Keynes (1951, pp. 140–41) reminds us that Marshall's double nature was a clue to his strength and weakness; he was a sage and preacher and a scientist too, but the scientist was at the service of the sage. Marshall's 'mixed training and divided nature furnished him with the most essential and fundamental of the economist's necessary gifts – he was conspicuously historian and mathematician, a dealer in the particular and the general, the temporal and the eternal, at the same time'.

And what about Arrow? Is there not a tinge of double nature in him as well? He too is a sage whose concern for the improvement of society's welfare, whose social conscience, dictate much of what he does. But in his case the sage is rather at the service of the scientist. Like Tinbergen, Arrow (1958, p. 89) is suffused with 'the warmth of a passion for social justice'. One could also well apply to him these lines that Arrow (1960, p. 186) wrote of Frisch:

> One has above all the impression of liveliness, of a passionate and deep concern with problems, both for their technical interest and for their effect on the welfare of humanity. I would speak of earnestness, did that word not seem to exclude the sparkling shafts of humor which appear repeatedly. My ... personal contact with Frisch gave the same impressions as the reading of his work; the man and his work are inseparable.

There are also numerous personal differences between Arrow and Marshall, aside from the overriding one of precision versus vagueness. The latter is not only a matter of approach to economic analysis, but has considerable pedagogical implications. It is important to be precise in order not to mislead students, but would not some fuzziness teach them a healthier outlook on the complexities of the real world? This is a difficult question, as Arrow points out in Chapter 2 of this volume. Whereas Marshall was somewhat pompous and fully conscious of the influence he wielded in his field, which he sometimes used to the detriment of others, Arrow (though fully aware of his abilities, his standing in the profession, and definitely not retiring) is relatively modest, straightforward, non-dictatorial, and leans over backwards to give credit to colleagues and predecessors alike.

How does the configuration of Arrow's particular qualities stack up against Keynes's 'ideal many-sidedness'? Certainly Arrow possesses a rare and extraordinary combination of talents, interests, and motivation. He is endowed with a brilliant mind,[2] combined with a warm heart. He is deeply committed to the improvement of human welfare in the best tradition of economics and philosophy. He brings to economics a native intuition and a phenomenal analytical and mathematical aptitude, honed with the skills of a modern mathematician and mathematical statistician. But he is much, much more than a master-technician; he has deep interests in moral philosophy, the theory of democracy (political theory), system design, communication theory, psychology, history, and, indeed, in many very diverse fields – a holism that is not always detectable in his writings. Indeed, in its modern setting the range of Arrow's interests is remarkable; he is a social scientist in the great polymath tradition of J. S. Mill.[3]

Although I have ventured to suggest that in some respects a comparison could be drawn between Arrow and Marshall, a much more obvious comparison, and I dare say much more palatable to many modern economists, is the one between Arrow and Walras. Nearly 50 years ago Samuelson (probably influenced by his teacher, Schumpeter) enjoined modern economics to exorcise the 'Marshallian incubus' and to draw its inspiration from Walras. Following in the Hicks-Samuelson path, Arrow has been in the avant-garde that has been most instrumental in this shift in modern economic theory. Schumpeter once quipped that Gustav Cassell was a Swedish Walras plus much, much water. In a somewhat similar vein Arrow can be called a modern Walras plus much, much sophistication. Aside from a close link with Walras on the subject matter of, and general approach to, their investigations, Arrow shares with him a certain *Weltanschauung* as well as deeply complex and not always consistent pursuits. Yet in many ways, especially in his propensity to look ahead to new problems, to open up new questions, Arrow is more like Marshall than like Walras.

An illuminating aspect of Arrow's vision of the economic process is what he calls 'g.e. thinking'. By this he means the notion of the pervading interdependence among all economic phenomena; the recognition that any specific economic change will have far ranging repercussions that may have far greater significance than the initial change. Basically, it is the simple, yet not always fully grasped, notion of a complex economic system where everything affects everything else.

The unwary may well be tempted to speak of the 'impossibility of Kenneth Arrow'. Although he is a phenomenon of our age, he has also been shaped by it. One can easily apply to him what he (1967, p. 737) said of Samuelson:

> A great leader of his field is not typical of his day; but neither is he outside it. Rather he is like a magnifying glass; not only are the accomplishments the best that the period can produce, but also the underlying conflicts and contradictions are brought out more sharply and separated from the mass of elementary error and shortsightedness.

In the age of narrow specialists and technicians who know more and more about less and less, Arrow is a versatile economist, social scientist in the old mold, and moral and political philosopher. In the age of axiomatization of economic theory and the flowering of neoclassical (mathematical) general equilibrium theory (in such great measure associated with his name); he remains interested in alternative approaches and is willing to learn from them no matter how much he disagrees with or criticizes them. In the age of mathematical economics, he appreciates institutionalist or literary economists. In the age of 'obsolescence' of history of economic thought, he cultivates an interest in this 'antiquarian subject', and periodically teaches a course in that field. In the age of 'self-sufficiency' among economists and of economic imperialists, he is strongly committed to promoting inter-disciplinary research, particularly to learning from psychology. In the age of economic science, he is also interested in political economy. In the age when economists ask primarily smaller questions and often tailor their visions to the tools at hand; he continues to demand rigorous proof, but does not lose sight of the broader visions of classical economists and moral philosophers. In the age of infatuation with the purest of pure abstract theory, mathematical reasoning and logic, and the aesthetics of the argument; he is also particularly sensitive to the usefulness of theory. In a world of exaggerated claims, he frequently points to the limits of economic analysis.

Arrow moves with grace and felicity from the exalted plane of abstract theory to the down-to-earth observations of reality. Though he may deduce rarified, internally consistent, abstruse theorems, their usefulness and relevance to reality is never far from his thinking. Whenever possible he takes great pains to explain the relevance and limitations of his abstract models. And once again what Arrow (1983d, pp. 28–9) said of Samuelson equally applies to him:

> His accomplishments both close chapters and open new vistas. I have not conveyed some other aspects of his influence: his striking sense of history, so that his works are to such a great extent the clear perception of immanent tendencies struggling for release, his fair-mindedness and respect for others even when they disagree, his exemplification of the compleat economist – at home simultaneously in mathematical rigor and probing of foundations and in practical policy formation with a full realization of their underlying unity – and his warmth as a human being and friend.

The creative tensions that beset this non-dogmatic neoclassical economist are attributes of a complexity developed under the influence of various impulses; they frequently prove to be advantages rather than apparent inconsistencies. While Arrow (1984b, p. 154) expresses 'unabashed admiration for the accomplishments of the neoclassical viewpoint', he recognizes the 'major scandals', openly and eloquently voices complaints, and influences directions of change. While much of his work is on the competitive model, he believes that we live in an imperfectly competitive world and he has contributed to our understanding of imperfect competition. While his forte lies in normative economics, he demonstrates strong interests in descriptive economics. While he has exhibited such high ability in the purest of pure theory, he has not resisted the urge to contribute significantly to reorienting applied economic theory (mainly motivated by a desire to focus on market failures). While he excels in mathematical analysis, he has a demonstrated intuitive flair. While he is primarily a contemplative theorist, he feels an urge to influence policy (but is unwilling to make the needed sacrifices). And, above all, Arrow feels deeply the tension between the demands of individual self-fulfilment, and the dictates of social conscience and action. In him the latter claims appear to be very strong, indeed. He is fond of quoting Rabbi

Hillel: 'If I am not for myself, then who is for me? And if I am not for others, then who am I? And if not now, when?'

Arrow is not only strongly committed to raising the standards of scientific inquiry in economics, but he has a passionate social concern for economics as the steward of humanity. Both of these facets of Arrow, the economist, are brought to bear on his work. It is from this perspective that we analyze the work of this modern Walras (with touches of Mill and Marshall) who has contributed so much to our understanding of the potentials and limits of organization, uncertainty, imperfect information, and all that.

Although with different perceptions and from different time perspectives, other economists will assess differently Arrow's achievements, it can be reasonably claimed that he belongs among the master-economists of all time. A versatile, pure and applied economic theorist in the mathematical mode and a social scientist *par excellence*, he, to such a remarkable degree, influenced and participated in the reorientation, reshaping and ascent of the economic science of our age. He shared in enlarging the domain and in transforming, reformulating, refining, and generalizing received theory.

Arrow contributed to changing the course of economics and, to some extent, of political science by a number of distinct contributions, but the sum total of his achievement far exceeds the individual components, partly due to the synergetic effect and to a great measure due to his influence on others (as exemplified by the various contributions to this and the companion volume). He has collaborated with many other economists and social scientists, some of whom have become leading figures in their own right. Also, Arrow's contributions have been gross value added due to his painstaking surveys of the literature that preceded him.

Arrow uses very effectively the axiomatic method. Whatever else needs to be said about it, this method demands rigor in reasoning. It is a fruitful way of verifying the logical consistency of theory and of zeroing in on underlying assumptions. It enables the scholar to sift through the received doctrine, to precisely spell out assumptions, to dispose of the superfluous and only technical assumptions and to retain only those that have precise economic meaning, and to rigorously define concepts and results. The very process of the proof is educational and focuses on important further problems requiring solutions. In an apt analogy Robert Aumann (1985, p. 42) views mathematical economics as an art form:

> The case for thinking of mathematics itself as an art form is clear. Mathematics at its best possesses great beauty and harmony. The great theorems of, for example, analytic number theory are reminiscent of Baroque architecture or Baroque music, both in their intricacy and their underlying structure and drive. Other sides of mathematics are reminiscent of modern art in their simplicity, spareness and elegance; the most lasting and important mathematical ideas are often also the simplest.

He speaks of the resistiveness of the medium in which the artist works.

> The resistiveness of the medium imposes a kind of discipline that enables – or perhaps forces – the artist to think carefully about what he wants to express, and then to make a clear, forthright statement.
>
> In game theory and mathematical economics, the resistive medium is the mathematical model, with its definitions, axioms, theorems and proofs. Because we must define our terms, state our axioms and prove our theorems precisely, we are forced into a discipline of thought that is absent from, say, verbal economics.

Not only is Arrow one of the landmark and prodigious founders of the new (post-Samuelsonian) era of mathematical economic theory, but his classic *Social Choice and Individual Values* created the new discipline of social choice that far exceeds the boundaries of economics.

In what follows we trace Arrow's contributions from his first *tour-de-force* accomplishment – the pathbreaking creation of the theory of social choice – through the making of modern g.e.t., to his contributions in applied g.e.t. In Section 2 we review 'new' welfare economics, Arrow's extension of the fundamental theorems of welfare economics, and we draw the relationship between the social welfare function and social choice theory. Section 3 discusses the coming of age of modern g.e.t. with the canonical Arrow-Debreu model and examines the Arrow-Hurwicz contributions to stability of general competitive equilibrium. Section 4 deals with the interrelationship between existence and efficiency and some of the more recent extensions of g.e.t. Sections 5 and 6 are closely interrelated and call attention to the fact that Arrow's interest in the extension of g.e.t. to transactions over time and under conditions of uncertainty is deeply rooted in his scientific and even practical training. Specifically,

Section 5 highlights Arrow's contributions to the theory of individual choice under uncertainty, measures of risk aversion, and his ingenious construction of contingent securities as a theoretical device for risk sharing. In Section 6 we examine Arrow's perception of the role of information as a key to many unresolved problems in economics, of information as a commodity, of uneven distribution of information (derived from his study of the economics of medical care), and of the economics of discrimination and we also examine his contribution to the centralization-decentralization debate. Section 7 follows Arrow's contributions to production, capital, and demand which are somewhat less cohesive. It focuses on Arrow's study of allocation of resources for invention; his specific formalization of the problem of learning as a function of the total past gross investment, his subsequent restatement of the technical progress question in terms of production, transmission, and growth of knowledge; his conceptualization (together with Chenery, Minhas, and Solow) of the now famous and controversial CES production function; his collaborative effort on optimal inventory policy and his closely related work on optimal capital policy; his elaboration (in cooperation with Kurz and also Lind) of the choice criteria for public investment as a problem of second-best optimality; his application of optimal control theory to economic growth; and finally his stand on demand as a limiting factor of production. The final Section (8) discusses critiques and vindications of mathematical economics and neoclassical theory and Arrow's participation as both critic and defender. The appendix attempts to place Arrow and modern economics within the context of the dynamics of economic thought, discusses some criteria of evaluation of progress in economics, contrasts the Walrasian and Marshallian approaches, and provides some glimpses of Arrow as a historian of economic thought.

2 WELFARE ECONOMICS AND SOCIAL CHOICE

Arrow's first, and in some sense unique, accomplishement in the social sciences was the creation of the modern theory of social choice – a concept that possessed him and towards which he had been groping for some time as he indicates in Chapter 2. Had he not produced anything thereafter, his place would have been secure, not only in the pantheon of economics, but in that of political theory and philosophy as well.

Unlike the subject of social choice which was fully his brainchild, Arrow's subsequent contributions were primarily centered on the logic and the potentials and limits of the g.e. system, in both an explanatory and a normative sense, thus on a subject that had an established tradition, though many of the central issues, such as existence, optimality, and stability of equilibrium remained gaping or only partly closed lacunae.

2.1 Coherence, Efficiency, and Optimality

The germ of the idea of g.e.t. can be traced back at least to the Physiocrats and to Adam Smith's 'invisible hand' (with clues traceable to the scholastic doctors and natural philosophers, if not antiquity – see Schumpeter, 1954, Chapter 2) – the idea that, contrary to what one might prima facie expect, the individual decisions of a multiplicity of diverse economic actors, acting in their own interest, do not result in utter chaos; rather they achieve not only a coherent, but also, in some sense, an efficient allocation of resources. This powerful and stirring idea took root and throve for over 200 years.

The grand notion of interdependence of the economic system is traditionally (but, as noted in the appendix, not universally) indentified with Walras,[4] who conceptualized and articulated the vision of general economic equilibrium. Arrow (1983b, p. 201) depicts it as follows:

> it was the fact that all agents in the economy faced the same set of prices that provided the common flow of information needed to coordinate the system. There was, so it was argued, a set of prices, one for each commodity, which would equate supply and demand for all commodities; and if supply and demand were unequal anywhere, at least some prices would change, while none would change in the opposite case. Because of the last characteristics, the balancing of supply and demand under these conditions may be referred to as *equilibrium* in accordance with the usual use of that term in science and mathematics. The adjective *general* refers to the argument that we cannot legitimately speak of equilibrium with respect to any one commodity; since supply and demand on any one market depend on the prices of other commodities, the overall equilibrium of the economy cannot be decomposed into separate equilibria for individual commodities.

However awesome Walras's accomplishments, the pioneer left many conceptual and technical problems unresolved, partly due to his crude analytical apparatus. What Schumpeter (1954, p. 968) called the Magna Carta of economics 'brought in a host of new problems of a specifically logical and mathematical nature that are much more delicate and go much deeper than Walras ... had ever realized. Mainly they turn on determinateness, equilibrium, and stability'. And Schumpeter (1954, p. 1026) points out that 'in the last analysis Walras' system is perhaps nothing but a huge research program'. It is into this research programme that Schumpeter (1954, p. 1026) describes as a basis for 'practically all the best work of our time' that the major part of Arrow's work fits in so well.

In an expository article for the *International Encyclopedia of the Social Sciences* (1968) (reformulated as part of Chapter 1 of Arrow and Hahn, 1971), Arrow (1983b, pp. 107–8) clarifies as follows the notion of economic equilibrium:

> There are perhaps two basic, though incompletely separable, aspects of the notion of general equilibrium as it has been used in economics: (1) the simple notion of determinateness – that is, the relations that describe the economic system must form a system sufficiently complete to determine the values of its variables – and (2) the more specific notion that each relation represents a balance of forces. The last usually, though not always, is taken to mean that a violation of any one relation sets in motion forces tending to restore the balance (... this is not the same as the stability of the entire system). In a sense, therefore, almost any attempt to give a theory of the whole economic system implies the acceptance of the first part of the equilibrium notion, and Adam Smith's 'invisible hand' is a poetic expression of the most fundamental of economic balance relations, the equalization of rates of return, as enforced by the tendency of factors to move from low to high returns ...
>
> Whatever the source of the concept, the notion that through the workings of an entire system effects may be very different from, and even opposed to, intentions is surely the most important intellectual contribution that economic thought has made to the general understanding of social processes.

Arrow and Hahn (1971, p. vii) also emphasize that one must realize how surprising the coherence aspect of the market mechanism must be to anyone not nurtured in this tradition.

> That quite a different answer has long been claimed true and has indeed permeated the economic thinking of a large number of people who are in no way economists is itself sufficient grounds for investigating it seriously. The proposition having been put forward and very seriously entertained, it is important to know not only whether it *is* true, but also whether it *could be* true.[5]

For more than 200 years much of the history of economic thought has centered on the explication of the workability and the desirable properties of the market mechanism. This has continued to be one of the most controversial issues and a considerable source of tensions. Basically, however (though with various emphases, shades of meaning, and interpretations and with all the difficulties involved in comparisons due to different time perspectives and various 'visions'),[6] the notion that economic actors, left to themselves (acting in their own interest and within a given framework that is variously interpreted by different writers), will in some sense promote general welfare or that perfect competition will in some sense achieve a maximum of individual satisfactions (or a maximum of production in Wicksell's formulation) – this notion runs through most of classical and neoclassical economic literature (see Koopmans, 1957, p. 41; Koopmans, 1970, p. 333; Samuelson, 1947, pp. 203–19; Whittaker, 1940, p. 141; and Wicksell, 1934, p. 142). As Arrow and Scitovsky (1969, p. 1) note,

> to the superficial observer, modern economics in its beginnings may have seemed like uncritical admiration of the work of the invisible hand of competition and a mere endorsement of the philosophy of laissez faire. Thoughtful economists, however, have always shown great critical discernment and attention to detail, hailing some, deploring other, consequences of competition, exercising choice, advocating policies, and so practicing welfare economics.

Some modern economists (for example, Hayek, 1967; Friedman, 1976, 1981; Stigler, 1982; see also the anthology by Klausen, 1965) have hailed the 'invisible hand' as the most substantive proposition in all of economics. Others (for example Joan Robinson, 1962; Dobb, 1973; Walsh and Gram, 1980, and Nell, 1984) consider it a kind of metaphysical sacred cow in defense of the status quo. And in the middle is a wide spectrum of varied interpretations that more or less converge on the view of the 'invisible hand' as in some sense co-ordinating and beneficent, but ill-defined, hopelessly entangled in a web of exaggerated claims, and enshrouded in neglect or underrating the 'breakdown of efficiency conditions' (see Samuelson, 1977b).

Virtually since Adam Smith, economic literature has abounded with various claims and misinterpretations of the coherence and efficiency of competitive *laissez faire*. To be sure, exceptions to the rule that perfect competition ensures an orderly and efficient allocation were increasingly recognized, and the rule itself came to be questioned. Over the years there has been a gradual refinement of the conditions under which the market might or might not achieve efficient allocation of resources. However, it is only about 50 years ago that a kernel of veracity was separated from the chaff of untruths and half-truths and the doctrine reinterpreted and reformulated by modern welfare economists.

Welfare economics is not a new subject: It goes as far back as economic theory itself. It took a long time to clarify its basic principles. To this day it is full of unresolved questions. As Hicks (1975, p. 307) argued, 'though Welfare Economics appears to have settled into the position of a regular, accepted, branch of economics . . . it remains to some extent a mystery. It has often been criticized, and its critics have never been fully answered; yet it survives'.

The official history of the subject commences with Pigou (1912, 1920) who gave it its name.[7] The roots of the literature on welfare economics are in utilitarianism and Pareto optimality. The utilitarian view[8] of the individual sees him as freely weighing his gains and losses, as deciding to sacrifice present benefits for even larger ones in the future, and as acting to attain his own greatest benefits and his own rational goals, at least when others are not 'affected'. In its rigorous formulation, Arrow (1983d, p. 16) sees utilitarianism as stating 'that each individual has a numerically defined utility function defined (in the most general case) over the entire state and that the aim of economic (or any other) policy is to maximize the sum of these utilities over all individuals'. The utilitarian view has found much favour with economists past and present. Indeed, as Hammond (1982, p. 85) notes, 'the whole study of welfare economics is founded more or less explicitly on utilitarian ideas, even when economists deal only with the idea of Pareto efficiency'.

Utilitarianism has also been extensively used in discussions of income distribution by such notable philosophers (and economists!) as Edgeworth (1881) and Sidgwick (1907). Here a parallel is drawn between the individual's welfare and that of society: In the same way as the individual's welfare consists of a sequence of satisfactions derived at different time periods of his life, the welfare of society can be constructed from the achievement of the aspirations of the individuals in the group. Since the individual is supposed to maximize his own welfare, society is supposed to accomplish the same for the group as a whole.[9] In his celebrated treatise on justice, the noted philosopher, John Rawls (1971, p. 22) summed up Sidgwick's formulation in these terms: 'The main idea is that society is rightly ordered, and therefore just, when the major institutions are arranged so as to achieve the greatest net balance of satisfaction summed over all the individuals belonging to it'.

Arrow (1983d, p. 16) comments that 'when coupled with a hypothesis of diminishing marginal utility of income (concavity of the utility function, as we would say today), utilitarianism implies a redistribution of income from the rich to the poor'. These implications were clearly perceived by Sidgwick and Edgeworth. Other economists, however, showed scant interest, 'in applying the sum-of-utilities criterion to economic or any other policy. Very possibly, the radically egalitarian implications were too unpalatable, as they clearly were to Edgeworth' (Arrow, 1983a, p. 121). And, Arrow (1983a, p. 121) adds, 'subsequent work on "welfare economics", as the theory of economic policy is usually known, tended to be very obscure on fundamentals (although very edifying in other ways)'.

With the advent of what Sir John Hicks (1976) has called the 'catallactic' approach, utility gained a stronger foothold in economics. It was now endowed with a dual function: that of explaining individual demand functions and that of a collective criterion for assessing economic policies and systems. And this 'duality clarified the intuitive perception that perfect competition was in some sense a mechanism for insuring social optimality' (Arrow, 1983d, p. 17).

In the early 1900s, Pareto (by no means a household name among economists of the Anglo-Saxon tradition then or for many years thereafter) dealt a shocking blow to utilitarianism (see Pareto, 1971), although as Cooter and Rappoport (1984, pp. 511–12) remind us, the ordinalist tradition goes at least as far back as Jevons. As Arrow (1983d, p. 17) see it, Pareto perceived

> that the cardinal concept of utility function was unnecessary as an

> explanation of demand behavior; the demand functions were invariant under a monotone transformation of the utility function. Hence, only the indifference surfaces mattered. The indifference surfaces can be thought of (at least ideally) as observable entities. To them can be associated a utility function (Pareto tried to introduce the new term, *ophelimity*, presumably to eliminate the cardinal overtones, but the neologism did not last) that will rationalize the indifference surfaces (that is, the indifference surfaces will coincide with the level surfaces of the utility function) . . . But any strictly monotone transformation of a given utility is also a utility function, in the sense of an index that rationalizes the indifference map.

If cardinal utility has no meaning, the collective criterion has even less. (To be fair, one should point out that others claim that it is useful in social choice theory. See Chapter 5 of the companion volume where Kemp and Ng argue that cardinal utility has to be involved in a Bergson-Samuelson social welfare function.) If we cannot measure an individual's utility, how can we expect to add up those of various individuals? Instead, Pareto introduced what Arrow (1983a, p. 122) calls

> a necessary condition for social optimality, which has come to be known as *Pareto optimality*: a social decision is Pareto-optimal if there is no alternative decision which could have made everybody at least as well off and at least one person better off. In this definition, each individual is expressing a preference for one social alternative against another, but no measurement of preference intensity is required. Pareto optimality is thus a purely ordinal concept.

The principal merit of this ordinal theory is, according to Arrow (1983a, p. 47), 'the operational, behavioristic, pragmatic character of its method'. But Pareto optimality is not a robust concept.[10] Many alternative, often unjust, allocations would satisfy this definition (see Samuelson, 1947, pp. 212–14; Koopmans, 1957, pp. 42–54; Dorfman, Samuelson, and Solow, 1958, p. 409; and Sen, 1985, pp. 1107ff.) As Arrow (1983d, p. 17) emphasizes, 'this definition explicitly ignores the distribution of income; it is compatible with running the entire economic system to maximize the well-being of one individual. There is an infinity of positions of the system that are all optimal in the sense of Pareto; whether Pareto himself understood this is not clear from the text'.

To a large extent *Pareto optimum* is a misnomer, for it has highly favourable connotations; that is, it implies more than it means.[11] From the standpoint of distributive justice it might not be optimal at all. Hence Pareto efficiency or allocative efficiency are more accurate descriptions (see Koopsmans, 1957, p. 49; Arrow, 1971, pp. 32, 178; Arrow and Hahn, 1971, p. 91).

Pareto's work made hardly a dent in mainstream economics before 1930. Pigou (1920), representative of the so-called 'old' welfare economics, only incidentally mentions the sum of utilities, but its shadow overlays the work.

> Although the whole work is devoted to optimizing, there is no explicit formulation of a maximand. For the most part, the criterion is increase in the national income ('national dividend' in Pigou's language). But he is at pains to point out national income is itself an imperfect approximation, though I am not clear what it was supposed to approximate (Arrow, 1983d, p. 18, see Pigou, 1912, p. 25).

Some of the economists who revolted against the 'old' welfare economics, and whose work laid the foundations of the 'new' (see Bergson, 1938; Hotelling, 1938; Hicks, 1939; Kaldor, 1939; Lange, 1942; Allais, 1943; Lerner, 1944; and Samuelson, 1947), rediscovered the concept of Pareto optimality.[12] According to Samuelson (1972, p. 646), this was 'in part because Pareto is himself obscure and a bit confused; because the issue is a deep one; and because this is the way gifted scientists operate'. Samuelson (1966, p. 1041) is emphatic that

> the 'new welfare economics' is not intended as a *substitute* for the 'old' . . . all pretensions notwithstanding. It is an attempt to derive *necessary* conditions whose validity is independent of value judgments as between individuals, or more accurately, whose validity depends only upon less restrictive, and less well-defined value judgments than had previously been assumed. It involves the implications of the relatively mild assumptions that (1) 'more' goods are 'better' than 'less' goods; (2) individual tastes are to 'count' in the sense that it is 'better' if all individuals are 'better' off.

However, he (1966, p. 1096) is prompt to add that the 'new' welfare economics is nothing but 'a set of *incomplete necessary* conditions whose whole *raison d'être* disappears if the additional ethical conditions are not adjoined'. But that is another story to which we shall return in due course.

In 1951 Arrow made his first contribution to g.e.t. – 'An Extension of the Basic Theorems of Classical Welfare Economics' (see Arrow, 1983b, pp. 13–45) – which focused on the relations between Pareto efficiency and competitive equilibrium. In his Nobel Lecture, Arrow (1983b, pp. 213–14) recalls how his thought processes were stimulated in that direction by the discussions in the late 1940s among economists about the inefficiencies of rent control and various proposals for taking advantage of efficiency benefits of the free market via some transitional route. The informal efficiency arguments underlined that rent control induced individuals to prefer inappropriate, excessively large, housing, 'It struck me', he recollects 'that an individual bought only one kind of housing, not several. The individual optima were at corners, and therefore one could not equate marginal rates of substitution by going over to a free market. Yet diagrammatic analysis of simple cases suggested to me that the traditional identification of competitive equilibrium and Pareto efficiency was correct but could not be proved by the local techniques of the differential calculus'. Shortly thereafter he attended a seminar in which Samuelson provided an exposition of the fundamental theorems of welfare economics. As Arrow (1983b, p. 14) recalls, 'I was about to ask his opinion of my conundrum when I realized from his diagram that the separating-hyperplane theorem supplied the answer'.

In a sense it is fitting that Arrow's first contribution to g.e.t., following immediately after his extraordinary *Social Choice and Individual Values*, was in welfare economics. It is also fitting, but rather remarkable, that this 1951 paper, presented at the Second Berkeley Symposium on Mathematical Statistics and Probability, largely coincided with one on which Debreu (1954) had independently and simultaneously worked. And another overlap occurred. At the same symposium

> Albert Tucker presented his famous joint work with Harold Kuhn on nonlinear programming. The Kuhn-Tucker results are of course more general in many ways (and different, because they use differentiability), but not completely so; they assumed concavity of the objective function and the constraints, whereas Debreu and I assumed only quasi-concavity of the utility function. (Arrow 1983b, p. 14).[13]

And Arrow (1983b, p. 14) muses that these overlaps are a classic case of multiple discovery so common in science when the general impetus is from the same source – in this case game theory.

Though intrinsically this 1951 paper was not his most important contribution to g.e.t., it has proven to be very influential in the successive developments of the subject and an educational experience for Arrow himself. He (1983b, p. 14) remembers that it was while writing this paper that he

> understood for the first time the difference between the necessity and the sufficiency conditions and also found that there could be problems with corner equilibria – in effect seeing, though without fully understanding, the possible discontinuity in the demand functions which later played a role in my joint paper with Gerard Debreu on existence of competive equilibrium.

Similarly, Debreu (1984, p. 269) also emphasizes that

> the restatement of welfare economics in set-theoretical terms forced a reexamination of several of the primitive concepts of the theory of general economic equilibrium. This was of great value for the solution of the existence problem.

Before Arrow came on the scene there was, as we mentioned, a rich and varied, but not satisfactory, wave of literature known as the 'new' welfare economics (see Arrow, 1983a, pp. 24–6, 30–44; Hammond, 1985; Hicks, 1981; Scitovsky, 1984). Probably the most succinct and refined formulation of the basic assumptions and propositions for optimal resource allocation under different interpretations of optimality was Lange (1942) which greatly influenced Arrow.[14] Arrow (1983b, p. 208) observes that, in general, this literature lacked a clear formulation of the relations between Pareto-efficient allocations and competitive equilibria. 'What had really been shown was that the necessary first-order conditions for Pareto efficiency were the same as the first-order conditions for maximization by firms and individuals when the entire economy is in a competitive equilibrium'.

To recall, using tools developed in game theory and linear programming, Arrow (1983b, pp. 15–45) helps overcome certain shortcomings of earlier formulations.[15] He re-examines, restates, refines, and generalizes the basic theorems of classical welfare economics. Essentially the nature of the conclusions is the same as in received theory but the cases in which they hold become much generalized (allowing for corner solutions).[16] Thus Arrow answers with greater precision a focal question of economic theory: In what sense and under what conditions do competitive markets achieve economic efficiency?

The central results are summarized in the formulated Two Fundamental Theorems of Welfare Economics:

1. If a competitive equilibrium exists at all (the subject matter of the next section) and under appropriate assumptions, every competitive equilibrium is Pareto efficient.
2. For every Pareto-efficient allocation there is a redistribution of endowments such that the given Pareto-efficient allocation is a competitive equilibrium for the new endowment distribution.

The Two Theorems, and in particular the more profound economic understanding of the close link between Pareto efficiency and competitive equilibrium (or the decentralization result) provide not only central insights for economic analysis, but also have fundamental policy implications. The First Theorem does not imply that such a state is a social optimum and ethically just, for there is nothing in the process that assures distributive justice. On the other hand, the Second implies that the questions of distributional judgements can be separated from efficiency considerations. If a decentralized market solution is adopted and alterations of existing distribution is desired, the analysis implies the possibility of varying the initial distribution of endowments and allowing the market to function unhampered.

Naturally, the two Theorems are valid only if certain crucial and highly exacting hypotheses are met – such as completeness of all intertemporal and contingent relevant markets (including those for externalities) and absence of significant economies of scale in production. (Actually the First Theorem is true even if there are economies of scale in production. It is just that it may be vacuous if the economies of scale are sufficient to prevent existence of equilibrium.) In the real world these hypotheses are frequently invalidated – but we anticipate. The Two Theorems do provide a framework within which the potential role of social policy can be identified.

All this, however, still leaves the question of income distribution unanswered. In this connection, echoing somewhat Little (1950) and others, Sen (1973, p. 6) repeatedly asks whether modern welfare economics can shed light on questions of inequality. His answer is negative. 'Much of modern welfare economics is concerned with precisely that set of questions which avoid judgements on income distribution altogether'. In fact, 'the concept of Pareto optimality was evolved precisely to cut out the need for distributional judgements'. Sen (1973, p. 7) points out further that where problems of distribution are involved 'Pareto optimality has no cutting power at all. The almost single-minded concern of modern welfare economics with Pareto optimality does not make that engaging branch of study particularly suitable for investigating problems of inequality'. Although welfare economics does not offer clear-cut distributive policy guidelines, Arrow (1971, pp. 178–9) observes:

> It is reasonable enough to assert that a change in allocation which makes all participants better off is one that certainly should be made . . . From this it follows that it is not desirable to put up with a non-optimal allocation. But it does not follow that if we are at an allocation which is optimal in the Pareto sense we should not change to any other. We cannot indeed make a change that does not hurt someone; but we can still desire to change to another allocation if the change makes enough participants better off and by so much that we feel that the injury to others is not enough to offset the benefits. Such inter-personal comparisons are, of course, value judgments. The change, however, by the previous argument ought to be an optimal state; of course there are many possible states, each of which is optimal in the sense here used.

Thus the literature on 'new' welfare economics that suggested that policy prescriptions could be founded on objective economic criteria independent of ethical questions of income distribution was misguided (see Hammond 1985, pp. 406–9). The necessary efficiency conditions have to be reinforced by distributional considerations in order to arrive at 'a sufficient set of conditions for an optimum' and to determine policy prescriptions. Thus ethical norms (or a 'social welfare function') have to be introduced from outside (see Samuelson, 1966, pp. 1102–3).

In a way, as part of the 'new' welfare economics wave, Bergson (1938), still a graduate student at Harvard, gave birth to the social welfare function and Samuelson was the midwife who assisted him in his travail.[17] For our purposes it is instructive to see how Arrow perceives what he refers to as the Bergson-Samuelson social welfare function (for an alternative view see Chapter 5 of the companion volume). Paraphrasing what he calls Samuelson's (1947, Chapter 8) 'masterly exposition', Arrow (1983d, pp. 19–20) notes:

> I will take the most general perspective about the objects of choice,

> to be termed 'social states'. A social state may be taken to be a very large vector, describing the private goods received by all individuals, as well as public goods. Each individual is thought of as having an ordering over the set of social states; let R_i be the ordering of the ith individual. Thus xR_iy means that individual i regards social state x as at least as good as social state y (either prefers x to y or is indifferent between them). This ordering over social states is the natural extension of the ordering of commodity bundles assumed in the usual theory of demand by the individual. There and here orderings are related to actual choices because orderings are hypothetical choices. That is, xR_iy can be interpreted to mean that *if* x and y were the only social states available and *if* individual i were to make the choice, he/she should either choose x or be willing to choose either.

Arrow (1983d, p. 20) further observes that the Bergson-Samuelson argument is for a system of social judgements in the shape of an ordering.

> It should specify the set of chosen alternatives from any feasible set (more precisely, any feasible set with reasonable topological properties, such as closure or compactness), and the choices should have the consistency properties we associate with an ordering (completeness, that is, some alternative will be chosen out of every pair, and transitivity, that is, if x is at least as good as y and y at least as good as z, then x is at least as good as z). Preferences for one policy over another are expressed in these systems of judgment.

Arrow (1983d, p. 23) admits that the limited goal set by Bergson and Samuelson can be achieved.

> It is logically consistent to have a social ordering which is utilitarian in the broad sense that social preference between two alternatives depends on the utility levels (or, equivalently, indifference classes) of the alternatives for all individuals, reflects individual preferences positively, and is at least compatible with a strictly ordinal view that no meaning attaches to any indication of individual values other than the indifference map.

The larger question, however, that Arrow (1983d, p. 25) asks is, 'Whose ordering does the social welfare function represent?' In accepting fully the ordinalist viewpoint, Bergson stresses the ethical judgements of a single individual. However, such an approach, Arrow (1983a, p. 123) notes, is bereft of the important feature of impartiality among individuals that characterizes most thinking on social welfare. 'In Bergson's theory, any individual's social welfare function may be what he wishes, and it is in no way excluded that his own utility plays a disproportionate role'.

In fact, Samuelson (1947, p. 221) admits that he does not inquire into the origins of the social welfare function, but starts his discussion from

> a function of all the economic magnitudes of a system which is supposed to characterize some ethical belief – that of a benevolent despot, or a complete egotist, or 'all men of good will', a misanthrope, the state, race, or group mind, God, etc. Any possible opinion is admissible, including my own, although it is best in the first instance, in view of human frailty where one's own beliefs are involved, to omit the latter.

And Samuelson (1981, p. 228) continues to show his lack of interest 'in the process by which particular social welfare functions arise and are deemed to be of interest or relevance. I have been satisfied to consider it not to be the task of economics as such to pass judgments on whether this social welfare function is in some sense more important then that social welfare function'.

At Samuelson's hands the social welfare function 'is a very austere device, making as few commitments as possible. This inevitably raises the possibility of alternative interpretations, which might extend its usefulness but at the same time increase intellectual risks' (Arrow 1983d, p. 25). Ths social welfare function could well be interpreted as a sum of utilities as Lange (1942) has done. Samuelson (1981, p. 227) blames Lange for not having 'freed himself from his mid-1930s misconception that cardinal measurement of utility was intrinsically necessary for welfare economics'. Arrow (1983d, p. 25), on the other hand, insists that if there are interpersonally meaningful utilities, we would be in a position to use the sum of utilities. 'But for each individual the cardinal utility function is an index of the indifference map, and the sum is certainly strictly increasing in each utility. Hence, the sum of utilities is certainly an admissible Bergson-Samuelson social welfare function'.[18]

2.2 Social Choice and Individual Values

Arrow (1983a, p. 26) emphasizes that the vantage point of social choice theory is quite unlike that of the Samuelsonian view of the social welfare function as functional. Social choice theory envisages 'all possible societies in the sense of all possible sets of individuals, each of whom may have any possible individual ordering (or whatever expression of individual values is considered meaningful, up to interpersonally comparable utilities)'. However, social choice theory does borrow from Bergson and Samuelson the notion that any society can have a social welfare function and searches for a rule that would attribute to any possible society a corresponding social welfare function. The questions posed by social choice theory are more pungent in that it assumes that there should be certain consistency conditions among the social orderings pertaining to various societies. Arrow (1983d, p. 26) insists that 'what does deserve stressing is the sense in which social choice theory was a child, if unwanted, of the Bergson-Samuelson social welfare function'.

In Chapter 2 of this volume, Arrow vividly depicts how he was bedevilled by, and wrestled with, the ideas behind the theory of social choice, and how often frustrating and full of blind alleys their birth was. It is interesting to note that only when he thought of the social welfare function in the context of voting which he had previously identified with ordinalism (that is, in an operational sense) did he see the light. And, though social choice theory is a child of the social welfare function, it was born on the wrong side of the blanket so to speak and it proved to be a subversive child at that.

In a nutshell, Arrow (1951a) shows that it is impossible to aggregate individual preference orderings in such a way as to achieve a social order that meets certain very natural conditions of reasonableness; he shows how difficult, if not impossible, it is to extend the concept of individual rationality prevalent in economic theory to collective or social rationality. Though the paradox of majority voting has a long, if obscure and patchy, literature, in many ways Arrow originated the question in a modern and novel context and provided some, even if largely negative, but challenging, answers. Arrow's Impossibility Theorem is not only 'a remarkable result, of great analytical beauty, it is also surprisingly robust, *given* the informational constraints' (Sen, 1982, p. 337).

Samuelson (1977a, pp. 938, 935) tells us that 'what Kenneth Arrow proved once and for all is that there cannot possibly be found . . . an ideal voting scheme. The search of the great minds of recorded history for the perfect democracy, it turns out, is the search for a chimera, for a logical self-contradiction'. And 'Aristotle must be turning over in his grave. The theory of democracy can never be the same . . . since Arrow'.

Social choice theory is admirably pursued by Hammond in Chapter 1B of the companion volume. At this point we shall only touch on its highlights as perceived by Arrow. A clue to the question Arrow (1951a) posed is in his differences with Bergson over the meaning of 'welfare judgement'.[19] For Arrow (1983a, p. 68) it means 'an evaluation of the consequences to all individuals based on their evaluations . . . The process of formation of welfare judgments is logically equivalent to a social decision process or *constitution*'. He (1983a, p. 69) further argues.

> that the appropriate standpoint for analyzing social decision processes is precisely that they not be welfare judgments of any particular individuals. This seems contrary to Begson's point of view . . . In my view, the location of welfare judgments in any individual, while logically possible, does not appear to be very interesting. 'Social welfare' is related to social policy in any sensible interpretation; the welfare judgments of any single individual are unconnected with action and therefore sterile.

Arrow (1951a; 1983a, pp. 4–5) asks whether it is 'formally possible to construct a procedure for passing from a set of known individual tastes to a pattern of social decision making, the procedure in question being required to satisfy certain natural conditions'. Hence, the key problem is to 'provide a normative rationale for making social decisions when the individual members of society have varying opinions about or interest in the alternatives available' (Arrow, 1983a, p. 115). In other words, the problem is to determine how to aggregate the vast number of individual preferences about alternative social actions.

> The individual plays a central role in social choice as the judge of alternative social actions according to his own standards. We presume that each individual has some way of ranking social actions according to his preferences for the consequences. These preferences constitute his value system. They are assumed to reflect already in full measure altruistic or egoistic motivations, as the case may be (Arrow 1985b, p. 141).

Thus the individual's preferences ordering is not only an expression of his goals for himself, but also for society, that is, his attitudes towards the kind of society in which he wants to live. 'The ordinalist viewpoint forbids us from ascribing a definite quantitative expression to this preference, at least a quantitative expression which would have any interpersonal validity' (Arrow 1983b, p. 223).

Arrow (1985b, p. 141) tells us that 'the theory of social choice, as it has developed in the last thirty years, but with earlier history reaching back into the eighteenth century, seeks to analyse the concept of rational choice as it extends from the individual to the collectivity'. The most obvious manner of aggregating individual preferences into a social choice is through voting.

> In a voting context, the ordinalist-cardinalist controversy becomes irrelevant, for voting is intrinsically an ordinal comparison and no more. (Indeed, the failure of voting to represent intensities of preference is frequently a major charge against it.) The theory of elections thus forcibly faced the problems raised by ordinalism long before it had been formulated in economic thought' (Arrow, 1983a, p. 125).

Arrow (1951a) deals with what he calls a *constitution* (to recall, logically the same thing as the formation of a welfare judgement) – 'a rule which associates to each possible set of individual preference orderings, a social choice rule. A social choice rule, in turn, is a rule for selecting a socially preferred action out of any set of alternatives which may be feasible' (Arrow 1983b, p. 223). The following four conditions are imposed on the constitution:

1. Collective rationality, 'that is, that all possible alternative social states should be capable of being ranked and then the social choice from any particular set of alternatives should be the most preferred alternative, according to the ordering, in the available set';
2. The Pareto principle;
3. Non-dictatorship; and
4. Independence of irrelevant alternatives, 'that is, the social choice made from any environment depends only on the orderings of individuals with respect to the alternatives in that environment' (Arrow, 1985b, p. 143).

Though some of these conditions are more controversial than

others, they all seem quite 'reasonable'. Yet Arrow (1951a) shows that they are mutually contradictory. Simply put, '*there can be no constitution simultaneously satisfying the conditions of Collective Rationality, the Pareto Principle, the Independence of Irrelevant Alternatives, and Nondictatorship*' (Arrow, 1983a, p. 72).

> That is, if we devise any constitution, then it is always possible to find a set of individual orderings which will cause the constitution to violate one of these conditions. In one special form, this paradox is old. The method of majority voting is an appealing method of social choice . . . But as Condorcet pointed out as far back as 1785, majority voting may not lead to an ordering. More specifically, intransitivity is possible.

Essentially the social choice paradox means that the result of a system that ranks choices by comparing pairs in accordance with majority rule can be inconsistent and the situation cannot be rationally accommodated; that is, without going round in circles. In a formal way, Arrow (1983a, p. 170) has restated the essence of the General Impossibility Theorem for Social Choice as follows:

> Suppose there is a social choice procedure, capable of making choices from any finite number of alternatives, which uses only ordinal information on individual preferences and satisfies the conditions of independence of irrelevant alternatives, positive response, nonimposition, and nondicatorship. Then there will be some set of individual preferences such that the resulting social preference relation is not an ordering.

Arrows's Impossibility Theorem has been acclaimed as a truly great feat. Samuelson (1972, p. 411) considers it 'a first-rate contribution to man's body of knowledge. In the middle of the twentieth century there are not to be found many new milestones in the history of ideas'. He ranks Arrow's contribution with von Neumann's theory of games and other such accomplishments.

> If the Muse of history has its wits about it and succeeds in doing justice – two hypotheses of a somewhat romantic nature – I believe that Kenneth Arrow's name will be long remembered for a new and important insight into the permanent problem of the nature of democracy . . .

> I must admit that my vanity as an economist is gratified that one of the soldiers in our regiment should have made a contribution of universal interest (Samuelson, 1972, pp. 411–12), which is to mathematical politics something like what Gödel's impossibility theorem is to mathematical logic (Samuelson, 1977a, p. 935; see also Sen, 1985, pp. 1078, 1147, and *passim*; Kelly, 1978).

In this light it is interesting to note, as Ted Anderson recalls in Chapter 26 of the companion volume, that when Arrow presented the analysis as a doctoral dissertation at Columbia, his supervisor, Al Hart, and a number of others on the committee were not convinced of the importance of the subject matter. (Tongue-in-cheek, Anderson tells us that since the award of the Nobel Prize to Arrow partly for this result, he has never been so sure of having made the correct decision in approving a PhD thesis). In a personal conversation, Gerald Kramer told me that in the early 1960s when he was a graduate student (of political science) at MIT he tracked down an *unused* copy of *Social Choice and Individual Values* in the economics department library. In fact, as Debreu (1972, p. 2) perceptively noted in introducing Arrow at the American Economic Association luncheon honouring him as a recipient of the 1972 Nobel Prize in economics, the *American Economic Review* had not published a review of *Social Choice and Individual Values* (which had been uniformly favourably reviewed by the *Economic Journal*, *Economica*, *Econometrica*, and *Journal of Political Economy* all of which correctly predicted its great impact). (One should add, however, that though hardly a review, S. Schoeffler's 'A Note on Modern Welfare Economics', which appeared in the December, 1952 issue of the *American Economic Review*, did relate closely to Arrow. One should also note that in 1956 the American Economic Association awarded Arrow the J. B. Clark Medal, in part for his work on social choice.) Debreu (1972, p. 2) asks: 'Is it conceivable that in 1951 the American Economic Association overlooked the first major work of its future president?'

Perhaps all this was due to the simple fact that Arrow's sophisticated and elegant proof was intrinsically difficult to comprehend. Samuelson (1977a, p. 938) reminds us that 'it used to be said that only 10 men understood Einstein's theory of Relativity. That was an exaggeration. But it is no exaggeration to say that only a score of scholars were able to follow Arrow's early researches'.

Indubitably the publication of *Social Choice and Individual Values* caused marked consternation in the discipline of welfare economics.

Some economists even went as far as to infer that the Impossibility Theorem sounded the death knell of welfare economics as it then was. Others, like Little (1952), Bergson (1954), Mishan (1957), and Samuelson (1972, pp. 411–21) claimed that it was of no relevance to welfare economics. Samuelson (1972, p. 412), in fact, relegates it to the 'infant discipline of mathematical politics': 'I export Arrow from economics to politics because I do not believe that he has proved the impossibility of the traditional Bergson welfare function of economics, even though many of his less expert readers seem inevitably drawn into thinking so'.

In the second edition of his magnum opus, Arrow (1964, p. 108) implies that this sort of criticism is actually hair-splitting. 'One can hardly think of a less interesting question about my theorem than whether it falls on one side or another of an arbitrary boundary separating intellectual provinces'. Since his critics accept the Bergson social welfare function as part of welfare economics,

> any attempt to divide welfare economics in their sense from the theory of social choice must be artificial. At the very least, welfare economics, no matter how defined, has something to do with the public adoption of economic policy, and it is hard to see how any study of the formation of social decisions can have 'no relevance to' or 'no bearing on' welfare economics (Arrow, 1963, p. 108).

Can this controversy be laid to rest? Recently, Samuelson (1981, p. 223) reaffirmed his admiration for, and belief in, the social welfare function, 'despite the quite confused rumors that Kenneth Arrow's Impossibility Theorem rendered Bergson's "social welfare function" somehow nonexistent or self-contradictory'. (For Samuelson's most recent reflections see Chapter 3 of the companion volume.) Surely the point at issue is not one of existence of the function, as Arrow (1983d, p. 21) is the first to acknowledge. He admits that if such rumours as Samuelson mentions do circulate, 'they are indeed "quite confused" '. The point is whether society can arrive democratically at a rational choice when certain reasonable conditions are imposed. Arrow's negative answer stimulated a vast outpouring of literature that sought to overcome the paradox.[20] As Sen (1973, p. 9) notes the 'justly celebrated' Impossibility Theorem 'has produced much awe, some belligerence, and an astounding amount of specialized energy devoted to finding an escape route from the dilemma'. In this way 'scholars all over the world – in mathematics, politics, philosophy, and economics – are engaged in trying to salvage what can be salvaged from Arrow's devastating discovery' (Samuelson, 1977a, p. 938). Arrow (1983a, p. 163) notes that 'although there is no thoroughly satisfactory resolution, and there probably can never be a truly all-embracing one, some of the recent contributions are illuminating and very likely hopeful'.[21]

As Sen (1985b, p. 1774) recently pointed out, one cannot overemphasize the fact that,

> Arrow's motivational focus has been on social problems of great depth and complexity. This is worth noting because the impossibility theorem also has amusement value and is often seen as a brainteaser. The logical beauty and the elegance of the results are certainly undeniable, but what ultimately makes social choice theory a subject of importance is its far-reaching relevance to practical and serious problems.

In his review of the first volume of Arrow's (1983a) collected essays, Sen (1985b, pp. 1774–5) further notes that nowadays there are not many students in economics who have not heard of the Impossibility Theorem:

> The important question is *what* they hear about it, and what they understand the motivation for social choice theory to be. If they viewed the impossibility theorem as a 'fiendishly clever' mathematical result, but no more, the great gains from Arrow's work would, to that extent, be wasted. This collection of Arrow's essays, presenting his motivations, objectives, questions, answers, and doubts, in this area of his work, can go a long distance to motivate and orient others.

The new wave of welfare economics, so illuminatingly surveyed by Hammond (1985), was in part inspired by Arrow.[22] Hammond (1985, p. 410) speaks of the resurgence of interest in welfare economics in the 1970s as a revolution consisting of three parts, of which the first two were the development of optimal tax theory and the theory of incentives.

> The third part was the emergence of a coherent theory of social choice with interpersonal comparisons, securely founded on the principles laid down by Arrow (1951) and suitably extended using ideas originally due to Suppes ... and Sen ... for incorporating

> interpersonal comparisons with Arrow's formal framework. This was the third part of the revolution, however, because it was not really until 1976 that Arrow's conditions were completely formulated in a new framework ... Indeed, the second and third parts of the revolution are so recent that, at the time of writing, there are still a number of important issues that remain unresolved.

Some of these unresolved issues have led Hammond to reject the 1976 formulation (see Chapters 1B and 4 of the companion volume). But, in some ways, the rejection (though it goes to Harsanyi's utilitarianism) owes even more to Arrow than does the 1976 formulation.

3 EXISTENCE AND STABILITY OF EQUILIBRIUM

3.1 Existence

In many ways the Arrow-Debreu (1954) (A–D) classic paper is a milestone in the cumulative growth of economic knowledge and in the accretive process of providing ever deeper solid foundations for g.e.t. However great the contribution of the founding father, however rich the contributions of other streams of g.e.t. (concerned primarily with other issues), however admirable the pursuits and partial solutions of Wald and others in the German-language literature, it is only with the canonical A–D model that g.e.t. came of age.

An inquiry into the existence of equilibrium can be at least on two levels: the empirical and the theoretical. Here we are not concentrating on the observed (non)existence of equilibria in actual markets, but on the logical consistency of the theory. In other words, our concern here is 'whether the model – extensively used to draw various conclusions about equilibrium – is capable of ensuring the possibility of an equilibrium under the conditions it specifies. If it is not, all conclusions drawn so far are vacuous' (Koopmans, 1970, p. 358). The question of logical consistency cannot be answered by referring to empirical observations of cases approximating competitive equilibrium. As Koopmans (1957, p. 55) points out.

> the test of mathematical existence of an object of analysis postulated in a model is in the first instance a check on the absence of contradictions among the assumptions made. If we assume that not all members of a body of contradictory statements can have empirical relevance, this logical test has to be passed before any

> question about the relation of a model to some aspect of reality can seriously be raised.

Furthermore, it is not overly illuminating to find that competitive equilibrium yields efficient allocation of resources, if one were to find that such an equilibrium is logically inconsistent.[23] Thus the question of logical consistency of the theory comes before that of empirical verification. As Koopmans (1979, p. 358) put it:

> The problem of the existence of a competitive equilibrium therefore arises prior to any question concerning the realism of the assumptions of the model of competitive equilibrium. It so happens that this is a question of greater mathematical depth than that of the connections between competitive equilibrium and Pareto optimality.

In the process of establishing the existence of equilibrium, the requirement of verifying the logical consistency of the theory is met. Arrow (1983b, p. 160) emphasizes that

> existence of equilibrium is of interest in itself; certainly a minimal property that a model purporting to describe an economic system ought to have is consistency. In practice, the development of conditions needed to ensure the existence of equilibrium turns out in many cases to be very revealing; until one has to construct an existence proof, the relevance of many of these conditions is not obvious.

In an elegant juggling of the empirical and the theoretical, Dorfman, Samuelson, and Solow (1958, pp. 350–51) reply to those who feel that proof of existence is a rather esoteric idea that teaches us little about economic behaviour (see Blaug, 1978, p. 609, and 1980, pp. 188–92), that we do know that the real economic world does exist, and that the equations that describe the economic system, therefore, are bound to have a solution.

> But to reason this way is to miss the point. In the first place, it is not so clear that the ever-changing, imperfect, oligopolistic world has a statically timeless, frictionless, perfectly competitive equilibrium. In the second place, we can't blithely attribute properties of the real world to an abstract model. It is the *model* we are analyzing, not the

> world. We wish to use the model or parts of it for studying real economies. It is important to know whether this collection of supply-and-demand relations really captures what is important about economic systems. One test is provided by the existence problem. Just because no *real* existence problem can occur, a system of equations whose assumptions do not guarantee the existence of a solution may fail to be a useful idealization of reality. This may be a minimal test, but it is a test with some cutting power.

Walras himself was keenly aware that if no meaningful solution could be found to his system of equations, g.e.t. would be vacuous (see Debreu, 1982, p. 697). However, the father of g.e.t. was neither a sophisticated mathematician, nor, had he been one, were the tools then available suitable for tackling the problem successfully. Walras's unpersuasive answer to the question of existence was the equality between the number of equations and unknowns – neither a necessary nor sufficient condition for the existence of a solution to the system of Walrasian equations. Surprisingly for more than 50 years it was not perceived that the question of existence of economically relevant equilibrium was far deeper and more complex than such an equality of equations and unknowns. The following statement of Wald (1951, pp. 369–70) is of more than historical interest:

> as a rule, economists have contented themselves with equating the number of equations and unknowns and have assumed, without further investigation, that the system of equations had a meaningful solution from an economic viewpoint, and that this solution was unique. But the equality of the number of equations and unknowns does not prove that a soluation exists, much less the uniqueness of a solution.

Wald (1951, p. 403) concludes that we should not be content 'to argue that a solution must exist on the basis of the economic meaning of the equations, for something may be overlooked all too easily. Only the strictest investigation is satisfactory in this matter'.

The problem of existence lay relatively dormant until the late 1920s. Not surprisingly, in view of the technical nature of the problem, the greatest insights have come from mathematicians or mathematically-sophisticated economists. However, as Koopmans (1957, p. 58) notes, it is 'surprising that the fundamental importance of the problem to the entire edifice of the theory of competitive markets does not seem to have been commented on or even recognized by economists generally'. Koopmans (1957, p. 58) admits that

> there is ample precedent in physics for the bypassing of questions of mathematical existence of analytical constructs by investigators anxious to explore the useful properties these constructs can be shown to have provided they exist at all. But the fruits of such studies are like predated checks until the noncontradictory character of their premises has been established.

Surprisingly, interest in the problem of existence flourished during the interwar period among a small group of economists and mathematicians in Central Europe, whose discussion in German centered primarily on Cassel's version of the g.e. system. Thus, however oversimplified is Cassel's vulgar textbook interpretation of the Walrasian system, it nevertheless performed an extraordinary service by sparking the German-language interwar literature on existence.[24]

Probably one of the first to show that a solution to the Walrasian system of equations may not exist was the German mathematician, R. Remak, whose 1929 paper was otherwise of little economic interest (see Baumol and Goldfeld, 1968, pp. 267–77). In the first half of the 1930s, there appeared independent papers by the noted German economists H. Neisser and H. von Stackelberg, the well-known Danish economist F. Zeuthen, and the Hungarian banker and amateur economist under self-exile in Vienna, K. Schlesinger (for the latter see Baumol and Goldfeld, 1968, pp. 278–80).[25] Their perceptive challenge to the solution of the Walrasian system of equations threw the question into a new light.[26] Their inquiries are not only valuable on their own merits, but also as a stimulus for Wald's investigations.[27]

Another Hungarian, Abraham Wald, whose home town of Cluj had come under Rumanian rule, frequented the corridors of Karl Menger's mathematical colloquium in Vienna. Menger (the son of the famous Carl, one of the founders of the marginal utility theory, who, incidentally was no special friend of mathematical economics) was a well-known geometer and topologist and Wald's teacher of mathematics. Wald who, as a foreigner in depression Vienna, had difficulties finding a job, in turn, instructed Schlesinger and Morgenstern in mathematics. Morgenstern also found employment for Wald at the Institute for Business Cycle Research where his interests shifted towards economic problems. Thus Wald was receptive to Schlesinger's invitation that he turn his high-powered mathematical skills towards the question of solution of the Walrasian system which had stumped Schlesinger's intuitive mathematical abilities.

Morgenstern (1968, pp. 51–2) recalls that the Wald-Schlesinger interaction concerned Schlesinger's modification of the Walras-Cassel version of the system of equations by considering all, and not only the scarce, production factors which propelled Wald towards his contribution to the question of existence. From the start Wald's work was inhibited, as Schumpeter (1954, p. 1014) remarks, by the fact that he was dealing with Cassel's rather than Walras's system. Commenting on Wald's pioneering attempts, K. Menger noted that Wald's work brings

> to a close the period in which economists simply *formulated* equations, without concern for the existence or uniqueness of their solutions, or at best, made sure that the number of equations and unknowns be equal (something that is neither necessary nor sufficient for solvability and uniqueness). In the future as the economists formulate equations and concern themselves with their solution (as the physicists have long done) they will have to deal explicitly with the deep mathematical questions of existence and uniqueness (Baumol and Goldfeld, 1968, p. 288).

Wald's contribution to the proof of existence was apparently contained in three papers and a fourth summary paper. The first two (see Baumol and Goldfeld, 1968, pp. 281–93) contain proofs of the solution of alternative models of production of the fixed coefficient variety. Regrettably the third paper, whose assumptions were apparently more general, was not published due to the closure of the journal and was lost in the vicissitudes of exile (see Chipman, 1965a, p. 720). The fourth expository article (Wald, 1951) omits the proofs.[28]

The pioneering nature of Wald's contribution is beyond dispute, although the nature of his complete proof remains a puzzle that cannot be solved. Wald did indeed provide a proof of existence of general economic equilibrium under stipulated conditions that were difficult to interpret and that, in retrospect, proved to be inordinately stringent. Moreover, the published proofs are cumbersome and forbidding complex, both in the application of an involved calculus apparatus, and in the complicated intricacies of the argument. Arrow (1983b, p. 113) points out that 'as they gradually came to be known among mathematical economists' Wald's papers 'probably served as much to inhibit further research by their difficulty as to stimulate it'. Similarly, Dorfman, Samuelson, and Solow (1958, p. 368) admit that Wald's proof 'is extremely intricate and opaque. Nevertheless, it is a beautiful achievement, perhaps the most difficult piece of rigorous economics up to that time'. Whatever the faults in execution, Wald's contribution is an exemplary application of the axiomatic method to economics.

> For a fruitful application of mathematics in economics it is essential, *first*, that all the assumptions on which the given mathematical representation of economic phenomena depends be enumerated completely and precisely; *second*, that only those conclusions be drawn which are valid in the strictest sense, i.e., that if they are valid only under further assumptions, these also be formulated explicitly and precisely . . .
>
> If these directions are strictly adhered to, then the only objection which can be raised against a theory is that it includes assumptions which are foreign to the real world and that, as a result, the theory lacks applicability. It must be admitted that in many areas of mathematical economics very substantial abstractions are being used, so that one can hardly speak of a good approximation to reality. But it should be remembered that, on the one hand, mathematical economics is a very young science and, on the other, that economic phenomena are of such a complicated, involved nature that far-reaching abstractions must be used at the start merely to be able to survey the problem, and that the transition to more realistic assumptions must be carried out step by step. If the above-mentioned directions are strictly adhered to, it will always be known precisely just where the assumptions are still so simplified and unrealistic that they must be replaced with better ones, so that ultimately theories will be derived that are well applicable to the real world (Wald, 1951, pp. 368–9).

Wald made economically unreasonable assumptions and, indeed, a rather peculiar one requiring the demand function to satisfy (in later terminology) the Weak Axiom of Revealed Preference. Essentially, he assumed that there is really only one rational consumer (see Dorfman, Samuelson, and Solow, 1958, p. 368; Hicks, 1983, pp. 250–51 and 280; Samuelson, 1966, p. 499). As McKenzie (1981, p. 819) notes, 'in a one consumer economy the existence of the equilibrium becomes a simple maximum problem and advanced methods are not needed'. It is puzzling what methods Wald used to demonstrate the proof of existence in the lost paper. The calculus methods he used in the previous two papers appear to have been incapable of leading him to a satisfactory proof in the third. When he refers to the lost paper in summary form, Wald implies that the proof requires modern mathematical methods – a clue that he may have used some variant of the fixed-point theorem. But we shall probably never know whether he did or not. It may be argued that since this paper did not see the light of day and was never found it could 'not directly influence the writers of the fifties' (McKenzie, 1981, p. 820). On the other hand, it is possible that an announced result may lead later researchers to try to rediscover the proof.

All else aside, Wald's work was outside the dominant Anglo-American tradition, and it is not surprising that the American mathematical economists were not only stumped by the forbidding and inelegant mathematics, but even more so by the German language. In the late 1930s and during the war a considerable contingent of economists came to the US from the German-speaking countries and through them a strong infusion of the ferment in economic thought in that part of the world took place in the US. Wald himself came to Columbia University as a mathematical statistician and it is in that capacity that he was one of Arrow's teachers.

Arrow cannot recall precisely how he became aware of the importance of the existence problem. As a fledgling graduate student in economics, he was enormously impressed by Hicks's *Value and Capital* and planned to improve on it. He believes that he was probably led to the centrality of the existence problem, that was yet perhaps only partially solved, but cannot remember by whom. Hotelling was probably his source for references to the German-language contributions of Wald. Wald, whose mathematical prowess Arrow valued as much above his own, discouraged him from approaching this subject by branding it as very forbidding indeed. Arrow remembers reading Wald's papers at the time and not understanding them too well, both due to linguistic deficiencies and to disenchantment with the intricacies of the argument.

In any case, the idea that here was an interesting, essentially unresolved, analytic issue only lay dormant in Arrow's mind a few years. It was triggered back to life by a concatenation of several streams of thought (game theory, activity analysis, and fixed-point theory) that were fermenting in the 1940s, and flourished in the 1950s, in some of which Arrow actively participated. Although Arrow stresses the relevance of von Neumann (1945–46) on the existence of balanced growth equilibrium, he identifies Nash (1950) as the catalyst that set him off on the road to the proof of existence. Initially, by adapting the mathematical tools (Kakutani's fixed-point theorem) that Nash employed, it was possible for Arrow to broadly stipulate under what conditions a solution to the equations defining g.e. existed.

Both Arrow and Debreu repeatedly stress that von Neumann (1945–46) had a stronger influence on them than did Wald. Arrow (1983b, p. 212) calls attention to three principal points in von Neumann:

1. The novel characterization of the structure of production.
2. Characterization of the maximum growth path as a sort of competitive equilibrium,
3. The method of proof that used a generalization of Brouwer's fixed-point theorem which gave rise to Kakutani's theorem. To be sure, to an economist the model seemed somewhat peculiar for consumption was not determined by optimization considerations.

Arrow (1983b, p. 113) emphasizes the paradoxical historical relationship between game theory and g.e.t.

> In principle, game theory is a very general notion of equilibrium which should either replace the principle of competitive equilibrium or include it as a special case. In fact, while game theory has turned out to be extraordinarily stimulating to equilibrium theory, it has been through the use of mathematical tools developed in the former and used in the latter with entirely different interpretations. It was von Neumann himself who made the first such application in his celebrated paper on balanced economic growth.

Speaking of his and Debreu's initial application of Kakutani's fixed-point theorem to the existence question, Arrow (1983b, p. 217) explains that an essential precondition for their study was

> the basic work of Tjalling Koopmans ... on the analysis of production in terms of activity analysis. In this he extended von Neumann's work into a systematic account of the production structure of the economy. He saw it as a set of activities, each of which could be operated at any level but with the overall levels

constrained by initial resource limitations. The crucial novelty was the explicit statement of the assumptions which ensured that the feasible set of output would be hounded for any finite set of initial resources. It turned out that this limitation is a 'global' property. That is, conditions on the nature of individual activities (for example, that every activity had to have at least one input) were not sufficient to ensure the boundedness of the economy as a whole. It was necessary to require that no combination of activities as a whole permitted production without inputs.

Debreu, who came from a different tradition from Arrow, recalls that Wald's proofs were not important to him in the creative genesis of his work on existence.[29] He traces his own development, through the strong influence of the rigour and sophistication of the axiomatic approach à la Bourbaki to mathematics and the allure of g.e.t. as he first discovered it in the works of M. Allais and F. Divisia who had kept the flame of the Lausanne school alive in France. But the counting of equations and unknowns in the Walrasian system went against the grain of the budding economist whose mind was cast in uncompromising mathematical rigor. Debreu recalls that the contentious question of existence kept recurring in his mind, but for him in the mid and late 1940s a number of essential elements of the solution were not at hand, and this interesting, unresolved problem also lay dormant in his mind. When he joined the Cowles Commission in 1950, Debreu became gradually aware of Kakutani's fixed-point theorem, von Neumann's model of growth, and Nash's 1950 note on the existence of equilibrium points in *N*-person games. It was these results, especially Kakutani's theorem, that set Debreu off on the road to solving the existence problem.

In 1951 Arrow and Debreu began independently, each in his own way, to solve the existence problem. Initially Arrow (1983b, pp. 58–9) approached the question by formulating competitive equilibrium as the equilibrium of a suitably chosen game.

The players of this fictitious game were the consumers, a set of 'anticonsumers' (one for each consumer), producers, and a price chooser. Each consumer chose a consumption vector, each anticonsumer a non-negative number (interpretable as the marginal utility of income), each firm a production vector, and the price chooser a price vector on the unit simplex. The payoff to a consumer was the utility of his consumption vector plus the budgetary surplus (pos-

> sibly negative, of course) multiplied by the anticonsumer's chosen number. The payoff of an anticonsumer was the negative of the payoff to the corresponding consumer. The payoff to the firm was profit and to the price chooser the value of excess demand at the chosen prices. This is a well-defined game. The existence of equilibrium does not follow mechanicaly from Nash's theorem, since some of the strategy domains are unbounded.

Koopmans, who was then director of Cowles, became aware that both Arrow and Debreu were working on the same problem and he put them in touch with each other. Early in 1952 they sent their manuscripts to each other and discovered essentially the same oversight in each other's work, namely, the neglect of the possibility of discontinuity in cases where prices vary to such an extent that some consumers' incomes are close to naught. They then joined forces and collaborated primarily by correspondence, somewhat complicated by Arrow's travelling in Europe during most of 1952. Debreu recalls that the results they achieved gave rise to a paper he published in October (Debreu, 1952) on the existence of a generalized Cournot-Nash equilibrium for an abstract social system.

Arrow (1983b, p. 59) recalls that in their finished joint product they 'followed more closely Debreu's more elegant formulation, based on the concept of generalized games, which eliminated the need for "anticonsumers"'. Debreu (1984, pp. 269–70) reflects that in the joint paper they formulated a competitive economy in the fashion of a social system presented in Debreu (1952). In this joint paper,

> the agents are the consumers, the producers, and a fictitious price setter. An appropriate definition of the set of reactions of the price setter to an excess demand vector makes the concept of equilibrium for that social system equivalent to the concept of competitive equilibrium for the original economy. In this manner a proof of existence, resting ultimately on Kakutani's theorem, was obtained for an equilibrium of an economy made up of interacting consumers and producers. In the early 1950s, the time had undoubtedly come for solutions of the existence problem.

On 27 December 1952 Debreu presented the Arrow and Debreu 'Existence of an Equilibrium for a Competitive Economy' at a joint session of the American Economic Association and the Econometric Society in Chicago (published in *Econometrica*, July 1954). Lionel

McKenzie,[30] who had independently been working along similar lines also using Kakutani's fixed-point theorem, presented his proof of existence on 28 December 1952 in 'On equilibrium in Graham's Model of World Trade and Other Competitive Systems' (published in *Econometrica*, April 1954). Debreu became aware of McKenzie's work only when he attended the session at which it was presented. And McKenzie says:

> I recall that Koopmans, Debreu, Beckmann, and Chipman were at my session. The Arrow-Debreu paper had been given the day before and I had stayed away. However, Debreu rose in the discussion period to suggest that their paper implied my result. I replied that no doubt my paper also implied their results. Debreu [has told me] he spoke up after asking Koopmans' advice before the session. Later in his office, Debreu gave me a private exposition of their results (quoted after Weintraub, 1983, p. 34).

At this point we should also note the independent contribution on existence by Nikaido (1956) whose publication was unfortunately very much delayed. As Nikaido (1956, p. 135) points out in a footnote appended to the title, 'the result of this paper has been obtained independently of the important work carried out by Professors Arrow and Debreu ... and prior to its appearance in Econometrica, although it should be expressly acknowledged that there is much intersection.' His paper deals with the classical multilateral exchange model and the existence of an equilibrium is rigorously proved by means of Kakutani's fixed-point theorem. Nikaido (1956, p. 135) also adapts 'the basic mapping formula so as to apply it not only to a model of world trade involving social welfare functions of participant countries, whose graphical analysis is due to Professor Leontief ..., but also to Graham's model treated recently by Professor McKenzie.' We should also mention here the paper by Gale (1955) where he refers to Wald (1951) and to A–D (1954). Gale (1955, p. 155) notes that he studies a model 'closely resembling' A–D (1954): 'However, where the latter makes use of some rather sophisticated results of algebraic topology, we shall obtain a simple proof of existence of an equilibrium using a well-known lemma of elementary combinatorial topology'.

According to A–D (1954), the study of existence of solutions is important for both descriptive and normative economics.

> Descriptively, the view that the competitive model is a reasonably

accurate description of reality, at least for certain purposes, presupposes that the equations describing the model are consistent with each other. Hence, one check on the empirical usefulness of the model is the prescription of the conditions under which the equations of competitive equilibrium have a solution.

Perhaps as important is the relation between the existence of solutions to a competitive equilibrium and the problems of normative or welfare economics. It is well known that, under suitable assumptions on the preferences of consumers and the production possibilities of producers, the allocation of resources in a competitive equilibrium is optimal in the sense of Pareto . . . and conversely every Pareto-optimal allocation of resources can be realized by a competitive equilibrium . . . From the point of view of normative economics the problem of existence of an equilibrium for a competitive system is therefore also basic (Arrow, 1983b, p. 60).

In this connection, the authors emphasize the necessity of careful specification of assumptions of a competitive economy[31] – a subject to which we return in Section 4 on existence and efficiency. As Arrow (1983b, p. 220 put it in his Nobel lecture,

once the broad approach to the analysis of existence was set, it could be applied in many different directions. One was the analysis of models which represented in one way or another imperfections in the competitive system. The requirement of proving an existence theorem in each case leads to the need for a rigorous spelling out of assumptions, a requirement which seems to be proving very fruitful. Much of this work is now going on, in such areas as the analysis of futures markets, expectations, and monetary theory.

As we know, the methods A–D (1954) uses are not those of differential calculus, but those of fixed-point theory and convex analysis – set-theoretical mathematical techniques that are not only more suitable for investigating the existence problem, but also that of the basic welfare theorems (see Debreu 1984, pp. 269–70). Two theorems that specify the general conditions for the existence of competitive equilibrium form the crux of A–D (1954):

Loosely speaking, the first theorem asserts that if every individual has initially some positive quantity of every commodity available

> for sale, then a competitive equilibrium will exist. the second theorem asserts the existence of competitive equilibrium if there are some types of labor with the following two properties: (1) each individual can supply some positive amount of at least one such type of labor; and (2) each such type of labor has a positive usefulness in the production of desired commodities. The conditions of the second theorem, particularly, may be expected to be satisfied in a wide variety of actual situations, though not, for example, if there is insufficient substitutability in the structure of production (Arrow, 1983b, p. 60).

Aside from the all important differences in techniques, in a number of respects the assumptions that A–D (1954) makes are less stringent and closer approximate reality than those made by Wald. Also, unlike Wald's models, the A–D model consists of an integrated system of production and consumption that embraces the circular flow of income. On the whole the A–D proof is far simpler and more general than Wald's proof.

While McKenzie (1954) also uses Kakutani's fixed-point theorem, in some respects his model appears to be less general; it is developed within the context of international trade, although the conclusion of the paper is devoted to the applicability of the proof to a more general case. Another difference is that McKenzie (1954) does not disaggregate the demand function of the economy and consumption is not obtained from the utility maximization of consumers under budget constraints. Arrow (1983b, pp. 219–20) considers that McKenzie (1954) 'simply assumed the existence of supply and demand functions rather than analyzing them in terms of the underlying production and consumption structures'. For this and other reasons the models are not readily comparable (see also Hildenbrand, 1983, p. 19).

What needs to be stressed is that more than advances in techniques and mathematical virtuosity were involved in A–D (1954). It provided a reconstruction, refinement, and clarification of the conceptual apparatus. The A–D model has become the standard or canonical model of g.e.t. It lays the foundation on which the subsequent edifice of g.e.t. has been built. in Radner's (1982, p. 925) words:

> One of the notable intellectual achievements of economic theory during the past 20 years has been the rigorous elaboration of the Walras-Pareto theory of value, i.e. the theory of the existence and optimality of competitive equilibrium. Although many economists

> and mathematicians contributed to this development, the resulting edifice owes so much to the pioneering and influential work of Arrow and Debreu that ... I ... refer to it as the 'Arrow-Debreu theory'.[32]

One should also note at this juncture that Debreu (1959) has provided the most complete, systematic and rigorous account of the existence conditions. This terse and elegant classic treats the subject

> with the standards of rigor of the contemporary formalist school of mathematics. The effort toward rigor substitutes correct reasonings and results for incorrect ones, but it offers other rewards too. It usually leads to a deeper understanding of the problems to which it is applied, and this has not failed to happen in the present case. It may also lead to a radical change of mathematical tools. In the area under discussion it has been essentially a change from the calculus to convexity and topological properties, a transformation which has resulted in notable gains in the generality and in the simplicity of the theory (Debreu, 1959, p. x).

Further clarifications (the irreducibility of the economy) were made by Gale (1960) and McKenzie (1959). A very general version of the existence theorem can be found in Debreu (1962). And the ensuing years saw many more refinements and reformulations.

The subsequent literature on g.e.t. is rich in re-examination, amendments, and weakening of the conditions under which an economic equilibrium exists. A proof of existence has become an essential component of a g.e. model and a basic test of its adequacy. Indeed, in an impressive survey, Debreu (1982) has listed some 350 papers that use a variant of the fixed-point theorem, or related approaches.[33] Debreu (1982, pp. 697–98) calls attention to four distinct, but closely related, approaches to the proof of existence question:

1. Application of Kakutani's fixed-point theorem that has remained of central importance.
2. Development of efficient algorithms of a combinatorial nature in the 1970s for the computation of approximate economic equilibria.
3. Use of the theory of fixed-point index of a map and the degree theory of maps.

4. More recent application of a differential process that generally converges to equilibrium (see also Scarf 1982, Dierker 1982, and Smale 1981).

In the last four decades or so there has been a striking increase in the sophistication of the mathematical tools of economic theory, from differential calculus and the calculus of matrices to convex analysis, general topology, algebraic topology, integration theory, differential topology, and global analysis. But there has been something of a 'renaissance of calculus' due in part to Debreu (1962) and his colleagues at Berkeley, Stephen Smale (1976b and 1981) and Andreu Mas-Colell (1985, see also Chapter 7 of this volume). As Debreu often emphasizes, different tools are used to tackle different economic problems. One should note Smale's (1976b, pp. 290–91) explanation of this renaissance, of which only excerpts can be given here:

> The existence theory of the static approach is deeply rooted to the use of the mathematics of fixed-point theory. Thus one step in the liberation from the static point of view would be to use a mathematics of a different kind. . . .
>
> I think it is fair to say that for the main existence problems in the theory of economic equilibria, one can now bypass the fixed-point approach and attack the equations directly to give existence of solutions, with a simpler kind of mathematics with dynamic and algorithmic overtones. . . .
>
> Behind my own work on the questions of dynamics in economics, lies certain fundamental work in the equilibrium theory in terms of calculus. . . .
>
> My own work, 'Global Analysis and Economics', has been to try to systematize the use of calculus in equilibrium theory. This can be justified on several grounds. First, the theory is brought closer to the practice. With calculus, one has in the derivative a linear approximation. It is these linear conditions that are so basic to practical economic studies. Comparative statics depend on derivatives; the same is usually true for stability conditions; dynamic questions are more accessible via calculus. When general equilibrium theory is developed on calculus mathematics, not only is theory brought closer to practice, but greater unity is achieved. Furthermore, recent work on approximation by differentiable

> functions in economics gives further justification to the use of calculus.

Some mathematical economists of the younger generation have implicitly criticized both Hicks's *Value and Capital* and Samuelson's *Foundations of Economic Analysis* for not seriously questioning whether competitive equilibrium exists or not. With hindsight, Hicks (1983, pp. 374–5) reflects that his contribution is not really affected by such criticism.

> Existence, from my point of view, was a part of the hypothesis; I was asking, if such a system existed, how would it work? I can understand that for those who are concerned with the defence of 'capitalism', to show the possibility of an arm's length equilibrium (an 'Invisible Hand') is a matter of importance. But that was not, and still is not, my concern.

Certainly A–D is not concerned with the defence of capitalism and Sir John's snide remark is perhaps a misunderstanding. And, in a slightly different vein, Hicks (1983, p. 361) remembers that in 1946 he visited the US, where he met Samuelson, Arrow, Friedman, and Patinkin who prized his *Value and Capital* as the 'beginning of *their* "neo-classical synthesis"'. With their more sophisticated mathematical skills, these economists and their contemporaries were refining the analysis that Hicks had only outlined.

> But I am afraid I disappointed them; and have continued to disappoint them. Their achievements have been great; but they are not in my line. I have felt little sympathy with the theory for theory's sake, which has been characteristic of one strand in American economics; nor with the idealisation of the free market, which has been characteristic of another; and I have little faith in the econometrics on which they have so largely relied to make their contact with reality. But I make no pretence that in 1946 I was even beginning to get clear about all this. It took me many years before I could even begin to define my new position.

Samuelson is ambivalent on the importance of the question of existence and its rigorous proof (see 1947, p. 257; Dorfman, Samuelson, and Solow, Chapter 13; Samuelson, 1966, pp. 493–504). He (1983b, p. 988) asserts that 'having lived as a scholar in both the pre-

and post-Debreu era, I can testify that the modern proofs are better than what used to pass muster for demonstration of determinate economic equilibrium'. But, at the same time, Samuelson (1983a, p. xix) is clearly dubious about the achievements of sophisticated mathematical techniques applied to economics.

> More can be less. Much of mathematical economics in the 1950s gained in elegance over poor old Pareto and Edward Chamberlin. But the fine garments sometimes achieved fit only by chopping off some real arms and legs. The theory of cones, polyhedra, and convex sets made possible 'elementary' theorems and lemmas. But they seduced economists away from the phenomena of increasing returns to scale and nonconvex technology that lie at the heart of oligopoly problems and many real-world maximizing assignments. Easy victories over a science's wrong opponents are hollow victories – at least almost always.

3.2 Stability

Having addressed the question of existence and welfare properties of competitive equilibrium, Arrow (in collaboration with Hurwicz and others) turned his attention to a systematic and rigorous study of the formidable question of stability of general competitive equilibrium; that is, 'whether or not the . . . time path converges to an equilibrium. Global stability means that convergence occurs for any initial conditions; local stability that the path converges for initial conditions sufficiently close to an equilibrium' (Arrow, 1983b, p. 125). As Chipman (1965b, p. 36) put it, 'the real content of the equilibrium concept is to be found not so much in the state itself as in the laws of change which it implies; that is, in the tendencies to move towards it, away from it, or around it' (see also Arrow and Hahn, 1971, pp. 263–4, 353, 386–8; Dorfman, Samuelson, and Solow, p. 408). Whatever interpretation one accepts, one need keep in mind that the concept of stability refers to the models of g.e. and in no sense to the real world.

The centrality of the question, whether there are endogenous processes at work in an economy that may drive towards equilibrium, was well articulated by Arrow (1984b, p. 157):

> Who exactly is it that is achieving the balancing of supply and

demand? Where in fact is the information on bids and offers needed for equilibration actually collected and stored? . . . It was Walras' auctioneer which proved to have the most enduring effect on subsequent theoretical development, and the stability theory which flows from that concept is still the subject of vigorous theoretical development, though very little empirical application. What is envisioned is a feedback mechanism in which errors in the price are successively corrected by reference to the disequilibria they generate.

Hicks's (1939b) generalization of Walras's much maligned treatment of stability (tâtonnements)[34] was essentially static and not derived from explicitly dynamic considerations, as Samuelson (1966, p.563) has so clearly shown (see also Arrow, 1983b, pp. 114, 124 and Arrow and Hurwicz 1977, pp. 332–5). Indeed, the genesis of the real dynamic stability analysis can be traced to Samuelson's specification, in his pioneering 1941 work on the relevance of dynamics for statics, of the necessary and sufficient conditions for stability.

Although not bereft of certain pitfalls, 'dynamic analysis has produced many useful results. In the field of pure theory, the important problem of *stability of equilibrium* is wholly a question of dynamics. For it involves the question of how a system behaves after it has been distrubed into a disequilibrium state' (Samuelson, 1966, p. 613). The problem of stability of equilibrium cannot be meaningfully considered without explicitly specifying the dynamics of the adjustment process (see Hahn, 1983).

It is of some interest to note how Hahn traces the development of the subject. In a recent tribute to Samuelson, Hahn (1983, p. 49) points out that

> it was not long after the publication of *Value and Capital* that Samuelson wrote the important paper noting that the Hicksian stability analysis lacked a true dynamics. Samuelson showed that neither *perfect* nor *imperfect* stability as defined by Hicks was necessary or sufficient for true dynamic stability. . .
>
> Since in the event Samuelson only dealt with local (asymptotic) stability and since he took equilibrium prices to be strictly positive, he did not worry about the behaviour of the system when some price was zero. But rather surprisingly, he gave no economic account of this model of the price-mechanism. *Tâtonnement* is not

listed in the index of the *Foundations* and is, as far as I have been able to discover, nowhere discussed by Samuelson. The excess demands are written as functions of prices only, that is, endowments are not included. And so it came about that he did not consider processes in which endowments are changing in the process of exchange, nor did he discuss this matter.

It is clear – especially with the hindsight of 1980 – that imperfect stability is a nonstarter for true dynamic stability. If we work with excess supplies, the condition can be translated into the requirement that the principal minors of order $(n-1)$ of the excess supply Jacobian should be of the same sign as the full Jacobian determinant. Clearly this is neither necessary nor sufficient for the real parts of the roots of the Jacobian to be positive (recall that we are dealing with excess supplies). Perfect stability, on the other hand, requires all the principal minors of the Jacobian to be positive. That this is not necessary for the local stability of Samuelson's price system is clear. Samuelson produced an example . . . to show that it was not sufficient either. The stage was set for the search of sufficient conditions that culminated in the famous papers by Arrow, Hurwicz, and Block.

In a landmark study in the late 1950s, Arrow and Hurwicz, followed by a sequel with Block (see Arrow and Hurwicz, 1977, pp. 199–228, 228–58), superseded the earlier literature and provided results that to this day essentially represent the standard formulation of global stability (see Fisher, 1976, p. 8; Negishi, 1962). They (Arrow and Hurwicz, 1977, p. 199) start out by noting significant gaps in the theory of economic dynamics, especially in stability of equilibrium. Though they praise Samuelson for his 'systematic treatment in the context of economic dynamics', they criticize him for not fully exploring 'the implications of the assumptions underlying the perfectly competitive model'. Like other contributors to the literature (for example, Lange, 1944; Metzler, 1945; and Morishima, 1952), Samuelson concentrated on the relationship between 'true dynamic stability' and the notion of Hicksian stability, instead of zeroing in on whether or not, under given assumptions, stability (in either sense) would come about. Though Hicksian stability cannot be identified with 'true dynamic stability', Arrow and Hurwicz (1977, p. 199) claim that it is of 'considerable interest' for two reasons: first

> there are situations where the two concepts are equivalent; second, because the equilibrium whose 'stability' Hicks studied is indeed *competitive* equilibrium... But again, little is known about conditions under which Hicksian stability prevails. There is thus a gap in this field and our aim is to help fill it (see also Arrow and Hurwicz, 1977, pp. 317–30).

The pathbreaking results of global (rather than local) stability of the competitive economy, under gross substitutability, are obtained by Arrow and Hurwicz by creatively adapting the Lyapunov method. The global approach is pursued wherever possible, but in certain cases only local results are obtained. Confining themselves only to the cases studied, they establish the stability of the system under the perfectly competitive (instantaneous or lagged) adjustment process. As they (1977, p. 205) put it:

> (a) where equilibrium is unique (as, for instance, in the gross substitution case) we have found global stability in some of the cases studied, while in others local stability has been proved (with the question of global stability remaining unresolved); (b) where there is a possibility of multiple equilibria ... we have found in the class of cases studied that the *system* is stable ... even though some equilibria may be locally unstable.

However, they warn that the study is fragmentary in character and, hence, provides no grounds for general assertions about the stability of the competitive system.[35] In this connection one must mention Smale's (1976a and 1976b) *tâtonnement* process as essentially solving the stability problem, though perhaps in an artificial way.

Arrow and Hurwicz (1977) contains a wealth of stimulating papers on the working of the economic system as a mechanism for optimal allocation of resources. Space limitation prevents us from a detailed study, but we would be remiss not to call attention to Arrow's germinal and influential 1959 paper on the foundations of price adjustment where he (Arrow and Hurwicz, 1977, p. 380) argues that there is a logical gap in the conventional models of competitive equilibrium – that is, 'there is no place for a rational decision with respect to prices as there is with respect to quantities'. He suggests a proposal to fill this gap which 'implies that perfect competition can really prevail only at equilibrium' and hopes 'that the line of development proposed will lead to a better understanding of the behavior of the economy in disequilibrium conditions'. Arrow (Arrow and Hurwicz, 1977, pp. 387–8) draws some interesting conclusions. Among them are the following: In any disequilibrium state there is a tendency to monopolize and to discriminate by prices. Also, 'the incomplete competitiveness of the economy under disequilibrium conditions implies a departure from the maximum of possible efficiency in the use of resources'. Furthermore, 'one would expect considerable departures from maximum efficiency in conditions of severe disequilibrium, such as inflation and depressions'.

For the sake of brevity we can do no better than to refer the reader to Chapter 4 of this volume where Hurwicz shares with us his interpretation of the significance of stability analysis and his reflections on the strengths and limitations of his contributions with Arrow and on the subsequent developments, particularly by Scarf and Gale, and his own research enterprise on design of economic systems that possess more universal stability properties.

Despite the progress made, stability analysis remains to this day the Achilles heel of g.e.t. The subject also seems to have gone out of fashion, perhaps because it is too difficult to tackle with the tools at hand. Radner (1982, p. 924) calls attention to a general agreement that

> even for the case of certainty, the theory of adjustment and stability of competitive markets is in a less satisfactory state than are the theories of existence and optimality of general equilibrium. The situation is no better for the case of uncertainty, where it is natural to pose the questions in terms of the convergence of a stochastic process to a stationary process (see also Mirrlees, 1979).

In a recent survey, Frank Hahn (1982, p. 747), one of the most adept practitioners of the fine art of self-criticism, concludes:

> A great deal of skilled and sophisticated work has gone into the study of processes by which an economy could attain an equilibrium. Some of the (mainly) technical work will surely remain valuable in the future. But the whole subject has a distressing ad hoc aspect. There is at present no satisfactory axiomatic foundation on which to build a theory of learning, of adjusting to errors and of delay times in each of these. It may be that in some intrinsic sense such a theory is impossible. But without it this branch of the subject can aspire to no more than the study of a series of suggestive examples (see also Hahn, 1973, p. 8).

4 EXISTENCE AND EFFICIENCY

The conclusive proof of the existence of equilibrium started a new phase in g.e.t. Now we can speak of three principal theorems of g.e.t.: (1) Under appropriate conditions, a competitive equilibrium exists, and (2) and (3) refer to the previously discussed First and Second Fundamental Theorems of Welfare Economics respectively (see also Maskin and Roberts, 1980). As Arrow (1983b, p. 290) put it, 'in particular, the close link between Pareto efficiency and competitive equilibrium is the central result for both analysis and policy'.

Essentially a notable achievement of A–D (1954) has not only been to demonstrate that a coherent and orderly economic allocation can be theoretically achieved, but to specify precisely what conditions must be satisfied to obtain this result. By elucidating the requisite conditions, they helped to show not only what the world would have to be like for the results to be achieved, but also allowed us to focus on the absence of some of these conditions in real-world configurations[36] and to attempt to remedy these situations by designing appropriate policy measures – at least to try. They have also helped us to spotlight the shifting nature of industrial organization and market structures.

Essentially, competitive equilibrium can be broadly depicted in terms of a set of non-negative prices (such that equate demand and supply on each market) for all commodities in an economy where there are two kinds of price-taking agents: households and firms. Each household is endowed with certain initial resources, possibly including claims to shares in producers' profits. It chooses its consumption mix from among all consumption possibility sets so as to maximize its utility at a given set of prices and subject to its budget constraint. Each firm chooses its production mix from a set of feasible production possibility sets so as to maximize profits at the same given prices. The chosen mixes must be compatible with each other so that aggregate consumption does not exceed initial resources plus aggregate net production. The underlying notion in this depiction is that the individual agent is bereft of market power. Hence key roles are played by the parametric function of prices and the identity of prices for all agents. Another crucial implication is that there are neither information nor transaction costs (see Arrow and Hurwicz, 1977, pp. 384–5).

In fairly simplified form (see Arrow, 1983b, pp. 115–20, 135–42, 160–72, 217–20) we can state that, subject to 'standard assumptions', a competitive equilibrium exists if convexity of household indifference maps and firm production possibility sets prevails, even if universality (completeness) of markets (including those for externalities) does not. If, however, universality of market prevails, the First Fundamental Welfare Theorem holds; that is, a competitive equilibrium is Pareto efficient. In addition, if both universality of markets and convexity of household indifference maps and firm production possibility sets prevail, then the Second Fundamental Welfare Theorem holds; that is, any Pareto-efficient allocation can be effected as a competitive equilibrium through an appropriate redistribution of initial endowments. (The Second Fundamental Theorem also requires continuous preferences, so that indifference maps do exist, and some interiority assumption to rule out Arrow's 'exceptional case' [Arrow 1983b, p. 39]. In Chapter 4 of his forthcoming *Welfare Economic Theory*, Hammond rules this out by considering only 'relevant commodities'.) In such a case criticism of the system can be narrowed down to dissatisfaction with income distribution. The price system determines income distribution only by maintaining the original state. If the original state is not considered satisfactory and if costless lump-sum, transfers can be accomplished, then a social mechanism for redistribution is required.

However, one must bear in mind that redistributive transfers are costly in terms of loss of incentives. Any proposed tax will as a rule cause a price distortion and the redistribution will cause an inefficiency even if the market's operation after the transfer is unhampered. Hence the concept of Pareto efficiency will have to be modified to account for the redistributive losses, as Arrow (1983b, pp. 290–302) sets out to do (see also Hammond 1985, pp. 418-22).

In his Nobel lecture Arrow (1983b, pp. 222–3) stresses that the main lesson of g.e.t. is to explain to what extent independent private decisions, co-ordinated through the market, can achieve a social allocation of resources. It also assures us that the result of the allocation is Pareto efficient. But he (1983b, p. 223) sees nothing in the process that

> guarantees that the distribution be just. Indeed, the theory teaches us that the final allocation will depend on the distribution of initial supplies and of ownership of firms. If we want to rely on the virtues of the market but also to achieve a more just distribution, the theory suggests the strategy of changing the initial distribution

rather than interfering with the allocation process at some later stage.

One should note, however, that the final allocation can in practice be achieved in some other institutional setting than the decentralized market mechanism, 'for example, by a computer which has been provided with all the relevant facts, the preferences and production possibilities for all individuals and productive units, and the initial endowments of all factors' (Arrow, 1983a, p. 176).

Another important question that Arrow (1967, p. 734) emphasizes is 'the relation between microeconomics and macroeconomics'. Moreover, in view of some of the other lacunae or shortcomings of the real world market system (such as the non-existence of all relevant markets and non-convexities), thrown into sharper relief in the light of the assumptions made in modern g.e.t., Arrow (1983b, p. 223) also sees 'a great many other situations in which the replacement of market by collective decision making is necessary or at least desirable'.

Convexity really does perform a crucial role in the proof of existence; it is also a very restrictive assumption and empirically very vulnerable. In production it rules out the presence of considerable indivisibilities or increasing returns to scale that usually characterize mass production technology and in consumption it disregards situations where extremes are preferred to mixed assortments. Thus how far these assumptions can be weakened is an extremely fruitful investigation. Though the convexity assumptions cannot be fully dispensed with, further research (see *inter alia*, Farrell, 1959; Rothenberg, 1960; Aumann, 1966; Starr, 1969; Arrow and Hahn, 1971, Chapter 7) has helped to relax them by suggesting weakened convexity assumptions if the indivisibilities are not large relative to the economy.[37] In other words, if each agent is small in relation to the whole economy, by choosing appropriate prices and composition of consumption and production assortments, the disparity between supply and demand can be rendered small relative to the size of the market. Surely households being relatively small fit this pattern best; here non-convexities in individual preferences do not significantly affect the existence of equilibrium. But increasing returns to scale over a large range relative to the economy may pose a threat to the existence of equilibrium and substantial increasing returns to scale are incompatible with the existence of a perfectly competitive equilibrium.

Obviously, only under the assumption of perfect competiton does a properly operating market system lead to efficiency. The proclivity to monopolize is an intrinsic characteristic of the profit system and hampers efficiency. Arrow feels strongly about the need to incorporate imperfect competiton into g.e.t. He not only reminds us constantly of this lacuna, but is at the forefront in attempting to go some way towards rectifying this unpalatable situation (see Chapter 2 of this volume).

In 1971, in a paper on the rigorous treatment of the (price-making) firm in g.e.t. and analysis of existence under varying sets of assumptions, Arrow (1983b, pp. 156–98) generated new results. He acknowledged that the firm is an amorphous entity in the standard A–D model. On the other hand,

> among the literary economists in the Anglo-American tradition, a kind of orthodoxy has emerged, in the U-shaped cost curve for the firm plus free entry. In more modern language, the production possibility set of the the typical firm displays an initial tendency toward increasing returns followed at higher scales by decreasing returns. The first phase is explained by indivisibilities, the second by the decreasing ability of the entrepreneur.

Arrow (1983b, pp. 157–8) reminds us that the A-D model treats the sets of firms as fixed and assumes the convexity of the production possibility sets, thus excluding the possibility of an initial phase of increasing returns to scale. But the model is compatible with either constant or decreasing returns to scale. The treatment of entrepreneurship in this model can be variously interpreted.

> In static theories of general equilibrium and in the absence of monopoly, then, the individual firm has been characterized by diminishing returns, a phenomenon associated with the vague concept of entrepreneurship. Kalecki ... suggested long ago that the reasons for limitation on the size of the firm might be found in dynamic rather than static considerations. Recent years have seen the beginning of dynamic analysis of the firm. From the point of view of realism and of interpretation of observations, these are a major advance. But on the production side they still retain the basic structure of the static model...
>
> However, dynamic analysis may have deeper implications if we depart from the analysis of stationary states. The firm must now

> serve some additional roles. In the absence of futures markets, the firm must serve as a forecaster and as a bearer of uncertainty. Further, from a general equilibrium point of view, the forecasts of others become relevant to the evaluation of the firm's shares and therefore possibly of the firm's behavior. The general equilibrium to be analyzed is, in the first instance, the equilibrium of a moment, *temporary equilibrium* in the terminology of Hicks (Arrow, 1983b, pp. 159–60).

Arrow (1983b, pp. 172–97) explores the exact relation of such a model of the firm to a generalized g.e. model. He formulates a model of monopolistic competitive equilibrium, with the firm as price maker, and analyzes it for existence. Arrow's model is a formalization of Chamberlin's case of monopolistic competition with large numbers. It makes weaker assumptions than those made in the previous notable formalization by Negishi (1960–61). Arrow does not explicitly treat product differentiation. Neither does he consider the notion of free entry. The significant question of conditions under which monopolistic behavior is continuous is left unanswered. Arrow's formulation is, in fact, very general and compatible with utility- and profit-maximizing behavior. The assumption of continuity may, however, be strong; in fact, it attributes no role to increasing returns as a barrier to entry. Moreover, this type of model neglects the oligopoly interdependence problem–the mutual recognition of power among firms. Also the model does not treat uncertainty. Whatever its merits, the model poses significant difficulties in interpretation.[38] Arrow's model was probably the first to draw out some of the problems in formulating equilibrium in a stock market – problems that Diamond (see Diamond and Rothschild 1978, pp. 211–25) avoided by a special assumption.

Some of these subjects are pursued in the innovative chapters on g.e. under alternative assumptions and on markets with non-convex preferences and production of Arrow and Hahn (1971, Chapters 6 and 7). Here the concentration is on existence of equilibrium extended to the troublesome cases of externalities, intertemporal economy with limited futures markets, and the ability of some firms to exercise monopolistic or monopsonistic power over certain markets.

In summing up, and as a background to what follows, we could do no better than to refer to Arrow's 1971, (pp. 144–5) answer to the question:

to what extent does perfect competition lead to an optimal allocation of resources? We know from years of patient refinement that competition ensures the achievement of a Pareto optimum under certain hypotheses. The model usually assumes among other things, that (1) the utility functions of consumers and the transformation functions of producers are well-defined functions of the commodities in the economic system, and (2) the transformation functions do not display indivisibilities (more strictly, the transformation sets are convex). The second condition needs no comment. The first seems to be innocuous but in fact conceals two basic assumptions of the usual models. It prohibits uncertainty in the production relations and in the utility functions, and it requires that all the commodities relevant either to production or to the welfare of individuals be traded on the market. This will not be the case when a commodity for one reason or another cannot be made into private property.

We have then three of the classical reasons for the possible failure of perfect competition to achieve optimality in resource allocation: indivisibilities, inappropriability, and uncertainty.

5 CHOICE UNDER UNCERTAINTY

To recall, A–D (1954) does not treat uncertainty.[39] Paradoxically at the time it was being written, Arrow was participating in a history-making conference in Paris on the foundations of risk bearing organized in June 1952 by the Centre National de la Recherche Scientifique. The star-studded cast of participants also included Maurice Allais, Milton Friedman, Pierre Massé, Jacob Marschak, and Leonard Savage. At that conference, Arrow (1983b, pp. 48–57) presented the path-breaking, ingeniously simple concept of contingent securities later extended and incorporated in the g.e. model by Debreu (1959). In this 1953 contribution, Arrow (1983b, pp. 48–57) essentially uses theory – in Vernon Smith's (1974, p. 97) felicitous turn of phrase – 'to derive the performance characteristics of non-observed economies and institutions suggested by a reinterpretation of the arguments and equations of a received theory, or by a mathematical formalism'. It very simply lifts the barriers of certainty that constrict the g.e. model by an artful dodge – the reindexing of commodity space which turns a given commodity today into another tomorrow and yet another the day after depending on the states of nature then.

Indeed, basically, until Arrow's 1953 *tour de force*, formal economic theory was strongly cast in terms of the certainty assumption. This, of course, does not mean that there was no recognition of uncertainty; only that there was no rigorous foundations for explicitly incorporating uncertainty into g.e.t.[40] As Drèze (1974, p. 4) notes, the present generation, reared in the field after 1952, can still get a full flavour of the *ancient régime* from Arrow's (1984a, pp. 5–41) masterful 1951 survey. Arrow's paper 'presents, in an orderly manner, a spectrum of approaches and results that could, at that time, be grasped only by those who had fully mastered a highly diversified literature'.

As an introduction to this section and the following one, which are so closely interrelated, we should call attention to the fact that Arrow's interest in the extension of g.e.t. to transactions over time and under conditions of uncertainty is deeply rooted in his scientific and even practical training. Even as an undergraduate he was strongly attracted to the field of mathematical statistics which he seriously pursued during his graduate work at Columbia. The concept of uncertainty and its relationship to information came naturally. As he (1984b, pp. 138–9) often points out, 'statistics is, indeed, the science of extracting information from a body of data. More specifically, in the theory of design of experiments, R. A. Fisher, Jerzy Neyman, Abraham Wald, and a long line of successors have grappled with the problem of allocating scarce resources to maximize the information attained'. Furthermore, 'statistical method was an example for the acquisition of information. In a world of uncertainty it was no great leap to realize that information is valuable in an economic sense. Nevertheless, it has proved difficult to frame a general theory of information as an economic commodity, because different kinds of information have no common unit that has yet been identified' (Arrow, 1984b, p.v.). After all, 'the most usual doctrine represents uncertainty by probabilities . . . It certainly is the only theory that has shown itself to be useful in deriving any results' (Arrow, 1984b, p. 198).

During the war, as a weather officer in the Department of the Navy, Arrow certainly was in constant close touch with uncertainty. To satisfy his 'depression-born' needs for job security, while he was a graduate student in economics he sat for the examinations of the

Actuarial Society of America. Earlier, in the summer of 1940, he had worked as an actuarial clerk in a small insurance company. During this brief encounter with the actuarial world he imbibed some of the concepts with which insurance practice was dealing (see infra pp. 80–1). These stood him in good stead in his perception of adverse selection; that information is unevenly distributed, which he derived from his study of medical care (Arrow, 1963). In fact, differential (asymmetric, imperfect) information is widespread throughout the economy. It has caused inefficiencies, but has also given rise to contractual arrangements and institutions to safeguard the less-well-informed participants. In these areas Arrow's contributions have been conceptual not technical; they have constituted rather a way of looking at relationships that has helped to set economic theory on different tracks. 'I laid out the basic problems for economic analysis suggested by differential information, though it remained for others to make a positive contribution to their analysis' (Arrow, 1984b, p. 78).

And yet another stream of thought that has led to the confluence, discussed in this and the next section, is Arrow's continuous preoccupation with individual choice as a basic element of, and closely linked to, the developments in g.e.t (and collateral to his great contribution to the theory of social choice). Whatever the reinterpretations, criticisms, and reservations, since Jevons, Menger, and Walras, the 'individualistic view', and the hypothesis that agents maximized utility subject to a budget constraint, has been a staple argument in mainstream economic theory. On the whole uncertainty was neglected, though a theory of choice under uncertainty was at hand since Bernoulli (1738) who argued that the economic agent acts so as to maximize the mathematical expection of his utility.

> Broadly speaking, utility theory is concerned with the problem of choice by an individual from a set of alternative possibilities available to him . . .
> The prices and income together limit the range of alternative commodity bundles among which the consumer may choose. They thus define what Pareto has called the 'obstacles'. The utility theory of choice states that the choice in any given situation depends on an interaction of the externally given obstacles with the *tastes* of the individual, and that the obstacles and tastes can be thought of as independent variables (Arrow, 1984a, pp. 117–18).

Pareto recognized that the subjective theory of value is a statement about the consistency of choices made under varying conditions (see Pareto, 1971, Chapters 3–5; Ricci, 1933; and Hicks, 1983, pp. 13 and *passim*). Arrow (1984a, p. 56) describes the so-called *rational model of choice under certainty* (or decision making)[41] as follows:

> an individual is assumed to rank all alternative logically possible decisions in order of preference; in any given situation, only some of the logically possible alternatives are in fact available, due to budgetary or other limitations, and the individual is assumed to choose among the alternatives available that one which is highest on his ranking. The ranking or *ordering* is assumed to have the usual consistency properties so that, if alternative *A* is preferred to alternative *B*, and *B* to *C*, then *A* is preferred to *C*.

Logically such a theory is not vacuous; but Arrow (1984a, p. 56) perceives it as generally not overly meaningful. He seems to agree with Herbert Simon that 'that more important part of the content of a rational model of choice in any particular context lies in the specification of the range of alternatives actually available, and, it might be added, in more specific hypotheses about the underlying ordering'.

The concept of rationality has become an intrinsic part of economic theory. Even in a world of certainty it is only a weak hypothesis. More recently, however, much stronger versions of this hypothesis have emerged applied to a world of uncertainty, especially in studying criteria for consistency in allocations over time, the expected-utility hypothesis of behaviour under certainty, and the so-called Bayesian hypothesis for learning. In his 1981 presidential address to the Western Economic Association, Arrow (1984a, pp. 261–70) reminds us that the rationality hypotheses were not only ridiculed by some economists (such as Veblen) as soon as they began to be employed by others and that they continue to be under strong justifiable attack (*inter alia*, by Simon),[42] but that 'an important class of intertemporal markets shows systematic deviations from individual rational behavior and that these deviations are consonant with evidence from very different sources collected by psychologists' (Arrow, 1984a, pp. 269–70).

Voicing his discontent with the existing state of economic theory, in yet another presidential address (to the American Economic Association in 1973), Arrow (1984b, p. 154) quipped that 'the uncertainties about economics are rooted in our need for a better understanding of the economics of uncertainty; our lack of economic knowledge is, in good part, our difficulty in modeling the ignorance of the economic agent'.

Obviously, uncertainty has its roots in the economic agents' imperfect knowledge of the future, but it is also a property of many current or short-run decisions.

> Certainly a most salient characteristic of the future is that we do not know it perfectly. Our forecasts, whether of future prices, future sales, or even the qualities of goods that will be available to us for use in production or consumption, are surely not known with certainty, and they are known with diminishing confidence as the future extends. Hence, it is intrinsic in the decision-making process, whether in the economic world or in any other, that the opportunities available, the consequences of our decisions are not completely known to us (Arrow, 1984b, pp. 136–7).

Economic agents make contemporaneous decisions without having all the relevant information about prices, quality of goods available, technologies, and the like, and they have to engage in costly search (see Arrow, 1984a, pp. 137–8, 165–6).

Basically, we need a special theory to explain behaviour under uncertainty because of two considerations:

> (1) subjective feelings of imperfect knowledge when certain types of choices, typically involving commitments over time, are made; (2) the existence of certain observed phenomena, of which insurance is the most conspicuous example, which cannot be explained on the assumption that individuals act with subjective certainty (Arrow, 1984a, p. 172).

Arrow (1984a, p. 60) has summarized the *rational model of choice under uncertainty* as follows:

> There are a number of possible states of nature and a number of possible actions we can take. We do not know which state of nature, among a certain class, is the true one. We have to take an action the consequences of which will depend upon which state of nature is the true one. The problem is to choose which action to take among those which satisfy the constraints of the situation. The consequences are completely determined by the action and the state of nature, and presumably are ordered as in the case of certainty.

When agents make choices in dynamic situations, expectations of the future – their impact on behaviour and the process of their formation – become relevant. In line with the rationality behaviour postulate, it is expected that expectation formation is a process of rational learning from experience. In other words, that the individual compares his expectations with the event after it has occurred and thus revises future expectations in the direction of the actual result. But experimental evidence only partly supports this postulate (see Arrow, 1984a, pp. 136–42, 264). A theory of expectations is needed to support utility theory when choice under uncertainty is involved. However, as Arrow (1984a, pp. 142–3) points out,

> some methods of forming expectations seem more rational than others, and, at least formally, one can treat the learning process itself as a process of successive choices by the individual. His domain of choice now is a *strategy* – that is, in each stage he finds his next step as a function of all the information available to him up to the present time.

Expected utilities do involve probabilities that are in the first instance subjective. Arrow (1984b, pp. 160–61) emphasizes that

> the economic agent observes his world and has the opportunity to learn from his experience, for there is a considerable degree of continuity. By Bayes's theorem or perhaps psychological learning theory, the probabilities, say of future prices, will gradually adjust so as to conform to the facts. If indeed the economic world exhibited the same structure in some sense from period to period, and if everybody observed everything relevant, then the probabilities ascribed by different individuals to the same events might be expected gradually to converge to the correct values and therefore be the same for all. In fact, of course, the basic economic facts are changing, partly endogenously because of capital accumulation in its most general sense, partly exogenously with predictable and unpredictable changes in technology and tastes; equally if not more important, though, is the fact that the dispersion of information which is so economical implies that different economic agents do not have access to the same observations. Hence, it is reasonable to infer that they will never come into agreement as to probabilities of future prices.

And one should not forget that the past influences the future, perhaps much more strongly than we would like to believe. It has been observed that 'individuals are unable to recognize that there will be many surprises in the future; in short, as much other evidence tends to confirm, there is a tendency to underestimate uncertainties' (Arrow, 1984a, p. 267).

Now, retracing our steps in a more orderly fashion, chronologically, over the landscape of Arrow's contributions to this field, we pause in awe in front of one of his early master works of technical skill, creativity, and logical simplicity: the concept of contingent securities – a theoretical device for risk sharing.[43]

For some time now economists have been aware that risk aversion is a strong trait among many individuals and that it may be helpful in explaining a number of real-world phenomena. However, this observation runs counter to another: individuals also have a propensity to gamble. In reconciling somewhat these two human proclivities, Arrow (1984a, p. 148) mentions but is agnostic about Friedman and Savage (1948), who have shown ad hoc that the expected-utility hypothesis is compatible with risk-averse behaviour when relatively large risks are at stake and a proclivity to gamble when smaller risks are involved, and by arguing that risk taking can be compatible with risk aversion when individuals evaluate risks subjectively. In Arrow's (1984a, p. 148) words, 'the gambler is one who believes the odds are more favourable to him than they really are; according to his *subjective* probabilities, the bet is favourable to him, but there is, for one reason or another, a divergence between the subjective and objective probabilities'. In one of his Yrjö Jahnsson lectures, delivered in 1963 in Helsinki, Arrow (1984a, pp. 147–71) elaborates on measures of risk aversion and shows that, together with expected-utility hypothesis, these measures can be employed for deriving quantitative, instead of only qualitative, results.[44]

When individuals are risk averse, institutions or markets for risk sharing develop. Risks are traded; they are shifted from those who benefit from sharing them, to those who benefit from bearing them, until costs and benefits are equated at the margin. Historically all kinds of insurance and the common stock market have been risk-shifting devices. So have been, in a way, the cost-plus contracts, bankruptcy and limited liability laws, and the building of large organizations (see Arrow, 1984b, pp. 78-86).

> When there is uncertainty, risk aversion implies that steps will be taken to reduce risks. This partly affects decisions within the firm,

> such as the holding of inventories and preference for flexible capital equipment, and partly leads to new markets which will shift risks to those most able and willing to bear them, particularly through the equity market. The rich development of inventory theory and portfolio theory in the last few decades reflects growing understanding of these matters (Arrow, 1984b, p. 160).

And Arrow's invention of the contingent market is another such, but theoretical, device for shifting risks, and for preventing uncertainty from destroying existing markets. In his (1984b, p. 165) words:

> There is an ultraneoclassical approach to the market treatment of uncertainties, in which I take some pride. That is the notion of a contingent market. Instead of letting uncertainty ruin existing markets, we can take it explicitly into account by buying and selling commitments to be carried out only if some uncertain event occurs. We could in principle imagine agreements to transact which will hold if and only if a given conceivable technological innovation does not take place, with a second market for transactions valid if the innovation does take place. Then we can restore the possibility of markets.

In other words, the contract for each contingent commodity specifies the delivery of a unit of a given commodity if a certain event has taken place. Given that the state of the world describes fully the demand and supply conditions, the contingent contracts can always be met since only what would be available in the state on which the contract is contingent has to be delivered. These contracts can specify prices. The commodity in the ordinary sense is replaced by a contingent commodity and the standard A–D model can be made to incorporate uncertainty. In Arrow's (1983b, pp. 221–2) words:

> Commodities in the ordinary sense are replaced by *contingent commodities*, promises to buy or sell a given commodity, if, and only if, a certain state of the world occurs. The market will then determine contingent prices. Clearing of the markets means clearing of the contingent markets; the commitments made are sufficiently flexible so that they can always be satisfied. It should be noted that preference orderings over vectors of contingent commodities contain elements of judgment about the likelihoods of different states of the world as well as elements of taste in the

ordinary sense. Other things being equal, one will invest less heavily in a demand contingent upon a state deemed unlikely.

In this manner, theoretically a set of contingent markets can be obtained.

> Each such market trades in contracts contingent upon the occurrence of one state of the world. The standard theorems of welfare economics would be valid in an economy with a complete set of contingent markets, if such an economy existed. Since there is a separate market for each contingency, the equilibrium allocation would be feasible. In fact, it would be Pareto optimal, in the sense that it would not be possible to find another allocation, feasible no matter what happens, for which every agent would have a higher expected utility (Arrow, 1981a, p. 112).

In view of the good deal of misunderstanding that surrounds this 'salvaging of the market under uncertainty', it cannot be overstressed that Arrow conceived the contingent market as a *theoretical* construct or benchmark designed to demonstrate how, as a logical proposition, the optimality properties associated with the competitive market can be rescued in an extended A–D economy.

More specifically, Arrow's pathbreaking paper on contingent securities (Arrow, 1983b, pp. 48–57)[45] extends the theory of optimal allocation of resources to conditions of subjective uncertainty. A pure exchange economy is considered (the appendix deals with extensions to production).[46] Each individual is assumed to act on the basis of subjective probabilities as to the states of nature. Optimal allocation of risk bearing can be solved by making such choices, under constraints, that no other choice will improve the welfare of every individual. The argument is that if markets for claims on all commodities exist, under certain hypotheses, the competitive market will result in an optimal allocation. Since in the real world risk bearing is allocated by money claims, Arrow shows that, again under certain hypotheses, competitive securities markets are, in fact, optimal for allocating risk bearing. One important implication of the hypotheses used is that the viability of competitive allocation of risk bearing is only guaranteed if individuals are risk averse.

In the appendix Arrow introduces production decisions in essentially the same framework. However, he notes that the definition of a commodity is significantly affected on the production side by the nature of the theory of uncertainty. If two units are to be considered as part of the same commodity, they have to perform the same function in production in any possible state of nature, which is not necessarily the case of machines, for example. Thus, for instance, if each machine has to be considered as a separate commodity, one can imagine that the number of commodities grows immensely and indivisibilities become much more common. In this manner, the g.e.t. that assumes convexity of the production structure becomes inapplicable and the welfare theorems and competitive allocation do not hold (see Arrow 1983b, pp. 55–6). And Arrow (1983b, p. 57) concludes on a realistic note:

> We have seen that it is possible to set up formal mechanisms which under certain conditions will achieve an optimal allocation of risk by competitive methods. However, the empirical validity of the conditions for the optimal character of competitive allocation is considerably less likely to be fulfilled in the case of uncertainty than in the case of certainty and, furthermore, many of the economic institutions which would be needed to carry out the competitive allocation in the case of uncertainty are in fact lacking.

Debreu (1984) praises the concept of contingent commodities as a classical illustration of the fruitfulness of the axiomatic method. In a paper he wrote while he was in France in 1953, on leave from the Cowles Commission, and published as Chapter 7 of his classic *Theory of Value*, Debreu, in turn, applied and extended Arrow's concept of contingent commodities.[47] Debreu (1959, p. 98) notes that he extends his analysis to

> the case where uncertain events determine the consumption sets, the production sets, and the resources of the economy. A contract for the transfer of a commodity now specifies, in addition to its physical properties, its location and its date, an event on the occurrence of which the transfer is conditional. This new definition of a commodity allows one to obtain a theory of uncertainty free from any probability concept and formally identical with the theory of certainty.

In Arrow's (1981a, pp. 108–9) words:

> The ideal picture of a competitive equilibrium with dated commodi-

> ties, as set forth . . . by Gerard Debreu, is one in which all markets open at the beginning of time. Sales and purchases for all future dates are made now and paid for in today's money. Once the markets close, there are no further transactions; future deliveries are made in accordance with the contracts already made, but there are no exchanges of goods for money. . .

> What is assumed is equivalent to nothing less than a universal regime of futures markets, now extended in all times and all commodities.

Arrow's elegant, simple, and yet novel concept has by now become a standard tool of analysis. But, with the benefit of hindsight, perhaps a further delving into its historical development might be helpful. During the eventful 1952 conference (and the preceeding year at an Econometric Society meeting) Allais (1953) presented an independently formulated model of g.e. under uncertainty by emphasizing the welfare optimality of g.e. There are a number of differences between Allais's and Arrow's contributions. Arrow accepted Bernoulli (1738) as updated by von Neumann and Morgenstern (1947) and Savage (1954) but he did not use the expected utility hypothesis throughout. Allais, on the other hand, strongly criticized this and accepted a variant of a general ordinalist position. Arrow, as he often does in some other cases, minimizes his own contributions and praises others. He (1983c, p. 22) notes that in his extension Debreu 'showed that the two models could be synthesized. A theory of general equilibrium in contingent contracts did not require the Bernoulli hypothesis; it was consistent with any utility function over the outcomes. Debreu also extended the theory to paths over time, in which the uncertainties are realized successively'.

Ever the pragmatist, Arrow is somewhat skeptical about the widespread use of this tool he has created.[48] He confesses to a slight unease about its being perhaps taken too literally at times. After all, he never perceived it as a realistic description of an actual economy, and intended only to provide an ideal standard against which the real-world conditions could be measured and the failures and departures assessed.[49]

> Clearly, the contingent commodities called for do not exist to the extent required, but the variety of securities available on modern markets serves as a partial substitute. In my own thinking, the

> model of general equilibrium under uncertainty is as much a normative ideal as an empirical description. It is the way the actual world differs from the criteria of the model which suggests social policy to improve the efficiency with which risk bearing is allocated (Arrow, 1983b, p. 222).

To recall, the existing forms of transactions that can be compared to contingent markets are insurance policies, cost-plus contracts, and the common stock market. But what about the futures markets? Arrow (1981a, p. 109) explains the futures contract as

> one in which a contract is made now for a future exchange of money against goods. In the intertemporal competitive equilibrium model, money now is exchanged against dated goods. It is easy to see that a complete set of markets for dated goods is equivalent to a complete set of futures markets plus one bond market for each maturity, in which money now is exchanged for money later. The bond market permits each agent to transfer income over time by buying and selling bonds of different maturities.
>
> This model, in either form, resembles the real world very little. It even omits a most important element in the understanding of actual futures markets, the existence of spot markets. Perhaps the real world has been missing a great opportunity for improved efficiency. But we know, of course, that many considerations have been omitted.
>
> I have spoken of the competitive equilibrium of this complete set of futures markets. We must be careful that all the assumptions implicit in this concept are met. One of these, taken almost for granted in our usual textbook presentations, is that the economic agents, the households and the firms, know their own tastes and their own opportunities for all the marketed commodities. These opportunities might be related in complex ways. In particular, the producers of the future commodites must know their supply conditions... It is also true that demanders must know the conditions under which they will use the goods. This requirement may be especially onerous for consumers that are not yet born.

The recent spread of futures markets, mostly on financial instruments, was expected to 'increase the efficiency of resource allocation, in particular because rational behavior on the part of participants would pool the information available and cause a futures price to be a best forecast, relative to the information available to the market. There has been considerable disappointment' (Arrow, 1984a, p. 265). One should note, however, that in some cases opening an extra asset market produces a Pareto-inferior allocation (see Hart 1975). Indeed, Arrow (1981a, p. 109) notes that 'the possibility of a complete set of futures markets, the ideal intertemporal competitive equilibrium, is vitiated by uncertainty'. And when uncertainty raises its head we squarely face the problems of information, its transmission, costs, and unequal distribution; the problems of information as a commodity 'with peculiar attributes, particularly embarrassing for the achievement of optimal allocation' (Arrow, 1971, p. 153).

6. INFORMATION, CENTRALIZATION, AND DECENTRALIZATION

6.1 Information as a Commodity

Economic literature abounds with praise for the informational parsimony of the market system. Indeed, in such a system the individual need know only his own motivation and production conditions (that is, his own utility function, production possibility set, and the prices of commodities he buys and/or sells), while the system encompasses huge quantities of information about other individuals that he need not know.[50] As Arrow (1984b, p. 158) put it:

> the apparent modesty of the information needed is one of the most appealing aspects of the neoclassical model, both in the descriptive sense that the individual's decision problems appear manageable for him and for the economist studying him, and in the normative sense that the system permits its members to spend their time and effort at producing goods rather than in unnecessary duplication of information.

The market system saves on information by encapsulating it in the form of the prices it transmits (see Hayek, 1940; Koopmans, 1970, p. 246). When the whole system is in equilibrium it appears to be very economical in processing information because we suspect that the process of conveying prices is considerably more streamlined and thus less expensive than the cumbersome process of conveying sets of utility functions and production possibilities. This point was actually at the heart of the interwar debate on the economic efficiency of socialism, to which we shall return later in this section. At this juncture, suffice it to say that though it was convincingly argued that the socialist system could use or rely on some version of the price system and thereby economize on information costs, no definitive measure of information and its costs was provided to evaluate the relative superiority of the decentralized price system over a centralized variant. In fact, though much has been clarified, such a measure is still not available (see Arrow, 1984b, p. 159).

Although this is not true of Arrow and many other economists, it appears that in the postwar years fashion in economics has shifted away from improving our comprehension of alternative designs of resource allocation (other than the genuine market) and towards a concentration on very tight versions of the market model. Be that as it may, Arrow (1981a, pp. 114–15) warns against the entirely too strong informational assumptions made by the sophisticated rational expectations models.

> We are all accustomed to the idea that the price system is an information mechanism, but really that term is usually a figure of speech. From the point of view of any agent in the system, prices determine opportunities and constraints. Only from the viewpoint of the economic analyst are the prices information. But some of the current models consider the price to be literally a source of information. The economic agents use it to make inferences. If the market price is higher than what a given agent expects on the basis of its private information, it infers that there are others who have different and more favorable information. This inference is itself information on the basis of which the agent modifies its demand behavior.
>
> Under some rather restrictive conditions, it is shown that the price which finally results from these considerations is in fact the same price that would appear if all the private information were made publicly available. It would in some sense be a statement that the futures markets are fully efficient mechanisms for aggregating information.

> I have some reservations about the descriptive power of these models and about their logical foundations. Indeed, the simultaneity of the process in which demands determine prices and prices alter the information which underlies the demands is troubling. It certainly leads to some paradoxical conclusions.

In a broad sense, this means that no true equilibrium exists: anybody who gathers information gains no benefit from it, so nobody is expected to gather information, so anybody who does gather some information can profit from it, so then everybody learns what that information is, and so on and so forth (see Grossman and Stiglitz, 1976).

If some sort of contingent markets, such as insurance against possible alternative outcomes do exist, uncertainty need not destroy the leading role prices play in resource allocation. As we know, such markets are scarce primarily due to the existence and distribution of information. Arrow (1984b, pp. 139–40) writes,

> Thus at a very minimum, recognition of the concept of information and its possible changes over time implies a considerable revision of the theory of general economic equilibrium in the form in which it has evolved over the last century and which has reached such a high level of power and depth at the hands of Hicks, Samuelson, Debreu, and others in the last several decades.

And, again shifting to the real-world economy, Arrow (1983b, p. 144) warns that because of high costs of transmission of information, uncertainty creeps into even basically certain situations. 'The typical economic agent simply cannot acquire in a meaningful sense the knowledge of all possible prices, even where they are each somewhere available. Markets are thus costly to use, and therefore the multiplication of markets, as for contingent claims as suggested above, becomes inhibited.'

Before proceeding any further, it may be useful to stress that in the last few years incomplete or asymmetric information has become one of the 'hottest themes in economic theory' (see Aumann, 1985, pp. 40–41). Whatever the final verdict of future historians on the 'information economics revolution' or on the effects of the explicit treatment of differential and costly-to-acquire information on the (non)-classical assumptions and results, it appears to have opened new channels of intellectual activity, raised serious questions, and provided important insights into the processes and organization of economic activity in this imperfect world of ours. The problems it poses often appear to be intractable and it is likely to remain one of the great and fruitful themes of economic research for years to come. It is important to stress how deeply the classical assumptions of perfect information were ingrained in the standard treatments in economics until quite recently, in order to appreciate the significance of the new research (see Green, 1985; Atkinson and Stiglitz, 1980, p. 349; Rothschild and Stiglitz, 1976).

Arrow has had an important impact in guiding research in these directions. In 1977 in the first annual lecture of the Geneva Association, Arrow (1984b, pp. 197–215) noted with satisfaction the burgeoning intellectual activity in the economics of information,[51] and the increasing recognition accorded to the concept of differential information as central to many features of economic organizations. He also surveyed some recent theoretical developments on the implication of differential information on the existence and efficiency properties of equilibria. Indeed, it is being increasingly recognized (see, *inter alia*, Rothschild and Stiglitz, 1976; Hildebrand (ed.,), 1982, pp. 95–120) that differential and costly information critically affects traditional competitive analysis and leads to fundamentally different and less robust results.

The individual agents' information structure (that is, both the state of knowledge at any particular time and the possibility of acquiring relevant information in the future) strongly influences the opportunities for risk sharing through the market. The information that the agent receives is transmitted as signals through so-called information channels. Each agent is supposedly able to receive some signals from the outside world, though his ability to do so is limited. This limitation is a key to understanding individual and organizational behaviour. Moreover, the agent has some expectations about the range of signals available to him and others at a given point of time and in the future and probabilities about receiving them. A signal can then change the agent's probability distribution and this alteration of probabilities is a part of the process of information gathering. Arrow (1984b, p.139) explains that he uses the statistician's model of information.

> The economic agent has at any moment a probability distribution over possible values of the variables interesting to him, such as

present and future prices or qualities of goods. Call these his *economic variables*. He makes an observation on some other variable; call it a *signal*. The distribution of the economic variables given the signal is different from the unconditional distribution. The decisions made depend, of course, on the distribution of economic variables; but if this distribution is in turn modified by the signals received, then economic behavior depends not only on the variables we usually regard as relevant, primarily prices, but also on signals which may themselves have little economic significance but which help reduce the uncertainty in predicting other as yet unobserved variables.

Signals that modify the distribution of economic variables include the past changes in the development of prices, past quantity movements, alterations in government economic policy, and the like. Thus, when taking information into account, we realize that non-price variables do play an important role in economic behaviour (see Arrow, 1983b, p. 280). Here we may find the way to explain the significance of quantity variables in the Keynesian system (see Clower, 1975; Neary and Stiglitz, 1983; Feiwel, 1985b, pp. 19–20 and *passim*). Arrow (1984b, p. 161) observes that

> it sometimes is held that in a neoclassical world only prices matter; in the absence of prices, presumably they are replaced by price expectations. But this is not strictly true. Under constant returns, at least, quantity information for the individual firm is needed even when neoclassical assumptions are strictly fulfilled. Neoclassically founded investment theories usually predict capital-output ratios or capital-labor ratios; they still need output forecasts explicitly or implicitly. This gives considerable, perhaps major weight to past quantity information in predicting the future and therefore in guiding current investment decisions. It is perhaps along these lines that Keynesian theory, with its overwhelming emphasis on quantity changes as equilibrating variables, can be founded firmly on individual optimizing behavior.

Non-price signals are important informational devices that lessen uncertainty and have economic relevance. However, Arrow (1984b, pp. 140–41) believes that two more implications of the presence of information that reduces uncertainty – namely, the economic value of information worth acquiring and transmitting even at a cost and the unequal distribution of information – have even more basic significance for reorienting economic theory.

> The economic value of information offers no great mysteries in itself. It is easy to prove that one can always do better, whether as a producer or as a consumer, by basing decisions on a signal, provided the signal and the economic variables are not independently distributed. But this remark has an implication for economic decisions; the economic agent is willing to pay for information, for signals (Arrow, 1984b, p.141).

Thus the agents seek to acquire more information of predictive value and others have an incentive to produce it. In this way an economic information industry appears with information gathering and producing activities. The operating efficiency of firms can no longer be reduced to productive efficiency; it has to encompass also predictive efficiency. Information then becomes, as Arrow (1984b, pp. 142–43, 162) points out, a commodity, but not quite. If for no other reason, information has at least two outstanding features that 'prevent it from being fully identified as one of the commodities represented in our abstract models of general equilibrium: (1) it is, by definition, indivisible in its use; and (2) it is very difficult to appropriate' (Arrow, 1984b, p. 142). Hence it would be fallacious to presume that in this case an unhampered interplay of market forces would achieve allocative efficiency. The government then plays a leading role in information gathering and processing.[52]

The two telling points that Arrow makes are worthy of elaboration:

1. For example, the same information about production methods is required no matter what the size of output is. Hence a mass producer has more incentive to gather higher-grade information and his per-unit costs of information gathering are lower. In this way information injects economies of scale which undermine the competitive economy.
2. The inappropriability characteristic can be found in practice in two cases referring to different kinds of information: (a) information is inappropriable because one does not lose it by transmitting it and (b) while transmission costs are often way below those of research, sometimes transmission costs are high and in such cases there is also inappropriability because the sale price fails to reflect the social value of the information. As we know from welfare economics primers, in the presence of inappropriability,

> public goods, decreasing-cost industries, and the like, private market decisions tend to go astray. The 'Invisible Hand' will fumble or tremble, the fundamental welfare theorems cannot hold, and there is a real threat of suboptimal production if not of disastrous outcomes.

It has often been stressed that in a competitive system the firm will tend to underinvest in research and development projects because the information thus acquired cannot be confined only to the firm that pays for the project and will spread throughout the economy (see Arrow, 1971, chapter 6; Nelson and Winter, 1982). On the other hand, if secrecy can be maintained overinvestment might occur as firms will covertly undertake similar research projects which, of course, will tax society's resources much more than if one project were undertaken and the information spread through the economy. Arrow (1984b, p. 143) makes the essential point

> that there will very likely be an overinvestment in the acquisition of information whose private value is to gain at the expense of others. One would suppose that the securities markets and the extensive apparatus for private information gathering there would exemplify this point. Further, the very acquisition of this information is apt to make the securities market less valuable as a means for risk sharing.

Traditionally, discussions of alternative mechanisms of resource allocation (whether economy-wide or within a large organization) tended to equivocate about the relative facility of the process of transmission of information. Whereas the desirability of decentralization presupposes that the transmission process is costly (were it not, all information about availability of resources and production technology could be transferred to one locus where the optimum allocation of resources could be instantly computed), the literature on the subject has been seeking algorithms that would reduce the amount of information to be transmitted but that would result in the fully optimal allocation of resources. If there were any real trade-off between information costs and other resource costs, an optimal allocation of resources that reckons with information costs would differ from one that does not (see Arrow, 1983e, p. 63).

Essentially, both information gathering and processing are costly endeavours. Any pedagogue is aware of the energy expanded in transmitting information and even more of the difficulties students encounter in absorbing it. Though some physical cost may be relatively low (such as buying a book), one must remember the major costs involved in coding the information for transmission and the limited channel capacity of the recipients.

The education system emits ability signals as a by-product of its main activity. The system may identify the more able individuals but not necessarily the more productive ones. In Arrow's (1984b, p.144) words:

> The educational system has become, partly inadvertently, an industry which sells signals for individuals to emit to the world. Its primary intended function is the acquisition of knowledge. But in the course of its own internal measuring of its success in this function, it automatically generates signals of ability in education. If it is in fact the case, or at least believed to be the case, that ability to produce is correlated with ability to absorb education, then the educational system does produce signals about productive ability.

In an innovative approach to the system of higher education in the early 1970s, Arrow (1984b, pp. 115–35) conceived of it as a filter; as a screening device for individuals of divergent abilities, and thus as a purveyor of information to the buyers of labour. Such a view of higher education does not entirely contradict the productivity-adding human capital theory. 'From the viewpoint of an employer, an individual certified to be more valuable is more valuable, to an extent which depends on the nature of the production function. Therefore, the filtering role of education is a productivity-adding role from the private viewpoint; but . . . the social productivity of higher education is more problematic' (Arrow, 1984b, p. 116). Arrow assumes that though the potential employer has information about the extent of a potential employee's education and has some statistical distribution of productivities given the information on hand, he cannot distinguish the productivities of two individuals about whom he has the same information. Also once the employees have been hired, the employer cannot really determine the marginal productivity of each individual and that is what he needs for allocative efficiency.

What is particularly important about the filter theory of education is that it is fully entrenched in Arrow's (1984b, p. 117) larger view that 'information in the real world is much more limited than that assumed in our usual equilibrium models'.

Arrow (1984b, pp. 145–7, 169–78) outlines some economic features of information. In the first place the individual is the primary input into the communication channels. It is through his sensory organs that information penetrates his brain and there is a processing capacity constraint on both. Though information may be stored in special devices, it has to be retrieved for decision-making (see Simon, 1982, pp. 171–85, 456). Arrow (1984b, p. 170) insists that he does not want

> to argue for fixed coefficients in information handling any more than in more conventional production activities; substitution of other factors especially computers, for the individual's mind is possible. But the individual's very limited capacity for acquiring and using information is a fixed factor in information processing, and one may expect a sort of diminishing returns to increases in other information resources.

Another important clue to information costs is that typically they are irreversible and in that sense are part of capital costs. Besides the physical investment in communications, in order to receive messages individuals have to make an investment in learning various codes (for example, languages and technical vocabularies) in which others have found it economical to send signals. Arrow (1984b, p. 171) formalizes the capital aspect of information as follows:

> A signal hitherto unheard is useless by itself; it does not modify any probability distribution. However, a preliminary sampling experiment in which the relation between the new signal and more familiar ones can be determined or at least estimated will serve to make valuable further signals of the new type. This experiment, which may be vicarious (education, scientific literature) is an act of investment.

The information stored in the individual's brain, though it can be transmitted to others, is not only irreversible, but it is also inalienable. It is, however, subject to depreciation. As in the case of other irreversible investments, the question of future demand for it emerges. Arrow (1984b, p. 171) ventures on two generalizations: 'One is that the demand for investment in information is less than it would be if the value of the information were more certain. The second, more important I would guess, is that the random accidents of history will play a bigger role in the final equilibrium'. Once the investment has been made and the information channels established, it is not only cheaper, but also more convenient, to go on using them. In fact, the established system may run into some danger of petrification in the long run. Arrow (1984b, p. 146) stresses that

> a communication channel is used to greatest capacity when it has an optimal code for transmitting messages. This 'code' need not be interpreted literally; the term refers to all patterns of communication and interaction within an organization, patterns which make use of conventional signals and forms which have to be learned. Once learned, however, it is cheaper to reuse the same system than to learn a new one; there is a payoff on the initial learning investment but no way of liquidating it by sale to others. If external conditions change, an originally optimal communication system may no longer be the one that would be chosen if the organization were to begin all over again. Eventually the communication system may be very inefficient at handling signals, and the firm may vanish or undergo a major reorganization.

Information costs are also characterized by non-uniformity in various directions. Individuals often find it easier to turn on some information flows rather than others that they have accumulated. The learning process generalizes felicitously and inexpensively in some areas, but not so in others. Communication is easier among people speaking the same language, the same 'technicalese', or belonging to similar occupations. Also in various occupations, individuals have different opportunities of learning by doing (Arrow, 1984b, pp. 171–2).

An organization overcomes the constraints on the individual's capacity by having each of its members perform different functions. In order to do this, communication channels have to be established within the organization and the information has to be co-ordinated. The benefits derived from organizational information processing reside in the fact that the information received can be reduced to just that amount needed for decision-making.

> It is this reduction in retransmission which explains the utility of an organization for information handling. Since information is costly, it is clearly optimal, in general to reduce the internal transmission still further. That is, it pays to have some loss in value for the choice

of terminal act in order to economize on internal communication channels (Arrow, 1984b, p. 177).

Manifestly, the choice of the best structure for information gathering and processing within an organization is an intensely complex matter. Later in this section we shall briefly explore team theory as a device for studying the question of economizing on information costs and also that of uneven distribution of information.

Internal communication channels are designed so as to cut down on the costs of processing information. The efficiency of channels is enhanced by appropriately chosen codes. Coding slows down, but does not arrest, the tendency towards increasing information costs as the organization expands. Coding also constitutes an intrinsic part of the organization's capital commitment. All this means that individuals will acquire various qualifications in information gathering and processing; they will learn in their areas of speciality and unlearn in others. These specialists sometimes find it difficult to communicate with each other. The codes become ever more complex and, as the organization expands, coding becomes more expensive.

To recall, learning a code is an act of irreversible investment for an individual and setting one up is a similar act for the organization. Once the organization has been established, therefore, it is endowed with a special character. Human capital theory emphasizes that a large part of the accumulation of such capital consists of skills that are firm-specific. This is particularly so where information is considered. 'If the function of labor is to cooperate in production with capital goods which are held widely by different firms, it would appear that virtually all training is general. But learning the information channels within a firm and the codes for transmitting information through them is indeed a skill of value only internally' (Arrow, 1984b, p. 178).

All this offers us another vital clue to Arrow's (1984b, p. 147) view of economic relationships:

> I see the communication-economical point of view as explanatory of the internal structure of firms and more generally of other economic organizations. The assumptions about the firm made in classical economic theory will have to be altered. It is assumed there to be a point; instead, it is an incompletely connected network of flows (see also Arrow, 1983b, pp. 156–98).

6.2 Beyond the Economics of Medical Care

Arrow's perception of the unequal distribution of information, of the problem of incentive compatibility can be traced to his influential study of uncertainty and the economics of medical care (see Fuchs, Chapter 29 of the companion volume) to which we now digress.

Arrow is very fond of this 1963 study. When he first started it (at the behest of the Ford Foundation) it somewhat lacked cohesion. He admits that he did not immediately perceive the cardinal question of incentive compatibility and, with the benefit of hindsight, deplores that it is not sufficiently emphasized in this contribution. Yet his work on medical economics goes far beyond applied economics and analysis of the special circumstances of medical care; it imaginatively poses new theoretical issues and problems, enlarges the vista of economic theory, prompts a novel conceptualization, and is full of highly suggestive ideas for further research. And, as Arrow recounts in Chapter 2 of *this* volume, it was for him an extraordinarily stimulating and fascinating learning-by-doing experience with applied work and theory interacting and stimulating each other.[53]

At the outset, Arrow (1963) states that, by comparing the specific characteristics of the medical care industry with the norms of welfare economics, one can deduce that the special economic problems of this industry can be seen as adaptations to the incidence of uncertainty in the occurrence and treatment of illness (see also Arrow 1976b, pp. 1–8).

> Where there is uncertainty, there is the opportunity for information, which is the reduction of uncertainty; and the commodity sold by the medical profession is, first and foremost, information. Not merely is there uncertainty, but there is a difference between the uncertainty of the patient and the lesser uncertainty of the physician; and both parties to the transaction know this. This means that the physician is the agent of the patient. The relation between them is one involving trust, not merely the arm's length relation characteristic of the commercial market (Arrow 1972b, pp. 396–97).

In cataloguing the special features of the medical care industry, Arrow distinguishes the irregularity and unpredictability of an individual's demand for medical care. This demand is also accompanied by considerable probability and serious risks; risks of death, of partial or full disablement, and of impaired or destroyed earning power. He also underlines the necessary element of trust in the patient-doctor relationship and the ethical restrictions on the physician's behaviour – a 'collectivity orientation', to use T. Parson's term, that distinguishes medicine from business, so that self-interest is not here the accepted norm. And, most importantly, In Arrow's (1963, p. 951) words:

> Uncertainty as to the quality of the product is perhaps more intense here than in any other important commodity. Recovery from disease is as unpredictable as is its incidence. In most commodities, the possibility of learning from one's own experience or that of others is strong because there is an adequate number of trials. In the case of severe illness, that is, in general, not true; the uncertainty due to inexperience is added to the intrinsic difficulty of prediction. Further, the amount of uncertainty, measured in terms of utility variability, is certainly much greater for medical care in severe cases than for, say, houses or automobiles, even though these are also expenditures sufficiently infrequent so that there may be considerable residual uncertainty. Further, there is a special quality to the uncertainty; it is very different on the two sides of the transaction. Because medical knowledge is so complicated, the information possessed by the physician as to the consequences and possibilities of treatment is necessarily very much greater than that of the patient, or at least so it is believed by both parties . . . Further, both parties are aware of this informational inequality, and their relation is colored by this knowledge.

The point is clearly made that the asymmetry of information does not really concern production methods about which the producer of a commodity always knows more than the buyer. In most cases, however, the buyer has a fairly good idea about the utility of the products, nearly as good as the producer. But in this case it is about the consequences of medical care that the patient is not as well informed as the physician.

The supply of medical care is influenced by the restrictions on entry in the form of licensing defended by the need for maintaining quality standards. Costs of medical education are high, and only fractionally borne by the students. Both the quality and the quantity of the supply of medical care are strongly conditioned by social non-market forces. Pricing of medical care is strongly differentiated according to the patient's ability to pay, and price competition is disparaged.

After comparing the significant deviations of the medical care industry from the competitive model under certainty, Arrow (1963, p. 961) takes uncertainty into account and examines the problems of insurance.

> The welfare case for insurance policies of all sorts is overwhelming. It follows that the government should undertake insurance in those cases where this market, for whatever reason, has failed to emerge. Nevertheless, there are a number of significant practical limitations on the use of insurance. It is important to understand them, though I do not believe that they alter the case for the creation of a much wider class of insurance policies than now exists.

One of the problems is moral hazard – essentially a problem of differential information, similar to the question of adverse selection. Since these standard insurance terms are not part of every economist's 'technicalese', it may be worthwhile to define them here in Arrow's (1984b, pp. 147–8) own words:

> The most striking category of market failure due to differential information is that known in the insurance literature as *adverse selection*. Suppose a population at risk, for example, in life insurance, is divided into strata with differing probabilities of an untoward event. Suppose further that each individual desiring insurance knows which stratum he belongs to and hence the probability of risk for him, but the insurers cannot distinguish among the insured according to risk and therefore are constrained to make the same offer to all. At any given price for insurance the high-risk individuals will buy more, the low-risk individuals less, so that the actuarial expectations will become more adverse than they would be with equal participation by all or than they would be in an ideal allocation with different premiums to different strata. The resulting equilibrium allocation of risk bearing will be inefficient, at least relative to that which would be attainable if information on risks were equally available to both sides. . . .
>
> Closely related to adverse selection is the occurrence of 'moral hazard', that is, the difficulty of distinguishing between decisions and exogenous uncertainty. (The adjective 'moral' is misleading in many contexts but is hallowed by long use.) An insurance policy, for example, may induce the insured to change his behavior,

> therewith the risks against which the insurance is written. Thus, insurance against fire will lead a rational individual to be less careful if care is at all costly. 'Health insurance', more precisely insurance against medical costs, is a currently important illustration; the insurance, once taken out, is equivalent to a reduction of the price of medical care, and therefore the rational individual will increase his consumption, which increases the amount of medical insurance payments and ultimately causes an increase in the premiums. This is a social cost, since an increase in medical expenditures by any individual increases the premium for all, and thus the use of both the services of risk bearing and those of medical care is inefficient.

The crux of the problem is that any system that insures economic agents against adverse outcomes tends to modify their behaviour in the direction of slackening care in avoiding risks; that is, it produces disincentive effects and impinges on sound decision-making (see Arrow and Hurwicz, 1977 part 4; Hildenbrand 1982, (ed.) Chapters 1 and 2). The insurer desires the event against which the insurance policy is contracted to be beyond the control of the insured, but such a distinction is difficult to make in practice. Insurance to cover costs of medical care really means a reduction of costs to the patient who may then be expected to increase his consumption, thus raising medical insurance payments. Ultimately premiums will increase and bear on social costs, because premiums for all will rise. Thus there is inefficiency in use of both risk sharing and medical care services. Another aspect of moral hazard in medical insurance is the weakened incentive for either physician or patient to search for cheaper hospitalization or surgical care.

From a risk aversion standpoint the insurance becomes more valuable as the risks against which it insures increase. This is usually the argument for stressing insurance for hospitalization and surgery costs. Despite the fact that insurance that would carry a maximum discrimination of risks would be socially most beneficial, there is, in fact, a proclivity to equalize premiums. Arrow (1963, p. 964) points out that 'this constitutes, in effect, a redistribution of income from those with a low propensity to illness to those with a high propensity. The equalization, of course, could not in fact be carried through if the market were genuinely competitive'. This may be considered an insurance with a longer time perspective that insures all against changes in their basic state of health.

And what does Arrow (1963, pp. 964–5) consider an ideal insurance?

> This will necessarily involve insurance against a failure to benefit from medical care, whether through recovery, relief of pain, or arrest of further deterioration. One form would be a system in which the payment to the physician is made in accordance with the degree of benefit. Since this would involve transferring the risks from the patient to the physician, who might certainly have an aversion to bearing them, there is room for insurance carriers to pool the risks, either by contract with physicians or by contract with the potential patients. Under ideal insurance, medical care will always be undertaken in any case in which the expected utility, taking account of the probabilities, exceeds the expected medical cost. This prescription would lead to an economic optimum. If we think of the failure to recover mainly in terms of lost working time, then this policy would, in fact, maximize economic welfare as ordinarily measured.

Since such insurance does not exist, other institutions to reassure the less well-informed patient have arisen; that is, the relationship of trust and confidence between patient and physician and the medical code of ethics to which the latter is bound to adhere. This is, in fact, an intrinsic part of the physician's services, though it cannot be verified by the patient. 'One consequence of such trust relations is that the physician cannot act, or at least appear to act, as if he is maximizing his income at every moment of time' (Arrow, 1963, p. 965). It is virtually understood that the physician is primarily concerned with the patient's welfare and will extend his services despite the latter's financial difficulties. Another consequence is that the patient is forced to delegate to the physician much of his freedom of choice. Arrow (1963, p. 966) emphasizes the general principle in this position of trust:

> Because there are barriers to the information flow and because there is no market in which the risks involved can be insured, coordination of purchase and sale must take place through convergent expectations, but these are greatly assisted by having clear and prominent signals, and these, in turn, force patterns of behavior which are not in themselves logical necessities for optimality.

Arrow (1963, p. 966) sees the rigid entry requirements in the medical profession as a social way of handling the problem of general uncertainty about the quality standards of medical treatment, as a way of reassuring the patients that the trust they place in the physicians is justified. These rigid entry requirements

> are designed to reduce the uncertainty in the mind of the consumer as to the quality of product insofar as this is possible . . . I think this explanation, which is perhaps the naive one, is much more tenable than any idea of monopoly seeking to increase incomes. No doubt restriction on entry is desirable from the point of view of the existing physicians, but the public pressure needed to achieve the restriction must come from deeper causes (see also Friedman and Kuznets, 1945).

Arrow (1963, p. 967) concludes:

> The failure of the market to insure against uncertainties has created many social institutions in which the usual assumptions of the market are to some extent contradicted. The medical profession is only one example, though in many respects an extreme one. All professions share some of the properties. The economic importance of personal and especially family relationships, though declining, is by no means trivial in the most advanced economies; it is based on non-market relations that create guarantees of behavior which would otherwise be afflicted with excessive uncertainty. Many other examples can be given. The logic and limitations of ideal competitive behavior under uncertainty force us to recognize the incomplete description of reality supplied by the impersonal price system.

Besides deriving from this work the important concept of incentive compatibility, Arrow was inspired to call for establishing codes of ethics and trust relationships in business, especially in cases of unequal information and where government regulation, taxation, and legal liability are inadequate and, of course, where the market fails (see Chapter 1A of the companion volume).

6.3 Theory of Discrimination

Fundamentally motivated by social concerns, but partly related to his work in the economics of information, Arrow attempts to demonstrate the use of an appropriately extended g.e. analysis to studying the vital issue of discrimination. The immediate spur for Arrow (1972b and 1973) was the national awakening in the US against discrimination and his eagerness to comprehend and reduce discrimination in employment on the market. On the whole he is less satisfied with the power of mainstream neoclassical analysis to explain this phenomenon than with its ability to explain medical economics.

Arrow (1972b, Chapter 2, p. 83) prefaces his study of job discrimination by stressing that the 'real subject' of his endeavour is economic theory itself:

> more precisely, the use and meaning of neoclassical price theory in application to the allocation of resources and the distribution of income in the real world. These are some reflections that have grown out of attempts to analyze the differentials in income between blacks and whites in the United States with the tools of economic theory. The phenomenon of income differentials is, after all, an economic phenomenon, however much it may be linked with other social dimensions. There is no reason to impose the burden of a full explanation upon economic theory, but it should provide insight into the links between the social, cultural, and individual facts on the one hand and the economic fact on the other, just as the theory of production is supposed to provide a link between the facts of technology and the uses and rewards of factors.
>
> My discussion will therefore be a programmatic and methodological one rather than a confident analysis. My intention is to present the deficiencies of neoclassical analysis, as brought out by the attempt to use it as a tool for the analysis of racial discrimination in the economic sphere, and by so doing to suggest the areas in which further research may be more fruitful.

Arrow considers discrimination only as it appears on the market; this involves the notion that personal characteristics of workers (such as race, ethnic origin, and sex) unrelated to productivity are also values on the market. Although he is specifically concerned with racial discrimination, his analysis can easily be extended to sex discrimination. His analysis relies as much as possible on neoclassial tools and, in that respect, enlarges upon the pioneering work of Edgeworth (1922) and the later study by Becker (1971), though Arrow relates his models more closely to g.e.t.

Although Arrow (1973, pp. 3–5) consistently retains the basic neoclassical assumptions of utility and profit maximization, in the course of his analysis he relaxes a number of others such as convexity of indifference surfaces, costless adjustment, perfect information, and perfect capital markets. Furthermore, he emphasizes that there are a number of economic phenomena that can only be explained by abandoning these assumptions and thus the steps he proposes are more far-reaching. They could be important elements of a more general theory for analyzing the effects of social factors on economic behaviour, without either combining them into the nebulous category of 'imperfections' or rejecting neoclassical theory altogether.

More specifically, Arrow (1973, pp. 9–10) shows that discrimination imposes higher costs on the firm. Competition tends to reduce the degree of discrimination on the market, especially so in the long run as capital flows to the more profitable firms which are also the less discriminatory ones.

> Only the least discriminatory firms survive. Indeed, if there were any firms which did not discriminate at all, these would be the only ones to survive the competitive struggle. Since in fact racial discrimination has survived for a long time, we must assume that the model just presented must have some limitation (Arrow, 1973, p. 10).

Proceeding from this argument Arrow (1973, pp. 13–20, 32–3) demonstrates that the usual assumption of convexity of indifference surfaces is inapplicable in the analysis of racial discrimination and, indeed, of many externality problems. More generally, his position in this respect is sufficiently important to need stressing. In Arrow's (1973, p. 13) own words;

> I have gradually become convinced that the usual assumption that indifference surfaces are convex is inapplicable to the case of racial discrimination and indeed to many other problems in the economics of externalities. Pollution provides another example; Starett has already pointed to the importance of nonconvexity in this context . . . Asumptions which seem very reasonable in the contexts of discriminatory behavior *necessarily* imply a nonconvexity of the indifference surfaces of the firms in the case of employer discrimination or of the firm's profit function in the case of discrimination by complementary workers.

> Actually my view is that nonconvexity of indifference surfaces is in fact a widespread phenomenon.

He (1973, pp. 20–23) also shows that long-run adjustment processes do not function as smoothly as usually assumed and that there are costs that restrain the firm's adjustment. In this context these costs are involved in hiring and firing, in training, and in administration and they discourage (or delay) firms from taking the necesary steps that would wipe out racial wage differentials. In Arrow's (1972b, Chapter 2, p. 92) own words:

> Thus, after building up a more or less reasonable mechanism that gives a rationale for linking economic discrimination with other social attitudes, I now argue that if the logic of the competitive system is accepted, discrimination should still be undermined in the long run. This forces us to reconsider the meaning of long-run competition . . . I must also remark that the negative discussion has so far only concerned discrimination by employers. I must also ask whether discrimination by other employees is also eroded over time. This raises some other questions of a more technical nature.

An important contribution of Arrow's (1973, pp. 23–32) analysis is his identification of imperfect information as reinforcing discrimination. In a nutshell, if employers prejudge that black workers (or females) have lower productivity, they would hire them only at lower wages. Verification of actual productivity is costly. Arrow (1973, p. 26) points out that

> beliefs and actions should come into some sort of equilibrium; in particular, if individuals act in a discriminatory manner, they will tend to acquire or develop beliefs which justify such actions. Hence, discriminatory behavior and beliefs in differential abilities will tend to come into equilibrium. Indeed, the very fact that there are strong ethical beliefs which are in conflict with discriminatory behavior will, according to this theory, make the employer even more willing to accept subjective probabilities which will supply an appropriate justification for his conduct.

He (1973, p. 27) also shows that becauses of this the worker who is discriminated against will be discouraged from developing the not overtly apparent attributes of high productivity; that is, the 'more subtle types of personal deprivation and deferment of gratification which lead to the habits of action and thought that favor good performance in skilled jobs, steadiness, punctuality, responsiveness, and initiative'. As Wan points out in Chapter 14 of this volume, this is a self-perpetuating vicious circle in which there is no real villain, only many victims.

One wonders whether collectively we are not villains in allowing discriminatory systems to persist, even though no individual in particular can be singled out for blame (except perhaps a small number of people with exceptional political responsibilities). Arrow's (1972b, Chapter 2, pp. 101–2) attitude to this particular subject is very revealing of the cool-headed economic analyst and the committed reformer:

> I have chosen a topic on which many of us feel the greatest moral outrage and have analyzed it most dispassionately. Neither the moral indignation nor the cool analysis is misplaced; their juxtaposition is one of those paradoxes inherent in the nature of human society of which only the naive are ignorant. Our mastery of ourselves as social beings needs all the reinforcement it can get from study of ourselves in all contexts. Indeed, in the absence of analysis from a self-imposed and sometimes painful distance, our moral feelings can lead us to actions whose effects are the opposite of those intended. This is not intended to imply that social action must wait on adequate analysis. Inaction may be, and in this case surely is, as dangerous as any likely alternative. Indeed, social action may be indispensable to increasing our knowledge when the consequences are subjected to adequate study. But a firm commitment to ends must not preclude a tentative, questioning attitude to particular means of achieving them.

6.4 Centralization and Decentralization

To recall, team theory was developed by Marschak and Radner (1972) as a device for studying the problems of most economical information processing and differential information within an organization. It is a major contribution to the field of system design. Team theory is a synthesis of statistical decision theory, the economics of decision-making under uncertainty, and the theory of organization. Broadly, it represents a novel and refined interpretation of the economic co-ordination problem (Arrow, 1981b, p. 337; and 1979, p. 505). In Arrow's (1983e, p. 63) view 'the theory of teams was introduced by Jacob Marschak precisely to bring information costs into the allocation process explicitly ... It does so in a way that is polar to the standard tradition. It assumes a fixed amount of communication in fixed channels. The "costs" of communication are modeled by scarcity'.

Team theory presupposes that some or all the fundamental parameters of resources or technology are unknown. But probable values of the parameters can be estimated on the basis of previous information. Henece, decentralized decisions can profit from this knowledge and counteract as much as possible erroneous decisions. Moreover, team theory envisages that various members of the team possess irreducible differences in information, and this also distinguishes it from the standard approach. In the latter, the individual members are only information sources, while the decisions are all ultimately made at the centre. *Per contra*, in team theory there is genuine decentralization for the allocations ultimately result from a multiplicity of individual decisions. In this sense, team theory is also closer to reality (see Arrow, 1983e, pp. 64–5).

A team is an organization composed of a number of members or agents. Initially each agent has some specific, if restricted, information that other agents do not have. The entire organization's (or economy's) information may well be restricted. All agents are decision-makers and choose various actions on the basis of their different information: The end result for the organization (or economy) as a whole depends on the decisions made and on some facts about the world. A central point of team theory is that it is a very special case: it abstracts from a variety of (possibly conflicting) interests of agents and assumes that all of them have the same preferences. Marschak and Radner (1972, p. ix) conceive of this as an 'intermediate case ... useful as a step toward a fuller and more complex economic theory of organization'. The problem then is to choose an optimal set of decision rules that would prescribe for each agent what decisions he is to make on the basis of the information at his disposal.

Although Arrow (1985c, p. 304) stresses the importance of incentives, he defends their neglect in team theory and his proclivity to use team theory for two reasons:

1. In order to 'emphasize the choice of the information structure, which is still of great importance in models with incentives and has been neglected; these models invariably take the structure as given.
2. The present incentive models take a very limited view of the information structure. In fact, within a firm there are many forms of information gathering . . . beyond those in our current models'.

As Arrow and Radner (Arrow, 1984b, p. 235) have described it, team theory is a novel way of perceiving the centralization-decentralization quandary (see Heal, 1973).

> On the one hand, it assumes fixed information and communication structures. In the simplest models there is an initial information pattern, which may be followed by one step in which some of this information is transmitted to some (possibly all) agents in the team. On the other hand, team theory relies more heavily on the *a priori* structure of the information concerning productive posibilities. Following the standard Bayesian approach, it assumes that there is a prior probability distribution over the production structures of all the processes. In the specific examples that have been worked out, a priori assumptions take the form of drawing the production structures from a finite-parameter family, with a probability distribution over the parameters. This prior distribution is known to the team when it is deciding on its decision and communication functions. At any given realization, each process manager knows the parameters which determine his production structure, but not anyone else's. A communication structure then determines that each firm manager transmits some of the parameters to some of the other agents. Each agent now has certain information, and takes the variables he does not observe to be distributed according to the conditional distribution obtained from the prior by conditioning on the information he has.

Radner (1972, p. 189) sees two basic questions in team theory, just as in statistical decision problems in general: '(a) for a given structure of information, what is the optimal decision function? (b) what are the relative values of alternative structures of information?' These problems can also be cast in the guise of questions facing an organizer: 'How should the tasks of inquiring, communicating, and deciding be allocated among the members of an organization so as to achieve results that would be best from the point of view of their common interests and beliefs, or of those of the organizer?' (Marschak and Radner, 1972, p. ix). This framework throws into sharper focus the essence of the concept of informational decentralization. Radner (1972, p. 188), for example, speaks of

> decentralization as a special case of division of labor, where the labor in question is that of making decisions. The organizer can regard the members of the organization as 'machines', receiving messages as inputs, and producing messages and actions as outputs, according to predictable (although possibly stochastic) modes of behavior.

He (1972, p. 188) then points out

> an organization is *information-decentralized* to the extent that diferent members have different information, and *authority-decentralized* to the extent that individual members are expected (by the organizer) to choose strategies and/or modify the rules of the game. With these concepts of decentralization, all but the simplest organizations are decentralized to some extent in both senses. This serves to emphasize that the crucial question usually is not 'how much decentralization', but rather 'how to decentralize?'

The system is amplified by communication (that is, agents transmit their specific information to one another). The essence of this approach is that transmission of information is scarce and costly. Thus the rules must be so formulated as to prescribe the cost of or the restrictions on the amount of communication (see Marschak and Radner, 1972, pp. 167–324). This was a major spur for the search for a better understanding of the economics of information.

The principal issues that underlie team theory – information economy and centralization-decentralization – are directly traceable to the interwar debate on the economic efficiency of socialism that involved such notable participants as H. D. Dickenson, M. H. Dobb, F. A. von Hayek, O. Lange, A. P. Lerner, L. von Mises, and F. M. Taylor and many indirect ones, including Arrow's mentor, H. Hotelling. The opening salvo of the debate was sounded in the 1920s by Mises (1951, pp. 385–6). He maintained that a condition for the existence of rational prices is a genuine market. The latter can only exist where means of production are privately owned. With the collectivization of the means of production, the market and market valuations for producer and consumer goods disappear. Hence, there can be no rational price system and no rational economic calculation essential for efficient organization of production. The socialist economy would 'grope in the dark' producing 'senseless output' by an 'absurd apparatus'. Without market valuations, indicating what and how to produce, there would be no intrinsic basis for the rationality of decisions which would become purely arbitrary.

In his reply, Lange (1938) followed up Pareto's (1971, pp. 266–71) view of the socialist system as one that would have to imitate the competitive process to arrive at optimal allocation and Pareto's stress on the market as a computing device for solving the Walrasian system of equations. Lange emphasized that in any society that faces choice between alternatives, to solve the allocative problem three sets of data are required: (a) a preference function to guide choice; (b) choice indicators, or 'the knowledge of the terms on which alternatives are offered'; and (c) production function. If the data under (a) (which may reflect consumers' or planner's preferences) and (c) are known, (b) can be determined. Hence, it is not a condition that an actual market must determine the scarcity price. The socialist economy can operate with rational prices established on a simulated market. Lange assumes consumers' and wage-earners' sovereignty, a genuine market for consumer goods and labour, but only a simulated market for producer goods.

Lange demonstrates that prices of producer goods do not have to be determined as a result of actual market transactions. Rational prices, derived as equilibrium values, can be determined by the condition that demand for each commodity is to be equal to its supply, and this is done by a series of successive trials/(*tâtonnements*). Lange's Central Planning Board can set initially any price at random, but as a rule the starting point for the successive trials would be 'historically given' prices. Should there be excess demand or supply the planners will adjust the price through increase or decrease respectively in order to equilibrate demand and supply. And, if this is not achieved, the price will be altered again and again until equilibrium is finally reached. This, of course, relates to our earlier discussion of *tâtonnement* stability.

The solution of the series of successive trials is based on the parametric function of prices; that is, every participant in the simulated market process is separately a price-taker and regards the price set by the planner as a datum beyond his power to change, adjusting his behaviour (quantity adjuster) to take advantage of the market situation confronting him and which he cannot control. Apart from performing the function of the market by setting the prices, the planner establishes and imposes on the managers of production the observance of rules of conduct for combining productive factors so as to minimize average production costs (which in most cases is equivalent to minimizing total costs, but does not hold when there is joint production, as minimizing total costs would) and for fixing the scale of the plant's output so that marginal cost equals the prices of the product. The managers of decreasing-cost industries would increase production, irrespective of the average cost, until marginal cost equals price. The aggregate investment volume is not dictated by market considerations, but is established by the planner to eliminate fluctuations and foster growth. Allocation of capital among enterprises relies on the interest rate that balances availability and demand for capital.

In his rebuttal Hayek (1940) argued, *inter alia*, that the *tâtonnement* process is inferior to a genuine market as far as rapidity and completeness of the adjustment is concerned. Such a market is handicapped by the absence of price competition, and by insufficient differentiation of prices according to quality of goods and circumstances of time and place. The actual mechanism for implementing equilibrium cannot even 'distantly approach' the efficiency of real markets where the required adjustments result from 'spontaneous action of the persons immediately concerned'. However, as we have seen in the preceding pages and shall see in the ensuing ones, the superior efficiency of the genuine market is questionable and cannot be taken for granted in all circumstances.

In 1960 Arrow and Hurwicz (1977, pp. 41–95) contributed a significant postscript to the interwar debate. Essentially they tackled the Lange (1938) problem through Samuelson's (1947, pp. 269–75) restatement of the Walrasian dynamic system, through Koopmans's (1951) view of production as a process rather than the usual production-function approach, and through the use of more sophisticated mathematical tools. In their (1977, pp. 42–3) words:

> Our aim here is to state more precisely than hitherto the dynamic system which is implied by the market mechanism, to give conditions under which the resource allocation determined by it converges to the optimal, where optimality is defined in terms of a single utility function for the economy, and to suggest modifications of the market mechanism which still preserve some degree of

decentralization for cases where the conditions in question are not satisfied. The conditions for convergence of the unmodified market mechanism are basically those of diminishing or constant returns in production and diminishing marginal utility (in a generalized sense) for the consumption of final demands. To study these dynamic problems, we will make use of a variety of mathematical tools, some of which have arisen in the theory of games and of linear and nonlinear programming and some of which are more classical applications of differential equations to maximization problems.

Arrow and Hurwicz (1977, p. 41) note that the question of optimal allocation of resources is one of choosing that combination of production processes that maximizes the utility function of the economy, by which they mean either a firm or a nation. A firm is better suited to the assumption that a single utility function represents the economy's goals. Though less applicable to a nation, the assumption nevertheless 'provides an introduction, at least, to the more complex problem raised by the presence of many individuals, each of whom judges the workings of the economic system in light of his own utility function'.

Arrow and Hurwicz (1977, p. 42) clearly express the nature of the centralization-decentralization dilemma:

> Of course, as soon as the problem of optimal resource allocation is formulated as the solution of a system of simultaneous equations (namely, the equations defining competitive equilibrium), the possibility arises of solving them by some centralized procedure involving the use of computing machines rather than the market ... A completely centralized organization would require a capacity for storage and processing of technological and other information that exceeds anything likely to be available. The competitive process, on the contrary, achieves *decentralization* ... At each stage in the market's process of successive approximations, any individual firm adjusts its tentative production plans making use of information only about the current tentative prices and its own technology. The adjustments of tentative prices, at the same time, depend only on the aggregate demands and supplies. These are simply a sum of the tentative production plans of the individual firms (and consumption plans of consumers) plus the originally existing supplies of basic resources.

> Thus the information needed by firms and consumers consists solely of their technologies or utility functions plus prices, while the adjustment of prices is based only on the aggregate of individuals' decisions. It is the minimization of information requirements for each participant in the economy which constitutes the virtue of decentralization.

Arrow and Hurwicz (1977, pp. 66–88) analyze the case of production under diminishing or constant returns with a strictly concave utility function where two dynamic systems that formalize the notion of the market mechanism are shown to emerge. They also concentrate on cases where unaltered market processes do not converge (especially that of increasing returns) and where three altered market mechanisms (one related to imperfect competition and another to speculation), that have some redeeming features, are proposed. Furthermore, some of these altered mechanisms are shown to solve the case of linear utility function and constant returns to scale, for which the unaltered market mechanisms do not converge.

Essentially, Arrow and Hurwicz provide a firm mathematical foundation for Lange (1938), and for the theory of decentralization within large firms. They state more precisely the dynamic characteristics of the market mechanism, they specify the conditions under which the allocation determined by the market converges to the optimal, and they provide alterations of the mechanism that still preserve some advantages of decentralization in situations where the required conditions are not met. Theirs has, in fact, become a standard formulation of the problem and is by now recognized in the literature as the Lange-Arrow-Hurwicz procedure of price-guided planning (see Heal, 1973, pp. 78–82 and Chapter 6; and Mirrlees, 1979).

An intrinsic part of this discussion is the view of the market as a computing machine – a view that can be traced back at least to Pareto who emphasized that a centralized solution to the multiplicity of equations would be impossible. This was so in his time but is not necessarily so now. Arrow (1984b, p. 159) articulates the controversial view that

> with the development of mathematical programming and high-speed computers, the centralized alternative no longer appears preposterous. After all, it would appear that one could mimic the workings of a decentralized system by an appropriately chosen centralized algorithm. Although there is more to the story than

these few remarks, they do make the point that if we are going to take information economy seriously, we have to add to our usual economic calculations an appropriate measure of the costs of information gathering and transmission (see Shoven and Whalley, 1984).

A similar position was taken by Lange in his last published work before his untimely death in 1965 (1966, pp. 448–54). Lange states that should he attack the (1938) problem now his task would be much simpler: his answer would be to programme the system of simultaneous equations on a computer. The solution would be obtained in less than a second. To him the market process, with its sluggish method of trial and error, seems to be outdated and can be considered a calculatory device of the pre-electronic era. The market mechanism and the *tâtonnements* method of his prewar essay actually perform the function of calculatory devices for a solution of the system of simultaneous equations. The solution is achieved through the iterative process, where a displacement is followed by a corrective movement restoring equilibrium (assuming convergence). The equilibrating process acts as a servo-mechanism.

However, even the most powerful computers have a limited capacity. There are economic processes so complex in the number of products and types of interdependencies that exist, that either no computer can cope with them, or the construction of one that could would be too costly. In such cases, Lange argues, there is no other alternative but to revert to the old-fashioned market mechanism. Furthermore, the market is an institutional arrangement that is already in place. It would be pointless to replace it by another calculatory device. The computer may be used for planning, but the plans must be verified by the market.

The essential limitations of the market are that the calculations are static by nature; there are no sufficient bases for solving the problems of growth and development planning. For example, current prices cannot be used for investment decisions. However, the theory and practice of linear and non-linear programming permit the adoption of rational economic calculation. Having determined the objective function and the state of constraints, it is possible to arrive at future shadow prices that could be used as choice coefficients for development planning. Computers are essential for long-term optimal planning. In this instance the computer is not a substitute for the market, for it performs functions that the market cannot discharge (see also

Koopmans, 1970, pp. 211–30; Dorfman, Samuelson, and Solow, 1958, Chapter 14).

As a final note one should point the reader to a fascinating and flourishing literature of modern system designers, of whom a leading representative is Leonid Hurwicz (see Chapter 4 this volume). In the normative spirit, the modern system designers repudiate the essentially passive approach to the system. They search for means of intervening with the system that would draw it as near to optimality as possible, while attempting to eschew Utopianism by recognizing that intervention and its results are subject to constraints. System designers build models that are not only oriented to aggregative or national economic systems, but are also highly relevant to modern large corporations or administrative agencies (see Arrow and Hurwicz, 1977, pp. 3–37 and part 4; Hurwicz, 1985). It is in this spirit that Arrow views organizations of all sorts as filling the gaps created in the system by either non-existence or failure of markets – a subject explored in Chapter 1A of the companion volume.

7 PRODUCTION, CAPITAL, AND DEMAND

Whatever else it is (or should be), much of economic theory, with shifting emphasis through time, is concerned with explaining the forces of production, organization, exchange, and distribution in human society under (non)market arrangements for resource allocation and utilization. While it is disputable whether there was a central theme, and if so what it was, classical economics was largely about production, productivity growth, expansion of the economy's productive potential, and the factors that promote or inhibit its expansion and utilization.

Adam Smith's great book was about economic growth. While to us wealth is a stock, by 'wealth of nations' he meant flow of production. He accentuated capital accumulation as the mainspring of economic growth under the institutional arrangements of a competitive private enterprise market economy. He perceived competion as part of the growth process and conceived the allocation problem within the context of a dynamic economy, with changing endowments of resources, techniques and tastes. Ricardo shifted the focus to the problem of distribution of national product among social classes. But it was not so much the question of income distribution that preocupied him as the consequences of shifts in distribution on the accumulation of capital. In contrast to Ricardo, Malthus was concerned with the accumulation-consumption dilemma: the detrimental effects of excessive accumulation on labour's will to produce and of excessive consumption on the economy's growth potential. Malthus is relevant to the contemporary focus of the welfare economics of production on how income redistribution is constrained by incentive effects and on the interrelations between distribution and production.

John Stuart Mill argued that separate laws govern production and distribution in contrast to the long-standing and perennially revived argument that inequality of income distribution (in favour of capital) is a necessary component of rapid growth.

Marx provided us with the enthralling vision of the complex capitalist system in motion, under its own steam and in historical time, increasingly hampered by class conflict. He treated the institutional arrangements and social relations as key determinants of the system's dynamics and as 'variables' in the problem of resource utilization. He also pointed to the difficulties of sustaining technical progress that would entail raising the capital-output ratio and a falling rate of profit. Some of those questions were reiterated by Schumpeter and are echoed in contemporary welfare economics of production and in industrial organization literature.

If classical economics was largely about economic growth, its determinants and mechanism, the perceptions of the propellers of economic growth and the benefits derived therefrom have shifted over time. Nowadays we pay much less attention to accumulation of physical capital and more to technical dynamism, to investment in human capital, to learning by doing, and to the non-investment sources of growth. The economy's *modus operandi* plays a significant role in affecting the willingness to produce, work performance, and the innovative and entrepreneurial activity of economic actors. Thus the powerful classical approach that assigned the key role to accumulation is extended by attributing varied strengths to such factors as scientific and engineering progress, investment in human beings, motivation of economic actors, systems of rewards and incentives, income distribution, resource allocation policies, macroeconomic conditions, and the entire framework of the economy's working arrangements.

Whether the so-called marginal revolution of the 1870s did occur and if so what it was all about is still a large and controversial theme (briefly pursued in the appendix to this chapter). At least the earlier 'neoclassical' economists or 'catallacticists' shifted the focus from production and distribution to exchange, though the subject was not fully neglected by various later writers in that tradition (notably the development of the neoclassical capital theory and the treatment of production by Marshall and Pigou). After the Second World War the resurgence of interest was stimulated by various factors and several distinct theoretical and empirical research programmes developed. The various approaches, their successes and failures, constitute a large subject; no more than very incomplete reference to the huge literature can be made here (see, *inter alia*, Koopmans, 1951, 1970; Sen, 1970, pp. 9–40; Malinvaud, 1972; Nelson and Winter, 1982; Joan Robinson, 1982; and Leontief, 1984).

Among factors that influenced Arrow was the new vista opened by activity analysis. (Indeed, Arrow participated in, and presented an important paper, as Jerry Green mentions in Chapter 28 of the companion volume, at the historic 1951 conference (see Koopmans 1951)). His work in production and growth is quite diffuse (as he notes in Chapter 2 of this volume); it consists of a number of contributions focusing on more specific issues such as the optimal accumulation of capital and inventories, the process of learning, and innovations. Aside from information and uncertainty, an important common theme of many of these contributions is the recursiveness of optimization, captured in general mathematical form as dynamic programming or control theory. More specifically, here we shall concentrate on Arrow's study of allocation of resources for invention, broadly interpreted as the production of knowledge; his specific formalization of the problem of learning as a function of the total past gross investment; his subsequent restatement of the technical progress question in terms of the production, transmission, and growth of knowledge; his conceptualization (together with Chenery, Minhas, and Solow) of the now famous and controversial CES production function; his collaborative effort on optimal inventory policy and optimal production scheduling, and his closely related work on optimal capital policy – both of which are an illuminating special case of general intertemporal equilibrium decision theory under uncertainty; his elaboration (in co-operation with Kurz and also Lind) of the choice criteria for public investment as a problem of second-best optimality; his application of optimal control theory to economic growth; and finally his stand on demand as a limiting factor of production and the macro questions of reducing the gap between potential and actual output.

There is strong empirical evidence for the contention that the larger share of rising economic growth cannot be explained by growth in conventional inputs, but by the 'residual' variously attributed to technical and organizational advances and the like (see Abramovitz, 1981; Jorgensen, 1984). Technological knowledge has not only been increasing historically, but it differs among nations. Arrow (1971, p. 165) finds it unsatisfactory for an economist to assert that the causes determining the amount of technological knowledge at any particular time and place, like the tastes determining consumption patterns, are outside his sphere of competence. After all private enterprise does spend considerable resources on research and development, and diffusion of technical advances, at least within a country, is partly motivated by profit seeking. Thus the body of technical knowledge can be viewed as both cause and effect of economic change, and, in this respect, it is similar to capital.

In a paper originally published in 1962, Arrow (1971, pp. 144–63) brought together two specific threads of controversy surrounding the allocation of resources for invention, namely, (a) the relationship between market structure and the incentives to innovate, and (b) the parts played by government and the patent system in spurring invention and its practical implementation and spread. In nearly a quarter century since it first saw the light of day, this contribution has remained a vital force and a starting point for researchers in the field (see, *inter alia*, Chapter 16 of this colume).

At the outset Arrow (1971, pp. 144–52) firmly roots the question surrounding invention in the economics of information and uncertainty.[53] First, he reminds us that because of indivisibilities, inappropriability, and uncertainty, the competitive system may fail to achieve optimality in resource allocation and he proceeds to the economic features of information as a commodity and specifically to invention as a procees for producing information. Then he shows that the three above-mentioned reasons are present in the case of inventions and undermine optimal allocation of resources for inventions.

More specifically, the economic aspect of research and development processes centers on the production of information. Manifestly invention is an activity that involves much uncertainty for its outcome cannot be perfectly predicted from the inputs. Hence, there is a built-in bias against investments in research and development. The moral hazard factor strongly militates against any insurance for risk sharing in this area. The risk component is somewhat mitigated by conducting research and development in large organizations where risk is spread among many ongoing projects. More serious problems of misallocation are due to the very nature of the product; that is, the fact that from society's standpoint a new production method, for example, should be disseminated to all. In this manner optimal utilization of the information would be ensured, but the incentives for research and development would be vitiated. Arrow (1971, p. 153) speculates that 'in an ideal socialist economy, the reward for invention would be completely separated from any charge to the users of the information'. In a private-enterprise economy, however,

> inventive activity is supported by using the invention to create property rights; precisely to the extent that it is successful, there is an underutilization of the information. The property rights may be in the information itself, through patents and similar legal devices, or in the intangible assets of the firm if the information is retained by the firm and used only to increase its profits (Arrow, 1971, p. 153).

Hence, in such an economy, for inventions to be profitable, resources have to allocated suboptimally.

Nevertheless, appropriation of information on a large scale is impractical. Patent laws cannot be sufficiently complex and subtle to take into account all the fine distinctions and, even if they could, they would not be enforceable. Inventive activities are essentially interdependent and they are likely to be seriously constrained if there is no free flow of information.

> To appropriate information for use as a basis for further research is much more difficult than to appropriate it for use in producing commodities; and the value of information for use in developing further information is much more conjectural than the value of its use in production and therefore much more likely to be underestimated (Arrow, 1971, pp. 154–5).

Essentially, Arrow (1971, p. 156) finds that, compared to an ideal, a free-enterprise economy is likely to underinvest in research and development. This is so

> because it is risky, because the product can be appropriated only to a limited extent, and because of increasing returns in use. This underinvestment will be greater for more basic research. Further, to the extent that a firm succeeds in engrossing the economic value of

the inventive activity, there will be an underutilization of that information as compared with an ideal allocation.

Arrow (1971, pp. 156–60) examines the incentive for inventive activity in monopolistic and competitive markets. He disregards the problems of appropriating information and concentrates on indivisibility. He considers only barriers to entry as *sensu stricto* monopoly, for the temporary monopoly created by a previous innovation which can be offset by other firms entering with inventions of their own (the Schumpeterian incentive to invention) is in the sense of his analysis more nearly competitive than monopolistic. He demonstrates that under monopolistic conditions there is less incentive to innovate than under competitive ones, and even here it is less than would be beneficial for society (see Hammond, 1984, pp. 45–6; Feiwel, 1985b, pp. 401–8). Arrow (1971, p. 160) shows that 'the potential social benefit always exceeds the realized social benefit' and that 'the realized social benefit, in turn, always equals or exceeds the competitive incentive to invent and, *a fortiori*, the monopolist's incentive'.

He (1971, pp. 160–61) closes his argument by concluding that

> for optimal allocation to invention it would be necessary for the government or some other agency not governed by profit-and-loss criteria to finance research and invention. In fact, of course, this has always happened to a certain extent. The bulk of basic research has been carried on outside the industrial system, in universities, in the government, and by private individuals. One might recognize here the importance of nonpecuniary incentives, both on the part of investigators and on the part of the private individuals and governments that have supported research organizations and universities. In the latter, the complementarity between teaching and research is, from the point of view of the economy, something of a lucky accident. Research in some more applied fields, such as agriculture, medicine, and aeronautics, has consistently been regarded as an appropriate subject for government participation, and its role has been of great importance.

This, of course, raises the questions of how to select the appropriate amount of resources to be earmarked for research and development and how to induce efficient use of these resources – questions common to any government involvement in economic activity.

Formally, of course, resources should be devoted to invention until

> the expected marginal social benefit there equals the marginal social benefit in alternative uses, but in view of the presence of uncertainty, such calculations are even more difficult and tenuous than those for public works. Probably all that could be hoped for is the estimation of future rates of return from those in the past, with investment in invention being increased or decreased accordingly as some average rate of return over the past exceeded or fell short of the general rate of return. The difficulties of even ex post calculation of rates of return are formidable though possibly not insuperable. (Arrow, 1971, p. 161).

In a later paper, Arrow (1983f) discusses the innovation process in small and large firms. He observes that though the indices of concentration have not risen much throughout the 1900s, there has been a conspicuous shift towards larger-scale firms. These are much more complex entities, with more involved information processing structures, high information costs, and greater central control. No matter how decentralized these firms might be, their capital allocation functions are highly centralized. Information about research and development as it travels to the central decision-maker tends to get distorted due to restrictions on lengths of communication channels and to incentives to present the project in a more favourable light. The larger firm has both more internal funds for financing such projects and greater access to external ones. The smaller firm, if it has to seek outside finance, will only get it at unfavourable terms. If the project is large, the small firm may not be able to secure financing at all. The larger firm will invest suboptimally in research and development because of information loss and the smaller firm because of financial difficulties. Information loss in larger firms will also make them less prone than smaller firms to invest in essentially novel projects.

The smaller firm can solve its financing difficulties by selling the research and development outcomes usually to larger firms in similar fields. Such possibilities, however, further reduce the research and development stimulus in larger firms. Arrow (1983f, p. 25) notes that on the whole 'one would expect firms to specialize in projects whose optimal development scales are correlated with the size of the firm'. However, he adds, 'projects anticipated to lead to large expenditures will on the whole be less than optimally funded, because large firms have higher transmission losses for information'. In conclusion, he (1983f, pp. 16–17) expects that less costly and more original innovations will come from small firms, and those involving higher development costs but less radical departures in principle will come from larger firms. This specialization creates opportunities for trade, as all specialization does; in this case, the trade will frequently be in firms as such – that is, takeovers and mergers.

Arrow's much acclaimed 'learning by doing' (1962, pp. 155–73)[54] should be viewed against the backdrop of the general interest in the 1960s in the determinants of rising factor productivity.[55] There was then a general disenchantment with the notion of exogenous technical progress and a fascination with certain manifest empirical increases in productivity that were not convincingly explained (see Rosenberg, 1982). Essentially Arrow's vision is one of technical advance as a learning process – a perceptible shift from the simplistic concept of the economic actor as instantaneously grasping and adopting the best solution to any problem. It is a process where the economic actor is perceived as bogged down in the morass of uncertainty from which he only gradually emerges as he slowly learns from the experiences he accumulates (see Hahn and Matthews, 1965, pp. 66–7). Arrow shows that one can express output as a function of experience, appropriately measured.[56] He elaborates a growth model on the basis of this production relation and on conventional savings-behaviour assumptions. He employs the growth model and the search for steady states in order to illustrate how learning by doing affects economic growth; that is, that, given certain predetermined expectations, a steady rate of growth, that is a multiple of the population growth rate, is possible, and the multiplier is conditioned by the shape of the learning parameter. But that is not a central theme in his analysis.

Arrow (1962, p. 155) starts out with the following provocative statement:

> I would like to suggest here an endogenous theory of the changes in knowledge which underlie intertemporal and international shifts in production functions. The acquisition of knowledge is what is usually termed 'learning' and we might perhaps pick up some clues from the many psychologists who have studied this phenomenon ... I do not think that the picture of technical change as a vast and prolonged process of learning about the environment in which we operate is in any way a far-fetched analogy; exactly the same phenomenon of improvement in performance over time is involved.

As a rule, psychologists accept the notion that learning is a product of experience, though they are no more prone to agreeing on specifics than are economists. Learning experiments have also shown that in order for the learning-from-experience process to result in steadily improved performance, the experiences cannot be merely repetitive, but rather steadily evolving ones. 'According to all theories of learning, not only contemporary mathematical theory, people learn from experience. Given a problem, the individual makes exploratory responses and observes what happens. He chooses and retains responses that satisfy; he rejects the responses that do not give satisfaction. It is the experience of problems that motivates learning, that is, the increase of knowledge' (Arrow, 1965b). Arrow (1962, p. 156) traces the observations of the role of experience in raising productivity to aeronautical engineers who noticed that the number of labour-hours spent on the production of an airframe is a decreasing function of the total number of airframes of the same type manufactured in the past.[57] Arrow (1965b) stresses that

> according to this point of view, knowledge is, so to speak, a *by-product* of production or of investment. In research, on the contrary, it can be said that knowledge is the primary product. The distinction between products and by-products is not important for ordinary goods, because in a competitive regime the marginal costs of the two must be equal. But since knowledge does not have the normal properties of an economic good, it is necessary to study each mode of its production.

Arrow (1962) focuses on the effect of economic activity on productivity and the economic consequences of the interaction between activity and technical change. In a nutshell, Arrow (1962, pp. 157–60) designs a simple model to bring into prominence the main hypothesis: 'that technical change in general can be ascribed to experience, that it is the very activity of production which gives rise to problems for which favorable responses are selected over time' (Arrow, 1962, p. 156).[58] Specifically, the model abstracts from capital-labour substitution. It differs largely from mainstream economic theory in that profits result from technical change, the rate of investment in a competitive system is suboptimal, and gross investment plays first fiddle, with net investment and the stock of capital in subordinate roles.

Arrow (1962, p. 157) uses cumulative gross investment as an index of experience. 'Each new machine produced and put into use is capable of changing the environment in which production takes place, so that learning is taking place with continually new stimuli. This at least makes plausible the possibility of continued learning in the sense, here, of a steady rate of growth in productivity'. He employs a vintage model (see Johansen, 1959; Solow, 1957; and Salter, 1960) 'in which technical change is completely embodied in new capital goods. At any moment of time, the new capital goods incorporate all the knowledge then available, but once built their productive efficiency cannot be altered by subsequent learning' (Arrow, 1962, p. 157). Arrow also assumes fixed coefficients of production and that the new capital goods are superior to the old ones, so that the newer machine will always be preferred to the old one. Although he concentrates on the full-employment case, Arrow admits of Keynesian and structual unemployment. With regard to distribution, he (1962, p. 159) points out that 'both capital and labor are paid their marginal products, suitably defined. The explanation is, of course, that the private marginal productivity of capital (more strictly, of new investment) is less than the social marginal productivity since the learning effect is not compensated in the market'.

Arrow (1962, p. 168) is emphatic that 'the presence of learning means that an act of investment benefits future investors, but this benefit is not paid for by the market'. He stresses again that in the competitive model studied the aggregate amount of investment 'will fall short of the socially optimum level'. He (1962, pp. 168–71) investigates in detail the divergence between the competitive model and what he calls the 'optimal solution'. He shows that though the socially optimal growth rate is the same as in the competitive model, the socially optimal ratio of gross investment to output is above that in the competitive solution.

In a 1964 lecture to the economists of the Commissariat Général au Plan (France), Arrow (1965b) elaborates on the learning-by-doing themes. He stresses that knowledge is an economic good,

> more precisely a factor of production, for there is a positive return to an increase in knowledge. But the market for knowledge as a good is not well developed. Strictly speaking, knowledge lacks two properties that are important for a good that is to be bought or sold freely on competitive markets: (1) it can be possessed only imperfectly, and it is difficult to prevent others from using it; (2) the use of knowledge in productive activities obeys the low of increasing

> returns, since the need for knowledge in a given activity is independent of its scale. It follows from these remarks that neither the demand for nor the supply of knowledge satisfies the conditions of a competitive economy.

In a later paper (written in 1969), Arrow (1971, p. 166) is somewhat critical of his 1962 model on the grounds that it does not 'capture the essential features of the creation and transmission of knowledge'. Arrow (1971, pp. 167–71) sees technical advances as primarily reducing uncertainty. The production of knowledge differs qualitatively from that of goods; it is useful only when it is initially produced, but useless when repeated. He (1971, p. 169) evolves a general formulation of the process of production of knowledge by using both the research and learning-by-doing approaches.

> In fact, the bulk of research and development expenditures are actual steps in the production process – design, engineering, tooling, and manufacturing and marketing start-up costs. . . Each stage involves uncertainties with regard to costs and, at the end, with regard to demand. At each stage, then, something is learned with regard to the probability distribution of outcomes for future repetitions of the activity. At the same time, the physical outputs are expected to be directly valuable.

He then proceeds to the microeconomic theory of research and development which involves statistical decision theory and poses difficult analytical questions. Building a macro theory on this basis is a particularly vexed question.

> Information at the individual level is describable either as the actual outcome of a particular activity or as a whole conditional distribution over states of nature, with the conditions being the actual outcomes. Such a probability distribution is hard to describe in any simple way, and aggregating this information over individuals is even harder (Arrow, 1971, pp. 169–70).

Arrow (1971, pp. 171–4) then concentrates on the process of transmission of knowledge. For him (1971, p. 172) 'the understanding of transmission of knowledge is of special importance in two of the key socioeconomic problems of our time: (a) international inequalities in productivity, and (b) the failure of the educational system in reducing income inequality'. In studying the problem of transmission he brings to bear the disciplines of information and communication theory, learning theory in psychology, and diffusion theory in sociology.

Arrow (1971, pp. 14–75) also calls attention to the basic differences between mainstream growth models and those of technological progress as information-seeking and transmitting. Namely, the former usually take some form of rate of growth of productivity as a variable of the system, typically ending up in a quasi-stationary state, with a constant productivity growth rate. The latter, on the other hand, usually end up with constant outputs. As Arrow (1971, p. 174) points out:

> There is a limit to what can be learned even with infinitely many opportunities. Actually with respect to the very long run, such a conclusion seems very reasonable. You cannot get something for nothing, ever, and it seems unreasonable to suppose that, by waiting a sufficient length of time, you can get any given output for arbitrarily small input. Eternal exponential technological growth is just as unreasonable as eternal exponential population growth.

Another related contribution is the paper Arrow co-authored with Chenery, Minhas, and Solow (1961) sometimes referred to in the literature as ACMS (or more irreverently as SMAC). The project originated with Chenery (then at Stanford) who had been comparing structures of national economies at various stages of development. If in all countries an industry's production function were Cobb-Douglas, the ratio of the wage bill to value added would be the same everywhere. Chenery and his then student, Minhas, observed that the value added per unit of labour in a given industry varies with the wage rate and differs among countries; that is, they found that the regression coefficient of value added per worker on wage rates was definitely less than one. They discussed the problem with Arrow who suggested that perhaps the production functions involved were other than Cobb-Douglas and began to search for the new production function ... and the rest is history, but not quite. They found (through the intermediary of another colleague, H. Houthakker, then also at Stanford) that Solow had also found such a function and he was invited to join the project.

The scope of ACMS is very wide; it touches on the pure theory of production, functional income distribution, technological change, international productivity variations, and sources of comparative advantage. Essentially, the CES production function – now so widely used in empirical studies – that they derived is a mathematical function that is homogeneous, exhibits constant elasticities of substitution between capital and labour, differentiated for various industries. It involves three parameters: substitution, distribution, and efficiency. The Leontief and Cobb-Douglas production functions are included in it as special cases. ACMS attempts to test the validity of the CES function by examining the incomplete data on direct use of capital and also the deviations from regression analysis. Though they lack comprehensiveness, the tests imply a working hypothesis that the efficiency parameter differs among countries, but that the substitution and distribution parameters are constant for each industry. Thus the CES function suggests that countries with divergent relative factor costs will exhibit predictable divergent structures of production and trade. ACMS investigates some of these differences by comparing the US and Japan. The findings suggest the extent of substitutability between capital and labour in the various sectors of the economy and corroborate the varying-efficiency hypothesis. ACMS (1961, p. 246) concludes:

> Although we began our empirical work on the naive hypothesis that observations within a given industry but for different countries at about the same time can be taken as coming from a common production function, we find subsequently that this hypothesis cannot be maintained. But we get reasonably good results when we replace it by the weaker, but still meaningful, assumption that international differences in efficiency are approximately neutral in their incidence on capital and labor. A closer analysis of international differences in efficiency leads us to suggest that this factor may have much to do with the pattern of comparative advantage in international trade.
>
> Finally, our formulation contributes something to the much-discussed question of functional shares. If, on the average, elasticities of substitution are less than unity, the share of the rapidly-growing factor, capital, in national product should fall. This is what has actually occurred. But in the CES production function it is possible that increases in real wages be offset by neutral technological progress in their effect on relative shares.

The CES production function is not without its critics on various grounds. It also appears that difficulties are encountered in extensions to include substitution among capital, labour, and intermediate inputs or substitution among intermediate inputs (see Jorgenson, 1984, pp. 104–41; Archen Minsol, 1968).

As we have already alluded, Arrow's next three contributions – optimal inventory policy, optimal capital policy, and optimal public investment – are somewhat interrelated; they deal with the recursive nature of optimization – an idea that Arrow (1949) first encountered in a study he prepared during the war for the Weather Division, US Army Air Force.[59]

The Arrow, Harris, and Marschak (AHM, 1951) contribution on optimal inventory policy is a milestone in a field that, if not neglected, was until then at least patchy and unintegrated. To this day it has remained a classic, in many ways a starting point and inspiration. (Indeed, Arrow was recently rewarded – if this is a reward (?) – for his pioneering work on inventory theory by being elected President of the International Society for Inventory Research.) Before proceeding to this and his other contributions to the field (see Arrow, Karlin, and Scarf (AKS), 1958), let us pause for a glimpse of the essential elements of inventory theory.

In broad terms, the sources of the inventory problem are uncertainty and lack of information. Arrow (AKS, 1958, p. 3) traces the neglect of inventory problems in economic theory to 'the emphasis on equilibrium situations, in which the holding of inventories in anticipation of price changes is ruled out by hypothesis'. He (AKS, 1958, pp. 3–15) compares the motivating forces behind the economic actor's decision to hold inventories to those behind the demand for money: the transaction, precautionary, and speculative motives. By the early 1950s, the ingredients of inventory theory were scattered about:

> The interrelation of decisions in different time periods and the possibility of changes in demand and supply conditions, whether known in advance or random, were recognized. The cost factors isolated include those of storage, penalty, and production or ordering, the last including possibly a cost independent of the size of the order. The possibility of lag in delivery appears clearly in some discussions of the transaction motive (AKS, 1958, p. 14).

Hence the research programme in which Arrow so prominently cooperated centered on integrating those ingredients into a consistent entity and on determining optimal policies using what were then very new and sophisticated techniques.

AHM (1951) grew out of a study conducted at the Rand Corporation on inventory problems in the military in the summer of 1950. The two summer visitors (Arrow and Marschak) co-operated with Harris, a probability theorist and permanent staff member. They soon became aware that the essential economic aspects of inventory holding were demand uncertainties, the lag betwen orders and deliveries, and the salvage value or cost of unused inventories and that formally the optimization problem is repetitious from period to period, irrespective of the initial value of inventory on hand. This brought to mind the sequential analysis of statistical data examined as an optimization problem on which Arrow had co-operated two years before with Blackwell and Girshick (see Arrow 1984b, Chapter 1).[60] Arrow (1984b, p. 2) recalls that the latter paper which 'sets forth explicitly the notion of recursive optimization' provided him 'with a model argument to be applied to the determination of optimal inventories' in AHM (1951). 'More important, it helped to suggest to Richard Bellman . . . the general principle of dynamic programming, which has found so many applications'. At the time, Arrow, Harris, and Marschak were not cognizant of Massé's (1946) earlier contribution that essentially utilized similar ideas.

In a nutshell, AHM (1951) proposes a method for deriving optimal rules of inventory policy for finished goods. Any policy maker (firm or government organization), with a given 'net utility' conditioned by certain variables or the relations between variables, can as a rule control the strategies and rules of action but cannot control other conditions that are determined by joint probability distribution. AHM regards the rate of demand for the policy maker's product as the only random uncontrollable condition. Other uncontrollable conditions, such as pipeline time, the cost of placing an order, the price paid in relation to order size, the relation between storage costs and size of inventory, are considered as constants or as relations with constant parameters (excluding thereby speculative inventories). It is believed that this formulation is 'a workable first approximation. By regarding the order size as the only controlled condition, and the demand as the only random noncontrolled condition, we do take account of most of the major questions that have actually arisen in the practice of business and nonprofit organizations' (AHM, 1951, p. 252).

At first AHM derives optimal inventory policy for a simple model under certainty. It then proceeeds to a study of static and dynamic uncertainty models where the demand flow is a random variable whose probability distribution is known. The optimal size (maximum) of stock and reorder point are functionally derived from demand distribution, the costs of placing the orders, and the stock-depletion penalties. Subsequently AHM was extended to linear ordering cost and to time lags and applied for machine repair parts (see AKS, 1958, Chapter 9, 10, and 13).

Arrow's work on the optimal expansion of the capacity of a firm (see AKS, Chapter 7) is closely related to that on inventories. Here, he Beckmann, and Karlin deal with a firm (policy maker) that knows its demand over a time span and builds up a stock of capital goods that at any given time determines its maximum output capacity. They also assume the irreversibility of capacity expansion. (In a perfectly competitive system the decision to expand or contract is entirely determined by the behaviour of markets now and in the near future; the firm would then always retain only that capacity needed to meet demand. In reality resale of capital goods is possible, but often with time lags and at a loss. The complete unsaleability postulated here is the other extreme). The authors seek a constructive algorithm for solving the problem similarly to the simplex method solution of a linear programing problem. This type of problem is closely related to game theory. They formalize the problem as a game from which they derive a characterization of the solution. They show that the optimal expansion policy involves the breaking up of the time span into shorter intervals each of which features one of the following three policies: no expansion, expansion with capacity equal to demand, and expansion at the maximum permissible rate. The authors provide a simple constructive algorithm for determining the optimal expansion policy from the demand function of time, the cost of building new capacity, and the rate of interest.

Using methods developed for optimal policies in deterministic inventory processes and the aforementioned contribution (AKS, 1958, Chapters 4–7), Arrow (AKS, 1962, pp. 1–17) studies a situation similar to AKS (1958, Chapter 7), but with somewhat differing assumptions, though the irreversibility of investment is preserved.

In a later contribution, Arrow (1968a) retains the assumption of irreversibility of investment which allows him to obviate the myopic quality of an optimal capital policy that assumes a perfect capital goods market at any moment of time. This contribution is technically more sophisticated than the preceding ones; he uses here the Pontryagin principle. For simplicity's sake Arrow (1968a) assumes only one type of capital good, while all other inputs and outputs are flows. In such a situation, at any moment of time there is, for any fixed stock of capital goods, a most profitable current policy towards flow variables. He assumes that the flow optimization has occurred and thus defines a function that relates operating profits as a function of the stock of capital goods – a function that may change over time as underlying demand and supply conditions change. He also assumes a perfect capital market, so that the firm aims at maximizing the integral of discounted (as market rates of interest) cash flows.

Arrow (1968a, pp. 17–18) points out that in econometric application the profit function is an expectation of future profits. Under the given model, at any moment the firm plans its present and future investments, but only the immediate investment decisions are actually executed.

> Hence, we observe at each moment the initial investment of a long-term investment program, with the profit function and the future course of interest rates which are believed in as of that moment. To determine the empirical implications of this model, it would be necessary to add a second relation, showing how the anticipated profit function and interest rates shift with time, possibly in response to new observations on market magnitudes (Arrow, 1968a, p. 17).

A significant qualitative implication is that the firm either maintains its desired stock of capital (defined by the profit function at the given time and the given interest rate) or there is no gross investment. The empirical validity of this implication can only be tested after the model is reinterpreted to suit the available data. Arrow (1968a, pp. 17–18) notes that

> loosely speaking the firm may be expected to hold the desired stock of capital until a point of time shortly before an anticipated business cycle peak. At this point, gross investment stops abruptly. The hypothesis therefore resembles that of the flexible accelerator which works on the upswing but not on the downswing, – but differs (a) by having a less rigid relation between the desired stock of capital and the level of output, and (b) by admitting the

possibility that the collapse of investment may occur because of anticipation of the end of the boom rather than its actual occurrence.

Arrow's (1968b) study of the applications of optimal control theory to economic growth, runs along similar lines. Here again he makes good use of Pontryagin's basic criteria for optimization of dynamic processes which he restates with emphasis on the special features of growth theory, namely, the assumption of infinite time horizon and the constrained choice of control variables.

Arrow (1968b, p. 92) uses the infinite time horizon (generally traced back to Ramsey, 1928) to underline that the process of capital accumulation for the entire economy is never-ending and that the economy's capital structure at any point of time will have repercussions in the future. 'Of course, the astronomers assure us that the world as we know it will come to an end in some few billions of years. But, as elsewhere in mathematical approximations to the real world, it is frequently more convenient and more revealing to proceed to the limit to make a mathematical infinity in the model correspond to the vast futurity of the real world'.

Arrow (1968b, p. 97) assumes that the system is controllable by policy instruments that include allocations of resources to various productive uses and to consumption.

> We take the viewpoint of a government which is in a position to control the economy completely and to plan perfectly so as to optimize with respect to all possible instruments of the economic system – in this case, only investment and consumption (which are subject to the constraint that their sum not exceed total ouput).

Therefore, 'given . . . the state of the system at some time . . . and the choice of instruments as a function of time . . . the whole course of the system is determined' (Arrow 1968b, p. 86). Alternative scenarios of the economic growth process can be drafted by choosing various values of instruments over time. These alternative scenarios can somehow be evaluated; that is, preferences about them can be expressed and these preferences 'can be given numerical value by a *utility functional* . . . The optimization problem is to choose the values of the instrument variables so as to maximize the utility functional subject to the constraints ... and the initial values of the state variables' (Arrow 1968b, p. 86).

Once again Arrow (1968b, p. 106) uses the concept of irreversible investments, although, in the future, consumption can be increased at the expense of investment by allowing the capital stock to depreciate without replacement.

Another interesting aspect of Arrow's exposition is his inclusion of the dual economy hypothesis; that is, the existence in underdeveloped countries of a progressive and a backward sector. Wages in the former are much higher than in the latter. Workers save nothing and all capital accumulation stems from the surplus of output over wage payments. Assuming that the backward sector produces no relevant product at all, it is possible that full employment of labour in the progressive sector may not be optimal for 'each additional worker creates more product, on the one hand, and a claim to a fixed portion of that product, on the other. Thus capital accumulation might be lower under full employment that with some unemployment' (Arrow, 1968b, p. 114).

Another related field of study is Arrow's preoccupation with the criteria for public investment projects which gave rise to a number of significant contributions. The subject arose when Arrow – on the staff of President Kennedy's Council of Economic Advisers during a part of 1962–3 – was asked to prepare a memorandum on criteria for public investment for the US delegation to the meeting of Senior Economic Advisers, UN Economic Commission for Europe, 9 May 1962 (see Arrow, 1965a). This was the beginning of an abiding interest in the criteria for public investment, especially in the choice of an appropriate discount rate. Arrow was particularly attracted to the choice of criteria for public investment when viewed in the perspective of economic theory and policy of second-best optimality; that is, the recognition of market imperfections to which the design of government policy must adapt (see also Arrow and Kurz, 1970, p. 121 and *passim*; Atkinson and Stiglitz, 1980, pp. 358–63; Haveman and Margolis, 1983).

Thus Arrow accepted an invitation from Resources for the Future to study the problems. He was later joined in the effort by Mordecai Kurz and the result (Arrow and Kurz, 1970) is not only an admirable achievement in technical formulation, but a penetrating analysis and explication of leading points in the theory and policy implications of intertemporal allocation in a novel context; a remarkable integration of the theories of public finance and growth. They provide a link between the determinants of private and public decisions concerning resource allocation and the attempt to set the economy as a whole on an efficient growth path. Their methods draw on Arrow's previous work in capital and inventory theory; in particular they systematically apply the methods of optimal control theory (the Pontryagin principle). They graft the problem of controllability onto public finance and growth theory – a significant theoretical step forward.

Arrow and Kurz (1970) captures, builds upon, and synthesizes commonly accepted principles so as either to resolve certain controversies or at least to clear the air around them. They include in public investment, the investment side of providing inappropriable capital goods. They stress that an investment act is part of a flow of public and private investment and that the same kind of rules apply to future as to current investments. They argue that one should assume the future principles for allocating national income among consumption and private an public investment to be the same as those currently employed.

Arrow and Kurz (1970, Chapter 1) do not address intragenerational distribution and assume the additiveness of utilities in successive periods and thus that the government maximizes a total of discounted utilities. They (1970, p. 11) suggest a criterion function for the achievement of an optimal policy that is

> an analytically manageable form of criterion function, or *utility functional*, which will (a) depend on the main factors determining the satisfaction derived by individuals from the entire economic system, including government investment, and (b) reflect value judgments about intertemporal distribution. We will not seek to represent the effects of government investment on income redistribution at a given period of time; this issue is assumed to be handled by government policies other than investment.

Furthermore,

> the flow of consumption and the services of government capital to each individual are assumed to yield a flow of what may be termed *felicity* . . . to each individual. The flow of felicity to society is the sum over individuals at a given time; the total utility from a policy is taken to be the sum over all time of the felicities of each time,

> discounted back to the present at a constant rate (Arrow and Kurz, 1970, p. 11).

Of course, social benefits diverge from private ones in that the former represent more strongly the benefits accruing to future generations. Private decisions then may well diverge from social goals. In order to narrow down these divergences, the government requires intruments to put its programme into practice. In most societies these instruments are a form of indirect intervention into the workings of the market. Much 'depends upon the range of instruments available to the government, the divergence between private and public objectives, and the imperfections of the markets in which the instruments are employed' (Arrow and Kurz, 1970, p. 117).

Essentially, the social discount rate – more about which later – cannot be identified with market rates because of

> (a) the divergence between private values and market behavior because of capital market imperfections; (b) the divergence between social values and private costs in the products of government investment activity; (c) the divergence between social and private values with regard to perspectives for the future. A fourth, more specific, problem has been mentioned prominently: the imperfections of the capital market that are a direct result of the corporate income tax (Arrow and Kurz, 1970, pp. xiv–xv).

Arrow and Kurz (1970, Chapters 4 and 5) differentiate the fully optimal policy in a centralized economy from the best achievable policy in a mixed economy. In a centralized economy, as they (1970, p. 115) observe, 'the problem of optimal public investments is rather simply defined: the central planning board sets up its objectives and then seeks those investment criteria that will maximize those objectives subject to the technological constraints and resource availability'. The problem is by no means so simple in a decentralized mixed economy. In this case,

> the government cannot directly control private investment or consumption, but it can influence them through its *instruments*, such as taxes and creation or retirement of debt. Hence, the government decision on public investment should be made jointly with a choice of instruments. Since a decision on the volume of public investment is implicitly a decision on its marginal productivity – i.e., on its rate of discount – this position is equivalent to the

more usual formulation that the social rate of discount depends on the mode of financing (Arrow and Kurz, 1970, p. xv).

In the mixed economy, the private economic actors, be they consumers or producers, make their decisions taking those of the government as given. Hence, the government decisions must take into account the feedback effect on the private sector.

An optimal government policy may be controllable – a situation that depends on how well the private markets work and what gamut of policy instruments is at the government's disposal. As Arrow and Kurz (1970, pp. 120, 121, (italics removed)) put it:

> A policy is said to be controllable by a given set of instruments if there exist values of the instruments, varying over time in general, which cause the private and government sectors together to realize that policy.
>
> A policy is said to be controllable with stable instruments if the policy is controllable, the value of the tax rates that achieve control converge to finite values, and the value of the ratio of debt to national income . . . also converges to a finite value.

They focus on the serious problems that arise when public optimal (or some variant thereof) policy is not controllable by a given set of measures. The government may well fail to control optimal policy mainly because capital was not optimally allocated between public and private investment or because national income was not optimally allocated between consumption and investment. More specifically, Arrow and Kurz (1970, pp. 131, 145, 151 (italics removed)) show the cases where there will be uncontrollability:

> If private savings are a fixed proportion of disposable income and the government balances its budget and imposes only an income tax, then neither the publicly optimal policy nor any other given feasible allocation policy is controllable in general.
>
> If private savings consitute a fixed fraction of disposable income and the government finances investment by borrowing and interest payments by taxes, then the publicly optimal policy is not in general controllable.

> Suppose that private savings constitute a fixed fraction of personal income. Then any feasible policy is controllable if the government finances its investment by (a) borrowing and an income tax, (b) borrowing and a tax on consumption, or (c) borrowing for the investment itself and taxes on consumption and savings to pay for the interest. In general, feasible policies are not controllable by borrowing and a tax on savings.

Faced with uncontrollability, the government has to maximize, to the extent possible, its criterion function and resort to second-best (best possible under the circumstances) policy.

Subsequently Arrow and Kurz (1970, p. 153) assume that the consumer behaves perfectly rationally in all respects. 'He looks ahead infinitely far with perfect foresight, he faces a perfect capital market, and he chooses the consumption-savings program so as to maximize the integral of discounted utility for himself and his descendants'.[61] The individual also encounters perfect capital markets (whose values may or may not guide the government). By choosing a suitable mix of tax policies and borrowing, the government implements its policy. 'By an *allocation policy* we mean a choice of feasible time paths for consumption, private capital, and government capital. The government may also seek to control the volume of its public debt over time; in that case, we speak of an *allocation and debt policy*' (Arrow and Kurz, 1970, p. 206).

The authors (1970, Chapter 8) find that if there is an initial debt, financing public investments (determined by an optimal policy) by borrowing is optimal. Income tax (in the ordinary sense) destroys optimality through double taxation of savings. The value of the initial debt may be altered through an initial capital levy that may be thought of as a limiting form of income tax. The most interesting case they study is one where a consumption tax is the only tax imposed. An optimal public policy can be implemented with a consumption tax whose rate is invariable over time, while the rest of public investment is financed by borrowing. Arrow and Kurz (1970, p. xxvii) provide a simple interpretation for the constant rate of the consumption tax:

> If *private wealth* is defined as the sum of government debt, private capital, and future wages discounted to the present according to the wages and interest rates implicit in the publicly optimal policy (wages equal to marginal product of labor), the consumption tax is then the ratio of private wealth to the total of future consumption

discounted to the present. The consumption tax rate will thus depend, among other things, on the initial level of debt.

Aside from deviation of private from social time preferences, Arrow and Kurz consider the issue of determining the social discount rate as revolving around specific imperfections in the market structure (such as inappropriability of the product of public investment, in initial debt that has to be financed, and imperfections of the private capital markets, reflected in the fixed savings ratio hypothesis). They implicitly assume an otherwise perfect market structure. If, however, they (1970, p. xxviii) add,

> there are imperfections elsewhere in the market structure – such as monopolistic price distortions, excise taxes, or the corporate income tax that falls on the fruits of some but not all private investments – then the analysis becomes far more complicated. Any suggested policy must be evaluated in terms of all sorts of cross-effects.

In his latest contribution to the subject, Arrow (1982) deals with the rate of discount on public investments with imperfect markets. He makes some assumptions along the lines of Arrow and Kurz (1970), but in certain cases varies them. For example, here he assumes the identity of utility functions and discount rates between the individual and the government; the anticipation of all future incomes, including the private returns on public investments; and public capital as an intermediary good (for example, research and development or highway construction) that boosts private productivity. Also here he stresses taxes on profits as the method for financing public investment. He (1982, p. 118) focuses his study on

> the second-best policies, where public investment is wholly or partly financed by profits taxes both with and without the additional possibility of financing by borrowing. I concentrate on the steady-state solutions and study the relations among the rates of return on public and private capital and the rates that would obtain in a fully optimal policy. Are the first two rates necessarily equal even if the policy is not fully optimal? Or is the rate of return on public investment equal to the fully optimal rate even when the private rate is not?

Arrow (1982, p. 131) warns that the conclusions he draws are unfortunately not definitive:

> Probably the most striking, to me, though others would regard it as obvious, is the conclusion that there is a strong case for equating the rate of discount in the public sector to that in the private sector to the extent that public investment is financed by taxes on profits. However, as should have been clear all along, if public investment is financed partly through nondistortive taxes, the public rate moves to the utility discount rate, that is, in the long run, the public rate moves to the consumer's rate, and indeed more rapidly than in proportion to the proportion of nondistortive taxes.

In 1970, Arrow (and his former student, Robert C. Lind) contributed (see Arrow, 1971, pp. 239–66) to the controversy surrounding the issue of an appropriate rate of discount for public investment, thus facing the issue of risk and uncertainty in the theoretical and policy analysis of public investment decisions – an issue that had been largely ignored in the vast literature on cost-benefit analysis for public investment decisions (see Haveman and Margolis, 1983, p. 151). Their conclusion – essentially that the government should be risk neutral towards any relatively small projects, upheld in Arrow and Kurz (1970), though much criticized, is representative of Arrow's views to date.

One of the positions in the controversy is represented by Hirshleifer (1965, 1966), see also Haveman and Margolis (1983, pp. 145–66) who argues that public investments should be evaluated individually and discounted at the same rate as private ones, for otherwise public investments would crowd out private ones yielding higher returns. Another position is represented by Samuelson (1964) and Vickrey (1964) (see also Haveman and Margolis, 1983, pp. 152–3) who claim that the government should act as if it were unaffected by risk because the government, by virtue of the multiplicity and diversity of its projects, is able to spread risk over a large pool of projects. Thus the government should use a riskless discount rate which is much lower than the one used in the private sector. Yet a third position is represented by Eckstein (1961) and Marglin (1963) who deny the bearing of individual preferences, revealed by market behaviour, on government decisions (or argue that in any case markets are so imperfect that not much relevant information can be garnered from them) which are dictated by public policy. The latter should establish the attitude towards risk and the appropriate discount rates, which again would reflect an indifference to risk (see Haveman and Margolis, 1983, pp. 3–104, 129–66).

Paradoxically, though Arrow's approach to the problem is quite close to Hirshleifer's, the results he obtains are not unlike those of Samuelson, Vickrey, Eckstein, and Marglin. Arrow's (1971, p. 244) approach is that 'individual preferences are relevant to public investment decisions, and government decisions should reflect individual valuations of costs and benefits'. He (1971, p. 244) demonstrates that

> when the risks associated with a public investment are publicly borne, the total cost of risk-bearing is insignificant and, therefore, the government should ignore uncertainty in evaluating public investments. Similarly, the choice of the rate of discount should in this case be independent of considerations of risk. This result is obtained not because the government is able to pool investments but because the government distributes the risk associated with any investment among a large number of people. It is the risk-spreading aspect of government investment that is essential to this result.

On various occasions Arrow addressed himself to the pregnant questions of the role of effective demand as a factor limiting production and of the classical dichotomy and its policy implications. Hence, he raised the great controvsial questions of macroeconomics.

> Neoclassical microeconomic equilibrium with fully flexible prices presents a beautiful picture of the mutual articulations of a complex structure, full employment being one of its major elements. What is the relation between this world and either the real world with its recurrent tendencies to underemployment of labor, and indeed of capital goods, or the Keynesian world of an underemployment equilibrium? (Arrow, 1967, p. 734).

And Arrow (1984b, p. 155) answers his own question:

> the recurrent periods of unemployment which have characterized the history of capitalism are scarcely compatible with a neoclassical model of market equilibrium. A post-Keynesian world in which unemployment is avoided or kept at tolerable levels by recurrent alterations in fiscal or monetary policy is no more explicable by neoclasssical axioms, though the falsification is not as conspicuous.

Whatever else needs to be said about Keynes (and Kalecki), he focused on aggregate effective demand as a factor constraining production and argued that endogenously generated (private consumption cum investment) demand will generally fall short of stimulating full utilization of existing productive potential. Thus, in his monetary theory of production, Keynes argued for making up this gap by exogenous demand. The question is of an appropriate mix of policies to bring about and maintain full employment. (In a broader interpretation, to use whatever policy instruments are most appropriate to influence and co-ordinate both demand and supply to keep the system reasonably close to a desirable full-employment growth path, while minimizing adverse side effects.)

The foundations of 'Keynesian' theory and policy have been perennially challenged by friends and foes alike. Among the recurring issues is Keynes's attack on the classical separation of value and monetary theories (the 'almost' complete separation of real and nominal magnitudes), on the neutrality of money, and on the 'absence of money illusion'.

In his contribution to the discussion, Arrow (1980, p. 773) observes that, contrary to the main thrust of mainstream neoclassical theory, 'there has been a long-standing doctrine that high levels of employment tend to be accompanied by inflation and that slack economic conditions in general can be relieved by increases in the supply of money'. Furthermore,

> the theory and practice of economic stabilization have been at variance with the main lines of economic theory. In the last ten years or so, there has been a tendency to argue that movements in output and employment are governed primarily by real measures. It is held that there is no systematic relation between employment and inflation and that monetary policy can have no predictable effect.

Arrow (1980, pp. 773–4) argues that whether one accepts the neutrality or non-neutrality viewpoints depends very much on one's views on the existence of involuntary unemployment:

> The view that only real magnitudes matter can be defended only if it is assumed that the labor market (and all other markets) always clear, that is, that all unemployment is essentially voluntary. In this theory, individuals may be unemployed because of errors of judgment – they believe that higher wages can be found by search or

> waiting. But, it is held, at each moment there is a going wage, and any worker who wishes to work at that wage can do so. The view that only real magnitudes matter even over the short periods of the business cycle can only be defended on this extreme view of smoothly working labor markets. If the contrary view is held, that actual unemployment is to a considerable extent involuntary, then monetary magnitudes retain some of their traditional importance for the analysis of and policy toward short-term economic fluctuations.

The fundamental issue, as Arrow (1980, p. 783) sees it,

> in determining whether changes in monetary magnitudes can have planned effects on real quantities, is whether the fluctuations in our economic system are best described by a model in which prices clear markets at every instant or by one in which market disequilibria persist over months or even years.

Thus the critical question is one's notion of the working of the market mechanism: Do present and future markets always clear? Or, do economic agents behave as if they expected markets to be in disequilibrium in the future? Recall, Arrow (1980, p. 781) questions the assertions of the leading exponents of the new classical macroeconomics which leave out important features of the system:

> One is the evidence of everyday observation that some people are unemployed and that some businesses would like to sell more at the current prices and cannot find customers. Another is the statistical observation that the economy is volatile in real as well as nominal terms. To meet this, it is necessary to suggest mechanisms whereby the equilibrium magnitudes may change rapidly from one period to the next. This is related to their emphasis on the importance of anticipation in economic life.

Indeed 'the critical question is whether the anticipation of future disequilibria is an important factor or not. If it is, then it is difficult to maintain the view that nominal magnitudes are unimportant or that money is neutral' (Arrow, 1980, p. 781).

Referring to the arguments presented by the new classical macroeconomists and the policy implications they draw, Arrow (1983b, p. 278) calls attention to a paradox:

> the emphasis on anticipations and stocks minimizes the role of markets as equilibrating mechanisms. The crucial empirical point is that markets for most future commodities do not exist ... But in their absence behavior on current markets largely reflects anticipations of the future if the present is unimportant. It is true that the rational expectations hypothesis implies that the outcomes on future markets are well anticipated, but it is hard to see why this should be true. The very concept of the market and certainly many of the arguments in favor of the market system are based on the idea that it greatly simplifies the informational problems of economic agents, that they have limited powers of information acquisition, and that prices are economic summaries of the information from the rest of the world. But in the rational expectations hypothesis, economic agents are required to be superior statisticians, capable of analyzing the future general equilibria of the economy.

In final analysis, Arrow (1983b, p. 276) finds that the stress on 'the fleeting nature of the present and the dominance of the anticipated future'[62] and on stocks and expectations 'as governing present behavior is a most salutary corrective to an exclusive preoccupation with flows such as marked much post-Keynesian thinking'. He suggests, however, 'that much too drastic consequences are being drawn', but he admits that exaggeration may well be 'a necessary tendency in any shift in theoretical understanding'.

Arrow (1983b, p. 287) supports the interpretation of disequilibrium theorists:

> At any moment of time there are really disequilibria; individuals are not able to carry out all the transactions they want to at the current set of prices. Most strikingly, workers are not able to sell in the market all the labor they would like to at the going wage. Hence the income on which they base their purchasing decisions is not the income they will receive by selling all the labor they want, as it would be in Walrasian or Marshallian equilibrium theory, but rather by selling the labor for which there is an effective demand.

Unlike in the competitive model, here firms tend to anticipate excess supply and perceive limits to sales. 'Most evidence suggests that prices cover normal costs of operation plus a markup. Why do firms not reduce their prices? One explanation clearly is that they feel their sales are rationed and that price cutting would have relatively little influence' (Arrow, 1983b, p. 288, see also Neary and Stiglitz, 1983). Arrow (1983b, p. 288) suggests that 'the hypothesis of rationally perceived quantitative constraints on sales of goods and of labor appears to be fruitful enough for further study'.

The anticipation of future disequilibria has particularly serious consequences for investment decisions. An investor who expects insufficient demand for his product will tailor the investment project to anticipated sales volume, rather than prices, for then the sales volume is no longer affected only by the firm's decisions but by the level of demand. This touches on the Keynesian theory of effective demand.

> Certainly, businessmen in their calculations consider their future sales as limited by demand; and most empirical work on investment has taken the anticipated output as one of the main determining variables. Neither of these observations is decisive, but they both give support to the idea that investment decisions do not depend solely on anticipations of relative prices and that firms do not anticipate automatic market clearing (Arrow, 1980, p. 778).

8 A SUMMING UP

If one looks, as we do, at g.e.t. as one of the truly great ideas and at its achievements as a more or less ascending trend (with the usual 'fluctuations around trend') towards a more and more general and useful theory, one can emphasize the great feats and failures of the past and the challenges and roadblocks ahead. In scholarly work, as in real life, it is the dynamics of the process that count. When looking through the prism of the process of accretion of knowledge, one should not identify the state of g.e.t. with the shortcomings of specific models, intended to highlight particular (previously neglected) issues, such as the implications of information costs and asymmetries or particular representations of the organization of economic activity, that oversimplify or introduce 'mad' assumptions that may well be wildly at variance with reality about other aspects that are not the central subject of the models (see Hart, 1984).

True there is no truly universal g.e. model or theory. It is even doubtful whether such an all-encompassing theory (with shifting aspiration levels, say, of dynamics and *modus operandi* of monetary economy under different institutional arrangements and social systems) can ever (or at least in the near future) be constructed. Admittedly, g.e. is not *the* theory of economics. One of the benefits of the progress in economics is that it has made us much more humble; more careful and precise in advancing claims and more aware of the limits of our analysis. It is to the credit of the makers of modern g.e.t. that they explicitly articulate the limits and potentials of the theory.

'The prestige status of the purest of pure economic theory has never been higher; and yet there is now, as there has always been, a pervasive scepticism about the descriptive power and normative utility of Walrasian or other varieties of the theory of general competitive equilibrium' (Arrow, 1985a, p. 107). In order to throw the critiques of g.e.t., especially of the competitive model, into a certain perspective, it might be helpful to look closer at its very nature, its usefulness, and the general methodological approach.

Unlike activity analysis which is essentially a pre-institutional type of analysis (see Koopmans, 1977 pp. 264–65), the model of competitive equilibrium is closer to the private enterprise market economy. After all, when it was originally only a glimmer of the fully developed system we now have, its source was observation of real world behaviour at that time. It takes note of producers and consumers and specifies for them simplified behaviour patterns. In this model the firm is endowed with only the specific characteristics required for establishing the existence and optimality of competitive equilibrium. However, to a large extent this model is pre-institutional in nature, for it remains indeterminate about the size of the firm (see Koopmans, 1957 pp. 148–49). In fact, it too tells us little about the institutional set up of the economy and like activity analysis could be a helpful tool of analysis under various decentralized social systems (see Malinvaud, 1972; Smale, 1976b, p. 289).

Arrow is interested in the competitive equilibrium model both for its descriptive and prescriptive power. He (1983a, pp vii–viii) cannot conceive of the 'study of economic phenomena from a purely descriptive or positivistic viewpoint'. After all, 'policy implications have been the direct or indirect concern of economists throughout the history of the subject'. He (1983d, p. 16) observes that 'even the most austere seeker after truth and logic has found it difficult not to speak out on occasion to make some recommendation or another, and any recommendation must involve a normative statement'. And, speaking of himself, with a perspicacity not commonly encountered in self-analysis, Arrow adds, 'even the unworldly author of these lines has felt the obligation to speak out'.

Koopmans (1957, pp. 63–64) differentiates the descriptive and prescriptive *applications* of the competitive equilibrium model as follows: In the former, 'markets believed to be competitive are observed and the model assures us that such markets achieve efficient allocation, if not necessarily a most desirable distribution, of resources'. In the latter, 'allocative efficiency is embraced as part of a given norm, and competitive markets, or administrative prices responded to as if they were market prices, are recommended as a means of achieving this norm'. He points to a Lange-type model of market socialism as an example of this, with the possibilities of intermediate cases such as 'a mixed economy with genuine competitive markets where technological conditions so permit and a controlled form of price-guided allocation elsewhere'. One could envisage many other prescriptive applications, more in line with Arrow's work on (re)design of organizations to take care of problems caused by the nonexistence or failure of markets (see Chapter 1A of the companion volume).

Recall, Arrow is steeped in the axiomatic method and his *Social Choice and Individual Values* is a classic in the axiomatization of economics and, more generally, the social sciences - one of the *differentia specifica* of the post-war period (save for such inter-war 'incursions' into the subject by mathematicians such as von Neumann and Wald). In the various evaluations of contemporary economics much depends on the evaluator's understanding of and attitude to the axiomatic method. Before the critics have their say, we have to listen to the defence's case. Gerard Debreu has long been among the method's chief defenders and speaks about its advantages with the authority of a great master. He has returned to the subject on several occasions, most recently in his Frisch Memorial Lecture (Debreu, 1985) to the Fifth Congress of Econometrics, where he points out that the axiomatization of economic theory resulted in a clarity of expression that was one of the principal gains. The very definition of an economic concept is usually subject to a substantial margin of ambiguity. An axiomatized theory substitutes for an ambiguous concept a mathematical object that is subject to entirely definite rules of reasoning. The complete specification of assumptions, the exact statement of conclusions, and the rigour of the deductions of an axiomatized study provide a secure foundation for the construction of economic theory. Another important attribute of axiomatization is the gain in simplicity.

> An axiomatized theory first selects its primitive concepts and represents each one of them by a mathematical object ... Next, assumptions on the objects representing the primitive concepts are specified, and consequences are mathematically derived from them. The economic interpretation of the theorems so obtained is the last step of the analysis. According to this scheme, an axiomatized theory has a mathematical form that is completely separated from its economic content. If one removes the economic interpretation of the primitive concepts, of the assumptions and of the conclusions of the model, its bare mathematical structure must still stand. . . .
>
> The divorce of form and content immediately yields a new theory whenever a novel interpretation of a primitive concept is discovered. A textbook illustration of this application of the axiomatic method occurred in the economic theory of uncertainty. The traditional characteristics of a commodity were its physical description, its date, and its location when in 1953 Kenneth Arrow proposed adding the state of the world in which it will be available. This reinterpretation of the concept of a commodity led, without any formal change in the model developed for the case of certainty, to a theory of uncertainty. . . .
>
> The exact formulation of assumptions and of conclusions turned out, moreover, to be an effective safeguard against the ever-present temptation to apply an economic theory beyond its domain of validity. And by the exactness of that formulation, economic analysis was sometimes brought closer to its ideology-free ideal. . . .
>
> Thus an axiomatic theorist succeeds in communicating the meaning he intends to give to a primitive concept because of the completely specified formal context in which he operates. The more developed this context is, the smaller will be the margin of ambiguity in the intended interpretation (Debreu, 1985, pp. 12–14).

In final analysis, Debreu, (1984, p. 275) believes that

> Axiomatization, by insisting on mathematical rigor, has repeatedly led economists to a deeper understanding of the problems they were studying, and to the use of mathematical techniques that fitted those problems better. It has established secure bases from which

exploration could start in new directions. It has freed researchers from the necessity of questioning the work of their predecessors in every detail.

Along similar lines, Koopmans (1957, p. 147) emphasizes that

> the best safeguard against overestimation of the range of applicability of economic propositions is a careful spelling out of the premises on which they rest. Precision and rigor in the statement of premises and proofs can be expected to have a sobering effect on our beliefs about the reach of the propositions we have developed.

The strife for increased rigor and precision in formulating the assumptions and propostions casts the lack of realism of the assumptions into sharper relief. 'As we succeed in recognizing and incorporating one aspect of the real world in our models, our failure to incorporate other aspects becomes more apparent' (Koopmans, 1957, p. 126). When confronted with a mathematical model designed to mimic reality, the non-mathematical economist asserts

> that it is 'oversimplified', that it 'does not represent all the complexities of reality'. In effect, he is saying that the symbolic language in which the mathematical model is expressed is too poor to convey all the nuances of meaning which he can carry in his mind (Arrow 1951b, p. 130).

A legitimate question then is: is rigor the enemy of realism? Arrow (1951b, p. 131) believes that even if it is, 'the advantages ... may frequently be worth a certain loss of realism. In the *first* place, clarity of thought is still a pearl of great price'. Koopmans (1957, pp. 142–43) answers this questions by referring to the sequence of models that step by step involve problems closer to complex reality – a method that Arrow follows in this work.

> At first these aspects are formalized as much as feasible in isolation, then in combinations of increasing realism. Each model is defined by a set of postulates, of which the implications are developed to the extent deemed worthwhile in relation to the aspects of reality expressed by the postulates. The study of the simpler models is protected from the reproach of unreality by the consideration that

these models may be prototypes of more realisitic, but also more complicated, subsequent models. The card file of successfully completed pieces of reasoning represented by these models can then be looked upon as the logical core of economics, as the depository of available economic theory (see Hutchison, 1984; Hart, 1984).

Another advantage of the axiomatic method worth mentioning is that it facilitates communication among the sciences and further cross-fertilization among them. Koopmans (1957, p. 145) observes that

> specialists in reasoning outside economics such as mathematicians, logicians, statisticians, and philosophers, will more readily contribute from their experience in other fields if they are enabled to examine the reasoning on which economics rests in isolation from the welter of facts, circumstances, and interpretations, which the economist must have in mind when appraising the value to him of these pieces of reasoning.

Debreu (1984, p. 275) conceives of the 'superbly efficient language of mathematics' as permitting economists

> to communicate with each other, and to think, with a great economy of means. At the same time, the dialogue between economists and mathematicians has become more intense. The example of a mathematician of the first magnitude like John von Neumann devoting a significant fraction of his research to economic problems has not been unique. Simultaneously, economic theory has begun to influence mathematics. Among the clearest instances are Kakutani's theorem, the theory of integration of correspondences . . ., algorithms for the computation of approximate fixed points . . ., and of approximate solutions of systems of equation.

This language of mathematics is 'distinguished from the other language habitually used by the social scientist chiefly by its superior clarity and consistency' (Arrow, 1951b, p. 129). Arrow (1983a, p. 46) also admits to being lured by the aesthetic satisfactions in the use of mathematics; 'the more general our study, and the larger our horizon, the more our artistic taste is satisfied. But it is still more important to show that certain complicated problems are in their essence, analogous to simple problems that are more transparent'. Debreu (1984, p. 275) speaks of the 'aesthetic appeal' of the simplicity and generality of an 'effective theory' which 'suffices to make them desirable ends in themselves for the designer of a theory. But their value to the scientific community goes far beyond aesthetics'.

Not every proposition, however, can be expressed in mathematical form – at least within the framework of presently existing mathematical theory. However, 'every mathematician realizes what a small part of all the potentially available mathematical knowledge is actually grasped at the present time' (Arrow, 1951b, p. 130). This raises the pregnant question of interaction of tools and problems awaiting solution. Is the further development of economic theory hampered by the non-existence of the required tools? Koopmans (1957, p. 170) tells us that

> if we look with a historian's interest at the development of science, however, we find that tools also have a life of their own. They may even come to dominate an entire period or school of thought. The solution of important problems may be delayed because the requisite tools are not perceived. Or the availability of certain tools may lead to an awareness of problems, important or not, that can be solved with their help. Our servants may thus become our guides, for better or for worse, depending on the accidents of the case. But in any case changes in tools and changes in emphasis on various problems go together and interact.

Almost at the beginning of his career as an economist, Arrow (1951b, p. 131) noted that among its sister social sciences, economics is the field where mathematical methods have been most successful. More than 30 years later, Samuelson (1983a, p. xviii) reports that Debreu commented to him that modern economic theory is the discipline that makes greatest day-to-day use of avant-garde mathematics. And, Samuelson adds, 'that is a sobering thought indeed'. Arrow (1984b, p. 154) attributes the longevity and 'persistence of neoclassical theory in the face of its long line of critics' to the fact that 'for some reason of mathematical structure, the neoclassical theory is highly manipulable and flexible; when faced with a specific issue, it can yield meaningful implications relatively easily' (see Smale, 1975b, p. 289).

Recall, 'the twin pillars of neoclassical doctrine are the principle of optimization by economic agents, and the co-ordination of their activities through the market' (Arrow, 1985a, p. 107). The first pillar is 'the notion of the individual economic agent, whose behavior is governed by a criterion of optimization under constraints which are partly peculiar to the agent, such as production functions, and partly terms of trade with the economic system as a whole. The other is the market; here, the aggregate of individual decisions is acknowledged, and the terms of trade adjusted until the decisions of the individuals are mutually consistent in the aggregate, that is, supply equals demand' (Arrow, 1984b, p. 154).

Criticisms of the neoclassical theory, and more specifically of the competitive model, are not new; it has been much maligned over the years for a host of reasons. In recent years no less scathing, but more fruitful and constructive criticism has come from its practitioners. Before turning to the dissatisfaction from within the citadel, let us briefly pose on the issues raised by the (dis)loyal opposition which focus not only on the very pillars of neoclassical theory and on the axiomatic method, but also on some very specific aspects of the competitive equilibrium model.

Rationality of the economic actor has been a concept central to mainstream economics and refined over successive generations. From the very beginning it has been strongly criticized for being empirically unsubstantiated. Among others, Veblen ridiculed those of his colleagues who imputed exceptional computational power and proficiency to the average economic actor (see Arrow, 1975, p. 6; 1984a, pp. 261–70). On the contemporary scene, Simon (1982) and others – descendants of the institutionalist tradition – have been stressing that neither do individual actors possess the computational abilities demanded of them for rational choices nor do we pay sufficient attention to custom or convention as factors in decision-making (see Feiwel, 1985a, pp. 44–62).

There are a good many other characteristics of g.e.t. for which it is being impugned;[63] it is blamed for being lifeless, motionless, barren and divorced from reality. At the cost of oversimplification, and mindful of all the pitfalls into which such an encapsulated version of the long litany of g.e.t. shortcomings must fall, we shall nevertheless brave them and list the salient objections both when they are right and when they are wrong.

G.e.t. (or its specific models) is commonly (mis)perceived as being elegant, but too abstract (or starting from the 'wrong kind' of abstractions), sterile and useless. The intellectual effort is considered to be wasted on the vacuous, intractable, or unrealistic conceptual world of timeless equilibrium. Moreover, strong normative overtones are read into it. At its heart are economic agents (transactors or other disembodied entities) who are perfectly rational, perfectly informed, omniscient, egoistic, and governed by greed, operating with perfect foresight in an essentially static environment that is bereft of any institutional content or structure, and of any economic role for the government. In this fancy world markets operate smoothly without frictions or exogenous shocks, lags, and imperfect or incomplete adjustments. The theory has little to say about how equilibrium comes about and who it is that changes prices. It emphasizes allocative efficiency at the expense of dynamic efficiency; that is, the creative function of market signals to transmit impulses for change or the Schumpeterian creative destruction. In the world of g.e.t. there allegedly are no increasing returns to scale, no indivisibilities, and no inappropriability. It focuses on information embodied in prices and disregards other costly information necessary for carrying out production and consumption activities and the non-price influences on demand. It stresses anonymity of market relations and disregards the pervasiveness of direct specific contracts. Above all, it is essentially without the concepts of market power, uncertainty, and historical time, and says nothing about income distribution.

The modern world is characterized by pervasive market power of all kinds which is in striking variance with the g.e. concept of decentralized competitive economy and poses serious conceptual problems for theoretical analysis (see Hahn, 1973, p. 32). Countless economists have criticized mainstream neoclassical economics for neither perceiving nor treating economic power as a central issue of the contemporary world, except, perhaps, none of them in the inimitable prose of John Kenneth Galbraith (1973, pp. 5, 11):

> Neoclassical economics is not without an instinct for survival. It rightly sees the unmanaged sovereignty of the consumer, the ultimate sovereignty of the citizen and the maximization of profits and resulting subordination of the firm to the market as the three legs of a tripod on which it stands. These are what exclude the role of power in the system. All three propositions tax the capacity for belief ... It tells the young and susceptible and the old and

vulnerable that economic life has no content of power and politics because the firm is safely subordinate to the market and to the state and for this reason it is safely at the command of the consumer and citizen. Such an economics is not neutral. It is the influential and invaluable ally of those whose exercise of power depends on an acquiescent public.

Concurrently the scathing attacks on the use of mathematical methods in economics, that flourished in the later 1940s and the 1950s, continue to this day (see Feiwel, 1985a, pp. 82–6). Mathematical economists continue to be accused of treating sophisticated model building as an end in itself. The long-standing challenge of irrelevance, incongruity, esoteric nature, and ephemeral substance of certain theories in explaining and improving economic processes ebbs and flows.

Samuelson (1966, p. 1760) once perceptively remarked that economists who *do not* know mathematics run the 'grave psychological risks' of increasingly resenting this method as they grow older. Is this not also true of those who *do* know mathematics? As exhibit A, one can submit Solow's (1985, p. 328) statement: 'I suspect that the attempt to construct economics as an axiomatically based hard science is doomed to fail'. And, as exhibit B, we submit his (p. 330) caricature of the modern economist:

> My impression is that the best and brightest in the profession proceed as if economics is the physics of society. There is a single universally valid model of the world. It only needs to be applied. You could drop a modern economist from a time machine – a helicopter, maybe, like the one that drops the money – at any time, in any place, along with his or her personal computer; he or she could set up in business without even bothering to ask what time and which place . . .
> We are socialized to the belief that there is one true model and that it can be discovered or imposed if only you will make the proper assumptions and impute validity to econometric results that are transparently lacking in power.

As exhibit C we dare offer Hahn (1970, pp. 2 and 1), the master self-critic, who views the situation in mathematical economics as unpalatable and disquieting, an 'unsatisfactory and slightly dishonest state of affairs'. Undoubtedly 'the achievements of economic theory in the last two decades are both impressive and in many ways beautiful. But it cannot be denied that there is something scandalous in the spectacle of so many people refining the analysis of economic states which they give no reason to suppose will ever, or have ever, come about'.

Leontief (1971, p. 1) is adamant that there is in fact a 'fundamental imbalance in the present state of our discipline. The weak and all too slowly growing empirical foundations clearly cannot support the proliferating superstructure of pure, or should I say, speculative economic theory'. Georgescu-Roegen (1970, p. 1) also reminds us that 'in our haste to mathematize economics we have often been carried away by mathematical formalism to the point of disregarding a basic requirement of science; namely, to have as clear an idea as possible about what corresponds in actuality to every piece of our symbolism'. The appraisal of Morishima (1984, p. 65), the renegade g.e. theorist, runs along similar grooves. He believes that the crucial factor responsible for the 'present remarkably 'anaemic' situation is that empirical institutional knowledge and mathematics have failed to sustain a good, co-operative relationship'.

Solow (1985, pp. 328–9), on the other hand, points to the dangers of empirical verification of various hypotheses, especially by means of statistical analysis of historical time series. 'The competing hypotheses are themselves complex and subtle. We know before we start that all of them, or at least many of them, are capable of fitting the data in a gross sort of way'. Thus we require *long* time series under *stationary* conditions. However,

> much of what we observe cannot be treated as the realization of a stationary stochastic process without straining credulity. Moreover, all narrowly economic activity is embedded in a web of social institutions, customs, beliefs, and attitudes. Concrete outcomes are indubitably affected by these background factors, some of which change slowly and gradually, others erratically. As soon as time-series get long enough to offer hope of discriminating among complex hypotheses, the likelihood that they remain stationary dwindles away, and the noise level gets correspondingly high. Under these circumstances, a little cleverness and persistence can get you almost any result you want.

Solow then concludes that

> there is enough for us to do without pretending to a degree of

> completeness and precision which we cannot deliver ... In this scheme of things, the end product of economic analysis is likely to be a collection of models contingent on society's circumstances – on the historical context, you might say – and not a single monolithic model for all seasons.

Morishima's (1984, pp. 51–2) criticism is often biting and specifically directed. He speculates that if the degree of systematic axiomatization is to be identified with scientific advancement, by this criterion 'the theoretical systems such as are being worked on by top mathematical economists in the 1980s bear favourable comparison with highly advanced theoretical physics, regarded as the queen of the natural sciences'. He then goes on:

> Students who have read works on social choice or Arrow and Hahn's monumental book *General Competitive Analysis* (1971) are likely to be surprised at the remarkable resemblance between such works and Spinoza's *Ethica Ordine Geometrico Demonstrata*. The Arrow and Hahn work in particular is poor in terms of empirical content ... Spinoza's work, which is at the same time metaphysics, epistemology, ethics and religious doctrine, persuasively demonstrates that axiomatization and scrupulous mathematical proof are by no means the monopoly of modern science, and that such techniques could also be used as weapons by the dogmatists, sophists and scholastics who were the enemies of modern scientists.

Of interest here is Debreu's (1985, p. 19) note of warning about the proliferation of mathematical models. 'Their sum is so large as to turn occasionally into a liability, as the seductiveness of that form becomes almost irresistible. In its pursuit, researchers may be tempted to forget economic content and to shun economic problems that are not really amenable to mathematization'.

Is there all that much difference between the visions of Arrow and Morishima? On many occasions we have stressed the importance of the interdependence of the economic system in the Arrovian vision (see also Chapter 2 of this volume). Morishima (1984, pp. 68–9) admits that, despite all its failings, he still believes 'general-equilibrium theory to be the theoretical kernel of economics'. He also regards 'general-equilibrium theory as being significant' in the sense of the whole economy being conceived of as a system.

> Without this sort of framework it is impossible to elucidate in any

> systematic fashion what sort of repercussions on what part of the economy will result from a disturbance arising in one part of the economy. What I mean by general-equilibrium theory ... is this sort of theory concerning the framework of the economy. This framework is likely to be different for different countries, and apt to change when times change. In my 'general-equilibrium theory', therefore, mathematics too is, to a certain degree, important, but more important are such things as knowledge and observation of the economic system itself and a considerable interest in history and sociology (Morishima, 1984, p. 69).

Arrow (1960, p. 175) perceives that extensive use of mathematical techniques involves the danger of 'cutting the lines of communication with economists who lack mathematical training, and a tendency to value mathematical technique over economically meaningful results'. But, one may well say of Arrow what he (1960, p. 175) has said of Frisch: in his work

> the sterile Byzantinism that might be implied by these dangers is completely avoided. At all points, there is an open-minded receptivity to economic ideas derived from all sources, whether or not expressed mathematically, and the focus of all research is the underlying economic issue, not the mathematics used. This does not, however, mean any reluctance to use difficult mathematics when it is necessary to the solution. At all times, the economic problem is the master; the necessary mathematics is neither complicated for reasons of elegance and generality nor skimped for reasons of unpopularity.

Some of the most constructive criticism of neoclassical theory has come from within; from the soul-searching of the practitioners. Much of the progress in the last 30 years is due to the benevolent and beneficial influence that Arrow wields within this rather close-knit fraternity and his untiring efforts to redirect investigations into what he considers the most pressing unresolved issues.

In the prologue to this chapter we have brushed in bold strokes Arrow's proclivity towards emphasizing certain social and structural factors in his efforts to understand the way the economic system works – factors that are missing in neoclassical theory. In his 1973 presidential address to the American Economic Association, Arrow (1984b, pp. 153–66) shares with his fellow economists his disquietude about the state of the art and science and his conviction about the need to reorient research.

At the outset, he (1984b, pp. 154–5) expresses his unswerving wonder at the feats of the 'much abused' neoclassical viewpoint. Even when utilizing for analysis the formal statement of equilibrium conditions of the individual agent and of the market, without inquiring how they come about, Arrow considers that important revelations into the resource allocation process are gleaned. As an example he offers the explanation (due to Medicare and Medicaid with price-inelastic supply of physicians and hospitals) for the higher rise in medical (in relation to other) costs since 1967. Another example that Arrow (1984b, p. 155) considers 'an insight of purely neoclassical origin' is 'the explanation of environmental problems as due to the nonexistence of markets'.

In another context (as a prologue to his work on labour discrimination), Arrow (1972b, Chapter 2, pp. 83–4) clarifies his attitude towards the fruitfulness and value of neoclassical theory:

> On the one hand, I believe its clarifying value in social thought is great. Especially when dealing with problems central to economics, the difference in approach between trained economists and others, however able, is enormous. The importance of the search for possible alternatives, the value of consistency in different contexts as a guide to judgment, and, above all, the appreciation that the workings of institutions may be such that the outcomes are very different from the intentions of the agents are among the lessons of economic theory. So long as scarcity is an issue and social organizations for coping with it are complex, these principles and their logical elaboration and empirical implementation will be important. Although this is not the place for an elaborate defense, I reject, on both logical and historical grounds, the widespread suspicion that neoclassical economics is simply an apology for the status quo.

Arrow (1984b, pp. 156–7) admits that the concept of optimization by economic agents ignores many important ingredients that enter into the individual's utility function and the limits on information gathering and processing. Nevertheless, for him,

> the optimization by individual agents has a sense of concreteness about it, for all the sophisticated mathematical ability with which we theorists endow the agents. They behave in ways whose logic we

> understand. They seek to achieve goals which are reasonable to postulate, and we can specify constraints which clearly are real ... The model is comprehensible, and the motives and constraints we deal with are real and important.

Arrow (1951b, pp. 138–40) also draws attention to the fact that statistical inference theory and game theory rely heavily on the rationality of the economic agent.

Over the years, Arrow (1984a, pp. 261–70) has become increasingly sceptical of the concept of rationality which applied to the static world of certainty 'has turned out to be a weak hypothesis, not easily refuted and therefore not very useful as an explanation, though not literally a tautology'. Recent investigations by psychologists have cast dark shadows over the expected-utility hypothesis of behaviour under uncertainty and the Bayesian hypothesis for learning. All this was happening while the new classical macroeconomists have increasingly relied on these hypotheses in their rational-expectations models. 'These hypotheses have been used widely in offering explanations of empirically observed behavior, though, as not infrequently in economics, the theoretical development has gone much further than the empirical implementation'.

The very essence of Arrow's (1985a, p. 109) reservations about the price system is well captured in the following passage:

> Modern economic theory has gradually refined the conditions under which the price system might not achieve efficient or optimal resource allocation. Many of the discussions have revolved around three classical reasons: indivisibilities, inappropriability, and uncertainty, and around such concepts as increasing returns, externalities, public goods, transaction costs, and market failures, pointing, *inter alia*, to the incompleteness or the limits on the theoretical validity of the price system whereby certain actions though they may lead to private good may result in social ill.

In his Nobel Lecture, Arrow (1983b, pp. 191–200) underlines the coherence of the system of interdependencies expressed on the market and the remarkable balance 'between the amounts of goods and services that some individuals want to supply and the amounts that other, different individuals want to buy'. But he never overstates the case:

> Most conspicuously, the history of the capitalist system has been

> marked by recurring periods in which the supply of available labor and of productive equipment available for the production of goods has been in excess of their utilization, sometimes, as in the 1930s, by very considerable magnitudes. Further, the relative balance of overall supply and demand in the postwar period in the United States and Europe is in good measure the result of deliberate governmental policies, not an automatic tendency of the market to balance.

For Arrow (1984b, p. 156), 'the existence of unemployment is clearly a direct contradiction to the notion of the smoothly clearing market'. Of course, the official measure of unemployment aggregates voluntary, involuntary, seasonal, and frictional unemployment. Arrow forcefully rejects the view that all unemployment is basically voluntary. Indeed, he believes that 'the official measure may underestimate the degree of disequilibrium in the labor market, particularly with regard both to underutilization of advanced skills and discouraged job seekers'. And, it is quite clear to him that 'statistical unemployment does correspond to a disequilibrium as that term is used in the basic neoclassical model'.

Another basic difficulty for the neoclassical model is uneven economic development among countries and among regions, as well as inequalities of income distribution which 'seem much too vast to be explained by factor differences. Indeed, in the presence of international trade and especially international capital movements, wage differences should be very strongly reduced' (Arrow, 1984b, p. 155). This is explained by differences in production possibility sets in various countries. What it actually means is that, in various countries, the access to productive knowledge varies. The same also applied to various workers within a national economy (see Arrow, 1984b, p. 156).

Here we re-enter the realm of asymmetric information and information costs. It has been stressed that the price system is highly valued for its informational economy. But this economy is often more apparent than real as vast quantities of non-price costly information are required for daily operation. In particular, as we know, very few futures markets exist for mainly two reasons: 'One is that contracts are not enforceable without cost, and forward contracts are more costly to enforce than contemporaneous contracts; the other is that because of the many uncertainties about the future, neither buyers nor sellers are willing to make commitments which completely define their future actions' (Arrow, 1984b, p. 163). Hence, there is a whole gamut of implications of costly dispersed information for decisions that involve the future (such as, for example investments), but these also bear heavily on decisions involving current actions because all information is not readily at hand.

> At a moment of time, prices of what would usually be thought of as the same commodity bought or sold by different firms can differ because buyers or sellers may not, in their ignorance and in the presence of costs of search, find it worthwhile to shop further. Obviously, the important application of this principle may be to the labor market. There are clearly important informational differences between the employees currently working for a firm and potential substitutes elsewhere, although these are interchangeable in pure neoclassical theory. Indeed, there are differences both in the information the firm possesses about its employees as compared with alternatives and the information which employees have about the economic opportunities and the specific production conditions of the firm as compared with outsiders. It appears that considerations of this type must play some role in understanding the continued possibility of unemployment and particularly the sluggish response of wages to market disequilibria (Arrow, 1984b, p. 166).

Another important issue is how the system arrives at equilibrium. An attempt to answer this question was made in the third section of this chapter. But, along with many others, Arrow (1984b, p. 157) considers the stability models to be 'far from adequate representations even of the dynamics of the neoclassical models, and – what may be connected – the results are by no means necessarily favorable to the stability of the adjustment process; and on the other hand, the motivations for the feedback to operate are obscure'.

Arrow (1984b, pp. 157–8) is uneasy about what he terms our 'unsatisfactory' understanding of the market as an institution, but he emphasizes that this should not prevent us from using 'the perfect market as a model, at least pending further development'. He finds this model curiously complementary to Keynesian theory.

> We have never been able to integrate Keynesian viewpoints into standard neoclassical theory, in terms of individual motivation, yet this theory, with its various modifications has been a most serviceable tool of prediction and control. In fact, it is useful in domains

> where competitive theory fails and vice versa. Neither theory is good, however, at predicting dynamic process, the short-run changes which are responses to disequilibria, and it is here that the pressure for a more satisfactory model arises (Arrow, 1984b, p. 158).

Another area where the competitive model comes to grief is its neglect of the concentration of economic power and its bias towards small firms and free entry. The analytical tools of neoclassical economics are not suited for deviations from perfect competition. There is no conflict between optimizing behaviour and market power, but there are difficulties in defining imperfectly competitive markets. Game theory, as Arrow (1983f, p. 17) remarks, 'has supplied a formal framework that, in principle, replaces markets by more general forms of interactions, but it has not yet succeeded in producing a *general* theory comparable in power to the theory of general competitive equilibrium'. But the standard competitive model cannot readily take account of increasing returns. 'Constant returns, on the other hand, is neutral toward the size of firms. If two firms merge, the owners will (under perfect competition) be neither better off nor worse off than they were before. Under perfect markets, including perfect capital markets, the profits of two different activities will simply be additive'.

To sum up, the unresolved central issues of modern neoclassical g.e. theory, according to Arrow (1985a, p. 110), include:

> (i) the relations between microeconomics and macroeconomics, (ii) the failures to incorporate imperfect eompetiton, and (iii) the failures to account for costs of transaction (essential to the theory of money and asset holding generally). Moreover, the integration of the demand and supply of money with general competitive equilibrium theory remains incomplete despite attempts beginning with Walras himself.

That g.e.t. is vastly incomplete is not a controversial issue. What is debatable is whether in future economics will develop through recasting and refinements of the received apparatus, or through a revolutionary change of paradigm. Koopmans (1974, p. 325) for one suggests a 'reformist' agenda for research; that is, to amend and extend the given special case by grafting other important aspects on to it', but he would not exclude entirely new approaches embodying other aspects of reality.

On the other hand, Morishima (1984, pp. 57–8) has a gloomier outlook. He strongly criticizes what he calls the 'highly sophisticated mock-ups' that the improvers of g.e.t. have produced. He attributes 'the continuing frustration which has beset the development of economic theory over the last 30 years or more' to 'the failure of economic theorists to carry out sweeping, systematic research into the actual mechanisms of the economy and economic organizations, despite their being aware that their own models are inappropriate to analysis of the actual economy'. Most damaging is the fact that 'the institutional foundation of these so-called highbrow economic theories is an extremely shaky one' (Morishima, 1984, p. 59). And he (p. 67) warns that 'however beautiful or however elegant the whole system may be, those who devote themselves to a learning which is useless are inevitably just playing at a pastime, and it is likely that before long its learning will come to a standstill'.

Arrow's (1967, p. 735 (emphasis added)) position is very clearly a reformist one, as we have traced throughout this chapter:

> Obviously, I believe firmly that the mutual adjustment of prices and quantities represented by the neoclassical model is an important aspect of economic reality worthy of the serious analysis that has been bestowed on it; and certain dramatic historical episodes ... suggest that an economic mechanism exists which is capable of adaptation to radical shifts in demand and supply conditions. On the other hand, the Great Depression and the problems of developing countries remind us dramatically that *something beyond, but including, neoclassical theory is needed.*

In his own work he has continually heeded this injunction. For example, in his exposition of the theory of discrimination (as we have seen in Section 6.3), Arrow (1973, p. 4) uses 'as far as possible neoclassical tools in the analysis of discrimination'. And, continuing in his own words,

> even though the basic neoclassical assumptions of utility and profit maximization are always retained, many of the usual assumptions will be relaxed at one point or another: convexity of indifference surfaces, costless adjustment, prefect information, perfect capital markets. As I will try to show, the abandonment of each of these assumptions is motivated by a clearly compelling reason in the theoretical structure of the subject. Personally, I believe there are

> many other economic phenomena whose explanation entails the abandonment of each of these assumptions, so the steps proposed here are not ad hoc analyses but should be important elements in a more general theory capable of analyzing the effects of social factors in economic behavior without either lumping them into an uninformative category of 'imperfections' or jumping to a precipitate rejection of neoclassical theory with all its analytic power.

And in the area of social policy (see Chapter 1A of the companion volume), Arrow (1985a, p. 109) believes that

> the price system does not always work and valuable though it is in in certain realms, it cannot be made the complete arbiter of social life. In fact, there is a great number of situations where it is necessary or at least desirable to replace the market by social decision-making.

In 1848, J. S. Mill (1909, book 3, Chapter 1, pr. 1) wrote: 'Happily, there is nothing in the laws of Value which remains for the present or any future writer to clear up; the theory of the subject is complete.' Yet, as we have seen, since then this view has been continually challenged. Each generation of economic theorists called attention to the lacunae and to the moving boundaries as it perceived them. All scientists, great and humble alike, work within the field of their vision – in the Schumpeterian sense (see Chapter 5 of this volume). In Chapter 1A of the companion volume we attempt to trace the influences that conditioned Arrow, the scientist and moral philosopher.

Like his humbler brethren, a great scientist does not work in a vacuum. His feet rest on the shoulders of all those other giants who came before him. And, as is often the case in the history of science, his contributions are sparked by a specific concatenation of ideas that have flowed somewhat before him and seem to simultaneously erupt on the scene as a powerful stream. So it must have been for Arrow in the late 1940s when the first impact of Samuelson (1947), game theory, activity analysis, statistical decision theory (and, of course, the more specific contributions or examples of Hotelling, Marschak, Ramsey, Wald, von Neumann, Nash, and Kakutani) was being absorbed. As Samuelson (1977a, p. 937) put it: 'In science, a culmination is a beginning. When the young Arrow came to economics in the late nineteen-forties – at Columbia, Chicago, and ultimately at Stanford where he made his great contributions – he faced problems opened up by the Hicksian breakthroughs.' And, one should add, the Samuelsonian breakthroughs. But, unlike his lesser brethren, the mark of the great scientist is that he adds to the edifice of knowledge. Contemporary and future economists have good reason to be grateful to Arrow for having provided them with 'new shoulders' to stand on.

> Creating a new theory is not like destroying an old barn and erecting a skyscraper in its place. It is rather like climbing a mountain, gaining new and wider views, discovering unexpected connections between our starting-point and its rich environment. But the point from which we started still exists and can be seen, although it appears smaller and forms a tiny part of our broad view gained by the mastery of the obstacles on our adventurous way up (A. Einstein, quoted after Sacks, 1972, p. 756).

The need for further development of economic theory was clearly enunciated by Arrow (1983b, pp. 207–10) in his Nobel Lecture and his current perception is discussed by him in Chapter 2 of this volume. In both these volumes we are calling attention to the advances made and the remaining lacunae.

APPENDIX: SOME ASPECTS OF THE HISTORY OF ECONOMICS

> I do not think that we can hope to understand the problems and policies of our own day if we do not know the problems and policies out of which they grew. I suspect that damage has been done, not merely to historical and speculative culture, but also to our practical insight, by this indifference to our intellectual past – this provincialism in time – which has become so characteristic of our particular branch of social studies (Robbins, 1978, p. 1).
>
> The study of scientific 'revolutions', in which one system of thought (or 'research programme') has given place to another, [is] . . . a powerful tool in the methodology of natural science. Economics also has had its 'revolutions'; it is fruitful to study them in much the

> same manner. I think however that when one looks at them comparatively, one finds that their significance is very largely different.
>
> That is a matter of importance, for economics itself. Economics is more like art or philosophy than science, in the use that it can make of its own history. The history of science is a fascinating subject – but it is not important to the working scientist in the way that the history of economics is important to the working economist. When the natural scientist has come to the frontier of knowledge, and is ready for new exploration, he is unlikely to have much to gain from a contemplation of the path by which his predecessors have come to the place where he now stands. . .
>
> Our position in economics is different; we cannot escape in the same way from our own past. We may pretend to escape; but the past crowds in on us all the same. To 'neoclassical' succeeds 'neomercantilist'; Keynes and his contemporaries echo Ricardo and Malthus; Marx and Marshall are still alive. Some of us are inclined to be ashamed of this traditionalism, but when it is properly understood it is no cause for embarrassment; it is a consequence of what we are doing, or trying to do (Hicks, 1976, p. 207).

Naturally, those who maintain their interests in the history of our subject do so for different reasons,[64] are influenced by divergent traditions, and have various predispositions towards theory, tools, institutions, history, and the like. The first distinction to be made is between the professional historians of economic thought and the 'working' (or theory-making) economists (like, for example, Arrow, Hicks, and Samuelson) who maintain an active and continuing interest in the history of their subject. Another broad distinction is between those who are interested in the traditional history or development of doctrines and those who (following Schumpeter) focus on and assign the greatest weight to analytical contributions. In Schumpeter's (1954, p. 242) words:

> the first discovery of a science is the discovery of itself. But this does not spell discovery of its fundamental problem. That comes much later. In the case of economics, it came particularly late. The scholastics had an inkling of it. The seventeenth-century businessmen-economists came nearer to it. Isnard, A. Smith, J. B. Say, Ricardo, and others all struggled or rather fumbled for it, every one of them in his own way. But the discovery was not fully made until

Walras, whose system of equations, defining (static) equilibrium in a system of interdependent quantities, is the Magna Carta of economic theory – the technical imperfections of that monument of constitutional law being an essential part of the analogy . . . The history of economic analysis or, at any rate, of its 'pure' kernel, from Child to Walras might be written in terms of this conception's gradual emergence into the light of consciousness.

Each generation rewrites its textbooks and changes the focus of historical treatment. In his presidential address to the American Economic Association, Samuelson (1966, pp. 1500–01) gave what he called an 'insider's view' of the dominant shift that had taken place and was to continue to influence contemporary economics. He (p. 1501) contrasts the 'different sets of standards' between his student-day bible, *The History of Economic Doctrines* by Gide and Rist, with Schumpeter (1954):

reading Gide and Rist you would be forgiven for thinking that Robert Owen was almost as important as Robert Malthus; that Fourier and Saint-Simon were much more important than Walras and Pareto. The A. Young in the index is, of course, Arthur Young, not Allyn Young.

In Schumpeter (1954), however, 'it is Marshall, Walras, Wicksell and such people who steal the stage. Of course, Adam Smith is given his due. But what a due! He is rather patronizingly dismissed as a synthesizer who happened to write the right book at the right time: his analytic contributions are certainly minimized' (Samuelson 1966, p. 1501).

In what follows we shall give prominence to Schumpeter's views on the history of economics, especially his attitude to and analysis of Walras and Marshall which have had a profound influence on the way we now perceive progress in economics. As is well known, Schumpeter views progress in economics essentially as improvements in the analytical apparatus – a view particularly stressed nowadays by Lucas (1981, pp. 272 and *passim*). Schumpeter extolled Walras as the greatest of all economic theorists and his theory of general economic equilibrium as his claim to immortality. While praising Marshall's achievements, Schumpeter denigrated him as a pure economic theorist. Indeed, the following passage, alluding to Marshall, is revealing of Schumpeter's (1954, p. 954) stance:

> The truth that economic theory is nothing but an engine of analysis was little understood all along, and the theorists themselves, then as now, obscured it by dilettantic excursions into the realm of practical questions.

His attitude, of course, prompts us to ask two more basic questions: What was Schumpeter's frame of reference and what legacy did he leave for contemporary economics?. Schumpeter (1954, p. 827) sees economics as a large vehicle whose passengers are endowed with incommensurate abilities and interests:

> However, as far as pure theory is concerned, Walras is in my opinion the greatest of all economists. His system of economic equilibrium, uniting, as it does, the quality of 'revolutionary' creativeness with the quality of classical synthesis, is the only work by an economist that will stand comparison with the achievements of theoretical physics. Compared with it, most of the theoretical writings of [the 1870–1914 period] . . . – and beyond – however valuable in themselves and however original subjectively, look like boats beside a liner, like inadequate attempts to catch some particular aspects of Walrasian truth. It is the outstanding landmark on the road that economics travels toward the status of a rigorous or exact science and, though outmoded by now, still stands at the back of much of the best theoretical work of our time.

It is for his static general theory of the economic universe and particularly for his mathematical approach and his comprehensive equations of g.e. that Schumpeter placed Walras at the apex of the totem pole of theoretical economists. Schumpeter (1951, p. 74) praised Walras's single-mindedness in his devotion of all his concentration to the problems of pure economics, without any deviations, so that the unity of the whole picture remains intact. It seems that Schumpeter (1951, p. 75) was particularly impressed by Walras's method rather than by his vision of general economic equilibrium. He (1954, p. 1004) points explicitly to Walras's awareness of the need to establish every point in his analytical construct by formal proof (whatever the success or defects of his proofs) which made him 'the teacher of all theorists of the future'. In a sense, he perceives the history of economic analysis as divided into two parts: the pre-scientific (or pre-Walrasian) and the scientific (or post-Walrasian).

Schumpeter (1954, p. 1015) grants that one may feel uncomfortable with the discrepancies between Walras's construct and real life processes, but, drawing his analogy from physics, Schumpeter asks whether we ever '*saw* elastic strings that do not increase in length when pulled, or frictionless movements, or any other of the constructs commonly used in theoretical physics; and whether, on the strength of this' we believe 'theoretical physics to be useless'. In the same breath, however, he stresses that 'it remains true . . . that both Walras himself and his followers greatly underestimated what had and has still to be done before Walras' theory can be confronted with the facts of common business experience'. Here, Schumpeter draws an all too obvious parallel between Walras and Marshall: 'We can learn from Marshall how to put flesh and skin on Walras' skeleton, although it does remain true that a more realistic theory raises a world of new problems that are beyond Walras' (and Marshall's) range'.

Schumpeter extolls Walras's 'brilliant' development of the theory of competitive exchange of two commodities and poses the question of alternative mechanism of reaction than that considered by Walras. He (1954, p. 1012) correctly emphasizes the deficiency of Walras's approach to production theory, and his imposition of 'heroic' assumptions to reduce the problem of production to manageability.

> We may balk at the assumptions. We may question the value of a theory that holds only under conditions the mere statement of which seems to amount to refuting it. But if we do accept these qualifications and assumptions, there is little fault to be found with Walras's solution.

Schumpeter adds:

> Those, who, like myself, do not go so far, must rate the pioneer performance as such very highly and see a merit precisely in the fact that Walras chalked out the work that had (in part still has) to be done in the future.

It is noteworthy that Schumpeter (1954, pp. 1006–7) emphasized the strictly static structure of Walras's theory and pointed out that

> Walras treated only a problem in pure logic of simultaneous determination of variables, and therefore neglected, e.g., all lags of any kind, the explanatory value of this part of his argument does not go beyond clearing up one of the many aspects that even pure theory must attend to.

Walras's scheme of instantaneously equilibrating markets and free competition is of great interest, not only for its own sake, but also because it sheds light on some recent developments in general equilibrium theory and in equilibrium business cycle theory. Schumpeter (1954, p. 1002) clearly realized that Walras's static logical skeleton of economic life is a highly artificial methodological fiction. Walras attempted to construct an equilibrium state from its inception, in such a manner as if 'smooth and instantaneous adaptation of all existing goods and processes, to the conditions obtaining at the moment, were feasible'.

It is of some interest to point out that, with considerable prescience of recent developments in macroeconomics, Schumpeter (1954, p. 999) strongly, and in my view incorrectly, emphasized 'that it is not correct to contrast income or macroanalysis of, say, the Keynesian type with the Walrasian microanalysis as if the latter were a theory that neglects, and stands in need of being supplemented by, income and macroanalysis'.

Walras's interpretation of pure competition includes the parametric function of prices (excludes price strategy) and Jevons's 'Law of Indifference'. With his profound insights into how our economy works, and a canny anticipation of later controversies about efficacy of adjustment and learning processes, operation of markets, competition, rationality of agents, futures markets, and the like, Schumpeter (1954, p. 973) observes:

> But exclude 'strategy' as much as you please, there still remains the fact that this adaptation will produce results that differ according to the range of knowledge, promptness of decision, and 'rationality' of actors, and also according to the expectations they entertain about the future course of prices, not to mention the further fact that their action is subject to additional restrictions that proceed from the situations they have created for themselves by their past decisions.

Though Walras (1954) was aware of these difficulties, and in certain places (particularly in the concluding part of the *Elements* – what Jaffé calls *Coda*) foresaw the future need for building dynamic schemata to take them into account, his self-appointed task, as Schumpeter (1954, p. 974) points out, was to simplify heroically.

Reading Walras and Jaffé's (1983) scholarly commentaries, one is under the impression of an integral unity of Walras's analytical structure and social vision, commitment to distributive justice, and the like. Walras himself did not seem to consider his mathematical approach as his principal mission; rather he looked at it as subjugated to his vision of social justice. On the other hand, Schumpeter (1954, p. 827–8) deplored the fact that Walras attached so much importance 'to his questionable philosophies about social justice, his land-nationalization scheme, his project of monetary management, and other things that have nothing to do with his superb achievement in pure theory'.

Here we can only allude to the Jaffé-Morishima controversy about the ultimate aims of *Elements*, the relation of the latter to the entire corpus of Walras's writings, what the kernel of *Elements* consists of, and Morishima's (1977) contention that Walras's general equilibrium construct was founded on a four-class view of society and Jaffé's (1983, chapter 19) retort that this is a figment of Morishima's imagination, as well as a number of other issues. Only two points can be made here:

1. One needs to distinguish between the historian's interpretations of what Walras actually aimed at or meant (Jaffé's search) and the approach that attempts to extend, amend, and refine Walras's pioneering analytical construct to make it more dynamic and bring it closer to real life (Morishima's quest).
2. Whatever the truth about Walras's four-class conception of society, I would only like to stress that his conception of the entrepreneur appears to be emaciated and the diametric opposite of that of Schumpeter, J. M. Clark, Frank Knight, and others (see Schumpeter 1954, p. 893).

Reflecting on the early development of neoclassical economic theory (c. 1870–1914), Schumpter (1954, p. 952) stressed the questionable proposition of fundamental unity:

> Numerous differences in details notwithstanding, Jevons, Menger, and Walras taught essentially the same doctrine. But, Jevons' and Marshall's analytic structures do not, in essence, differ more than the scaffolding differs from the completed and furnished house, and note XXI in the Appendix to Marshall's *Principles* is conclusive proof of the fundamental sameness of his and Walras' models.

He (1954, p. 953) then asks: why do the structures of these dominant figures look so different? Characteristically he attributes the differences to the many differences in techniques. As the key difference he identifies the use of the failure to use calculus and the system of simultaneous equations. He (p. 956) notes that both Walras and Marshall had a regular mathematical training. But whereas the former had more of it than he disclosed, the latter had less than he needed.

Schumpeter (1954, p. 836) spoke of Marshall as

> not only a high-powered technician, a profoundly learned historian, a sure-footed framer of exploratory hypotheses, but above all a great economist. Unlike the technicians of today who, so far as the technique of theory is concerned, are as superior to him as he was to A. Smith, he understood the working of the capitalist process. In particular, he understood business, business problems, and businessmen . . . He sensed the intimate organic necessities of economic life even more intensely than he formulated them.

But Schumpeter did not hold Marshall in high esteem as a theoretical economist and often spoke of Marshall's 'subjective originality'. In a passage to which many of us may object, Schumpeter wrote in 1941 (1951, p. 92) that 'in some sense Marshallian economics has passed away already. His vision of the economic process, his methods, his results, are no longer ours'. Whatever the great merits of Marshall's accomplishments, 'what matters is that his analytical apparatus is obsolete and that it would be so even if nothing had happened to change our political attitudes. If history had stood still and nothing except analysis had gone on, the verdict would have to be the same'.

Schumpeter (1951, p. 106) deplores the fact that though Marshall 'grasped the idea of general equilibrium he yet relegated it to the background, erecting in the foreground the handier house of partial or particular analysis'. He (p. 99; see Keynes, 1951, p. 183) speculates whether Marshall was fully aware of the grave shortcomings of partial equilibrium analysis and how dangerous it might be in unwary hands. Still he (p. 100) adds, when critically evaluating Marshall's handy tools 'we cannot fail to be struck by realism of his theoretical thought. Particular equilibrium analysis brings out the practical problems of the individual industry and of the individual firm. It is much more, of course, but it is also a scientific basis for business economics'.

Although the analytic kernel of Marshall's *Principles* is essentially static, as he worked out his theory, he always looked beyond it. As Schumpeter (1951, p. 100) points out, Marshall 'inserted dynamic elements whenever he could, more often, in fact, than was compatible with the static logic he nevertheless retained'.

To do justice to the *Principles*, Schumpeter (1951, p. 94) observes, one has to look beyond the kernel of the analytic apparatus:

> For behind, beyond, and all around that kernel there is an economic sociology of nineteenth century English capitalism which rests on historical bases of impressive extent and solidity. Marshall was, in fact, an economic historian of the first rank ... And his mastery of historical fact and his analytic habit of mind did not dwell in separate compartments but formed so close a union that the live fact intrudes into the theorem and the theorem into purely historical observations.

What really restricts Marshall's creative achievements in pure theory is, according to Schumpeter (1954, pp. 836–7), the dichotomy between Marshall's strictly static theoretical apparatus and his thoughts running in terms of evolutionary change – in terms of an original irreversible historical process. In fact, 'Marshall was one of the first economists to realize that economics is an evolutionary science ... and in particular that the human nature he professed to deal with is malleable and changing, a function of changing environments' (Schumpeter, 1951, p. 93; see also Nelson and Winter, 1982).

Schumpeter (1954, p. 985) does not consider most of the leading economists of the early neoclassical period as 'unquestioning addicts of laissez-faire', nor does he view them as 'unconditional eulogists of pure competition'.

He (1951, pp. 104–5) contends that

> Marshall was the first to show that perfect competition will not always maximize output. This, so far as I know the first breach in an ancient wall, yielded the proposition that output might be increased beyond the competitive maximum by restricting industries subject to decreasing, and expanding industries subject to increasing returns.

Schumpeter (1951, p. 105) questionably considers Marshall to be the father of the theory of imperfect competition. He also notes that the Marshallian concept of elasticity of demand may not quite merit all the praise that has been heaped on it. And he emphasizes the Marshallian principle of substitution as the chief purely theoretical difference between Marshall's and Walras's constructs (see Keynes, 1951, pp. 183–90).

Schumpeter belonged to a select group of economists of grand vision and multifaceted interests. He had a great appreciation not only for economic analysis, but also for economic history, econometrics, and social economics. His own contributions range through many areas of the vast territory. Yet it is puzzling that he attached such an extraordinary weight to the 'engine of economic analysis' and to advances in mathematization of economics when his own comparative advantages lay elsewhere. This puzzle might well be the key to the answer.[65] Schumpeter clearly admired in others what he himself was not. To some extent Samuelson (1982, pp. 1–2), that astute observer, supports this contention. Moreover, Schumpeter's admiration for mathematical economics may also have been somewhat influenced by Samuelson's early (1947) work which at the time was obviously dazzling in its technical sophistication.

Strong objections to Schumpeter's approach have been raised from various quarters. This is not the place for a full treatment. Notably Hicks (1976, p. 214–15) increasingly voices his discontent with what he calls catallactics:

> A superb example of the way in which commitment to a catallactic outlook can blind one to the importance of the alternative is to be found in Schumpeter's *History of Economic Analysis* (1954). There are countless ways in which Schumpeter deepens one's understanding of what economists – ourselves and our predecessors – have been doing. But it is impossible not to notice that he always judges economists by their contribution to theory in the catallactic sense. It is the great catallactists (Jevons, Walras and Menger, together with their forerunners such as Turgot and Say) who receive particular praise; while some who would usually be regarded as greater names (Smith, Ricardo, Marshall) are treated somewhat grudgingly. Why does he write them down? Because they belong on the political economy side.

Another critic, Sir Roy Harrod (1956, p. 313), speaks of the 'extremely narrow range of Walras' theoretical interests. He was just bemused by his own equations'. And, in comparing Marshall and Walras, he (pp. 311–12) accords the palm to Marshall, despite the fact that his 'original contributions to pure theory are admittedly limited'. Harrod (1956, pp. 315–16) notes that the results of Walras's

> great labours for factual economics are meagre; we only reach such propositions as that there is an equilibrium position and that an increase in demand tends to raise price. Walras was perfectly justified in concentrating his interest and labour in this manner. The harmful influence that his work may have exerted springs from the gloss that what is to be found in his *Elements* constitutes the main corpus of economic theory. Marshall has far greater scope and depth than Walras. But he too, in his work on principles, concentrated on the static equilibrium; he did not live long enough to write out even an intelligible summary of what may have originally been in his mind for his fourth volume . . . The consequence has been the neglect of dynamics for too long a period.

Friedman (1955; see Stigler, 1982) is critical of the Walrasian approach. He questions what he calls Schumpeter's 'extravagant' judgement. He grants that it was Walras's great contribution of construct a mathematical system that captures in considerable detail the interdependencies emphasized by Cournot, but Walras, as we know, did not show the solution for the system of equations. Basically, Friedman (1955, p. 909) acknowledges that Walras provided a framework for organizing ideas but, he contends, economics also needs

> ideas to be organized. We need the right kind of language; we also need something to say. Substantive hypotheses about economic phenomena of the kind that were the goal of Cournot are an essential ingredient of a fruitful and meaningful economic theory. Walras has little to contribute in this direction; for this we must turn to other economists, notably, of course, to Alfred Marshall.

And paraphrasing Mill, Friedman adds: 'A person is not likely to be a good economist who does not have a firm command of Walrasian economics; equally, he is not likely to be a good economist if he knows nothing else'.

Inspired by Joan Robinson's and Sraffa's criticism of g.e.t., Walsh and Gram (1980, p. 123) sharply differentiate between the classical and neoclassical theories of allocation. In the former the focus is on the allocation of surplus output so as to maximize growth and capital accumulation, whereas the latter center on how given resources are allocated among alternative uses.

> The classical economists would never have entertained the idea of

constructing an economic theory where inputs are an arbitrary job lot of 'resources', treated (to use modern language) as *parameters*, since the allocation of such a set of given resources would not have been recognized by them as the essential economic problem. For them, questions of allocation arise in connection with the reproduction of surplus, and the maximization of future surplus.

Whatever reservations one might harbour, there is something to Shackle's (1967, pp. 2–3) following argument:

> There is something to be said for the notion that theory prospers and marches forward in any subject if that subject happens to attract a particularly able group of many young contemporaries . . . In economics there have been at least three episodes of the kind. In the mid-eighteenth century our subject was founded as a distinct systematic discipline . . . In the last third of the nineteenth, it suddenly took on a new unity and elegance in the hands of a very remarkable group of men . . . who founded the notion of general equilibrium on the three pillars of subjective theory of value, the application of the differential calculus to moral science, and the conception of the univeral inter-penetrating influence of every economic quantity on every other. Their work and outlook were dominant for more than half a century, and, of course, it lies still at the heart of economics. But in the 1920s and 1930s it was suddenly found to be not enough. Attention was called by contemporary fact to the vagaries of money and the general price level, and then to the bewildering phenomenon of general heavy unemployment. These problems attracted a number of highly gifted minds from diverse scholarly beginnings, not only economics itself but mathematics, classics, and physics, and the result was a great ferment of new work at the heart of economic theory.

This brings to mind Boulding's (1971, p. 229) provocative comment that since Adam Smith much work in economics

> has, in fact, been talmudic, in the sense that it has clarified, expounded, expanded, mathematized, and translated into modern language, ideas which were essentially implicit in *The Wealth of Nations*. The whole of Walrasian, Marshallian, and Hicksian price theory, for instance, is clearly implicit in Adam Smith's concept of natural price, and in this respect one wonders whether any basic

new ideas have been added to Adam Smith, in spite of all the elegance and the refinements which the years have brought.

Boulding (p. 231) himself placates those of us whose ire might be aroused. He admits that 'as long as intellectual evolutionary potential remains yet underdeveloped in the early writers, the modern writers are a complement rather than a substitute; that is, we need both Samuelson and Adam Smith'.

Whether the so-called marginalist revolution took place at all is an open question (see Black, Coats, and Goodwin, 1973; Hicks, 1976) If it did, what did it amount to? Did it enrich our vision of the economic process? Did it create a new analytical engine? What are its consequences? All these are large questions on which economists will doubtless continue to differ sharply. Similarly an unresolved question is how and why neoclassical differs from classical economics. Even if neoclassical economics has some distinct meaning, as suggested by Arrow and others, the heterogeneity of approaches within it and changes in time and place make classifications difficult, if not doubtful (see Hicks, 1983; Leijonhufvud, 1981; Stigler, 1982). Tracing the history of the concept of equilibrium, Arrow (1983b, p. 108), like others, notes 'that Smith was a creator of general equilibrium theory, although the coherence and consistency of his work can be questioned'. Even more so can it be traced to Ricardo, Mill, and Marx who succeeded in filling some of Smith's logical gaps. Arrow (p. 108) stresses that Marx 'has indeed come in some ways closer in form to modern theory than any other classical economist, though of course everything is confused by his attempt to maintain simultaneously a pure labor theory of value and an equalization of rates of return on capital' (see also Samuelson, 1966, pp. 229–422).

But, according to Arrow, in a critically important sense, none of the classical economists really did have a genuine theory of general economic equilibrium, for none gave explicit cognizance to demand conditions in price determination. Admittedly, Mill, Cournot, and others do not disregard the influence of demand on prices; indeed, they pay verbal homage to it. But they lack true integration of demand with the essentially supply-oriented (long run) classical value theory. Here the essential neglect of demand is facilitated by the special simplifying and restricting assumptions, that at times are somewhat difficult to pin down, made about the conditions of production (see Arrow, 1983b, pp. 156, 229). To recall, modern g.e.t. is 'a theory about both the quantity and prices of all economic goods and services' (Arrow, 1983b, p. 229). From the modern vantage point, a system is incomplete if it says nothing about quantities. In classical economics, prices seem to be determined by a system of relations derived from the equalization of the rates of return into which quantities do not enter.

> This is clear enough with fixed production coefficients and a single primary factor, labor, as in Smith's famous exchange of deer and beaver, and it was the great accomplishment of Malthus and Ricardo to show that land could be brought into the system. If, finally, Malthusian assumptions about population implied that the supply price of labor was fixed in terms of goods, then even the price of capital could be determined (although the presence of capital as a productive factor and recipient of rewards was clearly an embarrassment to the classical authors, as it remains to some extent today).
>
> Thus, in a certain definite sense the classicists had no true theory of resource allocation, since the influence of prices on quantities was not studied and the reciprocal influence was denied. But the classical theory could solve neither the logical problem of explaining relative wages of heterogeneous types of labor nor the empirical problem of accounting for wages that were rising steadily above the subsistence level. It is in this context that the neoclassical theories emerged, with all primary resources having the role that land alone had before (Arrow, 1983b, pp. 108–9).

In a paper written with David Starrett, Arrow (1983b, Chapter 10) reiterates that Menger, Jevons, and Walras (and their precursors, Cournot and Gossen) understood the glaring omission of demand from the classical model. (*Stricto sensu* this is only true for internal trade. Demand was prominent in Mill's (and even Ricardo's) theory of international trade (see Arrow and Hahn, 1971, p. 3).) They took as an expository point of departure a polar opposite of the classical (production) model: the pure exchange (catallactic) model. They were not unaware of the significance of production. However, Menger and Jevons particularly stressed exchange as the essence of the economic system, with production appearing only indirectly as a way of exchanging initial endowments.

> If a classical model of production is completed by adding a system of demand relations, the prices are determined purely by technolo-

gical or cost considerations. Then the quantities are completely determined by the demands at those prices. In a model of pure exchange, the direction of causation is almost completely reversed. The total quantities of the goods are given; the demand conditions determine the prices as that set that will cause demand to equal the given supply for all goods (Arrow, 1983b, p. 231).

For Arrow's perceptive and lively comments on Walras and Marshall and on some of his own contemporaries, the reader is urged to look into Chapter 2 of this volume. Arrow maintains an abiding interest in the history of economic thought and his writings are replete with historical references.

Theoretical economists are often criticized for neglecting institutions and economic history. The only medicine suggested to 'cure this malaise . . . is for theorists to make a serious effort in the direction of the institutionalization of economics, in the sense of slowing the speed of all development towards mathematization and developing economic theory in accordance with knowledge of economic organizations, industrial structure and economic history' (Morishima, 1984, p. 70). But such a view is quite intransigent and restrictive; it would put all scholars in one mold. The very contributions that scholars can make spring from their independence and heterogeneity. It is difficult to disagree with Arrow's (1978, p. xii) following observation:

Scholars, like all other individuals, vary greatly in their tolerance for uncertainty and ambiguity. Some feel no comfort until they have a theoretical framework or at least a vision capable of explaining to their satisfaction the phenomena of interest in their field. The entertainment of alternative hypotheses is difficult for them. Others can contemplate with equanimity the possibility that our empirical knowledge and theoretical understanding are compatible with more than one view of the world, that only gradually will there be greater resolution.

Both types of scholars have their roles, and it is just as well that both types exist. The demand for certainty is a powerful incentive to developing the theory and empirical investigations that push the subject forward. The risk-tolerant scholar is more open to new ideas and, in particular, is liable to play a special role in synthesis, in the yoking together of ideas from disparate fields.

Much has been said in the preceding pages about the fruitfulness of the axiomatic method and the rising standards of scientific investigation in economics. The demands of such a method, however, may be inhibiting in many ways. The point is that it should not deaden imagination nor close doors on intuition or prevent the scientist from voicing half-baked ideas that may be picked up by others and subjected to rigorous investigation. This is not a license for loose thinking, but an appeal for more of the sort of thing that Arrow does so well.

For example, at a recent session of a meeting of the American Economic Association on economic history as a necessary though not sufficient condition for an economist, Arrow (1985d) draws an analogy between the relationship of physics and chemistry to geology, and of economic theory to history. He (1985d, p. 321) asks:

> Is economics a subject like physics, true for all time, or are its laws historically conditioned? The importance of history was on the rise throughout the nineteenth century, just when the abstract economic theory of David Ricardo was developed. Ricardo's doctrines were much attacked by contemporaries for lack of historical understanding. His disciple, John Stuart Mill, made clear that the laws of distribution were indeed historically conditioned; the classical laws of value held only in an economy in which exchange was governed by markets . . .
>
> Physics and chemistry have clearly been very useful to geology, interpreted as history. What does standard economic theory have to contribute to economic history? It could fail on several grounds. It might be so wrong that it is an obstacle to understanding.

His (p. 321) answer is that, despite claims to the contrary by some economists, theory is certainly not so powerful as to overwhelm history.

> In form, neoclassical theory is a statement of the implications of tastes, technology, and expectations for prices and quantities . . . There is plenty of room for historical specificity in the conditions even if economic theory were more reliable than it is in drawing conclusions from them. There is nothing in economic theory which specifies that tastes remain unchanged and a great deal of empirical knowledge about changes in technology. Indeed, it may be com-

plained rather that economic theory does not sufficiently constrain historical determination, particularly when the data are not sufficient.

Arrow (pp. 321–2) believes that historical investigations have been helped by using ideas and approaches of economic theory. Theory has helped historians ask new questions such as 'how economic institutions work in redirecting the flow of resources, not merely their intended workings'. Many of our views, for example, on the role of innovations in affecting the course of history or on the economic consequences of slavery have altered. 'Measuring the economic conditions of the masses of the population may have been driven by political aims as much as by modern welfare economics, but the appropriate measures and data have certainly been much clarified by the latter'. And, of course, our understanding of the past was assisted by using long time-series on national income – a concept derived from theory. But this is also an example of an inherent danger in applying economic theory to history. 'There is a bias towards flattening out the particularities of the past. The more one uses categories drawn from the need to generalize, the less marked is the difference among the institutions'.

And how can history help in the development of theory? There are many ways, but Arrow (1985d, pp. 322–3) singles out only two examples. 'One is simply the use of economic history as a source of empirical evidence for testing theories and estimating relations' – what he calls his 'naive view on the role of history. It is far from exhausting the content of history, but is is certainly one of its uses'. The second use that he sees for 'history in the development of economic analysis is a definition of its historical conditioning'. Despite much contradictory evidence, he finds 'some suggestion that the economic world of the past is not entirely different from that of our theories'. He also notes that historical conditioning of theory is inextricably intertwined with national and cultural conditioning. 'The cultural differences between nations, with all their implications for polity and economy, are precipitates of past events, sometimes from the far past. In an ideal theory, perhaps, the whole influence of the past would be summed up in observations on the present. But such a theory cannot be stated in any complex uncontrolled system, not even for the Earth . . . It will always be true that practical understanding of the present will require knowledge of the past'.

NOTES

1. Arrow (1976a, p.1) speaks of the 'inhibiting influence of Marshallian neoclassical orthodoxy'. But in another context, speaking of the complexity of the structure and interrelationships within the modern firm, he (1985c, p. 303) resorts to the common English platitude, 'it is all in Marshall'.
2. In personal conversations many of his peers have referred to him as a genius.
3. In his Inaugural Address as Rector of the University of St Andrews, John Stuart Mill (1867, pp. 27, 32, 34) provided remarkable, and still instructive, arguments for a liberal education and about the role, *inter alia*, of mathematics, logic and political economy:

   > It is a part of liberal education to know that ... controversies exist, and in a general way, what has been said on both sides of them. It is instructive to know the failures of the human intellect as well as its successes, its imperfect as well as its perfect attainments; to be aware of the open questions, as well as those which have been definitively resolved.
   >
   > In the operations of the intellect it is so much easier to go wrong than right; it is so utterly impossible for even the most vigorous mind to keep itself in the path ... Logic points out all the possible ways in which, starting from true premises, we may draw false conclusions ... Logic is the great disperser of hazy and confused thinking: it clears up the fogs which hide from us our own ignorance, and make us believe that we understand a subject when we do not ... Logic compels us to throw our meaning into distinct propositions, and our reasonings into distinct steps. It makes us conscious of all the implied assumptions on which we are proceeding, and which, if not true, vitiate the entire process. It makes us aware what extent of doctrine we commit ourselves to by any course of reasoning, and obliges us to look the implied premises in the face, and make up our minds whether we can stand to them. It makes our opinions consistent with themselves and with one another, and forces us to think clearly.
   >
   > The same persons who cry down Logic will generally warn you against Political Economy. It is unfeeling, they will tell you. It recognises unpleasant facts. For my part, the most unfeeling thing I know of is the law of gravitation: it breaks the neck of the best and most amiable person without scruple, if he forgets for a single moment to give heed to it. The winds and waves too are very unfeeling. Would you advise those who go to sea to deny the winds and waves – or to make use of them, and find the means of guarding against their dangers? My advice to you is, to study the great writers on Political Economy and hold firmly by whatever in them you find true; and depend upon it that if you are not selfish or hard-hearted already, Political Economy will not make you so.

4. And Isnard is identified as the isolated progenitor. See Baumol and

Goldfeld, 1968, pp. 253–7; Jaffé, 1983, pp. 55–77; and Arrow, 1983b, p. 227.

5. Sen (1982, p. 88), however, questions the underlying assumptions about the motivations of the economic agent. He notes that the point is not to what extent the postulated models of g.e. mimic the real world, but to what extent the 'answers to well-defined posed with preselected assumptions which severely constrain the nature of the models that can be admitted into the analysis' are accurate. He (p. 88) stresses that

> a specific concept of man is ingrained in the question itself, and there is no freedom to depart from this conception so long as one is engaged in answering this question. The nature of man in these current economic models continues, then, to reflect the particular formulation of certain general philosophical questions posed in the past. The realism of the chosen conception of man is simply not a part of this inquiry.

In his critique of the behavioural foundations of economic theory, Sen (1982, p. 87) scrutinizes, *inter alia*, the stylized view of man that forms part of Edgeworth's analysis (this was specifically geared to a particular controversy with Spencer and Sidgwick, addressing the abstract query in what sense and to what extent egoistic behaviour achieves the public good) and survives more or less intact in much of economic theorizing. Sen argues that the limited nature of the inquiry had a decisive impact on the choice of economic models and the conception of agents in them. Though Edgeworth enunciated as the first principle of economics that every agent is actuated only by self-interest, he himself felt that the concrete nineteenth-century individual is largely 'an impure egoist, a mixed utilitarian'. In his thought-provoking critique of the behavioural foundations of economic theory, 'Rational Fools', Sen (1982, pp. 84–5) asks why Edgeworth spent inordinate energy and talent in developing a line of inquiry the first principle of which he knew to be false.

> The issue is not why abstractions should be employed in pursuing general economic questions – the nature of the inquiry makes this inevitable – but why would one choose an assumption which he himself believed to be not merely inaccurate in detail but fundamentally mistaken? . . . This question is of continuing interest to modern economics as well.

6. Indeed, as Schumpeter (1954, pp. 888, 895) observes, contrary to the usual historical interpretations in the Anglo-American vein, most of the earlier (from 1870 to the early 1900s) leading neoclassical economists were certainly not unquestioning addicts of *laissez-faire*, nor were they 'unconditional eulogists' of pure competition. He (1950, p. 77) notes that the theoretical structure of Marshall and Wicksell

> has little in common with that of the classics . . . but it conserves the classic proposition that in the case of perfect competition the profit interest of the producer tends to maximize production. It even supplied almost satisfactory proof. Only, in the process of being more

correctly stated and proved, the proposition lost much of its content – it does emerge from the operation, to be sure, but it emerges emaciated, barely alive. (See also Samuelson, 1947, pp. 206–7.)

7. More influenced by Edgeworth and Sidgwick than by his teacher, Marshall, Pigou (1912, 1920) took the classical theory of production and distribution and turned it into the economics of welfare. '*The Economics of Welfare* is *The Wealth of Nations* in a new guise' (Hicks, 1975, p. 312). Pigou's concerns were the same as those of the classics; where he differed from them was in different methods of valuation. Pigou 'values not by cost, but by marginal utility. He is recasting the classical structure in terms of utility theory' Hicks, 1975, p. 324). Post-Pigovian or post-Paretian welfare economics 'is the allocation theory of the utility approach' (Hicks, 1975, p. 316).
8. The utilitarian view is found in scattered works of Bentham and through his influence in J. S. Mill. Sen and Williams (1982, p. 21) remind us that the origins of utilitarianism are in

    a distinctive psychological theory and, to some extent, a distinctive attitude to politics, though even in its earlier developments there were divergent conservative and radical applications of it. It is a strange but very striking fact that in its more recent existence as contributing to moral and economic theory it has lost those connections with psychological and political reality.

    This fact has implications not only for the credibility of utilitarianism but for the style of the debate about what, if anything, should replace it. Many utilitarians accuse other theories of 'prejudice', 'dogma', 'irrational tradition', and so forth, and similar charges are directed at some people who claim no theory, but only moral convictions or sentiments. In the absence of some concrete account of the psychology and politics of the utilitarian life, that rhetoric is totally empty and lacks the mass to dent anything.

9. Arrow (1983a, pp. 47–8) reminds us, however, that even Bentham had grave doubts about the additivity of utilities as long as no procedure for measuring them had been established.
10. 'Traditionally the Pareto principle has appeared to be a very mild requirement indeed, but it is clear that it has remarkable cutting power in excluding various natural formulations of rights and liberties precisely because they make use of non-utility information' (Sen, 1985, p. 1155).
11. In this context it is interesting to note Joan Robinson's (1962, p. 14) perception of economics terms as value impregnated: 'Bigger is close to better; equal to equitable; goods sound good; disequilibrium sounds uncomfortable; exploitation, wicked; and sub-normal profits, rather sad'.
12. For very interesting personal recollections of that period at the LSE see Hicks, 1983, pp. 357–9.
13. Arrow (1983b, p. 14) admits that this discrepancy caused him considerable disquietude – a problem that he and Enthoven (1961) tackled by

showing that, subject to certain limitations, the Kuhn-Tucker results could be extended to quasi-concave functions (see also Arrow, Hurwicz, and Uzawa, 1958).

14. Not surprisingly, Arrow and Scitovsky (1969, p. 5) call attention to the mathematical constraints that limit the generality of Lange's exposition where

    there is no place for corner equilibria (in which some goods may not be produced at all so that marginal rates of substitution for the producer need not equal the corresponding marginal rates for the consumer). Also, Lange did not explain carefully the distinction between necessary and sufficient conditions'.

15. 'The test of suitability of a tool of reasoning is whether it gives the most logical and economical expression to the basic assumptions appropriate to the field in question, and to the reasoning that establishes their implications' (Koopmans, 1957, pp. 182–3).

16. Since the A–D formulation has become the standard one, this rather long quotation from Arrow's 1951 paper (1983b, pp. 17–18) conveys his perception:

    The classical theorem essentially considers only the case where the optimal distribution is an *interior* maximum, that is, every individual consumes some positive quantity of every good, so that the restraint on the ranges of the variables are ineffective. Now if commodities are defined sharply ... it is empirically obvious that most individuals consume nothing of at least one commodity. Indeed, for any one individual, it is quite likely that the number of commodities on the market of which he consumes nothing exceed the number which he uses in some degree. Similarly, the optimal conditions for production, as usually expressed in terms of equality of marginal rates of substitution, are not necessarily valid if not every firm produces every product, yet it is even more apparent from casual observation that no firm engages in the production of more than a small fraction of the total number of commodities in existence.

    On the face of it, then, the classical criteria for optimality in production and consumption have little relevance to the actual world. From the point of view of policy, the most important consequence of these criteria was the previously mentioned theorem that the use of the price system under a regime of perfect competition will lead to a socially optimal allocation of economic resources. The question is naturally raised of the continued validity of this theorem when the classical criteria are rejected.

    It turns out that, broadly speaking, the optimal properties of the competitive price system remain even when social optima are achieved at corner maxima. In a sense, the role of prices in allocation is more fundamental than the equality of marginal rates of substitution of transformation, to which it is usually subordinated. From a mathematical point of view, the trick is the replacement of methods of differential calculus by the use of elementary theorems in the theory of convex bodies in the development of criteria for an optimum.

17. Bergson (1982, pp. 332–3) acknowledges that he benefited from Samuelson's helpful suggestions and interest when he was writing the paper on the foundations of welfare economics to which he attributes 'whatever claim to fame I may have as an economist'. Bergson recalls that he wrote that paper on his own, not for a course. 'It was only natural, though, that as my work progressed I should discuss it with Paul. He was, I think, the first person to whom I presented my idea of introducing a social welfare function into the analysis and using it to demonstrate the value judgments underlying previous formulation'. In his Nobel Lecture, Samuelson (1972, p. 16) recollects:

    Along with my close friend, Abram Bergson of Harvard, I have tried to understand what it is that Adam Smith's 'invisible hand' is supposed to be maximizing. Thus consider the concept which we today call Pareto-optimality – and which might with equal propriety be called Bergson-optimality, since it was Bergson . . . who, back in 1938, read sense into what Pareto was groping to say and who related that narrow concept to the broader concept of social norms and welfare function.

    More recently, Samuelson (1981, p. 223) credits Bergson with having pierced for him the veil of obscurity surrounding welfare economics. For Samuelson, Bergson's classic paper 'came like a flash of lightning': 'By sheer good luck, as a fellow graduate student and comrade at arms, I *was* in on Bergson's creation; but time has shown that I have not been able to do a better job of it; nor, I believe, has anyone else'. Samuelson adds: 'Mine was the best spectator's seat for Bergson's creative travail. I was the coarse stone against which he honed his sharp axe – the semi-absorbing, semi-reflecting surface against which he bounced off his ideas'.
18. Two subsequent developments should be noted here, namely, Vickrey (1945) and Harsanyi (1955). For Arrow's interpretation, see Arrow 1983a, pp. 123–5.
19. To his and our regret Abe Bergson was unable to provide the essay 'Welfare Economics and Social Choice Revisited' that he planned to write for this study of Arrow's contributions. For the Bergson-Samuelson position see, however, Chapter 3 of the companion volume.
20. Addressing himself to Arrow, Debreu (1972, p. 3) remarked:

    Since 1952 hardly a year passed by without several articles appearing on the problem of social choice as you formulated it. The statistics for *Econometrica* alone deserve attention. If we take the last fifteen years 1957–1971 and divide them into three five-year periods, we find that in the first of these periods 26 pages were devoted to the question of social choice, in the second 49 pages, in the third 118. A clear case of exponential growth with an alarming rate corresponding roughly to a doubling every five years.

21. For an up-to-date, comprehensive, and illuminating survey of social choice theory and an exhaustive bibliography see Sen (1985a).

22. Arrow's General (Im)Possibility Theorem (GPT) 'has been the prime mover in getting the discipline of social choice theory started, and though recently the focus has somewhat shifted from impossibility theorems to other issues, there is no doubt that Arrow's formulation of the social choice problem in presenting the GPT laid the foundations of social choice theory' (Sen 1985a, p.1078).

23. Addressing himself to the importance of the question of existence, Malinvaud (1972), p. 130) writes:

    Suppose we have established that a system of equations representing equilibrium has a solution, however the exogenous elements of the model may be specified. Then we can be certain that our model always provides a representation of equilibrium, a representation which may be true or false but exists in any case. On the other hand, if equilibrium does not exist for specifications of the exogenous elements, then the model is not valid in these cases; in a certain sense, it is inconsistent. We see why theoreticians, preoccupied with logic, ensure the existence of solutions to the systems of equations by which they represent competitive equilibrium.

24. Perhaps there is hope yet for modern textbook writers – the *bête noire* of Frank Hahn, who holds them responsible for many sins of misrepresentation and mis-statement, and generally for giving g.e.t. a bad image.
25. Quite aside from our interest in Schlesinger's work in this connection, it is worth noting that he has made some noted contribution to monetary theory in the Walrasian tradition. This work was largely neglected and prompted Schumpeter (1954, p. 1082) to remark that 'in our field first class performance is neither a necessary nor a sufficient condition for success'.
26. Schlesinger went further than the others. He intuitively understood that substitution of inequalities for equalities resolved the problems posed by Neisser and von Stackelberg. But he was aware that to tackle the problem successfully would require far greater mathematical sophistication than he possessed.
27. For A–D survey of the literature that preceded their contribution see Arrow 1983b, pp. 87-90 (see also Arrow, 1983b, pp. 111–13, 210–13). Among other interesting references are Baumol and Goldfeld, 1968, pp. 268–9; Dorfman, Samuelson, and Solow, 1958, pp. 357–88; and Weintraub, 1983, pp. 1–39.

28. The author has also investigated the question of the solubility of the equations of exchange in a market under perfect competition. Only the results of this investigation will be discussed here; the extensive exposition and the complete proof, for which subtle methods of modern mathematics had to be used, appear in No.8 of *Ergebnisse eines mathematischen Kolloquims* (Vienna: Deuticke, 1937) (Wald, 1951, pp. 379–80).

    Chipman (1965b, p. 720) reports that in the aforementioned issue, only the title of Wald's paper appeared on p. 84, with annotation that it could not be published due to lack of space, but that it would be published in a forthcoming issue. The journal was subsequently closed and no other issue came out.

29. Debreu (n.d., p.10) points to the obscurity of the German-language literature in which Wald wrote and to the novelty and complexity of his mathematical arguments as partial explanations of

   why no other work was done on the problem of existence of a competitive equilibrium for almost twenty years, and why his contribution received little attention until an English translation of the *Zeitschrift fur Nationalokonomie* article was published in *Econometrica* for October 1951. Actually, the paper that von Neumann wrote for the 1937 *Ergebnisse* on the existence of optimal balanced growth paths was far more influential in the period of the subject's development that was about to begin.

30. On the creative genesis of McKenzie's important contribution see Weintraub (1983, pp. 30–34) and McKenzie (1981).
31. For a detailed specification of the assumptions made see Arrow 1983b, pp. 62–8, 77–80. In successive developments of the theory the assumptions have been modified and relaxed as reflected in Debreu's (1982) authoritiative survey. For Arrow's restatement of the assumptions see, *inter alia*, Arrow, 1983b, Chapters 6 and 8; Arrow and Hahn, 1971, Chapters 5 to 8. For a comparison of assumptions made by various authors in the proofs of existence see Quirk and Saposnik, 1968, pp. 99–102.
32. This is particularly felicitously articulated in Chapter 11 (Wilson) in this volume.
33. Debreu (n.d. p. 11) points out that in the mid-1950s 'it became apparent that the complex proofs of Arrow and Debreu could be simplified if one replaced their approach, in which all the agents (including a fictitious market agent) simultaneously try to optimize their objective functions, by a more classical approach'. Furthermore, he (n.d. p. 12) elaborates: 'The proof of existence of a competitive equilibrium for an economy can be based on a lemma asserting the existence of a price-vector for which the associated excess demand set intersects the closed negative cone of the commodity space'. He stresses that this lemma was independently obtained by Gale (1955), Nikaido (1956) and Debreu (1956).
34. Walras's clumsy *tâtonnements* construct generated much heat and alternative proposals of so-called non-*tâtonnements* processes. See, *inter alia*, Arrow, 1983b, pp. 110–11; Arrow and Hahn, 1971, pp. 264–6 and *passim*; Hahn, 1982; Patinkin, 1965; Jaffé, 1983; and Morishima, 1977. Hahn (1982, pp. 745–6) points out that,

   the most popular form of modelling the price mechanism was, until recently, the *tâtonnement*. The device is resorted to for two reasons: the assumption of perfect competition (under which agents believe that they can trade what they want to at current prices) left no room for any actual agent to change price and so the fictitious auctioneer appears. Secondly, it seemed difficult to make the transition from planned trades and production to actual trades and production when plans were inconsistent. Moreover, to incorporate this transition into the formal analysis is very hard. Hence, no actual trading or production at 'false' prices was allowed in the process. While these reasons justify the tâtonnement as a first approach to a complex problem, it is obvious that it is incapable of providing a satisfactory answer to the stability question in most actual economies.

The *tâtonnement* is easiest to modify or abandon altogether in pure exchange economies. If one retains the auctioneer but introduces the assumption that at each date markets are *orderly*, ... one can show convergence to a competitive equilibrium whatever the exact form of the excess demand functions. Markets are orderly if no agent is restrained in his planned demand (supply) of a good when that good is an aggregate excess supply (demand). Convergence is proved by noting that the mechanism acts like a gradient process.

35. In the sequel paper with Block, Arrow and Hurwicz (1977, pp. 228ff.) present several extensions. For a brief summary of the development of stability analysis see Arrow 1983b, pp. 124–7. For surveys of the literature and issues involved see Negishi (1962), Fisher (1976), and Hahn (1982).

36. For example, Hahn (1973, pp. 14–15) stresses how useful the A–D model is when

one comes to argue with someone who maintain that we need not worry about exhaustible resources because they will always have prices which ensure their 'proper' use. Of course there are many things wrong with this contention but a quick way of disposing of the claim is to note that an Arrow-Debreu equilibrium must be an assumption he is making for the eeconomy and then to show why the economy cannot be in this state. The argument will here turn on the absence of futures markets and contingent futures markets and on the inadequate treatment of time and uncertainty by the construction. This negative role of Arrow-Debreu equilibrium I consider almost to be sufficient justification for it, since practical men and ill-trained theorists everywhere in the world do not understand what they are claiming to be the case when they claim a beneficent and coherent role for the invisible hand.

37. The study of the allocations achieved through forms of bargaining can be traced to Edgeworth's (1881) contract curve, reappearing in different forms in the theory of games, known in modern terminology as the core, which has become the subject of intensive investigations and a vast literature. See Aumann, 1985, pp. 49–54; Arrow and Hahn, 1971, Chapter 8; Hildenbrand (1982) and Debreu (1984, p. 272). Again, in the spirit of distributive justice, Sen (1982, p. 86) considers that being in the core

is not such a momentous achievement from the point of view of social welfare. A person who starts off ill-endowed may stay poor and deprived even after the transactions, and if being in the core is all that competition offers, the propertyless person may be forgiven for not regarding this achievement as a 'big deal'.

Similarly, in a critique of Nozick's entitlement theory of justice, Arrow (1983a, p. 188) points out:

> If one makes the assumptions of absence of externalities and of increasing returns to scale, then if the number of individuals in the economy is large (and no single one is large on the scale of the economy), the core shrinks to the competitive equilibrium. There is no problem of justice left!
>
> This is not precisely Nozick's conclusion, since he does not wish to assume perfect competition, but it is certainly complementary to it.
>
> My own view is that in some deep sense there are increasing returns to scale. The true basis for division of labor is the value of specialization, not merely in the economy but in society as a whole. Fundamentally similar people become different to complement each other. This vision informs the work of Adam Smith and also Rawls's concept of social union . . . If this is true, then the core remains large even with many individuals. There are significant gains to social interaction above and beyond what individuals and subgroups can achieve on their own. The owners of scarce personal assets do not have substantial private use of these assets; it is only their value in a large system which makes these assets valuable. Hence, there is a surplus created by the existence of society as such which is available for redistribution.

38. For an illuminating survey of imperfect competition literature in the g.e. tradition and rather discouraging conclusions see Hart, 1982.
39. 'If the Arrow-Debreu model is given a literal interpretation, then it clearly requires that the economic agents possess capabilities of imagination and calculation that exceed reality by many orders of magnitude' (Radner, 1982, p. 930).
40. As Hirshleifer and Riley (1979, pp. 1375–76) note in their survey 'until relatively recently there was no rigorous foundation for the *analysis* of individual decision-making and market equilibrium under uncertainty'. Without this foundation, 'the standard analytical models of our textbooks . . . made no explicit provision for uncertainty' (see also Shackle, 1967, pp. 4ff).

> Recent explosive progress in the economics of uncertainty has changed this picture. The subject now flourishes not only in economics departments, but in professional schools and programs oriented toward business, government and administration, and public policy. In the world of commerce, stockmarket analysts now regularly report measures of share-price uncertainty devised by economic theorists. Even in government and the law, formal analysis of uncertainty is beginning to appear in dealing with such problems as safety and health, allowable return on investment, and income distribution. And academic economists, armed with the new developments in the economics of uncertainty, are much more successfully analyzing previously interactable phenomena such as insurance, research and invention, advertising, speculation, and the functioning of financial markets . . .

> The theoretical developments that have brought about this intellectual revolution have two main foundation stones: (1) the theory of preference for uncertain contingencies and in particular the 'expected-utility theorem' of John von Neumann and Oskar Morgenstern . . . and (2) the formulation of the ultimate goods or objects of choice in an uncertain universe as *contingent* consumption claims (Hirshleifer and Riley, 1979, pp. 1375–76).

The state of analytical developments and the lacunae in the economics of uncertainty can also be gauged from Diamond and Rothschild, 1978 and from Machina's (1983) valuable survey of major developments in the economic theory of individual behaviour towards risk.

41. Arrow (1984a, p. 56) draws a distinction between choices and decisions.

> Psychologists frequently use the latter term only when conscious reflective choice is involved. Though economists are not always clear on this matter, I think it most consistent with the usual uses of choice theory to consider it applicable to unconscious or at any rate unreflective choices, as well as decisions in the narrower sense.

42. In an earlier paper on the usefulness of mathematical reasoning in the social sciences, Arrow (1951b, pp. 135, 137) discusses a number of objections that have been raised against the usefulness of the principle of rationality in economics and the Walrasian g.e.t. He notes that

> there is no single sweeping principle which has been erected as a rival to that of rationality. To the extent that formal theoretical structures in the social sciences have not been based on the hypothesis of rational behavior, their postulates have been developed in a manner which we may term *ad hoc*. (See also Diamond and Rothschild, 1978, pt 1; Aumann, 1985, pp. 35--9).

43. This has led Samuelson (1977a, p. 938) to declare that 'the economics of insurance, medical care, prescription drug testing – to say nothing of bingo and the stock market – will never be the same after Arrow'.
44. In 1962 Arrow offered a course on the economics of uncertainty (which he still teaches intermittently) emphasizing the issues of uncertainty, risk aversion, and liquidity preference emanating from Tobin's influential 1957 paper (see Tobin, 1971, pp. 242–71). Arrow (1984a, p. 147) felt that Tobin's results could be improved.

> I was especially concerned with deriving the comparive statics for demand for risky assets, analogous to the usual developments in ordinary consumer demand theory. It was in studying the wealth effects that I realized that the much-used quadratic utility function implied that risky assets were inferior goods, an empirically dubious proposition. This led to the general formulation of the two measures of risk aversion studied . . . which were developed independently by John Pratt.

Thus in literature we often encounter the Arrow-Pratt measure of risk aversion (see Yaari, 1969). For Pratt's own interpretation of the relationship between his invention and Arrow's see Pratt (1964).

45. The paper was first published in 1953 in a French translation (in which Arrow assisted) of what Arrow calls his 'hastily' written up notes. The original English version was published in 1963–4) by the *Review of Economic Studies* in what was dubbed the 'English translation'.
46. The appendix was added when the paper was republished in Arrow, 1971.
47. Debreu (1959, p. 102) notes:

> This chapter is based on the mimeographed paper, 'Une économie de l'incertain', written by the author at Electricité de France in the summer of 1953. The analysis of the theory of value under uncertainty in terms of choices of Nature originated in K. J. Arrow . . . where the risk-aversion implication of weak-convexity of preferences is established.

48. In his tribute to Arrow on the occasion of the award to him of the Nobel Prize, Debreu (1972, p. 3) notes that this 'beautifully simple discovery, or should one say invention, of commodities contingent on the states of nature' was not immediately picked up by the profession.

> It seems that between 1953, the year of its publication, and 1959, there was not a single reference to your contribution in the literature. Was this due to the fact that your original article was in French, to the fact that it appeared in the proceedings of a colloquium (a frequently inefficient means of communicating ideas), or simply to the fact that your paper came too early? In the sixties references rapidly became more and more numerous, notably after an English translation appeared in the *Review of Economic Studies* in 1964. However, by then you were yourself providing one of the most searching critiques of the idea you had offered in 1953.

49. A very friendly critic, Frank Hahn, has called the contingent commodities device a 'cavalier' treatment of time. Another ally, Vernon Smith (1974, p. 97) sees it as

> a remarkable commentary on the nature of the human mind that such a contribution (and it is indeed) should be considered to have solved a problem. In a sense one can say that it is a sleight-of-hand dodge of the problem, and it certainly constitutes what earlier generations of graduate students would have called an 'empty box'. On the other hand, I find it useful and insightful to imagine a world of Arrow certificates in which every good event has its price and every bad event has its insurance premium so that every portfolio is sharply tuned to individual attitudes toward risk. What is not a legitimate use of the state-contingent securities model is to make judgments to the effect that the real world economy is inefficient because there 'are not enough markets'.

50. In our usual textbook arguments, it is said that the market system is economical of information. Each agent knows its own tastes, technology, and endowment of assets, but neeed know nothing of these personal chacteristics, as we may term them, for other individuals. It is

then implied that individuals are in fact uncertain about most relevant matters, but in a competitive price system, this uncertainty does not matter (Arrow, 1981a, p. 110; see Hayek, 1940; Koopmans, 1970, p. 246).

51. Aside from Arrow's work there is by now a very rich theoretical literature on information which, however, does not converge into a coherent stream as it starts out from divergent sources, concerns itself with different facets, and even uses, to some extent, various terminologies. Curiously, however, it flows primarily from the neoclassical mainstream; that is, it is cast in a world where the individuals are self-seekers and have no appreciable market power and where the equilibrium allocations achieved are such that expectations are not falsified. See *inter alia*, Diamond and Rothschild, 1978, part 3 and Hirshleifer and Riley, 1979, and references therein.
52. The traditional welfare economics focus on market failures, that is, the need for correctives and design of policies to alleviate the defects in the market system by appropriate government intervention, has given way recently to a strong and fashionable counter offensive that emphasizes public sector inefficiencies and failures and the need to distinguish between an ideal and a bureaucratized-politicized government and to recognize a Schumpeterian 'march into socialism'. It is argued that market failures are not a sufficient justification for extra-market intervention for the consequences might be inferior to even the inefficient market solution. See Atkinson and Stiglitz, 1980, Chapter 10 and part 2; and Arrow, 1958.
53. With the benefit of hindsight, Arrow now considers that the paper suffers from an insufficient basis in the economics of uncertainty and information. Though nearly half of the paper is devoted to these subjects, Arrow probably means that the basis was then still underdeveloped.
54. Arrow used the term to remind the readers of his own generation of the doctrines of John Dewey and other leaders of progressive education in the interwar period. And those who are too young to have heard of it, might still find it of some interest.
55. On a personal note, I must confess to a partiality for this paper. Arrow expounded it in 1961 at a seminar in Berkeley where I was a visiting graduate student. It was, I think, the first time I encountered him.
56. Arrow now believes that the model should be redone with a more explicit focus on the dissemination of the information garnered from experience.
57. Arrow (1962, p. 156) also mentions Verdoorn's (1956) application of the learning curve to national outputs, Lundberg's (1961) 'Horndal effect', and others.
58. Haavelmo (1954) proposed a model not very much unlike Arrow (1962) where output was a factor of capital and the state of knowledge and investment was conditioned by output, the capital stock, and the state of knowledge. The latter was, in a simple version, a function of time and, in a more elaborate one, resulted from investment, while each investment

act had an educational effect that exponentially grew smaller as time went by.

59. Arrow (1968a, pp. 1–2) traces it historically:

> This recursive aspect of the production process simplifies analysis and computation, as was first recognized in the context of inventory theory in the magisterial work of Massé (1946) (unfortunately ignored in the English-language literature) and independently by Arrow, Harris and Marschak (1951). Subsequently, the mathematician Bellman ... recognized the basic principle of recursive optimization common to inventory theory, sequential analysis of statistical data, and a host of other control processes in the technological and economic realms and developed the set of computational methods and principles known as *dynamic programming*. Finally, the Russian mathematician Pontryagin and his associates ... developed an elegant theory of control of recursive processes related both to Bellman's work and to the classical calculus of variations. The Pontryagin principle ... has the great advantage of yielding economically interesting results very naturally.

60. That paper was originally presented at a meeting in the fall of 1948. Arrow (1984b, pp. 1–2) recalls that

> Abraham Wald developed the idea and methods of testing statistical hypotheses by sequential analysis at the Statistical Research Group, formed to develop statistical methods for use in the national defense in World War II. No doubt, as in other such efforts, many of the fruits were not available for use until after the emergency that called them forth was over. The memorandum (Statistical Research Group, 1945), originally marked 'Confidential', was circulated, and some of us at the Weather Division of Air Force headquarters were using it within a few months to test whether or not the long-range weather forecasts produced there were significantly better than chance. (They were not.) I became especially interested in Wald's more general formulations of statistical decision theory, both nonsequential and sequential.

During the summer of 1948 Arrow worked with Girshick at Rand. Girshick returned from meeting at which he heard Wald and Wolfowitz present

> some new results about the structure of sequential analysis when there were more than two alternative hypotheses. He returned with great excitement and stimulated David Blackwell and myself to join him in attempting to reconstruct the results in a more transparent form; the original presentation was certainly hard to understand, and its underlying logic unclear. The three of us grasped that the essential idea was the repetion of the decision situation at each step, though with varying values of the parameters. Hence the decision rule consisted in specifying regions in the parameter space, the same for all time. This point of view was of course implicit in the studies of Wald ... and of Wald and Wolfowitz ... but had not been made central (Arrow, 1984b, p. 2).

Arrow (1984b, p. 2) reveals that a rather unsavory episode surrounded his contribution with Blackwell and Girshick: 'a version was circulated that had inadequate acknowledgment to the work of Wald and Wolfowitz, and they felt that there was a challenge to their priority'. (See also Chapter 26 of the companion volume). For the formal acknowledgment of Wald's and Wolfowitz's work and a scrupulous tracing of similarities and differences that appeared in the published version of the Arrow, Blackwell and Girshick contribution see Arrow, 1984b, p. 1.

61. Of course, a more realistic approach is that of overlapping generations where each consumer maximizes utility over a lifetime and the government's policy goals protect future generations. The inevitable differences between private and social goals are mitigated by the recognition that individuals are concerned about their heirs (see Pestieau, 1974).
62. Characteristically, Arrow (1983b, p. 275) pays tribute to Alchian for advancing economic theory both when he is right and when he is wrong.
63. For a more detailed exposition of the criticism from various quarters, including those of Kaldor, Kornai, Morishima, Joan Robinson, and others, and references to the literature, see Feiwel, 1985a, pp. 27–38 and *passim*.
64. 'Of the many uses we can make of the past, one – but certainly not the only one – is to reask some of the questions older writers posed and to provide them with answers in terms of modern analytical methods and terminology' (Samuelson, 1966, p. 371).
65. We may well wonder whether Schumpeter's exhaltation of Walras and down-grading of Marshall was not also coloured somewhat by his well-known prejudice against Anglo-Saxon dominance in economics. But this suspicion may be unwarranted and unfair to the man. Viner (1958, p. 349) notes that Schumpeter's

> biases could take the form of exaggerated enthusiasm and praise as well as of undue disdain and contempt. He was basically generous, moreover, and there is much evidence of his disciplining himself to give appropriate praise to analytical work which was of a high quality even when executed by men who used it to support conclusions he did not like. The fact remains that in the case of some authors he emphasizes their defects as analysts and admits their merits only grudgingly whereas with others he draws attention only to their strong points and leaves unmentioned or strains himself to find some sort of defense for the weak points in their analysis.

REFERENCES

Abramovitz, M. (1981) 'Welfare Quandries and Productivity Concerns', *American Economic Review*, 71:1–17.

Allais, M. (1943) *A la recherche d'une discipline économique* (Paris: Ateliers Industria).

Allais, M. (1953) 'Generalisation des théories de l'équilibre économique general et du rendement social en cas de risque', *Econometrie: Colloques Internationaux du Centre National de la Recherche Scientifique*, 40: 81–109.
Archen Minsol (acronym of Arrow, Chenery, Minhas and Solow) (1968), 'Some Tests of the International Comparisons of Factor Efficiency with the CES Production Function: A reply', *Review of Economics and Statistics* 50: 477–9.
Arrow, K. J. (1949) 'On the Use of Winds in Flight Planning', *Journal of Meteorology*, 6: 150–59.
Arrow, K. J. (1951a) (2nd edn, 1963), *Social Choice and Individual Values* (New York: Wiley).
Arrow, K. J. (1951b) 'Mathematical Models in the Social Sciences', in D. Lerner and H. D. Lasswell (eds) *The Policy Sciences* (Stanford: Stanford University Press) pp. 129–54.
Arrow, K. J. (1958) 'Tinbergen on Economic Policy', *Journal of American Statistical Association*, 53: 89–97.
Arrow, K. J. (1960) 'The Work of Ragnar Frisch, Econometrician', *Econometrica*, 28: 175–92.
Arrow, K. J. (1962) 'The Economic Implications of Learning by Doing', *Review of Economic Studies*, 29: 210–28.
Arrow, K. J. (1963) 'Uncertainty and the Welfare Economics of Medical Care', *American Economic Review*, 53: 941–69.
Arrow, K. J. (1965a) 'Criteria for Social Investment', *Water Resources Research*, 1: 1–8.
Arrow, K. J. (1965b) 'Connaissance, Productivité et Pratique', *Bulletin SEDEIS*, Étude No. 909, Supplément (translated by Arrow for inclusion in Volume 5 of his collected papers).
Arrow, K. J. (1967) 'Samuelson Collected', *Journal of Political Economy*, 75: 730–37.
Arrow, K. J. (1968a) 'Optimal Capital Policy with Irreversible Investment', in J. N. Wolfe (ed), *Value, Capital and Growth*, (Edinburgh: Edinburgh University Press) pp. 1–20.
Arrow, K. J. (1968b) 'Applications of Control Theory to Economic Growth', in *Mathematics of the Decision Sciences* pt 2 (Providence: American Mathematical Society) pp. 85–119.
Arrow, K. J. (1971) *Essays in the Theory of Risk-Bearing* (Chicago: Markham).
Arrow, K. J. (1972a) 'Problems of Resource Allocation in United States Medical Care', in R. M. Kunz and H. Fehr (eds), *The Challenge of Life* (Basel: Birkhäuser Verlag) pp. 392–408.
Arrow, K. J. (1972b) 'Models of Job Discrimination', and 'Some Models of Race in the Labor Market', in A. H. Pascal (ed.) *Racial Discrimination in Economic Life* (Lexington, Mass.: Heath) chs 2, 6.
Arrow, K. J. (1973) 'The Theory of Discrimination', in O. Aschenfelter and A. Rees (eds) *Discrimination in Labor Markets* (Princeton: Princeton University Press) pp. 3–33.
Arrow, K. J. (1975) 'Thorstein Veblen as an Economic Theorist', *The American Economist*, 19(1): 4–9.

Arrow, K. J. (1976a) 'Tjalling Koopmans: An Appreciation', Harvard Institute of Economic Research, Discussion Paper, no. 509.

Arrow, K. J. (1976b) *Theoretical Issues in Health Insurance* (University of Essex: Noel Buxton Lecture).

Arrow, K. J. (1978) 'Jacob Marschak's Contributions to the Economics of Decision and Information', *American Economic Review*, 68: xii–xiv.

Arrow, K. J. (1979) 'Jacob Marschak', in *International Encyclopedia of the Social Sciences*, vol. 18, biographical supplement (New York: Free Press) pp. 500–06.

Arrow, K. J. (1980) 'Real and Nominal Magnitudes in Economics', *Journal of Financial and Quantitative Analysis*, 15: 773–83.

Arrow, K. J. (1981a) 'Futures Markets: Some Theoretical Perspectives', *Journal of Futures Markets* 1(2): 107–15.

Arrow, K. J. (1981b) 'Jacob Marschak's Contributions to the Economics of Decision and Information', *Mathematical Social Sciences*, 1: 335–8.

Arrow, K. J. (1982) 'The Rate of Discount on Public Investment with Imperfect Capital Markets', in R. C. Lind and others, *Discounting for Time and Risk in Energy Policy* (Washington: Resources for the Future) pp. 115–36.

Arrow, K. J. (1983a) *Collected Papers of Kenneth J. Arrow* vol. 1; *Social Choice and Justice* (Cambridge, Mass.: Harvard University Press).

Arrow, K. J. (1983b) *Collected Papers of Kenneth J. Arrow* vol. 2: *General Equilibrium* (Cambridge, Mass.: Harvard University Press).

Arrow, K. J. (1983c) 'Behavior Under Uncertainty and its Implications for Policy', in B. P. Stigum and F. Wenstop (eds) *Foundations of Utility and Risk Theory with Applications* (Dordrecht: Reidel) pp. 19–32.

Arrow, K. J. (1983d) 'Contributions to Welfare Economics', in E. C. Brown and R. M. Solow *Paul Samuelson and Modern Economic Theory* (New York: McGraw-Hill) pp. 15–30.

Arrow, K. J. (1983e) 'Team Theory and Decentralized Resource Allocation', in P. Desai (ed.) *Marxism, Central Planning, and the Soviet Economy* (Cambridge, Mass.: MIT Press) pp. 63–76.

Arrow, K. J. (1983f) 'Innovation in Large and Small Firms', in J. Roned (ed.) *Entrepreneurship* (Lexington, Mass.: Lexington Books) pp. 15–28.

Arrow, K. J. (1984a) *Collected Papers of Kenneth J. Arrow*, vol. 3: *Individual Choice under Certainty and Uncertainty* (Cambridge, Mass.: Harvard University Press).

Arrow. K. J. (1984b) *Collected Papers of Kenneth J. Arrow*, vol. 4: *The Economics of Information* (Cambridge, Mass.: Harvard University Press).

Arrow, K. J. (1985a) 'The Potentials and Limits of the Market in Resource Allocation', in G.R. Feiwel (ed.)(1985a) *Issues in Contemporary Microeeconomics and Welfare* (London: Macmillan) pp. 107–24.

Arrow, K. J. (1985b) 'Distributive Justice and Desirable Ends of Economic Activity' in G. R. Feiwel (ed.) (1985b) *Issues in Contemporary Macroeconomics and Distribution* (London: Macmillan) pp. 134–56.

Arrow, K. J. (1985c) 'Informational Structure of the Firm', *American Economic Review*, 75 (May): 303–7.

Arrow, K. J. (1985d) 'Maine and Texas', *American Economic Review*, 75: 320–27.

Arrow, K. J., H. B. Chenery, B.S. Minhas and R. M. Solow (1961), 'Capital-Labor Substitution and Economic Efficiency', *Review of Economics and Statistics*, 43: 225–50.

Arrow, K. J. and G. Debreu (1954) 'Existence of an Equilibrium for a Competitive Economy', *Econometrica* 22: 265–90.

Arrow, K. J. and A. C. Enthoven (1961) 'Quasi-concave Programming', *Econometrica*, 29: 779–800.

Arrow, K. J. and F. H. Hahn (1971) *General Competitive Analysis* (San Francisco: Holden-Day).

Arrow, K. J., T. Harris and J. Marschak (1951) 'Optimal Inventory Policy', *Econometrica*, 19: 250–72.

Arrow, K. J. and L. Hurwicz (1977) *Studies in Resource Allocation Processes* (Cambridge: Cambridge University Press).

Arrow, K. J., L. Hurwicz and H. Uzawa (1958), *Studies in Linear and Non-Linear Programming* (Stanford: Stanford University Press).

Arrow, K. J. and M. D. Intriligator (eds) (1981) *Handbook of Mathematical Economics*, vol. 1 (Amsterdam: North-Holland).

Arrow, K. J. and M. D. Intriligator (eds) (1982) *Handbook of Mathematical Economics*, vol. 2 (Amsterdam: North-Holland).

Arrow, K. J. and M. D. Intriligator (eds) (1985) *Handbook of Mathematical Economics*, vol. 3 (Amsterdam: North-Holland).

Arrow, K. J., S. Karlin and H. Scarf (1958) *Studies in the Mathematical Theory of Inventory and Production* (Stanford: Stanford University Press).

Arrow, K. J., S. Karlin and H. Scarf (eds) (1962) *Studies in Applied Probability and Management Science* (Stanford: Stanford University Press).

Arrow, K. J. and M. Kurz (1970) *Public Investment, the Rate of Return, and Fiscal Policy* (Baltimore: Johns Hopkins Press).

Arrow, K. J. and T. Scitovsky (eds) (1969) *Readings in Welfare Economics* (Homewood, Ill.: Irwin).

Atkinson, A. B. and J. E. Stiglitz (1980) *Lectures on Public Economics* (New York: McGraw-Hill).

Aumann, R. J. (1966) 'The Existence of Competitive Equilibria in Markets with a Continuum of Traders', *Econometrica*, 34: 1–17.

Aumann, R. J. (1985) 'What is Game Theory Trying to Accomplish?', in K. J. Arrow and S. Honkapohja (eds.) *Frontiers of Economics* (Oxford: Blackwell), pp. 28-87.

Baumol, W. J. and S. M. Goldfeld (eds) (1968) *Precursors in Mathematical Economics* (London: The London School of Economics).

Becker, G. S. (1971) *The Economics of Discrimination* (Chicago: University of Chicago Press).

Bergson, A. (Berg, A.) (1938) 'A Reformulation of Certain Aspects of Welfare Economics',, *Quarterly Journal of Economics*, 52: 310–34.

Bergson, A. (1954) 'On the Concept of Social Welfare', *Quarterly Journal of Economics*, 68: 233–52.

Bergson, A. (1982) Paul A. Samuelson: The Harvard Days', in G. R.

Feiwel (ed.) *Samuelson and Neoclassical Economics* (Boston: Kluwer) pp. 331–8.

Bergson, A. (1983) 'Pareto on Social Welfare', *Journal of Economic Literature* 21: 40–46.

Bernoulli, D. (1738) 'Specimen theoria novae de mensura sortis', *Commentarii Academiae Scientiarum Imperialis Petropolitanae*, 5: 175–92 (translation by L. Sommer (1954) 'Exposition of a New Theory on the Measurement of Risk', *Econometrica*, 22:23–6.

Black, R. D. C., A. N. Coats and C. D. W. Goodwin (eds.) (1973) *The Marginal Revolution in Economics* (Durham, N. C.: Duke University Press).

Blaug, M. (1978) *Economic Theory in Retrospect* (Cambridge: Cambridge University Press).

Blaug, M. (1980) *The Methodology of Economics* (Cambridge: Cambridge University Press).

Boulding, K. E. (1971) 'After Samuelson Who Needs Adam Smith?' *History of Political Economy*, 3(2): 225–37.

Chipman, J. S. (1965a) 'A Survey of the Theory of International Trade, Part 2', *Econometrica*, 33: 685–760.

Chipman, J. S. (1965b) 'The Nature and Meaning of Equilibrium in Economic Theory', in D. Martindale (ed.) *Functionalism in the Social Sciences* (Philadelphia: American Academy of Political and Social Sciences) pp. 35–64.

Clower, R. W. (1975) 'Reflections on the Keynesian Perplex', *Zeitschrift für Nationalökonomie*, 35: 1–24.

Coddington, A. (1975) 'The Rationale of General Equilibrium Theory' *Economic Inquiry*, 13: 539–58.

Cooter, R. and P. Rappoport (1984) 'Were the Ordinalists Wrong about Welfare Economics?' *Journal of Economic Literature*, 22: 507–30.

Debreu, G. (1952) 'A Social Equilibrium Existence Theorem', *Proceedings of the National Academy of Sciences*, 38:886–93.

Debreu, G. (1954) 'Valuation Equilibrium and Pareto Optimum', *Proceedings of the National Academy of Sciences*, 40: 588–92.

Debreu, G. (1956) 'Market Equilibrium', *Proceedings of the National Academy of Sciences*, 42: 876–8.

Debreu, G. (1959) *Theory of Value* (New Haven: Yale University Press).

Debreu, G. (1962) 'New Concepts and Techniques for Equilibrium Analysis', *International Economic Review*, 3: 257–73.

Debreu, G. (1972) 'Lunch in Honor of Kenneth J. Arrow at the Toronto Meeting of the American Economic Association', mimeo. (December.)

Debreu, G. (1982) 'Existence of Competitive Equilibrium', in K. J. Arrow and M. D. Intriligator (eds) (1982) *Handbook of Mathematical Economics*, vol. 2 (Amsterdam: North-Holland) pp. 697–743.

Debreu, G. (1983) *Mathematical Economics: Twenty Papers of Gerard Debreu* (Cambridge: Cambridge University Press).

Debreu, G. (1984) 'Economic Theory in the Mathematical Mode', *American Economic Review* 74: 267–78.

Debreu, G. (1985) 'Theoretic Models: Mathematical Form and Economic Content', mimeo., Frisch Memorial Lecture, Fifth World Congress of

the Econometric Society (August, 1985), to be published in *Econometrica*.
Debreu, G. (n.d.) 'Mathematical Economics at Cowles', mimeo. (To appear in a volume edited by H. Scarf.)
Diamond, P. A. and M. Rothschild (eds) (1978) *Uncertainty in Economics* (New York: Academic Press).
Dierker, E. (1982) 'Regular Economies' in K. J. Arrow and M. D. Intriligator (eds) (1982) *Handbook of Mathematical Economics*, vol. 2 (Amsterdam: North-Holland) pp. 795–830.
Dobb, M. H. (1973) *Theories of Value and Distribution* (Cambridge: Cambridge University Press).
Dorfman, R., P. A. Samuelson and R. M. Solow (1958) *Linear Programming and Economic Analysis* (New York: McGraw-Hill).
Drèze, J. H. (ed.) (1974) *Allocation under Uncertainty* (London: Macmillan).
Eckstein, O. (1961) 'A Survey of the Theory of Public Expenditure' and 'Reply', in National Bureau of Economic Research, *Public Finances* (Princeton: Princeton University Press) pp. 439–504.
Edgeworth, F. Y. (1881) (1953 reprint) *Mathematical Psychics* (New York: Kelley).
Edgeworth, F. Y. (1922) 'Equal Pay to Men and Women for Equal Work', *Economic Journal* 31: 431–57.
Farrell, M. J. (1959) 'The Convexity Assumption in the Theory of Competitive Markets', *Journal of Political Economy*, 67: 377–91.
Feiwel, G. R. (ed.) (1985a) *Issues in Contemporary Microeconomics and Welfare* (London: Macmillan).
Feiwel, G. R. (ed.) (1985b) *Issues in Contemporary Macroeconomics and Distribution* (London: Macmillan).
Fisher, F. M. (1976) 'The Stability of General Equilibrium', in M. J. Artis and A. R. Nobay (eds) *Essays in Economic Analysis* (Cambridge: Cambridge University Press).
Friedman, M. (1955) 'Leon Walras and his Economic System', *American Economic Review*, 55: 900–09.
Friedman, M. (1976) *Adam Smiths' Relevance for 1976* (Los Angeles: International Institute for Economic Research).
Friedman, M. (1981) *The Invisible Hand in Economics and Politics* (Singapore: Institute of Southeast Asian Studies).
Friedman, M. and S. S. Kuznets (1945) *Income from Independent Professional Practice* (New York: National Bureau of Economic Research).
Friedman, M. and L. J. Savage (1948) 'The Utility Analysis of Choices Involving Risks', *Journal of Political Economy*, 56: 279–304.
Galbraith, J. K. (1973) 'Power and the Useful Economist', *American Economic Review*, 63: 1–11.
Gale, D. (1955) 'The Law of Supply and Demand', *Mathematica Scandinavica*, 3: 155–69.
Gale, D. (1960) *The Theory of Linear Economic Models* (New York: McGraw-Hill).
Georgescu-Roegen, N. (1970) 'The Economics of Production', *American Economic Review*, 60: 1–17.
Green, J. (1985) 'Differential Information, the Market and Incentive Compa-

tibility', in K. J. Arrow and S. Honkapohja (eds), *Frontiers of Economics* (Oxford: Blackwell), pp. 178–99.

Grossman, S. J. and J. E. Stiglitz (1976) 'Information and Competitive Price Systems', *American Economic Review*, 66: 246–53.

Haavelmo, T. (1954) *A Study in the Theory of Economic Evolution* (Amsterdam: North-Holland).

Hahn, F. H. (1970) 'Some Adjustment Problems'. *Econometrica*, 38(1):1–17.

Hahn, F. H. (1973) *On the Notion of Equilibrium in Economics* (Cambridge: Cambridge University Press).

Hahn, F. H. (1982) 'Stability', in K. J. Arrow and M. D. Intriligator (eds) (1982) *Handbook of Mathematical Economics*, vol. 2 (Amsterdam: North Holland) pp. 745–93.

Hahn, F. H. (1983) 'On General Equilibrium and Stability', in E. C. Brown and R. M. Solow (eds), *Paul Samuelson and Modern Economic Theory* (New York: McGraw-Hill) pp. 31–55.

Hahn, F. H. and R. C. O. Matthews (1965) 'The Theory of Economic Growth: A Survey', in *Surveys of Economic Theory*, vol. 2 (London: Macmillan, pp. 1–124).

Hammond, P. J. (1982) 'Utilitarianism, Uncertainty and Information' in A. Sen and B. Williams (eds) *Utilitarianism and Beyond* (Cambridge: Cambridge University Press) pp. 85–102.

Hammond, P. J. (1984) 'Must Monopoly Power Accompany Innovation?' in C. Seidl (ed.) *Lectures on Schumpeterian Economics.* (Berlin: Springer-Verlag) pp. 45–56.

Hammond, P. J. (1985) 'Welfare Economics', in G. R. Feiwel (ed.) (1985a) *Issues in Contemporary Microeconomics and Welfare* (London: Macmillan) pp. 405–34.

Harrod, R. F. (1956) 'Walras: A Re-appraisal', *Economic Journal*, 66: 307–16.

Harsanyi, J. (1955) 'Cardinal Welfare, Individualistic Ethics, and Interpersonal Comparisons of Utility', *Journal of Political Economy*, 63: 309–21.

Hart, O. D. (1975) 'On the Optimality of Equilibrium when the Market Structure is Incomplete', *Journal of Economic Theory* 11: 418–43.

Hart, O. D. (1982) 'Imperfect Competition in General Equilibrium: An Overview of Recent Work', mimeo (November).

Hart, O. D. (1984) 'Comment' in P. Wiles and G. Routh (eds), *Economics in Disarray* (Oxford: Blackwell) pp. 47–50.

Haveman, R. H. and J. Margolis (eds) (1983) *Public Expenditure and Public Policy Analysis* (Boston: Houghton Mifflin).

Hayek, F. A. von (1940) 'Socialist Calculation: The Competitive Solution', *Economica* (N. S.) 7: 125–49.

Hayek, F. A. von (1967) *Studies in Philosophy, Politics and Economics* (New York: Simon and Schuster).

Heal, G. M. (1973) *The Theory of Economic Planning* (Amsterdam: North Holland).

Hicks, J. R. (1939a) 'The Foundations of Welfare Economics', *Economic Journal*, 49: 696–712.

Hicks, J. R. (1939b) *Value and Capital* (London: Oxford University Press).

Hicks, J. R. (1975) 'The Scope and Status of Welfare Economics', *Oxford Economic Papers*, 27(3): 307–26.

Hicks, J. R. (1976) '"Revolutions" in Economics', in S. J. Latsis (ed.), *Method and Appraisal in Economics* (Cambridge: Cambridge University Press) pp. 207–18.

Hicks, J. R. (1981) *Wealth and Welfare* (Cambridge, Mass.: Harvard University Press).

Hicks, J. R. (1983) *Classics and Moderns* (Cambridge, Mass.: Harvard University Press).

Hildenbrand, W. (1982) 'Core of an Economy' in K. J. Arrow and M. D. Intriligator (eds) (1982), *Handbook of Mathematical Economics*, vol. 2 (Amsterdam: North Holland). pp. 831–78.

Hildenbrand, W. (1983) 'Introduction' to G. Debreu (1983) *Mathematical Economics* (Cambridge: Cambridge University Press).

Hildenbrand, W. (ed.) (1982) *Advances in Economic Theory* (Cambridge: Cambridge University Press).

Hirshleifer, J. (1965) 'Investment Decision under Uncertainty: Choice Theoretic Approaches', *Quarterly Journal of Economics*, 79: 509–36.

Hirshleifer, J. (1966) 'Investment Decision under Uncertainty: Applications of the State Preference Approach', *Quarterly Journal of Economics*, 80: 252–77.

Hirshleifer, J. and J. G. Riley (1979) 'The Analytics of Uncertainty and Information – An Expository Survey', *Journal of Economic Literature*, 17: 1375–1421.

Hotelling, H. (1938) 'The General Welfare in Relation to Problems of Taxation and of Railway and Utility Rates', *Econometrica*, 6: 242–69.

Hurwicz, L. (1985) 'Information and Incentives in Designing Non-wasteful Resource Allocation Systems', in G. R. Feiwel (ed.) (1985a) *Issues in Contemporary Microeconomics and Welfare* (London: Macmillan) pp. 125–68.

Hutchison, T. (1984) 'Our Methodological Crisis' in P. Wiles and G. Routh (eds), *Economics in Disarray* (Oxford: Blackwell) pp. 1–21.

Jaffé, W. (1983) *William Jaffé's Essays on Walras* D. A. Walker (ed.) (Cambridge: Cambridge University Press).

Johansen, L. (1959) 'Substitution vs. Fixed Production Coefficients in the Theory of Economic Growth', *Econometrica*, 27:157–76.

Jorgenson, D. (1984) 'Econometric Methods for Applied General Equilibrium Analysis', in H. E. Scarf and J. B. Shoven (eds) *Applied General Equilibrium Analysis*, (Cambridge: Cambridge University Press) pp. 139–207.

Kaldor, N. (1939) 'Welfare Propositions of Economics and Interpersonal Comparisons of Utility', *Economic Journal*, 49: 549–52.

Kelly, J. S. (1978) *Arrow's Impossibility Theorems* (New York: Academic Press).

Keynes, J. M. (1951) *Essays in Biography* (London: Horizon Press).

Klausen, A. (ed.) (1965) *The Invisible Hand* (Chicago: Henry Regnery).

Koopmans, T. C. (1957) *Three Essays on the State of Economic Science* (New York: McGraw-Hill).

Koopmans, T. C. (1970) *Scientific Papers of Tjalling C. Koopmans*, M. Beckmann, C. F. Christ, and M. Nerlov (eds) (Berlin: Springer-Verlag).

Koopmans, T. C. (1974) 'Is the Theory of Competitive Equilibrium with It?' *American Economic Review*, 64 (May): 325–9.
Koopmans, T. C. (1977) 'Concepts of Optimality and their Uses' *American Economic Review*, 67: 261–74.
Koopmans, T. C. (ed.) (1951) *Activity Analysis of Production and Allocation* (New York: Wiley).
Kuenne, R. E. (1963) *The Theory of General Economic Equilibrium* (Princeton: Princeton University Press).
Lange, O. (1938) 'On the Economic Theory of Socialism', in B. F. Lippincott (ed.) *On the Economic Theory of Socialism* (Minneapolis: University of Minnesota Press).
Lange, O. (1942) 'The Foundations of Welfare Economics', *Econometrica*, 10 (July): 215–28.
Lange, O. (1944) *Price Flexibility and Employment* (Bloomington, Ind.: The Principia Press).
Lange, O. (1966) *O socjaliźmie i gospodarce socjalistycznej* (Warsaw: PWN).
Leijonhufvud, A. (1981) *Information and Coordination* (New York: Oxford University Press).
Leontief, W. (1971) 'Theoretical Assumptions and Nonobserved Facts', *American Economic Review*, 61: 1–7.
Leontief, W. (1984) *Input-Output Economics* (New York: Oxford University Press).
Lerner, A. P. (1944) *The Economics of Control* (London: Macmillan).
Little, I. M. D. (1950) *A Critique of Welfare Economics* (Oxford: Clarendon Press).
Little, I. M. D. (1952) 'Social Choice and Individual Values' *Journal of Political Economy*, 60: 422–32.
Lucas, R. E., Jr (1981) *Studies in Business Cycle Theory* (Cambridge, Mass.: Harvard University Press).
Lundberg, E. (1961) *Produktivitet och räntabilitet* (Stockholm: Norstedt).
Machina, M. (1983) 'The Economic Theory of Individual Behavior Toward Risk', Technical Report no. 433 (Stanford: IMSSS).
Malinvaud, E. (1972) *Lectures on Microeconomic Theory* (Amsterdam: North-Holland).
Marglin, S. A. (1963) 'The Social Rate of Discount and the Optimal Rate of Investment', *Quarterly Journal of Economics*, 77: 95–111.
Marschak, J. and R. Radner (1972) *Economic Theory of Teams* (New Haven: Yale University Press).
Mas-Colell, A. (1985) *The Theory of General Economic Equilibrium* (Cambridge: Cambridge University Press).
Maskin, E. S. and K. W. S. Roberts (1980) 'On the Fundamental Theorems of General Equilibrium', mimeo. (November).
Massé, P. (1946) *Les réserves et la régulation de l'avenir* (Paris: Hermann).
McKenzie, L. W. (1954) 'On Equilibrium in Graham's Model of World Trade and Other Competitive Systems', *Econometrica*, 22: 147–61.
McKenzie, L. W. (1959) 'On the Existence of General Equilibrium for a Competitive Market', *Econometrica*, 27: 54–71.
McKenzie, L. W. (1981) 'The Classical Theorem of Existence of Competitive Equilibrium', *Econometrica*, 49: 819–41.

Metzler, L. (1945) 'Stability of Multiple Markets: The Hicks Condition', *Econometrica*, 13: 277–92.
Mill, J. S. (1867) *Inaugural Address*, delivered to the University of St Andrews, 1 February, (London: Longmans Green).
Mill, J. S. (1909) *Principles of Political Economy*, Sir W. J. Ashley (ed.) (lst edn 1848) (London: Longmans Green).
Mirrlees, J. A. (1979) 'Review of *Studies in Resource Allocation Processes*', *Economic Journal*, 89: 146–8.
Mises, L. von (1951) *Socialism* (New Haven: Yale University Press).
Mishan, E. J. (1957) 'An Investigation into Some Alleged Contradictions in Welfare Economics', *Economic Journal*, 68: 445–54.
Morgenstern, O. (1968) 'Schlesinger, Karl', in *International Encyclopedia of the Social Sciences*, vol. 14 (New York: Macmillan) pp. 51–2.
Morishima, M. (1952) 'On the Laws of Change of the Price-System in an Economy which Contains Complementary Commodities', *Osaka Economic Papers*, 1:101–13.
Morishima, M. (1977) *Walras' Economics* (Cambridge: Cambridge University Press).
Morishima, M. (1984) 'The Good and Bad Uses of Mathematics', in P. Wiles and G. Routh (eds), *Economics in Disarray* (Oxford: Blackwell) pp. 51–73.
Nash, J. F. Jr. (1950) 'Equilibrium Points in *N*-Person Games', *Proceedings of the National Academy of Sciences*, 36: 48–9.
Neary, P. and J. E. Stiglitz (1983) 'Towards a Reconstruction of Keynesian Economics: Expectations and Constrained Equilibria', *Quarterly Journal of Economics*, 97 (supplement): 199–228.
Negishi, T. (1960–61) 'Monopolistic Competition and General Equilibrium', *Review of Economic Studies*, 28: 196–201.
Negishi, T. (1962) 'The Stability of a Competitive Economy: A Survey Article', *Econometrica*, 30: 635–69.
Nell, E. (ed.) (1984) *Free Market Conservatism* (London: Allen & Unwin).
Nelson, R. R., and S. G. Winter (1982) *An Evolutionary Theory of Economic Change* (Cambridge, Mass.: Harvard University Press).
Nikaido, H. (1956) 'On the Classical Multilateral Exchange Problem' *Metroeconomica*, 8: 135–45.
Pareto, V. (1971) *Manual of Political Economy*, translated A. S. Schweir from the French 1927 edn, A. S. Schweir and A. N. Page (eds) (New York: Kelley).
Patinkin, D. (1965), *Money, Interest, and Prices* (New York: Harper & Row).
Pestieau, P. M. (1974) 'Optimal Taxation and Discounting for Public Investment in a Growth Setting', *Journal of Public Economics*, 3: 217–35.
Pigou, A. C. (1912) *Wealth and Welfare* (London: Macmillan).
Pigou, A. C. (1920) (4th edn 1960) *The Economics of Welfare* (London: Macmillan).
Pratt, J. W. (1964) 'Risk Aversion in the Small and in the Large', *Econometrica*, 32: 122–36.
Quirk, J. and R. Saposnik (1968) *Introduction to General Equilibrium Theory and Welfare Economics* (New York: McGraw-Hill).
Radner, R. (1972) chapters 1, 9, 10, and 11 in C. B. McGuire and R. Radner

(eds), *Decisions and Organization: A Volume in Honor of Jacob Marschak* (Amsterdam: North-Holland).

Radner, R. (1982) 'Equilibrium under Uncertainty' in K. J. Arrow and M. D. Intriligator (eds) (1982), pp. 923–1006.

Ramsey, F. P. (1928) 'A Mathematical Theory of Saving', *Economic Journal*, 38: 543–59.

Rawls, J. (1971) *A Theory of Justice* (Cambridge, Mass: Harvard University Press).

Ricci, U. (1933) 'Pareto and Pure Economics', *Review of Economic Studies*, 1: 3–21.

Robbins, L. (1978) *The Theory of Economic Policy in English Classical Political Economy*, 2nd edn (Philadelphia: Porcupine).

Robinson, Joan (1962) *Economic Philosophy* (Chicago: Aldine).

Robinson, Joan (1982) 'Misunderstandings in the Theory of Production', in G. R. Feiwel (ed.), *Samuelson and Neoclassical Economics* (Boston: Kluwer) pp. 90–96.

Rosenberg, N. (1982) *Inside the Black Box: Technology and Economics* (Cambridge: Cambridge University Press).

Rothenberg, J. (1960) 'Non-convexity, Aggregation, and Pareto Optimality', *Journal of Political Economy*, 68: 435–68.

Rothschild, M. and J. E. Stiglitz (1976) 'Equilibrium in Competitive Insurance Markets', *Quarterly Journal of Economics*, 90: 629–50.

Sacks, O. (1972) 'The Great Awakening', *The Listener*, 30 November, p. 756.

Salter, W. E. G. (1960) *Productivity and Technical Change* (Cambridge: Cambridge University Press).

Samuelson, P. A. (1947) *Foundations of Economic Analysis* (Cambridge, Mass.: Harvard University Press).

Samuelson, P. A. (1964) 'Discussion', *American Economic Review*, 54 (May): 93–6.

Samuelson, P. A. (1966) *The Collected Scientific Papers of Paul A. Samuelson*, J. E. Stiglitz (ed.) 2 vols (Cambridge, Mass.: MIT Press)

Samuelson, P. A. (1972) *The Collected Scientific Papers of Paul A. Samuelson*, vol. 3, R. C. Merton (ed.) (Cambridge, Mass.: MIT Press).

Samuelson, P. A. (1977a) *The Collected Scientific Papers of Paul A. Samuelson*, vol. 4, H. Nagatani and K. Crowley (eds) (Cambridge, Mass.: MIT Press).

Samuelson, P. A. (1977b) 'A Modern Theorist's Vindication of Adam Smith', *American Economic Review*, 67: 42–9.

Samuelson, P. A. (1981) 'Bergsonian Welfare Economics', in S. Rosefielde (ed.), *Economic Welfare and the Economics of Soviet Socialism: Essays in Honor of Abram Bergson* (Cambridge: Cambridge University Press) pp. 223–66.

Samuelson, P. A. (1982) 'Schumpeter as an Economic Theorist', in H. Frisch (ed.), *Schumpeterian Economics* (New York: Praeger) pp. 1–17.

Samuelson, P. A. (1983a) *Foundations of Economic Analysis*, enlarged edition (Cambridge, Mass.: Harvard University Press).

Samuelson, P. A. (1983b) 'The 1983 Nobel Prize in Economics', *Science*, 222: 987–9.

Savage, L. J. (1954) *The Foundations of Statistics* (New York: Wiley).

Scarf, H. E. (1982) 'The Computation of Equilibrium Prices: An Exposition', in K. J. Arrow and M. D. Intriligator (eds) (1982) *Handbook of Mathematical Economics*, vol. 2 (Amsterdam: North Holland).

Schumpeter, J. A. (1950) *Capitalism, Socialism and Democracy*, 3rd edn (New York: Harper & Row).

Schumpeter, J. A. (1951) *Ten Great Economists* (New York: Oxford University Press).

Schumpeter, J. A. (1954) *History of Economic Analysis* (New York: Oxford University Press).

Scitovsky, T. (1984) 'Lerner's Contributions to Economics', *Journal of Economic Literature*, 22: 1547–71.

Sen, A. (1973) *On Economic Inequality* (New York: Norton).

Sen, A. (1982) *Choice, Welfare and Measurement* (Oxford: Blackwell).

Sen, A. (1985a) 'Social Choice Theory', in K. J. Arrow and M. D. Intriligator (eds) (1985) *Handbook of Mathematical Economics* vol. 3 (Amsterdam: North Holland)

Sen, A. (1985b) '*Social Choice and Justice*: A Review Article', *Journal of Economic Literature*, 23: 1764–76.

Sen, A. (ed.) (1970) *Growth Economics* (Harmondsworth: Penguin).

Sen, A. and B. Williams (eds) (1982) *Utilitarianism and Beyond* (Cambridge: Cambridge University Press).

Shackle, G. L. S. (1967) *The Years of High Theory* (Cambridge: Cambridge University Press).

Shoven, J. B. and J. Whalley (1984) 'Applied General-Equilibrium Models of Taxation and International Trade', *Journal of Economic Literature*, 22: 1007–51.

Sidgwick, H. (1907) *The Methods of Ethics*, 7th edn (London: Macmillan).

Simon, H. A. (1982) *Models of Bounded Rationality*, vol. 2: *Behavioral Economics and Business Organization* (Cambridge, Mass.: MIT Press).

Smale, S. (1976a) 'A Convergent Process of Price Adjustment and Global Newton Methods', *Journal of Mathematical Economics*, 3: 1–14.

Smale, S. (1976b) 'Dynamics in General Equilibrium Theory', *American Economic Review* 66 (May): 288–94.

Smale, S. (1981) 'Global Analysis and Economics', in K. J. Arrow and M. D. Intriligator (eds) (1981) *Handbook of Mathematical Economics*, vol. 1 (Amsterdam: North Holland)

Smith, V. (1974) 'Review of *Essays in Theory of Risk-Bearing', Journal of Business*, 47: 96–8.

Solow, R. M. (1957) 'Technical Change and the Aggregate Production Function', *Review of Economics and Statistics*, 39: 312–20.

Solow, R. M. (1985) 'Economic History and Economics', *American Economic Review*, 75: 328–31.

Starr, R. (1969) 'Quasi-equilibria in Markets with Nonconvex Preferences', *Econometrica*, 37: 25–38.

Stigler, G. J. (1982) *The Economist as Preacher and Other Essays* (Chicago: University of Chicago Press).

Tobin, J. (1971) *Essays in Economics*, vol. 1: *Macroeconomics*, (Amsterdam: North-Holland).

Verdoorn, P. J. (1956) 'Complementarity and Long-Range Projections', *Econometrica*, 24: 429–50.

Vickrey, W. S. (1945) 'Measuring Marginal Utility by Reactions to Risk', *Econometrica*, 13: 319–33.

Vickrey, W. S. (1964) 'Discussion', *American Economic Review*, 54:88–92.

Viner, J. (1958) *The Long View and the Short* (Glencoe, Ill.: The Free Press).

Neumann, J. von (1945–46) 'A Model of General Economic Equilibrium', *Review of Economic Studies*, 13(1): 1–9, translated by G. Morgenstern, from 'Über ein ökonomisches Gleichungssystem und eine Verallgemeinrung des Brouwerschen Fixpunktsatzes', *Ergebnisse eines mathematischen Kolloquiums*, 8(1937): 73–83.

Neumann, J. von and O. Morgenstern (1947) *Theory of Games and Economic Behavior* (Princeton: Princeton University Press).

Wald, A. (1951) 'On Some Systems of Equations of Mathematical Economics', *Econometrica*, 19: 368–403, translated by O. Eckstein from 'Über einige Gleichungssysteme der mathematischen Ökonomie', *Zeitschrift für Nationalökonomie*, 7(5): 637–70.

Walras, L. (1954) *Elements of Pure Economics*, translated from the definitive (1926) edn by W. Jaffé (1st edn 1874–7) (London: Allen & Unwin).

Walsh, V. and H. Gram (1980) *Classical and Neoclassical Theories of General Equilibrium* (New York: Oxford University Press).

Weintraub, E. R. (1983) 'On the Existence of a Competitive Equilibrium: 1930–1954', *Journal of Economic Literature*, 21: 1–39.

Weizsaker, C. C. von (1972) 'Kenneth Arrow's Contributions to Economics', *Swedish Journal of Economics*, 74(4): 488–602.

Whitaker, J. K. (ed.) (1975) *The Early Economic Writings of Alfred Marshall, 1867–1890*, (London: MacMillan).

Whittaker, E. (1940) *A History of Economic Ideas* (New York: Longmans Green).

Wicksell, K. (1934) *Lectures on Political Economy*, vol. 1: *General Theory*, translated by E. Classen, L. Robbins (ed.) (London: Routledge & Kegan Paul).

Williamson, O. E. (1975) *Markets and Hierarchies* (New York: Free Press).

Yaari, M. E. (1969) 'Some Remarks on Measures of Risk Aversion and their Uses', *Journal of Economic Theory*, 1: 315–29.

PART I
The Makers of Modern General Equilibrium Theory

2 Oral History I: An Interview

Kenneth J. Arrow

Feiwel: Let me first take you beyond your contributions to the making of g.e.t. How did you become interested in the subject of social choice?

Arrow: Clearly this was a recurrent theme with me and this is where I have to give a lot of credit to the unconscious. I first hit upon it this way: I was working on redoing Hicks. One of the observations was that real firms are owned by several people, in fact, lots of people. Theoretically, let us assume that the stockholders run the firm. How should they behave? You might say that they all want to maximize profit. There is nothing to disagree about here, but I was interested in investment. If you invest, your estimate of profit depends on your expectations of the future (as I said, I was following Hicks then). Essentially there are no markets for the future, only markets for the present. So there is nothing to make people agree on the future as there is on the present. Even though they might all agree on maximum profits, they might have different ideas as to which investment project will yield maximum expected profits. Again, I was following the Hicks certainty idea; I had not yet got to using decision theory under uncertainty. Then I asked myself, why do they disagree, what are the criteria? You know the rules, the majority wins. So then the natural thing is to say that investment project A is chosen over investment project B ... and you can see where this leads. I started playing around with this and it took me very little time to realize that there was a paradox there.

The minute I saw this I said to myself, surely this must be wrong. In fact, I thought I had heard it somewhere before. From that day to this I have never been able to establish whether I had really heard it or not. I now know the literature and there is certainly no way I could have read any of it. I certainly had not delved into things like an article in the Proceedings of the Royal Society, 1882. Nevertheless, it is still an idea that might have been repeated in a column or a book or something; that is conceivable. I have been unable to trace it.

It is possible that I made it up and only imagined that I heard it. Anyway, at that point I did not pursue it.

I then decided, well, all this does not seem very satisfactory, let us just assume that the firm maximizes weighted averages of the expected profits. But I really did not develop this at all. Of course, it is a lucky thing that I didn't, because I omitted the very elementary point, that Modigliani would later realize, that if you do not like the stock you can sell it. The whole argument was really wrong to begin with in that context. The stockholders can sell their stock, so it is not quite true that you have to go to the majority; the existing stockholders are not the whole story. If I think that a policy is bad, but there are a lot of people out there that think it is good and would vote for that policy, then I can sell my shares. So the model of the firm was not really right because I did not recognize stock transfer. It is a lucky thing I never published it. But that was the source of the idea.

Then somehow, while I was still at Cowles, in the spring of 1948 I began to think about elections. I was thinking of people on a left to right scale. I drew some diagrams. It was easy to see how the problem about majority voting disappears if you have single-peakness. I thought about that and decided to write up a little note. Then – Lo and Behold! – as I am writing the note I pick up the June 1948 issue of the *Journal of Political Economy* and there is the same idea, but done by Duncan Black!

This I still do not understand. I do believe in multiple discoveries, there are lots of them. But usually it is because the ground has been prepared. Something happened, perhaps for some other reasons someone developed something, and the next step was at least reasonable, it might not have been obvious, but at least reasonable. But what Black and I did could have been done 150 years earlier, there was no mathematical development, there was no intellectual development. Perhaps game theory in a very general way could be credited. Some people had written about elections as competitive devices; their approach was, however, different. For example, Hotelling had done so as an aside in one of his papers. Schumpeter did it at some length in *Capitalism, Socialism, and Democracy*, but not a real theory, just talk, as usual. But social choice theory is really different from electoral competition. Why Black and I hit on this at about the same time, I really do not know. It was actually sheer chance. He could have done it a year earlier, I could have done it a year earlier . . .

I was really disappointed in not having priority since I had not published anything yet that was worthwhile. I thought at least to get some little note and then I was scooped.

Well, that summer I went to Rand, and luck was with me. There was a philosopher there (the Rand Corporation was hiring philosophers and this fellow was a regular staff member), Olaf Helmer, whom I had actually met earlier. And, I digress: Helmer had translated a book by Alfred Tarski who taught at City College. He was visiting this country when he was caught by the outbreak of the war. They hired him through a very complicated chain of circumstances, involving Bertrand Russell. But that is another story. Tarski gave a course on the calculus of relations where I learned to think about relations. But in all fairness, I think, I would have learned it anyway. Now, Helmer translated Tarski's elementary textbook on logic and I proof-read it. Tarski used to ask me: 'Are you sure that is good English'? He could hardly speak English, but he had a sound intuition. He realized that a lot of these constructions were Germanisms translated into English; they were correct, but they were not good English. So this is how I got to know Helmer.

When we were at Rand together, Helmer remarked that there was something that bothered him about game theory or about its applications. We wanted to talk about the US, the USSR, and Western Europe as players, but they are not like people, in what sense do they have utility functions? How can we apply game theory where it is essential to have utility functions? Since when does the US have a utility function? 'Oh! I said, 'that is nothing, Abram Bergson has written on this type of thing'. 'Oh', he said, 'would you write an exposition of this?' Well, that was the thing that led to the social choice book.

I realized that I had several ideas in mind as to what was meant by voting. But when you put them all together it is very inconsistent. First I just experimented. And I remembered this majority voting and realized that majority voting won't work, but there are lots of other criteria. Then I sort of tried them out. None of them worked. It all took about three weeks once I got the question right.

Feiwel: How did you become interested in the problem of existence of general economic equilibrium? How did it become a joint paper?

Arrow: The answer is that I am not absolutely positive. Somehow, when reading Hicks, I got the idea that there was a question whether these solutions exist. I guess I had been exposed to enough mathematics to know that when one has a system of equations one worries about existence. I may have been thinking about the problem during the war, but it was after the war that I found out that Wald had worked on this problem. I asked him about it and all he said was: 'Oh, yes, that is a very very difficult problem'. I thought that if he found it a difficult problem, it was probably nothing for me to touch. But it sort of remained in the back of my mind.

Then I read, first von Neumann, but especially Nash's 1950 paper. It suddenly struck me: This is very much like the problem of competitive equilibrium. I thought about it on and off, until one day, when I had a few free hours, I thought how to interpret competitive equilibrium as a game. After a number of steps, you can take Nash's result and apply it. I finally wrote this up as a technical report in October or November, 1951. Then I went off to Europe on a Social Science Research Council Fellowship. Selma and I travelled through Europe. When I got to Rome just before or after New Year, I found at my mailing address a letter from Gerard Debreu whom I barely knew. We had never been at the same place at the same time. He wrote that he had been working on the same problem and he sent me his manuscript. In this letter he also said that he found an error in my proof. I could see that it was not an error. The next day there was another letter from Gerard awaiting me at the American Express (where I used to pick up my mail) admitting that that was not an error. Then I got a third letter saying that there was another error. And that was an error! On checking his manuscript I could see that he had made the same error; the error he had found in my paper was not really ruled out by his assumptions. I read his manuscript closely and I could see where we had both gone wrong. So I wrote back proposing that we make it a joint venture and circulate it for comments. His conception was essentially complete; he had a somewhat different way of doing it, and the final paper is much closer to his than to my version.

The problem of overcoming this error remained. There was one assumption that was obvious, but I thought that it was too strong and I ruined the rest of my trip to Europe by thinking how to overcome that error in a better way.

So that is how the paper came to be written. This was essentially an example of two people arriving totally independently at the same solution, and indeed by somewhat different methods, but both stemming from the Nash seminal paper.

Feiwel: You refer to Nash (1950) as one of the stimuli that set you on the road to proving existence. Would you comment on Raiffa's recollection (in Chapter 27 of the companion volume) that Nash was influenced by you?

Arrow: I am sure that he did pick up the phrase 'independence of irrelevant alternatives' from me since my work on social choice had been distributed as a Rand report in the fall of 1948 and was available to Nash. He visited Rand during the summers, as I did, and I know he knew of my results. However, I think he read my work somewhat carelessly, because his use of the phrase really differs from mine (his refers to variations in the set of opportunities, mine to variations in the preference orderings). The two uses are easy to confuse (I did myself in *Social Choice and Individual Values* at one point).

Feiwel: You have remarked that whereas in social choice theory you made a fundamental difference, g.e.t. would not today be much different without you. I do not want to be contrary, but it seems to me that in some fundamental sense you are wrong. Would you comment?

Arrow: I meant something quite simple by that statement: Here was Gerard who had exactly the same thing without me. McKenzie had almost exactly the same thing, not quite as good, but pretty much the same thing. Here we had at least two fine scholars with essentially the same idea and, I think, that if neither of them had existed, someone else would have appeared on the scene. Of course, the von Neumann-Nash tradition had created tools. Once the tools are there, somebody is bound to pick them up.

How can I answer your comment? It is possible that my exposition was a little closer to what economists would understand than what Gerard might have done had I left him to his own devices. I may have been able to relate it somewhat better to the mainstream of economic thought. But that is only of expository value. If I had not done it, somebody else would have. In fact, in Dorfman, Samuelson and Solow, *Linear Programming and Economic Analysis,* there is an existence proof (that came a little later) very much related to the main body of literature, though it is done by oversimplyfying, in my view. Nevertheless the idea was there and ready to be expounded and incorporated into the mainstream.

Let me be more specific. Unfortunately, I no longer have the manuscript that Gerard sent me, but it had a formulation that was in all important aspects identical to mine: he had the production, consumption and all that. Our language may have been somewhat different; as I said, I made more of an effort in writing to bring along the mainstream, to explain what the question is, and I was probably the one who suggested the intertemporal interpretation (the idea that you could have equilibrium over time, I thought, was a pretty obvious step). But in all other respects Gerard's interpretation was pretty identical with mine. Incidentally, both of us were influenced by Koopmans's formulation of production (activity analysis), that was another common ground, in this respect for the formulation, not the proofs. As far as consumer theory is concerned, we both started from the same point; it is all Hicks (and Hicks himself is not all that new in this respect).

Feiwel: Some critics have suggested that the question of existence is a trivial one. May we explore why this is not so?

Arrow: It is an interesting question and I must say that I could give you good arguments on both sides of it. Let me give you the argument why it may be considered trivial. There is a sense in which you might say, well, if the world is really governed by general equilibrium, then we know it exists. Given that we have a theory which we believe explains the world, let us say that we look at each part of it and say, yes, that is the way the household behaves, that is the way the firm behaves. We see that the world exists. Therefore, we say there will be some conditions under which general equilibrium exists; they may be very strong, very weak, whatever. Clearly those conditions are satisfied in the real world, why do we have to worry about what those conditions are?

The counter-argument is that since general equilibrium is a theory that relates some parameters to some outcomes (and by parameters I mean things like production, possibility sets, utility functions, and so forth and so on) it, therefore, asserts relationships. Now, presumably those parameters could be changing; in fact, they are changing and they could be different from what they are. If I am unable to produce a general existence theorem, then it is at least suspicious that the world could be different from what it is and, therefore, there would be no equilibrium. But that seems a little odd. And after all competitive equilibrium would probably not be a correct theory of the world if most of the time equilibrium did not exist. Then I would be wrong in assuming that the competitive equilibrium theory is the correct theory of the present world. Now, I could overcome that if I had enormously detailed empirical information which would prove beyond a doubt that competitive equilibrium theory is empirically valid. Then it would be less interesting. In the absence of that I would have to say, well, I cannot help; theory cannot be that well established. Therefore, I would like at least to be sure that it is a coherent theory. That does not prove that the real world is like that, but at least it gives me a chance.

Actually, I think that the benefits of general equilibrium theory are indirect rather than direct. You have to ask yourself, well, what is general equilibrium theory? It turns out that, if I may be immodest, until Arrow and Debreu, and to some extent McKenzie (somewhat less true for various reasons), there was no complete statement of the general equilibrium theory. In order to establish an existence theorem you have to specify it very carefully. We were, therefore, forced to specify the model really well in order to analyze it. We were thus able to see which assumptions are important for existence and which are not. If you go down the Hicksian lines based on calculus you could never get anywhere on the existence problem. I think that one of the consequences of what we did was to exhibit where the theory is of greatest value.

One of these things, for example, is to show that convexity is an essential feature of the assumptions. That is probably the biggest lesson that was learned. Now, in one dimensional diagrams you could see that convexity is important, but it it not easy to go from there to the general case. You find all sorts of misleading statements in the literature before this as to what does and does not permit competitive equilibrium to exist.

My own view of the matter is that the world is imperfectly competitive. I *do not* believe in the perfectly competitive view of the world, I think the general equilibrium theory is an imaginatively manipulative theory; one can get results out of it. It serves for many purposes as a good approximation for reasons that one does not fully understand. Therefore, it is a useful tool. It is not, however, a useful tool for various micro problems, even in something like international trade, for example, or questions of industrial policy. I think it is essential to remember the fact that in some industries there are increasing returns and, therefore, natural obstacles to competition. But if you look at the economy, so to speak, in the gross these exceptions are very small. That is, all these exceptions are small on the scale of the economy. On the whole, what the existence problem has done was to force us to think a lot more rigorously about what it is. That may be the biggest benefit, rather than the existence theorem itself.

There is another benefit of the existence theorem that I should mention. It turns out that the existence theorem implies an algorithm for solving general equilibrium. This is the line that Herb Scarf first took up. So that, in fact, we have now actually people who are solving general equilibrium systems and not merely postulating them. So as it turns out the existence theorem has a second implication of a practical nature.

Feiwel: What is the genesis and essence of your work on stability?

Arrow: That, of course, is more derivative than some of my other work. Stability theory is actually a very old theme, really discussed first by Mill. It is a standard theme in economics. The better formalizations of general equilibrium theory were due to Hicks and Samuelson. Samuelson provided a formalization that in fact captured in a general equilibrium sense the intuitive ideas of stability that had been expressed for the most part in a partial equilibrium context. Of course, Walras had made an attempt at a general equilibrium formalization of stability. So, in that sense, the problem had been set forth by Samuelson in his papers in 1941.

In a way, what Leo Hurwicz and I and others were trying to do was essentially to carry out the Samuelson programme and to extend it. Samuelson had a few classes of cases of stability; we tried to extend this in various ways (Metzler made a very important contribution there). One of the things that Leo and I were trying to do was to extend it to global analysis rather than local analysis. Actually, one of the immediate impulses was a somewhat different kind of stability, namely, in programming problems. That again was due to Samuelson. Samuelson had discussed stability, using economic ideas, in the context of linear programming methods. Of course, you are aware that there was an important strand of thought about stability in a socialist system which was in a way in between stability of a competitive equilibrium and stability of a programming problem which is a method of optimization. Paul had argued that if you apply straightforward methods in a linear programming system you get cycles.

Leo and I started out by re-examining that question and, in particular, to extend it also to non-linear programming. We got some important results in this simpler context of general equilibrium. Having done that we got interested in the stability concept in the broader context of general equilibrium theory. We used a standard method in stability theory that had not been used in economics – the so-called Lyapunov method for analyzing global stability.

The derivative of that was a number of stability results in specific contexts, particularly on questions of expectations. This was a question that Hicks had introduced, but it somewhat slipped out; it had not been picked up by Samuelson. Namely, supposing you have a system where your demands and supplies depend on future prices which, of course, are not there, but are only expectations. You then have to have another set of equations that determines expectations. This was actually stimulated by discussions I had with Alan Enthoven who was then writing a thesis for MIT. I met him at Rand. He had essentially a partial equilibrium analysis that covered *n* commodities and was trying to get stability. He talked to me about it and we pondered on it. We actually solved the problem, although it turned out to be a rather difficult and interesting one. After that I wrote a series of papers with expectations playing an important role. I no longer think that is so important, by the way, because we now have to think in terms of probabilistic expectations. That whole field of stability under expectations has to be reworked more in terms of forming probability judgements instead of point expectations.

Feiwel: In this connection, would you mind clarifying for us your conception of statics and dynamics?

Arrow: There are really two totally different things under the heading of dynamics. One is what you may call adjustment dynamics which is what we have been talking about, where you assume an equilibrium system and the world to be out of equilibrium and the question is: what happens? A totally different kind of dynamics, much more common in literature, is when we assume the world to be in equilibrium at all times, but equilibrium includes plans for the future and possibly contingent plans for the future. So in a sense you have a world where things you do today affect the future, such as research and development, capital formation, and the like. They not only affect the future, but the way in which they affect the future becomes part of your decision to invest in them with the expectation of returns. Then, if you have an equilibrium concept, you have to have an equilibrium of the present and the future, fully anticipated by everybody in the full general equilibrium context. That I would call genuine dynamics. The world is in one equilibrium, but the equilibrium itself is different from time to time depending on what is going to happen and may also be different due to chance.

Feiwel: With the benefit of hindsight would you reflect on your Haley *Festschrift* contribution and challenge to develop a disequilibrium price theory?

Arrow: It has turned out to be very difficult to take off the ground. I think that the challenge is a very sound one. It is an attempt to have an equilibrium-disequilibrium concept. Since then there has been a very rich development of rationing theory, one which I suggested in that particular paper. Namely, the idea that when prices are not equilibrium prices you also have to have rules for rationing either supply or demand. And when you do have that you also have, in effect, a kind of imperfect competition. So that even if the world were basically perfectly competitive, with all the necessary conditions, free entry, and so on, at a given moment of time the price decisions of the firm are real, they are not just imposed by the outside because of disequilibrium. Of course most of the rationing turns out to be rigid rationing so that there is no opportunity to get some extra business by cutting your price. Therefore, it does not directly answer the question. There has been some interesting literature (for example, Benassy), but these models turn out to be very complicated, they do not do very much. There is also the question of what you do in a dynamic context because I am afraid that if you impose the perfect foresight assumption (the rational expectations assumption, as we say today), you would probably get to equilibrium immediately. I am not sure about that. Of course, the story I had was one where people were continually surprised. That is not the way I would think now, nor is it the way most economists would think now. I am not sure that we have an answer to that question yet. I think that it has to do with incomplete markets, myself. But these future anticipations are not going to be worth very much if there is no way of trading them in the present. This is probably the clue to the answer, but it still has not been done.

Feiwel: To what extent have the modern (since Walras) achievements in g.e.t. improved our conception of the economic process?

Arrow: That is quite a controversial question. Some people will tell you that it has done nothing. It is almost taken for granted that no serious empirical work can be based on g.e.t. I think this is dead wrong. The important point about g.e.t. is that it teaches you that sometimes direct links are not the important ones. It is probably true most of the time that the primary impact of a change is the important immediate one and that it tends to dissipate as you go on. But this is just not always the case. What happens sometimes is that you have to look at the other side of the market; you have a shift in demand, the real impact is on the supply, and the repercussions may be quite changed. This is particularly true of, let us say, policy measures that are quite general in their formulation. Take the work on changes in the taxation of capital; the effect of changes in the corporate income tax. This is such a broad area that it is hard to see how one could study it without some kind of a general equilibrium model; it is probably not correct to study it without a reasonably disaggregated one. The same is true of other applications, such as studies of the effects of changes in welfare payments, which also have general equilibrium implications.

I think in the first place g.e.t. causes you to keep that in mind. In the second place, it actually provides a basis, a framework, for empirical interpretation. There is by now a fair body of literature of actually fitted g.e. models which certainly show results that you would not have gotten from a partial equilibrium point of view. The other thing is that it allows you to keep in mind a sense of what the economy is all about. As far as I can see, nobody within the neoclassical tradition can deny the validity of g.e.t. For example, no matter how much the Chicago school tends to stress the methodological advantages of the partial equilibrium approach, they cannot deny that what they are talking about is embedded in a g.e. world. Their only defense is that by limiting their scope they can do more practical things; that g.e.t. makes estimating anything so hard that one cannot do it. My personal feeling is that you get a lot of fallacies by partial equilibrium thinking because you can easily confuse supply and demand relationships. For example, whether the monetary history of the US is really explicable in terms of demand for money and an exogenous money stock requires the idea that the supply of money is endogenous. For me the evidence is clear, you cannot look at one side of the market. Furthermore, if you ask how money affects the system, we only dimly understand that. One needs a large degree of disaggregation.

Therefore, just thinking in terms of g.e. teaches you a lot about measuring the impacts of policy, measuring what the effects of changes in technology are, making international comparisons of competitiveness and comparative advantage, and the like. I believe that without g.e. thinking you would never get these insights.

Feiwel: Do you consider that thus far the questions asked by g.e. theorists have been sufficiently broad?

Arrow: Yes and no. One of the problems is that the questions have not been sufficiently detailed; another is of extending g.e. into new contexts, particularly in the directions of imperfect competition and incomplete markets (which includes externalities). It is not that there has been no work in these areas; there is by now a fair amount of literature, but these are difficult problems, and the literature does not cumulate so far. What cumulates has been g.e. under the most perfect conditions; here there is a very rich literature and it is mathematically an extremely tractable object. I do not disparage the difficulties involved; but you can get results, given the right brains and talents. It is in this area that people like Gerard and Hildenbrand have done some beautiful things. We have also got what you might call impossibility theorems; that is theorems that say that you cannot prove certain things. Namely, we have discovered that we cannot get stability analysis out of a general g.e.t. – by which I mean only a theory that makes the minimal degree of assumptions necessary to ensure existence (concavity, boundedness, and the like). It turns out, as Gerard and others have proved, that you cannot get any information essentially on aggregate demand functions: you cannot get any comparative statics, you cannot get any stability theory. The suggestion then is to add more hypotheses. The trouble is that, after the ones we adopt, none of the others are particularly compelling. It is also not easy to see how you can do this without empirical work.

What we could do, of course, is to model g.e.t. The empirical g.e. theorists do that. They model it for a specific purpose, thus bringing out certain specific aspects. For example, the energy crisis has generated a lot of g.e. models in which energy played a distinct role; it was not just another product, but was disaggregated everywhere. People like Jorgenson or Alan Mann (here at Stanford) have taken these concepts and made them very useful.

Feiwel: Without detracting from their contributions to g.e.t can you tell us in what sense the visions and techniques of Walras, Hicks and Samuelson were deficient?

Arrow: I have a very great admiration for all three of them. Walras is a curious case. He had a peculiarly cramped style and a very broad vision of the world which he enunciated with the greatest of understanding. It is really very hard to fault him after all these years. His analytic abilities were very low – it is quite interesting that the great patron saint of mathematical economics was a very poor mathematician, much inferior to Marshall, for example. His mathematics is everywhere very clumsy. But the important thing is that he asked many of the right questions. He even discussed the question of the future and capital formation in a very crude way, which is in fact logically inconsistent and gave rise to some very peculiar results. A lot of this was because he was trying to impose a particular way of approaching a problem that was in a way inconsistent with his g.e. view; he just did not understand about dated commodities. His stability analysis, I think, went pretty far for its day. He came to grief because he was claiming to prove things that were not true, but nobody has improved on that. In fact the real trouble is, as we know today, that these *tâtonnements* are not stable; it is not surprising that he was not able to produce a good proof of it. One could conceivably fault him for not getting the boundaries very clearly. For example, he has only a very brief discussion of public goods. He does not come to grips with what public goods are, why they differ from other goods. He does mention monopoly and he understands it as due to increasing returns – of course, that was already in Cournot. Not only is this not integrated into his system – which may be asking a lot – but he does not really come to grips with these problems. He did ask a very large number of interesting questions, nevertheless. The difficulty is that it is all couched in a very forbidding style which makes it hard to discuss any particular economic problem.

Hicks provided a very beautiful exposition of g.e.t. He had a dated commodity argument which he very clearly understood. He is a much better mathematician than Walras. We owe to him the revival of g.e.t. The subject was sort of known; everyone paid respect to the fact that Walras had stated the problem correctly, then ignored it completely. Hicks made a very commendable effort to make it a useful tool with which, I think, he had a number of great successes. He did not raise the existence question, or did he (I cannot recall, I have not re-read Hicks for a while)?

Feiwel: Recently, in the third volume of his collected papers, *Classics and Moderns* Hicks has added a summing up where he claims that he did not need a proof of existence.

Arrow: Well, one can put it that way. One can say 'Look, I am describing the world, and the world exists, therefore, the description is consistent. In other words, these equations describe the world, the world is there, so the solution must exist. Perhaps it is a mathematical question as to what conditions are needed. It is a possible attitude at which I would not sneer. I think that what Gerard and I essentially showed was that, with the asumptions Hicks was making anyway, in effect, explicity or implicitly, existence follows. By and large, there was no need for additional hypotheses.

Hicks raised the stability question. We tend to think now that it was a little too bound down to some Marshallian concepts; even if he made a g.e. out of it, it was not a genuine dynamic system. We are not sure yet that we have a good understanding of what the stability problem is: where do these differential equations come from? We can make a hypothesis about what an excess demand price is, but we do not know why. It is this *why* that I tried to answer in the Haley *Festschrift* paper, but not very successfully. Hicks also asked a number of other interesting questions. He was trying to get comparative statics results and he was trying to relate them to stability theory. Sometimes he succeeded, sometimes he failed. He has a lot of very interesting observations about capital. I think his elasticity of expectations has turned out to be much too mechanical. He introduced the future, but then he sort of eliminated it again by bringing in single-point expectations. Not only that; they also did not depend on the right things, they depended on current prices. But he did open up this very important question.

Samuelson has been less systematic than Walras or Hicks in his pursuit of g.e.t. His main contribution is really to adjustment dynamics, of which he provided a very coherent view. He has done a number of specific things that are part of g.e.t., like the so-called non-substitution theorem. This makes very specific hypotheses and the result is quite surprising about the nature and relations of prices and quantities. He has many contributions of this kind, but he has been less concerned about g.e.t. as such, except for his contribution to the stability concept.

Feiwel: Could you comment on the remark that some recent contributions to g.e.t. are damaging to neoclassical economics?

Arrow: This is exactly what I referred to before as a kind of impossibility theorem. It is damaging in the sense that one cannot conclude anything from g.e.t. about comparative statics. You see, Hicks was trying to provide a comparison. He said, if a price goes up, something happens, the quantity demanded will fall or something like that. Or if the production function shifts upwards, you can say at least that the price of the commodity falls, and the prices of substitutes fall, and all of that. It turns out that most of these things are false. In a sense, you can always find demand functions that will invalidate them. And then you can always state that the theory invalidates any set of demand functions.

It is damaging to neoclassical economics in the sense that it makes the statements weak. Basically, the trouble with economic theory is that it is weak. It may be false also, but even if it were true, it would still be weak. By itself it says nothing. But then the question arises: what do you mean? After all why bother with theory? Go out and estimate your demand functions, your supply functions, and all the rest of that and then calculate. The reason we do rely on theory is because we feel that these empirical estimates are not very good. But in principle, g.e.t. just says 'go out and calculate'; and, indeed, a lot of people are doing just that, they are using theoretical analysis, but of a different kind.

Some people are posing the following type of questions: Supposing we had a g.e.t., how do we find the solution? Is the solution unique? In general, we have very few theorems on this. There is one way of approaching so-called index theory, apart from mathematics, by which, under certain circumstances, you can count the number of equilibria. Unfortunately, you cannot always do it, but sometimes you can; and if you have a specific problem you can do certain calculations and they may, if you are lucky, tell you that this equilibrium is unique, or that there are, say, three equilibria, or something like that. And that may be very helpful.

There is an area of g.e.t. we have not touched upon – the area of bifurcation theory, catastrophy theory. It somehow seems to be relevant, in the sense that if you imagine the parameters of an economy changing, there will be places where there are abrupt changes in equilibria. This sounds as if it could be useful. Nobody has ever used it and there are a lot of claims for it that are ridiculously extreme. But, on the other hand, I am sure there is a useful place for it in systems in general, including economic systems.

Feiwel: What do you make of Joan Robinson's (and Hicks's) criticism that the concept of equilibrium arose from a misleading analogy with movements in space that cannot be applied to movements in time?

Arrow: I am not quite sure what that means. Equilibrium does apply to movements in time in mechanics. Supposing I have a bar with equal weights, then if I do not put the fulcrum at the right place, the bar will swing in one direction or the other; it can only be balanced in one place. That is an example of unstable equilibrium actually. Or, take a ball in a concave bowl, then presumably it will come to rest at the bottom of the bowl. And that is a movement in time, one starts anywhere and something is going to happen. It is true that the things that are moving are in space, but the analogy is not space versus time, it is commodities versus space. In other words, in both cases they are movements in time; in one case they are movements in space in a geographical sense, and in the other they are movements in the sense of changes in commodities. The thing is then not an opposition of space and time since both are movements in time; it is where the movement takes place, in one case it takes place in a physical space and in the other in an abstract commodity space. But that is true of a lot of physical reactions, by the way; they describe the mechanical reactions and if you want to use this kind of thing the dimensions are not spatial co-ordinates at all, they are different things.

Now, you may say the world is such that you never really are in equilibrium and that the equilibrium concept is empirically not good. It is true that if you are analyzing weather, to take my favourite example, it is not clear what equilibrium means. There are, however, equilibrium concepts for specific things in weather. If you look closely at the equation usually used to analyze the way the winds flow (the relation between pressure gradient and the wind flow), it is an equilibrium relationship. If you sort of stop the earth and then start it again the equation would not hold instantaneously. And there are other kinds of equilibrium relationships about vertical movements in the air, for example. There are certain stability considerations there that have to do with thermo-dynamic equilibrium. On the other hand, if you look at the weather in the gross, it never seems to come to rest. In fact, the description of that is not very good; it only solves a lot of differential equations and the solutions just are not restful solutions.

It may be that in economics we should be thinking in terms of dynamic systems. If you have a dynamic system, one of its characteristics is a movement in time of which a feature is equilibrium. It may well not be a very interesting characteristic. It happens all the time in turbulence phenomena; if you heat up a liquid and watch what happens to the bubbles, well, there is an equilibrium, but it may not be the interesting part of the story.

Feiwel: To follow this up, Joan Robinson, for one, emphasizes that Marshall was concerned with the long-term tendency of the system towards equilibrium, a much richer concept than that of modern g.e. theorists who, in her view, are concerned with the questions of rest, of the balance of forces. May we have your comment?

Arrow: I think this is a misreading of Marshall. I think that what Marshall says is exactly the same thing as g.e.t. Intertemporal g.e.t. *is exactly* the same thing as Marshallian theory properly spelled out. If you start with the disturbance of the system somehow, then in the first instance, for example, supply is fixed and that is Marshall's market price. And the price will rise if there is an increase in demand or a decrease in supply (for some reason, there are less fish, for example). The way Marshall tells this story, because the price increases, additional fishermen go out and fish, eventually they come back and then there is a kind of short-period equilibrium where the number of fishing boats is the same, but either there are more fishermen or they work harder; and then there is a longer-period equilibrium and the number of fishing boats increases. Actually in g.e.t. over time you have exactly the same thing. Marshall also emphasizes that in that story expectations matter. If you assume that the expectations are rational (which he does not exactly say, but he does not say the opposite either, however, he does mention that in the long run the expectations are rational), people will know that there is a period of time before the new boats can come in, therefore, they will find a problem with the fish. The people who are building the boats will know that the prices will gradually be coming down. What we then have is a time structure of prices, quantities, and investments, and in this way the Marshallian story is consistent with the story of g.e.t. over time.

There is something else in Marshall; a flavour not a theory. There are some economists who say the world is complex and, therefore, we should always be vague. Marshall is that way. John Maurice Clark, who is not as well known as he probably should be, and from whom I took courses at Columbia, was an extremist that way. At every point he would stop his logical exposition short and say, 'well we could continue with this, but that would be getting too exact'. For example, independent of Kahn, he figured out the multiplier analysis, but his typical method was to run through two or three rounds and then stop, on the grounds that by that time things would have changed. This, of course, is not a different theory, it is a matter of style. Now, one may be pedagogically more suitable, perhaps it teaches the students the right attitude – and I am not sure which, by the way, the vague or the precise.

However, coming back to the analytic core of Marshall, I must repeat that it is exactly the same as general equilibrium over time – a point that the Cambridge economists never seem to grasp. Imagine a sequence of prices, currently high and falling towards the long-run equilibrium, fully anticipated, and people are making decisions, some of which take time to realize. Marshall's story of all that (including some side remarks) is certainly totally compatible with intertemporal g.e.t. Except that he did not like to spell it out because he knew there was going to be another disturbance. On the other hand, he was ambivalent about the long run. Because of the complexity of long-run analysis, it is probably true that the Walrasians have led to more short-run thinking. The concept of g.e. is more like Marshall's market equilibrium or short-period equilibrium than it is long-period equilibrium. But g.e.t. over time encompasses all of these concepts. It may not be credible that people have these anticipations – that is what is wrong with that theory.

Joan Robinson, you see, knew all these things, except that she kept on insisting on the steady state. The steady state is not something that is real; it tells you something about the real world, but I have never understood what it was that it does tell you about the real world. If it is not there, why should I believe it? The argument is that it tells us something about how things would work out if they remained the same. Of course, steady state and equilibrium are not the same thing. That is an old story, Frisch said it in 1936. Joan kept twitting us that we did not understand it, but that is simply not so. I read Frisch when I was a graduate student and I knew all about it. There is an equilibrium concept that is not steady state; it is today's equilibrium and tomorrow's equilibrium will be different. Or, one can say there is one big g.e. over time.

Feiwel: Can we pursue your impressions of Marshall?

Arrow: When I was a graduate student I read a lot of the classics. I could not stand Marshall for two reasons: one was his vagueness, his refusal to write down a model as I interpreted it. Now I am a little more tolerant, I see that the model is there whether he chooses to present it or not. The other thing was an occasional pomposity of manner. He was very much laying down the law. In that case, the more I know about him the truer this appears to be. That impression which I derived from reading the *Principles* was not mistaken. Now I know much more of his writings and it is quite clear that he regarded himself as the supreme authority and was regarded as such by all the people around him who counted. Jevons, for example, was an outsider. Marshall never gave him sufficient credit and his review of Jevons was quite intolerable. Instead of recognizing that here was an extremely novel approach, he denied its validity, and somewhat ridiculed it; presumably because he had worked it out himself and felt scooped. Even if this is true, it shows a deplorable side of his character. There are some personal characteristics of Marshall that I find unpalatable.

On the other hand, he was a remarkable intellect, able to see through quite complex problems. He certainly did emphasize the question of adjustment over time that none of the others did. He did stress (although again vaguely) the second kind of dynamic economics; time adjustment due to things like lags, capital formation, and so on. And that is an insight that I really have not detected anywhere before him. He also perceived the problems of externalities which again he did not do right. But he did see the difficult problem of the industry's supply curves being different from the firm's supply curves which, had he forced himself to write down an explicit model, he would have been able to tackle better. It created a lot of confusion. He got Pigou all mixed up – which is quite apparent in the first edition of *Wealth and Welfare*.

There is an interesting story about this. Krishna Bharadwaj (who is visiting this year at Stanford) got hold of Marshall's copy of *Wealth and Welfare* in which he wrote copious marginal notes that he would not even show Pigou. By the way, in fact, he says in there, 'I do not even think it is for four eyes'. Incidentally, what kind of relationship there was between Marshall and his star pupil I do not really understand. Now, the errors Marshall found were correct. For example, he criticizes Pigou for confusing pecuniary and technological externalities, but, I think, that was because Marshall was sufficiently vague in his original work that he got Pigou off on the wrong track. Later, of course, Pigou straightened this out, but the man who set him straight was Allyn Young, not Marshall who should have done it. It seems to me that, aside from all else, there is a real price to be paid for this vagueness. There is something wrong with Marshall the pedagogue if his best purpil cannot get the concept right.

So there are these essential irritants in Marshall. On the other hand, we cannot help but admire him for being willing to ask much harder questions. Walras cleaned up a certain well-controlled area, but he did not look ahead the way Marshall did to new problems. But that again is not quite fair to Walras; he did open up some questions of capital theory.

Feiwel: How can historical time be taken meaningfully into account?

Arrow: That is a considerable problem. One way of looking at it is that g.e.t. over time already allows you to take time into account. The state of the world today, which is the beginning of the future, is the result of past or particular accumulations. We got here by a set of contingencies in the past, but only one of these contingencies was realized. The present is dictated by those contingencies and not by others that might have taken a different course. So, in some ways, one could tell the story of history by saying that the present is the sort of concrete deposit of the particular contingencies that happened in the past. In other words, there were a lot of possibilities at random, but a particular one came to be and not something else, and in that sense we can formulate it. Now, whether this is deep enough I do not know.

There is a counter-argument which is that we cannot allow for it in a perfectly competitive world; we cannot allow for it in a world of constantly diminishing returns. The argument is that small effects have large consequences. Basically if that is true it has a non-concave situation. That is one way of interpreting it; that is the way, for example, that my colleague Paul David now likes to interpret history.

For example, at the December 1984 American Economic Association Meeting, Paul David (*American Economic Review*, May 1985) pointed to the example of the typewriter keyboard. There is every evidence that the particular layout of the typewriter keyboard is definitely not the most efficient one. Others have been devised and trained people can do 15 per cent better or so on these alternative keyboards, yet the standard one has persisted. The argument is that though it could have been replaced by a more efficient one, because people get trained in the standard keyboard, human capital has developed. Therefore, there are vested interests, and at no stage do these people want to switch to another system. By now there are millions of typists in the world and computer operators who know this keyboard and do not want to switch to another. So here is an illustration of this small effect, presumably this non-concavity problem. There is the other possibility: in a concave world you have, say, ten different keyboards and some people like one and some another. But because you have to move from one typewriter to another, you cannot quite have that. And this poses an interesting question about standardization in general. The counter-argument is, of course, 'this is a small matter, who cares?' But does it not apply to essentials as well?

There is some evidence that the economies of different countries are not convergent. For example, Canada and the US, which are very similar, are systematically different in certain ways. In Canada productivity is usually somewhat lower than in the US, trade union membership is higher, the industrial structure differs somewhat, the distribution of firm size is different. What answer do we get from economic theory to this quandary? Well, it should have to do with tastes and technology. Economic theory, of course, does not say what is going to happen, it only says that, if certain tastes and technology prevail, one can expect certain consequences, and a certain path of history. But this is not necessarily so. The history of

Canada is different from that of the US and because Canada started out different it is going to remain different. This suggests that one will not get convergence; it contradicts the usual view that there is going to be *an* efficient allocation of resources and, therefore, all countries should eventually converge to the same thing. The neoclassical growth model of the 1960s generally wound up with all countries on the same path; years ahead or years behind, but the same steady state path.

There is one other example of this thing that intrigues me and it has to do with languages, but there is something very peculiar here. Take romance languages – an example that is usually used for all other languages – an evolution that usually took place in the historical time we know, unlike others on whose development in time we can only conjecture. Here presumably you have one language that became many languages. In terms economists like to use, they were all trying to solve the same problem of efficient communication. For example, one of the things that may have been desired was that frequently used words should be short. Now, how is it that people all talking Latin, eventually wound up, some talking French, some Spanish, and so on? Why did they not all preserve the same language? We all understand that languages change over time, but even that is something of a mystery. If a language is optimal, why does it change? We do seem to have trends in languages. Why should a language change at all? To be sure one needs new words, but not a new language. But these changes do occur. Take, for example, the way vowels are pronounced in English. We now, in effect, have great difficulties reading Chaucer because the vowel sounds have since changed. It took a long time to realize that in Chaucer's time vowels were pronounced the way they are in Italian, not the way they are in modern English at all. They were very big open vowels. Sometimes during that period and, say, the seventeenth or eighteenth century there was a great steady shift in vowel pronounciation (with the Shakespearian period an intermediate one). But why? According to economics, this has always been part of an optimizing process. Language is like economic trade. One could say that there are pressures for standardization. If some people shift, then others have to as well just to be able to communicate. Still, it is not easy for me to understand why the shift occurred in one particular direction. Why do they not shift back and forth? And why, starting from a similar base, do languages diverge from each other? Take, for example, people speaking the same language, some of them go on the other side of a mountain range and after a while they no longer speak the same language. The conditions are not particularly different on one side of the mountain range from the other.

What I am trying to say is that there seems to be an elusive law of history. By the way, biologists seem to be saying the same thing with the concept of the molecular clock: that is, that the genetic content as expressed in proteins of animals seems to move linearily. But why? If it is an adaptive thing (presumably an adaptation to a new environment) why does it do that? One school seems to think it is not adaptive at all. But then why do they not all change in different directions? I do not understand that. Yet the evidence is pretty strong that there is a molecular clock.

To come back to our subject after this long excursion, the usual g.e.t. economics tends to predict convergence. Not exactly because if you do with more detail, the convergence will be very slow, since all countries have very different capital structures. Even in a neoclassical environment, it may take a very long time, and by that time other things are changing. Perhaps if one did g.e.t. very seriously, one might discover that it does not predict convergence, but that, of course, would mean that it predicts even less than we originally thought it did.

Feiwel: Can g.e.t. be extended to incorporate asymmetry of information?

Arrow: We now have g.e. models with asymmetric information, but we do not have a general formulation. That is, we have a lot of specific g.e. models with asymmetric information, but we do not have a general formulation of g.e.t. with asymmetry of information and what that implies. There have been some attempts; there are papers that claim to have done it, but if you look at them closely they are much more specific. But that may be just a question of time, I think.

Feiwel: Can class, power, conflict, and other human relations in the production–exchange process be satisfactorily grafted on neoclassical theory?

Arrow: I do now know. I have thought about this a bit. Of course, some kinds of conflict are in g.e.t. The process of competition is a conflict situation, after all. What class has to do with neoclassical theory is very hard to interpret. There was recently an article by two neo-Marxist economists, Resnick and Wolf I think, in the *Monthly Review* which attacked neoclassical economics via Gerard's Nobel Prize. It tried to explain why Marxist economic theory was different from neoclassical theory. My curiosity was aroused. The authors kept repeating the word 'class' over and over again – that was the big difference. But I really found it difficult to understand just what they meant. Were they saying that the prices will be different because of class considerations or that the quantities bought will be different? Or, were they saying that there are social classes and they were not discussing so much the correctness of theories, but the subject matter? I am not quite sure that the class concept is a real one. I understand that people are different. Was it not Fitzgerald who said that the rich are different, they have more money? But presumably he was interested in the fact that the rich are qualitatively somehow different. Well, an economist has no difficulty in believing that people's consumption patterns are different in a trivial way and that there is inequality. There is no question that there is inequality and economic theory predicts that inequality will manifest itself in different life styles, consumption patterns, and the like. There is nothing particularly mysterious about that. The mystery may be how we can have such large income inequalities within a neoclassical framework. But that is an empirical question. The empirical substratum is so weak that it is compact. It just says that some people are vastly more able than others or that in a world of chance some people can make more money than others. There are things that are compatible with that story. I personally find the *degree* of inequality a little hard to understand, but I cannot say that there is a formal contradiction.

There is some evidence, for instance, in British data, that working-class people have different consumption patterns from white-collar workers even though their income is the same; they consume more food, spend less on clothing, and the like. It is also true that there are considerable differences in national consumption patterns. (By the way, the one problem you did not mention in your question is nationality.) Nationality is a question that intrigues me. You see on that issue neoclassical economics agrees with Marxist economics; they both treat it as if it were of no consequence. And they are both equally wrong.

As I said before, I do not know the answer to this question. Part of the answer is that neoclassical economics, being rather generous or rather weak, in other words, is really compatible with a lot of these stories. It does not illuminate them, but it does not contradict them either.

Feiwel: Have developments in g.e.t. met with your expectations? Have you revised your aspiration level?

Arrow: I do not develop strong expecations. I believe that in research things happen. It is a mistake to say in advance there is a right road and a wrong road and to expect this or that to happen. I do remember one thing: around 1962, partly because I was doing empirical work, I kept on feeling that g.e.t. had reached about as far as it was going to go, because the need was for more specific developments. That was just before the theory of the core, the continuum models, the theory of algorithms; that is, it was just before one of the richest periods in the development of g.e.t. So I was dead wrong; I could not have made a worst prediction. I suppose, then, that I could say, if I look at my expectations at certain periods, the achievements far surpass them.

Feiwel: Is there a 'love-hate' relationship between g.e. and game theorists? If so, what are the major issues involved?

Arrow: Hate is probably too strong a word. They get along fairly well. But it is quite true that there is a certain difference in viewpoints. In a way the relationship is a bit like that between g.e. and partial equilibrium theorists. The g.e. theorists want something that can apply to the whole economy. The game theorists have a much more complex set of tools and they tend to apply them to specific questions. They really tend to discuss partial equilibrium theories of the economy. Their theories are general in a methodological sense, but they are not general in the sense of trying to formulate the whole economy as a game. Some people have tried that, but by and large the games tend to be very specific. On the other hand, they, therefore, are much more complex and much more nuanced.

It turns out that if you look for a general theory, that is, a theory that is always applicable, the competitive model is the answer. The competitive model will give you a *kind* of answer to any question; it may not be the right answer, but it will be an answer. Most of the other modelling methods, including game theory, really require that you take a problem, understand what it is, and then model that. Now, one might say, 'why not; this is the right way of approaching it'. But the difficulty is that since all the parts are interconnected, these partial models are not the full answer to the whole question. And that is an old and continuing dilemma.

Feiwel: Returning now to more specific questions about your work, what is the genesis of your work on uncertainty?

Arrow: As I have mentioned elsewhere,* when I was an undergraduate I had taken a sort of cookbook course in statistics. I was also studying mathematics. I discovered a book in statistics that had a lot of references to the mathmetical literature. It was all very new then. In fact, it was being worked on and new stuff was coming out daily. So I got very interested in this economics of uncertainty and probability theory. The new statistical theory that was being worked on by Neyman, Pearson, and later Wald, was very close to economics; it had an economic flavour. In fact Wald was very explicit about it, and Neyman and Pearson were not, but their work showed it. The idea that there was a rational sort of behaviour under uncertainty was something that intrigued me very much.

When I got to Columbia I took a lot of courses in statistics. I was very serious about it. I had this strong statistical background which was very much in the area of uncertainty. It was not difficult to see that the economics literature needed to bring in this new material. I was not the only one to perceive this; a lot of others did as well. Marschak, for example, was aware of this and was bringing in statistical methods into economics. I cannot claim any special priority in this area, but I was one of those who were attracted to the problem and it has remained a constant theme with me to this day.

Feiwel: What do you think of Frank Hahn's comment that the concept of contingent commodities is a 'cavalier' treatment of time?

Arrow: Well, that is a deep question. I think it was Hermann Weil who said that a deep truth is a statement whose opposite is also true. If you think of time as embodying creativity, novelty, there is a sense in

* In Chapter 23 of the companion volume.

which an uncertainty theory generally (and contingent commodities is only a straightforward application of uncertainty theory to economics) is inadequate. We recognize that new things can happen, we know that they do happen, so there is a kind of sense in which they cannot be a genuine novelty. One does not really have room for saying, 'Well, I never thought of that'. In a way it is not clear to me that there ever can be a theory about things whose possibility one cannot even envision. In a sense, I do not know how to answer you. It is 'cavalier' in the sense that all the calculations of all the possible events are already there.

I think that a very large fraction of what we mean by novelty in the future can be formally encompassed in a statement that these things are conceivable. We do not know whether they are going to happen or not, but we assign some kind of probability weight, and as time goes on the evidence accumulates and you can make a sort of bet contingent upon those events.

There is a sense in which it does not meet our deepest needs for a theory of genuine novelty. This is, of course, a point that is usually attributed to Schumpeter (I do not think that his thinking was all that deep); the way innovations are brought out as brand new ideas. Schumpeter does not say, 'if an individual is investing does he take account of the fact that there might be an innovation?' He never discusses that question. In his attack on historicism, the idea that the future is predictable, Karl Popper does not fully address the question whether the world is unpredictable; we know that it could happen, not that it will happen. He does argue that you cannot know, for example, that there will be an innovation because it would take longer to figure out the innovation than the innovation itself. Whether or not there is real proof of that I do not know, I have my doubts . . . Anyway, it certainly is a legitimate argument. To put this argument to rest, perhaps I should mention that computability may have something to do with this. It may be that one can anticipate everything, but it takes so long to do it, that it is not worthwhile. And we do not have a satisfactory theory of it.

Feiwel: What is the genesis and essence of your work on the theory of production and growth?

Arrow: My work in that area is quite diffuse. I have worked on a number of topics, and in a sense have contributed to a large and ongoing literature. I do not think I have any strikingly novel approaches, but I have tried to solve a number of highly specific or more general problems. I have helped in diffusing the optimal control theory into economics. By example, and by expository work, I have taken the Pontryagin methods and shown their general applicability. I am at least one of those who contributed to promoting their use. But that is not a novel idea of mine; I have applied optimal growth theory in a number of cases.

Somewhat different was an empirical study (with Chenery, Minhas, and Solow) that generated a new type of production function (CES). Actually it was not all that new; it was in the literature, but we did not know about it, we invented it . . . again. We showed that the CES function empirically fitted a lot of facts somewhat better. Probably one of the most useful things was that by having a standard form we were able to ask a number of questions about international comparisons in productivity. By the way, I am surprised that that work has not been used more in the international trade context which seems to me the most interesting area of application. It was used right away in the dissertation by Minhas here at Stanford, but it does not seem to have been picked up. A lot of the international trade literature still acts as if all countries were identical. I think that this was one thing we proved cannot possibly be the case.

One particular form of this work is the application to growth with public goods which I have stated in the form of criteria for public investments, the rate of return. It is a topic on which I have written a number of papers. Usually these things get interesting when you assume that you do not have a perfect equilibrium concept; that there are incomplete markets in terms of my previous discussion. Then you have the question of reconciling different possible rates of interest.

Feiwel: You said that in your early years you were interested in economic planning – a task that you envisaged would synthesize g.e.t., statistical methods, and social choice criteria. Do you feel that such a synthesis can now, or in the near future, be achieved? Are you still interested in that type of planning? How realistic is its achievement?

Arrow: I guess I am probably more modest about it now. I understand the complexities of the task a lot better than I did then. I have learned over the years about the difficult problems of political decision-making. In effect, in the tradition of most theorists of economic planning, I thought that planners were engaged in optimization. Lange, Lerner, even Kalecki when he was thinking in terms of theory, and others, were thinking along similar lines. We did not think of the extent (essentially consistent with some of my other views) to which we have to think of everybody making rational decisions with some kind of degree of personal self-interest or some sort of local or national self-interest. So that there is no guarantee that decisions in the political sphere will be made in accordance with the kind of rules that we are talking about. Nevertheless, I am still very interested in the problem. I still think it is an important component. I think it is important to try and develop standards of decision-making in the public sphere that are relatively impersonal, unless subject to bias. This is why I have been involved in benefit–cost analysis for environmental and other projects. I think that one should not take this as a propaganda viewpoint; that environmental restrictions are always better, but as a genuine decision-making strategy, so that in some cases we say 'Yes' and in others 'No'. When I look at the sheer complexity of the matter, it seems much more likely that we are going to get an improvement within a little domain than a global improvement. I guess I am much more cautious. I suppose it is typical of the aging process. When I was young I used to despise older people who used to say, well, when you are my age you will understand the practical limits. And now I am saying just that! I suppose it is part of the human cycle. It is probably a mistake for a 25-year-old to accept those limits and just as much a mistake for a 60-year-old not to accept them.

But I think that we now have a better appreciation of the fact that this is not a task that can be closed in any way. In some ways conceptually, the real challenge is the idea of politics as a branch of economics; politics as a deterministic subject. In a sense, if political decisions (or the decisions made by some kind of a planning body) are themselves the result of some kind of social forces, whether they be self-interest or something else, then it is interesting what the question is. If the world is deterministic then you really have no strategies to choose. I do not like to think of it in those terms, but I have not fully thought that problem out yet. I am not quite prepared to accept the consequences of this. On the other hand, I think it is very fruitful to analyze collective decisions by analytic techniques and regard them as predictable in the same sense as economic decisions are ... which is not all that much either.

Feiwel: What led you to work in applied economics?

Arrow: Primarily two factors: social conscience and an attempt to be a complete economist. Somehow I always had this idea that one ought to be socially useful. Economic theory to a large extent seemed like self-indulgence. When I began to take economics seriously, I always looked for topics that I could tackle from a practical point of view, and that also meant an empirical point of view. Indeed, one of the reasons why it took me so long to find a dissertation topic was because I felt that I should be doing something that leads to empirical work quickly. Social choice, which in a way was a sort of dream interlude, something I began to think about without any serious intentions, is quite far removed from empirical work, though it does have some empirical implications. And I felt somewhat guilty about it. I had this recurrent feeling that one should always be interested in practical affairs. As long as one is going to be an economist, one has to be interested in empirical work just to know what the problems are. And because of the nature of the subject, policy is in some sense very basic to it. Historically it has been very basic, and, in a sense the subject is about policy – private policy or public policy. Therefore there is a kind of dualism there; when we talk about studying people, we also talk about advising them. This dualism is very deep in the subject. It is somewhat different in economics from a number of other fields.

Now, the actual applied work that I have done has tended to be in response to instigation from the outside. But I *was* responsive whereas others might not have been. For example, when Hollis Chenery and one of his students, Minhas, came to me and said, 'We have this empirical irregularity that we found, does it deserve theoretical interpretation?' Well, I could not resist getting involved in it. I got obsessed with it. I knew right away it had to do with the production function, but it took me two weeks to figure out why and how. As usual, I made a couple of slips in the process ... But I really got excited about it. In fact, I have to tell you that a good part of the empirical work in that paper was due to me. I kept on saying, 'Well, we could test the hypothesis this way, and that way'. I was the one who was pushing for more empirical work. That is why the paper has this complex structure, showing how one can do things in several different ways.

Another example of this responsiveness was my involvement in the social rate of discount. When I was at the Council of Economic Advisors, I was somewhat involved in the area of water resources which was then the standard place connected with the study of the social rate of discount. I was asked to write an expository paper for a US delegation to a meeting in Europe which I did. This got me very much interested in the subject. I was then approached by Resources for the Future . . . and the rest is history.

Another, even better, example is my study of medical economics. To this day I have not been able to figure out why the Ford Foundation thought that I would be able to do interesting work in the medical field. Even though until 1960 my work had been totally abstract, somehow I must have been felt to be somebody sympathetic, because whoever made the decision at the Ford Foundation (and I really never knew on whose advice it was) asked me if I would be the theorist to look at medical insurance. (They had this idea of having a theorist and an empirical worker in each of three fields.) That turned out to be very exciting. I started out writing a survey of the literature. I was very dissatisfied because I had no unifying thread. Then the idea came to me the way uncertainty had deeper consequences than I had allowed up to that point, because of these ideas of moral hazard and the like. My slight brush with the actuarial world brought back these phrases to my mind; in fact, it was very helpful.

Feiwel: Your work and comparative advantage are predominantly in the purest of pure economic theory. Your remarkable performance far transcends theory – a characteristic that many of us greatly value. Is there some opportunity cost in not confining oneself to one's comparative advantage?

Arrow: Oh, I feel it all the time. I do feel very much torn up. I am always doing little theoretical calculations and then I go off and do something applied, and increasingly so. Of course, one view I have, by the way, is that theory does not feed on itself. Even if one's aim is to have solely interesting theoretical problems, one should look at the applied problems because they will generate theoretical problems. My study of medical care is a good example of that, because it generated an idea that is essentially one of incentive compatibility. While people were coming to this idea from other directions, I think I was the first one to enunciate it. I was laid to this problem by looking at an applied problem and asking, 'What is the theoretical problem at the core?' Obviously, my work in applied economics is only good to the extent that I find a theoretical problem. I am not good at forming a judgement on a mass of concrete data unless I can find a theoretical structure to it. But other people are. In other words, I am not saying that this is the only way of doing things; I am only saying, given my talents, this is the only way I can make sense of it. In many instances I have done scattered reading here and there; then I put two and two together and I get a theoretical structure. Sometimes one can get very far away from the applied problem from which one started. Take my work on capital theory or public investment which got very far removed from empirical applications, with ideas like irreversibility and the like. I really do think that in order to keep theory alive we have to have empirical work.

Feiwel: Frequently the scholar's own ordering of the importance of his work differs from that of the profession at large. Has it been so in your case? Which of your contributions do you consider the most important and why? What were your greatest disappointments?

Arrow: Partly yes and partly no. To your question of what I consider the most important, my answer, without any ordering, is social choice theory, which I think has been highly appreciated, I cannot complain one bit; existence theory in which Gerard and I shared, and which has also been fully acknowledged; and I would also add the extension of the equilibrium concept to contingent securities, because whether you accept it or reject it (which I do myself on occasions) it is that which you reject. It is the basis; the thing from which you deviate. Before that we did not have a coherent theory. Incidentally, its history is interesting. It was written in French and it was not picked up at all in the English language literature – the only one who picked it up was Gerard! But then after it appeared in English translation it became a standard. Perhaps Gerard's exposition of it played a bigger role in its diffusion. The medical care paper is one that I value very highly. I think it has had a significant influence, perhaps not as much as I think it should have had.

There are two papers that I would not actually place at the top of any list, but that should have had more influence than they actually did. There is one on statistical decision theory (that I wrote for the statistics *Festschrift* for Hotelling, published in 1960)* in which I argued for distinguishing the statistical significance and economic significance and actually suggested a relatively practical procedure – the use of the *t*-test. And now, finally, after 20 years people have begun to refer to that article! Not very much, to be sure ... The methods used to test the significance in the ordinary sense, I think, are very misleading. This is not the place to give an exposition. My argument was not stated in a very general theoretical way; it was rather specific, I took the *t*-test and argued how it should be interpreted and how levels of significance should be calculated. I think it was a rather good paper that was overlooked. Another paper that I published relatively recently (in the *Festschrift* for Bergson)† that I think should have received more attention than it did, was on optimal income distribution or income redistribution. I argued that if you allow for such externalities as utility, in some sense for large populations the egalitarian solution is the only Pareto-optimal solution. I thought it was a rather striking result, but I am afraid my opinion is not shared; it seems to be quite ignored in the literature. In these cases I was a little disappointed, but on the whole I certainly have no reason to complain.

Certainly a more serious disappointment was that the paper on contingent securities was not picked up more rapidly than it was. I was quite young at the time and it was an embarrassing situation. I should have published it in English, of course, as well as in French. I felt at the time that once it had been published it would have been a little vulgar to publish it a second time, even in another language. In fact, I did not publish it in English until an editor actually asked me for it. I simply could not bring myself to do it. This was really a disappointment because I think that paper provided a clear answer to a question that bothered a lot of people.

Feiwel: Some of us feel that your work on choice theory was underappreciated. How do you feel?

Arrow: It has certainly been surpassed by Sen and Richter. They always acknowledge my work, so I have nothing to complain about. I provided another way, a more abstract way, of looking at the matter

* Now Chapter 5, vol. 4 of Arrow's collected papers.

† Now Chapter 15, vol. 1 of Arrow's collected papers.

than the revealed preference approach of Samuelson, which is essentially very much confined to the competitive world, whereas mine was a more general formulation. My work in this field is still being referred to, Sen certainly does when developing his own work. Whatever I have done has by now been already incorporated in later work.

Feiwel: Allow me now to ask you some very general questions. How, in your view, does economics differ from the natural sciences?

Arrow: In December 1984 I spoke at a session on economic history at the American Economic Association meetings. I made an analogy between economic history and geology. Geology, of course, is a historical subject; it is not a science of general principles like physics, though, of course, there are lower-level generalizations within in, such as plate tectonics. I was trying to pursue the analogy between economic theory and physics or chemistry. But I firmly believe that there are limits to that story.

Of course, economic theory may well be culturally bound. There is no reason why the principles of competitive equilibrium, if they are applicable to our world, need to be applied to all societies at all times. Presumably behind that there should be some meta-economics which would specialize in each particular case. But we do not have that meta-economics. Of course, it is also true that even in a most non-competitive world we can always find that the kind of things that we call economics does operate. Take the height of feudalism, when the Black Death wiped out a good fraction of the labouring population, wages *did* rise (as the competitive model would predict) even though it was not a competitive world, with the serfs bound to the soil and all that. I guess the answer is that some of these forces operate but perhaps in very strained ways.

I do not know enough about this, but some people believe that in the ancient world, for example, the modern economic principles were completely inapplicable. Moses Finley, who is probably the leading classicist of the day, is very firm in that opinion. Other economic historians take a completely different view. Rostovtzeff, whom I read when I was un undergraduate, argued that the Roman empire of the second century A. D. was a kind of capitalist country, with workers moving from job to job, merchants maximizing profit, that sort of thing. Incidentally, one can also discuss slavery under capitalism, slaves being bought and sold at the point of maximum profit. There is, in fact, a very rich literature that argues that you can apply capitalist principles of a competitive economy to the Anti-bellum South.

On the other hand, one can presume economic history to be culturally bound the way the natural sciences are not. Although this again is not quite true. Take geology again: the principles that govern modern geology may not be the same principles as the ones that governed geology when the earth was a good deal hotter. For example, plate tectonics is not a universal principle; there was a pre-tectonic era, also we do not seem to find tectonics on the other planets. Unfortunately we do not happen to have unconnected economies for experimental purposes. There is a little bit of that in the studies of primitive economies, but it provides very little ground for comparison.

There is also the fact that our attitude towards economics is different because, as I said before, *we are* part of the economy. There is no question that a good deal of the shaping of our opinions comes from the fact that we are part of the system. We have what the sociologists call in German a *Verstand.* I think it is nonsense to say that eonomics is a purely positivistic science as the Chicago school would like to think. That is just not true and I do not think that they behave in a way that supports their position.

Economics is also a very complex subject. At the cost of repetition, let me underline that everything is connected with everthing else, which means that you do not have the opportunity for a careful study of isolated bodies, one of the main foundations for the study of natural sciences. Now, there are many natural sciences which are complex in the same sense as economics such as astronomy, geology, a good deal of chemistry, and biology. By and large we know how plants and animals evolve, but there is the human being, for example, so in some sense biology is temporally bound.

Feiwel: What is your position on the famous controversy about methodology (Friedman v. Samuelson, Kooopmans, and others)? How do you feel about the realism of assumptions?

Arrow: I do not believe that you can do without theoretical presuppositions. In some ways this is so standard in the history of our science that it is almost an orthodoxy. Your perceptions at any moment are filtered by the views you inherit from the past. Whether you should do a lot of thinking before you fit empirical data, as Koopmans was implying, or whether you should go ahead and measure with only vague theories in mind, as the National Bureau was doing, I think is more a matter of art than a matter of genuine controversy. It is a matter of what works.

Friedman's argument about the realism of assumptions is something that I really do not understand at all. One of the consequences of an assumption is the assumption itself. Presumably, he says, you should test the validity of assumptions – not by their realism – but by how well they predict. But one thing that an assumption will predict is that it itself is true. If it is false, then I do not understand this. I think that there is a tendency in Friedman's methodology to say, 'here is a particular problem, I will make a set of assumptions, and here are the consequences; ah! yes in this case they worked out well'. But I say, if these assumptions are true, they should also be true for the next problem. In other words, there is a tendency to look only at the consequences that one happens to be studying at that moment, and not asking whether these assumptions can imply something quite different, whether they can be used in another field. In other words, it is not enough to test the assumptions in one field, one has to test them in others as well – something that Popper, for instance, would insist on.

It is legitimate to question the realism of assumptions. If the assumptions are dead wrong, there is no point in discussing them. There is a problem, however, when it comes to assumptions that have a considerable degree of validity about them. I am willing to entertain that one look at the consequences, that one use them as a sort of tool. It is, of course, not the highest degree of understanding, but perhaps it may be the best we can do in our present state of ignorance. It is very difficult to insist that at every stage everything be realistic. People who do empirical work also gloss over big deviations, by the way. If they find that something does not fit, they often say, 'well, it fits in the long run, or it fits in the short run, or this or that'. Now, the relation between the money supply and the price level, for example is just very far from an invariant. The longer you take your spans, the better it looks.

I would say that there is one problem with the modelling approach; it is a psychological one. Namely, it encourages people to think in terms of models, and discourages them from thinking in terms of data. Data becomes less important. Now, I have to admit there was one thing I liked about the National Bureau approach. In fact, when Koopmans wrote his critical article I did tell him that I thought he had made a mistake, not because he was wrong, but because the Bureau, in the mistaken belief that you have to pile more data on more data and then the truth would emerge, was, therefore, getting a lot of people to collect a lot of data that were very useful to the model builders. So I could not see why we should discourage them from this task when they were providing us with such useful fodder. By now, I think that the demand for data has been sufficiently good that my fears were not warranted.

Frequently we have models that cannot be fitted on existing data, but could be fitted in principle. Such models have created demand for specific data; in particular, I am thinking about intertemporal relationships. One of the consequences, for example, has been the accumulation of life-time or at least long-time histories of labour force participation. That is the result of models that say that your work today may determine your expectations about your work tomorrow. If that is your model, you cannot do much about it unless you actually have a time series. I do think such models have had a positive effect by creating a demand for data that is not available at a given time. My view of the matter is much more pragmatic.

Feiwel: Would you care to classify by order of importance the most significant contributions to economics in the last 50 years?

Arrow: Let me give you some answers in the order in which they come to my mind which is not the same thing. I would still put the development of Keynesian economics at the top of the list; the vision if not the theory contained therein. Second would be the development of the economics of uncertainty and information; I am really amalgamating a couple of topics under that heading, but I think there has been a total change both in the theories that we apply and in our understanding. Thirdly, I must say, is the elaboration of g.e.t.; I am quite unrepentant on that score. Fourthly is a whole series of developments which may be called 'taking economic theory of a relatively sophisticated kind and making it applicable to more specific cases'. A primary example of that is the theory of consumption depending on intertemporal contexts such as permanent income, life cycle, bequest motive, all this sort of thing that is a combination of theoretical and empirical inquiry. This section also includes such less striking examples as the theory of demand for money which is somewhat less well developed than consumption theory. Another example would be the application of econometric models based on production, theories of investment, and production based upon taking economic models, whether they be CES or trans-log, and applying them to concrete situations and getting workable models. And a fifth is a very general one, it is just the very large simultaneous accumulation of data and applications of a great number of specific models of varying degrees of sophistication.

Feiwel: Your writings offer telling and moving glimpses of the impact of the Great Depression on your thinking and motivation. While you appear to have accepted Keynes's fundamental message, would you enlarge on your initial and subsequent reactions to the *General Theory?*

Arrow: I did not really come across the *General Theory* until five or six years after it was published: that is, until I began to seriously study economics. I always had difficulty reconciling it with the g.e. position. To put it another way, it was an obvious criticism of why prices were not always adjusted, why such large amounts of unemployment existed, why wages do not go down, and so on. Nevertheless, the idea that this was an important part of the world seemed to me quite well established. Subsequently, I felt, people began to bring back into the *General Theory* considerations based a little more on economic theory. Most generally it was the kind of thing that you might call the world of assets, the world of time: that consumption does not depend merely on present income, but on the past and on the future expectations of income; that investment is a stock-flow relationship, that is, it is not only a function of the rate of interest, but it depends on existing capital. Various modifications of that sort took place over the years which, of course, have culminated in the kind of ultimate resurgence of neoclassical economics that says there is no such thing as unemployment – a point that I find completely unacceptable. There really are imbalances between supply and demand and we still have not thought these things through.

Feiwel: To follow up, however briefly, what do you think are the weakest links in the Keynesian revolution and what do you think of the neoclassical synthesis?

Arrow: I think that the weakest links are in conception, rather than in implementation. I always found the neoclassical synthesis a somewhat vague concept. In fact, I objected to it in my review of

Samuelson's collected papers, and I have not rethought the question since then.

Feiwel: Recently you expressed a regret for the revival of single-market thinking both among monetarists and some of the younger applied economists. Would you care to enlarge upon it?

Arrow: Working within the g.e.t. framework is very demanding on applied economists. There is no question that g.e.t. makes it harder to do empirical work because it says 'Look, you have overlooked this and that'. It is very inhibiting. In consequence we have a lot of empirical work being fitted based on one or two variables and then somehow this is identified as a structural relationship of some kind or another, with invariant characteristics. Now, g.e.t. and its statistical counterpart, simultaneous equations estimation, emphasize that any observed empirical relationship can be essentially a mixture of a lot of structural equations and, if any one of them changes, the derived equation changes. So finding a good fit by itself is not a real proof of anything and may well even lead to embarrassment. You see, anytime you really rely upon some of these simple relationship equations, they invariably turn out to be wrong. The monetary equations, for example, as fitted to the past have behaved very badly in the last four years. In their terminology, the velocity of money has been well below what past history indicated and, therefore, the effects of monetary expansion have been less than expected. So, in fact, they have been very poor predictors. I think that methodologically it is wrong and misleading to use this approach, and to base policy on it is just as bad.

Feiwel: What is your opinion of the new classical macroeconomics (the Lucasian equilibrium business cycle theory)? Do you consider this to be some sort of misreading of your work?

Arrow: I am not sure that it is either a reading or misreading of my work: it is not necessarily reacting either for or against me. On the one hand, we have an elaborate theory in which the world is always in equilibrium and this means taking account of expectations and contingent markets and all the rest of it. In the strict model actually, there are no expectations, all future contingent prices are known. Presumably, we think of approximating that by a world where there is perfect contingent foresight, and this is supposed to fit the world we live in. They take this very seriously. I personally feel that there is evidence of substantial deviations, at various points of time, from such a depiction. I feel that their picture of the world simply does not fit the facts except by a good deal of strained interpretation.

Now, it must be said for them that they are making a very serious and scholarly effort. They have a very interesting approach; they do not want to fit their business cycle theories by looking at business cycles, rather they try to fit them by looking at long-run data, and then say that the business cycle derives from that. In effect, when their theories fit at all, it is a kind of big credit and they do get things which, in a vague way, do resemble business cycles. But, as I say, only in a vague way; the fit is quite poor. On the other hand, it must be said that models fitted in a Keynesian manner, which exploit the data much more thoroughly, nevertheless do not achieve a very good fit either. Therefore, my last comment is not a very striking repudiation of equilibrium business cycle theory.

Anything that is essentially positivistic tends to be somewhat misleading. Another way of putting it is that they are not using all the data they can. They claim to be fitting data, by which they mean data on prices, quantities, output, unemployment, and the like. They never really ask for qualitative phenomena. For example, there are people out there looking for jobs. That is a fact, it is a perfectly good, hard, empirical fact. But it is not one of the facts that economists of that positivistic school tend to use. I think that one of the troubles with the positivistic school is that in a sense, perhaps, it is not following its own logic. Its economists restrict the data they are talking about and make it much harder, for example, to test things like discrepancies from equilibrium. My whole point is that there *really is* this disequilibrium.

Perhaps the best defense of the new classical macroeconomics that I ever heard was from Stan Fischer. His position is that the theories may not be very good, but what does really happen in the business cycle? From peak to trough output may vary by about 10 per cent. We cannot expect to predict within 10 per cent anyway! Now, that is a kind of defense. In other words, it is not an argument that the world really is in equilibrium all the time, but that pretending it is may well be the best you could hope to do anyway.

I do think it is an interesting development in macroeconomics. I take it seriously, perhaps a little more seriously than some of my colleagues. But I do believe that it is fundamentally wrong: There is unemployment – that is a fact!

Feiwel: What do you think of the concepts of satisficing and bounded rationality?

Arrow: My problem is not with the underlying reality they are trying to capture. I think that, in a way, the economics of information is trying to get some of these ideas across. As we put it, we do not know everything, it is too costly to find out, and knowing would mean computing as well as acquiring information. But what economists like myself try to do is to put it into a rational framework, we say that behind that there is optimization, optimization of the amount of information. Economists of the Simon school, on the other hand, do not even want to ground it in rationality; they do not want to say that bounded rationality is itself rational at a higher level, as I would say it is. It is rational when you take account of the costs of information; it then becomes rational not to be too rational. In other words, it is rational not to be too well informed or to know too much because it is expensive. The fact that it is costly to find information is, I think not only a fact of the world, but a very, very central one. One way of looking at it is this: when defining the price system, it is customary in neoclassical economics to point out how economical prices are in the transmission of information. That in itself implies that information is costly. But once this is accepted, it has be to be accepted in other contexts as well.

The bounded rationality school has no trouble with information costs which are not used as an explicit analytic category; rather it points to the limits on people's rationality. Essentially, I have the same difficulty here as I have with any kind of partial analysis. I keep on thinking that economic theory ought to be sort of all-ambracing. I do not know what to do with a theory that says, 'Well, let us look at it in this context, here we mean by bounded rationality that *A* does not know *B* and does not bother forecasting *C*, and things like that'. Then I would worry, as one does in Marshallian analysis, is not there a chance for a sharp arbitrageur, of one order of intelligence higher, who would take advantage of the others? Of course, once you go down that route, you are led to rational expectations and all the rest of that devil's trap, but it is hard to avoid it. I am trying to do just that by stressing the cost of information. I am trying to show that you cannot *really* have rational expectations – they are rational given the information at hand, but they are not rational taking account of all one might know – and yet result in optimizing decisions.

I have similar difficulties with the hypotheses that come out of cognitive psychology, like prospect theory on which Tversky and Kahneman have worked. If I believe it, I do not know what to do with the theory next. It would help me if I tried to predict that X would do on the next bet in my experiment. But it is not of much use to me if I try to explain the behaviour of the securities market. I cannot use that kind of theory extensively, perhaps only to a limited degree. I have tried to touch on it in some of my papers. But I feel that one can only get so far and then these theories just do not tell one anything. For example, if you have an individual who invests with an uncertain outcome and then is planning to reinvest the proceeds, it turns out that these prospect theories just do not tell one anything. One could tell several stories that are compatible with that.

Feiwel: What are your impressions of the Chicago school?

Arrow: Actually I think I have revealed some of them in my previous answers. The Chicago school seems to have this idea that, on the one hand, they can take neoclassical economics and apply it to very specific models of a small scale nature, which means that they are not looking at g.e. implications. They fit empirically small-scale versions and simple relationships. Since I have a general view of the world that is complex and very highly interrelated, I find these to be unsatisfactory in their methodology. On the other hand, they are helped in their endeavours by assuming perfect competition. In fact, they have an assumption that goes beyond perfect competition: it is a view that there is no such thing as unexploited opportunities for gain. I say it goes beyond perfect competition, because the latter means to me that we have complete markets, but these people do not necessarily assume complete markets and yet they assume that. I think it is rather easy to argue that in many cases people can be irrational in a way, according to their criteria, and yet there is no possibility of someone else taking advantage of that; that there just are not that many opportunities for arbitrage. I think they have a somewhat naïve methodological view both from the standpoint of theory and of empirical work; an unwillingness to look at the complexity of the world.

However, I must say that some very good specific work has come out from that school, from among the traditional Chicago economists. I am saying 'traditional' because some of the younger ones do not quite fit into this mould. For instance, neither Lucas nor Grossman are traditional Chicago economists. This is a different group; Lucas is a general quilibrium theorist. There is no question that removing the inhibitions of g.e. thinking does give economists a certain degree of freedom. And once in a while, like in the case of the permanent income hypothesis, they do come up with a sensational victory for that kind of effort.

Feiwel: As the creator of social choice would you comment on the Public Choice Society and trends within it? Why have you never participated in any of its meetings?

Arrow: It is true that I have not participated in any of the meetings . . . I have no particular objection to it, I have been wanting to go; in fact, I have certain guilt feelings about it. They always hold their meetings in the spring – a time when I am exceedingly busy and when one more trip just seems to be more than I can take. And one of these years I do mean to show up.

Public choice, as you know is much more of a descriptive theory than social choice. They have done some very good work and some rather silly work, but that is true about most other branches of economics, I think. Sometimes they tend to get involved in an exceedingly small problem and then generalize on it. There is a tendency – which on the whole has been good – of using individual rationality models to explain collective public behaviour. I think that is inadequate. I simply think that an explanation of the Interstate Commerce Commission solely in terms of preventing the railroads from monopolizing just does not get to the heart of the matter; there is a lot more to it than that. I am sure that they are quite right in pointing out that this played a role, but it certainly was not the only motivating factor.

I believe there are collective norms – something that sociologists talk about – that are very important in social action. People just do not maximize on a selfish basis every minute. In fact, the system would not work if they did. A consequence of that hypothesis would be the end of organized society as we know it. Of course, not all people behave according to these collective norms; there are always people who violate them. And we do not have a good theory of how these norms come into existence. We do have some ideas about that, but it is a little hard to formalize. People are always writing papers and then starting all over again from the beginning. There is no consistent thread for this sort of thing.

Feiwel: In general, do you feel that modern (post-Second World War) economists ask smaller questions? Do you consider that addressing the grand classical themes is dangerous because of our limited technical abilities? Is such an inquiry futile?

Arrow: Not really – and I know this is contrary to what everybody says. There is a very profound observation of Wittgenstein's, and I paraphrase, that on which you have nothing to say you should keep silent. Now if you look at the grand themes and at what was said about them, it was all wrong. What was the most portentous prediction of nineteenth-century economics? Surely, that the population was going to rise to choke off any growth in posperity; any growth in capital would be met by a corresponding growth in the labour supply. This is a bit of a caricature; but, as we know, a fairly incorrect prediction. It is very interesting because its economic logic is really pretty good. The fact that it has not come about is another story. There are still a lot of people who think that *now* we are in the Malthusian era. But I am skeptical about this.

Marshall begins to stay away from these grand issues; he does not talk that much about them. Perhaps there is a big theme in Marshall: free enterprise as the salvation of the world, but he is as equivocal about that as he is about everything else. What is this marvellous quotation? 'I believe in *laissez-faire*, let the state be up and doing'. That is Marshall all over again. His book is full of reasons why the free enterprise system is not perfect. Keynes may be said to be talking about a grand theme. He and Schumpeter were probably the last of the big thinkers. Keynes was a big thinker about unemployment; he and others have suggested that stagnation is a recurrent property of the capitalist system. The evidence says that is wrong; what we have is periodic stagnation, but I see no evidence that there is a secular trend towards stagnation. Not as an economist, but in some of his social writings, Keynes was very broad and speculative. For instance, he conjectured that if we really saved, at full employment, we would saturate all our needs in two generations. This is certainly poppycock; it was even poppycock when he wrote it. This is sometimes the fate of most of these broad statements.

Schumpeter supplies us with a kind of vision, if you like, that there is a lot of innovation in the world; it is a steady flow. Once stated this seems to be self-evident, but it is probably an insight you do not get from others before him. The classical writers talk about inventions, but each invention happens and works itself out. Even Marshall does not say that there is going to be a steady stream of these inventions. I am not quite sure that Schumpeter faced up to the consequences of what he said. He connnects it with the business cycle which is probably only a minor contribution to the truth. He has a different line, along similar grooves as the public choice people, namely, in his *Capitalism, Socialism, and Democracy*. This is, by the way, a fascinating book in many ways, but full of odd judgements on actual politics. For instance, he did not even take Naziism very seriously, and compared Roosevelt unfavourably to Hitler. It just goes to show how even the best and brightest can falter in their estimations of the big pictures. Schumpeter was obviously a very intelligent man; I do not think he was at all disciplined and that probably permitted him to talk about these topics. By and large his predictions are wrong. Take his inevitability of socialism; perhaps it is going to come, but certainly the history of the last 30 years has not been along the lines Schumpeter was talking about. Perhaps it is just as well that we no longer seek these big concepts.

On the other hand, looking from a somewhat different, and perhaps more circumscribed vantage point, I see that our vision of the economic world has been changed by the idea of scarcity of information presented in many different forms, whether it be by Marschak, Simon, or others. I see this as a basic and distinct alteration in our picture of the world whose consequences are not yet fully understood. In my conception this is a big topic, a grand theme, if you like. Of course, it takes the form of models on absolutely microscopic issues. But there is a common picture that emerges which may be as much a transformation of the way we see the world as anything else.

I think that the biggest thing we got out of nineteenth-century economics was not these big issues like the future of the economy, the stationary state, or the population trap; it was the picture of the economy – the vision of the Invisible Hand. What emerged as most important was this vision of the world, not the predictions about big issues.

By the way, a lot of the grand classical themes were neither grand nor classical, nor were they worth addressing. The long-run predictions about the future of society have no operational meaning anyway. We are not going to do anything about them. It may be very nice to know that the end of days, whether one gives it a religious or economic interpretation, is going to take place in this or that form, but there is nothing operational about it.

Feiwel: In connection with the 'Invisible Hand', would it be fair to say that the classical economists were speaking about a dynamic system, the modern welfare economists are mainly speaking in static terms?

Arrow: I think it is a matter of style; we are essentially saying the same thing. I do not know how dynamic Adam Smith's conception was. Those passages about the 'Invisible Hand' are very scattered about. One gets the feeling that it is not the analytic core of his work. His system is dynamic in the sense that he talks about the flow of capital to places where it is put to the highest use, but presumably the equilibrium state is one where the capital is in the highest use and nowhere else. If one talks about micro-models that ask what is going to happen tomorrow, these two things may be different, but nobody ever uses it this way anyway. If you talk about a picture, one of them says, 'When the dust is settled you are in an optimal state', and the other one says, 'People are going to go from the lower use to the higher use'. One sounds dynamic and the other sounds static, but they are both saying the same thing. And, all the more, if one is not willing to commit oneself on what the dynamics really are; that is, how fast does the capital flow and the like, then, it seems to me, that the only statement being made is about equilibrium.

What would be more genuinely dynamic would be the arguments that have been read into Schumpeter (I do not think they are explicitly there) that monopoly is better for innovation. That would be an argument, probably best interpreted as a second-best argument, that says that the theorems of welfare economics do not apply, because research is indivisible and the technical conditions are not satisfied.

Feiwel: What do you think of the work of such modern economists as Galbraith and Myrdal who address themselves to the larger questions?

Arrow: This question does suggest a sense to the term 'larger questions' that is somewhat different from what we discussed before. It is the sense that an economy cannot be explained in terms of itself. Most economic thinking, be it partial or general equilibrium, tends to explain the economy in terms of itself. Now these people and I think this is truer of Myrdal than it is of Galbraith, argue that the economic system somehow involves these 'other' considerations. I personally think that economics strictly speaking, or at least the neoclassical paradigm, in a sense does admit the importance of other things; it puts them in the exogenous variables. In other words, what does it say? It says 'from tastes, technology, and endowments I can predict the world'. This means that there is plenty of room from the outside to affect tastes, technology, and maybe endowments (the latter are a bit of a mixture of endogenous and exogenous). How hard people work, for example, depends on their willingness to trade off goods for leisure. So you can say if an economy is poor it is because the people do not like to work, and that is a question of tastes which, in turn, have a cultural interpretation. Let us ask the anthropologists questions like that. One danger of that is that anthropologists do not ask questions in the form that economists can use. Even if the idea is sound, it looks as if the economist is going to have to measure tastes as he sees them, for nobody else will measure them that way, in terms of demand functions, utility functions, or whatever. Then the argument is: does it matter whether tastes are culturally formed or not? Well, from a certain point of view, certainly from the descriptive point of view, it does matter, providing we know what they are. Another argument is that there is a feedback: and here we have Galbraith sort of picking up on Veblen, that tastes are formed by the economic system as well as forming it. So it is a two-way street; tastes are not really exogenous. Here it is not so much that other things determine economics, as that economics determines other things which, in turn, determine economics. That is the logic of that.

I am afraid that I have not read the *Asian Drama*, those fat three volumes are somewhat offputting. I am surprised that development economists do not refer to it more often. Myrdal is, of course, a man of extraordinary breadth who has produced some first-rate work. His work in macroeconomics is of the first order. We cannot help but admire an economist who, at the height of his power, would spend time studying the American Negro. He has been going around attacking economists for not addressing larger issues of interrelationships between economics and 'other' things. I think that in principle he is right, but the trouble is that I have never found anything useful in these things.

It is quite clear, for example, that culture affects economic performance. I think that it affects it through communciation structures – a problem that we have not fully addressed yet. Comparisons between the U.S. and Japan suggest that different communication structures have to do with different degrees of efficiency. I am obviously pushing this down the line in which I am interested. It is obviously in a naïve way that different tastes produce different production structures, if only different things are produced. The question to what extent technology is exogenous or endogenous is not easy to answer. Does building up a scientific culture in a country increase technology? The answers turn out to be complicated and not at all self-evident.

My feeling is that the principle of addressing larger issues in this sense is very important, but I have not seen much constructive work in this area.

Feiwel: Is modern economics pursuing seriously the large issue of income distribution?

Arrow: In a sense this is purely an economic issue. People are poor because what they have to sell does not get a high price. Nevertheless, as I have hinted before, one does worry about the adequacy of our explanations of income distribution. To what extent is it self-perpetuating from generation to generation? To what extent is it recreated? It does seem to be recreated each generation; bequests do not play that large a role.

It is quite true that throughout its history, economic analysis, on the whole has paid very little attention to the distribution of income. Now, you will probably tell me, 'What about Ricardo?' But what does he mean by income distribution? He means what we would call today the functional distribution of income. And what does this matter? In his model all wage-earners get the same income. He concedes, by the way, that they do not, but then ignores it resolutely. Also, he does not address the question why some landowners are richer than others nor, for that matter, why some capitalists are richer than others. Since in his model everybody is making the same rate of return on capital, the only way one can explain that some capitalists are richer than others is because they started with more capital. But that is not an explanation. Ricardo does not explain income inequality among wage-earners nor among capitalists. Today, at least most income inequality *is* among wage-earners. His explanation of income distribution among classes – that people with land and capital are richer than the others – does not really address the major inequality issue today. Neither does Marx. There is no doubt that today in the U.S. the very richest people are capitalists, but if you look at the total amount of income received by people who are essentially capitalists, it is not a very large fraction of the total. And those who are capitalists *became* capitalists somehow or other. So that economists who did talk about income distribution, like Ricardo and Marx, did not really explain it. The naïve question is, 'If it is so nice to be a capitalist, why does not everybody want to be one?' Of course, you cannot become a capitalist without capital. In addressing the question, Marx says there had to be original accumulation and that was done by force, theft, and fraud. That certainly happended; but the idea that the bulk of the industrial fortunes that were developing in his own time, not inherited, could be explained that way is a little inconsistent.

On the other hand, neoclassical economists have not really addressed themselves to the question at all. There is a little sub-branch of economists who study income distribution, but there are not many of them. I think it is one of the great disgraces of modern economics.

That is a big issue! And it is a big issue for yet another reason. Not only is it in itself extremely important, but if one asks, 'What does the economic system produce?', the answer is that it produces the distribution of income. The average is, of course, one very interesting characteristic, but it is only *one* among many. The other is that, I think, the distribution of income has, in turn, consequences for the running of the economy. The practical models tend to assume that everyone has the same income. Most of the models are built on a representative consumer. Or, if you are looking at savings models, on a representative saver. The fact is that people have vastly different wealth and, I think, the fact that most saving is done by a relatively small number of people gets lost in such a model. You see, the bulk of the income is held by the poor and the middle class and, I would guess, that that is not where the bulk of the savings is. Take a study of the effects of social security on savings. It turns out that most of saving is done by people to whom social security is a minor matter. So the explanation makes no sense.

The question of income distribution in the modern context is a two-way one: Why is income distribution the way it is? What is the effect of income distribution on savings, investment, consumption, and the like? That, as I said, is a big issue which nobody seems to be addressing.

Feiwel: If economics were an Aristotle Republic and you the benevolent dictator, what directions of research would be encouraged and what criteria would be used to judge the quality of work?

Arrow: That is a bad idea right off; power always corrupts and absolute power corrupts absolutely. I may believe in government intervention in the economy, but when it comes to economics I am a great believer in *laissez-faire*. You have to let people develop as they see fit, let research develop naturally. There is always a problem in judging. One man's wild-eyed abstraction is another man's mainstream. Interestingly enough, however, there is not that much difference; there is something of a consensus. In fact, economics may be overly 'standardized', and economists much too unified in their judgement: they agree far more than sociologists do, for example. I have been on a number of committees where we were supposed to rank people. You would be surprised, no matter how heterogenous the committee (composed of abstract theorists, empirical data collectors, or what not) most members tend to agree on the ranking of the top five or six candidates. Within this economics republic there is a kind of common language, common understanding. In fact, I think it may be excessive; that much agreement is itself rather disturbing.

There are many detailed pieces of research that I would like to see done, but that is not what you mean. To come back to what I said before, the one field that I feel has been grossly neglected is income distribution. Comparative economic systems is another. In fact, I just realized this recently when I was writing the paper for the economic history session for the 1984 AEA meetings. I suddenly realized that all the things that history is supposed to do are also done by comparative economics (such as a different perspective, a discussion of the extent assumptions are culture-bound). About 30 years ago comparative systems was a well-established field in the economics curriculum; it seems to have dropped out. I am not quite sure why this happened; part of it might have been due to the fact that to some extent it attracted superficial work. But there is obviously a real hard core in the field which should be plowed. To some extent economic development touches on similar topics, making comparisons between the underdeveloped and developed countries. But it, too, is a field that is less stressed than it used to be. Perhaps one of the problems is that we do not have very much to say about it. More generally, there is a whole question of cultural influences on economics to which I alluded before. The only trouble with that is that the people who work on it do not come up with much. Their work turns out to be rather banal and of a journalistic flavour, in the genre of 'the French do a lot of formal thinking, the Japanese do a lot of consensus-building' and the like. These are probably true statements, by the way, but one cannot build anything analytically out of them.

I would tend to trust the market and peer evaluation. It is true that in the US much of the research in economics, like in other fields, is funded by the government. We have a problem that there is a chance that this may influence the direction of research. To some extent this is mitigated by the fact that peer review has remained important. But there are priorities. . . It is quite true that studies on income distribution do not enjoy priority funding.

Feiwel: You have argued that something more, but including neoclassical economics, is needed. What would it be? Where are we to look for it? And, if an alternative approach is constructed, what role would neoclassical theory play?

Arrow: One of the important ingredients is, of course, asymmetric information, which I think has really changed the way we are looking at the world. Even though it is still a theory with a lot of flaws in it, a lot of incompleteness, it has provided us with an outlook which has made other complex phenomena more understandable. It is also bringing together somewhat different strands of economic thought, for example, people like Ollie Williamson who is somewhat outside the neoclassical tradition. It has also changed our ideas of whether the numbers are large or small. It turns out that if you look at it globally, there are a lot of people out there, most industries have many firms and so on. But if you look closely at the relations between employers and workers, the numbers are not very big. The workers do not automatically move from firm to firm. At any given moment the workers are not facing a market. There is this market out there and it is important, but you do not move to it costlessly. So I think that when you talk about things like imperfect information and imperfect competition, which I think are closely related, there are grounds for rather serious departures from neoclassical economics.

It may well be that you will never get a good theory. If you take the formal game theory, it tends to have a lot of indeterminateness. It also makes great demands on rationality, well beyond those that neoclassical theory imposes. There is a possibility that we might not solve these problems by way of rationality–and this is a Simonesque kind of argument.

Feiwel: What criteria would you use to evaluate the soundness of an alternative theory?

Arrow: Persuasiveness. Does it correspond to our understanding of the economic world? I think it is foolish to say that we rely on hard empirical evidence completely. A very important part of it is just *our* perception of the economic world. If you find a new concept, the question is, does it illuminate your perception? Do you feel you understand what is going on in everyday life? Of course, whether it fits empirical and other tests is also important.

Feiwel: What problems in economics fascinate you most at this time?

Arrow: The main thing I am working on is communication and computing. I should really put it this way; I would like to go into computing. I have not done anything in that area yet, in fact, I am not quite sure there is a field there. But certainly the work on communication and information gathering has implications for economics. I am taking a line that is a little different from the standard one today. Everybody is now into incentive compatibility and I want to say that the communications structure itself is a variable. In other words, everybody says, 'You have a given communications structure, the principal can see so much about his agent, but no more'. What I want to do is make what is observed a variable. In my heart of hearts I believe this has deep implications for macroeconomics, but I am still very far away from being able to discuss it in those terms. At this stage it is a belief and a motivation that the business cycle has a lot to do with all of this. It is basically the question of information-gathering in private and collective spheres that I am concerned about.

3 Oral History II: An Interview

Gerard Debreu

Feiwel: In accepting the Nobel Prize you implied that the logical rigour, the generality, and the simplicity of mathematical general equilibrium theory satisfied deep personal intellectual needs. But it also contributed to promoting the social interests of the scientific community. Why is the question of existence of general economic equilibrium so profoundly important?

Debreu: Since I have not seen your question discussed in the terms I would like to use, I will not give you a concise answer. Take the Walrasian model in its contemporary form. It tries to explain the observed state of an economy as an equilibrium resulting from the interaction of agents through markets. The model would be empty without the specification of assumptions that guarantee the existence of the central concept of the theory, that is, the concept of general economic equilibrium. In other words, in proving existence one is not trying to make a statement about the real world, one is trying to evaluate the model.

When Kenneth Arrow and I started working on the existence problem in the early 1950s, we did not know how strong those assumptions would have to be. If they had turned out to be extremely restrictive, I believe that the model would be of little value. Over the last three and a half decades the assumptions have been gradually weakened. We now understand that they basically require convexity of preferences and of production sets. And even convexity of preferences can be dispensed with, as we have learned from the introduction of a continuum of agents by Robert Aumann. If you have a large number of economic agents, all of them insignificant relative to their totality, then preferences need not be convex.

There remains the matter of convexity of production sets; that is one point on which the theory of general economic equilibrium is least satisfactory. When you deal with a small number of giants dominating an industry you have to resort to other theories, such as oligopoly theory and game theory, in attempting to explain economic equilibrium.

In any case one result of the work of the past three and a half decades has been to show that the assumptions required to prove the existence of a general economic equilibrium are far weaker than could have been anticipated 35 years ago.

The necessity of proving the existence of equilibria is now recognized, and authors who propose an equilibrium concept either in economic theory or in game theory feel compelled to specify assumptions guaranteeing existence of the concept.

Feiwel: Can you provide some examples of, say applied or policy problems that would be intractable without prior solution of the problem of existence?

Debreu: In the process of obtaining existence proofs the model has been streamlined. It was made substantially more general and simpler, and this is of interest to the general economic theorist. The model, as it is now formulated, is easier to grasp than 30 or 40 years ago. Therefore, to the extent that the theory of general economic equilibrium is first an intellectual frame of reference, economists have a better analytical tool as a consequence of the recent insistence on rigor, generality, and simplicity.

Several men who were close to the center of economic action during the past decades were thoroughly versed in the theory of general economic equilibrium, for instance Pierre Massé, who was Commissaire Général au Plan in the de Gaulle government; Marcel Boiteux, now President of Electricité de France; and Edmond Malinvaud, currently Director of the Institut National de la Statistique et des Etudes Economiques and former advisor to ministers of economics and finance. Those are remarkable examples of men who knew the theory of general economic equilibrium well and who used it as an intellectual framework in the analysis of the day-to-day problems that they faced.

Consider also the applied general equilibrium models that have become popular. They have received strong impetus from algorithms for the computation of approximate equilibria, an area in which Herbert Scarf played a leading role. The development of those algorithms grew naturally out of the work on existence. Their combinatorial character, in particular, reflects the influence of the prior theoretical studies. That seems to be one of the clearest examples in economics of abstract theory eventually leading to important concrete applications.

It is true that in the early 1950s few economists had any sympathy for the study of existence. It was often seen as an abstract problem, possibly without any interest. Yet gradually it has led, for instance via the development of algorithms for computing economic equilibria, to a large number of applications, for example, in public finance, economic development, and international trade.

Take still another example of the indirect ways in which abstract theory may eventually lead to the clarification of concrete issues. The law of demand, in its simplest form, says that if the price of a commodity increases, there results a decrease in the aggregate quantity demanded. This is undoubtedly one of the most widespread economic beliefs. In a more sophisticated form, one considers aggregate demand, a vector with l co-ordinates if there are l commodities, as a function of l prices, and one asserts that the Jacobian of the aggregate demand function is negative semi-definite. It is worth noting that this statement, in any of its forms, had not been validated by economic theory until the recent past.

The development of ideas in this area started with the characterization of aggregate excess demand functions. The question was formulated by Hugo Sonnenschein who also provided a first solution. In its general form, the confirmation of Sonnenschein's conjecture says that any function from the strictly positive orthant of R^l to R^l that satisfies homogeneity of degree zero, continuity, and Walras's law can be generated as the aggregate excess demand function of an economy. This is a negative statement indeed. But this negative statement led to a reformulation of the problem in the following terms: What assumptions must we make about the distribution of the characteristics of economic agents in an economy to ensure that the law of demand will prevail? An important contribution to its solution was made by Werner Hildenbrand in *Econometrica*, 1983. the calculus proof provided by Hildenbrand in the latter part of his article could have been given by any one of the thousands of economists who have looked at the Slutzky relation. It was not found earlier for lack of a general research programme.

Feiwel: There appears to be, at least in the popular press, a misunderstanding of your contributions. In straightening this out, would it be fair to say that you have given us arguments both for and against the market, because, if in the real world the conditions for existence are not satisfied, we could investigate whether such conditions could be created and, if not, where else we should look?

Debreu: One of the common dangers of economic theorizing is the easy temptation to apply conclusions of vaguely formulated theories in cases in which they do not hold. The exact formulation of assumptions that goes with axiomatization gives some protection against that danger.

The theory that we are discussing tries to be ideologically neutral. It deals with problems that are basic and common to all economic systems, for instance the efficient allocation of resources through decentralized procedures. Theorems of Welfare Economics provide solutions for those problems and point to an intrinsic character of prices. Some proponents of *laissez-faire* policies find comfort in their conclusions, while opponents can point out the extent to which their assumptions are not satisfied.

Economic decisions must be decentralized. Mathematical models of the economy help to analyze the optimal extent of this decentralization. The risk of misinterpretation of conclusions in situations that are out of the range of the theory is lessened by the uncompromising exactness of the modelization.

Feiwel: Mainly for the benefit of the 'uneducated' would you kindly distinguish between the use of the terms 'efficient' and 'optimal' in your writings, because at times they are misinterpreted?

Debreu: I have distinguished them in writings but not in this interview. Technically the word 'efficient' has been reserved for production problems in which consumers do not appear explicitly. Production is said to be efficient if one cannot increase simultaneously the output of all commodities. In contrast, Pareto optimality considers a set of consumers characterized by their preferences. An allocation is said to be optimal if one cannot simultaneously increase the utility of all consumers. Thus in one case one puts the accent on production, as in Koopmans's activity analysis, in the other the accent is on allocation among consumers.

Feiwel: Without going into the definition of terms, would you kindly elaborate on your use of the term 'general' and on your predilection for 'simple' economic theory?

Debreu: Simplicity appears in many forms. Consider the definition of the concept of a commodity in which one includes its physical characteristics, its date, its location, and even the uncertain state of the world in which it is available. By using this extremely general concept one covers a multitude of phenomena, including interest, location, transportation, risk. One can deal with all of them by working in the commodity space, a space having a dimension equal to the number of commodities and in which the action of an agent is represented by a point.

As another instance, look at the study of consumer behaviour by means of the differential calculus where you find a complex formulation in terms of decreasing marginal rates of substitution. In contrast, the convexity analysis approach is not only simpler, it is also more general since the boundary of a convex set does not have to be smooth.

Feiwel: For the benefit of the uneducated, what do you mean by 'primitive' concepts?

Debreu: 'Primitive' is used in the sense of axiomatic theory. Those are the concepts that you do not have to define. They can be given different interpretations. A good example is the introduction of the idea of contingent commodities by Kenneth Arrow. Thanks to a new interpretation of the concept of commodity it was possible to extend the existing theory of general economic equilibrium so as to cover a host of new phenomena without any further deductive work. In this sense 'primitive' means not 'naïve' but applies to a concept beyond which no further logical reduction is sought.

Feiwel: Speaking of the exciting early 1950s at Cowles you said that one of the leading motivations of research on general equilibrium theory was to make it 'rigorous, to generalize it, to simplify it, and to extend it in new directions'. You were good enough to discuss rigor, generality, and simplification for us. May we have your impression of extensions?

Debreu: Extending the theory in new directions was indeed an important aspect of the work done on the theory of general economic equilibrium. These extensions have included, in a list that does not attempt to be exhaustive, the theory of the core, the computation of equilibria and applied general equilibrium models, the theory of regular economies, externalities, indivisibilities, public goods, the characterization of excess demand functions.

Feiwel: May we explore the question of creative genesis in general?

Debreu: Creativity is an obscure process marked by the sudden emergence of ideas. I have mentioned two specific examples in my Nobel Lecture. Those ideas usually come after long periods of hard work, of unsuccessful groping. And suddenly everything falls into place. One of the two examples to which I alluded is the ride from the San Francisco airport to Palo Alto in Herbert Scarf's car during which one of us provided a significant part of the solution of a problem in the theory of the core and the other immediately provided the other part.

Feiwel: More specifically, how did you become interested in the problem of existence of general economic equilibrium?

Debreu: It seems fairly straightforward, at least with hindsight. You must remember that I was trained as a mathematician. When I learned about the theory of general economic equilibrium in the works of Allais, Divisia, and Walras (listed in the order in which I read them, which happens to be the reverse of the order in which they were written), the standard argument for existence was equality of the number of equations and the number of unknowns. For somebody schooled in the mathemtical tradition of Bourbaki this was unconvincing if the system is not linear, in fact even if it *is* linear, and if there *are* inequality constraints. Therefore at that time, that is, in the mid- and late 1940s, I was not satisfied with the pseudo answer that I read. But I must add that the problem of existence looked forbiddingly difficult then and that I did not do any serious work on it in those years.

It was only after I joined the Cowles Foundation in June 1950 that I became gradually aware of works like Kakutani's fixed point theorem, von Neumann's model of growth, and Nash's note of 1950. Their results, especially Kakutani's theorem, turned out to be crucial for the existence problem, and they led me to start thinking about it again in 1951. On his side Kenneth Arrow, who was on the Stanford faculty at the time, had also begun working on the same problem. Tjalling Koopmans, who was then the Director of Cowles, knew what I was doing and learned what Kenneth was doing. He put us in touch with each other at the beginning of 1952. From then on we worked together on the paper published in *Econometrica* 1954, without meeting until December 1952. Things were complicated by the fact that Kenneth was travelling in Europe during the greater part of 1952, which did not make for quick correspondence.

The papers by Wald that gave the first proof of existence in the early 1930s did not happen to be important for me. The work of von Neumann on growth turned out to be much more significant since, in particular, it led to Kakutani's theorem.

Feiwel: Would you comment about Lionel McKenzie's work along somewhat similar lines about the same time?

Debreu: I learned about Lionel McKenzie's work at the meeting of the American Economic Association and the Econometric Society in December 1952 in Chicago, where I presented the results that Kenneth and I had obtained. The day after I presented our paper I attended Lionel's presentation of his, and that is how I became aware of his work. His paper was also published in *Econometrica* 1954. It puts emphasis on an international trade formulation of general equilibrium. It uses Kakutani's fixed-point theorem which has remained to this day the main tool for proofs of existence.

Feiwel: Would you care to comment about Arrow as an economist, friend and collaborator?

Debreu: Kenneth is a great economist and a great friend. I have only admiration for many of his intellectual and personality traits. He has had great influence through his first book. His Impossibility Theorem has given rise to a vast literature. We have collaborated on existence. We have worked separately on optimality. He has introduced contingent commodities which I have generalized. Clearly he has been a major figure for his generation and for the younger generation of economists.

I have written only one paper in collaboration with Kenneth. Leonid Hurwicz who has written many probably would have more to say about Kenneth as a collaborator. I always found it wonderfully easy to have a dialogue with him. He is a good talker, but he is also a good listener. We always got along extraordinarily well.

Feiwel: Would you reflect on the profession's positive and negative reactions to your work?

Debreu: In the early 1950s mathematical economics was not widely practiced, and Kenneth and I were certainly in a minority. But that may have been all to the good. There is an irritant, and stimulating factor in a minority position. Moreover we were left alone to do our work. There is no doubt that the reaction of the profession to proofs of existence was not enthusiastic. I would have been surprised had it been otherwise.

In fact, I have seen this occur several times. For example, when Bob Aumann introduced the idea of a measure space of agents, or of a continuum of agents, a number of mathematical economists did not immediately accept his use of measure theory in economics.

Similarly the introduction of non-standard analysis into economic theory by Donald Brown and Abraham Robinson met with substantial resistance. This is a perfectly natural process. There may even be occasionally something suspicious about ideas that are readily accepted.

Feiwel: I have always admired you for pursuing the fields in which your great strength lies, that is for applying the theory of comparative advantages, and for not getting side-tracked into other fields as most economists are apt to do. For the inspiration of other scholars can you share with us what it is in your make-up that makes you follow this route?

Debreu: Comparative advantage is a sound economic principle, and your description is accurate.

Feiwel: Are some of the recent advances in general equilibrium theory damaging to neoclassical economics, as has been suggested, for example, by Mas-Colell, in particular, with respect to the definition of perfect competition and the number of agents?

Debreu: The assumption of perfect competition has found its natural formulation in measure spaces of economic agents or alternatively in the use of non-standard analysis. Those models provide a good approximation of what happens in the consumption sector and a bad approximation for a number of industries. When one is dealing with large agents who have enough power to influence the market, one has to resort to a variety of theories. One of the major goals of game theory when it was introduced was the explanation of oligopolistic behaviour. It has succeeded to a limited extent.

Feiwel: You have not used the term 'perfect competition' in your classic *Theory of Value*?

Debreu: I did not find it necessary to use the expression. I assumed that the agents were price takers, that is, that they behaved as if prices were given. The behaviour required explanation, and this was done by the theory of the core developed shortly afterward. It was necessary to go through the limit theorems and the measure theoretical approach to give a satisfactory account of what one meant by perfect competition, namely of the circumstances in which agents act as price takers.

Feiwel: You have pointed to game theory as the beginning of a golden age of mathematical economics. Morgenstern, who probably played a lesser role in it, accused the general equilibrium theorists of misusing the term 'competition', that competition means rivalry, bluffing, creatvie activity, and the like, rather than price-taking behaviour. May we have your thoughts on this?

Debreu: So you approve of the fact that I did not use the term 'perfect competition'!

I have said that the publication of *Theory of Games and Economic Behavior* was a symbol of the beginning of a golden age. I must be more precise. I did not mean that the framework and all of the central concepts of game theory had to be taken literally. I meant that there was in the book of von Neumann and Morgenstern a reformulation of economic theory, that new mathematical tools, in particular convex analysis, were introduced, that mathematical rigor was adhered to, that the theory of games provided in many ways a powerful intellectual stimulus. The theory of games has not yielded exactly the results that von Neumann and Morgenstern expected. The main concept of their theory, the concept of a solution, which in modern terminology is a stable set, has not turned out to be fruitful. Two of the most fruitful solution concepts in game theory, the Nash equilibrium and the core, are not stressed in their book. The influence of their work has been great, but in many cases it has been indirect and was felt in ways that were unanticipated by the two authors. That may, however, be typical of scientific work of great importance.

Feiwel: Is the mathematical theory of general equilibrium *the* theory of economics; in other words, the general or universal theory of economics?

Debreu: It is a theory of an important aspect of economic reality. Economics is an extremely complex subject and the best we can hope for is to throw some light on a limited area by using a theoretical model. The theory of general economic equilibrium focuses on the interdependence of many agents via many markets which is indeed an essential aspect of economics.

Any model can only go so far. Clearly it cannot encompass the whole of economics. A general theory with that scope will not be available in the near future, if ever. We should not hope in economics for a synthesis similar to that provided by physics at the end of the nineteenth century.

Economists must be conscious of the limits of what they can achieve. At the same time, in my optimistic view, the insights that have been gained are impressive, given the complexity of the phenomena that they concern.

Feiwel: Would you care to comment on Frank Hahn's statement that in the world of Debreu there is no Keynesian problem?

Debreu: If the assumptions of the theory to which Frank referred were fully satisfied in the real world, that would be true. But they are not. Let us note, however, that there have been recent, important attempts to base macroeconomics on microeconomic foundations, attempts that I have not discouraged in Berkeley. Various theories have been advanced: a theory of temporary equilibrium, a so-called theory of disequilibrium (a misnomer since it is a theory of equilibrium under new constraints). They show, if it were needed, that the concept of equilibrium is an organizing intellectual concept of great generality with which it is difficult to dispense in the social sciences. That one may wish to introduce constraints that were overlooked at first is perfectly legitimate.

I do not consider either that the present formulation of general economic equilibrium will remain unchanged forever. I usually stress to my students at the beginning of my course that what I want to teach is not certain specific topics, certain theorems, but methods. In 50 years economic theory will look different. But I believe that the use of mathematical models, and the rigor, the generality, the simplicity for which they induce one to strive will stay.

Feiwel: Static and dynamic aspects of general equilibrium theory and the treatment of time are controversial. Recently, also, a sharp differentiation has been drawn between classical and neoclassical general equilibrium theory. Would you kindly address yourself to some of the issues involved?

Debreu: Dynamic economic processes have not lent themselves to an easy mathematical formalization. The question of stability gives an instance of the treatment of time in economics which is not convincing. First, if one considers an economic system out of equilibrium, one must not expect every commodity to have a well-defined price. Many authors then write a differential equation that equates the derivative of the price-vector relative to time with a function of aggregate excess demand which itself is a function of prices. This equation seems to have been inspired too readily by classical mechanics. What we lack in economics, even in the most favourable circumstances, when we attempt to write down a differential system of that type, is a way of estimating the lags of the reactions of agents.

Feiwel: Is it your opinion that every economic question requires a specific analytical or mathematical apparatus to tackle it?

Debreu: Since economics gives a central role to quantities of commodities and prices, the use of mathematics seems entirely natural. This use does not have to be at an extremely sophisticated level. A brilliant original idea may be present in the simplest mathematical model. Take the example of Walras. He did use simple mathematics, because the main ideas of his model could not be formulated, could not be given substance, without the use of mathematical symbols. But his assumptions were far too strong, his mathematics was neither elegant, nor rigorous. Nevertheless, his contribution was of the first rank.

Yes, I tend to see theorizing in economics as being essentially mathematical in nature. But it does not mean that higher mathematics is required in order to do good economic theory. In fact, there is an ever present danger of doing bad economic theory by using mathematical tools that are more sophisticated than needed.

Feiwel: Could you enlarge on this?

Debreu: One can take a certain theorem in economic theory and try to extend it to the most general kind of commodity space. The relevant question is whether this extension is necessary in order to obtain new economic insights. The use of powerful mathematics may, however, be required as in Aumann's introduction of the concept of a measure space of economic agents. This enabled him to show in the context of an atomless economy the identity of two equilibrium-concepts, each one of them of basic importance, namely, the set of Walras equilibria and the core.

Feiwel: Would it be fair to say that the motivation of your generation of mathematical economists is different from that of some of the younger practitioners who often maximize mathematical sophistication and have little interest in gaining economic insights?

Debreu: There is now an enormous number of papers written in mathematical economics compared with the situation prevailing 30 years ago. Inevitably there is some work of the kind you have mentioned. But there is also innovative work in which new economic concepts are the main concern. In economics as elsewhere a number of papers extend in a purely formal way, sometimes without yielding new insights, previously developed results.

Feiwel: Would it be fair to say that mathematical economics has progressed from the engineering mathematics of Samuelson to your sophisticated mathematics?

Debreu: The change of mathematical tools in economic theory is a natural unending process. Several generations of economists worked with certain tools, and after the Second World War those tools were replaced by convexity theory, set theory, topology, and so on. Differential calculus, however, came back into its own albeit in a different context, that of global analysis, and in order to answer different questions, such as the discreteness of the set of equilibria, and the continuity of the set of equilibria as a function of parameters of the economy.

Feiwel: The following is a question I often get from students – 'Could you explain to me to what extent our view of the economic world has been enriched by using advanced mathematics, compared not only with calculus but also with more primitive tools?'

Debreu: In a way I have already answered this question. The characterization of excess demand functions is an example. The problem had not been formulated, had not even been perceived. Yet it seems important to know that *any* aggregate excess demand function can be generated by an economy and more important still, as a consequence of this negative finding, to redirect research on aggregate demand functions. Another example is the theory of the core of an economy. The concept itself was not discussed after Edgeworth's work of 1881 on the 'contract curve' until Martin Shubik's paper of 1959. Other examples include models of applied general economic equilibrium. All these were closely linked with the reformulation of the theory of general economic equilibrium and with the introduction of different mathematical tools in economic theory.

Feiwel: Have developments in general equilibrium theory met with your expectations? Have you revised your aspiration level?

Debreu: You realize that my expectations of about 35 years ago were vague. I did expect the theory to become more general, simpler, and more rigorous. I also expected it to develop in new directions but clearly I did not anticipate its specific developments, several of which have gone far beyond my vague expectations. It was a mark of optimism to believe that there was a large amount of work to be done.

Feiwel: Would you care to reflect on the Chicago Department of

Economics during the period when you were at the Cowles Commission in Chicago?

Debreu: My personal situation was not typical. As you may know, in the 1940s and early 1950s the Cowles Commission was not part of the Department of Economics of the University of Chicago, whereas after 1955 the Cowles Foundation was part of the Department of Economics at Yale. My position in Chicago was that of a junior research associate of the Cowles group. I did teach a small number of advanced courses, but it was on the basis of an informal arrangement. I never attended a meeting of the Department of Economics of which I was not a member. I was left alone to do my work during the five years from 1950 to 1955, a marvelous opportunity that I tried to use fully.

Feiwel: How do you react to the criticism from some quarters that modern economic theorists do not address themselves to the grand classical themes and concentrate rather on questions of a limited technical nature?

Debreu: I understand the impatience of many economists and of the general public in their concern with the pressing issues of our times, but the essence of scientific work is to proceed by small steps. Galileo could have been ridiculed by many of his contemporaries when he was rolling balls on an inclined plane, but that was the way to begin a study of mechanics. One could also have been impatient 50 years ago with the fact that the medical sciences were not making faster, greater progress in the treatment of some diseases. Science must proceed gradually and attack problems that are not intractable at a given time. Solving the grandest problems of the universe, preferably all at once, has been attempted repeatedly in the prescientific period, without notable success.

Feiwel: What lies ahead? If economics were an Aristotle Republic and you were its benevolent dictator, what directions of research would you encourage?

Debreu: Since I do not wish to be a dictator, even a benevolent one, I will simply tell you two of the questions that are of greatest interest to me at the present time. Both of them are broad. One is to try to push further the idea that one must make assumptions on the distribution of the characteristics of economic agents in order to explain the properties of aggregate demand. The other is the recent work on complexity theory, or on the theory of algorithms, which may influence the economic theory of information. In 1985–6 at the Berkeley Mathematical Sciences Research Institute, the two main research subjects will be complexity theory and mathematical economics. I eagerly hope that there will be a great deal of fruitful interaction between the two groups.

4 Oral History III: An Interview

Leonid Hurwicz

Feiwel: In the preface to volume 2 of his collected papers (on general equilibrium), Arrow identifies you as one of the four major contributors to modern general equilibrium theory and acknowledges the collaborative effort. Can you outline for us the areas in which you worked together?

Hurwicz: There were three major areas of collaboration between Ken and myself. Our first area of collaboration was not in general equilibrium theory; rather, it had to do with certain extensions of the Kuhn-Tucker theorem in non-linear programming. It was started in the early 1950s and a paper along these lines was published in one of the Berkeley Symposium volumes edited by Jerzy Neyman (see Arrow and Hurwicz, 1956). The second area was the problem of stability; it resulted in two papers in *Econometrica* (one with H. D. Block). The third area was the application of results in the first two areas to the design or construction of resource allocation mechanisms (see especially 'Decentralization and Computation in Resource Allocation').

The three areas were closely related, at least in their technical aspects: While the first topic dealt with the *static* aspects of non-linear programming, we then proceeded to the *dynamics* of linear and non-linear programming (and various papers on this subject were contained in Arrow, Hurwicz, and Uzawa, 1958). When we shifted to a study of stability of competitive equilibrium, we started out with the thought of applying the techniques we had developed in the context of linear and non-linear programming, namely the so-called gradient method. (It was Samuelson who pioneered the use of the gradient method in programming models.) We thought that that method, originally designed for the programming problems would also work in the context of competitive equilibrium and would enable us to determine whether, and under what conditions, competitive equilibrium is or is not stable. So we sort of got into competitive equilibrium theory through programming theory, and we got into dynamics through our initial work on statics. Furthermore, as it turned out, in order to handle dynamics, some of the static theory also had to be extended. Thus, as you see, these matters were very much interconnected. And in connection with the third topic mentioned (that is the design of mechanisms), it was natural to interpret the dynamics of programming as a certain kind of mechanism for resource allocation. It then became clear that this interpretation brought us very close to the earlier work of two groups of economists.

One group was composed of people who talked a lot about stability, the main ones being Hicks and Samuelson; the other group consisted of people like Lange and Lerner who were designing a certain kind of economic system. As we started looking at the work of the first group we were struck by the following: On one hand, you have the work of Hicks which did utilize the concept of competitive equilibrium (that is, utilized the properties of competitive equilibrium such as the Walras Law), but whose concepts of stability were not in accordance with the modern notion of what stability means in the dynamic sense. On the other hand, the work of Samuelson was modern in spirit as far as the dynamics were concerned, but it did not exploit fully the specific properties of stability of a competitive equilibrium, as distinct from stability of any other kind of equilibrium. We noticed that there was a gap in the economists' understanding of this problem; that one had to bring together the modern theory of stability in the dynamic sense on the one hand, and what is known about the specific properties of competitive equilibrium as distinct from other kinds of equilibria on the other. We were not the only ones who perceived this. In this very early period, in addition to Ken's and my work, there were two other contributions whose precise timing eludes me, but very close to simultaneous, namely one paper by Frank Hahn and at least one by Lionel McKenzie. And, as long as I am mentioning names, I should add that the second of our two papers on stability also had the collaboration of a mathematician whose name was H. D. Block and whose role was very significant (see Arrow, Block, and Hurwicz, 1959).

Feiwel: In your seminal paper with Ken on stability you noted that major feats were accomplished 'on what one may call the static aspects of competitive equilibrium, its existence, uniqueness and optimality.' But 'with regard to dynamics, especially the stability of equilibrium, much remains to be done.' Could you explain the portent of your contribution on stability?

Hurwicz: If you look at the history of the concept of stability before the economists ever got into it, a topic on which I did some research some years ago but never published, you will find that physicists treat this problem typically with the following type of comment: Only stable equilibria are of interest, because one is, in fact, very unlikely to observe an unstable equilibrium. For example, if you have a walking stick, theorectically there is a certain position of vertical equilibrium such that if you put it ideally vertically it will stay vertical. But have you ever seen a stick standing upright by itself? Thus the view expressed by physicists and others who have studied these problems is that unstable equilibria are really of no interest in interpreting observed reality. That may be too strong an interpretation, but I am mentioning this because it is common to sciences in which the concept of equilibrium itself was studied; to them the only equilibria that are worth talking about are the stable ones. This was the first point I wanted to make. The second is related to welfare economics aspects.

A stable equilibrium is a point towards which you tend even if you are not going to have a chance to get there. Suppose that it has been proven that under certain conditions competitive equilibrium is optimal. Well, we do not know anything about the optimality of disequilibrium positions. Generally speaking, they are not going to be optimal. But one can argue that under reasonable conditions the closer you are to an equilibrium that is optimal, the closer you are to being optimal or efficient. So that the optimality of equilibria, which is what recommends the competitive mechanism, is only of interest if there is a tendency to go towards them rather than, for instance, away from them. These then are among the reasons for one's interest in the stability of equilibria. But there is still a further reason that is of relevance in the planned or computational counterpart of this problem.

Imagine that you have centralized economy that operates by collecting information, computing what should be done, and then issuing commands. (This is an idealized version of a planned economy.) Well, then the question is: How do you solve the problem of optimization centrally, supposing that you even have all the data? As a practical matter, most problems, if they are of any sufficient degree of complexity, as economic problems are, can only be solved by some iterative method. That is, you adopt some sort of trial value and then repeatedly apply a certain operation to get closer to the correct solution. But an iterative process of computation would be of no interest unless it has a tendency to converge to the correct answer. But what is that convergence if not stability of the iterative process? So this is another reason why I think stability is a very central concept.

One additional point comes to mind: What we did could be reduced to two aspects: First, formulating the *concept* of stability of the system and, second, identifying certain *categories* of stable systems. We got away from talking about the stability of a particular equilibrium point (since there can be multiple ones) and instead formulated the notion of *stability of the system* as a whole which does not ask whether you converge to a particular equilibrium but rather whether there is some equilibrium to which you converge.

Having so formulated the problem, our techniques of analysis involved the use of Lyapunov functions. (These had hardly been used previously be economists; at least I cannot at this moment think of a prior use. Typically, stability was studied through the properties of characteristic roots.) The advantage of this method is that you do things globally rather than starting from the neighbourhood of an equilibrium. This means that you can study the stability of a system even when it is subject to some big shocks and not only very slight perturbations. This was one accomplishment. The other is that we were able to identify certain categories of economies in which, in fact, a competitive system would have this property of global system stability. For example, a competitive system is stable when all goods are gross substitutes. We tried to get more general results and we also tried to see whether there are cases in which there is no stability. But we did not carry the work that far.

There were two successors who, in fact, constructed examples of instability, Herb Scarf (1960) and David Gale (1963). Their work was in a very fundamental sense complementary to ours because while we mapped out some categories of economies that were 'good' (in the sense of being stable), they mapped out some areas that were 'bad' (in the sense of being unstable).

A question left open at that stage was: Can you draw the boundary between these two categories more precisely? Even now there is a huge no-man's-land. Another problem was this: If the competitive system is not satisfactory from this point of view because it has these areas of instability (and by areas I mean categories of economies in which instability can arise), and if one would like the economy to be stable, there arises the need for design. Namely, can one in some sense 'design' the economic system so that it would have a more universal property of stability? That problem has been studied more recently, in particular in some of the work of Smale, Simon and Saari and a few others. But much of this work goes in the direction of designing a convergent *computational* system rather than of designing a mechanism that could be applied in a real economy. In any case such work is in the normative sphere rather then trying to describe the way that an actual economic process works. By contrast the study of stability of the competitive system may be viewed as a first step in understanding the workings of actual economies.

Feiwel: Do you agree that stability has different meanings in general equilibrium theory and Keynesian economics? (For example, Franco Modigliani, in his Presidential Address to the American Economic Association, observed that a private enterprise monetary economy needs to be stabilized, can be stabilized, and thus should be stabilized.)

Hurwicz: If I were describing the same issue that I think Franco Modigliani was talking about I would do it without using the word stability at all. I would rather say that what Keynes was pointing out was the possibility for an economy to get stuck in the wrong place. That is not a phenomenon of instability. If anything it is the wrong kind of stability. You see, if unemployment equilibrium were unstable, it would mean that things don't tend to stay there; they would tend to get away. But the Keynesian problem is that you can have equilibrium with involuntary unemployment and there is not an endogenous natural tendency for the system to get out of it. So to me it means rather stability in a 'bad' place, not instability. However, Franco may have had something else in mind. I am just reacting to your quotation of his comment.

Feiwel: Could you clarify for us the notions of equilibrium and dynamics?

Hurwicz: Dynamics deals with the laws of motion and change of the system. What is the meaning of the terms equilibrium and stability in terms of modern dynamics? All equilibrium is simply a position of rest. That means a position of the system such that if the system happened to start from there, it would stay there. Whereas the question of whether the equilibrium is stable or not is a question of what would happen if you were *not* to start from a position of equilibrium. And there we would have to distinguish, and I was doing it tangentially a moment earlier, between the stability of a particular equilibrium point and the stability of the system as a whole, as defined in our work with Arrow.

The stability of a particular equilibrium point is the traditional concept used in much of physics and traditional dynamic theory. It is usually defined this way: We say that a point of equilibrium is stable, if it is true that when you start from somewhere else you will tend towards that point. There are many variants of this concept, but two in particular: *local* stability means that if you start from somewhere – but not too far away – you tend to go to that point; and then there is *global* asymptotic stability of a given equilibrium point that says that no matter where you start you will be going to that point. But this kind of global stability of a particular equilibrium point can only occur if you have a unique equilibrium.

Now, in economic applications typically we do not have a unique equilibrium. There are special classes of cases (such as the gross substitutes models), with unique equilibria, but in general we do not have uniqueness. So you cannot hope to have global asymptotic stability of any particular equilibrium point. It was for that reason that we generalized the notion. We said: We are not asking about any particular equilibrium point, we are not looking at this equilibrium or that, we are only asking the following: Suppose you start from an arbitrary point (say arbitrary price, labour, quantities, or whatever), is it true that the system will converge to some equilibrium point (no matter which)? Well, in the class of situations that we studied the answer was 'Yes'. It may converge here or there, depending where it started, but it will converge to something. We then say that the *system* is globally stable; even though one or more of its equilibria are unstable, the *system* is stable. On the other hand, the examples that were constructed by Scarf (1960) and Gale (1963) had the property that, at least for certain initial positions, the system would cycle forever and would not tend to converge to anything.

Feiwel: What is the relationship of this to business cycle theory?

Hurwicz: In a formal sense, the kind of example that was constructed by Scarf (1960) could be referred to as a business cycle theory. Namely in the sense that if the economy satisfies the conditions that he assumed (a high degree of complementarity between goods, and so on) then if you trace the diagram with prices as co-ordinates they will just be going in a circle; this means that if you drew the same diagram as a function of time, it would be going up and down just like a business cycle. Thus, in a formal sense, one could call it a theory of the business cycle. But no one could seriously regard it as a theory of the real business cycle of a modern industrial economy because while it has cyclicity (which, of course, is an essential element of business cycle theory), it, so to speak, has it for the wrong reasons.

The factors that cause the cyclical fluctuations in the Scarf model are not the ones that most economists would regard as being responsible for business fluctuations in a modern economy. I am still old-fashioned enough to believe that some of the elements that Kalecki had in his model (including the lag on the construction side, and so on), while not a complete explanation of the business cycle, are pretty important. That is, I believe that investment is an important aspect of the business cycle, whereas the Scarf example does not even have production, let alone investment: his is a pure exchange model. What I am saying is that though this kind of example gets cycles, they are not really business cycles in the usual sense of the term. But from the point of view of pioneering techniques for constructing models in which one could get cyclical fluctuations (perhaps of a more appropriate kind), I regard the Scarf and Gale examples as important contributions.

Furthermore, in my opinion at least, a relevant kind of business cycle theory has to take explicitly into account the role of random fluctuations, random shocks. I myself once wrote a very brief note criticizing certain aspects of Kalecki's model (not the original Kalecki model but the later one) because I felt that if one added to it the stochastic fluctuations in a way that one ought to do it, one would not get fluctuations of stable amplitude, but an explosive phenomenon. Thus, ignoring the role of random shocks can seriously vitiate a business cycle model.

I do not feel competent to comment in detail on recent business cycle theories that you find in Lucas and others because, first, these models do involve the stochastic element that we did not have in the work with Arrow and Block and, second, because they involve the ('rational') expectational element, even though we actually had expectations in some of our papers.

In any case, speaking now of Arrow's contribution, I think that it laid a foundation for bringing together the theory of competitive equilibrium and the theory of expectations. Incidentally, that was quite natural against the background of Hicks's *Value and Capital* which has competitive equilibrium as well as a multi-period model involving expectations, although it did not have what we regard as the right kind of dynamics. But I do not believe that any of that earlier work had built into it the kind of rational expectations hypothesis that Lucas and others typically use.

For me the problem of how to study stability or cycling in multi-period models involving capital accumulation is not just a matter of finding out how the model works when these expectations are rational or self-fulfilling because the system is already in equilibrium. Rather, I would ask the following question, 'Suppose that initially people's expectations are not "rational" ' (in other words, if those expectations continued to be held, they would not, in fact, be fulfilled); presumably people notice that their expectations are not being fulfilled, therefore, they learn from those observations and modify their expectations or the way of forming their expectations. The question then is, 'In that kind of situation, will this "learning" process converge to rational expectations?' There is no reason to expect that initially the expectations are rational. But if you have burnt your fingers a couple of times and if you keep learning about things, will you finally learn and will your expectations conform to the way the world works? That is indeed likely to happen if you are dealing with an unchanging exogenous world; that is with the physical world. But the situation is different when your learning about things modifies your and others' behaviour. Because other people's behaviour has changed, what would have previously been for you the correct behaviour, no longer is. It is then not obvious that this learning process will actually converge to rational expectations. I know that there exist in the literature some contributions concerning the learning process in the context of multi-period models but I have not studied them in detail. I think such work will ultimately form the counterpart, for a multi-period economy, of the stability studies for the kind of one-period economy that Arrow and I undertook in the 1950s and 1960s.

Feiwel: With the benefit of hindsight, can you reflect on the creative genesis, on the co-operative effort, and on the strengths, weaknesses, and impact of your work with Ken?

Hurwicz: I really cannot distinguish between our respective contributions to our joint work. Nor can I tell you how we first got into this stability problem; I mean at what exact moment we started thinking about it. Perhaps Ken remembers it better than I do. I do know, however, that it emerged from our study of the statics of the programming problem.

But there is one antecedent that is worth mentioning: As you know, our original interaction took place during a summer that we both spent in Santa Monica at Rand. The work of Kuhn and Tucker and some of the other programming work, to a considerable extent, centered around Rand. Of course, much of it was done at the Cowles Commission, but that (the work of Koopmans and others) was also partly subsidized by Rand. One paper that is relevant here was written as a Rand research paper and I am not sure whether it was ever published (except in Samuelson's collected papers, see Samuelson, 1966, pp. 425–92). This was a Samuelson paper that (in part, at least) was related to gradient methods. It dealt with dynamics, because gradient methods are dynamics. In particular, Samuelson tried to apply gradient methods to linear programming models. What he found was that they were non-convergent, there was no stability. As I think now, this may have been one of the stimuli for our work, because what we did was to show how, by modifying that process in a certain way (called modified Lagrangean gradient process), one could get convergence. And there was also a rather obvious relationship of the linear programming and activity analysis models to the Lange-Taylor model (and also to the much later work by Malinvaud, which involved a similar model). So you see, you have here again the intertwining of the programming problem, stability problem, and also the design of a mechanism. Definitely this part of the Samuelson paper was at least one of the stimulating factors.

Interestingly enough, our modification of the standard Lagrangean gradient method (see, in particular Arrow and Hurwicz, 1960) turned out to be the counterpart of introducing an element of imperfect competition into the socialist economy. (Nowadays this is sometimes called non-linear pricing.) It amounted to saying, 'If the economy has strictly decreasing returns (strictly convex production sets), then the kind of thing that Lange and Lerner were proposing, with parametric prices, would work fine'. And ordinary competitive mechanism may have the right properties of convergence. But if you have constant returns (which is the linear case) or increasing returns (which is the non-convex case), what Lange and Lerner had proposed was marginal cost pricing. Now that may work out statically, but it might not have the right stability properties. Also, it might not have the right incentive properties because you are asking people to operate at a level that would result in losses. Inefficiencies could result because if you subsidize all deficits, the firms have no reason to be efficient. So we wanted to find a mechanism stable under increasing returns, and with better incentive properties.

Specifically, in our mechanism you would have the firms in the socialist economy maximizing profits, which under increasing returns is different from marginal cost pricing. If you have firms maximizing profits, their motivation is better, and if we could also make the system stable, you would have both incentives and stability in the right place. Well, it turned out that that can be accomplished (for small deviations from equilibrium) if you replace the usual model in which the price proposed by the center, is fixed and everybody treats it as a given parameter (parametric treatment of prices), if you replace it with a system in which the center proposes not just a single price but a schedule of prices varying according to the quantity you buy. Typically in our model this variation was the reverse of the usual quantity discount: The more you buy, the more you pay per unit. Locally (that is for small deviations from equilibrium) at least, this approach resulted in the proper kind of convergence. The idea may have had some antecedents in the paper by Kahn (1935), although I would have to think it through to say exactly what they were. In fact, if you start looking for antecedents, there are always quite a few. (This is as much as I can say about genesis at this time.)

Now, as to strengths, weaknesses, and impact. I have already mentioned the worthwhile aspects of these contributions. Now the weaknesses, or rather the questions that were left unanswered; well, the most immediate question that our work left unanswered was whether there were examples of instability. This was a gap which was filled by Scarf and Gale. But then, once it was noted that there can be instabilities, this opened the question whether one could think of alternative stable mechanisms that one could consider either from a normative, descriptive, or computational point of view. That work got started quite a bit later perhaps in the mid-1970s. It is by no means completed even now.

Recently two new kinds of dynamics have appeared in mathematical theory: One is the catastrophe theory and the other the dynamics of chaos. Of course, nothing is more appropriate for economics than a combination of catastrophe and chaos! I, myself have not done any work in that area, but I would mention Grandmont's two very interesting papers. One could argue that this work is filling one of the many gaps that our original work leaves.

Some of the subsequent work can be regarded as at least partly due not so much to what people found unsatisfactory in the earlier work as to what the earlier work showed concerning competitive equilibrium. (When I say here 'earlier work', I mean not just my work with Arrow and Block, but also that of Scarf, Gale, as well as other contributions.) That is, people sort of said, 'Well, it is really shocking that you economists have been talking all the time about a mechanism, namely perfect competition, that is unstable. Therefore, we must find something else, look for other mechanisms'. So, the impact was in terms of showing what still needs to be done. The reason for dissatisfaction was that cases for which we showed the system to be stable involved assumptions (for example, substitutability) that economists did not always want to make about the economic system.

My own view is that a synthesis has not yet occurred. That is, if one were to construct a plausible model of the economy, including in a meaningful way capital accumulation phenomena, I do not think we know yet whether it would be more realistic that this model be stable or unstable. Hence we should not commit ourselves to stability as a necessary feature of a descriptive (as distinct from normative) model. I think there is still an important gap there.

Feiwel: Can you trace for us the directions in which your own work has gone since your collaboration with Arrow?

Hurwicz: Since our earlier work together, our paths have somewhat diverged. In a sense, Ken's subsequent work, at least much of that which I have followed, has been more oriented towards the relevant applications in the kind of economy in which we actually live. Thus, for instance, he has done work relevant to health economics, relevant to various kinds of externalities, and on cost-benefit analysis. He has, in particular, looked at such phenomena as externalities or other non-conventional economic situations (what I call non-classical environments) to see how one can apply the economic techniques to provide some answers.

On the other hand my own work has gone somewhat in a more abstract direction, but the abstraction is perhaps only a superficial characteristic. The point is that my interest has been in a broad class of situations, broader than the advanced industrial market economies, including situations in third world countries and in countries attempting some kind of socialist approach to their problems. I have been interested in studying how one can construct efficient mechanisms that have the decentralization features similar to a market economy but that do not necessarily resemble a market. For this purpose, I formulated the notion of an informationally decentralized economy of which perfect competition is just a very special case. We know that, in certain cases, perfect competition would not work. Therefore, rather than to look for something *ad hoc* to paste on to it, so to speak, I am asking the following question, 'Supposing that I am willing to look at anything that will satisfy this criterion of decentralization (including a competitive market, but including also a lot of other things), will it at all be possible to decentralize in a given non-classical situation?' Perhaps there are situations where you cannot decentralize, no matter what you try. In fact, we know that that is the case under certain circumstances.

Of course, in order to carry out such analysis you have to have a very general notion of what you mean by decentralization. I say general, because you cannot just point to the market system and say, well, that is decentralized. (That is as if someone were to ask you what is a mammal, and you would point to a dog and say, a dog is a mammal. This, or course, does not help answer the question whether an elephant is a mammal or not.) If you are going to prove either a possibility or an impossibility theorem concerning decentralizability, you must provide a general description of what would qualify as decentralized. If you do not have a rigorous answer to that question, how can you know whether it is possible to decentralize in a given situation?

So questions that I tend to ask have been of this general nature.

They have led me to the consideration of many constructs which according to my definition are mechanisms, although they may not resemble any economic mechanism that exists or even one that I would seriously propose. I use these constructs, however, in order to explore the underlying concepts, very much as, in mathematics, people define, say, a continuous function. This definition may lead them to classify as continuous a function (say the Peano curve) that is so peculiar that intuitively you would not have thought of it as continuous. Such counter-intuitive examples help clarify the concepts.

When I say that our paths have diverged somewhat, I do not mean that Ken has not recently done a lot of theoretical work. Of course, he has. In particular, subsequent to our collaboration, is his work in the area of social choice and justice, temporal and risk aspects of resource allocation, information theory, as well as the various chapters in Arrow and Hahn (1971). This book has a lot of ideas that are at the fundamental level and go beyond what had been known before both in statics and dynamics. But its focus is on perfect competition, rather than on a more general category of mechanisms.

However, let me underline that while there is this kind of divergence in terms of the subject or area of study, even in my later work I have been influenced by Ken, especially by the structure of his possibility (or impossibility) theorem in welfare economics. What had struck me at some point about his approach was this: You define a certain concept – in his case a social welfare function – a concept that aids you in classifying outcomes of the socio-economic process as being either good or not good. You define it rigorously. Say, a social welfare function is a certain kind of function whose domain is a class of preference profiles; then you formulate some postulates, some desiderata (some attributes you would like this function to have), and this enables you to answer rigorously the question whether it is logically possible to reconcile these desiderata. Of course, the answer may be positive or negative depending on exactly how you define the concept. The first time that things had been done this way in economics was by Ken in the context of social welfare function theory. Of course, this was very important in terms of what we wanted to know about the concept of social welfare. However, beyond this, at least for me, it was also a kind of blueprint (although I was not aware of it when I started my work) for the way to proceed when developing other concepts in other areas – such as mechanism or decentralization.

In my case the concept that I was dealing with was that of a mechanism, which had never been (and this is perhaps where I will sound conceited) rigorously formulated in general. Of course, we economists talked about particular mechanisms, such as central planning, competition, but we did not have a general concept of an economic mechanism. Thus one had to define this animal that one is talking about, that is, answer the question, 'What is a mechanism?' This required the construction of a certain kind of model of the economic process. Once you have this concept, but not before, you can formulate some axioms that it might or might not obey. The mechanism's property of being decentralized – is an example of such an axiom. Once you have defined decentralized mechanisms, you can ask the question, 'Is it possible to have such a mechanism, say under specified conditions, and with efficiency? Well, if you claim it is possible, exhibit an example'. And I did that for certain cases. For example, in my earliest paper in this area (see Hurwicz, 1960), having defined mechanisms and informational decentralization, I asked whether it is possible to have an efficient decentralized mechanism even though there are indivisibilities and increasing returns. It turned out that I was able to construct a mechanism with these properties. This construction could be regarded as the proof of an existence theorem. I called this mechanism the 'greed process'. The basic idea of the 'greed process' is that whatever the other side offers you take as a minimum and then you ask for more. (Its origin was an old Polish Jewish anecdote about a young man who went to buy a suit. But he had never bought anything before. So his father told him, 'Whatever they ask, always offer half'. So when he was asked, let us say 100 zloty, he said 50 zloty. When the tailor went down to 80 zloty and he retorted 40 zloty. At the end the tailor is really disgusted, wants to get rid of him, and tells him he can have the suit free. The young man then retorts, 'Can I have two pair of pants?' The 'greed process' in somewhat similar in spirit.)

My work in this area started around 1950–51 when I was still at the Cowles Commission. I was writing a more or less expository paper dealing with activity analysis, on which I was then working, and happened to use the term 'decentralization' which was then often applied to the market mechanism as a sort of a selling point. But when I used the word 'decentralization' I thought I should explain what it meant. So I made a footnote mark, went to the bottom of the page, and began writing 'By decentralization we mean . . .' But then it struck me that I did not in fact know what we mean by decentralization. That was the beginning of many years of work trying to clarify the concept, because I thought that if we think this property is so important, we should be able to define what it is.

I then wrote a paper defining and dealing with decentralized mechanisms; it had many failings. If was very difficult to read. It could have happened (as it often happens with my papers) that it would have been in my desk drawer for many years, but Ken asked me to present a version of it at a symposium at Stanford in the spring of 1959 which resulted in Arrow, Karlin, and Suppes (1960). Since I was under the gun, so to speak, I really had to write it up. A feature of the volume was that all papers were required to be no longer than 20 pages. So the exposition had to be compressed but rigorous and complete. The limitation made it a much better paper than it otherwise would have been, but not easy to read.

I should say that the notion of desirability of decentralization was implicit in work that Ken and I did together, such as Arrow and Hurwicz (1960). In this paper we proposed a variety of mechanisms, including this imperfectly competitive socialism, and clearly what we were trying to do was to construct mechanisms that would still have the decentralization virtues of the market. I might add that at that time (certainly this was true of my work but I think perhaps for both of us) the focus was on the informational aspects of mechanisms, in particular on the parallelism of the relationship between market processes and their stability on one hand, and the convergence of iterative computational procedures on the other. We paid much less attention to the incentive aspects of the mechanisms. (However, imperfectly competitive mechanisms did involve profit maximization which from an incentive point of view is better than marginal cost pricing.)

This emphasis on information aspects was true of my own work until the late 1960s. But then I noticed that whenever I was asked to present some of my work, I would start by saying, 'Of course, the incentive problem is very important, but I will assume that people are angels and whatever you tell them to do, they will do'. Thus I was ignoring the incentive aspect and instead asking the following question, 'Could we give the decision-makers (say managers) the kind of instructions that, if followed, would make the economy run well?' But at some point I decided that since I know people are not angels, perhaps I should not completely ignore the incentive aspect.

At that stage I tried to see how one can formalize the incentive issue. Initially I was thinking of it in rather informal terms, something along these lines: Les us say a country has some economic problem, for instance its balance of payments is in bad shape, as in pre-war Poland. What would it do? It might, say, introduce exchange controls (you must not export money, and so on). But what happens then? People figure out ways of exporting money, one has an uncle in London, others overinvoice or underinvoice . . . all the usual tricks. You could of course put them in jail or shoot them. But that is a distinct failure of economics, isn't it? Because what economists should be able to do is to figure out a system that works without shooting people.

So this led me to the notion of incentive compatibility of an economic system. What I meant by this was a system of rules designed in such a way that people would have an incentive to obey these rules. If the system is incentive compatible, you do not have to threaten criminal punishment in order to get compliance. But this does not necessarily mean just maximizing profits. So the question is, 'Could one design a system (a combination of taxes, subsidies, trading rules, and what not) that would work as one would want it to work (that is, achieve its goals) even without coercion or compulsion?'

Two questions arose, 'Where does such a problem come up in standard economics?' and, 'What are the analytical tools to analyze it?' As for where it comes up in standard economics, there were two areas. One, most fashionable, was Samuelson's work on public goods where he said that the Lindahl solution for public goods would not work because people will lie, but also stated more generally that no decentralized system will work. Of course, as soon as I see the word 'decentralized' I am aroused, especially when such a strong negative assertion is made. So this was one thing that started me.

The other area where the issue arose had to do with managerial incentives in the Lange-Lerner mechanism. There the managers of state firms were told: Even if you are a monopolist, behave as if you were a perfect competitor (that is, be a price taker). Well, if I am such a manager I have two possibilities. One, if I am on a fixed salary, I ostensibly do what Lange and Lerner tell me, but I am not going to knock myself out to be efficient. So that is not so good.

Alternatively, the state could say, 'We want you to maximize profits while treating prices parametrically, and to encourage you to do it, we will give you 10 per cent of the profits'. In fact, that is what is happening now in many socialist countries. Now, if you do that, the manager really wants to maximize profits. Since he wants to maximize profits, he would be better off to behave like a monopolist, rather than a perfect competitor. But the rules prohibit it, they require that he act as a price taker. The question then is whether he could ostensibly (by the books) behave like a competitor (price taker), while in fact behaving like a monopolist (price setter). It turns out that he could do precisely that. Thus this led me into this study of the question whether, generally speaking, especially with the problem of fewness of numbers, perfect competition is incentive compatible, as some have tended to assume. Well, that was the other area in which I then got involved.

In both areas the basic analytical tool I used was the concept of Nash equilibrium.

Feiwel: In that connection, do you believe there is a 'love-hate' relationship between game theory and general equilibrium?

Hurwicz: There certainly is no conflict between the game theoretic approach and this kind of 'generalized general equilibrium'. Here I would like to make a clarifying comment. Many people, when talking about 'general equilibrium theory', mean 'general *perfectly competitive* equilibrium theory'. Whereas I mean a theory of equilibria for *whatever mechanism* one happens to be dealing with, not necessarily of the perfectly competitive mechanism. If one is using certain kinds of responses to differences between supply and demand, then it is a perfectly competitive equilibrium. But one might be using some other rules of the game, and one would still have general equilibrium theory, but no longer general perfectly competitive equilibrium theory, of course. But when we speak of *general* equilibrium theory, we mean this as distinct from what? Well, as distinct from *partial* equilibrium where you do not take into account the roundabout feedbacks through the impact on the rest of the economy.

In that sense, I would certainly classify what I am doing as general equilibrium theory, because it is a theory of the whole economy and it takes into account the indirect feedbacks as well as the local, immediate, first-order feedbacks, but again it is not just *general* competitive equilibrium. I mean it is not necessarily competitive although some of my models provide a game theoretic interpretation (through Nash equilibrium) of Walrasian (that is, competitive) equilibrium. In these models the mechanism is different from the usual competitive mechanism, that is the rules of the game are different, but the outcome of the game is precisely what Walras would have liked. That is, at the rest point of that mechanism the resulting resource allocation is precisely the same as if people played according to the Walrasian rules. (That the rules of the game are different from the usual Walrasian ones is not surprising because it has been shown that the classical Walrasian mechanism is not incentive compatible with a finite number of economic agents.) So, as I see it, there is no conflict between game theory and general equilibrium.

Feiwel: You were one of the first to write a classic review of von Neumann and Morgenstern (1944). I would like to ask you to comment on Morgenstern's attack of Arrow-Debreu general equilibrium models for misusing the term 'competition' which to him (like in Adam Smith) should be used in a dynamic sense of rivalry, game, bluff, and so on.

Hurwicz: I would like to distinguish between the question of terminology and the question of substance. As far as terminology is concerned, I would tend to agree with Morgenstern. His comment is not a valid criticism of the substance of the Arrow-Debreu theory, but this theory does use the term 'competition' in a way that is quite different from traditional usage. In fact, for that reason, say, in my teaching (and especially when I was lecturing in China), I do not use the term 'competitive equilibrium'. Rather I use the term 'parametric price equilibrium'. The advantage is that unless the audience heard my definition, it would not have a clue as to what this term means. So they are not misled by the traditional meaning of the term competition. But my definition of parametric price equilibrium is the same as the definition of competitive equilibrium used by Arrow, Debreu, and Koopmans. So the question is, 'What is the relationship between the two concepts?' I agree that the kind of thing that I call parametric price equilibrium (which is not just Arrow-Debreu, it goes back to Walras) is not really competition in the everyday sense of the term.

You see, a basic story, underlying the Arrow-Debreu contribution, that is most frequently told is the 'auctioneer story.' There is an auctioneer who announces prices; he asks people, 'If this were the price how much would you buy, how much would you sell?'; he adds up the responses, and if they do not balance adjusts prices. This then is the 'Walrasian' idea of the competitive or market process. But I agree that it does not have that element of competition that expresses some notion of rivalry. So, for example, when someone says 'you know you live in a very competitive world' it means not only that I have to be clever, but I have to be a little more clever than the other fellow; there is an element of rivalry, absent from the Walrasian auction. However, when it comes to the notion of what kind of equilibrium prevails, I would argue that if Morgenstern had formalized his idea of a (rivalrous) competitive economy, it would have turned out to have the same equilibrium that Arrow-Debreu or Walras have. so that even though the term 'competitive' may be misleading when applied to the kind of *scenario* that is being told about it, I do not think it is misleading when we think of the equilibrium *position* of an economy that is perfectly competitive in the sense used by earlier economists. We can ask ourselves what would have been classically an essential element – not of the competitive *process* but of the competitive *equilibrium*. Certainly, that supply has to be equal to demand, right? You cannot do without that. Secondly, if you talk about perfect competition, it involves the assumption that no one firm or individual can significantly influence market prices. So, that means you treat prices parametrically. And certainly, all these models involve selfish behaviour; that is profit maximization and utility maximization. The equilibrium that you will get out of that, when that process comes to rest, will be the same as the equilibrium that Arrow, Debreu, and Koopmans are talking about. But if you wanted to get a scenario of a competititive process, it would look very different.

There is one additional point, a kind of technical footnote. In earlier times when people talked about the perfectly competitive market, in order to justify the assumption that individual economic units could not affect the price – and that they knew that they could not – it was assumed that there were very many economic units and that they were all relatively small as compared with the market as a whole. (The term was: an 'atomistic' market. Today the term, taken from measure theory is 'non-atomic.') On the other hand, the Arrow-Debreu theory is applicable even if you had only two consumers and three firms, or any other number, such as one consumer and one firm. What then is the difference? What Arrow and Debreu are saying is the following: If it were so that *for any reason* people treated prices parametrically (even though in fact they could influence prices, but supposing they do not take advantage of that power and instead act as price takers), then such and such would happen at equilibrium. So then you might well ask: Is this price taking behaviour likely to happen in a capitalist economy in sectors with few firms? The answer is 'No'. So where is the theory applicable? Well, it is applicable in an 'atomistic' (= 'non-atomic') economy, and in principle also in a Lange-Lerner economy – because in such an economy the managers are instructed to ignore their market power even if they have it, and it is assumed that they obey the instructions. From that point of view, what is called a competitive equilibrium in the Arrow-Debreu sense, if you do not assume large numbers and infinitesimal units, is really a theory of equilibrium in a Lange-Lerner economy. But it happens that the relevant properties of such an equilibrium are the same whether you have three firms or a million firms. So the Arrow-Debreu theorems are valid both for Lange-Lerner economies and also in what traditionally would have been called competitive 'atomistic' markets.

Feiwel: What do you make of Joan Robinson's criticism that neoclassical theory stresses exchange and ignores production?

Hurwicz: I really do not think that this is true. Certain aspects of production important for the accumulation process used not to be taken into account by the earlier neoclassical models. However, there are now many models of capital accumulation. Some of them, take into account the irreversibility of investment. Also, these models do not always assume decreasing returns everywhere; some use what in my time was called a Knightian curve; that is, a production function first with increasing returns and then with decreasing returns. Still in their general approach these models are neoclassical, but with this term more broadly interpreted. So, I would say that if this comment or criticism was ever valid, it is not valid now. It may be that there are still some aspects of the capital accumulation process, such as time dimensions, that are not adequately taken into account. But as far as the emphasis on exchange is concerned, this is mainly true of elementary microeconomic textbooks, because that is the easiest part to teach.

Feiwel: do you consider the 'Sraffian revolution' a challenge or merely a subset of neoclassical theory?

Hurwicz: I have at various times tried to study Sraffa's model. I know that there are individuals or even centers where people are just devoted to this approach. (That was and perhaps still is, for example, true of the Department of Economics in Bombay.) I think people with Marxian inclinations find that model to be a bridge between the verbal formulations of Marx and the more mathematized type of formulations that we use now. It did play that role. But I do not see it as a 'revolution'; I do not think it is part of the mainstream. I think that it appeals to Marxists, or 'radically'-inclined economists, among others, for the following reason: It is an incomplete model. It has left in it an element of indeterminacy as between the wage rates and profit or interest rates, this indeterminacy to be resolved by non-economic forces, by some sort of power struggle – which I think accords with their sociological view of the capitalist system. But I feel that a model must be complete to be analyzable. Also, the Sraffa model is limited because it postulates linearity everywhere. It may have stressed certain points to which we should have paid attention, but is not sufficiently complete to be used for general development of theory.

Feiwel: Some economists have differentiated between the classical and neoclassical general equilibrium theories. Do you consider this valid?

Hurwicz: Of course, different people use different terminologies. One place where you can see a lot of reference to classics is Keynes's *General Theory*. Depending on when you live you can draw the distinction between classical and something else. Say, for people who lived in the early 1900s it would have been natural to say that Smith was a classic, but Walras was a neoclassic. When I hear the term 'neoclassical model' now, I think of a production function that is strictly concave, twice differentiable, has the value of zero at zero, . . . a very nice, smooth curved kind of model that is not at all like the Walrasian which was mostly linear. so I would not call Walrasian neoclassical.

Feiwel: One possible distinction that has been suggested is that the classics were concerned with the problems of surplus, growth, and the like, whereas the neoclassics are concerned with allocation of existing resources between alternative uses. Do you agree?

Hurwicz: I would say this: It is certainly true that in the early phases of this more recent work, whether you call it neoclassical or whatever, attention was focused on *a*temporal models. For example, that is the case of the Arrow-Debreu paper. But starting already with the Malinvaud paper in 1953, and continuing through a tremendous literature by Majumdar, Cass, and a variety of other people, there is by now a very rich body of work that is considered to be neoclassical, dealing not with some given resources but with the problem of efficient or optimal capital accumulation. (It still is not a business cycle theory.)

I would say the distinction you mentioned is based on a somewhat narrower interpretation of neoclassical economics than what I understand it to be. If the comment you quote had been made in 1952 I might have considered it justified, but by 1984 I would think it invalid.

However, there is still another problem. When attacking questions that have not previously been studied, the easiest setting in which to study them may well be a pure exchange economy. Thus the history of such investigation is such that when you have a new kind of problem, one that perhaps requires a new set of analytical techniques, you start out by studying it in a pure exchange economy; then you build into it production, but still only as a one-period problem; and only then do you go to intertemporal models. In particular, this has been true of my own work in the theory of economic mechanisms.

Since I do not accept the interpretation of the term neoclassical as atemporal and confined to pure exchange, the question is what is my concept of neoclassical and in what sense can neoclassical economics (as I interpret the term) be regarded as narrow? Where I think it is narrow, is that typically it makes assumptions such as continuity and convexity, and rules out externalities, indivisibilities, and increasing returns (although, as I mentioned, there are by now models using Knightian production functions.) But a theory that rules out externalities and indivisibilities is not a good basis, for say, giving advice to countries like India or China as to how they should run economies in which externalities and indivisibilities are very important.

For these reasons, I myself feel that neoclassical theory (even in my interpretation) is not as broad as economics should be, and part of my own work has been an effort to get out of those confines. So that while I may still be using some of the techniques, I do not confine myself to the neoclassical world. I ask: What would be a good way of running the economy if we did have indivisibilities. Well, there is virtually nothing in the neoclassical framework that will tell you anything about that. So, the kind of theory of mechanisms in which I am interested, at least some parts of it, deal precisely with the problem of what happens when you go outside of the neoclassical framework.

Feiwel: Would that also apply to the question of relaxation of the assumptions of maximization and of perfect rationality (bounded rationally)?

Hurwicz: Well, this is a very different kind of question. There are two aspects to assumptions of maximization. On the one hand, maximization may be a descriptive behavioural assumption, in the spirit of 'positive' economics. We may assume for instance, that consumers try to do something that we call utility maximization subject to the budget constraint. That kind of behavioural assumption I tend to maintain in my own work. On the other hand, there may be raised the question of assumptions concerning rules to be followed by managers of large enterprises, or of bodies supplying public services, in order to achieve efficiency of the economy as a whole. Here I am in the normative sphere and there I do not necessarily retain the assumption of profit maximization, because the question of what rule the managers should follow is precisely the unknown of my problem.

I do not know the proper way of providing public services, of running the infrastructure, of running the biggest chunks of our industry which are highly indivisible, and so on. There I am asking, 'What should we do?' To say that it should be done by perfect competition begs the question. Under increasing returns you could not do it even if you tried. There a competitive equilibrium does not at all exist. But even where competitive equilibrium is logically possible, the question is what 'rules of the game' would lead us to it. That is the problem of 'implementation.'

I think that the neoclassical approach has arrived at a point where it has a large body of mutually consistent ideas, so it is, if nothing else, a sort of fairly complete toy. We know more about that kind of world than other ones. Even though our assumptions are not realistic, we know at least how the world would run if it operated under those assumptions.

The point I am making is this: We know that there are oligopolies, bilateral monopolies, and the like, but we really do not have (perhaps for technical reasons) a generally accepted theory telling us, say, to what extent taxes are shifted to consumers in the presence of imperfections. I do not mean to say there is no general imperfect equilibrium theory. We have a few models, as for example Negishi's. But all that is much more controversial; it involves disputes about the appropriateness of Nash equilibrium or some other kind of equilibrium and so on. So we are on much less secure ground here. For that reason there are a great many problems which it is easiest to tackle, at least at first, in the neoclassical framework.

Here is an analogy: There is this special strain of mice that have been bred for many years, a very pure strain, but perhaps not very viable in the outside world; however, they can live in the laboratory, and you can try all kinds of experiments on them. The results of such experiments can be valuable provided we do not try to apply them directly to ordinary mice. I have a similar view of the neoclassical model. I think the neoclassical model is of great intellectual importance, but it is not ready or appropriate to be sold 'as is' to an imperfect outside world.

Feiwel: In this connection, I would like to ask you a general question. If I would have to explain to students to what extent you, Arrow, and Debreu have enriched our knowledge and understanding of the economic system, how should I go about it?

Hurwicz: Well, let me talk about Arrow and Debreu. I think to appreciate what they (and McKenzie) have done is to compare the situations that existed before their work and since. Suppose that you want to study the question of how sales taxes are shifted in a certain economy. You want to take into account various indirect repercussions, income effects, and the like. Therefore, you have to have a general equilibrium system. So, you take pencil and paper and you try to set up some kind of either model or diagram or equation system to study this. Of course, before you can reach any kind of conclusion you have to make some assumptions (whether the production function is convex or concave, and other things like that). Imagine that you have a list of these assumptions and you are going to reason from them. Now, it is quite possible that, in the kind of world that you have postulated, competitive equilibrium would not in general exist, that is, that the assumption of prevalence of (perfect) competition is inconsistent with some of the assumptions that you have made. In that case all your conclusions are of no interest because from an inconsistent set of assumptions any conclusion can be drawn. Essentially what Arrow and Debreu have done, and this may seem like only a technical contribution but it is a very fundamental one, is to teach economists how to set up systems of assumptions about which they could be sure that they are not vacuous. I would say that this is their most fundamental contribution.

Secondly, if you look at the optimality problem, you know we have these classic propositions as to relationship between optimality and economic equilibrium. Walras was actually the first who tried to treat this subject in an analytical manner, but he did not have the tools that we now have. In particular he did not have the concept of Pareto optimality. As a result, his approach was considered, and I think with some reason, to be tautological. In other words, Walras defined optimality as having certain elements of competitive equilibrium, so naturally, what came out as optimal was competitive equilibrium. Schumpeter, criticized him for that in the early 1900s. Then in the 1930s, the so-called new welfare economics developed. Somewhat slowly people tried to develop an argument about the conditions under which competitive equilibrium would be optimal. But if you wanted to know what assumptions are actually needed in order to be able to make this claim, there simply was no coherent statement, although there were some inklings already in Pigou. The first statement that actually was in the modern spirit was that of Lange (1942), except that it used the tools of calculus rather than those of topology and convex sets and was therefore at a lower level of generality. But the clear and complete relationships between optimality and competitive allocations are first found in the equilibrium results due to Arrow (1951 [*2nd Berkeley Symposium*]), Debreu (1951, 'The Coefficient of Resource Utilization', and 1959 [*Theory of Value*]), and Koopmans (1957 [*Three Essays*]) and constitute a basic part of this neoclassical framework. If you look at where we were, say, before 1940 as against where we have been since 1960, there simply is no comparison.

There is still a further point. As we know, there are two basic theorems of welfare economics. The first one that says that if it is a competitive equilibrium, it is optimal. But that proposition could again be vacuous, because, for instance, if you have increasing returns, it is not possible to have a competitive equilibrium. Then one question is, 'When is this theorem non-vacuous?' This is answered by the existence theorems. But there is still another problem. Suppose that your social value judgements tell you that you would want to have not just any Pareto optimum, but a particular Pareto optimum (for example, one characterized by a certain degree of equality or equity or fairness or whatever you wish to call it). Then the question is: Is it possible to accomplish this objective through the competitive mechanism? An answer is to be found in the second theorem of welfare economics. This proposition, found already in Lange (1942), although not in its most modern form, then in Arrow (1951), as well as in Debreu, Koopmans, and some others, tells us under what conditions it would be possible, at least with the help of lump sum taxes, subsidies, and asset transfers, to achieve, at a competitive mechanism equilibrium, an arbitrary Pareto optimal resource allocation. At present we are more sophisticated and say, lump sum tax is not good enough. (It may be impossible to avoid incentive effects.) But the formulation and proof of the two theorems was a major step toward developing a theory that would enable one to analyze the question of the extent to which it is possible to bring about some sort of equity together with efficiency.

Nothing like that existed until these theorems appeared. I do not mean to say that there were not some ideas. But, for instance, if you study Pigou – who was the father of welfare economics – in his writings in the 1920s and 1930s – you will find that the criterion he used for optimality was the maximization of what he called national dividend or ideal output. The trouble with that was that in order to talk about national dividend (roughly what we call GNP or NNP) you need prices to construct it. Well, what kind of prices are you going to use? If you are going to use competitive prices you are really begging the question because if you do not know that competition is good, how do you know that competitive prices are the appropriate ones for evaluating national product? So I think that there was nothing that was philosophically acceptable until these welfare economics theorems were rigorously formulated in the modern way. But it is true that if one looked very hard, early forms of these ideas, could already be found in Pareto or in Edgeworth. However, it was not done in what we now consider a 'right' way until the period starting in the early 1940s and ending in the 1950s.

Then, the same kind of problem began to be studied in the capital accumulation theory, namely the relationship between the market mechanism and efficiency or optimality in intertemporal capital accumulation models. It was Malinvaud who already in his 1953 paper showed that profit maximization in intertemporal models with infinite horizons is not sufficient to guarantee efficiency, in contrast to the situation in atemporal models. Well, no one ever knew that, prior to this kind of rigorous mathematical analysis. Similarly, until the Scarf (1960) instability model was constructed, people who did not think very much about it, took it for granted that somehow competitive equilibrium has to be stable. Even now in popular expositions, people advocating free markets argue that if preferences or technology change, there will be an adjustment towards the right kind of equilibrium. Rigorously expressed, this popular recommendation for the market process is equivalent to asserting the stability of the competitive process. Well, if it were not for the question first having been posed, and then knowing under what conditions there is stability and under what conditions there is not, we would be completely at a loss to know to what extent or under what circumstances this assertion is justified.

Not everything that has come out of this work is a total surprise, but prior to it there was no coherent, logical setup that was known to be internally consistent and that would allow rigorous analysis. For example, if one wants to study the impact of taxes, one essentially grafts taxes on to a kind of Arrow-Debreu model. That is actually how it is put on the computer. As I said earlier, I do not think that such procedures are always adequate because, in fact, we have elements of imperfect competition. Therefore, I feel a perfectly competitive model is not good enough for many applications. But prior to the Arrow-Debreu work one could not have at all analyzed the problem in a general equilibrium framework, even for a perfectly competitive economy.

Feiwel: To what extent has Arrow and Hurwicz (1960) enriched our understanding of the Lange-Lerner economy?

Hurwicz: I would say that we provided a possible dynamics. This had not been previously analyzed in a systematic way because in the mid-1930s, when Lange and Lerner were writing about socialism, there was no theory of general equilibrium dynamics. What we did was to apply gradient-type dynamics which, as I mentioned earlier, had at least some parentage in the Samuelson analysis. We showed under what conditions you could have that kind of a system if people were willing to follow the rules (in other words, ignoring the incentive issue) and that, in fact, you could arrange it so that at least under certain conditions the process would converge to the right solutions. This had not been done before. On the other hand, it was only the first such attempt and it had its weaknesses although there was nothing wrong with it logically or mathematically. A short time later Malinvaud, for example, proposed an alternative to our dynamics. The reason he gave for wanting an alternative was to make sure that you should be able to stop the iterative process, so to speak, anywhere in the middle and still be sure that you are at a feasible resource allocation. Our process did converge, but if you stopped it at an arbitrary step of the iteration you might find yourself in an infeasible zone. Of course, our process was of *tâtonnement* nature, so only asymptotic feasibility was claimed for it. One can argue for one or the other approach, because in using the Malinvaud approach there are certain other (informational) difficulties. But in any case, I would not want to overstate the enduring value of the particular dynamics that we proposed. We showed, however, that one can rigorously analyze Lange-Lerner type economies not only statically, but also dynamically. If you know that the equilibria are OK, you would naturally ask, 'But how will we ever get to it?' Depending on our interpretation of the iterations, we need either an economic mechanism or a computational process to get to a desirable equilibrium from an arbitrary initial (disequilibrium) position. What we proposed could be interpreted either as a decentralized economic mechanism or as a certain kind of computational process, although as a computational process it would not now be regarded as sufficiently speedy or efficient. At least we showed how to construct this kind of a procedure. That I think is what is useful about it.

Feiwel: Without detracting from their contributions to general equilibrium theory, can you tell us in what sense the visions and techniques of Walras, Hicks, and Samuelson were deficient and how did they differ from Arrow and Debreu?

Hurwicz: Well, I would not accept that 'deficiency' characterization. I would rather talk in terms of stages of development. We could define three such stages: The pre-Samuelson calculus period (in particular Hicks, but also Kaldor and a few other people), then the era of Samuelson, Lange, and some others, and then the new era that started with Arrow, Debreu, Koopmans and others. The question is of the difference between these periods. Let me try to answer this in an indirect way.

When I was myself doing mathematical economics (equilibrium, dynamic stability) around 1945, I was following the methods due to Lange and Samuelson and this approach was giving sensible answers. Then there came the linear programming models, in particular those of Koopmans and Dantzig, and then Kuhn and Tucker who branched out into non-linear models. Initially, to me at least, the linear programming model seemed totally unrelated to the kind of things that economists do. You know, economists always had nice curved production functions while linear programming models had everything straight or angular. And some economists had said, that if you have constant returns to scale, things become indeterminate and that is not a good model to work with. Yet the linear programming people seemed to be getting interesting results with their models. So I thought, well, maybe this is good for those who have to solve a particular kind of programming problem, but it is not economics.

But the field continued to develop in several ways. Samuelson provided economic interpretations of linear models. Then non-linearities were introduced (by Kuhn and Tucker) and this already looked more like traditional economics–you could have decreasing returns and conventional utility functions. Also, linear programming had dual variables which could be thought of as prices. This enabled Koopmans and others to interpret certain rules as profit maximization. So this looked more and more like the economics of the market process. At the same time those models, especially in the linear phase, were simple enough. They did not use any calculus at all. It looked like elementary geometry or algebra or, at most, geometry of convex sets. However, we (at the Cowles Commission) had the good luck to be associated with first-rate mathematicians who would not accept the idea of just looking at a diagram. Rather, they would say, first of all we have to see whether your system of inequalities has a solution at all, and so on. So the habit of rigor, of establishing the non-vacuousness of a model, of checking whether or not a solution is unique, became a part of the regular procedure. And this habit carried over into situations of greater mathematical complexity.

At that point there were two tracks: One where you had very formal ways of doing things, but in a model that did not quite yet seem like ordinary economics, and initially without the use of calculus. The other, of the Samuelson-Lange variety, using (advanced) calculus, with less insistence on formalism. This is what underlies, for instance, Hicks's appendix and Samuelson's *Foundations*. (Of course we should remember that Samuelson's work dates from the late 1930s, even though it was published later.) When it became clear that the linear programming models are dealing with the same phenomena as traditional economics, the qestion was whether it would be possible to have a synthesis. The need for it was clear. For example, by calculus techniques, you could not do anything that would involve a production function with a straight line up to a point, then a kink, then another straight line. And yet such a function might have come out of engineering analysis. Through those linear models you could handle that kind of thing, but by the techniques of traditional theory, you could not.

So two things had to be done. One was to integrate the two kinds of worlds, the two sets of assumptions, the other to combine the greater power and flexibility of the calculus kind of analysis, characteristic of the Samuelson-Lange approach, with axiomatic structure and rigor characteristic of the work in linear models. (When I refer to the flexibility of calculus methods, I mean that you could use the techniques of calculus to determine say the impact of a sales tax or, more generally, for various questions of comparative statics, while activity analysis techniques would be an awkward tool for such problems.) So, the problem was how to synthesize these two approaches. One step in that direction was the Kuhn and Tucker paper, which provided theorems of which one special case was the linear activity analysis model, while another special case was the kind of situation that could have arisen in traditional production and economic theory. However, it only dealt with programming models, not general equilibrium.

The first aspect of synthesis in a general equilibrium context was carried out in the Arrow-Debreu paper (1954) and Arrow (1951) with Wald and von Neumann as precursors; there the general equilibrium linear model was one special case, and the traditional general equilibrium model that Hicks, Samuelson, or Lange had in mind was another. Arrow and Debreu (1954) showed the essential common features of these two types of models and made clear that, say, the presence or absence of a kink in a production function is quite unimportant if we want to know whether or not equilibrium exists, whether or not it is optimal.

This synthesis covered many kinds of models in addition to those two special cases. For instance, you could have a production function with a piece that is linear and a piece that is curved. Furthermore, this synthesis used the tools of convex set theory and topology with precisely the same rigor that previously had only been characteristic of the linear models. This was the foundation of a rigorous approach to general equilibrium theory, hence a major advance.

Let me make one more point. The original contributions were contained in a few papers in *Econometrica* and other journals. They were then popularized in several books such as Debreu (1959), Koopmans (1957), and Arrow and Hahn (1971). What is characteristic of all these contributions is that they have roughly the same level of generality. In particular, they hardly ever use smoothness (that is existence and continuity of derivatives, absence of kinks, and so on) as one of the assumptions. In particular, therefore, they do not use calculus, except in dynamics. As far as describing equilibrium is concerned, you will not find a symbol of the derivative. That, of course, is a very extreme contrast to the previous Samuelson-Lange generation.

But then, starting in the late 1960s, a new period began, actually initiated by Debreu himself, perhaps partly under the influence of mathematicians a floor above him in Evans Hall. What he and some others found at that point was this: While certain theorems (such as existence and optimality) can be proved with great generality without using any smoothness assumptions, other questions that one might want to ask cannot be answered without postulating smoothness. Using smoothness assumptions means that the conclusions will be applicable to a narrower class of situations, but you will be able to say more about them. One example of a problem where smoothness assumption was used was the question of how many equilibria there could be. So, this more modern theory (perhaps you can call it neo-classical), that started roughly with a presidential address by Debreu in 1969 (Debreu 1970) has gone back to using calculus, but based on rigorous topological foundations. Instead of being at the level of an advanced course in differential geometry and topology; it is more complex, more difficult to follow, but also more powerful. And it has given us back the advantages of flexibility that goes with the use of calculus.

In my own experience, when I teach certain parts of welfare economics or a microeconomics course, I still, very often, use the Samuelson type analysis. I find it is much closer to the intuitive understanding of what is going on and, if I know what I am doing, it will provide me with correct answers. But the general theory that came later will tell me where I am safe and what I should not try to do. Also, this general theory tells us where we can get by without making strong specializing assumptions that previously might have seemed necessary. Thus the power of our analysis has been greatly increased both in theoretical and applied fields.

The level of mathematics used in economic theory has increased steadily. Also, new branches of mathematics were created by mathematicians and were found particularly appropriate in economics.

The lag between their introduction in mathematics and utilization in economics has shortened a great deal.

To illustrate this let me go back to the problem of existence of equilibrium. This problem was posed by Walras (although there may have been precursors). Hicks, more than half a century later, pointed to what he called this 'sterile' business of Walras–counting the number of equations and unknowns. Well, the reason why Walras was doing this was that he wanted to make sure that his system had a unique solution, that it was neither overdetermined nor underdetermined. But the only way that he knew how to do it was by what we would now regard as elementary college algebra where a first step in determining the solvability of a linear equation system is to count the number of equations and unknowns. (But this is not quite enough; you have to check whether certain determinants are not zero.) The great merit of Walras was that he perceived what seemed to be the more general problem. If you had asked him, 'What if some equations are not linear', he might have said, 'It probably works roughly the same'. Now Walras had a very limited mathematical education. But suppose he had been very sophisticated and suppose that he had tried to do something as Arrow and Debreu did in the 1950s. Well, the basic tool they used was a so-called fixed-point theorem. But this theorem did not exist in the nineteenth century. The first fixed-point theorem was proved by Brouwer, around 1910 or 1915 I think. And actually it was not good enough for the economist's purposes. Arrow and Debreu used the Kakutani theorem for multi-valued functions. That appeared much later, I think in 1941. So the point is, that the kind of problem that was posed by Walras with respect to existence could not really be solved by the mathematics that existed in his time, at least not with the generality that was needed.

Now if you ask about stability theory, the local stability of equilibrium was studied from ancient times on, beginning with Aristotle (or his students) and Archimedes. Later Lagrange did important work, but the classic foundation of our modern studies is a paper by Lyapunov that was published in the Annals of Toulouse, about 1907 or 1908. This is also much after Walras. So, it is not surprising that Walras (as well as, independently, Marshall) only studied stability in a very intuitive way, in a very simple case and only for a one-commodity market. Subsequently, Hicks tried to generalize stability analysis to multi-commodity markets, but without using what by then did exist, namely the Lyapunov theory of stability. So

Walras had a much better excuse than did Hicks, although he failed to use even those stability techniques that were already known in his time.

Basically, it was Samuelson who acquainted the world of economics with modern dynamics and stability theory. I think that he was the first economist who knew the Lyapunov-type theory, and that, initially, at least, most other economists learned it from him. However, Samuelson was not the first economist to study dynamics rigorously. The first three I am aware of were Kalecki, Tinbergen, and Frisch. Of Frisch's dynamics work I only know a simple macromodel. Kalecki analyzed stability mostly in a geometric way, basically by a stairway (cobweb) kind of diagram. Tinbergen also had a very simple, essentially cobweb, type of model dealing with the cycles in shipbuilding. But in my view, as a branch of general equilibrium, economic dynamics did not exist before Samuelson. He was the first one, for instance, to write down the differential equations of what we now call the dynamic Walrasian (as well as Marshallian) dynamic *tâtonnement* models, with the rate of change of prices an increasing function of the difference between demand and supply (dually for the Marshallian process). This was a major step forward.

Even though Samuelson did not primarily study business cycle theory, he constructed in 1939 a simple but self-consistent (Keynesian) model of a business cycle theory (Samuelson, 1966, pp. 1107–10). He showed how, with two simple difference equations, you could algebraically explain in three minutes why you would have continuing fluctuations and how the nature of these fluctations depends on the magnitude of the marginal propensity to consume.

REFERENCES

Arrow, K. J. (1951) 'An Extension of the Basic Theorems of Classical Welfare Economics', in J. Neyman (ed.), *Proceedings of the Second Berkeley Symposium on Mathematical Statistics and Probability* (Berkeley: University of California Press) pp. 507–32.

Arrow, K. J. (1979) 'The Property Rights Doctrine and Demand Revelation Under Incomplete Information', in M. Boskin (ed.), *Economics and Human Welfare* (New York: Academic Press) pp. 23–39.

Arrow, K. J., H. D. Block and L. Hurwicz (1959) 'On the Stability of Competitive Equilibrium II', *Econometrica*, 27:82–109.

Arrow, K. J. and G. Debreu (1954) 'Existence of Equilibrium for a Competitive Economy', *Econometrica*, 22:265–90.

Arrow, K. J. and F. Hahn (1971) *General Competitive Analysis* (San Francisco: Holden-Day).

Arrow, K. J. and L. Hurwicz (1956) 'Reduction of Constrained Maxima to Saddle-point Problems', in J. Neyman (ed.), *Proceedings of the Third Berkeley Symposium on Mathematical Statistics and Probability* (Berkeley: University of California Press) pp. 1–20.

Arrow, K. J. and L. Hurwicz (1958) 'On the Stability of Competitive Equilibrium I', *Econometrica*, 26:522–52.

Arrow, K. J. and L. Hurwicz (1960) 'Decentralization and Computation in Resource Allocation', in R. W. Pfouts (ed.), *Essays in Economics and Econometrics* (Chapell Hill: University of North Carolina Press) pp. 34–104.

Arrow, K. J. and L. Hurwicz (1977) *Studies in Resource Allocation Processes* (Cambridge: Cambridge University Press).

Arrow, K. J., L. Hurwicz and H. Uzawa (1958) *Studies in Linear and Non-Linear Programming* (Stanford: Stanford University Press).

Arrow, K. J., S. Karlin and H. Scarf (1958) *Studies in the Mathematical Theory of Inventory and Production* (Stanford: Stanford University Press).

Arrow, K. J., S. Karlin and P. Suppes (eds) (1960) *Mathematical Methods in the Social Sciences* (Stanford: Stanford University Press).

Arrow, K. J. and M. Kurz (1970) *Public Investment, the Rate of Return, and Fiscal Policy* (Baltimore: The Johns Hopkins Press).

Debreu, G. (1951) 'The Coefficient of Resource Utilization', *Econometrica*, 19:273–92.

Debreu, G. *Theory of Value* (New Haven: Yale University Press).

Debreu, G. (1970) 'Economies with a Finite Set of Equilibria', *Econometrica*, 38:387–92.

Debreu, G. (1972) 'Smooth Preferences'. *Econometrica*, 40:603–15.

Gale, D. (1963) 'A Note on Global Instability of Competitive Equilibrium', *Naval Research Logistics Quarterly*, 10:81–87.

Hurwicz, L. (1960) 'Optimality and Informational Efficiency in Resource Allocation Processes', *Mathematical Methods in the Social Sciences*, K. J. Arrow, S. Karlin and P. Suppes (eds) (Stanford: Stanford University Press).

Kahn, R. F. (1935) 'Some Notes on Ideal Output', *Economic Journal*, 45:1–35.

Koopmans, T. C. (1957) *Three Essays on the State of Economic Science* (New York: McGraw-Hill).

Lange, O. (1942) 'The Foundations of Welfare Economics'. *Econometrica*, 10:215–28.

Malinvaud, E. (1953) 'Capital Accumulation and Efficient Allocation of Resources', *Econometrica*, 21:233–68.

Neumann, J. von and O. Morgenstern (1944) *Theory of Games and Economic Behavior* (Princeton: Princeton University Press).

Samuelson, P. A. (1966) *The Collected Scientific Papers of Paul A. Samuelson* J. E. Stiglitz (ed.) 2 vols (Cambridge, Mass.: MIT Press).

Scarf, H. (1960) 'Some Examples of Global Instability of the Competitive Equilibrium', *International Economic Review* 1:157–72.

Wald, A. (1936, 1951) 'Über einige Gleichungssysteme der mathematischen Ökonomie', *Zeitschrift für Nationalökonomie*, 7:637–70, translated by O. Eckstein, 'On Some Systems of Equations of Mathematical Economics,' *Econometrica*, 19:368–403.

PART II
Vision, Method, Application

5 Arrow's Vision of the Economic Process

Christopher Bliss

1 INTRODUCTION

The concept of *vision* is due to Schumpeter (1954). A writer reveals his vision through his approach to economic problems and by the problems which he selects for close investigation. It follows that a vision is not typically located in the explicit assumptions of economic theory, although its trace can be seen there, but more typically it is to be found in the unstated assumptions, what critics often call the 'implicit assumptions', which characterize a writer's work. As Schumpeter (1954, p. 41) puts it:

> Obviously, in order to be able to posit to ourselves any problems at all, we should first have to visualize a distinct set of coherent phenomena as a worthwhile object of our analytic effort. In this book, this preanalytic cognitive act is called Vision.

Although it is sometimes supposed that the implicit is somehow underhand and disreputable, this idea cannot be conceded. Every argument must take something for granted, and a complete lack of selectivity concerning what to pick out and emphasize would lead nowhere.

We talk of vision in connection with great economists, those of the highest standing in their time. This is first, because it is only possible to distill out a vision when an economist has thought long and deeply, and when his thoughts have given rise to a considerable body of literature. And secondly, it is worthwhile to do so only when there is a measure of greatness. Clearly Kenneth Arrow, as one of the leading economic theorists of the present time, is in the category of writers whose vision should be considered.

Before embarking on the examination of Arrow's vision we must consider the possible objection on the grounds that the concept was developed by Schumpeter in connection with the discussion of historical figures, in most cases no longer alive when Schumpeter wrote, and that to apply it to a contemporary economist, indeed to a man still writing at a formidable rate, amounts to an abuse.

In assessing this objection one should distinguish between the claim that it is illegitimate to talk of vision where a living figure is concerned, and the separate claim that certain difficulties are encountered when a writer is a contemporary. To the first point one need only answer that if the idea of vision is useful and insightful in considering the work of Ricardo or Marshall, then it is very difficult to see why it should not eventually apply to the work of Arrow. The second point, however, has some force. There are problems in looking at the work of an economist from too close a vantage point. What seems to us significant and interesting may not appear so in 100, even 50 years' time. Probably some contemporaries of Stanley Jevons, for example, thought that it was for his sunspot theory of the trade cycle that he would chiefly be remembered. But the risk of writing what may in the future seem dated is one worth taking where the subject is as interesting as the work of Kenneth Arrow.

2 THE CONTENT OF A VISION

Evidently the notion of a 'preanalytic cognitive act' may embrace many different kinds of orientation and it would be unfortunate to restrict the application of Schumpeter's concept to the consideration of only some kinds of vision. True, for Schumpeter the idea of a vision is very much tied up with the elusive and subtle question of the relation between ideology and economic theory. But even this permits one vision to differ from another, not simply in what it posits, but also in *what kind* of point of departure it represents. However, two particular subjects of vision are encountered so frequently that we may reasonably take them to be of central importance. They are:

1. Assumptions concerning the institutional nature of the economy.
2. The selection of the questions which are taken to constitute the central economic problem.

It is useful to borrow Schumpeter's telling phrase 'Vision of facts and meanings' to distinguish between (1) and (2) above. Thus institutional presumptions will be referrred to as *vision of facts* and theoretical standpoints as *vision of meanings*. Naturally these two concepts are not necessarily disjoint and the vision of a particular writer will typically contain elements of both. John Maynard Keynes's vision is held by Schumpeter to have already been 'clearly formulated in the first pages of the *Economic Consequences of the Peace* (1919)', and is described by Schumpeter (1954, p. 1171) in these terms: 'the arteriosclerotic economy [of England] whose opportunities for rejuvenating venture decline while the old habits of saving formed in times of plentiful opportunity persist.' Leaving aside the question of whether this is the right description of Keynes's ideas, what we have here is the attribution to Keynes of a particular vision of facts.

Examples of visions of meaning are readily obtained from the examination of the history of economic thought. Of crucial importance is the conception of what we now call *general equilibrium*. To quote Schumpeter (1954, p. 242) again:

> Now Cantillon and Quesnay had this conception of the general interdependence of all sectors and all elements of the economic process in which – so Dupont actually put it – nothing stands alone and all things hang together.

But there are other visions of meaning as well. Concerning Marx, Schumpeter (1954, p. 573) writes:

> Based upon a diagnosis of the 1840's and 1850's that was ideologically vitiated in its roots, hopelessly wrong in its prophecy of ever-increasing mass misery, inadequately substantiated both factually and analytically, Marx's performance is yet the most powerful of all. In his general schema of thought, development was not what it was with all other economists of that period, an appendix to economic statics, but the central theme.

It is hoped that this broad introductory discussion will have made clear what is meant by a vision, and it will have shown how this concept provides a valuable way of viewing an economist's work. The time has come to apply the concept to Kenneth Arrow.

3. ARROW'S VISION OF MEANING

There is no precise manner of determining the content of a man's vision, for the exercise is inherently a somewhat subjective one. But it is clear how one should go about the exercise. The evidence is the corpus of writing of the economist concerned which is examined to determine which institutional aspects of reality have particularly made themselves felt, and which view of the economic problem, meaning the problem of economic analysis, emerges. After reading widely (which very often was re-reading, of course) Arrow's copious writings, and thinking about the question, I have come to a clear view in my own mind of what Arrow's vision amounts to. I offer it as an impression without any suggestion of authority or finality. It is indeed particularly difficult to make any statement which would be good for all of Arrow's work for its breadth and variety is one of its extraordinary features.

It comes as no surprise, with an economist of Arrow's breadth and stature, to discover that his vision encompasses both fact and meaning. Here I am concerned with meaning, what it is that is taken to be the problem for economic analysis. Arrow's view of economics I shall argue is the view of a *planner*. By this designation I do not intend to imply that he is a proponent of economic planning as it is usually understood. He is not, for example, an advocate of the direction of economic activity by a centralized state apparatus, although some of his work impinges directly on the question of how such a means of organizing economic activity could be made effective (see Arrow and Hurwicz, 1977). But if one considers what the problem of economic planning amounts to, then one may see how much of Arrow's way of doing economics falls into that approach.

Arrow himself seems to lend support to the idea that economic planning was an important component of his vision from the outset when he writes (1984a, p. vii) about his early orientation in the subject:

> My ideal in those days was the development of economic planning, a task which I saw as synthesizing economic equilibrium theory, statistical methods, and criteria for social decision making. I was content to work on the separate pieces of this task and not seek a premature synthesis.

It is striking indeed to consider that these words describe how Kenneth Arrow viewed the economic problem as a young graduate economist. They could easily be taken as a retroactive description of what was to be his life's work.

The economic planner must first clarify his objective, and secondly he must design a means of implementing that objective, translating it, that is, into an allocation of resources. The planner's objective is what economists call a *social welfare function.* The feasible allocation of resources is a requirement of *general economic equilibrium.*

The connection between economic planning and the social welfare function was quite explicit in the development of Arrow's thought. In an autobiographical note which prefaces his paper on 'A Difficulty in the Concept of Social Welfare' as included in Volume 1 of his collected papers, Arrow (1984a, p. 3) writes

> I was invited for the summer of 1948 to the then-new RAND Corporation, which was trying to develop game theory as a tool for analysis of international relations and military conflict. During one of the coffee breaks (which frequently provided more intense intellectual challenge than the work in one's own office), Olaf Helmer, one of several logicians at RAND, told me he was troubled by the foundations of this application. Game theory was based on utility functions for individuals; but when applied to international relations, the 'players' were countries, not individuals. In what sense could collectivities be said to have utility functions?

Arrow volunteered the Bergson social welfare function as a solution to this problem. Olaf Helmer asked him to write an exposition showing how this would be achieved. Three weeks later Arrow knew that it could not be achieved and he knew exactly why. The essential form of the argument of the thesis that eventually became *Social Choice and Individual Values* (Arrow, 1951) was already complete.

4. THE MARKET AND PLANNING

If a competitive equilibrium exists, and if it is the state to which the economy will take itself, then the market system is, in the broad and general use of the word 'planning', an instrument of planning. This is the idea which gave rise to the concept of 'market socialism'. However, notice that a capitalist market system is a planning system of a restricted kind.

Economic planning involves the allocation of available resources in such a manner as to maximize an objective – the social welfare function. The market system, however, allocates without waiting to be given its objective function. We know that special assumptions are required to ensure that the market system will allocate well, even on the basic test of Pareto efficiency. But even allowing those assumptions which then define an ideal case, the market allocates as if it had been given a particular objective function, one which it defines itself simultaneously with the solution to the allocation problem.

Given N agents, each with a concave utility function defined over his final allocation, and given initial resources and the transformation possibilities implied by production technology, we may derive a *utility possibility set* U that consists of the levels of utility for the individual agents which may be feasibly attained subject to resource constraints. This set U is convex[1] and may be supported by a hyperplane at any point on its boundary. The coefficients of the support plane at a point on the boundary of U are weights such that an allocation giving rise to the utility levels corresponding to that point maximises the weighted sum of utilities, using those weights, subject to production possibilities.

If we start with a given distribution of resources, skills, etc., and let the system find a competitive equilibrium, we have, in effect, solved a planning problem the objective function of which is defined implicitly, in the manner described above. With the usual assumptions of no externalities or absent markets, the efficiency in the sense of Pareto of this equilibrium is assured, but its optimality is highly questionable. For allocation through the competitive market reflects strongly the principle 'to them that have shall be given'. How well a family will do and what weight will be given to its utility, will be much influenced by the resources or skills which it has at its disposal, by their quantity and by their scarcity.

In the judgement of a good many, these features of the market system condemn it from further consideration. In reading Arrow one encounters the sense of this innate failing of the market. The questions of redistribution and of economic justice are ones to which he often alludes and frequently returns. However, the aversion which any sensitive observer must feel when confronted with the market's patent disregard of the interests of those who cannot pay up for what they need, is balanced in Arrow's writing by two clear recognitions.

First there is the recognition, amounting almost to an awe, of the possibilities for the efficient allocation of resources which the decentralized market system represents. This, of course, is the market's role as a solver of the problem of economic planning. The second recognition follows from Arrows clear understanding of the difficulties that confront the attempt to give to our general and intuitive ideas concerning just distribution and redistribution a precise and finished shape.

To take this last recognition first, Arrow's liberal and egalitarian sentiments cannot be doubted. There is no connection between his reticence concerning redistribution and the active principled hostility to redistribution that marks the writings of Robert Nozick (see Nozick, 1974). Instead there is a gap between what one feels Arrow would like to be able to show, and what can be shown. Indeed, for Arrow, it is not fortuitous that there should be a difference between his private and individual tastes in matters of general economic allocation and anything that would earn the title 'social welfare function'. As he trenchantly expresses the point (Arrow, 1967a):

> Indeed, I would go further and argue that the appropriate standpoint for analyzing social decision processes is precisely that they are not the welfare judgments of any particular individuals ... 'Social Welfare' is related to social policy in any sensible interpretation; the welfare judgments of any single individual are unconnected with social action and therefore sterile.

The claim that Arrow's view is the view of a 'planner' has seemingly been somewhat undermined by the conclusion, very much his own, that a well-defined and appropriate objective function – an essential feature of planning as it has been described – cannot be derived. However, the recognition that the social welfare function is a highly problematical construct still leaves us with the allocative role of the market system, and the potential of the market as an *efficient* allocator is unaffected by those problems.

That Arrow is impressed by the allocative function of decentralized markets is clear from his writings. He has, of course, submitted economic equilibrium to as ambitious and refined analysis as it has received at the hands of any economist. But some economists never really consider their models as more than toys, though those toys may occupy years of study. Such is not Arrow's philosophy. In a fascinating review of the first two volumes of Samuelson's collected papers, Arrow, (1967b) chides the great man for the smallness of his faith in 'the relevance of neoclassical price theory'. In a subsection of that paper headed of 'The Usefulness of Neoclassical Price Theory', Arrow writes with evident feeling:

> Obviously, I believe firmly that the mutual adjustment of prices and quantities represented by the neoclassical model is an important aspect of economic reality worthy of the serious analysis that has been bestowed on it; and certain dramatic historical episodes – most recently the reconversion of the United States from World War II and the postwar European recovery – suggest that an economic mechanism exists which is capable of adaptation to radical shifts in demand and supply conditions. On the other hand, the Great Depression and the problems of developing countries remind us dramatically that something beyond, but including, neoclassical theory is needed.

It is a curious feature of contemporary economics that if one were to attribute to Arrow the view that the allocative role of the price system is to be taken very seriously, without giving the game away be revealing his name, many people would imagine someone whose attitude to the market system fell little short of idolatry. For the view is rife that the market system is not merely an important allocator with great potential, but a *perfect allocator*. This is not and never has been Arrow's view. That it is not is in part a reflection of his exact and meticulous study of equilibrium theory. It sometimes seems that the touching faith in the market system is more the product of a process resembling religious conversion than of deep study. To understand fully Arrow's refusal to advance extravagant claims for the price system we need to examine another aspect of his vision.

5. ARROW'S VISION OF FACTS

The second essential element of Arrow's thought, his vision of facts, has to do with the way in which he views the institution of *markets*. This view is closely tied up with his feeling for the importance of *information* and *communication* in economic systems. And this in turn is the view of the *economic planner*. So it is, after all, that visions of fact and value are never wholly separate or clearly distinguishable.

To some theorists a market is an abstraction, no more; an idealized representation of the process of exchange. Arrow's vision concerning the market is different: it is realistic and institutional. This is not to say, of course, that Arrow is uninterested in frank idealizations of markets. Such could hardly be supposed of the great co-architect of what has come to be known as 'The Arrow-Debreu model'. Yet there is no doubt that pure general equilibrium theory is not for Arrow an end in itself. Its interest for him springs from its role as a point of reference for the evaluation of the performance and potential of real world markets.

For Arrow 'market imperfections' are not an accidental irritation which the theorist must do his best to brush aside; they are an essential and normal feature of economic life. I remarked above that if the only clue to my subject's identity were to be that he takes very seriously the allocative role of the market mechanism, then few would guess his name. If, on the other hand, the clue were to be that the following are his words, then most economists would at once say 'Kenneth Arrow'. And it would not be from a recognition of the text of a lecture to the Federation of Swedish Industries (Arrow, 1973):

> There is an element of trust in every transaction; typically, one object of value changes hands before the other one does, and there is confidence that the countervalue will in fact be given up. It is not adequate to argue that there are enforcement mechanisms, such as police and courts; these are themselves services bought and sold, and it has to be asked why they will in fact do what they have contracted to do.

It is because Arrow recognizes what it is that the market system is required to do, and here his guide is the Arrow-Debreu model, that he is so painfully conscious of the shortcomings of real world markets. Arrow the planner feels satisfaction when he considers the received model of consumer behaviour, a satisfaction that his vision of facts, and his theoretical acumen, prohibit him from extending to decentralized allocation through markets. As he puts it in his Presidential Address to the American Economic Association (Arrow, 1974a):

> It can be and has been correctly objected that our models [of consumer behaviour] are too simple; we ignore other arguments in the utility function – power, status, social approval, or whatever – that also motivate individuals, and we ignore some constraints,

> capacity for calculation and social controls. But the model is comprehensible and the motives and constraints we deal with are real and important
>
> The market, on the other hand, is a much more ethereal construct. Who exactly is it that is achieving the balancing of supply and demand? Where in fact is the information on bids and offers needed for equilibration actually collected and stored? Right from the beginning of neoclassical theory, the difficulty of explaining markets in terms of individual self-seeking behavior was perceived.

6. CONCLUSION

Classification has a way of glorifying the inessential. A catalogue of Beethoven's musical innovations does not explain in what way he was greater than his contemporaries – the music tells that story. Similarly, Arrow's vision, even if I am right about its content, is the least important aspect of his work. Some indifferent scribbler could well think like an economic planner and see real markets as imperfect realizations of the Walrasian ideal. One waits to know, what did he do? It is not for his vision that we revere Arrow, but for what that vision gave rise to. Indeed the nonentity who thinks like an economic planner, and so forth, will hardly have a vision, more a style and some opinions.

A vision is something grander, more refined. No doubt it is true that the shape of a vision is formed while an economist is young. With Kenneth Arrow that certainly seems to have been the case. But only hard work, and much thinking and writing, builds the early orientation into a finished vision. The relationship between vision and writing is one of fruitful interplay. The vision guides the work and selects the path, but the work itself feeds back to the vision and makes it solid.

It has been said of John Stuart Mill that he believed too much in the rationality of his fellow men. Arrow is too clear-headed to nurse illusions but he might be said to share Mill's weakness for rationality. To borrow his words (Arrow, 1974b):

> I want to discuss here the relation between society and the individual in, I would like to say a rational spirit, but let me be more particular, in the spirit of an economist. An economist by training thinks of himself as the guardian of rationality, the ascriber of rationality to others, and the prescriber of rationality to the social world. It is this role that I will play.

One could go further. What I have called planning is much the same as rationality applied to the allocation of economic goods. And when he refuses a fairy-tale specification of how markets function Arrow has *reasons*. His work stands as a monument to what unbending rationality can achieve in economics.

NOTE

1. Given two allocations of resources A_1 and A_2, a convex combination of A_1 and A_2, denoted A_3, involving the same convex combination of the allocation for each agent, is feasible if the production technology is convex. But as the utility functions are concave, the utility levels of A_3 are not less than the same convex combination of the utility levels of A_1 and A_2. Hence U is convex, as required.

REFERENCES

Arrow, K. J. (1951) *Social Choice and Individual Values*, Cowles Commission monograph no. 12 (New York: Wiley).

Arrow, K. J. (1967a) 'Values and Collective Decision Making', in P. Laslett and W. G. Runciman (eds), *Philosophy, Politics and Society*, 3rd series (Oxford: Basil Blackwell) reprinted in Arrow (1984a).

Arrow, K. J. (1967b) 'Samuelson Collected', *Journal of Political Economy*, 75:730–37.

Arrow, K. J. (1973) 'Information and Economic Behavior', reprinted in Arrow (1984b).

Arrow, K. J. (1974a) Limited Knowledge and Economic Analysis, *American Economic Review* 64, reprinted in Arrow (1984b).

Arrow, K. J. (1974b) *The Limits of Organization*, The Fels Lectures, 1970–71, Norton, p. 16.

Arrow, K. J. (1984a) *Social Choice and Justice*, vol. 1. of Arrow's collected papers (Oxford: Basil Blackwell).

Arrow, K. J. (1984b) *The Economics of Information*, vol. 4. of Arrow's collected papers (Oxford: Basil Blackwell).

Arrow, K. J. and L. Hurwicz (1977) *Studies in Resource Allocation Processes* (Cambridge: Cambridge University Press).

Nozick, R. (1974) *Anarchy, State and Utopia* (New York: Basic Books).

Schumpeter, J. (1954) *History of Economic Analysis* (New York: Oxford University Press).

6 Economic Theory and Mathematical Method: An Interview

Robert J. Aumann

Feiwel: Would you say that Arrow has a mathematical bent of mind?

Aumann: Absolutely. He is an extraordinarily clear thinker. His mathematical acumen never ceases to amaze me. Very deep and complex kinds of mathematics are not his forte, but he both understands and is able to produce subtle mathematical arguments; he is a very good mathematician. Several of the most important ideas of this century in mathematical economics are due to him.

Take the existence of competitive equilibrium, which has by now become a commonplace. When it was discovered in the early 1950s it was an extraordinary tour de force of deep mathematical thinking. Of course, that was done by Arrow and Debreu, but it was actually discovered independently by each. That idea alone is one that identifies Arrow as a first class mathematician – the very idea of applying a fixed-point theorem in the way in which it is applied, the making of that connection, that is an extraordinary idea.

In my opinion the important mathematics is not necessarily the most complex, involved gymnastics that one can do. The really important pieces of mathematics are those that can be reduced to at most a few pages. An idea that is more complicated than that will eventually be forgotten. Arrow's mathematical work falls into that lasting category of things that are very far from obvious but are still basically simple – simple, not in the sense of easy, but in the sense of clean, like the best modern architecture.

Feiwel: How have these aesthetic and profound mathematical ideas improved our comprehension of the economy and society?

Aumann: Your question, of course, does not relate to Arrow in particular but to all of mathematical economics. It is a subject on which one cannot say much that is sensible in the framework of an interview. In *Frontiers of Economics* (edited by Arrow and Honkapohja) I have an article entitled 'What is Game Theory Trying to Accomplish?' in which mathematical economics is also treated. Very briefly, if one tries to do economic theory without using mathematics – that is, purely verbally – one gets the impression that one can reach any conclusion. Anything can be done with words, but afterwards one is not sure where one stands, what has been shown, what has not been shown, and what it is all about. When one presents economic theory in a formal model, then one can show that certain assumptions necessarily lead to certain conclusions. Mathematics imposes a discipline of thought; it forces one to think clearly.

Mathematics has been called the language of science. That also sums up its relation to economics very well.

There is another aspect that bears mention, and that is the interdependence, what could be called the ecology. In an economy, like in a biological environment, all things hang together; change one, and everything else will change, usually in ways that are far from obvious. One of the tasks of mathematics is to try to see, at least qualitatively, where such changes might go.

Of course, one must add immediately that once one has a model, and one has a set of assumptions and a conclusion, if it remains in mathematical form, it is not worth very much. You have to be able to translate it back into words. But then at least you have something to back up the words, so that if someone asks you, 'Now just what do you mean by that?', it is easy to say precisely what you do mean. If you cannot explain it in words, it is not worth very much; but if you can *only* explain it in words, it also is not worth very much.

Feiwel: Is there a fundamental difference in approach between game theory and g.e.t.?

Aumann: There are probably two fundamental methodological differences. The more important one is that the theory of games is much more general. It refers to any situation of human interaction. A specific situation like a market would be an application of the general theory of games. G.e.t. refers only to a specifically defined situation and does not apply any further than that. So that the domain of game theory is much more general. The other, less important, difference is that by definition, g.e.t. is not specifically interactive; that is, the protagonists react to prices rather than reacting to each other in the way that they do in game theory. What differentiates game theory from economic theory in general is that economic theory consists of a number of specific models tailored to specific situations with no wider applications, whereas game theory is a sort of unifying theory that in principle covers everthing.

Feiwel: What do you think has been the influence of game theory on Arrow?

Aumann: Arrow has done a lot of work in applications of non-co-operative game theory to specific economic environments, as distinguished from works in a general game theoretic set-up. The only one of that kind – and it is, of course, an extremely significant exception – is the work on social choice theory, which is basically axiomatic, co-operative game theory. It is, of course, one of the great milestones of his life.

Arrow is fundamentally an economist. He is interested in economic problems. He has contributed an enormous amount to information economics, and that is very closely tied into game theoretic ideas. So there is another link.

Feiwel: Are the young mathematically sophisticated economists shifting away from g.e.t. towards game theory?

Aumann: There is some of that. Arrow would be one of the first to emphasize the limitations of the g.e. model. In fact, he feels a little uncomfortable with the g.e. model, also because of its anti-socialist implications. The idea that the market leads to efficiency is something that is foreign to Arrow's emotions, so that he is happy to see the limitations of the model and to see that there are many ways in which the market can fail (information, public goods, what have you). He emphasizes that one of the lessons of modern economics is the manifold ways in which the market mechanism can fail to yield efficiency, the ways in which the imperfections manifest themselves.

As I said before, game theory provides a tool that allows one to analyze just about any interactive situation; that would include all the various aspects of market imperfections that will lead away from efficiency. All these are amenable to game theoretic analysis. Perhaps this is a reason for the shift. Basically, game theory is a wider ranging tool than the g.e. model, which is quite limited in the kind of situations with which it can deal.

Feiwel: Would you care to comment on Arrow's views of the selfish motive, co-operation and trust?

Aumann: There is one theme in game theory that lately has been getting increased attention and that is: What is the connection between selfishness and co-operation? Can one derive co-operation from purely selfish motives? That is related to the interaction that has recently been growing between evolutionary biology and game theory. One would like to think of the selfish motive and co-operation not as being opposed to each other, but as dovetailed; of co-operation as the consequence of selfishness.

But it is not at all certain that Arrow would go along with that. His point of view, as I read it, is that co-operation, helping other people, the socialist ideal, that sort of thing, is a supreme value that he would like to take as a starting point. Whereas he is too wise to take it for granted that everybody behaves in this way, there is something deep inside him that hopes that people do behave that way, and he sometimes acts as if that hope were a reality.

Here is an anecdote: An issue that comes up perennially in the Econometric Society is the method of electing fellows. That, of course, is a jewel of an issue for the Econometric Society; it is social choice in the home of the social choice experts. Lately one of the issues that has come up in that connection is that of strategic voting. This means taking into account how others might vote, rather than simply voting one's true preference. For example, in the US in 1980, somebody who preferred Anderson, but voted for Carter because he thought Anderson had no chance, was voting strategically.

There is a sort of counterpart to Arrow's famous impossibility theorem, due to Gibbard and Satterthwaite, that says that whenever there are more than two alternatives, *any* non-dictatorial election method is subject to strategic voting. In addition to its great theoretical interest, this has important practical implications. Strategic voting introduces noises into the system; rather than voting what they think, people try to outguess the other voters. The result may well involve significant distortions. Practically, one would like to build the incentives so as to minimize these distortions.

Specific, practical, real-life implications of theory have always fascinated me; the problem of minimizing strategic voting in the election of fellows caught my imagination. It seemed paradoxical and incongruous that just the Econometric Society would ignore incentive effects in its own voting mechanisms; the message seemed to be, 'theory is OK for making a living, but for heaven's sake, let's not take it seriously in practical affairs'. I discussed the matter with Arrow, expecting to find a sympathetic ear from the founder of social choice theory. He did express interest, but little real enthusiasm for the issue. He himself does not vote strategically; somehow he feels that it is unbecoming that, as scholars and gentlefolk, the Fellows of the Society should engage in such practices. I have assured him that I do; I play the game by its rules and I see nothing even remotely immoral or unethical about it. But whereas intellectually he recognizes that some people do vote strategically, emotionally there is something in him that rejects this. He does not want to bother with that kind of thing and expressed surprise at my involvement. As an economist he recognizes the importance of incentives; but as a humanist, he cannot get terribly excited about them in a practical context.

I have dwelt on this at some length because it illustrates nicely the dualism, the intellectual tension in the man.

Feiwel: Does game theory assume much greater rationality of agents than g.e.t. and if so why?

Aumann: No, I would not buy that. I think that the amount of rationality assumed is basically the same. Obviously it is too much. One of the purposes of the 1985–86 programme at the Mathematical Sciences Research Institute (Berkeley), of which Arrow is a member, is to explore the consequences of bounded rationality. But before one does that, one has to formulate precisely the idea of bounded rationality. On the other hand, perhaps full rationality is not such a bad assumption; it is a sort of idealization, like the ideas of perfect gas or frictionless motion. Idealizations have always been very fruitful in science. To some extent people do behave rationally; the idea of full rationality is no less valid than any other scientific idealization.

Feiwel: Specifically, what do game theorists mean by rational behaviour?

Aumann: Utility maximizing behaviour, just as economists do. Each person maximizes against the given situation as he perceives it. This does not imply full information; no matter what your information is, you have to have some estimate as to what might happen, and you maximize against that.

Feiwel: Am I correct that you are not overly impressed with 'satisficing' and 'bounded rationality' in Herb Simon's sense?

Aumann: My criterion for judging any piece of science is how effective it is, where it leads, whether it leads to insights, to a considerable body of work, to better understanding. There are two different criteria: One is, how plausible are the assumptions? The other is, where do the conclusions lead? Many people use the first criterion – *a priori* plausibility of the model – as the criterion for judging a piece of work. But I prefer the second criterion: Where does it lead? The usual assumptions of utility maximization have led to practically all of economic theory, and at least some of that helps us to understand the world. The idea of satisficing and other ideas of that kind that abandon the model of full rationality are extremely attractive as hypotheses. If I ask myself, do I satisfice or do I maximize utility? I have to answer that I satisfice. So the concept is very attractive as an assumption, but I do not know of any general conclusions to which it leads. It is not that the concept *cannot* lead to anything. A coherent model of bounded rationality could very well lead to interesting results, and people are beginning to generate such results now. But up until now they had not led to any significant body of theory or indeed to anything very startling.

Feiwel: Did game theory revolutionize our understanding of how the economy really works?

Aumann: The revolution has been in method, in the way we think about economic problems. Game theory is a tool, not a product. There have been hundreds of applications. Take the idea of Nash equilibrium; it is a method, a tool of analysis; it is not in itself an economic insight, but it leads to economic insights. For example, there is an enormous amount of interest in auctions nowadays. How do you analyse auctions? You formulate them as incomplete information games and you look for their equilibria; Nash equilibria, perfect equilibria, sequential equilibria, and various related ideas. You apply them to specific, real-life auctions and you get outcomes. These things are very important. Oil-lease auctions are held in which the values of the properties easily reach 100 million dollars in one auction. Game theory contributes in a very practical, down-to-earth way, in addition to providing general, theoretical insights.

We talked before about Arrow's work in game theory. One of the pieces of work he did about a dozen years ago was the application of game theory to analyzing racial discrimination in the job market. It is enormously important to understand what part of discrimination is just cussedness and ignorance, and what part of it is really rational given the circumstances. And if it is rational given the circumstances, how can we change those circumstances? What can we do about it? How can we change the situation, so that the incentives are structured against discrimination? The tools one uses are game theoretic.

Game theory also enables one to attack better such problems as the economics of health insurance, labour relations, etc. In cooperative game theory you have core analysis. For example, Al Roth recently discovered that the way that interns are assigned to hospitals in the US is described exactly by an algorithm for finding a point in the core of the corresponding market. Another example is the application of the Shapley value to voting situations where you try to get representation for various districts in accordance with the 'one man – one vote' rule. It is a methodology that enables you to analyze all kinds of situations, and in that sense it has indeed revolutionized our ways of thinking.

Feiwel: Since your work on the continuum of traders figures prominently in this volume, can we overcome your natural reluctance to talk about yourself and explore the creative genesis of this work?

Aumann: One day I received in the mail an article written by Milnor and Shapley – an analysis of voting in a situation in which there are some large voters and what they called an 'ocean' of small voters. Afterwards Shapley wrote an article applying this to a corporation with two large stockholders; the many small stockholders constitute the 'ocean'. It was an analysis, using the Shapley value, to investigate power relationships. The idea caught my imagination; it was a beautiful paper. This was in the winter of 1960–61. Then in the summer of 1961 there was a conference on Recent Advances in Game Theory at Princeton University. Herb Scarf gave a paper there that was a forerunner of the Debreu-Scarf paper on the core of an economy, and an outgrowth of previous work by Shubik (and by Edgeworth). Scarf's model had a denumerable infinity of traders, divided into a finite number of types, and he got an equivalence theorem between the core and the competitive equilibrium. However, this model had various defects. For example one had to be careful about how one defined the sum for this denumerable infinity. I remembered the paper by Milnor and Shapley about 'oceanic' games when hearing Scarf's model and said to myself, 'surely, the continuum just *has* to be the right way of doing that'. It was really putting these two ideas together that was the genesis.

A few minutes ago we were discussing applications of game theory. The continuum was a purely game-theoretic idea. The way Milnor and Shapley originally thought of it was not at all in an economic context and had nothing to do with the core. Then came Scarf's model of the core in an economic context. So ideas coming from one place fit nicely into another, completely different, place. That kind of interaction is one of the most important ways in which game theory contributes to economics. Since game theory is not constructed with a specific application in view, it is sufficiently broad so that ideas from one context apply to others as well. One is able to tie things together, to see the common underlying principles. Indeed, it is one of the significant ways in which science operates in general – making connections, seeing the big picture.

Feiwel: In your paper 'What is Game Theory Trying to Accomplish?' you have a wonderful passage about game theory and mathematical economics as art forms. Could you enlarge on this idea?

Aumann: The best art is something that strikes a chord with the viewer or listener. It expresses something that the viewer or listener has experienced himself and it expresses it in a way that enables him to focus his feelings or ideas about it. You read a novel and it expresses some kind of idea with which you can empathize, or perhaps something that you yourself have thought about or experienced. Take a sculpture or a cubist painting. It expresses some reality, some insight, in an ideal way. That is what the best mathematical economics does. It is a way of expressing ideas, perhaps in an ideal way.

Feiwel: In the same paper you mention that 'our fields are by no means the only ones in science that are not strong on predictions and falsifiability; in which the measure of success is "does it enable me to gain insight?" rather than "what will be my observations?" Similar in this respect are disciplines like psychoanalysis, archeology, evolution, meteorology and to some extent even aerodynamics'. Can we explore this further?

Aumann: This is a theme that Arrow has expressed repeatedly. One of his favourite examples is meteorology. We are good at explaining what makes the weather, but we are not very good at predicting it. We have not become much better since Arrow did meteorology in the Second World War. We are significantly better, but the significance is only three or four percentage points. With all our satellites and the like we still cannot predict the weather. And that is what is happening in economics. Perhaps we understand economics a little better, but we are still not very good at predicting what will happen.

In this connection, let me tell you an anecdote. I was on the Hebrew University committee that oversees the doctoral theses in the experimental sciences. I came across this thesis in meteorology explaining and predicting the weather on a perfectly round island in an otherwise empty ocean extending over an infinite plane. Well, I thought, that is wonderful. Like many people in economic theory, I have a tendency to breast-beating. After seeing that thesis, I thought, 'welcome to the club'. The author was not at all bothered by such questions as the realism of assumptions. This kind of work makes an important contribution, however, because once we understand how the weather behaves in such a situation, perhaps we can understand how the weather behaves in different situations, where the island is not perfectly round and the ocean not infinite. Perhaps it provides us with some qualitative insights that are applicable elsewhere.

Feiwel: A few sentences before the cited paragraph you mention that 'the sciences are the children of our minds; we must allow each one of them to develop naturally, and not force them into molds that are not appropriate for them'. Could you enlarge on that theme?

Aumann: We should not try to think of economics as physics or chemistry. Ernst Mayr has written a book entitled *The Growth of Biological Thought* (which, by the way, I first saw in Arrow's office and borrowed from him). Mayr makes the point repeatedly that biology is not physics and that one should not try to apply to it criteria like falsifiability, that grew out of the philosophy of physics. They are inappropriate for biology, and I think that they are inappropriate for economics also. One cannot get very far applying that sort of criterion in economics. We have to understand that in physics one generally expects a unique result from any given situation. Even in theory one cannot make that kind of prediction in economics. Thus we often have situations where all kinds of circumstances, in addition to those described as economic ones, are operative and are going to affect the outcome. When you have a competitive equilibrium that is not unique, how can you say even in theory which one takes place? A lot of economics involves index numbers of various kinds, indexes in the sense of averages. You can say something about how you estimate a situation without being able to make a clear prediction.

There are many areas where falsifiability is not the criterion. When you study evolutionary biology you are totally unable to falsify anything. You are explaining the past; it is important to understand the past also. Falsifiability is definitely not the only possible criterion for a useful scientific theory.

Feiwel: I understand that in physics the fundamental question of existence of equilibrium was only explored much later after the concept of equilibrium had been in use for some time (similarly as in economics). Can we have your reflections on the importance of the question of existence in economics?

Aumann: Existence is an important issue, but not a *primary* one. Your model must have interesting substantive implications before it makes sense to study existence. Sometimes people introduce a new concept, discuss the definition a little, prove existence, and then call it a day. I do not find that kind of work very interesting.

Once one has a model or concept of established interest or usefulness, like competitive equilibrium, then it becomes very interesting and even vital to establish conditions for existence, to delineate the domain of the concept. It is the boundary of the domain that is important. Non-existence is as important as existence; one needs to understand what kind of conditions can be destabilizing. In the study of competitive equilibrium, it is as important to know that non-convexities or discontinuities can lead to non-existence as to have the existence theorem itself.

Feiwel: Are there any developments in mathematics at present that are likely to have a profound influence on economics?

Aumann: One answer is suggested by the particular marriage we have this year (1985–6) at the Mathematical Sciences Research Institute (Berkeley) between mathematical economics and complexity theory; the implication being that complexity theory – a relatively recent development in mathematics – will have an important influence on economic theory. But I think that it is often very difficult to tell beforehand what kind of discipline will have a significant influence. In the past we have had the influence of global analysis, differential geometry, measure theory, convex analysis, and the like, and nobody could have guessed it before it happened. It is really difficult to foretell.

Feiwel: What is complexity theory?

Aumann: Basically it is concerned with the difficulty or length of time involved in doing some kind of algorithm. How fast can one solve some kind of problem, such as linear programming, for instance? How many additions and subtractions does it take? Complexity usually has to do with computations of various kinds. In other words, if you are given a problem, what is the maximum number of steps that might conceivably be required to solve that problem? An example of the kinds of ways in which complexity theory may be useful in economics could be the following: If you limit your agents to being able to perform only a certain number of steps, and they have to reach a decision based on that, how would they do it? What would be the best kind of decision they could reach?

Feiwel: Is computer technology involved?

Aumann: In theory yes, because when, for example, you are asking about the complexity of linear programming, it gives you an idea of how large a computer you have to have to solve the problem. But sometimes the algorithms suggested by complexity theory are, for one reason or another, not practical. Sometimes they are, but often not. Complexity theory is a sort of theoretical background for computer technology. The relationship is somewhat similar to that between microeconomics and macroeconomics.

7 Transformation in General Equilibrium Theory and Methods: An Interview

Andreu Mas-Colell

Feiwel: To what extent have modern developments in g.e.t. improved our understanding of the economic world?

Mas-Colell: It is fair to say that economics is a discipline where the tools, methods and analytical instruments evolve more than the fundamental questions. It can be said that many of the fundamental questions were already in Adam Smith. If you ask me, 'In general terms, do we understand better Adam Smith's economy than Adam Smith did?' a likely answer is 'No'. But if your question is, 'Do we have more analytical tools to study the economy in finer detail than Adam Smith had? then the answer is, 'Yes'. G.e.t., the development of certain kinds of mathematical tools, the axiomatic method – all these together have, I believe, contributed much to our tool box and to clarity of thought and clarity of models. I do not think that anyone could now write analytical economics in the way it was done before the Second World War. Things have to be much more precise now.

Feiwel: To what extent have there been fundamental changes in g.e.t. since the Arrow-Debreu landmark article on existence?

Mas-Colell: It depends on what one perceives as fundamental. It also depends where exactly one places the frontiers of g.e.t. Let me just mention a few of the topics that have been clarified since that article; whether or not they are fundamental I leave to you. First, the full implications for welfare economics were not yet clear at the time. Although Arrow had already written his French article on state contingent commodities, the full comprehension of that came later. Secondly, there has been the development of g.e.t. in incomplete markets that has opened the way towards a treatment of time; that is the study of sequential economies and the like. Thirdly, there has been the work on the foundations of competition (for example, the so-called equivalence theorems). Finally, public goods have also been incorporated, stability has been studied, the whole issue of uniqueness and the lack of uniqueness of equilibrium, and many other developments, have occurred within g.e.t. Last but not least, g.e.t. has also become an applied, computational discipline.

Feiwel: How do you perceive Kenneth Arrow's impact on economics?

Mas-Colell: The obvious answer is – enormous. Economics would not today be the same without him. What else can one say? I admire his breadth and his ability to focus his mind so creatively on so many topics. It is remarkable in how many fields he has initiated the questions; how many fields he has revolutionized. G.e.t. is just one of them: here he is, of course, one of the founding fathers.

Feiwel: In perusing your instructive *The Theory of General Economic Equilibrium: A Differentiable Approach*, I understand that the question of existence is merely a subset of the larger question of determinateness of which uniqueness, stability, and the like are all a part. Is this a correct inference?

Mas-Colell: Absolutely. Personally, the problem of determinateness of equilibrium is one on which I am pursuing research. Existence is only a starting point. If one is going to talk about equilibrium one has to know whether one is talking about something that is not vacuous. But, ideally, a theory that does not predict a unique outcome is an incomplete one. How seriously incomplete it is depends on exactly what it does predict. If it predicts just a discrete set of equilibria, then its incompleteness is probably not that serious. History may help determine exactly what we see. I am certainly not one to believe that we live in the only possible world.

However, things do become serious as soon as we have a continuum of equilibria. Now, here is an interesting point. For a while there has been a feeling that we could show, with considerable generality, that the g.e. model and many other economic models will have this discrete equilibrium property. In the last three or four years researchers have begun to see that things are much more complicated. That there are whole classes of very interesting models that do not seem to have this property – and that is very disturbing. The famous overlapping-generations model is just one example. Incomplete markets is another. The same also happens in game theory: correlated equilibria, sun spots, etc. Those are non-pathological models where competitive theory just does not seem to narrow down equilibria to something determinate. And that is very bothersome, especially if we do theory for comparative statistics or policy purposes where the idea is to predict what will happen if we change the exogenous conditions. With locally unique equilibrium it is reasonable to expect that one stays there, but with a whole continuum, it is difficult to see what one can say. It just looks as if one would get into an equilibrium drift. We do not yet understand that development very well; that particular topic is not yet fully clarified. But it will soon be because a younger generation of g.e. theorists (for example, T. Kehoe, D. Levine, J. Geanakoplos, M. Woodford, etc.) is hard at work on it.

Feiwel: For the benefit of the non-mathematical economist, would you be kind enough to convey the gist of your new book, *The Theory of General Economic Equilibrium: A Differentiable Approach?*

Mas-Colell: I look at this book as a summary of my work and that of others, and I do emphasize: the work of others. The substantive economic problem is that of determinateness of equilibrium; that is what goes beyond existence: uniqueness and local uniqueness. It provides the appropriate mathematical and technical setting for applying the traditional method of the counting of equations and unknowns; that is the mathematical theory of transversality – a sophisticated and relatively new part of advanced calculus.

Besides this it covers quite a number of topics. It tries to illustrate the use of new techniques by working out representative examples of applications to classic economic problems. For example, there is a very extensive treatment of the welfare theorems. It also illustrates the use of first- and second-order conditions. This is another technique that one recovers for g.e.t.

Feiwel: I noticed that 'typicality' and 'genericity' play a very important role in your book. Could you enlarge on this?

Mas-Colell: Part of the lack of rigour of the traditional calculus approach was that in order to apply differentiability tools, one had to assume a multitude of regularity-like conditions, postulated at equilibrium. But equilibrium is something endogenously determined, so how could one postulate that at equilibrium some matrix has full rank if one did not even know where the equilibrium was? The generic approach lets one out of this quandary by providing rigorous ways to assert that 'typically' the regularity conditions are satisfied.

Feiwel: Is g.e.t. sufficiently general to be the theory of economics?

Mas-Colell: We have here a problem of definitions: the Arrow-Debreu model in itself, no; but a theory of economics will have to be a g.e.t. As is well known, the Arrow-Debreu model is not able to accommodate what we today call asymmetric information phenomena. It is partly because of this that Baysian game theory has become so popular. It offers a technical framework that allows, to some extent, the handling of asymmetric information. Every technique has its own demands and inner directions. Eventually, however, I would expect the final theory to emerge as g.e. I do not believe it is going to be partial equilibrium.

Feiwel: What directions of development do you foresee for g.e.t.?

Mas-Colell: Let me give you two complementary answers: one relating to the direction of the inner logic of the theory and the other to outside intellectual forces. In the first aspect developments in the next ten years or so will probably go in the direction of incorporating imperfections of all kinds (imperfect competition theories and the like), a good understanding of the determinateness issues, development of the theory in an infinite-dimensional setting (for example, infinitely many commodities) and others of that kind. In the second aspect I would expect a sharpening and intensification of relations with game theory. Some of that is already happening. Thus one can already see g.e. work that is strongly influenced by the asymmetric information revolution. I would expect more and more of this – and it is very important.

As I said before, the Arrow-Debreu model cannot handle asymmetric information. We do have models that can handle it, but they tend to be restricted; that is, where competition takes place between two or three players, while the g.e. vision of the world is thousands of players competing. Hence, I do expect a synthesis of these two approaches to take place: asymmetric game theory broadening towards incorporating more and more agents and bringing in some of the standard considerations of g.e.t. and g.e.t. developing towards endogenous formation of markets and things like that.

Feiwel: What about integration of social choice theory and g.e.t.?

Mas-Colell: They are certainly not incompatible. Some of the practitioners of the two are the same persons, starting with Arrow. It seems to me that social choice theory has two branches: One is a theory of ethics, and as such it is part of welfare economics. For this branch your question could be rephrased, 'Is welfare economics going to be synthesized with g.e.t.?' The answer, of course, is that it has been there from the very beginning and will continue to be. The second branch of social choice theory is descriptive political theory. Here again there is no conflict. Since I do not know this field well, I cannot predict what will happen to descriptive political theory. There is, however, a general trend in economics, not only in g.e.t., but also in macroeconomics or in industrial organization to incorporate explicitly the political instance. In macroeconomics this interaction is very clear: One has to predict what the government will do and that depends on the results of elections.

But I would like to emphasize that, as I see it, these days social choice theory does not seem to be a unified discipline. It is split into these two very distinct branches. To mention only two of the leading figures: Sen is not in the slightest interested in the properties of elections and Kramer is not interested in the slightest in the consistency of axioms of moral choice.

Feiwel: One of the aims of this study is to convey the developments of g.e.t. beyond the Arrow-Debreu model. Could you kindly overcome your innate modesty and discuss some of the areas in which your work has helped to extend and refine the g.e. model?

Mas-Colell: Let me select a couple of items, not quite at random, that are in g.e. but are not at all related to the local uniqueness or the regular economies approach.

One of the topics on which I worked is the extension of g.e.t. to a framework where preferences may not satisfy one of the standard axioms such as completeness and transitivity. An anecdote in this connection is very revealing of the logic of the axiomatic method. My research aim was to get rid of the completeness axiom for existence-of-equilibrium purposes. It just seemed to me that in general in our decision theory (including decision under uncertainty) the completeness axiom is by far the most restrictive. It turned out that this could be done, but in the process, and unexpectedly, I had also eliminated transitivity. Because it was surprising, what struck most people then was the elimination of transitivity, whereas I did not think that conceptually this was so important. I do not think that one can go very far in decision theory without transitivity. I do believe in this axiom but certainly not in completeness. I should add, however, that the elimination of transitivity turned out to be very useful for technical reasons because many problems with externalities and with other complicated interactions can be looked at as traditional problems without transitive preferences.

Another extension of the g.e. model in which I take some pride is the formulation of a g.e. model of product differentiation which provides the foundations to study things such as hedonic pricing. I do not think this is the place to go into details. Let me just say that in the Arrow-Debreu model the commodities are simply labels. It is preferences that determine whether two commodities are very close to each other. Those preferences decide which goods are substitutes among themselves. I replaced this with a more explicit treatment.

Feiwel: May we have your comments on the development of mathematical techniques in economics from the calculus (derided by Debreu in *Theory of Value*) through advanced convexity and topology (used by Arrow and Debreu) to the renaissance of calculus (due to Debreu himself in the early 1970s and now so well exposited in your book)?

Mas-Colell: Your question is a good summary of what has happened. I do not wish to see things as ups and downs. There were good reasons for the take-over by topology and convexity at a certain moment. The pressing problems at that time seemed to require those tools which, at that point, lent themselves to more rigorous treatment. But there is no doubt, as I think Gerard would agree, that he exaggerated a bit in that well-known sentence on calculus. As I point out in my book, there were two weaknesses in the traditional application of calculus. Indirectly they both referred to inequalities. One of them was the counting of equations and unknowns as a way of proving existence. The other was boundary equilibria and inequalities. Calculus has an inner logic towards concentrating on interior solutions. This is, of couse, constrictive. To take a limit case, with linear inequalities everything happens at boundaries.

So there were reasons for the switch to convexity and topology, but those also had their limitations. For example, Arrow and Hurwicz kept using differentiability in the study of stability. There was no choice. But even they went to enormous lengths to get rid of it in some of their results. For example, in their analysis of gross substitutability they succeeded in getting the whole theory without differentiability. In the 1960s there was a perception of considerable accomplishment if one did not use differentiability. One can still see the influence of this today and it can be overdone.

Feiwel: May we have your reflections on the axiomatic method?

Mas-Colell: The axiomatic method is still all pervasive in economic theory but I would not venture to say that it will be so forever. I do not know what our subject will be like in 50 years, but I would not be astounded to find that the computer revolution would have changed the character of what we do and how we do it, or, for that matter, what the mathematicians do. Just the other day I read a quote from a well-known mathematician (G. C. Rota) to the effect that 'the axiomatic method itself will now be rendered obsolete'.

Feiwel: Do you see any limitations of the axiomatic method?

Mas-Colell: For the present I am still a staunch defender of the axiomatic method. I think that it is extremely helpful in clarifying ideas. As any labour, it can be performed with or without artistry. As any approach it has its own dangers. One of the dangers of the axiomatic method is the following: You have three interesting phenomena that give the striking impression that something common is going on. You then succeed in building up a theory where the three phenomena are unified under four characterizing axioms – that is very good and a clear pay-off of the axiomatic method. Now, as soon as you have four axioms this gives you 16 different combinations of axioms; you take two at a time, three at a time, four at a time, etc. A further advantage of this method is that you may not have thought of any of these 16 theories, and it may turn out that one or two of them are quite interesting, so that you have discovered something. But the danger is that the other 14 may be utterly uninteresting, but still the inner logic of the method compels you to spend time building up every one of these 16 theories. Where to stop is a matter of judgement for which there is no rule; it is an art to discern the interesting combinations of axioms to explore from the uninteresting one that should not be pursued. Certainly the axiomatic method has this lurking drawback, but all things considered, it is by far less dangerous than the literary method. One of the alleged virtues of the literary method tends to be its lack of precision. This seems to me intellectually perverse. Fortunately there is no magic formula to entirely mechanize intellectual discourse. Though the axiomatic method may become obsolete, we shall certainly not go back to literary economics. We shall probably progress to something that will be very computer-intensive.

Feiwel: Are there any new developments in mathematics that are likely to change mathematical economics?

Mas-Colell: Of course, there are many new developments in mathematics and mathematical economics is very much influenced by what the mathematicians do. Let me mention a couple of things that already have, and are bound to have, even greater influence. One is the recent upsurge in the mathematical theory of dynamical systems (the term 'chaos' is a catchword usually associated with this). It is already having an impact on economics. I do not know what will come out of it, but I understand that there is some big battle shaping up between the linear stochastic and the non-linear deterministic approaches to business cycle theory. There has been something of a rebirth of non-linear models of the business cycle (the old Goodwin-Kaldor-Hicks models) combined with rational expectations. There is no doubt that this has been very directly influenced by progress in mathematics. Some of the initial economics papers in this area are almost direct lifts or transcriptions of results in mathematics (and I do not mean this as a criticism). The study of dynamics in economics is going to greatly benefit from progress in dynamics in mathematics. Another area is complexity theory; that is the progress in mathematics in evaluating what are inherently more complex computational methods. So it is just possible that this may have some influence in evaluating economic decision processes. Here the economic applications are in their infancy.

There are also other areas which, within a narrower scope, are having a direct impact on economics. For example, progress in functional analysis is essential for the construction of an infinite dimensional g.e.t.

8 Theory and Method – Second-Generation Perspective: An Interview

Hugo Sonnenschein

Feiwel: You are 20 years younger than Arrow. Much of his fundamental work on general equilibrium theory and social choice theory had already appeared by the time you started to study economics. Can you tell us your initial reaction to his work?

Sonnenschein: Despite the fact that I did not get to know Ken until several years after the start of my study of economics, in a surprising way he is responsible for my getting into economics, and I hope that you will not consider it too much of a digression for me to tell you the story. As an undergraduate at the University of Rochester, in order to fulfill a social science distribution requirement, I signed up for a course titled 'Statistics for Economists'. At the time I was set to go off to graduate school in mathematics; I am embarrassed to add that the little bit of economics to which I had been exposed had not gone down too well. Upon discovering that my mathematics background was substantial, the instructor informed me that I would be ill served by his course and strongly suggested that I find a more suitable alternative. I countered that I was more interested in mathematics than in social science and made it clear that I had no interest in looking elsewhere. He proposed a compromise: I was to go to the library and find the journal *Econometrica*. Next I was to identify one or two papers from the journal and write critical reviews. I agreed, and an article by Blau that was concerned with the proof of the General Possibility Theorem immediately caught my eye. This quickly led me to Ken's *Social Choice and Individual Values*. Mathematical economics was a very active area at the University of Rochester, and three graduate students, Amano, Drandakis, and Takayama, were very supportive of my interest. I fell in love with

Ken's little book; the very idea of formalizing the aggregation of preferences excited me a great deal. This got me started.

Granted my story is rather personal; hoever, I would suggest that it contains elements that are common to the explanation of how many people of my age got into mathematical economics. Because of Ken's work, and let me add the work of Koopmans, McKenzie, Uzawa, Debreu, Hurwicz, von Neumann and Morgenstern, and the other pioneers, economics came to be done in a style that was attractive to students with a mathematical background. I simply cannot conceive of how I might have been attracted to economics in the late 1940s. Despite the fact that I had always found social relations, social equilibrium, notions of justice, and political issues fascinating, I do not believe that I would have been bold enough to enter our discipline before it became clear that economic argument could be carried out in ways that would satisfy my need for formal and rigorous presentation. The post-Second-World-War developments were very much of a pre-condition for my becoming an economist. As you can see, I feel an enormous debt to Ken specifically, and also to his fellow pioneers.

Feiwel: What is it like to be a younger colleague of Ken?

Sonnenschein: I'm amused by the way you put the question. While Frank Hahn still refers to me as 'young Sonnenschein', as I look around in seminars these days I'm constantly reminded that nine out of ten active theorists are now younger than I am. But I do understand the question.

Let me say that my acquaintance with Ken has largely been professional. Since I am here at Stanford for the year, I have had the good fortune to see him on a regular and less formal basis. In addition to learning from Ken's work, I have on several occasions been exposed to his quick and generous criticism. It is impressive to see him run through the collection of ideas that I had at the beginning of an investigation and to quickly wind up at the point where he is suggesting next steps and alternative interpretations. The first time this happened to me was soon after the completion of my thesis work (who was I?), when the mail brought a letter from Ken describing how a paper I had written – it concerned consumer's demand without assuming the transitivity of preference – could be adapted for proving existence of a majority decision. And Ken still continues to help. After grilling me at lunch last month on my current work on dynamic monopoly, he asked whether the possibility of increasing returns could serve as an instrument for monopolists to make credible the commitment not to lower prices in the future. After some reflection I realized that the answer was 'Yes', and this has important implications for my research.

My conversations with Ken have always borne great fruit, and judging from the substantial number of people I have seen with him, one at a time, at lunch, after seminars, and so on during the past year, it is easy to see that this is true for many others as well. Ken doesn't discriminate by age, and he has the intellectual vitality to always be open to the ideas of the young.

Feiwel: What are the main influences of Ken's work on modern economics?

Sonnenschein: This is a difficult question to put one's arms around. There is so very much. First, Ken is the father of social choice theory, and this is an area, where in addition to economists, significant contributions have been made by political scientists, game theorists, and psychologists. Then, there is general equilibrium theory, with and without uncertainty. Also, the theory of individual consumer choice under uncertainty. There is in addition Ken's work on the stability of competitive equilibrium and on decentralization and control in large organizations. His papers on the welfare economics of medical care and the evaluation of public investments are classics as are some of his papers on programming. And this list attempts only to organize his contribution in terms of *substance*. When you take into account Ken's profound influence on the *methods* that are used in economics you have the beginning of an outline of why one might claim that from 1950 on we have been in the 'Arrow era'.

Feiwel: Okay, I can see that my question left too much open. Let me ask you this: In the long run, which of Ken's many fundamental contributions do you believe will be most lasting?

Sonnenschein: You take me from the frying pan into the fire! Let me attempt a two-pronged answer.

First, I believe that the influence of Arrow and Debreu on the methods used in economic analysis has been profound and will be very long lasting. In his work on economic growth, von Neumann used rather high-powered techniques, and several of the early general equilibrium theorists used set theoretic methods to deal with the problem of the existence of competitive equilibrium, but the volume of Arrow and Debreu's contributions, and more than this, the variety and appropriateness of the mathematics employed, makes their role special. Nobody can question that the mathematics of convex sets is the appropriate vehicle for studying the efficiency of a price system. There is no doubt that the representation of preferences as orderings on an abstract space is the correct starting point for a theory of preference aggregation, and so on. With the work of Arrow and Debreu we have, in bulk, the demonstration that the appropriate formulation of economic phenomena requires a variety of mathematical structures.

The second contribution I wish to single out is somewhat more difficult to articulate. In much of Ken's work, and especially in his collaborations with Leo Hurwicz, there is the view that an allocation mechanism is very much an object of choice. The possible advantages and disadvantages of an economic system should be taken into account. To me their thinking takes an important conceptual step beyond what I can find in the work of, for example, the Utopian socialists, von Mises, Lange, F.N. Taylor, Hayek, Lerner, and early Jacob Marschak. Rather than speaking of *particular* allocation processes and *particular* methods for forming social values, Arrow and Hurwicz have taught us to speak about the *set* of methods for forming social values. Socialism and capitalism are but *examples* of allocation mechanisms, and their particular advantages, can be constructed.

Allow me a small digression: shortly before leaving graduate school at Purdue for a position at the University of Minnesota, which by the way was initially funded by Leo Hurwicz's N.S.F. contract, I was taken aside by a wise and senior member of the Purdue faculty and told that 'while this Hurwicz fellow is really quite brilliant, his work on abstract resource allocation mechanisms and their properties really has the wrong balance between definitions and theorems'. Since Stan Reiter, a major contributor to mechanism theory was my thesis supervisor at Purdue, and since I was about to leave for Minnesota and Leo Hurwicz, this faculty member was plainly worried that I might catch a disease.

From the start the issue of the balance between assumptions and results has been a problem for mechanism theory, but this is at least in part due to the difficulty of the problems that are being addressed. And now, with a variety of interesting mechanisms at hand, we have a very much improved understanding of some of the essential limitations on resource allocation. This feeds into the economics of incentives, but in conception it goes far beyond what is offered there. I would hold that it is difficult to underestimate the potential fruits of the point of view that has the allocation mechanism as a matter of choice, and again it is Ken, in this case with Leo Hurwicz, who has been the leader.

Feiwel: How important is Ken's work for the non-mathematical economist?

Sonnenschein: I believe that Ken's work is fundamental, period. It is simply not a matter of mathematical economics. Let me make this point with two examples. First, I think that most economists would agree that the single most important development in macroeconomics during the past 25 years has been the Lucas model of the business cycle with his incorporation of the notion of *rational expectations*. Whatever one thinks of the Lucas theory, and there are powerful minds on both sides, there is very little doubt that it has directed attention to a vital set of issues. And what is it that makes the Lucas model possible? To paraphrase Lucas, it is the observation by Arrow and Debreu that the theory of value could incorporate uncertainty by making delivery of goods contingent on the state of nature.

My second example is very different and demonstrates the direct influence of Ken's work in an applied area. I am no expert on the economics of medical care, but I cannot imagine that any paper on the subject is cited more often than Ken's 1963 classic, 'Uncertainty and the Welfare Economics of Medical Care'. This paper contains his important result on the optimality of 'full coverage above a deductible minimum', and the general implications for applied economics are both basic and frequently exploited.

Ken's work is even important for me as a consumer. This is very applied economics and a true story. As the result of an automobile accident, I was recently sued for one million dollars. This is a very large amount of money, and you might well ask whether or not I was insured for this amount. Foreunately, the answer is 'Yes' – I hold a so-called umbrella policy – and it is Ken's paper that many years ago convinced me to buy it.

Feiwel: How would you contrast Samuelson's approach to economics with Ken's?

Sonnenschein: I feel a bit as if I am being put on the spot here. As is said in Ecclesiasticus, 'Let us now praise famous men'. Samuelson's *Foundations* is a 'how to' book and so a large amount of his contribution has to do with 'method'. His seminal pure consumption-loan model is very much general equilibrium theory and lays the foundations for a monetary general equilibrium theory as well as for a theory of bequests. And again there is so much more: the work on public goods, the non-substitution theorem, and so on. Both Samuelson and Arrow have made the greatest contribution, but I suppose that the approach is somewhat different. Perhaps it comes back to what we were speaking about before. By and large, for Samuelson the economic system is a given, while for Arrow it is the object of choice.

Feiwel: In the historical introduction to the *Handbook of Mathematical Economics*, Ken mentions 11 topics that have been important to the development of mathematical economics since 1961. One of these concerns the characterization of aggregate demand functions. You were responsible for the first argument suggesting that aggregate demand functions are not restricted by the condition that the individual demand functions arise from utility maximization. Can you reflect on the creative genesis of this work, and how you believe it has changed general equilibrium theory?

Sonnenschein: When I was a graduate student my teachers Jim Quirk and Rubin Saposnik pointed out to me that, because of Walras's identity, not all demand functions could be linear. As I recall, they posited the question of whether all but one could be linear, and this must have initiated my interest in the subject of aggregate demand. I saw rather quickly that for two commodities and two agents there were no restrictions on aggregate excess demand beyond homogeneity and Walras's law. My treatment of the case of *n* commodities was somewhat awkward, and in any event my characterization theorem was quickly improved upon by Mantel and Debreu.

This work was great fun. I often find myself beginning with the hypothesis that the king has no clothes. In my education the Slutsky restrictions on individual demand were a big thing, and the major importance of the utility hypothesis was to give structure to demand functions. The mere hint that these restrictions could disappear in the aggregate appealed to me very much. I can only believe that a large number of theorists could have proved the theorem more quickly than I did if they had conjectured the result.

I believe that the effect of the characterization theorems on general equilibrium theory has been rather important. For example, the work of Scarf and his colleagues on the computation of economic equilibrium was essentially redefined as a problem of fixed-point computation. Also, I believe that the characterization theorems are sufficiently striking that they have clarified for empirical researchers the nature of the misspecification involved in the assumption that the aggregate demand function is an individual consumer demand function. Good results blow away myth and change the way that people think. The characterization theorems have had some of this effect.

Feiwel: Why is the question of existence of general equilibrium so profoundly important?

Sonnenschein: First, one must realize that the manner in which value depends *simultaneously* on preferences, technology, and the distribution of ownership is fairly subtle, and for a long time was not well understood. To this day, a major challenge in teaching the introductory course in economics is to help students to see that although value depends on relative costs of production, it also depends on tastes and the distribution of wealth, and that indeed relative costs of production depend on what is being produced of all commodities and thus on the demand for other commodities, and so on. It is the general equilibrium that determines value, and the observation that all of the requirements of equilibrium can be satisfied for an arbitrary economy is no less trivial than the observation that a continuous map from the n-ball into itself has a fixed point. Of course n corresponds to one less than the number of commodities, and for $n \leqslant 4$ the result cannot, by any stretch of the imagination, be considered obvious. Economists who hold that it is 'obvious' that our partial equilibrium notions of consumer and firm maximization can be fitted together to form a coherent determination of value simply do not know what they are talking about. Colleagues who make this claim, almost by definition, either do not understand the interrelatedness of it all or deny the importance of interrelatedness.

The existence theorem provides a test of whether, for an arbitrary specification of the economy, it is possible to simultaneously satisfy all of the conditions that have classically been demanded for equilibrium. It also to some extent tests whether the classical notion of equilibrium is sufficiently complete to determine value. To be sure, it is a theorem about models, but it concerns our most basic models. How else could we as economists test the coherence of our view of the determinants of value other than by an existence theorem?

Allow me a small postscript. The methods used by Arrow and Debreu in their 1954 existence result generalize very nicely to prove the existence of competitive equilibrium when there are, possibly externalities in consumption, externalities in production, commodity taxes, non-transitive preferences, certain kinds of public agencies, and much more. This is emphasized in my work with Wayne Shafer. Also, Farrell and Rothenberg pointed the way to the formal demonstration that the convexity of individual firm production sets and individual consumer preferences is not essential for the coherence of the competitive theory of value. Convexity can be replaced by the assumption that economic agents are insignificant relative to the markets in which they participate. As a result of these advances we have come to understand that the competitive view is coherent for a much wider range of situations than one might have believed. To be sure, conditions are needed and we really don't know how to deal with bankruptcy – McKenzie's important notion of resource relatedness notwithstanding – but by now it is fair to say that the conception of an economy with a large number of price-taking and maximizing agents is, at the least, consistent.

Feiwel: What do you make of Morgenstern's contention that equilibrium theory misuses the notion of competition for it does not grapple with the essence of competition (that is, struggle, fight, maneuvring, bluff, and the like)?

Sonnenschein: Let me take the easy way out and treat the issue as a matter of semantics. Perfect competition à la Arrow-Debreu is a technical term, which has as its defining property the requirement of price-taking behaviour. Perfect competition does not attempt to model competitive haggling, bluff, manoeuvring, and the like. Cournot's limit theorem, Novshek's limit theorem, and the Edgeworth-Debreu-Scarf limit theorem formally express the idea that non-co-operative competitive forces may, in the appropriate setting, lead to the perfectly competitive result. I think of Morgenstern's remarks as calling for an analysis of when the result of real competition is that agents effectively lose their ability to make a price. In such cases they behave *as if* they are price takers. This is an important research topic, perhaps one that requires a specification of institutions, and Martin Shubik and his co-workers certainly accord it the highest priority.

Feiwel: Is there a love-hate relationship between general equilibrium theory and game theory?

Sonnenschein: I really don't believe so; in fact, I have tried to indicate how they complement each other. Let me begin with an example from Ken's work. According to Ken's own account, his original approach to the problem of the existence of competitive equilibrium was to associate with each economy a game for which the Nash equilibrium would be a competitive equilibrium of the economy. This is the way that the Arrow-Debreu existence theorem goes, and it, of course, uses Debreu's lemma on the existence of equilibrium in generalized games. So we have a case in which game theory ideas led to a première result in general equilibrium theory. And it goes the other way too. The existence theorem does only a partial job of solving the problem of the determinateness of equilibrium. For some time economists have been aware of the existence of non-pathological economies with a continuum of equilibria. Debreu showed that such economies are exceptional and the key idea was to study the correspondence from economies to equilibria rather than to examine an individual economy. Recently, in order to understand better certain inadequacies in the concept of Nash equilibrium, game theorists have begun to study the correspondence from games to their equilibria. From a mathematical point of view the exercise is not so very different than the one undertaken by Debreu. Here it looks as if a mathematical idea developed in the context of important economics will be of substantial service in game theory.

Feiwel: In some of the game theory models you are speaking of it appears that more rationality and sophistication is required of economic agents than is customary in the general equilibrium theory of Arrow, Debreu, and McKenzie. Is there a fundamental tension betweeen the general equilibrium theory and the new game theory models?

Sonnenschein: All that an agent needs to know in the perfectly competitive theory, in order to make the decision that is ascribed him by that theory, are prices plus his own private characteristics. One thinks of perfect competition as *decentralized and efficient in its use of information*. Of course, someone must set prices, but an auctioneer who mechanically adjusts prices in response to the magnitude of aggregate excess demand would at least have some chance of guiding the economy towards an equilibrium. (One might, for example, consider the possibility of an auctioneer for each market.) In game theory the situation is quite different. In order for a player to decide on the appropriate action in a non-co-operative game, he must know not only his own characteristics, but the characteristics of all other agents as well. Bayesian equilibrium formulations capture the idea that one may be uncertain regarding the characteristics of other agents, but then the distribution of this uncertainty must be common knowledge. The bottom line is the same; for game theory, in addition to one's own characteristics, one must know the random characteristics of all other agents. In some cases one cannot help but be chilled by the comprehensive knowledge ascribed to agents in game theory models. Furthermore, we sometimes find ourselves attributing behaviour to agents that would appear to require an unbelievable amount of computational ability. This is a problem. Sometimes I worry that the current emphasis on game theory approaches will obscure issues of decentralization and cost of information transfer and processing. Of course, the hope is that game theory will lead to a more explicit consideration of informational factors; the framework for such an analysis is at least there.

Feiwel: How does economics differ from the natural sciences?

Sonnenschein: The distinguished physicist Richard Feynman has written that 'the test of all knowledge is experiment'. Recently in economics there has been a good deal of interest in laboratory experiments, but meaningful experimentation remains difficult. One of the great challenges in economics is to figure out ways to test our ideas, and I feel that for us a more pluralistic approach is indicated than is appropriate for the natural sciences. In particular, we must be on the lookout for cases in which nature or the political process runs an experiment for us. Hurricanes and increases in defense spending can add important data points! In addition, in the social sciences introspection can sometimes be valuable. A molecule of liquid cannot answer the question, 'How do I react when things heat up'; however, a banker might provide a useful answer.

Feiwel: This leads me to ask whether or not you feel that the realism of assumptions is important.

Sonnenschein: As I said, critical laboratory experiments are not so readily available in economics, and data is difficult to interpret. With many models we cannot tell whether or not they successfully mimic the workings of actual economies. In using such models for prediction, I take comfort when the assumptions of the model prescribe behaviour that strikes me as plausible. But let me add that I find traps in this question. Economists do more than describe and predict; we also recommend institutions and figure out what is possible. To make a connection with Ken's work, the general possibility theorem tells us that there is no method for aggregating preferences that satisfies three simple axioms: unanimity, non-dictatorship, and the independence of irrelevant alternatives. The result is fundamental for the problem of preference aggregation and thus is fundamental for determining the class of feasible resource allocation mechanisms. The theorem gives a limitation on what is possible, and the realism of the axioms is simply not an issue.

We should be skeptical of all existing theories and test them in every way possible: formal models, controlled experiment, historical experience, introspection, and the realism of assumptions are all important. A major barrier to the advancement of our discipline is that it is hard to discredit our guesses of how the economic world works.

Feiwel: Why is not the young generation of mathematical economists generally more interested in questions of stability?

Sonnenschein: Well, it is true that there is no longer much interest in the *tâtonnement* dynamics. But in all fairness one must keep in mind that the *tâtonnement* has obvious conceptual problems: in a market economy there is typically no auctioneer who adjusts the price in response to excess demand. Is *tâtonnement* a story of dynamics for economies with market makers or bureaucratic control of prices? Do trades actually occur before equilibrium is reached? Are there real buffer stocks to absorb the excess demand? Does the *tâtonnement* attempt, in a reduced form, to capture the way that enterprises will change prices after an economy is shocked?

Actually, I find the part of the Walrasian *tâtonnement* that the Samuelson-Arrow-Block-Hurwicz literature ignores to be more descriptively relevant than the part they study. This has to do with differences in profit or factor rewards leading to the movement of resources, and eventually leading to the equality of factor rewards and profits. But having said all of this, I want to emphasize that I see an increasing interest in real economic dynamics. This work tries to get at the same questions that the stability theory addressed, but in a more fundamental manner.

When I was a graduate student, Cournot duopoly dynamics and Cournot stability were essentially as they were in 1838: you iterated the responses given by the duopoly reaction functions. Now, the chic thing to do is to look at the repeated Cournot game with discounting and examine the subgame perfect trajectories. The old way had its embarrassing aspects – agents were continually surprised – but the new way also has its problems in that it requires the duopolists to know each others characteristics and to make very sopohisticated computations. This is the trade off between decentralization and rationality that I alluded to before.

In any case, dynamic theory is quite the rage and with models that are explicitly dynamic there is less of a role for the stability analysis of reduced form static models.

Feiwel: How do you react to the various attacks on mathematical economics?

Sonnenschein: Does this really go on? To be serious, I don't see very much of it. Gerard, in his Nobel Lecture, was quite marvellous regarding the role of mathematics in economics. He emphasized rigor, simplicity, and generality as attributes of an effective theory, and pointed out how these attributes are fostered by the mathematical method. Because of the success of the mathematical method there is the danger that research will be judged by the level of mathematics used, but it really is unfair to blame this on the mathematical approach. It is not uncommon for older researchers to resist the techniques that go beyond the ones that they themselves introduced or the ones that they learned as young scholars. This is, of course, one of the ways in which Ken, Gerard Debreu, Leo Hurwicz, and Lionel McKenzie remain special; they are always open to the latest ideas and technologies.

Feiwel: How do you feel about Frank Hahn's observation that in practical application the Chicago economists have taken general equilibrium theory far more seriously than its present state warrants and that paradoxically they are rather hostile to its abstract foundations.

Sonnenschein: I have been pleased to see the ideas of general equilibrium incorporated into macroeconomic theory. One of Frank Hahn's major contributions has been to point out that in a model with money there will be a nonmonetary equilibrium – an equilibrium in which money is not used – and as a consequence the problem of the existence of a monetary equilibrium is quite delicate.

The rational expectations approach has used some of the framework of general equilibrium theory – in particular the idea of an economy with contingent claims; however, this is not its defining characteristic. Rational expectations equilibrium requires that consumers use information intelligently and not ignore opportunities to increase their welfare. The approach forces us to be more faithful to our neoclassical heritage, and it has led to a re-evaluation of the foundations of the Keynesian theory. The criticism offered by the rational expectations school has been of first-order importance.

I know some of these Chicago economists, as you have called them, quite well. Lucas has never struck me as hostile toward the abstract foundations of general equilibrium theory. Certainly, he is more interested in economic policy than are most general equilibrium theorists; however, his work is very abstract and mathematically difficult. I am amazed at the extent to which macroeconomic theory has gone 'high tech' during the past 20 years, and by any account Lucas and his co-workers are very much responsible for this event.

Feiwel: What in your opinion are the major unsolved problems of general equilibrium theory?

Sonnenschein: I don't know the answer. I'm not at all sure that the major unsolved problems in theoretical economics are general equilibrium in nature. There are many puzzles out there that I feel are important to resolve and on which we have made a bit of a start: Does the fact that we see delayed agreement in bargaining, that is strikes, contradict rationality? What is the economic role of repeated relationships? At the same time, there are aspects of our most basic formulations that leave me unsatisfied: Is Nash equilibrium at all satisfactory when there are several Nash equilibria? What are the appropriate welfare criteria when there is asymmetric information? Part of understanding economic theory is to realize how very much there is to learn, even in the realm of obtaining the most basic knowledge.

Feiwel: Well then, why in your opinion have mathematical economists been content to ask such small questions?

Sonnenschein: Rigor and precision limit one to questions that can be well formulated and to answers that are at the least internally consistent. Generality means that we are not satisfied by examples. In economics it is simply quite hard to develop rigorous and general theory. For example, bilateral bargaining is essential to economics and it is an institution that has been around since ancient times. But how can one give a rigorous and general analysis of bargaining without the notions of strategy, game, equilibrium, time preference, and perhaps even subgame perfection? The mathematical approach is not the approach of the impatient. In physics it was necessary to solve small general problems – such as to explain why objects fall when dropped – before bigger topics could be intelligently addressed – such as how and when did the universe begin? You must understand the theory of gravitation and a good deal more before you can reasonably analyze the 'big bang'. The discovery of DNA is a necessary step towards understanding how life begins, but in context it is one of many small steps.

In mathematical economics we take small steps. For most interesting and important questions economists simply do not have very good and complete answers, but often we have some learning that is more or less relevant. For example, we may know what happened 30 years ago in a situation similar to what is being analyzed at the moment. To form a conclusion based on such evidence involves a large and nonrigorous step – a leap of faith, an uncontrolled lunge, whatever. It may be the best that can be done, and it may at the moment provide the best guide for action, but it is not the style of mathematical economics. All that one must believe is that our patient style is a valid means for discovering truth. I have no doubt that this is so, but at the same time one can see why the mathematical economics approach seems peculiar to those only interested in the problems of the day.

9 Interaction Between General Equilibrium and Macroeconomics: An Interview

Lawrence R. Klein

Feiwel: I understand that during the early post-war years at Cowles there was a strong connection between empirical and theoretical work. May I take you back to the exciting period of your early career as an economist? Would you share with us some of the creative genesis of your work?

Klein: As an undergraduate and graduate student I was much preoccupied with fulfilling requirements, passing examinations. In student-teacher relationships you never get the full flavour of what people will do when they are in a professional situation. So I would rather date things from the time I took my first job at the Cowles Commission, although, like most people I have been and continue to be much influenced by what I have learned from my teachers. I do not mean in any way to detract from my teachers by starting my recollections from the beginning of my professional career.

When I went to the Cowles Commission it was against the advice of Paul Samuelson who thought that I should go to the Federal Reserve. I took a smaller salary, but I took the job because I had met Marschak and Koopmans at an Econometric Society meeting – the first professional meeting I had ever attended. Marschak said to me, 'What this country needs [meaning the US] is a new Tinbergen model'. Sometimes things strike you in the face, and that struck me. Marschak wanted me to come to the Cowles Commission and to work on that problem, and that was exactly the problem that attracted me. So I was completely comfortable in accepting that position even though I was advised to do something else and the stipend was smaller.

The important thing to realize – something that is really not well known by the outside world – is the extent to which we all worked together as a team at Cowles in those days. Everybody had a specific job. Marschak and Koopmans were working on statistical theory and the computation techniques for the problem of model building. I was set to work on the formulation of a model using contemporary macroeconomics, collection of data, and statistical measurement. Hurwicz was, in a sense, the gadfly; he worked on everybody's problems in a very pointed and penetrating way, but he did not have, as I recall, a special assignment. Haavelmo came to us from the Norwegian Embassy and he was working on the joint problems of statistical theory and model testing.

It was impressed on me from the very beginning that everything we did in building the model should have roots in economic theory. That is why I got interested in the problems of specifying a theory of economic behaviour of the firm, a theory of economic behaviour of a household, and their translation into computable equations, together with a collection of data tailored to those specifications. Now, I noticed in the presentation of the work of the Cowles Commission on its 50th Anniversary, dealing with macroeconomics and model-building, that outsiders, so to speak, really failed to realize how closely we interacted in those days on the problems of economic theory and on the problems of model estimation and testing. At Cowles macroeconomics was an integrated branch, blended into the whole programme in a distinctive way.

Marschak made the point that all the equations in the model should be deducible from theory. He made a related point that we should build a bridge between microeconomics and macroeconomics. That got me into what was called the aggregation problem. I think that we never had a perfect explanation in this case, but it was a reasonably good one, of how you would make measurements in terms of index numbers to relate the kinds of equations we have in macroeconomics to the kinds of equations that we have in microeconomics.

Now, in later life some people have said to me that they really admired the way I presented this kind of concept in the Cowles Commission monograph, *Economic Fluctuations in the United States*. At that time, however, a prominent economist, Evsey Domar, came to Chicago on a year's scholarship as I was leaving. He reviewed the manuscript I had left and said, 'Well, you just have equations that seem intuitively plausible, and you are going to estimate them anyway, why do you go through this whole process of trying to relate them to economic theory?' Here was an outsider who did not participate in the discussions we had had in this formative period and who, of course, did not appreciate it.

In my opinion, we were extremely theoretically oriented in those days. We were theoretically oriented both in the terms of the concepts of lags, adjustments, and expectations, and in terms of the concepts of neoclassical equilibrium and the concepts of Keynesian economics – whether an unemployment equilibrium existed or not. We explored all those kinds of theoretical problems of micro and macroeconomics at the same time as we were experimenting with the simultaneous equation method of estimation and building our systems, using the latest methods of statistical inference.

This was, then, our entire frame of reference at that time. To some extent, that has stuck with me all the time. I think it is wrong, therefore, for the present generation of economists to criticize macroeconometrics on the grounds that it lacks theoretical foundations or that it pays no attention to theoretical specification, because that is really how we got started, and this is really the basis for the macroeconometric work that is now being done. However, we should not be slavish is this application and fail to take account of aggregation error or the time shape of lag adjustment or other things that may cause what we find in practice, to deviate from the theoretical specifications.

If one used the models in a completely mechanical way, they broke down. Perhaps it was because the data series were too short; that is the samples were small. Perhaps it was because of our inexperience. And perhaps it was because of something that I learned later in life, namely, that one cannot walk away from a statistical model without caring for it on a regular basis. One has to live with it and keep it in touch with reality virtually every day. To use a common expression, one has to keep it tuned up to present circumstances, and that is a consequence of the small sample proposition in economics. Now, in my opinion, many of my colleagues at Cowles got turned-off from model-building and application at an early stage. Either they found it too much work, too tedious, or they found it not to work mechanically well enough. They went into other highly varied areas: Kenneth went into social choice, Koopmans went into activity analysis, Marschak went into team theory, Haavelmo went into more theoretical and speculative ideas about economic growth and economic philosophy, Anderson went back to his work on statistical inference, and Patinkin went into pure macro theory. Our team then fell apart, but while it was together it was very productive. We all discussed in the greatest detail the most intricate problems of economic theory as they arose in those days, and the problems of statistical measurement.

The later work that I did in model-building at Michigan, and subsequently at the Wharton School, was very fundamentally set on the basis of that early experience. Things were added to the models. For example, at Michigan I added survey information and the possibility of introducing direct measurements of anticipations. When data became more available on a quarterly basis, we tried to make finer business-cycle estimates. The computer, which was always a bottleneck – for example, during the Cowles Commission days everything was done by hand – suddenly opened up new horizons for us.

I regard these things as evolutionary developments in the kind of work in which I was mainly engaged; that work started at the Cowles Commission and, with new facilities, new information bases, and new thinking, it evolved into the kinds of systems we have eventually been able to build. But I think it is a pity that we could not hold the old group together. On the other hand, however, we were extremely fortunate to find all that talent together at that period of time. I do not know whether one could ever recreate such a group of people; people who have been so successful in later life, all together in their twenties and thirties working as a team. It was quite an experience! At the 50th Anniversary celebrations of Cowles it was said that there were just a number of episodic efforts in macroeconomics at Cowles during its Chicago days. But those were not episodic things; it was all part of a co-ordinated effort and, I think, it worked very well.

At Cowles we were taught respect for Simon Kuznets. Kuznets was a close friend of Marschak and he visited us there. I think that one of the big breakthroughs in the work that I did later was the ability to use social accounting systems and the data generated by them. Without tailoring his work to our needs, Kuznets really produced the kind of basic materials that we needed.

The same was true of Leontief. I had seen a fair amount of him when I was a student at MIT and he was teaching at Harvard. I found the Cowles group a little flippant about Leontief's work. In later life I found the Leontief organization and interpretation of the data in the input-output framework as fundamental as the Kuznets interpretation in national income accounting. Those two formed the basis for the evolutionary work that I did after leaving the Cowles

Commission. The third thing was the electronic computer, but that had nothing to do with economics or with economists. My argument is that if you put all these things together – the computer, Kuznets, Leontief, and the work we did at Cowles – then you get all the ingredients for what came afterwards.

Being in Chicago, the Cowles Commission was at the center of the country in a transportation sense in those days. John von Neumann used to come through Chicago on regular train trips between Princeton and Los Alamos and always changed trains in Chicago. He consulted a lot with Koopmans and others on the computational problems, but he also made brilliant contributions in our general discussions. That, of course, was of considerable benefit to the work at Cowles. We also benefited very much from the work of Abraham Wald who came out from time to time but not regularly. He contributed greatly to statistical development, much more so than to other subjects.

A third influence was really on the side lines – it was that of the Hungarian physicist, Leo Szilard, who was also a good friend of Marschak and who had done unusually noteworthy work in getting Jewish scientists out of Germany by organizing a large network, of which Marschak was a part, for financing the exodus of scientists, and locating them either in England or the US. Szilard was working on the atomic bomb project in the greatest of secrecy, but he was also an amateur economist. He used to come to Cowles quite regularly. He used to spend a lot of time in the evenings with me, Hurwicz, and others. He had very clever ideas about structuring an economy that was cycle-free. He demonstrated this by means of a game. I and others helped him in building the basic parameters of the game; how much the player representing trade unions should have, how much the player representing business should have, how much the player representing government should have, and the like. Szilard used to say to me, 'I am going to prove to Hayek, von Mises, and the other free-marketeers, just why their ideas are wrong and what you need to do to get an economy that is cycle-free'. His technique was to have two kinds of money, money for spending and money for saving, red money and green money, the relative circulation rates of which would govern the stability of the economy.

It was being in contact with the thinking of this brilliant group, Wald, von Neumann, and Szilard, that made a great impression on my own development, in addition to the rather more fundamental economics work of Kuznets and Leontief.

After I left the Cowles Commission, I drew heavily on these early impressions in perfecting each successive phase of model-building; that dominated my own career.

Feiwel: Would you be good enough to enlarge on the various phases of the development of your work subsequent to the Cowles Commission?

Klein: The new thing during the Michigan phase was, as I have previously indicated, to build a system that had some content from the surveys that were located at the University of Michigan, and to try to correct some of the flaws of the models we had built at the Cowles Commission. I think that, for their times, the systems that we built then were quite good as precursors of the later models.

By the time I went to Pennsylvania, however, quarterly data had become readily available and we could do better work on the business cycle characteristics of systems. In this connection, the impressive work that Irma and Frank Adelman did, at about that time, on the stochastic nature of cyclical fluctuations became the focal point of a lot of our research in Philadelphia. Furthermore, in the Wharton models we carried out much more explicitly the surveys of anticipations that we had started to use at Ann Arbor. The models that we built at Wharton carried on in a continuing stream of thought.

This was the point at which the electronic computer entered in the early 1960s. It enabled us to do so many things that we had always wanted to try out.

Curiously enough, each time in the development after the Cowles Commission, that we thought we had a breakthrough, we were somewhat disappointed. Shifting to quarterly data became necessary, but it was no breakthrough. Using anticipatory data was helpful, but it was no breakthrough. Using the computer to make sophisticated analyses was interesting and important, but it was no breakthrough. In the end I found that nothing was a breakthrough, but by being persistent, by building a model and having a computer available so that we could use it every day, so that we could keep it up to date, so that we could follow the latest trends in the business community, so that we could have a dialogue with people with their ear to the ground in the business community, we could make some real progress. The models were considerably improved by better data, in touch with reality, and daily operation of the models. All the other things were interesting and carried on in an improved fashion after the Cowles days, but none by itself brought the breakthrough for which we had hoped. In a sense you could say that it was hard work and a lot of 'tender loving care' that were important rather than any single brilliant idea.

The next stage for me in model-building after I came to Pennsylvania was not only the application of the computer to the general solution of the problem, but, in connection with the Brookings model project, the discovery of a technique for solving or simulating models. That was a joint effort between myself and Gary Fromm in our work on the Brookings model, and Ed Kuh in his computer research work at MIT. I found that interesting because it represented collaborative work in different institutions, using different approaches, and suddenly everything fell into place. Once we had developed a computer algorithm, where Ed Kuh had a lot of the ultimate insight, we then found that we were in a position to use the computer in a way to solve models quickly, frequently, and cheaply – and to do it in a way that allowed us to instruct a clerk to run it. This freed us to do much experimental work, to consider a broader range of alternatives, and to present the user with a broad range of options. It also made possible the delivery of results in highly readable tables and charts.

The next stage in this was the integration of input-output methods with final demand models. That really was the inspiration for my Presidential Address to the American Economic Association 10 years later, in which I pointed out that what this country now needed was a Keynes-Leontief model – a system where we put together in one model the Leontief input-output system and the final demand-income generated through the system of Keynes. This was really put into place during the 1960s as a kind of speculative venture of the Brookings model. We saw how it worked and then put it together as a major model. In my opinion that was the best way of approaching the energy crisis; to have a model with many sectors in which the energy component aspect of intermediate production could be traced, so that we could see its strategic importance in the economy.

The final phase, the one in which I am now, developed at Pennsylvania, involves international model-building. When I was in England, when I was in Japan, when I was in Israel, wherever I went, I had a hand in developing some models. The concept of the Brookings model (of having many experts-specialists of each department of the economy putting a model of the economy together) had run its course. We then asked the question, 'why can't we take a British model-builder in London, a French model-builder in Paris, a German model-builder in Bonn, a Japanese model-builder in Kyoto or Tokyo and put them all together to work on a world trade and world modelling system. This idea that we developed starting in 1968 working with Bert Hickman, Aaron Gordon and Rudolf Rhomberg, flourished. At first we were able to bring in the model-builders from the major industrial powers. Then we were able to extend it to all the industrialized countries and simultaneously to the communist countries. The present stage is to bring in the model-builders from the LDCs.

This is where I stand at this moment. We have reached a point at which we have tried to put together principles that drew on the work that started at the Cowles Commission and evolved through the work at Michigan and Pennsylvania, and which is now centered at Pennsylvania but has a world-wide scope. One of the interesting things that I soon discovered was that the problem of modeling countries along the concept of the world trade matrix, in which different countries are related to each other, was a complete analogue of the problem of putting an input-output model into a macro system in which the different branches of the domestic economy are related to one another. Many of the techniques that were developed for handling the world trade matrix then became techniques that we also used simultaneously in the Keynes-Leontief model as I call it, and vice versa: they fed upon each other.

I doubt that I will ever get to it, but the last problem that I would like to tackle, beyond the international one that has unlimited dimensions, is to build a model in which there is a flow of funds system and an input-output system and a national income system. That, in my opinion, will be the ultimate model. We have, by now, built flow of funds systems with national income systems, we have built input-output systems with national income systems, but the task ahead is to put the three together. In my opinion the ultimate model for a national economy will be a system built on these three great social accounting frameworks. But at the present time I am heavily involved with the LDC modeling. This is a very big thing to tackle and it is going to take up my energies for some time to come. I regard all that as a very natural evolution from the first job I had when Marschak told me that the US needed a new Tinbergen model.

Feiwel: Could you enlarge on the comments in your Presidential Address to the American Economic Association historically relating your work to the Walrasian system?

Klein: You see, Leontief always pointed out that his work was Walrasian. It is in that spirit. But as I look at Walras, I see that he had a technical production set, not unlike the Leontief set, but Walras also had demand for money, goods, consumer behaviour, and producer behaviour, which I do not see in the usual rendition of the Leontief system. So where is inventory behaviour, where are interest rates, or where is demand for money? Thus, Keynes plus Leontief is a closer approximation to Walras than anything else, but Leontief alone is only the technical production part of Walras. Indeed, parts of the flow of funds would probably be in Walras.

The Walrasian conception is interesting because it is a simultaneous equation approach, and the Keynesian system is also a simultaneous equation approach. The Keynesian system is a macro simultaneous equation approach, whereas the Walrasian system is a completely micro simultaneous equation approach. The Keynesian and Walrasian systems are similar in that they both use simultaneous equation systems to explain how economic magnitudes get determined. But there is enormously more detail in the Walrasian system. The closest we have come to that in applied work is, in my judgement, the combination of the Keynes-Leontief systems.

You see, the way we have implemented that in the Wharton group was by taking a 56-sector breakdown of the economy in the Leontief input-output system and adding many components of demand-income generation, interest rates, prices, and money holding. That became a total system of 3000 equations. Now, many modern models are being criticized for being so big and almost unintelligible. My answer to this is that in the end what we really should be after is the Walrasian system; that is the ultimate, and everything we do is some kind of an approximation. And the best approximation that we have been able to devise is still very tiny in relation to a true Walrasian system.

Feiwel: If memory serves, earlier in your career your were critical of the Leontief system?

Klein: I wrote a review of a book that Leontief published in the 1950s on input-output systems. The thing that I was critical of was the constancy of the technical coefficients, not of the system itself. I was critical of the thought that it was Walrasian because, as I see it, it is only one part of Walras. I was also critical of the idea that the technical coefficients remain constant. However, the thing that we discovered in the late 1960s in our work on the world trade matrix is that there is a way of generating the movement of the technical coefficients as prices change. Now, Leontief rejects that. He says that estimates of the elasticity of substitution between inputs are not good enough to use as a basis for changing these coefficients. I say that the price signals are the best signals we have to go by. So my view of the Leontief system is of a system with changing production coefficients where the changes depend on the price system. And if you build a total system you have to explain the prices together with the flows of production. I got close to that in the early stages, in the 1950s, when I wrote a paper on the interpretation of the Leontief system as value ratios. I had an exchange about this with Morishima in the *Review of Economic Studies*. I still like my interpretation; it could be classified as a giant Cobb-Douglas interpretation of Leontief. And now we have gone to giant CES or giant trans-log interpretations, which are generalizations.

Feiwel: You mentioned that the Leontief system was not thought of too highly at Cowles. Could you enlarge on that?

Klein: One day I met Kenneth in the hall and I said something favourable about the Leontief system, that some problem or other should be analyzed with it. Kenneth replied that he thought this was just an accounting system. To people at Cowles, accounting identities were something to take into account but they did not get one anywhere. Kenneth was saying that this would not get me anywhere. I think that, although the production coefficients change, they do not do so immediately, overnight, so that it does get you somewhere. But the Cowles group did not want to structure the system that we were then building along Leontief lines. I did not press the point either, I only thought about it. It was in the early 1960s, when we were building the SSRC-Brookings model, that I pushed the point that we should include an input-output framework. I suggested that when we allocate investment behaviour to Jorgenson, housing activity analysis to Maisel, the monetary sector to De Leeuw, prices to Charlie

Schultze, and so on, we should allocate the input-output model to Karl Fox. Once we got into discussions within the group putting that model together, we began to see how input-output fitted into the total picture. It was towards the end of the 1960s that we were able to put together consistent models that had an input-output framework as a central part.

Feiwel: However great the theoretical merits of Kenneth's work on general equilibrium, does this have any tangible repercussions on the work that you are doing?

Klein: When I was at the Cowles Commission we discussed the Wald paper on existence of solutions to general equilibrium systems. We were interested in that problem as an intellectual question. Our models were always simultaneous equations. We acknowledged that the idea of simultaneous equations is a Walrasian one, But all that Walras did was to say you can view the economy as a solution to a set of simultaneous equations. That was our whole framework at Cowles. We wanted to develop each piece, but we saw the world as a solution of an equation set and we were aiming to build a model that worked. Naturally in that work we would question whether the solution to the constructed equation set exists. I personally thought that Wald had a very deep proof of that proposition, because in order to prove it he had to invoke economic behaviour of households. Economic decision-making, together with the existence of simultaneous equations, was part of the proof that showed the conditions under which a solution would exist. Kenneth's and Gerard's work was to specify the system more meaningfully, and to generalize and improve that proof.

They also taught us another thing. They taught us a way of looking at the role of the price system. Other people might retort that that is obvious: Friedman, for example, would be one of those. In the modern generation Barro appears to say that there is no such thing as macroeconomics, there is only microeconomics and one adds up the totals and that is that: so freshmen should only be taught microeconomics. Now, I do not accept those views, but I do accept the idea that the meaning of the price system is not so obvious – Kenneth and Gerard have taught us that meaning.

One could say that the whole statistical apparatus at the Cowles Commission did not pay off. We thought it would, but it did not.

There was no breakthrough in accuracy or precision for macroeconometric modeling, but we were taught a way to look at the structure of the models. In the same way, one could say that the general equilibrium existence theorem has not shown us how to go out and calculate prices for the detailed economy, but it did teach us the meaning of a price system. In more recent times, Herbert Scarf has worked out algorithms for computing approximate equilibria.

I remember that in the mid-1950s there was a series of answers to a question raised in the *Review of Economics and Statistics* (November 1954) by David Novick, about the usefulness of the mathematical method in economics. I was one of the dozen or so responders, and I pointed to the work on general equilibrium theory and activity analysis as having taught us the function of prices in bringing about equilibrium; it has explained to us the underlying meaning of prices. To me, that is the main contribution, in addition, of course, to the sheer intellectual achievement.

One could also say that game theory does not solve any problems. I remember, for instance, Marschak saying that six more books like von Neumann and Morgenstern and the future of economics is assured. Well, that is not the way that things have worked out. But one could say that game theory was a milestone, an achievement in the history of thought. In the same way the solution to the existence of equilibrium puzzle was a great achievement in the history of economic thought.

Feiwel: Arrow and Debreu have greatly advanced the techniques of economic analysis. Have they in your view also enriched deeply our understanding of the way the economic system works?

Klein: They enriched the axiomatic approach. They showed how the axiomatic approach could be used in economics. Along the way they solved problems that bothered us a lot. At the Cowles Commission we worried about the problem of homogeneous systems. This became a real problem because one of the techniques that Keynes used, to establish the existence of underemployment equilibria was to make one of the equations in the system inhomogeneous – it was the money illusion in wages. I always thought that that was a totally wrong-headed way of going about it: it had no behavioural support. Workers had no money illusion at all, except perhaps for very small amounts. Certainly after the Second World War everybody was superconscious of the way inflation ate up wage gains.

Well, we worried a lot because homogeneous functions really throw away one variable. We wondered about the system being overdetermined or underdetermined. This gave rise to the Patinkin question. The whole Patinkin problem grew out of our daily discussions at the Cowles Commission. Haavelmo, Patinkin, Rubin, Marschak, I, and others, were always around the blackboard puzzling about these issues. Haavelmo had a great idea: he said that there are systems that have a solution when they are dynamic and they are inhomogeneous, but when you stop them at a point of time and you try to take them to the steady state you force them to be homogeneous. So you say rational economic behaviour of an equilibrium sort has no money illusion, but there are speculators and people trying to make short-term gains in the actual economic world. The dynamic process is inhomogeneous. So you say there is a homogeneous core to an inhomogeneous system, and that the inhomogeneous system is the dynamic part.

Now I posed this question to Hurwicz and perhaps also to Kenneth. I asked, 'Does the system of dynamic equations that shows stability of prices according to the interpretation in Lange's appendix to his *Price Flexibility and Employment* also deal with this problem of system homogeneity in the long run steady state?' Indeed, Leo and Kenneth took up that question in a whole series of joint papers (reprinted in their *Studies in Resource Allocation Processes*). So, here is a problem that they worked out theoretically, in terms of the stability of the system, that bothered us in our specifications of the practical systems we were building. Their work implied that, yes, we could have systems that have Haavelmo's properties and can be stable and reach steady state equilibrium with homogeneity.

Feiwel: Is it a misrepresentation or misunderstanding, in your view, to say (as Franco Modigliani has in his Presidential Address to the American Economic Association) that the essence of the Keynesian problem is that the economy is unstable, that it can be stabilized, and hence should be stabilized?

Klein: You see, early Keynesian theory said that the economy could reach a stable equilibrium with persistent unemploymnent, perhaps not forever, but at least for long periods of time. Keynes did not say that the system was so much unstable; he said that if you let it alone, if the authorities back off and just let the market find a solution, it could be one of an underemployment equilibrium. Keynes then said that economic policy could guide the system back to full employment, but otherwise it would get bogged down in an underemployment equilibrium. Now, this does not suggest instability; it just suggests the impotency of the price mechanism in bringing about full employment.

Keynes was not arguing so much about the instability of the system as about the equilibrium of the system. I think that those are two points that always have to be kept separate, the equilibrium position – the existence of an equilibrium position – and the stability of the path of getting to equilibrium. Keynes did not deal very much with the exact path, he dealt mainly with the equilibrium position which was one of long-run unemployment, unless we intervene and change the system, or unless we intervene and change the nature of the equilibrium. But he did not say that the system is unstable, he might have said that it oscillates, but not that it is unstable.

Feiwel: To what extent did the work of Arrow, Hurwicz, and Block contribute to understanding the question of stability?

Klein: It certainly did clarify it in a very abstract sense. One of the critics that often visited at Cowles was Gerhard Tintner. He was mainly critical of our particular econometric approach. However, he had a theory of the business cycle that was really quite simple. He suggested that if you take a Cassel version of the Walrasian system, make it dynamic; say that you have *n* equations (*n* excess demand functions) and you make the rate of change of price a function of excess supply or demand; then that gives a dynamic system that has motion, and, he said, it might have some imaginary roots. Those imaginary roots would be sine and cosine functions. He then claimed that an explanation of the business cycle is the existence of this system. Now, that was a provocative point, very much like the Walrasian one that says that you can take a system of simultaneous equations and describe the economy as their solution. Tintner was saying, you can take a system of simultaneous equations, you can dynamize them, and you can say that if there are some imaginary roots, then we shall have cyclical fluctuations in the system. The real question is: are there imaginary roots? What are the conditions? What is the nature of these roots? Are they damped or explosive?

You could say that all the explorations of Arrow, Block and

Hurwicz and Arrow and Nerlove (with some kind of expectations mechanism) were investigations of some of the dynamic properties of that system. From the point of view of economics, what Tintner did was analogous to what Walras had done, in the sense of presenting us with a system of equations that had to be further investigated.

Feiwel: Is there, in your opinion, a fundamental difference in approach between Paul Samuelson and the Cowles people?

Klein: Paul did not really believe at the time in the formal transition between micro and macroeconomics; he did not believe in the approach that I took to the aggregation problem. I thought that he always took the easy way out, that is to say the Hicks way, which says that if all prices change in the same proportion then one can compute things as one would in the standard macrosystem, or that the macroequations have the same form as the microequations. Paul also used to say that one should take a macroeconomy as it is and you cannot derive it as an analogue of optimization.

When I first went to Cowles, Marschak pushed me into the aggregation problem, saying, 'Well, if you are going to pose this consumption function, this investment function, show me how you derive it from consumer theory and from the theory of the firm'. As you know, I was Samuelson's student. I wrote him a letter about what we were doing on production function estimation and how we were relating it to marginal productivity in the theory of the firm. He wrote me back saying this was a dead end that would not prove to be fruitful. I do not know whether I ever convinced him; he was always sceptical, not antagonistic. He was sceptical about the use of neoclassical theory and aggregation theory as a basis for our models. In a way his attitude was similar to the reaction of Domar, that I mentioned earlier on reading the monograph that I wrote, advising me just to write down the equations without justifying them by economic theory arguments. The Cowles group said, no you do have to justify them. Later Koopmans argued that the mechanical breakdown of the models was due to a lack of adequate economic theory. I did not accept that argument, but I did accept the insistence that they had to be theory-based. I think that Samuelson was sceptical about the validity of that. And he might still have that scepticism.

I have just reviewed for McGraw-Hill the Samuelson-Nordhaus twelfth edition of the textbook – the macro chapters only. They introduce early on an aggregate supply function and an aggregate demand function, both being functions of the general price level. My comments as a reader were: Where do these functions come from? I pointed out that one could explain the consumption function as they do by Engel curves and by going back to fundamental household decision-making, but one cannot simply pull a supply function out of thin air and say that there is a relation between GNP and the price level; one has to relate it back to the theory of the firm in the same way that one relates the consumption function to Engel analysis and the theory of the household. I think that their position is that macroeconomic relationships exist by themselves.

You see, in my own work I have always refrained from relying on Okun's law. I disapprove of the use of Okun's law. I do not challenge the numbers; everyone uses the law and I know what they are talking about. But it is just an empirical relationship between unemployment and GNP. One cannot derive it from fundamental behaviour particularly at the microeconomic level. It allots no role to capital. It just does not fit into the neoclassical interpretation.

Feiwel: Why does it have to be derived from neoclassical precepts?

Klein: Well, you see, if we break the line here and allow people to pull equations out of thin air, so to speak, without theoretical substantiation, then people will put models together with no guidance. They will simply say that these things are empirically related, that, for example, Okun has observed that unemployment moves when GNP moves: unemployment is one of the variables of our big system and GNP is another. The law shows how they have moved together. This reasoning skirts the problem of capital. One way of treating the problem of capital, through the back door, is in the same mistaken manner that Keynes did, by saying that we could treat the stock of capital as given. Well, the stock of capital cannot be given logically if you simultaneously have non-zero investment. And once you have investment and capital, there really is no simple relationship between output and unemployment. I regard Okun's law as a 'synthetic' relationship, and it cuts corners.

As I mentioned, the Cowles Commission wanted to be very fundamental. By and large I am wedded to the Cowles Commission approach. It is again a way of thinking about the economy and, from my point of view, it is a fruitful one. It keeps you from getting into troubled waters.

Feiwel: Would you say that the Cowles approach is more Walrasian, whereas Samuelson's approach is more Marshallian, though Paul insisted about the need of 'exorcizing the Marshallian incubus'?

Klein: Perhaps that is so. But the Cowles approach is also more neoclassical. Samuelson, of course, is a neoclassicist, but when he gets to macroeconomics, especially in the twelfth edition of the textbook, he says, well, that is the Keynesian approach to macroeconomics. The Cowles group, on the other hand, used no shortcuts. For example, the fundamental problem today is the high budget deficit related to high interest rates. The Secretary of the Treasury said that there is no correlation between budget deficit and interest rates. Well, that is a correct statement, but it does not tell us anything because there is no shortcut behavioural relationship between deficits and interest rates. They are both parts of a big system.

In the Cowles group we were always taught to think about the economy in terms of an interrelated system, even if that system involved 10, 20 or 1000s of equations. One was not supposed to cut corners and say that there was a relationship between two variables – that is what Okun's law is all about – that is what the budget deficit debate is all about. I find that I am not on the same wave-length as many of the Washington-based macroeconomists because they want to take shortcuts. You see, in my view, there is hardly any bivariate relationship in economics that is stable and robust. The real world is quite complicated. I think that this was the fundamental point of view at Cowles.

One of the other famous bivariate relationships is the quantity theory of money that poses a relationship between money and nominal GNP. There is no such stable relationship by itself; it is just a definition of velocity which is a variable. In the same way, there is no simple fundamental relationship between unemployment and GNP. Anybody who uses these 'great rules' is going to come to grief at one time or another. For example, velocity went all to pieces in the last few years – that was a breakdown; Okun's law was in abeyance for some time – that was a breakdown. These oversimplifications are very dangerous.

Feiwel: In what way, do you think, introductory courses in econometrics should be taught?

Klein: Actually, the book I wrote called *An Introduction to Econo-*

metrics is, in my opinion, the way the subject should be taught. Of course, not all the chapters of the book stand up because it was after all written in 1962, nearly a quarter of a century ago. Teaching econometrics after a background chapter in statistical methods, which is not truly econometrics, involves the blending of economic analysis with the statistical approach and it is not a pure exercise in statistics. However, nowadays the most popular textbooks in econometrics tend to be pure exercises in statistics. I think that they tend to be more like cookbooks. The students look to them for, say, what test to use, how to make calculations; they do not provide the students with ideas about how to go about making economic interpretations of their estimates. You do need both approaches, but up front you need economic analysis. Essentially you need the kind of economics that is in Henderson and Quandt, right up front, just behind the statistical chapter. This is not the usual way that the textbooks are written, nor is it the usual way that the courses are taught.

Feiwel: Would you comment on your observation that economic theory is deterministic and the world is stochastioc?

Klein: Economic theory can be stochastic. In his PhD thesis at Pennsylvania, Roy Weintraub analyzed the Arrow-Hurwicz stability analysis with the stochastic element added. In econometrics the stochastic element is very important; it conditions what is done with the problem; it conditions the outcome. Economic theory could go that route but it rarely does. Without the stochastic element economic theory is simpler to do, but, I think, much less revealing.

Feiwel: How do you envisage future developments in economics?

Klein: I think it will probably explore the expectations issue much more. We already have good ideas about how firms or households optimize, and more attention will have to be paid to how expectations are formed. That is one direction. Also, economic theory will probably become more stochastic and, in general, more dynamics-oriented.

Feiwel: May we have some of your personal observations about Kenneth Arrow as economist, scholar, and friend?

Klein: Kenneth is an old friend from the Cowles days. He has always been very smart. Now, you have to realize that I was very attached to Samuelson and he, too, is very smart. Friedman was around Chicago during my time at Cowles and he, too, is very smart. Another person at the Cowles Commission – a young kid at the time, named Herman Rubin, is also very smart. And Kenneth fitted into that group. But there is something else about him, he is quick. Kenneth is mathematically sophisticated, he can see through problems very rapidly. In some sense he was then a young genius. The question is: how did he stack up against Samuelson, Friedman, and Rubin? Kenneth has a much more balanced judgement than the others. I think that Friedman and Samuelson are more worldly than Kenneth. But he is just great in discussions, he can see through problems rapidly, he can unravel puzzles and provide quick answers. There are some theorists with whom one can talk very comfortably and Kenneth (and Gerard Debreu) is among them.

PART III
Theory of Resource Allocation

10 On the Non-existence of Equilibrium: From Thornton to Arrow

Takashi Negishi*

1 INTRODUCTION

Among the many contributions to economic science made by Arrow, one of the most important is certainly the proof of the existence of an equilibrium for a competitive economy.[1] The case where no equilibrium exists even though indifference curves, production functions, and so on, are fairly well behaved is a useful one to show the necessity of proving the existence of equilibrium. Mill (1869) indicates that one of the first examples of the non-existence of equilibrium consists of the counter examples to equilibrium theory given in W. T. Thornton's *On Labour* (1869) though Thornton himself was concerned not so much with the non-existence of equilibrium as the possibility of trade at disequilibrium prices. The Thornton-Mill examples of the non-existence of equilibrium are remarkable because they are due to the discontinuity of demand curves; other unsuccessful attempts to show the non-existence of equilibrium failed because of their assumption of continuity. The Thornton-Mill examples, as well as the example of Wald (1951), are, however, not so serious to equilibrium theory, if we consider, not the Walrasian *tâtonnement* with recontract, but the non-*tâtonnement* without recontract. From such non-*tâtonnement* point of view, a truly important example of the non-existence of equilibrium is the one given by Arrow, that is, the case where a Pareto optimal allocation cannot be viewed as a competitive equilibrium.[2]

*I must thank Professor K. J. Arrow for invaluable suggestions and warm encouragement given to my early studies of general equilibrium theory. It was in 1957 when I was a first year graduate student at Tokyo that I dared to write to him to discuss an alternative proof of the *existence* of equilibrium based on *Pareto optimality* of a competitive equilibrium, which was later published in *Metroeconomica* (1960). Subsequently, I joined the Office of Naval Research project at Stanford, where I began my studies of the *non-tâtonnement* stability problem.

2 THORNTON'S EXAMPLES

Thornton's *On Labour, Its Wrongful Claims and Rightful Dues, Its Actual Present and Possible Future* (1869) is famous in the history of economic science because it made J. S. Mill recant the wages fund doctrine.[3] It is, however, not only an attack on a specific equilibrium theory of the wages fund doctrine, but also a criticism of equilibrium theory in general. As Mill (1869) recognized, Thornton presented at least three counter examples to the theory that the equations of supply and demand determine prices.

The first example given by Thornton is that of Dutch and English auctions for fish.

> When a herring or mackerel boat has discharged on the beach at Hastings or Dover, last night's take of fish, the boatmen, in order to dispose of their cargo, commonly resort to a process called Dutch auction. The fish are divided into lots, each of which is set up at a higher price than the salesman expects to get for it, and he then gradually lowers his terms, until he comes to a price which some bystander is willing to pay rather than not have the lot, and to which he accordingly agrees. Suppose on one occasion the lot to have been a hundredweight, and the agreed price twenty shillings. If, on the same occasion, instead of the Dutch form of auction, the ordinary English mode had been adopted, the result might have been different. The operation would then have commenced by some bystander making a bid, which others might have successively exceeded, until a price was arrived at beyond which no one but the actual bidder could afford or was disposed to go. That sum would not necessarily be twenty shillings; very possibly it might be only eighteen shillings. The person who was prepared to pay the former price might very possibly be the only person present prepared to pay even so much as the latter price; and if so, he might get by English auction for eighteen shillings the fish for which at Dutch auction he would have paid twenty shillings. In the same market, with the same quantity of fish for sale, and with customers in number and every other respect the same, the same lot of fish might fetch two very different prices.[4]

Thornton's second and third examples of the failure of supply and demand as the law of price are those of horses and of gloves.

Suppose two persons at different times, or in different places, to have each a horse to sell, valued by the owner at £50; and that in the one case there are two, and in the other three persons, of whom every one is ready to pay £50 for the horse, though no one of them can afford to pay more. In both cases supply is the same, viz., one horse at £50; but demand is different, being in one case two, and in the other three, horses at £50. Yet the price at which the horses will be sold will be the same in both cases, viz., £50.

When a tradesman has placed upon his goods the highest price which any one will pay for them, the price cannot, of course, rise higher, yet the supply may be below the demand. A glover in a country town, on the eve of an assize ball, having only a dozen pairs of white gloves in store, might possibly be able to get ten shillings a pair for them. He would be able to get this if twelve persons were willing to pay that price rather than not go to the ball, or than go ungloved. But he could not get more than this, even though, while he was still higgling with his first batch of customers, a second batch, equally numerous, and neither more nor less eager, should enter his shop and offer to pay the same but not a higher price. The demand for gloves, which at first had been just equal to the supply, would now be exactly doubled, yet the price would not rise above ten shillings a pair. Such abundance of proof is surely decisive against the supposition that the price must rise when demand exceeds supply.[5]

3 MILL'S INTERPRETATIONS

Mill (1869) misinterpreted Thornton's example of auctions for fish that 'the demand and supply are equal at twenty shillings, and equal also at eighteen shillings'. Mill argued that the case may be conceived but in practice is hardly ever realized as it is an exception to the rule that demand increases with cheapness. In the second edition of *On Labour* (1870), Thornton reproduced the same example but changed prices from twenty and eighteen shillings to eight and six shillings and made a rejoinder to Mill.

In this particular case it would not be possible for supply and demand to be equal at two different prices. For the case is one in

> which demand would increase with cheapness. A hawker who was ready to pay 8 *s.* for a hundred herrings, would want more than a hundred if he could get a hundred for 6 *s.* There being then but a given quantity in the market, if that quantity were just sufficient to satisfy all the customers ready to buy at 8 *s.*, it follows that it would not have sufficed to satisfy them if the price had been 6 *s.* If supply and demand were equal at the former price, they would be unequal at the latter.[6]

In this example, therefore, there is an equilibrium price that equalizes demand and supply, that is, the price established by Dutch auction. If English auction is adopted, however, trade takes place at a lower price with demand larger than supply and unsatisfied demand remains after trade is over. The reason is, first, that there is no competition to bid up the price since no one except the actual purchaser is willing to buy any at that price. Secondly, the actual purchaser himself would not bid up the price even though he wants to buy more than the quantity supplied since he knows that the supply will not be increased. The lesson from this example is not the possibility of the non-existence of equilibrium but the possibility that Walrasian equilibrium can be established either through Walrasian *tâtonnement* or by Dutch auction, but not by English auction, if the supply is constant. Similarly, we can construct an example where Walrasian equilibrium can be established either through Walrasian *tâtonnement* or by English auction but not by Dutch auction when demand is constant but supply increases as the price rises.

Mill (1869) correctly recognized the examples of horses and gloves, given by Thornton as counter-examples to the law of demand and supply, as those of the non-existence of equilibrium:

> At £50 there is a demand for twice or three times the supply; at £50.0*s.* 01/4*d.* there is no demand at all. When the scale of the demand for a commodity is broken by so extraordinary a jump, the law fails in its application; not, I venture to say, from any fault in the law, but because the conditions on which its applicability depends do not exist.
>
> Mr. Thornton has shown that the law is not fulfilled – namely, when there is no price that would fulfil it; either the demand or the supply advancing or receding by such violent skips, that there is no halting point at which it just equals the other element.

The reason for the non-existence of equilibrium is, of course, the discontinuity of the demand (or supply) curve, in the case of present examples, caused by the indivisibility of a horse and a pair of gloves, as was pointed out by Chipman (1979). In both examples, each identical demander wants a minimum unit of commodities, that is, a horse or a pair of gloves, so that no price rise can clear the excess demand, that is, equate demand with the given positive supply.

Although Thornton's original (1869) aim was to show the possibility of trade at disequilibrium prices by the use of all of his three examples, he later (1870) recognized that the examples of horses and gloves show also the non-existence of equilibrium.

> Mr. Mill does not deny that in every single instance in which I have represented the law of supply and demand as failing, it does actually fail. Nay, he goes so far as to admit that in one of my classes of cases 'the conditions on which the applicability of the law depends do not exist' – that, whereas in those cases the law is that the price will be one which equalises the demand with the supply, I have shown not only that the price arrived at does not equalise them, but that there is no price whatever that could. And of another set of cases he similarly admits that fulfilment of the law therein is 'in the nature of things impossible'.[7]

4 UNSUCCESSFUL EXAMPLES

Thornton-Mill examples of the non-existence of equilibrium are remarkable in the sense that they are due to the discontinuity of demand curves while other unsuccessful attempts to show the non-existence of equilibrium failed because of their assumption of the continuity of demand and supply curves derived from well-behaved indifference curves and production functions.

Henderson and Quandt (1958) considered the case of a backward-bending supply curve for a factor of production such as labour in a two-commodity system of a consumption good and labour. It is shown as curve *ce* in Figure 10.1 where the price *p* of a commodity (labour) relative to the other (consumption good) is measured vertically and the demand *D* and supply *S* of the commodity, horizontally. If the demand curve for labour is like *fg*, equilibrium cannot exist since 'the quantity of labor that consumers offer is less than the quantity that entrepre-

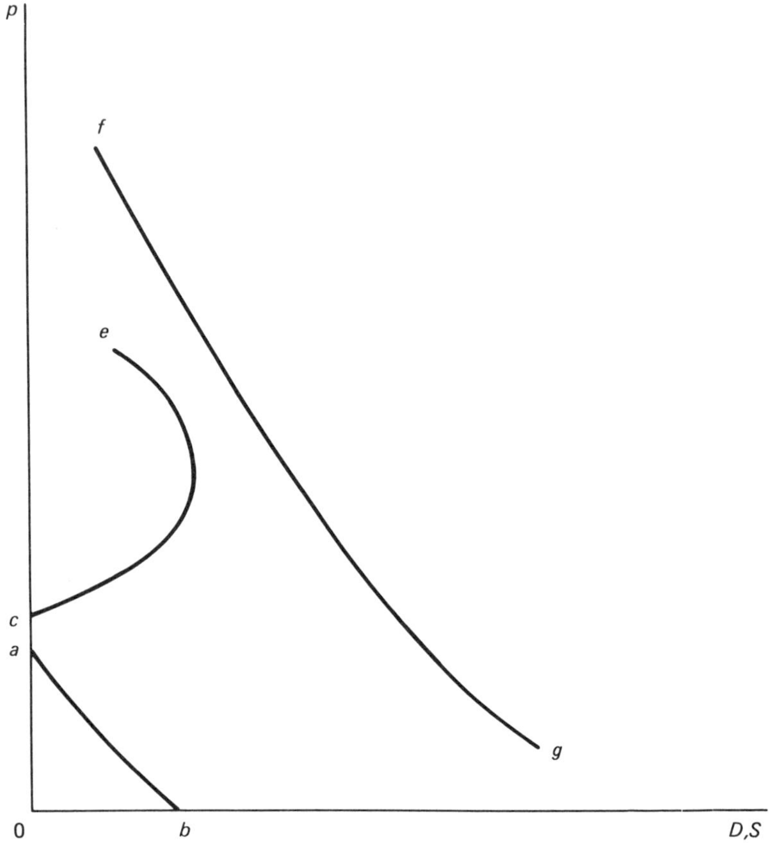

Figure 10.1 The case of a backward-bending supply curve for a factor of production in a two-commodity system of a consumption good and labour

neurs demand at every wage rate'. An example of a quadratic excess demand function for labour

$$D - S = p^2 - 14p + 53$$

is given, which has no real roots for $D = S$.[8] A backward-bending supply curve of labour can be derived from well-behaved indifference curves between leisure and consumption. Although no detailed descriptions of the behaviour of consumers and entrepreneurs and of the relations between them are given, demand and supply curves are considered as continuous and no sufficient conditions required in modern theorems of the existence of a competitive equilibrium are explicitly excluded. Henderson and Quandt's example of the non-existence of equilibrium has, therefore, no choice theoretic foundations.

According to Jaffé, Walras was aware of the possibility of non-existence of equilibrium, that is, of 'no solution' in his theory of exchange of two commodities for each other. What Walras showed is the case of a demand curve *ab* and a supply curve *ce* in Figure 10.1.[9] Chipman (1965b) correctly argued that this is a play on words, for what characterizes Walras's example is not the fact that there is no solution, but rather that there is no trade.[10] The demand curve should be considered not as *ab* but as *pab*, and the supply curve, not as *ce* but as O*ce*, so that any *p* located between *a* and *c* is a solution.

Morishima (1977) insists, however, that a no-trade equilibrium cannot be regarded as an essential equilibrium of exchange. Certainly, the essentiality of equilibrium is very important in the other three problems of Walras, that is, equilibria of production, capital accumulation, and money. If no commodity is produced at all, the equilibrium involving the possibility of production is not essential and reduced to an exchange equilibrium. Similarly, the equilibrium involving the possibility of capital accumulation is not essential and reduced to a simple production equilibrium if no net investment is made, and the monetary equilibrium is not essential and reduced to real economic equilibrium if the price of money is zero.[11] In the case of exchange equilibrium, however, the inessentiality of equilibrium (that is, no trade) is not so serious as in the case of inessentiality of other equilibria, since whether trade exists or not depends on the distribution of endowments of commodities among traders, which itself is changed through trading out of equilibria. The aim of trade is to make no further trade necessary, and no-trade equilibrium implies, not so much that no trade can take place, as that no trade is necessary, since a Pareto-optimum is already achieved, possibly through trading out of equilibria. In other words, Walras's example of the non-existence of an essential equilibrium can be important only if we stick to Walrasian *tâtonnement* which rules out any trading out of equilibria. Even then it should be noted that an essential exchange equilibrium becomes an inessential one after the equilibrium trade takes place.

5 NON-*TÂTONNEMENT* POINT OF VIEW

Not only Walras's example of an inessential exchange equilibrium, but also Thornton-Mill examples of the non-existence of equilibrium are not serious from the point of view of non-*tâtonnement* theory which introduces trading out of equilibria.[12] As a matter of fact, the original intention of Thornton's attack on equilibrium theory is to demonstrate not so much the non-existence of equilibrium, as the possibility (in the case of auctions for fish) or the necessity (in the cases of horses and gloves) of trading out of equilibria, that is, at disequilibrium prices.

Certainly £50 is not an equilibrium price of a horse, since only a horse is supplied while two or three horses are demanded. If a horse is sold at this disequilibrium price of £50, however, a Pareto-optimum is achieved, since unsatisfied demander(s) and the supplier do not evaluate a horse at more than £50 while the satisfied demander does not agree to sell back the horse just bought at £50. Even though there still remains excess demand of one or two horses at £50 after this trading, both demand and supply can be made zero by a slight rise of price from £50, so that an inessential exchange equilibrium is achieved. In the case of gloves, similarly, a Pareto optimal inessential exchange equilibrium is established at a price slightly higher than 10 shillings for a pair, after 12 pairs are sold to 12 persons at 10 shillings for a pair, even though another 12 persons remain unsatisfied.

If we stick to Walrasian *tâtonnement* where trading out of equilibria is ruled out, neither an essential nor inessential equilibrium exists in the examples of horses and gloves. In the case of fish, however, there exists an essential equilibrium at the price of 20 shillings (or 8 *s.*) which can be achieved through Walrasian *tâtonnement*. Even then, such an equilibrium cannot be established if we adopt the English auction. Suppose, as in the example of Thornton, the single person who is prepared to pay 20 shillings (or 8 *s.*) is the only person prepared to pay 18 shillings (or 6 *s.*) which is arrived through the English auction. At the latter price there is an excess demand, since this person wants more fish than at the former price. If fish are sold to this person at the latter price, however, the result is a Pareto-optimum which can be made an inessential equilibrium by raising the price up to 20 shillings (or 8 *s.*) after trading.

If, unlike in Thornton's examples, commodities are divisible, the result of trading out of equilibria can even be an essential equilibrium in the sense that at least the last step towards a Pareto optimum is an equilibrium trade. This can be seen by considering an example of the non-existence of equilibrium constructed by Wald (1951). Wald considered an exchange economy of three persons and three commodities. Marginal utilities of the *j*-th commodity for the *i*-th person U_{ij}:

$i = 1, 2, 3, j = 1, 2, 3$, are given as

$$
\begin{aligned}
u_{11}(x_{11}) &= 1/x_{11}, & & \\
u_{12}(x_{12}) &= (b - x_{12})/x_{12}^2 & & \text{for } x_{12} \leqq b \\
&= 0 & & \text{for } x_{12} > b \\
u_{13}(x_{13}) &= 2(c - x_{13})/x_{13}^2 & & \text{for } x_{13} \leqq c \\
&= 0 & & \text{for } x_{13} > c \\
u_{21}(x_{21}) &= 1/x_{21}^2 & & \\
u_{22}(x_{22}) &= 1/x_{22} & & \\
u_{23}(x_{23}) &= 0 & & \\
u_{31}(x_{31}) &= 1/x_{31}^2 & & \\
u_{32}(x_{32}) &= 0 & & \\
u_{33}(x_{33}) &= 1/x_{33} & &
\end{aligned}
$$

where x_{ij} signifies the amount of the *j*-th commodity held by the *i*-th person, and the initial holding a_{ij} of the *i*-th person of the *j*-th commodity is given as

$$
\begin{aligned}
a_{11} &= a, & a_{12} &= 0, & a_{13} &= 0, \\
a_{21} &= 0, & a_{22} &= b, & a_{23} &= 0, \\
a_{31} &= 0, & a_{32} &= 0, & a_{33} &= c,
\end{aligned}
$$

where a, b, c are given positive constants.

Wald skilfully demonstrated that no Walrasian equilibrium exists in this economy. Suppose, however, that trading out of equilibria is possible provided that it is Pareto improving, that is, no one's utility is decreased and someone else's utility increased by such a trade.[13] Since only the first and second persons are interested in the second commodity, and only the first and third persons are interested in the third commodity, and clearly the initial distribution of commodities (a_{ij}'s) is not Pareto optimal, the first and second commodities are exchanged between the first and second persons, and the first and third commodities are exchanged between the first and third persons, until a Pareto optimum is reached. The last (possibly infinitesimal) trade towards a Pareto optimum is an equilibrium trade at prices proportional to the first person's marginal utilities at the Pareto optimum, in the sense that demand and supply are equalized for each commodity at such prices, provided that the Pareto optimum is an inessential equilibrium. In this case, the Pareto optimum achieved is an inessential equilibrium. If $x_{12}=b$ and $x_{21}=0$ at such Pareto optimum, then $u_{11}>0$, $u_{12}=0$ while u_{21} is positive but finite and u_{22} is infinitely large so that conditions for a Pareto optimum are not satisfied. Therefore, $x_{12}<b$ and $x_{22}>0$. Similarly, $x_{13}<c$ and $x_{33}>0$. Then, positive (x_{11}, x_{12}, x_{13}) is the most preferred among the commodity bundles equally or less valuable at positive prices proportional to marginal utilities, u_{11}, u_{12} and u_{13}. Since $u_{11}/u_{12}=u_{21}/u_{22}$ and $u_{11}/u_{13}=u_{13}/u_{33}$, positive (x_{21}, x_{22}) and (x_{31}, x_{33}) are also the most preferred respectively among the commodity bundles equally or less valued.

Thornton seemed to admit these arguments, though he insisted that the law of demand and supply can then be applicable only in a trivial sense.

> it would be but a mere fraction of the whole stock of goods that would be sold at equation price, by far the greater part being sold at prices at which supply and demand were unequal ... the price at which the last lot of any commodity is sold must be one at which supply and demand are equal – one at which, there being of course but one customer desirous of purchasing left, that last customer could get as much of the commodity as he desired – the truth might be rather worth knowing than not; still, seeing that every lot of the commodity except the very last would have been sold at prices at which supply and demand were not equal, it is not easy to conceive a piece of knowledge more barren of practical utility.[14]

6 ARROW'S EXAMPLE

Our considerations suggest that an example of the non-existence of equilibrium which does really matter for the equilibrium theory is the one of Pareto optimum, either given as the initial distribution of commodities or achieved as a result of trading out of equilibria, which is not an inessential equilibrium. Such is the celebrated example given by Arrow.[15]

Figure 10.2 is the so-called Edgeworth box diagram, where the first commodity is measured horizontally, and the second commodity

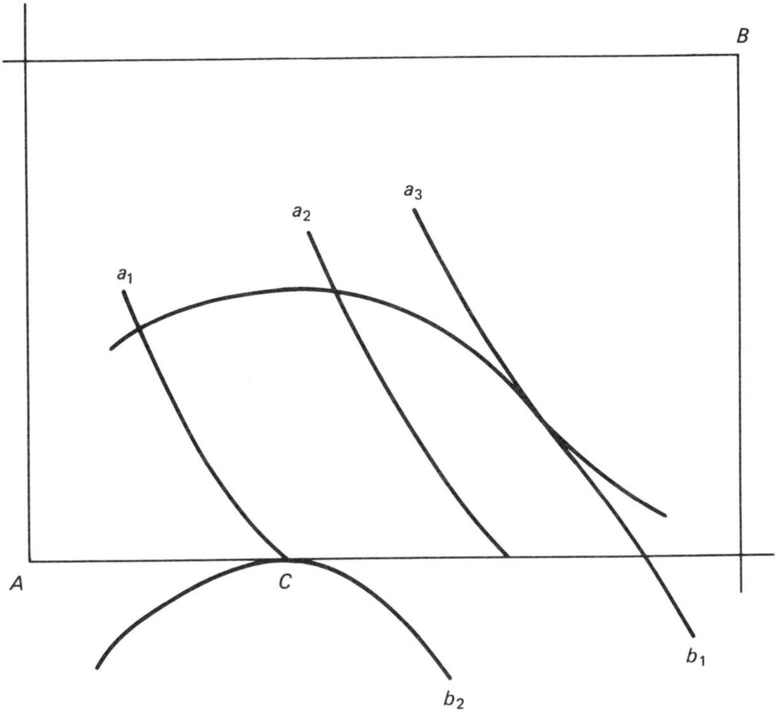

Figure 10.2 The Edgeworth box diagram

vertically. Commodities allocated to person *A* are measured from the origin *A*, and those allocated to person *B*, from the origin *B*. Curves a_1, a_2, a_3 are indifference curves of person *A* and curves b_1, b_2 are those of person *B*. Point *C* is clearly a Pareto optimum where the marginal utility of the first commodity is zero for person *B*. If the first commodity is free, the price line through *C* is horizontal and *A* demands an infinitely large amount of the first commodity while *B* does not supply any of the first commodity, so that *C* is not an equilibrium. If the first commodity is not free, the price line through *C* is not horizontal and *B* demands more of the second commodity while *A* does not supply the second commodity, or even demands it, so that again *C* is not an equilibrium.

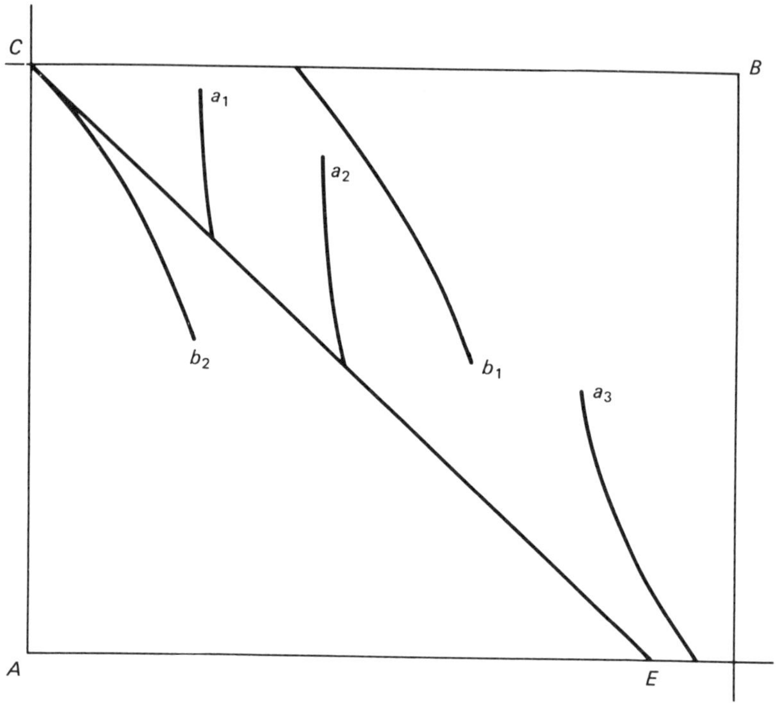

Figure 10.3 The Edgeworth box diagram (modified)

In Arrow's example, the demand curve for the first commodity is discontinuous when its price is zero, since the demand is infinitely large when the price is zero while the demand is zero when the price is even infinitesimally positive. Similar discontinuity exists also in Wald's example. This is partly the reason for the non-existence of equilibrium. An example of a demand curve discontinuous at some positive price can be constructed by a slight modification of Arrow's example. Figure 10.3 is an Edgeworth box diagram similar to Figure 10.2, except that the area *ACE* does not belong to the consumption set of *A*.[16] Suppose the first commodity is a consumption good and the second commodity is labour. *A* has *AC* of the maximum amount of labour to be supplied and *B* has *BC* of consumption good. To supply labour it is physiologically necessary to consume the consumption good and the line *CE* indicates the minimum necessary consumption required by A to supply different amounts of labour. When the price of the consumption good in terms of labour is AC/AE or lower, A demands AE or more of the consumption good while A does not supply labour and does not demand the consumption good when the price is higher than AC/AE. The demand curve for the first commodity is discontinuous at the price of AC/AE and a Pareto optimum C is not an equilibrium, since B does not supply the consumption good when its price is AC/AE or lower and demands labour when the price is higher than AC/AE.

NOTES

1. See Arrow and Debreu (1954); Arrow and Hahn (1971), pp. 107–28.
2. See Arrow (1951). Chipman (1965b) gave an interesting interpretation with referrences to classical debates on the possibility of glut.
3. Mill (1869); see Negishi (1985) for Mill's recantation of wages fund theory.
4. Thornton (1869), pp. 47–8, quoted from Mill (1869); see also Thornton (1870), pp. 56–7.
5. Thornton (1869), pp. 49, 51–2, quoted from Mill (1869); see also Thornton (1870), pp. 59, 61–2.
6. Thornton (1870), pp. 57–8; see also p. 60.
7. Thornton (1870), p. 68. 'One of my classes of cases' is the case of horses and 'another set of cases' is the case of gloves.
8. Henderson and Quandt (1958), pp. 155–7. Fortunately, this example was withdrawn in the subsequent editions.
9. Walras (1954), pp. 108, 502.
10. Chipman (1965a) argued, however, that Walras 'seems to assume that both traders start out with more of everything than they want, so that there is really no economic problem', which is clearly not the case, since the price is positive and finite.
11. See Morishima (1977), pp. 17–18; Hahn (1965).
12. See Arrow and Hahn (1971), pp. 324–46, and Negishi (1972), pp. 207–27.
13. This seems to be the most plausible rule for trading out of equilibria in a moneyless model of an economy; see Hahn (1962); Morishima (1964), pp. 43–53; Uzawa (1962). For the so-called Hahn rule which is applicable to monetary economy, see Arrow and Hahn (1971), pp. 337–45.
14. Thornton (1870), p. 65. See also Thornton (1869), p. 53.
15. See Arrow (1951), Figure 2 and Quirk and Saposnik (1968), p. 133, Figure 4.8. In the latter figure, however, the contract curve is wrongly drawn.
16. For the definition of consumption set which is independent of preference, see Debreu (1959), p. 51.

REFERENCES

Arrow, K. J. (1951) 'An Extension of the Basic Theorems of Classical Welfare Economics', in J. Neyman (ed.) *Proceedings of the Second Berkeley Symposium on Mathematical Statistics and Probability* (Berkeley: University of California Press) pp. 507–32.

Arrow, K. J. and G. Debreu (1954) 'Existence of an Equilibrium for a Competitive Economy', *Econometrica*, 22: 265–90.

Arrow, K. J. and F. H. Hahn (1971) *General Competitive Analysis* (San Francisco: Holden-Day).

Chipman, J. S. (1965a) 'The Nature and Meaning of Equilibrium in Economic Theory', D. Martindale (ed). *Functionalism in the Social Sciences* (Philadelphia: American Academy of Political and Social Science) pp. 35–64.

Chipman, J. S. (1965b) 'A Survey of the Theory of International Trade, Part 2', *Econometrica*, 33: 685–760.

Chipman, J. S. (1979) 'Mill's "Superstructure": How well does it stand up?' *History of Political Economy*, 11: 477–500.

Debreu, G. (1959) *Theory of Value* (New Haven: Yale University Press).

Hahn, F. H. (1962) 'On the Stability of Pure Exchange Equilibrium', *International Economic Review*, 3: 206–13.

Hahn, F. H. (1965) 'On Some Problems in Proving the Existence of Equilibrium in a Monetary Economy', in F. H. Hahn and F. P. R. Brechling (eds) *The Theory of Interest Rates* (London: Macmillan) pp. 126–35.

Henderson, J. M. and R. E. Quandt (1958) *Microeconomic Theory* (New York: McGraw-Hill).

Mill, J. S. (1869) 'Thornton on Labour and Its Claims', in *Collected Works of John Stuart Mill*, vol. V (Toronto: University of Toronto Press) pp. 631–68.

Morishima, M. (1964) *Equilibrium Stability and Growth* (Oxford: Oxford University Press).

Morishima, M. (1977) *Walras' Economics* (Cambridge: Cambridge University Press).

Negishi, T. (1972) *General Equilibrium Theory and International Trade* (Amsterdam: North-Holland).

Negishi, T. (1985) 'Comments on Ekelund "Mill's Recantation of the Wages Fund",' *Oxford Economic Papers.*

Quirk J. and R. Saposnik (1968) *Introduction to General Equilibrium Theory and Welfare Economics* (New York: McGraw-Hill!)

Thornton, W. T. (1869) *On Labour, Its Wrongful Claims and Rightful Dues, Its Actual Present and Possible Future* (London: Macmillan).

Thornton, W. T. (1870) ibid, 2nd edn (London: Macmillan).

Uzawa, H. (1962) 'On the Stability of Edgeworth's Barter Process', *International Economic Review*, 3: 218–32

Wald, A. (1951) 'On Some Systems of Equations of Mathematical Economics', *Econometrica*, 19: 368–403

Walras, L. (1954) *Elements of Pure Economics*, translated from the definitive (1926) edn by W. Jaffé (1st edn 1874–7) (London: Allen & Unwin).

11 On Equilibria of Bid–Ask Markets

Robert B. Wilson*

Among his many contributions to economic theory, Kenneth Arrow's studies of general equilibrium are especially important to the continuing development of the fine structure of market-mediated allocation processes. The paradigm of efficient decentralized allocation via market clearing prices developed from the Walrasian model in the long line of research given its greatest impetus by Arrow, Gerard Debreu, and their colleagues. The demonstration that 'perfectly' competitive complete markets, characterized by universal price-taking behaviour, can in principle (absent non-convexities, and so on) attain an efficient allocation set the cornerstone of the theory of markets. By establishing the standard against which further studies of imperfectly competitive and incomplete markets are compared, this accomplishment continues to shape the agenda of continuing research on competitive processes.

Building on the foundation established by the theory of Walrasian models of general equilibrium with perfect competition, subsequent studies have aimed to elucidate the mechanisms of price formation in imperfectly competitive markets. One approach has been experimental and the data have strongly confirmed the predictive power of the Walrasian model, particularly in the case of pure exchange via publicly announced bid and ask prices, even with relatively few participants. In replicated markets most of the gains from trade are realized and the

* This work was supported by grant SES 83-08-723 from the National Science Foundation and contract ONR N00014 79 C 0685 from the Office of Naval Research. I am indebted to Peter Cramton for inspiration and the insights that made this research possible, and to Drew Fudenberg, David Kreps, John Ledyard and John Roberts for discussions, though none of these are responsible for my errors.

I gladly dedicate this chapter to my friend and colleague Kenneth Arrow. Over a span of 20 years I have benefited continually from Ken's unbounded creativity, sparkling intellect, and professional leadership. I have always thought of him as the finest example of the humane concerns of the scholar. This chapter is a small token of my great appreciation, I only wish that it achieved the definitive solution so often attained in Ken's work.

trading prices converge quickly to or near the Walrasian price. A second approach has aimed to establish game-theoretic foundations for imperfectly competitive markets, focusing mainly on models of oligopoly and monopolistic competition but also recently on the extreme case of pure exchange represented by models of bilateral bargaining.

In this chapter we undertake an exploratory analysis of the connection between bilateral bargaining and the multilateral bargaining that is inherent in trading processes such as bid–ask markets. The theme suggested is that the theory of bilateral bargaining has a natural extension to multilateral trading in bid–ask markets, and then this extension generalizes naturally to encompass models of nearly perfect competition with many buyers and sellers. Our results are not complete, since we only examine certain necessary conditions and merely speculate on the appropriate sufficiency conditions, but nevertheless, the internal consistency of the construction is encouraging.

Our analysis is based entirely on extrapolation from the important results obtained by Cramton (1984) for a model of bilateral bargaining between a buyer and a seller, with a crucial exception. Generalizing from the work of Rubinstein (1982) on a model with complete information, Cramton derives an equilibrium for a model with incomplete information in which each party's reservation price for the item to be traded is privately known. A main conclusion from this work is that the parties' impatience for an agreement, reflected in the interest rates they use to discount future payoffs, are major determinants of their bid, ask, and acceptance strategies. Moreover, trading takes time because each party needs to signal credibly his or her reservation price, and delay in offering or accepting proposed prices is an important credible signal.[1]

In generalizing Cramton's construction to multilateral markets, we propose to omit the role of impatience in the form of discounting in order to show how impatience arises endogenously from the competitive pressures among multiple buyers and among multiple sellers. That is, in multilateral situations a buyer or seller is impatient to trade lest a competitor usurp the opportunity with an earlier bid or ask that might be accepted. In doing so we obtain some notational and analytical simplicity in an otherwise very complicated formulation, while at the same time we illustrate starkly the endogenous generation of impatience among the traders. A price we pay, however, is that the results are further incomplete due to the absence of a theory of the associated endgames that result when only one buyer or one seller remains who has not previously traded, and who is therefore not subject to competitive pressure. (The possible resolutions of this difficulty are discussed in Section 5.)

Showing that competitive pressure suffices to create impatience contributes to the second part of our agenda, which is to argue that bid–ask markets with many buyers and sellers approximate perfectly competitive markets; for example, the equilibrium strategies imply near exhaustion of the gains from trade at prices approximating the Walrasian clearing price. This agenda requires that strong competitive pressures create overwhelming impatience so that trade proceeds quickly and little is lost in delay costs if in fact the participants have positive interest rates. One hopes to establish eventually, though not here, that with very many traders the market clears nearly immediately at prices predominately close to the Walrasian clearing price – thereby establishing a game-theoretic foundation for the Walrasian model of perfect competition in the case of pure exchange with incomplete information. Such a construction would at the same time yield an answer to von Hayek's long-standing conundrum as to how it is that information dispersed among the traders is manifested in prices.

The execution of this agenda lies far beyond what will be accomplished in this chapter, and indeed its premises might still be found false. Nevertheless, here we take the first steps to construct the hypothesized form of the equilibrium.

1 INTRODUCTION

The bid-ask market is a common form of market organization, prevalent for instance in the commodity exchanges that are often used as the chief examples of perfectly competitive markets. It has been the subject of several experimental studies, some of which are reviewed by Plott (1982) and Smith (1982). These experiments use the format of an oral double auction. In the simplest version, each trader is assigned a role as either a seller or a buyer, with an inelastic supply of, or demand for, one unit at a privately known reservation price. A limited duration is allowed in which at each time each trader can post an ask or a bid price, or accept one of the previously posted prices and thereby conclude a trade. A trader's payoff is the difference between his or her reservation price and the accepted price, or zero if the trader fails to trade. A prominent feature of the experimental results is that frequently most of the gains from trade are realized. Our aim is to show that this feature and others of interest would also obtain if the traders used strategies of the form derived by Cramton in the case of bilateral bargaining. Moreover, we will verify that such strategies satisfy at least the necessary conditions for an equilibrium.

The purpose of this chapter, then, is to construct a proposed equilibrium for a model of an oral double auction. The model used is somewhat stylized; for example, time is taken to be continuous. Moreover, the equilibrium has the special form derived in prior work by Cramton (1984) for the special case of one seller and one buyer; no attempt is made here to find other equilibria.[2]

Our main result characterizes the proposed equilibrium as a multilateral sequential bargaining process in which sellers and buyers are endogenously paired off to trade until the gains from trade are nearly exhausted. If there are many sellers and buyers then there is a small chance that a profitable trade will be missed, and if so the unrealized gains from trade are small.

The price at which each pair trades is determined by the prospect of competition from other sellers and buyers. This feature differs from Cramton's characterization in which each trader's impatience to reach an agreement derives from an exogenously specified interest rate at which future payoffs are discounted.

The model is formulated in Section 2.[3] The proposed equilibrium is then described informally in Section 3, and its main implications are derived. In Section 4 we undertake a more detailed construction and specify the traders' strategies completely except for contingencies far from the 'equilibrium path'. The special case of one seller or one buyer (that is, an ordinary auction) is discussed briefly in Section 5 without specific results, since in this case it is necessary to add some exogenous source of impatience to sustain the form of strategy of a monopolist trader. Concluding remarks are in Section 6.

A caution about terminology: we use the term 'equilibrium' in what follows even though we examine only whether the proposed equilibrium satisfies certain necessary conditions. The reader is urged to remember that it may yet be found that the construction fails because our assumptions or the necessary conditions prove to be insufficient.

2 FORMULATION

The following data of the game are common knowledge among the players. There are $m+n$ traders divided into m sellers and n buyers, and a single traded good to be exchanged for money. Each seller $i=1, \ldots,$

m has an inelastic supply of one indivisible unit at any price not less than his privately known reservation price u_i, which we call his *valuation*. Similarly, each buyer $j=1, \ldots, n$ has an inelastic demand for one unit at any price not exceeding his privately known valuation v_j. Thus, if seller i and buyer j trade at the price p then their payoffs are $p-u_i$ and v_j-p respectively. The traders' preferences are linear in these payoffs; neither risk aversion nor wealth effects are present. The traders' valuations $U=(u_i)_{i=1,\ldots,m}$ and $V=(v_j)_{j=1,\ldots,n}$ are jointly distributed according to the distribution function

$$F(a, b) \equiv \Pr\{U \geqslant a \;\&\; V \leqslant b\} \tag{1}$$

with a positive density on the support $[u^*,1]^m \times [O,v^*]^n$. (Note that F is a right-cumulative distribution in terms of U; all other distribution functions used will be left cumulatives.) Suppose that $u^* < v^*$ so that gains from trade are not precluded. Assume that (U,V) are affiliated (see Milgrom and Weber, 1982), and symmetrically distributed in the sense that $F(a, b)=F(aa, \beta b)$ for any two permutations α and β on m and n characters respectively.[4] Associated with F is the expectation operator $\mathcal{E}\{\cdot\}$ and the various conditional expectation operators $\mathcal{E}\{\cdot|\cdot\}$; for example, the one relevant for seller i is $\mathcal{E}\{\cdot|u_i\}$ which conditions on his valuation u_i. These operators can be conditioned further on observations of public events, interpreted for their informational significance using the traders' equilibrium strategies.

Remark: A special case of such a distribution arises naturally in our construction and the reader may find it useful for interpretive purposes. Suppose that the buyers' valuations are independent of the sellers' valuations, and for illustration consider only the joint distribution of the buyers' valuations. Suppose that the buyers' valuations are conditionally independent and identically distributed given the value of a random variable $z \in [0,v^*]$, each with the distribution function F_B and the distribution function G for z. Unconditionally it is known only that the buyers' valuations do not exceed z, so that

$$\Pr\{V \leqslant b\} = \int_0^{v^*} \Pi_j F_B(\min\{b_j, z\}) dG(z).$$

Such a case arises if the buyers' valuations were known initially to be independent but midway in the trading process it is inferred that those buyers who have not yet traded are those with valuations less than the ones who have already traded, but the minimum z among the valuations of those who have previously traded is not observed. Note that the distribution G is then the distribution of the rank order statistic appropriate to the number of buyers who have previously traded [see equation (5) below].

As usual in game-theoretic formulations, the traders' equilibrium strategies are assumed to be common knowledge. The following trading rules are also common knowledge: Play is confined to a duration 1 and time, which runs continuously, is indexed by $t \in [0,1)$; since trade ceases at $t=1$ there are no 'final offers'. At each time each trader who has not previously transacted can post an ask or a bid price or accept a posted price: sellers post asks and accept bids, buyers post bids and accept asks. Acceptance fixes that price for both the poster and the acceptor and these two traders are inactive thereafter; recontracting is excluded. All posted prices and acceptances are observed by all traders, and each trader has perfect recall.

A *strategy* for a trader specifies at each time he is active (that is, has not yet transacted) his action conditional on the common knowledge, his observations to date, and his valuation. His action is either his posted price, if any, or his acceptance of a posted price, thereby concluding his activity.

A *belief system* for a trader specifies at each time he is active a probability distribution over the other active traders' valuations, conditional on the common knowledge, his observations, and his valuation – starting with F at time $t=0$ conditioned on his valuation. An assignment of strategies and belief systems to the traders is *consistent* if the belief system is a conditional probability system satisfying Bayes's Rule wherever applicable (that is, the most recent conditioning event is not null).[5]

We present a special kind of Nash equilibrium called *a sequential equilibrium* by Kreps and Wilson (1982). A sequential equilibrium is a consistent assignment of strategies and beliefs to the traders such that for each trader, conditional on the time, his observations, and his valuation, his strategy for the remainder of the game is optimal given his current probability assessment and the other traders' strategies. We are interested, moreover, in a special kind of sequential equilibrium, called *Markov perfect* by Maskin and Tirole (1983), having the property that a trader's strategy at each contingency depends on the current history only through his current beliefs; that is, his current beliefs are a sufficient summary of the history. Interest in such an equilibrium stems from the fact that if other traders' strategies do not depend on the details of the prior history then a trader obtains no advantage from conditioning his strategy on these details. We shall also specify that the equilibrium is *symmetric*; all sellers (and buyers) use the same strategy and belief system. Because their valuations differ, however, different sellers (or buyers) generally take different actions in similar contingencies.

Assume that each trader is indifferent as to the time he transacts; a trader does not discount future payoffs. We are thus able to construct the equilibrium so that it is independent of any particular interpretation of clock time. That is, it suffices to describe the strategies as implicit functions of time and then to allow that the actual equilibrium is obtained from any parameterization of time that is common knowledge among the traders; this technique is illustrated in section 4. Since time runs continuously, moreover, the time index can be re-started at zero after each transaction. For example, if the first trade occurs at $t=0.5$ then the remaining $m-1$ sellers and $n-1$ buyers enter a 'subgame' with a new clock that runs twice as fast as the original clock, so that both clocks register 1 and close the market at the same instant. (In practice there is a natural parameterization of time derived from the rate at which postings and acceptances are recorded; here we ignore this feature of the transaction technology.) The construction is designed in this way so that we need to describe only the strategies for a typical 'subgame' similar to the original game except for the number of traders and the conditioning of probability assessments.

Several technical specifications complete the formulation. First, we choose to exclude retention of posted prices; the posted prices at each time are those offered at that instant. Secondly, ties are resolved by some tie-breaking rule. The natural rule is a randomization: (a) multiple asks (or bids) at the same price at the same time are resolved by choosing one by an independent, uniform randomization; and (b) multiple acceptances of a single posted price are similarly chosen randomly. This natural rule complicates formulas, however, so here we opt in favour of the (admittedly impractical) rule of choosing the seller with the least valuation or the buyer with the greatest valuation. Thirdly, multiple postings of different ask prices (or bid prices) at the same time are excluded; only the least ask (or the greatest bid) is posted. Similarly, an acceptance is interpreted as acceptance of the least current ask (or the greatest current bid); and posting, say, an ask less than, or equal to, the current posted bid is interpreted as acceptance. Further ambiguities can arise from the continuity of time and we resolve these by imagining that each instant is an infinitesimal interval that allows traders to respond to each other's actions: for example, a seller's strategy can specify in some contingency that he asks the minimum of his 'intended' price p and the least among the prices asked (if any) by competing sellers and not exceeding his valuation (for example, if several sellers do this then the resulting posted price is the second lowest valuation, posted by the seller with the least valuation). As we shall see, these technical specifications have little effect on the particular equilibrium that is constructed.

Lastly we mention some notational conventions. The notation $x \bigcap y$ where x is a scalar and y is a vector indicates the vector $(\min\{x,y_j\})$, and similarly $x \bigcup y$ indicates the vector of maxima. Functions of time are shown in **boldface** type to indicate that they depend on the parameterization of time. Expectations and probability distributions that are conditioned on the publicly observed history up to time t are denoted by $\mathcal{E}_t\{\cdot|\cdot\}$ and F_t. We use similar notation to represent conditioning on a seller's valuation $[F(\cdot|u_i)]$ and a buyer's valuation $[F(\cdot|v_j)]$; no confusion should result. $\bar{F}_t(\bar{v})$ is used to indicate the distribution function of the maximum $\bar{v}$ among the buyers' valuations, and similarly for the distribution of the minimum of the sellers' valuations. Each distribution can be conditioned further on publicly observed events or inferences from the traders' strategies. We use a semi-colon to separate conditioning on a valuation and conditioning on an extreme valuation; for example, $\bar{F}_t(\bar{v}|u;\tilde{u})$ is the distribution function of $\bar{v}$ at time t conditioned on one seller's valuation being u and the *minimum* among the *other* sellers' valuations being $\tilde{u}$.

The exposition is eased by supposing that a trader who fails to trade in the game actually trades elsewhere at a reservation price equal to his valuation. Thus, the payoff of a seller with the valuation u can be interpreted as either his transaction price or, if he fails to trade, then his valuation u; similarly a buyer with the valuation v obtains either his transaction price or his valuation v. Following this convention, we use $U(u)$ to indicate the expected price obtained by a seller (so in the original formulation his payoff is $U(u)-u$), which he wants to maximize, and $V(v)$ to indicate the expected price obtained by a buyer (so his payoff is $v-V(v)$ in the original formulation), which he wants to minimize.

After two traders transact they become inactive and the remaining active traders enter an ensuing 'subgame'; the typical notation uses F° to indicate the conditional probability distribution they carry into the ensuing 'subgame' (restricted to the support of the active traders' valuations conditioned on the history of observations, though this conditioning will not always be explicit), U° and V° to indicate the expected payoffs of a seller and a buyer in the ensuing subgame, and so on. (This is a non-standard use of the term 'subgame', equivalent to the notion of a *subform* used by some authors to indicate what would be a subgame were it not for the effects of the incomplete information regarding the initial assignment of valuations to the traders. Here we induce a particular continuation game that the remaining active traders play by specifying their probability assessments as determined by conditioning on the prior history of play. However, later we shall allow that prior history can influence beliefs off the equilibrium path; see Section 4. Hereafter we use the term subgame without apology.)

3 THE EQUILIBRIUM: DESCRIPTION AND IMPLICATIONS

In this section we describe the equilibrium informally in order to convey its structural features, and then derive its main implications. The precise specification is deferred to Section 4.

The significant aspect of the equilibrium is that sellers and buyers are sequentially matched for transactions via an endogenous process that continues so long as there is a chance that gains from trade remain and time has not expired. Moreover, the price at which each pair transacts is determined by the competitive pressures from other sellers and buyers who are alternative trading partners. The following description sketches the workings of this process. We concentrate on the results of play according to the equilibrium strategies (that is, along the 'equilibrium path') and mention only briefly the consequences of deviations, which will be elaborated in Section 4.

A key property of the equilibrium is that each strategy is a monotone function of the trader's privately known valuation. This property has several important consequences. First, given our choice of the tie-breaking rule (see Section 2), traders are matched in order of their valuations: the seller with the lowest valuation transacts first (if at all) with the buyer having the highest valuation. Consequently, each transaction moves the remaining active traders into an appropriately specified subgame that is *similar* to the original game; for example, the numbers of active sellers and buyers are reduced from m and n to $m-1$ and $n-1$, time is again initialized at zero, and the remaining active traders' probability assessments are conditioned on the accumulated observations. Since the equilibrium is sequential, the strategies for the remaining active traders must constitute a sequential equilibrium for this subgame. By an induction argument, therefore, along the equilibrium path it suffices to describe the equilibrium for a typical subgame. However, the terminal subgames having only one seller or one buyer are special, because competitive pressure is absent, so their description is referred to Section 5.

Secondly, in a typical subgame a price offered by one trader allows others to infer information about his valuation. The form of the equilibrium we construct is essentially characterized by this inferential process, which is derived from the prior work of Cramton (1984). It is useful to distinguish between *non-serious* and *serious* ask and bid prices. An ask so high or a bid so low that it has zero probability of being accepted (according to the equilibrium strategies) is non-serious, and serious otherwise. For example, an ask is non-serious if it exceeds a posted ask or if there is no other serious ask offered and the ask exceeds the highest price that any buyer would accept according to the equilibrium strategies. We construct an equilibrium in which the traders' beliefs and strategies do not depend on the magnitudes of non-serious offers; similarly, not posting any offer is interpreted as the same as offering a non-serious price. Interest in such an equilibrium stems from the fact that a trader has no incentive to choose a particular non-serious offer from the many available unless it has some special significance as a signal; if other traders make no inferences from the numerical magnitudes of non-serious offers then a trader is indifferent as to which non-serious offer he makes. Since we seek a Markov perfect equilibrium in which the details of the history have no special significance along the equilibrium path we want to exclude the possibility of signalling and thus rule out any inferential process that would motivate a trader to prefer one non-serious offer over another.

With this convention, the inferential process allows two possibilities after a trader makes an offer. The trader either makes a serious offer and the others then infer his valuation by inverting his strategy, or he makes a non-serious offer and the others infer only that his valuation is insufficient to prompt a serious offer. In the case of a seller, for example, if his ask price exceeds the maximum serious ask price then others infer only that his valuation exceeds the maximum valuation that would have led him to offer a serious price in that contingency. (Later we reinforce this approach further by requiring that also off the equilibrium path other traders infer that a trader's valuation is no less extreme than the most extreme that can be inferred from the entire history of his serious offers; for example, others infer that a seller's valuation is no more than the least valuation consistent, according to the equilibrium strategies, with any one of his serious ask prices.)

This inferential process has strong incentive effects, as we shall see. Each trader prefers to delay his first serious offer so as to prevent others from inferring that his valuation is more extreme than in fact it is. A seller, for example, wants to avoid the inference that his valuation is lower than it actually is. He does this by delaying his first serious offer until it signals correctly his valuation – and competitive pressure, the prospect that another trader will usurp the opportunity to trade, will make him delay no longer.

This form of the equilibrium implies that a typical subgame divides into two phases. In the *initiial* phase no serious offers are proposed and as time passes each trader continuously truncates the support of the probability distribution of the others' valuations as he infers that no trader has a valution sufficient to induce a serious offer. We shall see that this initial phase continues until time expires only if the probability and magnitude of gains from trade are both sufficiently small. Otherwise, it terminates with an initial serious offer that, by inference from the equilibrium strategies, reveals the posting trader's valuation. Since the offer is serious there is a positive probability that it is accepted immediately. If it is not accepted then the *second* phase ensues and the posting trader improves his offer until he obtains an acceptance or time expires.

Before describing the ensuing second phase it is useful to see the equilibrium strategies for the initial phase that are depicted schematically in Figure 11.1. The time t is represented along the abscissa and the traders' valuations are represented along the ordinate. Shown in the figure are the valuations $\mathbf{u}^*(t)$ and $\mathbf{v}^*(t)$ of the sellers and the buyers respectively that prompt their first serious offers $\mathbf{p}(t)$ and $\mathbf{q}(t)$ at time t; the difference between these is denoted by $\Delta(t) \equiv \mathbf{q}(t) - \mathbf{p}(t)$. Initially $\mathbf{u}^*(0^+) \geqslant u^*$ and $\mathbf{v}^*(0^+) \leqslant v^*$; one (or both) of these is an equality and the figure illustrates the case that $\mathbf{u}^*(0^+) = u^*$ and $\mathbf{v}^*(0^+) < v^*$. When time expires $\mathbf{u}^*(1) \equiv \hat{u}$ and $\mathbf{v}^*(1) \equiv \hat{v}$. For example, if a seller i has the valuation $u_i < \mathbf{u}^*(t)$ then he makes his first serious offer before time t, but if $u_i \geqslant \hat{u}$ then he never makes a first serious offer in this subgame. As shown in the figure, $\mathbf{S}(u)$ and $\mathbf{T}(v)$ denote the times that a seller with the valuation u and a buyer with the valuation v make their first serious offers. At each time t the maximum serious ask and the minimum serious bid are $\mathbf{p}(t)$ and $\mathbf{q}(t)$ respectively. If, say, the serious ask price $\mathbf{p}(t)$ is offered at time t by a seller with the valuation $u = \mathbf{u}^*(t)$ then each buyer with a valuation in the interval between $\mathbf{v}^{**}(t)$ and $\mathbf{v}^*(t)$ proposes

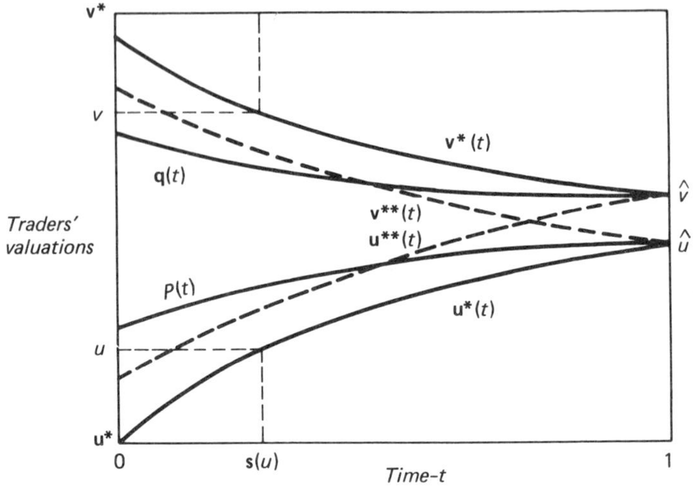

Figure 11.1 Equilibrium strategies in the initial phase

to accept; according to our tie-breaking rule the one with the highest valuation is selected for the transaction. Accordingly, the other traders infer the seller's valuation to be $\mathbf{u}^*(t)$ and infer that it is a lower bound on the other sellers' valuations. If there is an immediate transaction then they infer that the buyer's valuation is between $\mathbf{v}^{**}(t)$ and $\mathbf{v}^*(t)$ and that it is an upper bound on the other buyers' valuations. Similarly, if the initial serious ask is not accepted then the traders infer that no buyer has a valuation exceeding $\mathbf{v}^{**}(t)$. When time expires $\mathbf{p}(1)=\mathbf{u}^*(\mathbf{1})=\mathbf{v}^{**}(1)=\hat{u}$ and $\mathbf{q}(1)=\mathbf{v}^*(1)=\mathbf{u}^{**}(1)=\hat{v}$; for example, if a seller with the valuation $\hat{u}$ asks $\mathbf{p}(1^-)=\hat{u}$ just before time expires, then it is accepted by any buyer with a higher valuation.

The fact that there is an interval of buyers' valuations implying willingness to accept a first serious ask price is another manifestation of a buyer's incentive to delay making a first serious offer. The benefit of delay is assurance that others will not infer that his valuation is too high, and the cost is the risk that another buyer will intervene earlier with a serious bid and capture an opportunity to trade; when this cost is removed buyers, with valuations appreciably lower than the level prompting a serious bid, are ready to accept. On the other hand, the fact that a seller about to conduct an auction among the buyers prefers to reveal his valuation is an instance of a general result due to Milgrom and Weber (1982, theorems 17, 18).

Note that no serious offer occurs if no seller has a valuation below $\hat{u}$, and no buyer has a valuation above $\hat{v}$. In this case time expires without a transaction even though there is a positive probability that gains from trade are possible; however, the possible gain from a trade is bounded by the difference $\delta \equiv \hat{v} - \hat{u}$ and the probability is correspondingly small. That there is a positive difference between $\hat{v}$ and $\hat{u}$ is a necessary property of an equilibrium of this form since it is known that no trading rule can ensure that all gains from trade are realized; for example, see Wilson (1983). We shall see that it is also necessary that $\Delta(1) \equiv \mathbf{q}(1) - \mathbf{p}(1) \equiv \delta$ is positive.

The equilibrium strategies in the second phase are depicted schematically in Figure 11.2 for the case where a seller with the valuation u offered a first serious ask price $\mathbf{p}(t)$ at time $t = \mathbf{S}(u)$ that was not accepted. In the ensuing play this seller conducts a Dutch auction in which he continuously lowers his ask price $\mathbf{A}(t;u)$ until it is accepted by some buyer, or his ask price declines to his valuation u as time expires and there is no trade. Initially $\mathbf{A}(\mathbf{S}(u);u) = \mathbf{p}(\mathbf{S}(u))$ and when time expires $\mathbf{A}(1;u) = u$. Shown in the figure is the valuation $\mathbf{v}^{\circ}(t;u)$ of the buyer who would accept at each time $t > \mathbf{S}(u)$, starting with $\mathbf{v}^{\circ}(\mathbf{S}(u);u) = \mathbf{v}^{**}(\mathbf{S}(u))$ and ending at $\mathbf{v}^{\circ}(1;u) = u$. As time passes without a transaction, therefore, the traders infer at time t that no buyer has a valuation exceeding $\mathbf{v}^{\circ}(t;u)$, and if the ask price $\mathbf{A}(t;u)$ is accepted at time t then the remaining active traders infer that the accepting buyer's valuation is $\mathbf{v}^{\circ}(t;u)$. Along the equilibrium path the other sellers make no serious offers and the probability assessment of their valuations remains unchanged. The fact that the two curves $\mathbf{A}(t;u)$ and $\mathbf{v}^{\circ}(t;u)$ coincide at the valuation u when time expires at time $t = 1$ is a general requirement of a sequential equilibrium: if the seller planned to keep his ask above his valuation then near the end he would want to cut his price to increase his chance of trading, and similarly for a buyer who plans when to accept. Thus in this second phase failure to trade indicates an absence of gains from trade (this is consistent with the general theory since the seller's valuation has already been inferred by the other traders). [Off the equilibrium path the strategies in the Dutch auction are actually more complicated than is shown in the figure: if another seller intervenes with a lower ask price then play immediately reverts to

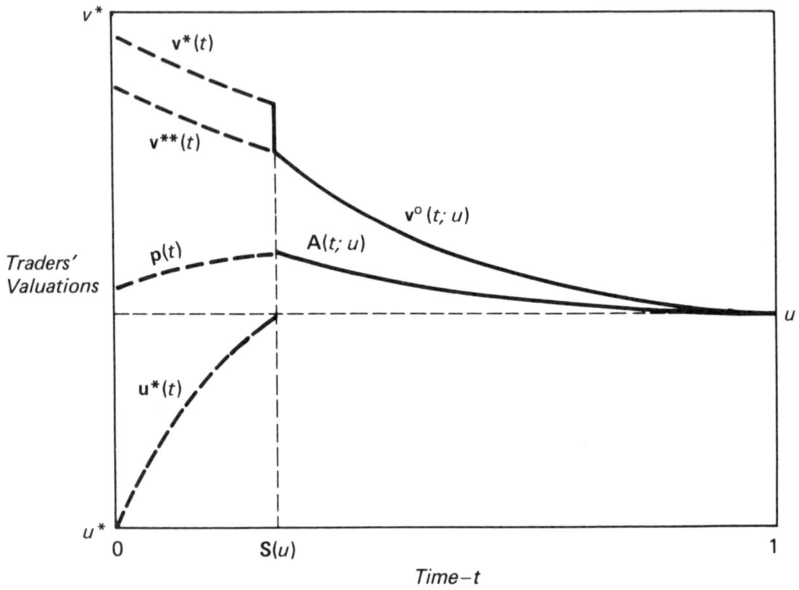

Figure 11.2 Equilibrium strategies in the second phase, after a first serious ask by a seller

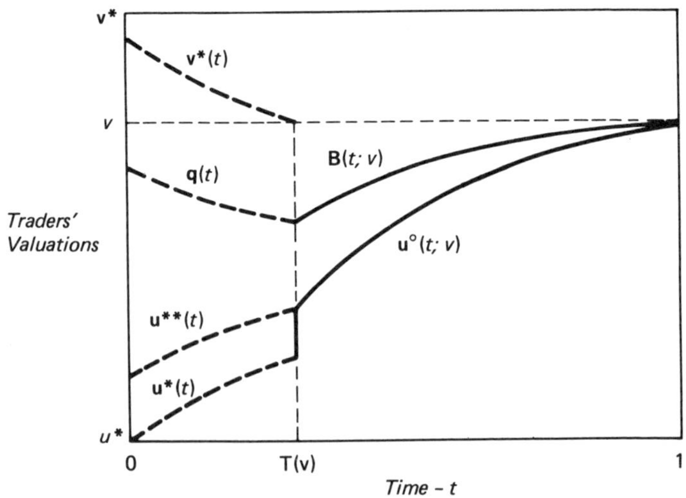

Figure 11.3 Equilibrium strategies in the second phase, after a first serious bid by a buyer

a Dutch auction conducted by the intervening trader, whose valuation is presumed revealed by his offer by inference from the equilibrium strategies – Section 4.]

Figure 11.3 depicts schematically the analogous strategies in the case that the first serious offer was made by a buyer with the valuation v and not accepted.

In the following paragraphs we outline some of the consequences of an equilibrium of this form.

3.1 Probability Assessments

The inferential process in the two phases of a subgame is summarized as follows: As time passes without a serious offer in the initial phase, the traders continuously truncate the support of the probability distribution to reflect the inference that no trader has a valuation sufficient to prompt a serious offer. Based on the generally observed history, therefore, the distribution for the traders' valuations is

$$F_t(a,b)=\frac{F[\mathbf{u}^*(t)\bigcup a,\mathbf{v}^*(t)\bigcap b]}{F[\mathbf{u}^*(t)\mathbf{1},\mathbf{v}^*(t)\mathbf{1}]} \tag{2}$$

at time t in the initial phase, where $\mathbf{1}$ denotes a vector of 1s. This is equivalent to the expectation operator $\mathcal{E}\{\cdot|\bar{u}\geqslant\mathbf{u}^*(t),\bar{v}\leqslant\mathbf{v}^*(t)\}$, where $\bar{u}=\min_i\{u_i|1\leqslant i\leqslant m\}$ and $\bar{v}=\max_j\{v_j|1\leqslant j\leqslant n\}$; of course, each trader further conditions on his valuation.

The first serious offer is interpreted as revealing precisely the valuation of the trader who proposes it. Taking the case of a seller, let $F(a,b|u)$ be the conditional distribution function given the seller's valuation u; then upon offering his first serious ask at time $t^*=\mathbf{S}(u)$ the distribution function for the traders' valuations becomes

$$F_{t^*}(a,b)=\frac{F[\mathbf{u}^*(t^*)\bigcup a,\mathbf{v}^*(t^*)\bigcap b|\mathbf{u}^*(t^*)]}{F[\mathbf{u}^*(t^*)\mathbf{1},\mathbf{v}^*(t^*)\mathbf{1}|\mathbf{u}^*(t^*)]} \tag{3}$$

This is equivalent to the conditional expectation operator $\mathcal{E}\{\cdot|\bar{u}=\mathbf{u}^*(t^*),\bar{v}\leqslant\mathbf{v}^*(t^*)\}$. If the first serious offer is not accepted then again the traders truncate the support to reflect the inference that no trader has a valuation sufficient to induce acceptance according to the equilibrium strategies.

Similarly, as time passes without a transaction in the second phase, the truncation reflects the inference that no trader has a valuation sufficient to accept the offer in the Dutch auction. At time $t > t^*\mathbf{S}(u)$, therefore, the distribution function for the traders' valuations becomes

$$F_t(a,b) = \frac{F[\mathbf{u}^*(t^*) \bigcup a, \mathbf{v}^\circ(t;u) \bigcap b \,|\, \mathbf{u}^*(t^*)\,]}{F[\mathbf{u}^*(t^*)\mathbf{1}, \mathbf{v}^\circ(t;u)\mathbf{1} \,|\, \mathbf{u}^*(t^*)\,]}. \tag{4}$$

This is equivalent to the conditional expectation operator $\mathcal{E}\{\cdot|\bar{u} = \mathbf{u}^*(t^*), \bar{v} \leqslant \mathbf{v}^\circ(t;u)\}$. If a transaction occurs then the remaining active traders move into a subgame with a probability assessment that depends on the circumstance.

If the first serious ask was accepted then the ensuing subgame is initialized with the probability assessment

$$F^\circ(a,b) = \int_{\mathbf{v}^{**}(t^*)}^{\mathbf{v}^*(t^*)} \left[\frac{F_{t^*}(a, \bar{v} \bigcap b \,|\, \bar{v})}{F_{t^*}(\mathbf{u}^*(t^*)\mathbf{1}, \mathbf{v}^*(t^*)\mathbf{1} \,|\, \bar{v})} \right] d\bar{F}_{t^*}(\bar{v}) / [1 - \bar{F}_{t^*}(\mathbf{v}^{**}(t^*)\,)\,] \tag{5}$$

on the support $[\mathbf{u}^*(t^*),1]^{m-1} \times [0,\mathbf{v}^*(t^*)\,]^{n-1}$ for the remaining active traders; here $F_t(a,b|v)$ represents the further conditioning of F_t on a buyer's valuation v, and $\bar{F}_t(\bar{v})$ is the marginal distribution (derived from F_t) of the maximum valuation $\bar{v}$ among the buyers. This is equivalent to the conditional expectation operator $\mathcal{E}\{\cdot|\,\bar{u} = \mathbf{u}^*(t^*), \bar{v} \in [\mathbf{v}^{**}(t^*), \mathbf{v}^*(t^*)\,]\,\}$.

If the seller's later ask in the Dutch auction at time $t > \mathbf{S}(u)$ is accepted then the ensuing subgame is initialized with the distribution

$$F^\circ(a,b) = \frac{F_t(a, \mathbf{v}^\circ(t;u) \bigcap b \,|\, \mathbf{v}^\circ(t;u)\,)}{F_t(\mathbf{u}^*(t^*)\mathbf{1}, \mathbf{v}^\circ(t;u)\mathbf{1})} \tag{6}$$

on the support $[\mathbf{u}^*(t^*),\mathbf{1}]^{m-1} \times [0,\mathbf{v}^\circ(t;u)\,]^{n-1}$ for the remaining active traders. This is equivalent to the conditional expectation operator $\mathcal{E}\{\cdot|\,\bar{u} = \mathbf{u}^*(t^*), \bar{v} = \mathbf{v}^\circ(t;u)\}$. In either case, the distribution F° that initializes the ensuing subgame satisfies the requirement that the subgame is similar to the original game: the remaining active traders' valuations are affiliated and symmetrically distributed (Milgrom and Weber, 1982).

3.2 Subgame Payoffs

The implications of these strategies for the expected payoffs obtained by a trader, say a seller i, are depicted in Figures 11.4, 11.5, and 11.6 for three ranges in which his valuation u can lie. Figure 11.4 represents the situation if $u < \hat{u}$ so that he plans to offer a serious ask price at the time $\mathbf{S}(u)$ if no other trader does so earlier. The abscissa $\tilde{u}$ represents the minimum among the *other* sellers' valuations and the ordinate $\bar{v}$ represents the maximum among the buyers' valuations. The three regions shown correspond to the three cases that there is no trade in this subgame (his payoff is his valuation u), some other seller trades with a buyer (his payoff is the expected payoff U° in the ensuing subgame, depending via F° on $\tilde{u}$ and $\bar{v}$ for the transaction that occurs), and the case that he trades with the buyer having the valuation $\bar{v}$ at a price $P(u,\bar{v})$. This price is defined by

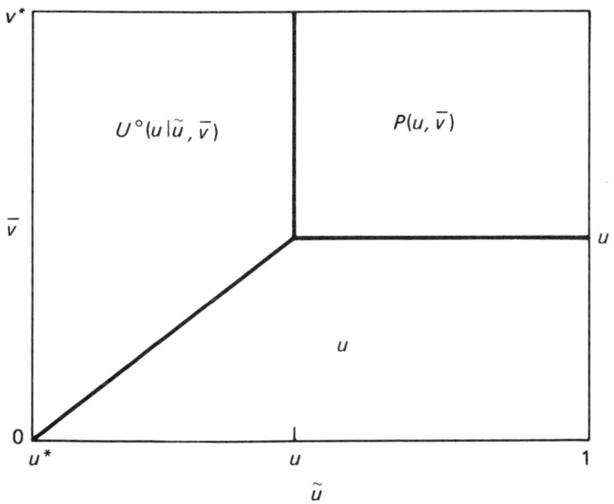

Figure 11.4 Subgame payoffs for a seller if $u < \hat{u}$

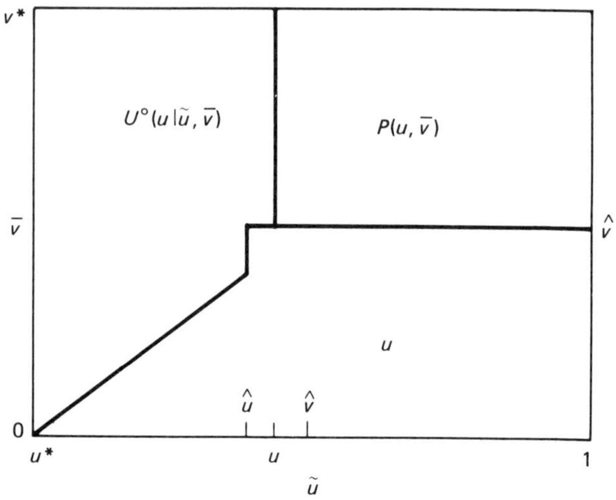

Figure 11.5 Subgame payoffs for a seller if $\hat{u} \leqslant u \leqslant \hat{v}$

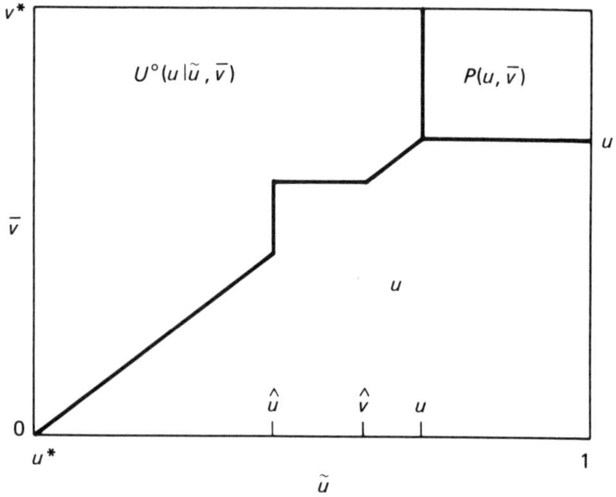

Figure 11.6 Subgame payoffs for a seller if $\hat{v} < u$

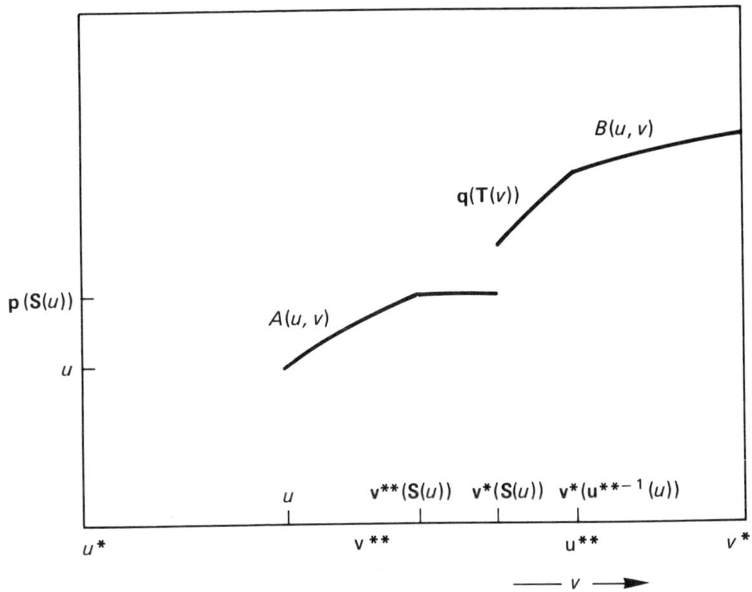

Figure 11.7 The transaction price $P(u,v)$

$$P(u,v) \equiv \begin{cases} \mathbf{p}(\mathbf{S}(u)) \text{ if } \mathbf{S}(u) < \mathbf{T}(v) \ \&\ v \in (\mathbf{v}^{**}(\mathbf{S}(u)), \mathbf{v}^{*}(\mathbf{S}(u))), \\ \mathbf{A}(t;u) \quad \text{if } \mathbf{S}(u) < \mathbf{T}(v) \ \&\ v = \mathbf{v}^{\circ}(t;u) < \mathbf{v}^{**}(\mathbf{S}(u)), \\ \mathbf{q}(\mathbf{T}(v)) \text{ if } \mathbf{S}(u) > \mathbf{T}(v) \ \&\ u \in [\mathbf{u}^{*}(\mathbf{T}(v)), \mathbf{u}^{**}(\mathbf{T}(v))], \\ \mathbf{B}(t;v) \text{ if } \mathbf{S}(u) > \mathbf{T}(v) \ \&\ u = \mathbf{u}^{\circ}(t;v) > \mathbf{u}^{**}(\mathbf{T}(v)). \end{cases} \tag{7}$$

Figure 11.7 shows how the transaction price $P(u,v)$ varies with v. The notation $A(u,v) \equiv \mathbf{A}((\mathbf{v}^{\circ})^{-1}(v);u)$ and $B(u,v) = \mathbf{B}((\mathbf{u}^{\circ})^{-1}(u);v)$ is used. Note the discontinuity where $\mathbf{S}(u) = \mathbf{T}(v)$, or equivalently $(u,v) \equiv (\mathbf{u}^{*}(t), \mathbf{v}^{*}(t))$.

As shown in Figures 11.5 and 11.6, these regions are more complicated when the seller is uncertain that a serious offer will be made, since there is a small triangular region in which gains from trade are missed. Table 11.1 summarizes the features shown in Figures 11.4, 11.5, and 11.6. An analogous table describes a buyer's contingent subgame payoffs.

Using this description of a seller's contingent subgame payoffs, we develop a general formula for the expected subgame payoff of a seller. At time t let $\bar{F}_t(\bar{v}|w;\tilde{u})$ be the distribution function of the maximum $\bar{v}$ among the buyers' valuations conditional on one seller's valuation

Table 11.1 A seller's contingent subgame payoffs

	$\bar{v} \leqslant (u \cap \tilde{u}) \cap \hat{v}$	$\bar{v} > (u \cap \tilde{u}) \cap \hat{v}$ $\bar{v} \leqslant (u \cap \tilde{u}) \cup \hat{v}$	$\bar{v} > (u \cap \tilde{u}) \cup \hat{v}$
$\tilde{u} < u \cap \hat{u}$	u	U°	U°
$u \cap \hat{u} \leqslant \tilde{u} < u$	u	u	U°
$u < \tilde{u}$	u	u if $u \geqslant \hat{u}$ $P(u,\bar{v})$ if $u < \hat{u}$	$P(u,\bar{v})$

being w and the minimum among the other sellers' valuations being $\tilde{u}$; and let $\bar{F}_t(\tilde{u}|w)$ be the conditional distribution function of the latter. Also, let $U^\circ(u|\tilde{u},\bar{v})$ be the expected payoff of a seller with the valuation u if he remains active in the ensuing subgame after a transaction between another seller with the valuation $\tilde{u}$ and a buyer with the valuation $\bar{v}$. The dependence of U° on $(\tilde{u},\bar{v})$ is via its dependence on F° as in (5) and (6). Corresponding to the three rows of Table 11.1, define

$$\Gamma^1_t(u|w;\tilde{u}) = \int_0^{\tilde{u}} u\,d\bar{F}_t(\bar{v}|w;\tilde{u}) + \int_{\hat{v} \cup \tilde{u}}^{\mathbf{v}^*(t)} U^\circ(u|\tilde{u},\bar{v})\,d\bar{F}_t(\bar{v}|w;\tilde{u}),$$

$$\Gamma^2_t(u|w;\tilde{u}) = \int_0^{\hat{v} \cup \tilde{u}} u\,d\bar{F}_t(\bar{v}|w;\tilde{u}) + \int_{\hat{v} \cup \tilde{u}}^{\mathbf{v}^*(t)} U^\circ(u|\tilde{u},\bar{v})\,d\bar{F}_t(\bar{v}|w;\tilde{u}), \tag{8}$$

$$\Gamma^3_t(u,\check{u}|w;\tilde{u}) = \int_0^{\check{u}+\xi(\check{u})} u\,d\bar{F}_t(\bar{v}|w;\tilde{u}) + \int_{\check{u}+\xi(\check{u})}^{\mathbf{v}^*(t)} p(\check{u},\bar{v})\,d\bar{F}_t(\bar{v}|w;\tilde{u}),$$

where

$$\xi(u) \equiv \begin{cases} \hat{v} - u \text{ if } \hat{u} \leqslant u \leqslant \hat{v}, \\ 0 \quad \text{otherwise} \end{cases} \tag{9}$$

Observe that this notation distinguishes between the seller's actual valuation u, the valuation w upon which he conditions his probability assessment, and the valuation $\check{u}$ upon which he conditions his strategy, although in equilibrium these must all be identical.

With this notation we specify a general formula that is useful later. The seller's expected subgame payoff if he conditions his probability assessment on w and his strategy on $\check{u}$ is

$$\check{U}_t(u,\check{u}|w) = \int_{\mathbf{u}^*(t)}^{\hat{u}\cap\check{u}} I_t^1(u|w;\tilde{u})d\tilde{F}_t(\tilde{u}|w) + \int_{\hat{u}\cap\check{u}}^{\check{u}} I_t^2(u|w;\tilde{u})d\tilde{F}_t(\tilde{u}|w) + \int_{\check{u}}^{1} I_t^3(u,\check{u}|w;\tilde{u})d\tilde{F}_t(\tilde{u}|w), \tag{10}$$

at each time $t < \mathbf{S}(u)$ before any serious offer. In equilibrium, of course, the actual expected subgame payoff is $U(u) = \check{U}_0(u,u|u)$. A similar formula can be constructed for a buyer.

It is important to note that potentially there could be a discontinuity in $U(u)$ at $u = \hat{u}$ where ξ is discontinuous. In fact, however, continuity is assured since $P(\hat{u},\bar{v}) = \hat{u}$ for all $\bar{v} \in (\hat{u},\hat{v})$ due to the specifications $\mathbf{p}(1) = \hat{u}$ and $\mathbf{v}^{**}(1) = \hat{u}$ for the equilibrium strategies. That is, since continuity is generally necessary, the positivity of the difference $\Delta(1) \equiv \mathbf{q}(1) - \mathbf{p}(1)$ is a corollary of the positivity of the difference $\delta \equiv \hat{v} - \hat{u}$, and indeed $\Delta(1) = \delta$.

3.3 The Revelation Game

A crucial test of whether the specified strategies and beliefs are a sequential equilibrium is obtained by analyzing the 'revelation games' they induce. At each time t the induced revelation game allows a trader the option of selecting the valuation on which his strategy is conditioned. A seller, for example, can condition his strategy on any valuation $\check{u}$, possibly different than his actual valuation u. An equilibrium in the original game necessarily has the property that each trader prefers to condition his strategy on his actual valuation, since otherwise in the original game he would have preferred a different strategy. In the next paragraphs we derive the necessary conditions implied by this requirement. We consider only the case of a seller with the actual valuation u; the case of a buyer is analogous.

First consider the situation at a time $t > \mathbf{S}(u)$ in the second phase after the seller has made the first serious offer. Using the notational scheme introduced above, the seller's expected payoff according to the specified strategies is

$$\check{U}_t(u,\check{u}|w) = \int_0^{\check{u}} u d\bar{F}_t(\bar{v}|w) + \int_{\check{u}}^{\mathbf{v}^\circ(t;u)} P(\check{u},\bar{v}) d\bar{F}_t(\bar{v}|w), \tag{11}$$

if he conditions his subsequent strategy on $\breve{u}$ and his beliefs on w. At this time, of course, he is conducting a Dutch auction with

$$P(\breve{u},\bar{v}) = A(\breve{u},\bar{v}) \equiv \mathbf{A}((\mathbf{v}^\circ)^{-1}(\bar{v});\breve{u}); \tag{12}$$

moreover, in this case $P(\breve{u},\bar{v})$ is an increasing function of $\breve{u}$ and $P(\breve{u},\breve{u}) = \breve{u}$. From these two properties it follows that $\breve{U}_t(u,\breve{u}|u)$ is maximized by the choice $\breve{u} = u$ as required; for example, $\delta\breve{U}_t(u,\breve{u}|u)/\delta\breve{u} = 0$ at $\breve{u} = u$.

Second, consider the situation at a time $t > \mathbf{T}(\bar{v})$ in the second phase after the first serious offer has been made by the buyer with the valuation $\bar{v}$, and assume that both u and $\breve{u}$ are less than $\bar{v}$. According to the specified strategies the seller's expected subgame payoff, conditional on the maximum of the buyers' valuations being $\bar{v}$, is

$$\breve{U}(u,\breve{u}|w;\bar{v}) = \int_{\mathbf{u}^*(t)}^{\breve{u}} U^\circ(u|\tilde{u},\bar{v})d\tilde{F}_t(\tilde{u}|w;\bar{v}) + \int_{\breve{u}}^{1} P(\breve{u},\bar{v})d\tilde{F}_t(\tilde{u}|w;\bar{v}), \tag{13}$$

if he conditions his subsequent strategy in this subgame on $\breve{u}$ and his beliefs on w. In this case, of course, the buyer is conducting an ascending Dutch auction with

$$P(\breve{u},\bar{v}) = B(\breve{u},\bar{v}) \equiv \mathbf{B}((\mathbf{u}^\circ)^{-1}(\breve{u});\bar{v}); \tag{14}$$

moreover, $P(\breve{u},\bar{v})$ is an increasing function of $\breve{u}$ and $P(\bar{v},\bar{v}) = \bar{v}$. A necessary condition for the requirement that $\breve{U}_t(u,\breve{u}|u)$ is maximized by the choice $\breve{u} = u$, is therefore that the corresponding derivative is zero:

$$0 = [U^\circ(u|u,\bar{v}) - B(u,\bar{v})]\tilde{F}_t'(u|u;\bar{v}) + \frac{\delta B(u,\bar{v})}{\delta u}\int_u^1 d\tilde{F}_t(\tilde{u}|u;\bar{v}). \tag{15}$$

The seeming dependence of this condition on the time t can be eliminated by expressing it in terms of the 'hazard rate'

$$\varphi(u;\bar{v}) \equiv \tilde{F}_t'(u|u;\bar{v}) \Big/ \int_u^1 d\tilde{F}_t(\tilde{u}|u;\bar{v}), \tag{16}$$

so as to cancel out the common proportionality factor; see (4). Thus, the relevant condition is

$$0=[U^\circ(u|u,\bar{v})-B(u,\bar{v})]\varphi(u;\bar{v})+\frac{\delta B(u,\bar{v})}{\delta u}. \tag{17}$$

Invoking the boundary condition $B(\bar{v},\bar{v})=\bar{v}$ mentioned earlier, this implies that

$$B(u,\bar{v})=\frac{\bar{v}\Phi(\bar{v};\bar{v})-\int_u^{\bar{v}} U^\circ(x|x;\bar{v})d\Phi(x;\bar{v})}{\Phi(u;\bar{v})} \tag{18}$$

where $\Phi(u;\bar{v})\equiv\exp\{-\int_{u^*}^{u}\varphi(x;\bar{v})dx\}$. For example, if the sellers' valuations happen to be independent with the distribution function G then $\varphi(u)=[m-1]G'(u)/[1-G(u)]$ and $\Phi(u)=(1-G(u))^{m-1}$. In general, if there are many sellers then one with the valuation u accepts a bid close to his continuation value $U^\circ(u|u,\bar{v})$ in an ensuing subgame.

Similarly, a parallel analysis yields a differential equation for $A(\bar{u},v)$ that determines the traders' strategies during a seller's descending Dutch auction:

$$0=(A(\bar{u},v)-V^\circ(v|v,\bar{u}))\psi(v;\bar{u})+\frac{\delta A(\bar{u},v)}{\delta v}, \tag{19}$$

where

$$\psi(v;\bar{u})\equiv \tilde{F}_t'(v|v;\bar{u})/\int_0^v d\tilde{F}_t(\tilde{v}|v;\bar{u}), \tag{20}$$

using an obvious transposition of notation. Invoking the boundary condition $A(\bar{u},\bar{u})=\bar{u}$, this implies that

$$A(\bar{u},v)=\frac{\bar{u}\Psi(\bar{u};\bar{u})+\int_{\bar{u}}^{v} V^\circ(y|y,\bar{u})d\Psi(y;\bar{u})}{\Psi(v;\bar{u})}, \tag{21}$$

where $\Psi(v;\bar{u})\equiv\exp\{-\int_v^{v^*}\psi(y;\bar{u})dy\}$. Again, if there are many buyers then the hazard rate is large and a buyer accepts an ask close to his continuation value $V^\circ(v|v,\bar{u})$.

It will be mandatory in the next section that we verify that $A(\bar{u},v)$ and $B(u,\bar{v})$ satisfy these two relationships. We show, in fact, that these relationships completely characterize the traders' strategies along the equilibrium path during the second phase.

Lastly, consider the situation at a time $t\leqslant \mathbf{S}(u)$ in the initial phase before any serious offers have been made. Assume that both u and $\check{u}$ are less than $\hat{u}$, and in particular $\xi(\check{u})=0$. According to the specified strategies, the seller's expected payoff is then

$$\check{U}_t(u,\check{u}|w)=\int_{\mathbf{u}^*(t)}^{\check{u}} I_t^1(u|w;\tilde{u})d\tilde{F}_t(\tilde{u}|w)+\int_{\check{u}}^{1} I_t^3(u,\check{u}|w;\tilde{u})d\tilde{F}_t(\tilde{u}|w), \tag{22}$$

if he conditions his strategy on $\check{u}$ and his beliefs on w. A necessary condition for the requirement that $\check{U}(u,\check{u}|u)$ is maximized by the choice $\check{u}=u$ is therefore that the corresponding derivative is zero (and decreasing):

$$\begin{aligned}
0&=[I_t^1(u|u;u)-I_t^3(u,u|u;u)]\tilde{F}_t'(u|u)+\frac{\delta}{\delta\check{u}}\int_u^1 I_t^3(u,\check{u}|u;\tilde{u})d\tilde{F}_t(\tilde{u}|u),\\
&=\int_u^{\mathbf{v}^*(t)} [U^\circ(u|u;\bar{v})-P(u,\bar{v})]d\bar{F}_t(\bar{v}|u;\tilde{u}=u)\cdot\tilde{F}_t'(u|u)\\
&+\int_u^1\left\{\int_u^{\mathbf{v}^*(t)}\frac{\delta P(u,\bar{v})}{\delta u}d\bar{F}_t(\bar{v}|u;\tilde{u})+\Delta(\mathbf{S}(u))\bar{F}_t'(\mathbf{v}^*(\mathbf{S}(u))|u;\tilde{u})\right\}d\tilde{F}_t(\tilde{u}|u),\\
&=\int_u^{\mathbf{v}^*(t)}\left\{[U^\circ(u|u;\bar{v})-P(u,\bar{v})]\tilde{F}_t'(u|u;\bar{v})\right.\\
&\left.+\frac{\delta P(u,\bar{v})}{\delta u}[1-\tilde{F}_t(u|u;\bar{v})]\right\}d\bar{F}_t(\bar{v}|u)\\
&+\Delta(\mathbf{S}(u))[1-\tilde{F}_t(u|u;\mathbf{v}^*(\mathbf{S}(u)))]\bar{F}_t'(\mathbf{v}^*(\mathbf{S}(u))|u).
\end{aligned} \tag{23}$$

Here, the second equality again uses the property that $P(u,u)=u$; also recall that $\Delta(t)\equiv\mathbf{q}(t)-\mathbf{p}(t)$ is the jump discontinuity in P at $t=\mathbf{S}(u)=\mathbf{T}(\bar{v})$. The third equality uses the identity

$$\bar{F}_t'(\bar{v}|u;\tilde{u})\tilde{F}_t'(\tilde{u}|u;v)\equiv\bar{F}_t'(\tilde{u}|u;\ v)\bar{F}_t'(\bar{v}|u),$$

according to the rules of conditional probability.

The condition (23) must hold at all times $t\leqslant\mathbf{S}(u)$ but note that it is sufficient that it holds where $\mathbf{u}^{**}(t)\geqslant u$ since at earlier times (15) assures that the integrand within the curly brackets in (23) is zero for $\bar{v}>\mathbf{v}^*((\mathbf{u}^{**})^{-1}(u))$; that is, in this region the buyer with the maximum valuation makes the first serious offer and the seller does not accept it, so an ascending Dutch auction ensues.

At the time $t = \mathbf{S}(u)$ when the seller makes his first serious offer we have $\bar{F}_t(u|u;\bar{v}) = 0$ and $\bar{F}'_t(u|u;\bar{v}) = \varphi(u;\bar{v})$; consequently a special case of (23) is

$$0 = \int_u^{\mathbf{v}^*(\mathbf{S}(u))} \left\{ (U^\circ(u|u;\bar{v}) - P(u,\bar{v})]\varphi(u;\bar{v}) + \frac{\delta P(u;\bar{v})}{\delta u} \right\} d\bar{F}_{\mathbf{S}(u)}(\bar{v}|u;u)$$
$$+ \Delta(\mathbf{S}(u))\bar{F}'_{\mathbf{S}(u)}(\mathbf{v}^*(\mathbf{S}(u))|u;u). \quad (24)$$

At this time $\bar{F}_{\mathbf{S}(u)}$ is conditioned on $\tilde{u} \geq u$ (indicated by the semi-colon) by inference from the other sellers' strategies.[6] Also $\delta P(u;\bar{v})/\delta u$ is properly interpreted here as the derivative from the left, and in particular in the relevant range of $\bar{v}$:

$$P(u,\bar{v}) = \begin{cases} A(u,\mathbf{v}^\circ(\mathbf{S}(u);u)) & \text{if } \mathbf{v}^\circ(\mathbf{S}(u);u) \leq \bar{v} \leq v^*(\mathbf{S}(u)), \\ A(u,\bar{v}) & \text{if } u < \bar{v} < \mathbf{v}^\circ(\mathbf{S}(u);u). \end{cases} \quad (25)$$

The condition (24) essentially determines the seller's planned time $\mathbf{S}(u)$ of his first serious offer. Alternatively, it can be interpreted as determining the upper bound $v^*(\mathbf{S}(u))$ of the support of the buyers' valuations that prompts the seller to make his first serious offer. If there are many sellers so that the hazard rate φ is large, then a seller plans to make his first serious offer early. If (24) holds then also (23) does since it corresponds to an expectation of (24). In the next section it will be mandatory to verify that these conditions, and their analogues for a buyer, are satisfied.

An examination of the various conditions derived above for the revelation game reveals that there is one less equation than is required to determine all the functions entering the specification of the equilibrium strategies. Later we show that the missing condition is that $\mathbf{v}^{*\prime}(t) = \mathbf{u}^{*\prime}(t)$ at all times $t \in (0,1)$; that is, the supports of the buyers' and sellers' valuations contract at the same rate during the initial phase.

3.4 Monotonicity

Each of the formulas (10), (11), (13), and (22) for a seller's expected payoff have the property that $\delta \breve{U}_t/\delta u$ is precisely the seller's conditional probability that he fails to trade (using an evident induction on the subgames): this is necessarily so since u is his payoff if he fails to trade. Additionally, the revelation conditions associated with each one ensure that $\delta\check{U}_t/\delta\check{u}=0$ at $\check{u}=u$. Finally, affiliation implies that $\delta\check{U}_t/\delta w\geqslant 0$. Combining these results yields the requisite property that $dU(u)/du\geqslant 0$; that is, a seller's expected payoff is a non-decreasing function of his valuation u. The analogous property holds for buyers as well.

The various formulas also involve a seller's continuation value $U^\circ(u|\tilde{u},\bar{v})$ in an ensuing subgame. Again, affiliation implies that $\delta U^\circ/\delta\tilde{u}\geqslant 0$. For example, $U^\circ(u|u,\bar{v})$ as in (15) or (24) is a non-decreasing function of the seller's valuation u, and the analogous property holds for a buyer.

3.5 Inefficiency

Condition (24) gives the illusion that it is possible that all gains from trade are realized, as would be the case if $\mathbf{v}^*(1)=\hat{u}$ and $\Delta(1)=0$ at the close of the market. This is not possible, however, since it is the larger of two roots of (24) that corresponds to the optimal choice for the seller. To see this, interpret (24) as the condition that determines the seller's optimal choice of $v^*(u)\equiv\mathbf{v}^*(\mathbf{S}(u))$, in which case the second-order condition requires that the first term on the right of (24) is decreasing. If $v^*(\hat{u})=\hat{u}$, however, the derivative of this term with respect to $v^*(u)$ at $\hat{u}$ is

$$\left\{(U^\circ(\hat{u}|\hat{u};\hat{u})-P(\hat{u},\hat{u}))\varphi(\hat{u};\hat{u})+\frac{\delta P(\hat{u};\hat{u})}{\delta u}\right\}\bar{F}'_1(\hat{u}|\hat{u})\geqslant 0, \tag{26}$$

since $U^\circ(\hat{u}|\hat{u};\hat{u})=P(\hat{u},\hat{u})=\hat{u}$ and $\delta P(\hat{u};\hat{u})/\delta u\geqslant 0$.

This concludes our description of the equilibrium (along the equilibrium path) and its main consequences. In the next section we construct the equilibrium strategies as solutions to the traders' personal optimization problems, given that each anticipates that all other traders will be using the specified strategies.

4 THE EQUILIBRIUM: CONSTRUCTION

We divide the construction between characterization of the equilibrium path and analysis of off-the-equilibrium-path behaviour. In the first part we are mainly concerned with establishing that the characterizations derived in the analysis of the revelation games are valid. We concentrate on the necessary conditions that specify formulas for the strategies, but make some references to the sufficient conditions. In the second part we delineate off-the-equilibrium-path beliefs that are sufficient to support the equilibrium by deterring deviations.

It is sufficient to characterize only those features of the strategies that are independent of the parameterization of time, since the remainder can then be determined once a particular parameterization has been selected. For the second phase of a subgame we characterize the price $A(u,\bar{v})$ at which a seller making the first serious offer subsequently trades with a buyer having the highest valuation $\bar{v}>u$. In this case the parameterization of time can be taken to be the specification of the valuation $\mathbf{v}°(t;u)$ of the buyer accepting the ask price $\mathbf{A}(t;u)$, subject to the conditions that $\mathbf{v}°$ is a declining function of time and that $\mathbf{v}°(1;u)=u$; thus, knowing the parameterization we obtain $\mathbf{A}(t;u)=A(u,\mathbf{v}°(t;u))$. Alternatively, one could specify the temporal sequence $\mathbf{A}(\cdot;u)$ of declining ask prices subject to $\mathbf{A}(1;u)=u$ and then derive $\mathbf{v}°(t;u)$. Similarly, we characterize the price $B(\bar{u},v)$ at which a buyer making the first serious offer subsequently trades with the seller having the lowest valuation $\bar{u}<v$, and then $\mathbf{B}(t;v)=B(\mathbf{u}°(t;v),v)$. Knowing these functions also enables us to specify that if $\mathbf{S}(u)=t=\mathbf{T}(v)$ then $\mathbf{p}(t)=\mathbf{A}(t;u)$ and $\mathbf{q}(t)=\mathbf{B}(t;v)$, and also $\mathbf{u}^{**}(t)=\mathbf{u}°(t;v)$ and $\mathbf{v}^{**}(t)=\mathbf{v}°(t;u)$. For the first phase, therefore, it remains only to characterize the times $\mathbf{S}(u)$ and $\mathbf{T}(v)$ of the first serious offers of a seller and a buyer with the valuations $u<\hat{u}$ and $v>\hat{v}$.

4.1 Strategies in the Dutch Auctions

We study the ascending Dutch auction by a buyer in a market with more than one seller ($m>1$); a descending Dutch auction by a seller is analogous.

On the Equilibrium Path

A seller with the valuation u anticipates the sequence $\{\mathbf{B}(t;\bar{v})|\mathbf{T}(\bar{v})<t<1\}$, of bid prices after the first serious offer by a buyer inferred to have the valuation $\bar{v}>u$, and that any other seller with a valuation less than

$\mathbf{u}^\circ(t;\bar{v})$ will accept any bid price above $\mathbf{B}(t;\bar{v})$. At a time t this seller prefers to wait a further interval $\epsilon>0$ if the current bid is less than the expectation of the price he can obtain by waiting. This subsequent price is either his expected price in an ensuing subgame, with the probability

$$Q_t(\epsilon|u,\bar{v})\equiv\int_{\mathbf{u}^\circ(t;\bar{v})}^{\mathbf{u}^\circ(t+\epsilon;\bar{v})} d\tilde{F}_t(\tilde{u}|u;\bar{v}) \tag{27}$$

that another seller accepts in the interim, or the subsequent bid $\mathbf{B}(t+\epsilon;\bar{v})$ with the complementary probability. That is, he prefers to wait if there exists $\epsilon>0$ such that

$$\begin{aligned}\mathbf{B}(t;\bar{v})<\mathcal{E}_t\{U^\circ(u|\tilde{u},\bar{v})|\mathbf{u}^\circ(t;\bar{v})<\tilde{u}<\mathbf{u}^\circ(t+\epsilon;\bar{v})\}Q_t(\epsilon|u,\bar{v})\\ +\mathbf{B}(t+\epsilon;\bar{v})(1-Q_t(\epsilon|u,\bar{v})).\end{aligned} \tag{28}$$

Conversely, if the seller is willing to accept at t then

$$\lim_{\epsilon\to0}\frac{\mathbf{B}(t+\epsilon;\bar{v})-\mathbf{B}(t;\bar{v})}{\epsilon}\leqslant[\mathbf{B}(t;\bar{v})-U^\circ(u|u,\bar{v})]\cdot\lim_{\epsilon\to0}\frac{Q_t(\epsilon|u,\bar{v})}{\epsilon}. \tag{29}$$

Thus, an equilibrium requires that $u=\mathbf{u}^\circ(t;\bar{v})$ only if

$$\begin{aligned}\frac{\delta B(u;\bar{v})}{\delta u}&\equiv\frac{\mathbf{B}'(t;\bar{v})}{\mathbf{u}^{\circ\prime}(t;\bar{v})}=(\mathbf{B}(t;\bar{v})-U^\circ(u|u,\bar{v}))\tilde{F}'_t(u|u;\tilde{u}\geqslant u,\bar{v})\\ &=[B(u,\bar{v})-U^\circ(u|u,\bar{v})]\varphi(u;\bar{v}).\end{aligned} \tag{30}$$

At this time one conditions $\tilde{F}$ on $\tilde{u}\geqslant u$ since the seller infers that his valuation is the smallest among the sellers; hence,

$$\lim_{\epsilon\to0}\frac{Q_t(\epsilon|u,\bar{v})}{\epsilon}=\tilde{F}'_t(u|u;u,\bar{v})\mathbf{u}^{\circ\prime}(t;\bar{v})=\varphi(u;\bar{v})\mathbf{u}^{\circ\prime}(t;\bar{v}).$$

The differential equation (30) is therefore the same as (17), as required. A sequential equilibrium requires that this differential equation for B must be satisfied; moreover, the boundary condition $B(\bar{v},\bar{v})=\bar{v}$ must be satisfied as we mentioned earlier, so the solution is given by (18). If

$\bar{v}=v^*(t)$ then (30) can be interpreted as an equation for u whose solution is $u=\mathbf{u}^{**}(t)$.

That (30) is a sufficient condition for a solution of the seller's optimization problem is assured since **B** is an increasing function of time. In the alternative case that $\bar{v}\leqslant u$ no bid from the buyer will exceed the seller's valuation and clearly the seller's optimal strategy is never to accept in this subgame.

This entirely characterizes the behaviour along the equilibrium path during an ascending Dutch auction by a buyer. It is in fact the standard condition for a sequential equilibrium of an ordinary Dutch auction, and since the sellers' valuations are affiliated and $U^\circ(u|u,\bar{v})$ is increasing with u it is known to be sufficient as well as necessary (compare Milgrom and Weber, 1982).

It is worth mentioning that our specification of the strategies during the second phase is substantially motivated by the need to be explicit in the construction. It would be adequate for some purposes to allow greater generality, requiring only that, say, $B(u,\bar{v})$ is the price at which a buyer with the valuation $\bar{v}$ expects to trade with a seller with the valuation u, rather than tying it to the specific temporal sequence of serious bids $\mathbf{B}(\cdot;\bar{v})$ made by the buyer. In this case it would be sufficient merely to specify the seller's strategy in the form that he plans to accept the first bid exceeding $\mathbf{B}((\mathbf{u}^\circ)^{-1}(u);\bar{v})\equiv P(u,\bar{v})$.

Off the Equilibrium Path

During the second phase there are several ways that play can depart from the equilibrium path. In all of these we follow a principle developed by Cramton (1984) in more detail than we shall do here. The principle is that non-serious offers are ignored, whereas new serious offers are interpreted by the other traders as equilibrium offers according to revised probability assessments. As we shall see, this specification is sufficient to induce all traders to adhere to the equilibrium strategies. Moreover, it enables an economy of presentation by allowing that behaviour in any circumstances can be determined by reference to the equilibrium strategies in that circumstance according to the traders' revised beliefs. We consider only the case of an ascending Dutch auction by a buyer; the case of a descending Dutch auction by a seller is analogous.

We first consider the buyers' behaviour, and begin with the buyer conducting the Dutch auction. He can deviate by bidding either lower or higher than the equilibrium strategy requires. If he bids lower then this is a non-serious offer and the other traders expect him to revert to the equilibrium strategy; clearly he has nothing to gain by this deviation. If he bids higher then the other traders infer that his valuation is higher than they previously estimated and they expect him to continue with the sequence of bids corresponding to this higher valuation, and in particular to continue raising all the way to this higher valuation if necessary to make a transaction; in addition, subsequent reversion to his equilibrium strategy will be interpreted as non-serious, so a deviant higher bid represents a permanent commitment. Again it is fairly clear that this deviation is disadvantageous (for example, if the initial deviant bid is accepted then he has missed a chance of transacting at the lower price specified by the equilibrium strategy), but we refer to Cramton (1984, pp. 119–22) for additional details.

Other buyers who intervene with bids less than the auctioneers' bids gain no advantage since their bids are non-serious. A higher bid, however, is serious and the other traders immediately infer that the intervening buyer has a correspondingly higher valuation and expect him to continue with the equilibrium strategy. Along the equilibrium path such a buyer actually has a lower valuation and, by a repetition of the previous argument, sees such an intervention as disadvantageous. This is true even if he fails to trade in this subgame, since in a subsequent subgame he will be treated as having the higher imputed valuation.[7]

The previous paragraph describes only one of the possible specifications. Another is that the auctioneer's strategy is actually in the form that he bids the maximum of the equilibrium bid and any intervening serious bids by other buyers, up to the limit of his reservation price. With this specification an intervener with a lower valuation has no chance of making a transaction in this subgame, but jeopardizes his terms of trade in any ensuing subgame.

Among the sellers an ask price above the auctioneer's bid is non-serious and is ignored, while an ask equal to or less than the bid cannot be more advantageous than accepting the bid. Alternatively, one can simply specify as part of the rules that an ask no greater than an offered bid is construed as an acceptance of the bid.

All of these disequilibrium specifications are innocuous except for the key feature that a new higher serious bid induces other traders to revise their assessment of the auctioneer's valuation, and thereafter he is unable to lower this assessment by reducing his bids; that is, the auctioneer is essentially 'locked in' by the expectations of the other traders. This is the essential determinant of the form of the equilibrium derived by Cramton, since in anticipation of this feature in the second phase, delay in making a serious offer in the initial phase can function effectively as a signal of a trader's valuation.

4.2 Strategies in the Initial Phase

On the Equilibrium Path

Consider a seller with the valuation u contemplating a first serious offer at a time $t < \mathbf{S}(u)$ in the initial phase. If he offers the serious ask price $\mathbf{p}(t)$ then other traders infer that his valuation is $\check{u}(t) = \mathbf{S}^{-1}(t) \equiv \mathbf{u}^*(t)$ and expect that the subsequent ask price $\mathbf{A}(\cdot;\check{u}(t))$ will decline towards $\check{u}(t)$ at time 1. A buyer with the valuation v, therefore, plans to accept the first ask that is $\mathbf{A}((\mathbf{v}^\circ)^{-1}(v);\check{u}(t)) \equiv P(\check{u}(t), v)$ or less. Anticipating this behaviour, the seller's expected payoff is

$$\mathcal{E}_t\{\int_{u \bigcup \check{u}(t)}^{\mathbf{v}^*(t)} P(\check{u}(t),\bar{v}) d\bar{F}(\bar{v}|u,\tilde{u}) | \tilde{u} \geqslant u^*(t)\} \tag{31}$$

if he conducts the Dutch auction, but of course stops at his valuation $u > \check{u}(t)$, and if no other seller intervenes.[8] Midway in the Dutch auction he could revert to his equilibrium strategy $\mathbf{A}(\cdot;u)$ but these would be non-serious offers: the key point is that having allowed the inference that his valuation is $\check{u}(t) < u$ the seller has no later opportunity to induce other traders to revise their assessments upwards; thus, (31) represents the best that he can achieve in the second phase. If another seller intervenes this seller gets the expected payoff in the ensuing subgame with his valuation assessed to be $\check{u}(t)$.

His only other alternative (other than the trivial one of offering an ask less than $\mathbf{p}(t)$, which is clearly disadvantageous), is to delay making a serious offer for an interim period, which we take to be infinitesimal to preserve some brevity in the notation. Compared to the first alternative this option obtains an expected gain of

$$\begin{aligned} G(t;u) = {} & \Delta(t)\bar{F}'_t(\mathbf{v}^*(t)|u;\tilde{u} \geqslant \mathbf{u}^*(t)) \cdot |\mathbf{v}^{*\prime}(t)| \\ & + \int_{u \bigcup \check{u}(t)}^{\mathbf{v}^*(t)} \frac{\delta P(\check{u}(t),\bar{v})}{\delta \check{u}} d\bar{F}_t(\bar{v}|u;\tilde{u} \geqslant \mathbf{u}^*(t)) \cdot \check{u}'(t), \end{aligned} \tag{32}$$

where $\bar{F}'_t(\mathbf{v}^*(t)|u;\tilde{u} \geqslant \mathbf{u}^*(t))$ is the probability that in the interim the highest valuation buyer makes a first serious bid $\mathbf{q}(t^+)$. Note here that delaying enables the seller to improve the other traders' assessment $\breve{u}$ of his valuation, and this helps in the second phase. Offsetting this gain, however, is the expected loss from the chance that another seller (with the valuation $\tilde{u} = \mathbf{u}^*(t)$) will make the first serious offer:

$$L(t;u) = \int_{u \bigcup \breve{u}(t)}^{\mathbf{v}^*(t)} (P(\breve{u}(t),\bar{v}) - U^\circ(u|\mathbf{u}^*(t),\bar{v}))\,\tilde{F}'_t(\mathbf{u}^*(t)|u,\bar{v})\,d\bar{F}_t(\bar{v}|u)\cdot\mathbf{u}^{*\prime}(t). \tag{33}$$

Thus, at time t the seller with the valuation u prefers to wait an infinitesimal period if $G(t;u) > L(t;u)$. An equilibrium requires, therefore, that $G(t;u) \geqslant L(t;u)$ for all times $t < \mathbf{S}(u)$, and at the prescribed time $t = \mathbf{S}(u)$ for his first serious offer that $G(\mathbf{S}(u);u) \leqslant L(\mathbf{S}(u);u)$.

Recall now that $\breve{u}(t) \equiv \mathbf{u}^*(t)$ and therefore $\breve{u}'(t) = \mathbf{u}^{*\prime}(t)$; consequently, the condition derived here that, say, $G(\mathbf{S}(u);u) = L(\mathbf{S}(u);u)$ in equilibrium is equivalent to the optimality condition (24) in the corresponding revelation game if and only if $|\mathbf{v}^{*\prime}(\mathbf{S}(u))| = \mathbf{u}^{*\prime}(\mathbf{S}(u))$. This, then, is the missing condition that knits together the equilibrium by connecting the time parameterizations of the buyers and sellers during the initial phase. This condition must hold at all times that a first serious offer might be made by either a seller or a buyer. Hence, for an equilibrium such as we have specified in which all times have the potential for first serious offers, it is necessary that

$$\mathbf{v}^{*\prime}(t) + \mathbf{u}^{*\prime}(t) = 0$$

at each time $t \in (0,1)$.

Off the Equilibrium Path

Deviations from the equilibrium path in the initial phase can be of the following types: A trader can make a serious offer too early or too late, in which case our analysis for off-the-equilibrium-path behaviour in the second phase applies; too early saddles the trader with other traders' too-favourable assessment of his valuation; and too late, as we have just seen, forgoes a profitable opportunity. A trader can make a serious offer that is better than the expected serious offer, but this is clearly disadvantageous. Lastly, when another trader, say a seller, makes a serious offer then a buyer cannot accept though the equilibrium strategy says he should; again, by construction, this is unprofitable.[9]

4.3 Construction of the Equilibrium Strategies

We now show how the various conditions that have been derived combine to determine each of the functions that specify the equilibrium strategies.

First, one can determine $\hat{u}$ and $\hat{v}$ by invoking (24) at $u=\hat{u}$, and its analogue for a buyer at $v=\hat{v}$. For brevity we display only the seller's condition:

$$0=\int_{\hat{u}}^{\hat{v}}\left\{[U^{\circ}(\hat{u}|\hat{u},\bar{v})-\hat{u})\varphi(\hat{u};\bar{v})+\frac{\delta A(\hat{u};\hat{u})}{\delta u}\right\}d\bar{F}(\bar{v}|\hat{u};\tilde{u}\geqslant\hat{u},\bar{v}\leqslant\hat{v}) \tag{35}$$
$$+(\hat{v}-\hat{u})\bar{\bar{F}}'(\hat{v}|\hat{u};\tilde{u}\geqslant\hat{u},\bar{v}\leqslant\hat{v}),$$

using $P(\hat{u},\bar{v})=A(\hat{u},\hat{u})=\hat{u}$ for $\bar{v}\geqslant\mathbf{v}^{\circ}(1;\hat{u})=\hat{u}$, $\Delta(1)=\hat{v}-\hat{u}$, and so on. Of course this condition and its analogue for the buyer are to be solved for the solution with $\hat{v}>\hat{u}$ rather than the trivial solution $\hat{v}=\hat{u}$, as mentioned in section 3.

Next, as in Figure 11.1, if it is $\mathbf{u}^*$ that is continuous at $t=0$, then it suffices to parameterize time in the initial phase so that

$$\mathbf{u}^*(t)=u^*+t\cdot[\hat{u}-u^*],\ \mathbf{S}(u)=\frac{u-u^*}{\hat{u}-u^*};$$
$$\mathbf{v}^*(t)=\hat{v}+(1-t)\cdot[\hat{u}-u^*],\ \mathbf{T}(v)=1-\frac{v-\hat{v}}{\hat{u}-u^*}; \tag{36}$$

which ensures that $\mathbf{v}^{*\prime}(t)+\mathbf{u}^{*\prime}(t)=0$. Note that the magnitude of the discontinuity at $t=0$ is

$$v^*-\mathbf{v}^*(0^+)=[v^*-\hat{v}]-[u^*-\hat{u}]; \tag{37}$$

if this were negative one would parameterize so that $\mathbf{v}^{*\prime}(t)=\hat{v}-v^*$, and so on.[10]

The remaining step in the construction of the initial phase is to determine $\mathbf{u}^{**}(t)$ and $\mathbf{v}^{**}(t)$, and this is done by invoking (24) again for the seller and the analogous condition for the buyer. Without displaying the long formulas, observe that (24) for the seller depends on $\mathbf{v}^{**}(t)\equiv\mathbf{v}^{\circ}(t;u)$ for $t=\mathbf{S}(u)$ via (25).

We presented in (18) and (21) the construction of the reduced forms of the buyers' and sellers' strategies in the second phase. To obtain extensive-form representations for, say, a seller's Dutch auction it suffices to adopt the convenient parameterization of time in which the offers $\mathbf{A}(\cdot;u)$ decline at a constant rate from $A(u,\mathbf{v}^{**}(\mathbf{S}(u)))$ down to u over the interval $\mathbf{S}(u)<t<1$:

$$\mathbf{A}(t;u)=\frac{1-t}{1-\mathbf{S}(u)}A(u,\mathbf{v}^{**}(\mathbf{S}(u)))+\frac{t-\mathbf{S}(u)}{1-\mathbf{S}(u)}u. \tag{38}$$

One can then solve for the buyer's acceptance strategy $\mathbf{v}^{\circ}(\cdot;u)$ by using (21) and the condition that $\mathbf{A}(t;u)=A(u,\mathbf{v}^{\circ}(t;u))$.

These constructions all depend on the traders' expected payoffs U° and V° in ensuing subgames with one less seller and one less buyer. Thus the construction actually begins with the case in which there is a single seller or a single buyer and then proceeds inductively to compute the strategies and expected payoffs in markets with successively larger numbers of sellers and buyers. In the next section we address the special case of the 'endgame' market in which there is only one remaining active trader on one or both sides of the market.

5 THE ENDGAMES

We first consider the case of an endgame in which there is a single seller and several buyers; the case of a single buyer and several sellers is analogous. This case is degenerate in that there is no competitive pressure on the seller that determines his strategy. Referring to (33) one sees that in the initial phase the seller suffers no loss from delaying a serious offer, since there is no chance that another seller intervenes with a serious offer in the interim. Similarly, in the second phase after a serious offer by a buyer the seller again incurs no loss from delay, as indicated by (28), and prefers to wait for the buyer's ask to decline. Further, since each buyer sees no chance that the seller will make a first serious offer in the initial phase, and expects that delay will not function as a signal to improve his terms of trade with the seller in the second phase, a buyer obtains no gain from delay. He does, however, expect to lose by delay since there is a chance that another buyer will capture the opportunity to trade with the one remaining active seller. (For these conclusions one can examine the analogues of (30) and (33) for a buyer.) After a serious bid is offered, moreover, other buyers in the second phase are not deterred from intervening; thus the serious bids in the second phase are immediately driven to the second-highest valuation among the buyers. Thus an apparent extension of the specified equilibrium to the endgame has the following scenario: all the buyers open with serious offers, and immediately the maximum serious bid is driven up to the second-highest valuation. That is, the endgame is much like an ascending English auction, but compressed into the first instant.

This is an unsatisfactory model of the endgame unless it is elaborated further.[11] It seems better to dispense with the continuity of time at the initial moment, since all the action takes place there, and to model explicitly the trading process in finer detail. We have the benefit of the results obtained by Milgrom and Weber (1982, theorems 11, 13, and 15): the seller prefers an English auction to a Dutch auction (and to several variants), and the seller prefers to reveal his private information.[12] These results permit an endgame specification that is consistent with the specification of the equilibrium for the other subgames, although fanciful in one aspect. If the seller reveals his valuation u and the buyers bid in an ascending English auction then the endgame's expected payoff for a buyer with the valuation v is $V(v) = \mathcal{E}\{v \bigcap (u \bigcup \tilde{v}) | v\}$, and the seller's expected payoff is $U(u) = \mathcal{E}\{u \bigcup v_{(2)} | u\}$, where $v_{(2)}$ is the second-highest among the buyers' valuations. The fanciful aspect, of course, is the source of the credible signal that his valuation is u. From Milgrom and Weber we know that if the seller can signal credibly that his valuation is u then he will do so, but the present formulation does not include any such signalling mechanism in the absence of competitive pressure on the seller. To allow the possibility of credible signalling in the absence of competititve pressure, given that it is in the seller's interest, it suffices to introduce an auxiliary feature. The simplest device is to allow a final instant in which the seller can either accept the outstanding bid or ask a final take-it-or-leave-it price before the market closes. Another alternative is to introduce an additional source of impatience, as described below. In any case one expects that whatever refinement is used to resolve the indeterminancy in the endgame will have only a slight effect on the construction of the specified strategies in the earlier subgames with more numerous traders.[13]

An additional degeneracy is introduced if the endgame involves only one seller and one buyer, corresponding to the case where the market opened originally with equal numbers of sellers and buyers ($m = n$). This case is essentially one of pure bargaining, and there is no formulation that is directly consistent with the construction adopted for the subgames with more traders in which competitive pressure determines the signalling mechanism. One could, of course, adopt the expedient of assuming that the traders split the gains from trade, if any, according to some maintained hypothesis. For example, if the endgame consists only of division of the gains according to an offer by one party that is either accepted or rejected by the other, then a focal-point equilibrium suffices and any one can be specified as the common-knowledge expectation of both traders; this is essentially the model studied in the bargaining experiments by Roth and Schoumaker (1983).

A preferable model allows that a positive rate of interest makes the traders impatient for conclusion of a transaction, as in the bargaining model of Cramton (1984). In this case, impatience resurrects delay as an effective signal of a trader's valuation.

We do not present here the alterations in the construction entailed by a positive interest rate, but refer the reader to the exposition by Cramton (1984) for the case of one buyer and one seller. The main conclusion is that if the interest rate is positive then the endgames are quite like all the other subgames and require no special treatment. Admittedly this is not fully satisfactory for studies of experiments in which the duration of the market, typically measured in minutes or hours, is too short to make plausible values of the interest rate an important determinant of the traders' strategies, but it has the advantage of unifying the theory of the endgames with the other subgames in the construction. Optionally, one could interpret the interest rate in the endgame as infinitesimal compared to the competitive pressure (that is, the hazard rates) in the earlier subgames, or in an experimental situation one could interpret the interest rate as a generic impatience (for example, fatigue) with behavioural origins. In some experimental designs the time of the closing of the market is uncertain and in this case the hazard rate of termination serves the same role as an interest rate.

In general, any source of impatience suffices for delay to be an effective signal, and here we have concentrated on the role of competitive pressure as a source of impatience, so the endgames necessarily present significant degeneracies.

6 REMARKS

The sequential equilibrium proposed and partially verified here is likely only one of many possibilities. Its form derives primarily from the presumed role of delay in making or accepting a serious offer as the sole signal of a trader's valuation. Underlying the construction is Cramton's key distinction between serious and non-serious offers, the special character of the off-the-equilibrium-path beliefs, and the Markov-perfect character of the on-the-equilibrium-path beliefs. One can reasonably conjecture that there are many other equilibria that accomplish signalling by different mechanisms; for example, by using history-dependent strategies. The one presented here is interesting mainly because it invokes delay to exploit directly the temporal features of the trading process. It is, moreover, relatively simple and tractable to analyze, particularly since we can draw on the previous insights of Cramton for the special case of one seller and one buyer. For purposes of comparison with experimental results it is a useful first step in providing a testable model of equilibrium behaviour.

The deficiencies of the model for use in experimental work are severe nevertheless. Most of the experiments that have been conducted allow that each trader may demand or supply several items, the subjects could plausibly be supposed to be risk averse, and so on. The crucial deficiencies, however, are inescapable consequences of the game-theoretic formulation. These are, first, that the probability distribution of the traders' valuations is common knowledge (which is rarely controlled in experiments); and secondly, that the subjects are able to know or compute equilibrium strategies and select one equilibrium in a way that is common knowledge (including, for example, the parametrization of time). Ledyard (1984) emphasizes that nearly any undominated strategies can be justified as equilibrium behaviour if there is no control on the risk aversion of the traders. Easley and Ledyard (1983), moreover, describe simple behavioural (non-equilibrium) rules-of-thumb that suffice to explain the experimental data to a substantial degree. It remains an open question, therefore, whether a game-theoretic hypothesis such as the one pursued here will prove to be the most useful explanation of the experimental data.

Some of the implications of our model and the specified equilibrium are, in fact, too strong to fit the data well. For example, the equilibrium predicts that traders transact in order of their valuations, and that no traders with extra-marginal valuations (for example, sellers' valuations above the Walrasian clearing price) succeed in trading. As Easley and Ledyard (1983) report, these properties are often contradicted by experiments. One must be cautious, however, since such experiments are a test of the compound hypothesis that the common knowledge structure (as well as the equilibrium strategies) is the one specified.

On the other hand, the implications of the equilibrium for theoretical studies of price formation and the micro-structure of markets are favourable. In particular, the equilibrium presented here offers a specific interpretation of the trading process that lends substance to the Walrasian model of markets when there are many traders on both sides of the market. If there are many buyers and sellers then the competitive pressures (measured by the hazard rates) drive all traders to offer and accept prices approximating their continuation values in ensuing subgames; since the gains from trade will be nearly exhausted these continuation values must approximate, say for a seller, the maximum of the Walrasian price and his valuation. That is, asymptotically $U(u) \to p^0 \bigcup u$ as $m \bigcap n \to \infty$, where p^0 is the asymptotic Walrasian clearing price.[14]

Bid-ask markets are familiar in commodity exchanges and it seems plausible to extrapolate from the present results that near exhaustion of the gains from trade, at prices approximating the Walrasian price, are predictable features of these markets. Even with small numbers of traders (as in the usual experimental designs), to the extent that gains from trade are nearly exhausted it is predictable that transaction prices converge over time to values close to the Walrasian price.

The suggested equilibrium also offers a concrete explanation of the mechanism by which the dispersed information about traders' valuations is manifested in the prices at which transactions are consummated. The mechanism, according to the present hypothesis, is multilateral sequential bargaining in which the traders are endogenously matched for transactions via a signalling process using delay as the primary signal. Other signalling mechanisms may be possible, but it appears that delay suffices and therefore this provides a presumptive hypothesis from which further studies can proceed.

All of the above remarks must, of course, be taken as speculative until the theory of affiliated random variables is applied, as in Milgrom and Weber (1982) for the case of ordinary auctions, to determine whether or not the proposed equilibrium strategies also satisfy the requisite global optimality properties that would be sufficient to establish the validity of the equilibrium. The satisfaction of the necessary conditions as established here and the internal consistency of the construction do, I think, lend encouragement to the expectation that an equilibrium of this form will obtain. If so, it unifies a spectrum of market structures ranging from bargaining to perfect competition.

NOTES

1. See also Rubinstein (1985) for a related model with one-sided incomplete information about one party's discount factor.
2. See also the related results by Chatterjee and Samuelson (1984).
3. Apologies are offered for the complex notation, most of which stems from the feature that traders' reservation prices are *not* assumed to be independent: the generality is necessitated by the fact that, even if independence were assumed initially, it would be lost as trading proceeded, as shown in equation (5) on page 390.
4. For example, it suffices that the valuations are stochastically independent and the sellers' valuations are identically distributed and so are the buyers' valuations. Affiliation also allows positive correlation among the valuations. If the proposed equilibrium is to be verified it seems certain that affiliation will prove to be the relevant sufficiency condition, judging from the results established by Milgrom and Weber (1982).
5. This definition of consistency is loosely stated; see Kreps and Wilson (1982) for a complete statement. In the present context the only null event involves histories that have zero probability according to the strategies. For a formal definition of a conditional probability system in this context see Myerson (1984).
6. If the buyers' valuations happen to be independent with the distribution function H then $\bar{F}'_{s(u)}(\bar{v}|u;u)=nH'(\bar{v})/H(\mathbf{v}^*(\mathbf{S}(u)))$.
7. Such an ensuing subgame is not of the form initially assumed, since the buyer's valuation is assumed (incorrectly) to be known. We address this exception in the obvious way by specifying that in the ensuing subgame he is expected to open immediately with a serious bid.
8. Actually one could allow that he stops at some higher ask, essentially turning the auction over to another seller or buyer, and gets the expected payoff in an ensuing subgame, but this option plays no role subsequently so we omit the corresponding notational refinements.
9. As usual in games of timing, as here in the initial phase, the disequilibrium analysis is essentially trivial, since delay is the only signal with informational content and each disequilibrium action has an equilibrium interpretation.
10. Alternatively one can retain the parameterization (36) and instead set $\mathbf{v}^*(t)=v^*$ for $t<t^0\equiv 1-(v^*-\hat{v})/(\hat{u}-u^*)$. In this case, only the sellers signal their valuations by delay in the initial interval $(0,t^0)$. In one way this is a preferable specification since it reduces the reliance of the equilibrium on the tie-breaking rule.
11. For comparisons with experimental results, one should note that the exact formulation of the endgame is immaterial to the extent that it is unlikely that the market will arrive at an endgame before the gains from trade are exhausted or time expires.
12. Their theorems 18 and 19 do not apply here since a reserve price other than the seller's valuation is inconsistent with a sequential equilibrium.
13. If the buyers' valuations happen to be independent in the endgame then the following device will also suffice, since in this case a Dutch auction is

equivalent to an English auction for the seller: the seller conducts a Dutch auction, as in (21), and the buyers infer his valuation from the *rate* at which his ask prices decline.

14. For example, if the sellers' and buyers' valuations are distributed independently according to the distribution functions G and H then $G(p^0) + H(p^0) = 1$.

REFERENCES

Chatterjee, K. and Samuelson, L. (1984) 'Infinite Horizon Bargaining with Alternating Offers and Two-Sided Incomplete Information', Technical Report (Pennsylvania State University).

Cramton, P. C. (1984) *The Role of Time and Information in Bargaining*, PhD thesis, Graduate School of Business, Stanford University.

Easley, D. and Ledyard, J. O. (1983) 'A Theory of Price Formation and Exchange in Oral Auctions', Technical Report 249 (Cornell University) revised.

Kreps, D. M. and Wilson, R. B. (1982) 'Sequential Equilibria', *Econometrica*, 50: 863–94.

Ledyard, J. O. (1984) 'The Scope of the Hypothesis of Bayesian Equilibrium', Technical Report 532 (California Institute of Technology).

Maskin, E. and Tirole, J. (1983) 'A Theory of Dynamic Oligopoly, I: Overview and Quantity Competition with Large Fixed Costs', Technical Report 409 (IMSSS: Stanford University).

Milgrom, P. R. and Weber, R. J. (1982) 'A Theory of Auctions and Competitive Bidding', *Econometrica*, 50: 1089–122.

Myerson, R. B. (1984) 'Sequential Correlated Equilibria of Multistage Games', Technical Report 590 (Kellogg Graduate School of Management: Northwestern University).

Plott, C. R. (1982) 'Industrial Organization Theory and Experimental Economics', *Journal of Economic Literature*, 20: 1485–1527.

Roth, A. E. and Schoumaker, F. (1983). 'Expectations and Reputations in Bargaining: An Experimental Study', *American Economic Review*, 73: 362–72.

Rubinstein, A. (1982): 'Perfect Equilibrium in a Bargaining Model', *Econometrica*, 50: 97–109.

Rubinstein, A. (1985) 'A Bargaining Model with Incomplete Information about Time Preferences', *Econometrica*, 53: 1151–1172.

Smith, V. L. (1982) 'Microeconomic Systems as an Experimental Science', *American Economic Review*, 72: 923–55.

Wilson, R. B. (1985) 'Incentive Efficiency of Double Auctions', *Econometrica*, 53: 1101–1116.

12 General Equilibrium Analysis of Imperfect Competition: An Illustrative Example

John Roberts*

1 INTRODUCTION

While Kenneth Arrow's contribution to the general equilibrium analysis of perfect competition is so fundamental that the standard model bears his name, he has also been one of the leaders in developing the analysis of imperfect competition in a general, multimarket framework. Indeed, in 1967 he labelled the failure to incorporate imperfect competition into the neoclassical general equilibrium model as one of the major 'scandals' of equilibrium theory (Arrow, 1967, p. 734), and by 1971 he published two path-breaking pieces, 'The Firm in General Equilibrium Theory', Arrow (1971), and 'General Equilibrium Under Alternative Conditions', which constituted Chapter 6 of Arrow and Hahn (1971). Moreover, in part under Arrow's influence, over the next few years, a number of other authors also developed general equilibrium models with imperfectly competitive elements.[1]

This work was very much in the spirit of standard competitive general equilibrium theory. The prototypical paper consisted of an Arrow-Debreu model to which was added some collection of firms that were assumed to recognize their influence over the prices of certain prespecified goods. These firms were taken to behave non-co-operatively toward each other with respect to the non-competitively supplied goods, while all agents (both competitive and non-competitive) treated

* I am grateful to Kathy Roberts and Bob Wilson, both of whom made very important contributions to this work, and to the National Science Foundation, which supported my research.

the prices of the remaining goods parametrically. The key result usually was an existence theorem.

This research involved important contributions, and in particular it raised and illuminated a number of subtle issues in the modelling of imperfect competition that were far from evident – or had not arisen at all – in partial equilibrium analyses.[2] In this regard, this work served the same important role as had earlier general equilibrium analyses of perfect competition. However, it turned out that these treatments, while in the spirit of the Arrow-Debreu general competitive analysis, did not quite measure up to its high standards of avoiding *ad hoc* assumptions and of deriving all results from conditions on the fundamental data of the economy.

In particular, the papers of this literature fell into two classes; in one the demand that the imperfect competitors used in their profit calculations was assumed to be the actual demand relationship and in the other some perceived demand. The existence theorems offered in both types of models required that the optimizing choices for each firm define a continuous function (or upper hemi-continuous, convex-valued correspondence) of the strategic choices of the other imperfect competitors, so that Brouwer's (or Kakutani's) fixed-point theorem could be applied to yield a pure strategy equilibrium. In the perceived demand models, this was achieved by assuming that the perceived total profit function was concave in the firm's choice variables, while in the actual demand models the requisite continuity was assumed directly.[3]

The first of these approaches was obviously *ad hoc*, for no explanation was offered of the origin of the demand perceptions, let alone why they should be so nice mathematically. The second, too, turned out to have problems, since it was shown by Roberts and Sonnenschein (1977) that there were no obvious, natural conditions that could be placed on the fundamental data of the economy that would yield continuous best reply functions. In fact, imperfectly competitive pure strategy equilibria were shown not to exist in some very simple, non-pathological examples. The essential feature of these examples was that non-concavities in the profit functions resulted in best response correspondences that were not convex-valued. This in turn allowed the graphs of these correspondences to be disjoint.[4,5]

Of course, in such situations it is common for game theorists to consider mixed strategies and expected utility or profit maximisation, although economists often reject this approach. The examples given by Roberts and Sonnenschein have not been explicitly studied in this context, although one might expect that mixed strategy equilibria would exist. Moreover, given that one could never determine by actual observation of choices whether mixed strategies were being employed in a particular game, the common basis for economists' aversion to mixed strategies – that they seem 'unrealistic' – is inappropriate. Indeed, the recent literature on purification of mixed strategies (Radner and Rosenthal, 1982; Aumann *et al.*, 1983; Milgrom and Weber, 1980) suggests that so long as we are not convinced that we have modelled everything in an economic stiuation, *including payoff-irrelevant information*, then mixed (or even correlated) strategies should be the fundamental concept for analysis. Thus, it would seem that the failure of existence of pure strategy equilibria should not, except for the increased difficulty of working with mixed strategies, deter work on general equilibrium models or market power.

Unfortunately, there has in fact been relatively little work recently on general equilibrium models of imperfect competition. Moreover, most of what work has been done has focused on justifying the competitive model as an approximation to the outcomes of imperfectly competitive behaviour when there are enough imperfect competitors.[6] This latter work has also produced many illuminating insights and has given a much firmer justification for our profession's traditional reliance on the competitive model. It has not, however, given us much insight into the workings of economies where the market power of individual firms is non-trivial. Indeed, on this dimension we know relatively little more than we did a decade ago.[7]

While it seems extreme to label this situation as still being scandalous, it is certainly unfortunate. It is indisputable that modern economies are marked by large firms with few direct competitors, unions with the power to monopsonize labour supplies, natural resource cartels, and other institutions that might plausibly be thought to be able to influence prices and to be aware of this power. Yet we have little understanding of the workings of even the simplest, 'toy' models of a *general* economic system incorporating such features, let alone of reasonably rich representations of actual economies.

At the same time, our understanding of the nature, structure and behaviour of the firm and of rivalry between firms has increased substantially over the last decade, although in a partial equilibrium context. But, as Arrow long ago noted, recognition of 'the fact that the economic world [is] a *general* system, with all parts interdependent, ... [is] ... an essential of good analysis' (Arrow, 1963–64, p. 91). Thus, one must wonder whether our intuition, based as it is on results obtained in a partial equilibrium framework, can successfully be carried over when the full interrelationships between markets are modelled.

This chapter is intended to encourage further work on imperfectly competitive equilibrium. It consists largely of an example that is too simple to take very seriously in itself; indeed, most of the possible features that could make for serious difficulties have been assumed away. Yet the example does offer a vehicle for discussion of issues that are important in modelling, and, moreover, its simplicity allows us to solve explicitly for equilibria. This solution reveals some surprising phenomena that suggest that our partial equilibrium intuition is likely to be inadequate and that the rewards to studying explicit general equilibrium models might be significant. In particular, it turns out that in a world of monopolies, imperfectly competitive equilibrium prices may be lower (relative to numeraire) than under perfect competition. Moreover, depending on the fine structure of the institutions in the model, we may go from a situation with a unique equilibrium to one with multiple equilibria that are Pareto-ordered by the level of economic activity and are parameterized by the 'level of consumer confidence'.

2 AN ILLUSTRATIVE EXAMPLE[8]

The economy in the example consists of four agents, five marketed commodities, and two non-marketed commodities. One of the marketed commodities is a non-produced good, M, which is universally desired. Each agent is assumed to hold a positive (and sufficiently large) amount of this good. The other marketed commodities consist of two kinds of output, X_A and X_B, and two sorts of labour input, L_A and L_B. Output X_A (respectively, X_B) is produced under constant returns to scale from L_A (respectively, L_B). By our choice of units, we set the input-output coefficients at unity.

The four agents in the economy consist of two producer-consumers, A and B, and two worker-consumers, 1 and 2. Only producer A has access to (knows) the technology for converting L_A into X_A, and similarly only B can convert L_B into X_B. Each producer derives utility solely from consumption of M, the universally desired, non-produced good. Worker 1 is endowed with $\bar{l}_1$ units of time, in addition to his holdings of M, and can convert this time into either non-transferable and non-marketed personal leisure activities, R_1, or into marketable labour services L_B. This worker derives utility from consumption of X_A,

R_1 and M. Similarly, worker 2 can supply L_A and derives utility from X_B, R_2 and M.

This example has numerous special features, some of which merit particular notice. First, the existence of only one universally-desired good, M, makes it a natural candidate for numeraire, and we will take it to have this role. Of course, if one wishes to think of this as fiat money, then one must come up with some reason for its being desired. Chapter 13 of Arrow and Hahn (1971) gives a discussion of some of the issues involved. Further, our specification of the utility functions for the producers as depending only on numeraire will insure that utility-maximizing and profit-maximizing behaviour coincide. In a richer modelling, where producers would be less obsessive in their interests, the normal goal of utility maximization would not necessarily correspond to profit maximization, because owners might prefer to use the firm to influence the prices of goods they consume. Moreover, if we were also to admit the possibilities of joint ownership of firms by several agents and of any agent owning parts of several firms, as in the standard Arrow-Debreu framework, then assuming profit maximization would be even more questionable. It is only if the firms are individually unable to influence prices (at least for the goods entering the utility functions of the firm's decision-makers) that the separation of production and consumption decisions is valid, and this condition seems out of place in the context of imperfect competition (see, however, Oliver Hart (1985a) for an example where the condition does make sense). Moreover, if markets are incomplete, then even if the owners of a firm care only about profit maximization, they might still disagree about which production plans were maximizing. If one were to pursue these directions in generalizing, the literature on coalition production economies and the vast literature on principal-agent models and incentives within the firm should be considered. The former addresses the problem of reconciling the divergent interests of multiple owners, while the latter considers the problems of motivating managerial decision-makers to work in the owners' interests.

Note too that the single-ownership and producer-preference assumptions obviate the need to deal with the impact of the distribution of profits on demand. If profits are distributed to consumers or input suppliers, then the dependence of demand on the firm's choices becomes quite complicated. Moreover, a modelling issue arises of whether firms ought to be treated as recognizing this influence (see Hart, 1985b). The intuition is that perhaps a very large firm in a relatively small economy ought to recognize this influence, but that a corner grocery store should not. However, it seems that ideally this determination should be endogenous: a firm should ignore this influence if, and only if, it is negligible.

The example includes no intertemporal features, no uncertainty and no informational asymmetries or incompleteness: there is only one time period, there is only one state of the world, the whole structure described earlier is common knowledge amongst the agents, and no unobservability problems give rise to moral hazard. Thus, almost all the elements that have been central in the burgeoning partial equilibrium literatures on imperfect competition and on the nature of the firm are absent. All this means that the example has no claim to any label of 'the firm in general equilibrium'. Indeed, even constant returns have been assumed, whereas one often thinks of imperfect competition as arising from increasing returns. Here the source of imperfect competition is the inelasticity of the supply of entrepreneurship: only one agent knows the technology for producing each of the outputs.[9]

Despite all this, the example can yield some insights into the impact of imperfect competition. Before attempting to indicate these, however, let us first specify both the data of the economy more formally and then the operation of the economy.

The four agents are labelled A, B, 1 and 2. The commodity space can be taken to be R^5 by treating the non-transferable leisure activities as residuals. A typical commodity space vector will be written as (m, x_A, x_B, l_A, l_B), where lower case letters refer to quantities of the corresponding commodities. The agents are specified by their endowments e, consumption sets C, and utility functions U:

Firm A:

$$e_A = (\bar{m}_A, 0, 0, 0, 0),\ C_A = R^5_+,\ U_A(m, x_A, x_B, l_A, l_B) = m;$$

Firm B:

$$e_B = (\bar{m}_B, 0, 0, 0, 0),\ C_B = R^5_+,\ U_B(m, x_A, x_B, l_A, l_B) = m;$$

Consumer 1:

$$e_1 = (\bar{m}_1, 0, 0, 0, \bar{l}_1),\ C_B = \{(m, x_A, x_B, l_A, l_B) \in R^5_+ \mid l_B \leqslant \bar{l}_1,\ x_B = l_A = 0\},$$
$$U_A(m, x_A x_B, l_A, l_B) = x_A + ln(\bar{l}_1 - l_B))ln(m);$$

Consumer 2:

$$e_2=(\bar{m}_2, 0, 0, \bar{l}_2, 0),\ C_B=\{(m, x_A, x_B, l_A, l_B)\in R^5_+ | l_A\leqslant \bar{l}_2,\ x_A=l_B=0\},$$
$$U_B(m, x_A, x_B, l_A, l_B)=x_B+ln(\bar{l}_2-l_A)+ln(m).$$

The production sets are

$$\{(m, x_A x_B, l_A l_B)\in R^5 | x_A\leqslant l_A,\ l_A\geqslant 0,\ m\leqslant 0,\ x_B\leqslant \subset l_B\leqslant 0\}$$

and

$$\{(m, x_A, x_B, l_A, l_B)\in R^5 | x_B\leqslant l_B,\ l_B\geqslant m\leqslant 0,\ x_A\leqslant 0,\ l_A\leqslant 0\}.$$

Note that this example meets the conditions of the existence theorem in Arrow and Hahn (1971, Chapter 4), so that the existence of a competitive equilibrium for each specification of endowments with $\bar{m}_i>0$; $i=A, B, 1, 2$ and $\bar{l}_i>0$, $i=1, 2$ is guaranteed. More specifically, we can compute the demands from agent 1 corresponding to a price vector $(1, p_A, p_B, w_A, w_B)$ to be as in Figure 12.1: (note $x_B\equiv l_A\equiv 0$) and those for 2 are as in Figure 12.2, where $x_A\equiv l_B\equiv 0$:

Note that we have only weak gross substitutes here. Nevertheless, the additive separability of 1 and 2's preferences allows us to show that there is a unique equilibrium allocation for each endowment. For relatively small endowments the equilibrium leaves one or both outputs not produced, but once endowments are large enough, equilibrium involves positive outputs of both produced goods and uniquely defined prices:

$$p_A=w_A=[\bar{m}_1(2+\bar{l}_1)+\bar{m}_2(1+\bar{l}_1)]/[3+\bar{l}_1+\bar{l}_2]$$

$$p_B=w_B=[\bar{m}_2(2+\bar{l}_2)+\bar{m}_1(1+\bar{l}_2)]/[3+\bar{l}_1+\bar{l}_2]$$

$$x_A=l_A=\bar{l}_2-r_2=(w_A\bar{l}_2-p_B)/w_A$$

$$x_B=l_B=\bar{l}_1-r_1=(w_B\bar{l}_1-p_A)/w_B$$

$$m_1=p_A,\ m_2=p_B$$

For example, if $\bar{m}_1=\bar{m}_2=\bar{l}_1=\bar{l}_2=a$ (which we shall refer to below as the 'equal endowments case'), then for $a\leqslant 1$, the competitive equilibrium allocation is the endowment point, while for $a>1$ it involves both outputs being produced in amount $a-1$, with all non-numeraire prices and wages equalling a.

We now turn to specifying the operation of the economy under imperfect competition, that is, the institutional framework within

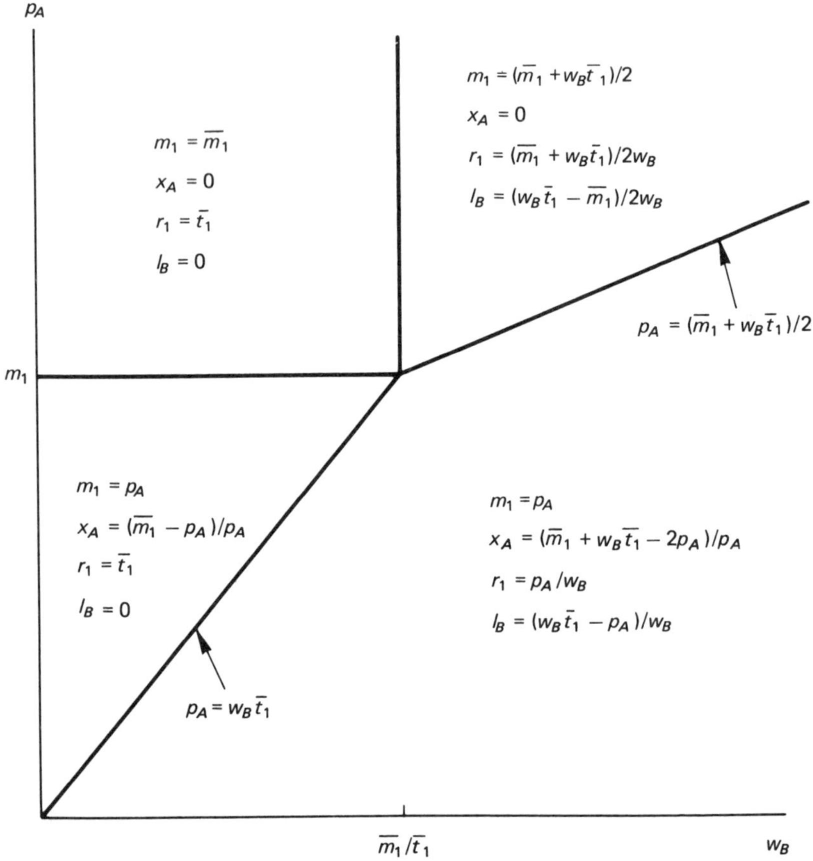

Figure 12.1 Supply and demand from consumer 1

which economic activity occurs. The intuition we have developed from the study of partial equilibrium models suggests that (except in very large economies) the institutional setting matters fundamentally in the determination of the outcomes that will obtain. This in turn suggests that the institutions should themselves be modelled as the outcome of agents' choices rather than being specified exogenously. Such analyses have, of course, begun to appear in partial equilibrium. However, attempting them in general equilibrium seems premature, and so we will content ourselves with an exogenous specification.

A complete specification of the institutions in (a model of) an economy would indicate the actions that are available to the various agents at any time, the information that they have when choosing

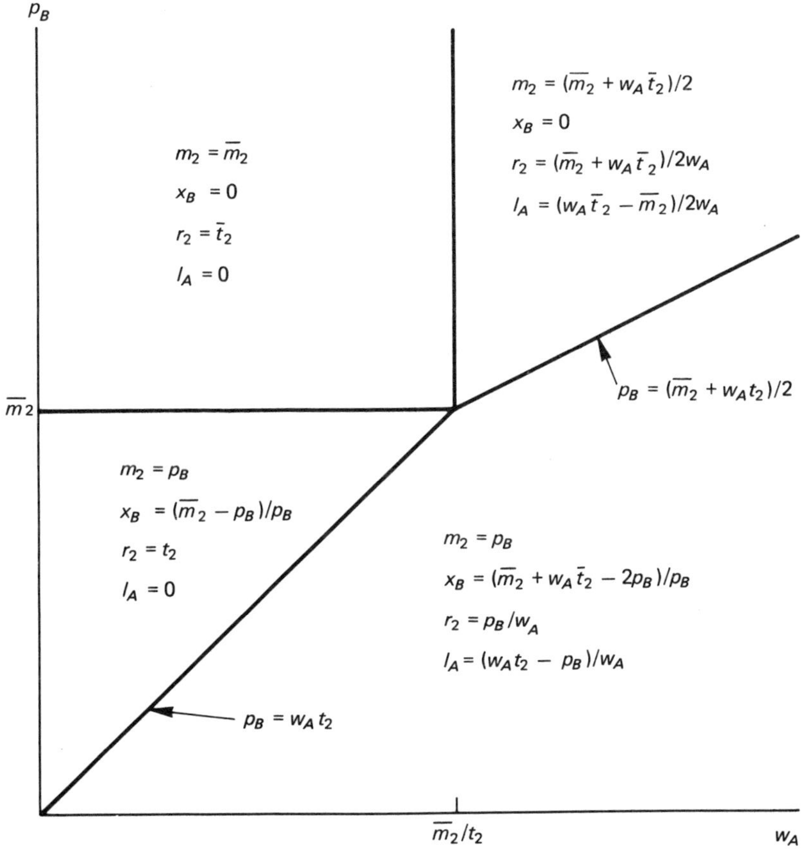

Figure 12.2 Supply and demand from consumer 2

among these actions, and the actual outcomes that result from any list of choices. Thus, as Martin Shubik in particular has often accentuated, specifying the institutions of the economy and specifying a game in extensive form to be played by the agents in the economy are equivalent.

Note that many of the papers that have sought to incorporate imperfect competition into the Arrow-Debreu model have not offered a complete institutional specification. In particular, the process by which quantity choices (in either perfectly or imperfectly competitive markets) give rise to prices has not typically been modelled. Now the various lines of work on large economies have shown us that asymptotically such an incomplete specification is adequate, because the outcomes predicted by the Arrow-Debreu model arise from a broad spectrum of institutional specifications.[10] However, there is no solid reason to expect that the operation of economies where small numbers are a factor should be institution-free: indeed almost everything we have learned from partial equilibrium analyses suggests the opposite hypothesis. Moreover, in contrast to most of the models where the institutions have not been carefully specified, those models in which a full specification has been given have been quite successful in that they have yielded not only existence theorems but also some specific results on the nature of equilibria.

With this as motivation, we will in fact give a full specification of the institutions. Further, the specification will be one in which each price (except that of the numeraire) is an actual choice variable for some agent. This approach has the double advantage of 'explaining' price formation and of matching behaviour in at least some 'real world' markets tolerably well.

The game then is as follows: The data of the economy given earlier, as well as the following specification, are common knowledge. The two firms (agents *A* and *B*) simultaneously announce the prices they each will charge for their outputs and the wages they will offer for the inputs they are willing to hire. Thus, *A* announces a value for p_A and w_A, while *B* announces p_B and w_B. The consumers (agents 1 and 2), knowing these price announcements, then simultaneously state the amounts of the outputs they wish to buy from each firm and the amounts (not exceeding the maximum feasible) of labour services they wish to sell to them. Thus 1 announces $x_A \geqslant 0$ and $l_B \in [0, \bar{l}_1]$ and 2 announces $x_B \geqslant 0$ and $l_A \in [0, \bar{l}_2]$. The firms are then obliged to hire all the labour made available to them and to produce output using the hired labour services, so that output equals labour supplied. If the volume of output from either firm weakly exceeds the demand for it, then the demand is met and any excess is costlessly destroyed. If either output level falls short of demand, then the available output of that good is provided to the consumers in proportion to their demands. In particular, since only one consumer ever demands a particular output, the entire supply, up to the quantity demanded, goes to that consumer. Payments at the announced prices and wages are then made in terms of numeraire, and the resulting outcome is evaluated in terms of the specified utility functions.

This structure provides a well-defined outcome for any specification of choices by the four agents. However, this outcome may not be feasible because one or more agents might end up with negative amounts of *M*. Assuming that the initial endowments of numeraire are 'sufficiently large' for *A* and *B*, the two firms, insures that they will not fall into bankruptcy provided we place an upper bound on the wage offers they are allowed to make. Then, once it is assured that A and B can meet their obligations, the form of the utility functions for 1 and 2 insures that they will never violate their (implicit) budget constraints: any strategy that led to a positive probability of $m<0$ would yield negatively infinite expected utility and can be ruled out.[11] Thus, with 'sufficiently large' endowments of M, we have a feasible allocation resulting from each specification of choices, and with the agents' utilities providing us with the associated payoffs, we have a well-defined non-co-operative game.

Several points are worth noting about this game. First, the structure of the game itself has special features of importance:

1. We have limited the firms to using uniform prices and wages. This is obviously an undesirable restriction, since in such a world non-linear pricing would be both straightforward and profitable. Our only justification is the need for tractability; as we shall see, even this linear pricing case is not exactly trivial to solve.
2. The specification significantly restricts the opportunities for communication. The two firms do not co-ordinate the price and wage offers they make, the consumers do not co-ordinate their decisions, and firms and consumers cannot bargain but, instead, the consumers are simply price-takers. These features are justified, if at all, by an appeal to the idea that, in a real economy, there are many firms (even if each has market power) and a huge number of worker-consumers, and that in such a world the sort of communication we have ruled out would be too expensive to justify any gains it might afford. However, it would certainly be desirable to relax these specifications in a framework that would explicitly include larger numbers of agents and to see if this intuition is justified.
3. Firms are obliged to buy all the labour time offered to them rather than any amount less than or equal to this. This specification simplifies some aspects of the problem, since the workers know how much they will work and earn and what their budget constraints will be, but it is not evidently more realistic than the alternative. Below we will discuss the impact of allowing firms to ration employment.
4. The rationing rule for output is explicit, although trivial. With more than one buyer for each good, the particular rationing scheme used would become important. In this case, one would need to be especially careful in specifying the scheme, and ideally it too should be endogenous. (Note that, in contrast to the labour side, the requirement on each firm to meet product demand, if possible, is not

a binding constraint, so long as its announced price exceeds its announced wage.)

5. Finally, the set-up, while explicitly modelling the temporal sequence of events, is essentially static. There is no recontracting, no possibility of the firms' reacting to each others' choices, no opportunity for adjusting prices if markets don't clear, and so on. This seems to me to be a reasonable first step in modelling, but only that.

The second set of remarks relates to the outcomes that this game can generate:

1. Given the price and wage choices by the firms, the various agents' choices of quantities are made in a fixed-price framework very similar to that considered in the macroeconomics literature. Thus, in these subgames, arbitrary quantity choices will typically result in rationing. For example, if one worker chooses not to work, then the other will be unable to find any of the output he would like to be able to purchase. Note, moreover, that although unemployment (in the sense that labour supply exceeds hiring) cannot arise here because we have required firms to absorb the full amount of labour offered, such unemployment might well arise under alternate specifications (see below).
2. In a standard sort of partial equilibrium model based on this economy, the demands and supplies facing each firm would be independent of each other and of those of the other firm. However, the income effects in a general equilibrium framework generate significant interactions. For example, if firm A increases its employment, it increases the income of B's customers and thereby the demand facing B. If, in turn, this leads to B increasing its output and employment, A's demand is increased.[12] We shall see that such effects can mean that the general equilibrium can be very different from what a partial equilibrium model would predict.

We now turn to explicit analysis of the example. First, for a basis of comparison, let us consider the partial equilibrium optimizing choice of firm A, say, when firm B has selected the competitive price and wage levels, supposing that for whatever price and wage that A announces, the consumers respond according to their demand functions. In particular, suppose $\bar{m}_i=\bar{l}_i=a>1$, $i=1, 2$, so that the competitive equilibrium values of prices and wages are $p_A=p_B=w_A=w_B=a$. Firm A now is considered to select $p_A\geqslant 0$ and $w_A\geqslant 0$. Since $w_B=a$, if $p_A\geqslant a(1+a)/2$, then, as we see from Figure 12.1, the demand for A's output will be zero, so we will have the optimal choice $\tilde{p}_A \leqslant a(1+a)/2$. Similarly, $\tilde{w}_A$ will be at least 1, since otherwise no labour will be supplied. Then A's problem is to select p_A, w_A to maximize its profit

$$p_A\left(\frac{\bar{m}_1+w_B\bar{l}_1-2p_A}{p_A}\right)-w_A\left(\frac{w_A\bar{l}_2-p_B}{w_A}\right)=2a+a^2-2p_A-aw_A$$

subject to the condition that its production not exceed the amount of labour supplied to it:

$$\left(\frac{\bar{m}_1+w_B\bar{l}_1-2p_A}{p_A}\right)-\left(\frac{w_A\bar{l}_2-p_B}{w_A}\right)=\left(\frac{a+a^2-2p_A}{p_A}\right)-\left(\frac{w_Aa-a}{w_A}\right)\leqslant 0$$

and subject to the bounds given above.

The solution to this problem is

$$\tilde{p}_A=\frac{(a+a^2)[a+\sqrt{2(a+a^2)}]}{(2+a)\sqrt{2(a+a^2)}};\quad \tilde{w}_A=\frac{a+\sqrt{2(a+a^2)}}{(2+a)}.$$

For $a>1$, we have $\tilde{w}_A<a<\tilde{p}_A$, as our intuition would suggest: the firm raises its price and lowers its wage when it recognizes its market power. For example, if $a=2$ then the competitive price and wage are both also 2, but the monopoly solution involves $\tilde{p}_A=2.36$, $\tilde{w}_A=1.37$ and yields profits (in terms of numeraire) of 0.54 versus the competitive profit of zero.

Now let us examine what happens when both firms recognize their market power. To do so, we need a prediction of behaviour, that is, a solution concept for the game. The natural one to use here is subgame perfect equilibrium in the game that we specified above. This means, in the first instance, that each of the two consumers, 1 and 2, has a strategy that specifies the individual's choice of the quantities of output to demand and of labour to supply contingent on the price and wage choices of the firms, and that, for each price–wage vector these strategies are best responses to one another, given the mechanism by which any such choices result in an allocation of resources. Further, the price and wage choices of the two firms each have the property of being best responses to one another, given that consumers will respond to any price–wage configuration according to their subgame equilibrium strategies.

Thus, to solve the game, we must first solve the game between consumers 1 and 2 that arises for each vector (p_A, w_A, p_B, w_B). This is a time-consuming process, but quite straightforward. The sole complication rests in recognizing that the labour supply choice of one consumer determines an upper bound on the availability of the output that the other consumer desires and in factoring this into the analysis. Here the requirement that the firms hire all the labour offered to them is extremely helpful, since the consumers need not be concerned that not all of their labour supply offer will be accepted. Note that this would not be so if firms were free to buy only a fraction of the labour offered. Then each consumer would need to forecast the product demand that would be forthcoming from the other consumer, because this will determine the amount of his labour offer that is accepted and thus will influence the amount of output he wishes to commit to buying. We would thus face a rather messy simultaneity problem that, as we shall see below, could naturally give rise to a multiplicity of equilibria in the subgames.

As an illustration of the computations involved in finding the subgame equilibria, consider the equal endowments case with $a=2$ discussed above, and suppose $p_A=3, w_B=3, p_B=5, w_A=2$. Then the demand functions in Figures 12.1 and 12.2 give

$$x_1 = \frac{\bar{m}_1 + \bar{w}_B \bar{l}_1 - 2p_A}{p_A} = \frac{2}{3}$$

$$l_1 = \bar{l}_1 - \frac{p_A}{w_B} = 1$$

$$x_2 = 0$$

$$l_2 = \bar{l}_2 - \frac{\bar{m}_2 + w_A \bar{l}_2}{2w_A} = 2 - \left(\frac{2+4}{4}\right) = \frac{1}{2}.$$

If the consumers were to announce these choices, 2 would be able to realize his plans, because he would sell $\frac{1}{2}$ unit of L_A to firm A, buy none of X_B, and consume $\frac{3}{2}$ units of leisure and $\bar{m}_2 + l_2 + l_2 \cdot w_A = 3$ units of numeraire. However, 2's supply of labour is inadequate to allow 1's unconstrained demand for X_A to be met. Thus, 1 actually faces the problem of maximizing $x + ln(2-l) + ln(2+3l-3x)$, subject to $0 \leqslant l \leqslant 2$ and $0 \leqslant x \leqslant 1/2$, the solution of which is $x=1/2$, $l=11/12$. The resultant profits of the two firms are $\pi_A = (p_A - w_A)x_A = 1/2$, $\pi_B = p_B x_B - w_B l_B = 5.0 - 3 \cdot \frac{11}{12} = -\frac{11}{4}$.

Note that we could carry out this constrained optimization for A alone, without worrying about B, because B does not wish to purchase any output and so faces no availability constraint that could ever be binding. At price–wage vectors where both A and B have positive nominal or unconstrained output demands, both might end up being rationed on their output demand choices by the other's labour supply choice. This happens, for example, with $p_A = p_B = 1$ and $w_A = w_B = 2/3$, where nominal output demands are 4/3 and labour supplies are 1/2. Note too that a standard partial equilibrium analysis, such as that given above, ignores the possibility of such rationing.

Despite this possibility of rationing, so long as the labour supply choices are unconstrained (except by the endowments), one can check by further calculations that there actually is a unique subgame equilibrium for each choice of prices and wages. Thus, the profits accruing to any pair of price and wage choices are well defined. Thus too, the search for a general equilibrium reduces to solving the induced game between the two firms, where each firm simply picks its price and wage.

Clearly not all price–wage configurations can be equilibria. For example, each price will weakly exceed the corresponding wage at any equilibrium. Moreover, for sufficiently large endowments, at equilibrium we can be sure that both the demand announced to any firm and the labour supplied to it will be positive and equal. That they will be equal is seen by noting that if they are not, the firm can reduce its wage slightly (if labour supply exceeds output demand) or increase its price (if labour supply will not allow the firm to meet output demand) and increase its profits. That they will be positive is clear, since if demand and labour supply are both zero, then the firm can earn positive profits by lowering its price and raising its wage (while keeping $p > w$) so as to elicit positive quantities and profits. This all means that p_A and w_B must, in equilibrium, lie in the region in the lower right of Figure 12.1 while p_B and w_A lie in the corresponding region of Figure 12.2. Further, we can also assure that neither consumer is rationed in equilibrium, although here the argument is more delicate.

First, suppose only one consumer, say 1, is rationed. Then, a slight increase in p_A will leave 1's unconstrained demand still greater than his announced demand, and will also increase his labour supply. This latter fact means that 2 remains unconstrained and so continues to supply as much labour to A as before. This in turn means that A can still produce and sell the same amount but receives a higher price. Thus in equilibrium we cannot have only one consumer rationed.

If both are rationed, then it turns out that a pair of simultaneous linear equations with non-zero determinant characterizes the subgame equilibrium, with the resultant profits of firm i being a strictly increasing function of p_i. Thus, the firm can increase its price and thereby increase its profits so long as we remain in the region where both consumers are constrained. Moreover, as we raise p_i, we eventually hit a region where at most one consumer is constrained, and we have already seen that one being constrained is not an equilibrium.

All this means that equilibrium, if it exists, can be found by limiting our search to price–wage configurations where neither consumer is constrained, where each price exceeds the corresponding wage, and where quantities are positive. This suggests that, in hunting for an equilibrium, we look for a simultaneous solution of the problems:

$$\max_{p_A, w_A \geqslant 0} \quad p_A \left[\frac{\bar{m}_1 + w_B \bar{l}_1 - 2p_A}{p_A} \right] - w_A \left[\frac{w_A \bar{l}_2 - p_B}{w_A} \right]$$

subject to

$$\left[\frac{\bar{m}_1 + w_B \bar{l}_1 - 2p_A}{p_A} \right] = \left[\frac{w_A \bar{l}_2 - p_B}{w_A} \right]$$

$$p_A \leqslant \min \left(w_B \bar{l}_1, \frac{\bar{m}_1 + w_B \bar{l}_1}{2} \right)$$

$$w_A \geqslant \max \left(\frac{p_B}{\bar{l}_2}, \frac{2p_B - \bar{m}_2}{\bar{l}_2} \right)$$

and the corresponding profit maximization problem for B, given p_A and w_A.

For the equal endowments case we obtain

$$p^*(a) = \frac{a[(5a^2 + 16a + 16) + \sqrt{[(5\alpha^2 + 16\alpha + 16)^2 - 4(2\alpha + 4)(2\alpha^3 + 5\alpha^2 + 8\alpha + 16)]}}{2(2\alpha^3 + 5\alpha^2 + 8\alpha + 16)}$$

$$w^*(a) = \frac{(2+a)}{2a} p - \frac{1}{2} - \frac{1}{2a} \sqrt{a^2(1-p)^2 - 4ap + 4p^2}$$

as a solution to the first order conditions. Further, one can check that these are the unique solutions over the region (defined by the second and third constraints) in which the forms of the demand and supply equations are as assumed in the calculations.[13] This means these expressions yield the only candidate for symmetric equilibrium.

Finally, of course, we need to check that these values for p and w actually are equilibria, that is, that no deviation by one firm is profitable given that the payoffs from such a deviation are determined by playing out the ensuing subgame.

The likelihood of rationing results in a complicated correspondence between the choices of the firms and the resulting payoffs. This, in turn, means that checking whether the vector $p_A = p_B = p^*, w_A = w_B = w^*$ is actually an equilibrium is not a simple matter. (Indeed, I was reduced to direct verification of the unprofitability of an exhaustive set consisting of several dozen possible sorts of deviations.) However, it turns out that the values given by these equations actually do constitute equilibrium.

Table 12.1 gives values of $p^*(a)$ and $w^*(a)$ for various values of a, along with the profits per firm divided by a. Note that, as $a \to \infty$, $p^*(a)$ converges to 2, $w^*(a)$ converges to zero, $aw^*(a)$ converges to 4 and π/a converges to unity. This means that, in the limit, the entire 'national income' is absorbed by profits.

Perhaps more striking is the fact that for all $a \geqslant 2$, the imperfectly competitive equilibrium price is strictly less than the competitive price,

Table 12.1 Eqilibrium prices, wages and profits

a	$p^*(a)$	$w^*(a)$	π/a
2	1.727607	1.106339	0.136197
3	2.034224	0.973567	0.321925
4	2.151388	0.825693	0.462153
5	2.193609	0.703968	0.561278
10	2.179906	0.386548	0.782009
25	2.093032	0.159103	0.916279
50	2.049965	0.079887	0.959000
100	2.025830	0.039986	0.979742
1 000	2.002658	0.004000	0.997997
10 000	2.000267	0.000400	0.999800
100 000	2.000027	0.000040	0.999980
1 000 000	2.000000	0.000004	0.999998

which is a. In fact, $p^*(a)/a$ goes to zero as a goes to infinity. (Of course, $p^*(a)/w^*(a)$ goes to zero, while the competitive price/wage ratio is constant at unity.) This is surely a result which we would not have expected from partial equilibrium modellings.

The origin of this result is in income effects operating across markets. Consider the partial equilibrium computation made above, where it was shown that the best response by one firm when the other announced competitive prices and wages was to raise its price and lower its wage offer. Doing this has an impact on both the demand facing the other firm and the supply of labour to it. Specifically, the higher price reduces the labour supply while the lower wage reduces the demand for the other firm's product. These effects, if we work through a Cournot-type dynamics, would ultimately lower both prices below the competitive level. In fact, as we have seen, for each a the partial equilibrium price exceeds the competitive level, which is unbounded in a, while the general equilibrium price is bounded.

This interdependence between the firms should lead to equilibrium prices that do not yield joint profit maximization, since neither firm recognizes that its choices affect the other's profits. This raises the possibility that co-operatively set prices might exceed the competitive levels (as our partial equilibrium intuition would suggest), but this is not the case. Indeed, collusive prices are even lower than the imperfectly competitive equilibrium levels, while wages are higher. For example, if $a = 2$, then the joint profit maximizing prices are 1.707107 while the wages are 1.207107, yielding profits of 0.292893 per firm, and for $a = 10$ the figures are 1.761976, 0.557186 and 8.238024. These relationships arise because the interdependence is in its effect equivalent to a complementarity. (Note: in the collusive solution, $p = a(1+2w)/(2+\alpha)$ and $w = (\alpha^{\frac{3}{3}} + 2\alpha + 2\alpha^{\frac{1}{2}})/(4+\alpha^2)$.) As one would expect, however, with both the equilibrium and the collusive prices and wages, the level of employment and output is lower than at the competitive equilibrium.[14] Thus, a public programme of wage and price subsidies would seem to be Pareto-improving if financed out of lump sum taxes. Note, however, that such taxes could cause real problems out of equilibrium since they might possibly yield infeasible outcomes.

While there is classic, monopolistic underemployment here, we do not have the sort of multiple equilibria that are Pareto-ordered by the level of employment that were found by Heller (1984) and that have figured in the macroeconomics literature. However, if we change the specification of the institutions in the model in a natural way, this possibility arises.

Specifically, suppose that, once the firms have announced prices and wages and the workers have announced the amounts of labour they want to supply and of goods they want to purchase, the firms need not employ all the labour offered but rather can hire any amount less than or equal to the supply. These choices are made simultaneously and independently by the two firms, which then convert the labour into output. Consumers are required to buy all the goods they ordered, provided production is at least as large as demand, and otherwise they must take the total production. As before, all accounts are then settled simultaneously via payments of M.

With this formulation, the consumers might easily be forced into bankruptcy unless their endowments of M are large. However, they can (and, given their preferences, will) protect themselves against this possibility by restricting their demands.

The game that results from this specification of the institutions has an extra stage compared with the original model where there was no hiring choice by the firms. As suggested earlier, this means that the consumer-workers face more complex strategic decisions in choosing the quantities to demand and supply, since they must forecast not only the amount of output that will be available but also the amount of their labour that will be hired. For example, the problem facing consumer 1, given prices and wages, is to maximize

$$x + ln(\bar{l}_1 - l) + ln(\bar{m}_1 - p_A x + w_B l)$$

subject to $x \leqslant x^*$, $l \leqslant l^*$, and $l \leqslant \bar{l}_1$, where x^* is the amount of X_A that he expects will be supplied and l^* is the amount of his labour that he expects will be hired.

Now, the conditions of sequential rationality imply that if a firm's announced price exceeds its announced wage then it will produce as much as possible, so that its hiring and output will be the smaller of the amount of labour supplied to it and the quantity of output demanded from it, while if it has announced a price less than its wage it will hire and produce zero. This means that, in effect, the consumers must forecast each other's choices, since (except when a firm's price and wage are equal) these choices uniquely determine the outcomes. Thus, solving the subgame that arises given $p_A > w_A$ and $p_B > w_B$ reduces to finding values x_1, x_2, l_1 and l_2 such that (x_1, l_1) maximizes $x + ln(\bar{l}_1 - l) + ln(\bar{m}_1 - p_A x - w_B l)$ subject to $0 \leqslant x \leqslant l_2$, $0 \leqslant l \leqslant x_2$ and $l \leqslant \bar{l}_1$ and also (x_2, l_2) maximizes $x + ln(\bar{l}_2 - l) + ln(\bar{m}_2 - p_B x + w_A l)$ subject to $0 \leqslant x \leqslant l_1$, $0 \leqslant l \leqslant x_1$ and $l \leqslant \bar{l}_2$.

It is easily seen that there may be a continuum of equilibria to this subgame. For example, consider the symmetric equal endowments case with $a = 2$ and suppose prices and wages are set at their equilibrium levels from the original formulation:

$$p_A = p_B = p^*(2) = 1.727607 \text{ and } w_A = w_B = w^*(2) = 1.106339.$$

Then, among the solutions to the subgame are any vectors $x_1 = x_2 = x$, $l_1 = l_2 = l$ with $x = l \leqslant .438447$, which is the activity level at the equilibrium of the original formulation. At such a vector, each consumer would like to work more and consume more output, but the expectation that the other will not demand more output than x limits the amount of his labour he expects to sell and, simultaneously, the low level of labour provision that he expects from the other limits the amount of output he expects to be available.

This multiplicity of subgame equilibria means that there may be multiple equilibria in the overall game. Among these are any price and wage choices followed by quantities of $x_A = x_B = l_A = l_B = 0$. Consumers never expect to be able to find either output to buy or employment, and the system is then stuck. Moreover, there are other equilibria with positive but low levels of activity. For example, consider the equilibrium prices p_A^*, p_B^*, w_A^* and w_B^* in the original formulation and the corresponding quantities x_1^*, x_2^*, l_1^* and l_2^*. Now let $x_1 = l_2 \leqslant x_1^* = l_2^*$ and $x_2 = l_1 \leqslant x_2^* = l_1^*$. Then these allocations can be full equilibrium outcomes: simply have customers expect that x_1, x_2, l_1 and l_2 will be the choices at these prices and that all quantities will be zero at other prices. Clearly, too, we can have other patterns of off-the-equilibrium path beliefs that would also support this outcome, and, moreover, we can have equilibria at other prices.

This extreme multiplicity of equilibria has some positive and negative aspects. On the one hand, the predictive power of the model is minimal. On the other hand, the multiplicity of equilibria may suggest an explanation of various possible levels of economic activity all being consistent with equilibrium. In this context, the role of consumer expectations in sustaining these equilibria points to a crucial role for measures of 'consumer confidence' in predicting economic activity.

3 CONCLUSIONS

Several lessons for future work on imperfectly competitive general equilibrium seem to emerge from the example. First, as has already been demonstrated by other researchers working in both partial and general equilibrium contexts, in analyzing imperfect competition it is important and perhaps absolutely crucial to adopt an explicit game-theoretic model of the economy. In particular, the formation of prices should not be left unmodelled, and one must be careful about treating such issues as the ordering of actions, the availability of information at any decision point, and other features of apparently fine detail. In this regard, the great success of the competitive model may have been costly for economics. Despite its failing to treat these issues explicitly, it has worked extremely well, and this has prevented economists from fully realizing that other institutions cannot be successfully analyzed in such a casual way.

Secondly, it would seem that our intuition derived from partial equilibrium models of monopoly or oligopoly may be seriously wrong. Thus, unless one believes not only in the prevalence of Bertrand competition, contestable markets, or other institutions which (in partial equilibrium) result in essentially competitive outcomes, but also in the efficacy of these institutions in general equilibrium, then explicit general equilibrium analyses of imperfect competition should be welcomed and encouraged.

Finally, although I must admit that analyzing the example here took much longer than I had anticipated, we see that we can solve interesting examples, even if we do not have general pure-strategy existence theorems. Moreover, it would seem important to obtain (mixed strategy) existence theorems and to attempt to characterize the equilibria so that we can better understand the workings of an economy where individual agents have market power.

NOTES

1. The first papers in the field are by Negishi (1961, 1972). The first of these predates Arrow's work. Later important contributions include Gabszewicz and Vial, 1972; Fitzroy, 1974; Marschak and Selten, 1974; Nikaido, 1975; Laffont and Laroque, 1976; Cornwall, 1977; Benassy, 1976; and Silvestre, 1977a, 1977b, 1978. A seminal contribution to a radically different approach to the general equilibrium analysis of imperfect competition was Shubik (1972).
2. We will indicate some of these below, but for a balanced survey, see Hart (1985b).
3. In fact, Arrow's own contributions do not fall neatly into either of these two classes, since profit maximization is not assumed. However, in terms of the assumptions used to obtain existence, Arrow's work fits in the mode of the 'actual demand' models.
4. These examples were different from those recently produced by Dierker and Grodal (1982). They consider a model of the type introduced by Gabszewicz and Vial (1972) in which the imperfectly competitive firms

select quantities treated as adjustments to the owners' endowments. The competitive prices for the exchange economy corresponding to these adjusted endowments are then used to evaluate the firms' choices. Dierker and Grodal show that there may be neither pure nor mixed strategy equilibria in these games. Their result depends on the non-uniqueness of the equilibrium prices and the dependence of the payoffs on the method by which prices are normalized. It is not clear that these results apply to a model in which price formation is explicitly modelled.

5. One should note that the work growing out of Shubik (1972) is immune to the Roberts-Sonnenschein criticism. I will suggest below that the explicitly game-theoretic approach taken in this work is not only a key to its success but is also crucial to making further progress on general equilibrium with imperfect competition. At the same time, the particular institutions assumed in the Shubik-style work are not obviously the most natural ones to consider.
6. See, in particular, the papers in Mas-Colell (1980) and the dissertation by Simon (1981).
7. An important exception to this comes from the explicitly game-theoretic work mentioned above based on Martin Shubik's model of commodity exchange. Shubik himself has been the major contributor in this area, beginning with Shubik (1972) and Shapley and Shubik (1977), but various others have also used this approach successfully to analyze imperfect competition in general equilibrium (see, for example, Okuno, Postlewaite and Roberts, 1980). Recent insightful contributions in a more traditionally neoclassical framework that also avoid pitfalls with existence are Hart (1985a) and Heller (1984).
8. After this work was completed I received a copy of Heller (1984). This very interesting paper considers an example with many features in common with that considered here.
9. This assumption is not completely standard, but, as Arrow (1971, p. 69) has pointed out, 'the notion of an infinite supply of entrepreneurship is no more reasonable than that of an infinite supply of anything else'.
10. See, for example, Dubey, Mas-Colell and Shubik (1980) and Dubey and Neyman (1984) for axiomatic treatments of this question, as well as Green (1981).
11. Bankruptcy is thus essentially assumed away here. In other models, including especially those in the Shubik mold, the bankruptcy problem has been a major focus of the analysis.
12. The discussion here sounds dynamic, but, as noted above, the model is static. However, the effects discussed can still occur.
13. The key is first to show that, on the relevant region, the first order conditions under symmetry yield a pair of well-defined, differentiable functions $w_i(p)$, $i=1,2$, then to check that $w_1(p)-w_2(p)$ is monotone and so has a unique zero.
14. Asymptotically, the ratio of the collusive wage to price is 1, so that the competitive and collusive levels ultimately agree, while the equilibrium gives approximately one half this level.

REFERENCES

Arrow, K. J. (1963–64) 'The Role of Securities in the Optimal Allocation of Risk-Bearing', *Review of Economic Studies*, 31: 91–6.

Arrow, K. J. (1967) 'Samuelson Collected', *Journal of Political Economy*, 75: 730–37.

Arrow, K. J. (1971) 'The Firm in General Equilibrium', in R. Marris and A. Wood, *The Corporate Economy: Growth, Competition and Innovative Potential* (Cambridge, Mass.: Harvard University Press).

Arrow, K. J. and F. H. Hahn (1971) *General Competitive Analysis* (San Francisco: Holden-Day).

Aumann, R., Y. Katznelson, R. Radner, R. Rosenthal and B. Weiss (1983) 'Approximate Purification of Mixed Strategies', *Mathematics of Operations Research*, 8: 327–41.

Benassy, J. P. (1976) 'The Disequilibrium Approach to Monopolistic Price Setting and General Monopolistic Equilibrium', *Review of Economic Studies*, 43: 69–82.

Cornwall, R. (1977) 'The Concept of General Equilibrium in a Market Economy with Imperfectly Competitive Producers', *Metroeconomica*, 29: 57–72.

Dierker, H. and B. Grodal (1982) 'Nonexistence of Cournot-Walras Equilibrium in a General Equilibrium Model with Two Oligopolists', Discussion Paper 95, University of Bonn.

Dubey, P. (1982) 'Price–Quantity Strategic Market Games', *Econometrica*, 50: 111–26.

Dubey, P., A. Mas-Colell and M. Shubik (1980) 'Efficiency Properties of Strategic Market Games: An Axiomatic Approach', *Journal of Economic Theory*, 22: 339–62.

Dubey, P. and A. Neyman (1984) 'Payoffs in Nonatomic Economies: An Axiomatic Approach', *Econometrica*, 52: 1129–51.

Fitzroy, F. (1974) 'Monopolistic Equilibrium, Non-Convexity and Inverse Demand', *Journal of Economic Theory*, 7: 1–16.

Gabszewicz, J. J. and J.-Ph. Vial (1972) 'Oligopoly "á la Cournot" in General Equilibrium Analysis', *Journal of Economic Theory*, 4: 381–400.

Green, E. J. (1981) 'Continuum and Finite-Player Noncooperative Models of Competition', mimeo. (California Institute of Technology).

Hart, O. (1985a) 'A Model of Imperfect Competition with Keynesian Features', *Quarterly Journal of Economics*, 96: 109–38.

Hart, O. (1985b) 'Imperfect Competition in General Equilibrium: An Overview of Recent Work', in K. J. Arrow and S. Honkapohja, *Frontiers of Economics* (Oxford: Blackwell).

Heller, W. P. (1984) 'Coordination Failure with Complete Markets in a Simple Model of Effective Demand', Discussion Paper 84–16, Department of Economics, University of California, San Diego.

Laffont, J.-J. and G. Laroque (1976) 'Existence d'un Equilibre Général de Concurrence Imparfaite: Une Introduction', *Econometrica*, 44: 283–94.

Marschak, T. and R. Selten (1974) *General Equilibrium with Price-Setting Firms* (Berlin, Heidelberg, and New York: Springer-Verlag).

Mas-Colell, A. (ed.) (1980) 'Symposium: Non-Cooperative Approaches to the Theory of Perfect Competition', *Journal of Economic Theory*, 22: 121–376.

Milgrom, P. and R. Weber (1980) 'Distributional Strategies for Games with Incomplete Information', Discussion paper 428, Northwestern University. Forthcoming in *Mathematics of Operations Research.*

Negishi, T. (1961) 'Monopolistic Competition and General Equilibrium', *Review of Economic Studies*, 28: 196–201.

Negishi, T. (1972) *General Equilibrium Theory and International Trade* (Amsterdam: North-Holland).

Nikaido, H. (1975) *Monopolistic Competition and Effective Demand* (Princeton: Princeton University Press).

Okuno, M., A. Postlewaite, and J. Roberts (1980) 'Oligopoly and Competition in Large Markets', *American Economic Review*, 70: 22–31.

Radner, R. and R. Rosenthal (1982) 'Private Information and Pure Strategy Equilibria', *Mathematics of Operations Research*, 7: 401–9.

Roberts, J. and H. Sonnenschein (1977) 'On the Foundations of the Theory of Monopolistic Competition', *Econometrica*, 45: 101–13.

Shapley, L. and M. Shubik (1977) 'Trade Using One Commodity as a Means of Payment', *Journal of Political Economy*, 85: 937–68.

Shubik, M. (1972). 'Commodity, Money, Oligopoly, Credit and Bankruptcy in a General Equilibrium Model', *Western Economic Journal*, 10: 24–38.

Simon, L. (1981) *Bertrand and Walras Equilibrium: A Theory of Perfect Competition for Finite Economies*, PhD thesis (Princeton University).

Silvestre, J. (1977a) 'A Model of General Equilibrium with Monopolistic Behavior', *Journal of Economic Theory*, 16: 425–42.

Silvestre, J. (1977b) 'General Monopolistic Equilibrium under Non-Convexities', *International Economic Review*, 18: 425–34.

Silvestre, J. (1978) 'Increasing Returns in General Non-Competitive Analysis', *Econometrica*, 46: 397–402.

13 Incentive-based Decentralization: Expected-Externality Payments Induce Efficient Behaviour in Groups

John W. Pratt and Richard Zeckhauser*

1 INTRODUCTION

1.1 Endowment Contributed by Kenneth Arrow

Thirty-five years ago Kenneth Arrow asked a profound question: Is it 'formally possible to pass from a set of known individual tastes to a pattern of social decision-making, the procedure in question being required to satisfy certain natural conditions'? (Arrow, 1951, p. 2). He laid out an appealing set of conditions and demonstrated that the answer was 'No'. The vast literature that followed, frequently played musical chairs with his requirements while it tiptoed along the border of infeasibility.

A second major strand of Arrow's work on collective choice processes examines the circumstances under which the market can serve as an effective decentralised decision mechanism. Arrow and Debreu (1954) assume that individuals' preferences are unknown, hence the

* Pratt's research was supported by the Associates of the Harvard Business School. Zeckhauser's research was supported by NSF grant SOC77-16606 and by the Energy and Environmental Policy Research Center, Harvard University. Valuable comments were provided by Roy Radner, John Riley, and participants in the NSF–NBER Seminar on Decentralization, San Diego, in the 8th Management Science Colloquium of the Kansai Economic Research Institute, Osaka, where the research was originally presented, and subsequently, in various seminars at the University of Chicago, Harvard, MIT, and Stanford.

process must elicit the requisite information. However, they allow for a medium of exchange, for transferable utility. (A monetary measuring rod – quite appropriate in this context – violates the Independence of Irrelevant Alternatives Condition of Arrow's aforementioned impossibility result.) Arrow and Debreu and their successors demonstrated that if all relevant markets can be established, and if preferences and production sets are not too ill behaved, then efficient competitive outcomes will be generated by market processes (see also Arrow and Hahn, 1971).

In quite separate lines of important and still continuing inquiry, Arrow has addressed many of the major issues of welfare economics related to market performance in the presence of such imperfections as externalities and asymmetric information. (His work is surveyed in the introduction to this volume.)

1.2 Decentralization

These three bodies of work together illuminate a central question of microeconomics: 'Under what conditions and with what mechanisms can we allocate resources efficiently in our society?' A vast literature on topics ranging from business management to socialism has addressed this question. Within economics it has taken the form: 'When and how can local decision units be induced to provide information and to take actions that co-ordinate appropriately and are in the interest of a company, an organization, or society as a whole? In other words, how can we effectively decentralize decision-making responsibility?' This paper addresses that question allowing for externalities and for asymmetric information, quite possibly about preferences, but permitting monetary transfers among the participants.

Effective decentralization is a major concern for both public and private organizations. The government, for instance, may seek to induce the industrial firms in a particular geographic region to make appropriate trade-offs between environmental quality and production cost. A business firm with many subordinate decision-making units will try to develop mechanisms to ensure that the units undertake actions that support the profits of the firm as a whole. To maintain a firm-wide reputation for product quality, for example, some prodding from headquarters is needed to give each self-interested profit centre sufficient encouragement to maintain or raise its own quality level. Another example: architects' fee schedules should be designed so that they have an appropriate interest in holding down construction costs.

If all agents had a common objective, it could be maximized by a team, whose members observe information and follow strategies formulated by a central authority (Marschak and Radner, 1972). Because interests are fully shared, team members have an automatic incentive to co-operate in achieving the team optimum, subject to whatever information-transmission constraints and costs the world imposes. The centre assesses the joint distribution of information the agents will observe and then specifies what messages each agent should send and what actions he should take depending upon the information he has, so as to maximize the joint payoff for the team. (Hurwicz, 1959, is a classic paper on the more general subject of informational efficiency in resource allocation.)

If objectives differ, there are still circumstances in which efficiency might be achieved, even without transfers. Under *laissez-faire*, self-interested maximizing decisions by each agent maximize total welfare unless there are interdependencies (externalities) whereby one agent's choice directly affects the welfare of another. (This holds even when agents have information useful to one another, providing they signal honestly when it costs them nothing to do so.) Alas, the market cannot always work its miracles: externalities do occur.

Despite interdependencies and differing objectives, a ruthless dictator could maximize total welfare if there were no uncertainty or if all information were eventually public or verifiable at negligible cost. Death to him who does not act to maximize total welfare. Equivalently, a central authority providing sufficient financial incentives could 'pin' the optimum.

But information may not be monitorable. The important literature of demand-revealing processes, starting with Vickrey's (1961) contribution, shows that interdependencies can be handled even in some situations with asymmetric information. The primary question it addresses is how can we simultaneously: elicit information from individuals about their valuations of goods, and use that information to allocate resources efficiently?

The procedures rely on financial incentives. The now-recognised guiding principle (see Tideman and Tullock, 1976), is to charge each individual the cost to all others of his choice, or pay him the benefit. Thus, in a Vickrey auction, the high bidder pays the valuation of the person who is denied. In a binary public choice, any individual who changes the decision, say from 'build' to 'not build', must pay the net valuation of all other individuals in favour of the opposite course. Groves (1973) employs and extends this approach, showing its applicability to a class of situations in which individuals signal to a centre, the centre replies, and then all choose their actions. These mechanisms make truthfulness a dominant strategy for each participant by paying or charging him for his revealed externality, that is, the actual net benefits or costs his action conveys to the other participants as implied by their actions and/or statements.

Besides the limited range of problems handled, a significant disadvantage of demand-revealing processes is that the incentive payments ordinarily create a deficit or surplus that must be absorbed by some external party. Is there a way to balance the incentive-payment budget? In many situations only the procedure just described makes truthfulness a dominant strategy (see Green and Laffont, 1979, and references therein). A weaker type of equilibrium must be accepted. And it can be implemented in some circumstances, given that if knowledge is probabilistic then incentives need only reward truthful revelation on an expected-value basis.

1.3 Arrow's Related Contribution

Once again it is appropriate to start with the work of our honoree. The work most closely related to ours is Arrow (1977, 1979) and d'Aspremont and Gérard-Varet (1975, 1979).[1]

Arrow includes a discussion placing his problem in the context of recent developments in economic theory:

> I wish to suggest a different approach to demand revelation, which achieves efficiency and avoids the waste of resources in the incentive payments. As might be expected, it makes stronger assumptions, in this case, assumptions about the expectations that each agent has about each other's valuations. (Arrow 1979, p. 27).

Arrow formalizes the collective decision problem as a game of incomplete information with one stage of revelation, a collective decision rule, and incentives induced by transfer payments. He assumes no income effects, specifically, utility functions linear in income whose expectations the players seek to maximize. He uses an equilibrium concept in extensive form, which he observes precludes reduction to normal (strategy) form because 'the second player is optimizing given all previous history', making the equilibrium perfect. He describes perfection as 'the game-theoretic counterpart of the principle of optimality in dynamic programming' (Arrow, 1979, p. 29; see note 2 for further discussion). Except for this sequential refinement, the solution concept is essentially Nash equilibrium, but it is often called Bayesian as well, since it relies on expected values defined by a common original prior distribution.

For a collective decision, assuming agents' information is one-dimensional and continuous, Arrow derives the first-order conditions that the transfers must satisfy locally to make truth-telling an equilibrium, and second-order conditions for a local maximum. He shows that the first-order conditions can be integrated – that is, there exist transfers satisfying them – if the agents have probabilistically independent information. He also shows that the second-order conditions are satisfied if the collective decision rule has a property he calls 'responsive' and that maximizing the sum of the agents' utilities, assuming truth-telling, has this property, namely, an agent's expectation of the product of his marginal utility for the public good and the marginal change in decision induced by a change in his information is always positive under truth-telling.

1.4 The Central Question

We are concerned more broadly with problems involving externalities, uncertainty, private information, and differing objectives among players, making team theory inapplicable, dictatorship and other 'pinning' mechanisms inadequately informed, and *laissez-faire* also inefficient. Furthermore we consider multi- as well as single-stage contexts.

Efficiency may still be achievable if appropriate financial incentives can be created to induce agents to take actions that are optimal for the group. The incentives we consider are transfer payments that may take the form of penalties, subsidies, compensations, taxes, and so on. We refer to our co-ordination mechanism as *incentive-based decentralization*. Our central research question is:

Under what circumstances can a group using incentive-based decentralization achieve as high an expected value as a team?

1.5 Description of a Group

We use the term *group* to signify that the decision-making units of concern are neither as cohesive as a team nor totally unco-ordinated. A group is composed of self-interested agents together with a central authority which implements a scheme of transfers among them intended to induce collectively desirable behaviour.

The scheme may be designed by the agents acting collectively and drawing up contracts and incentive agreements. The central authority is then merely a referee and clearing house. It monitors publicly available information and collects and dispenses payments on the basis of that information. Alternatively, the central authority might also design and impose the incentive scheme, if it has the power to do so. It could also be, at the same time, one of the agents. It is not, however, an external source of funds. The funds for making the transfer payments are extracted from and paid to the agents in the group. Thus the transfer budget must always balance. (A surplus could not be efficient.)

Our primary interest is in situations where the central authority can monitor agents' observations incompletely if at all. For this reason, among others, we seek here a scheme of incentives and penalties that is just powerful enough to bring each agent's objective into alignment with the group objective. The use of such gentle incentives may also be advantageous from the standpoint of fairness, individual initiative, public acceptability, and robustness against errors in assumptions. (For a variety of policy-relevant contexts, Schultze (1977) has outlined the attractive features of using incentives, in contrast to 'command-and-control' approaches, to promote public purposes.)

1.6 The Model

The model we shall consider is general with respect to uncertainty, private information, externalities, and agents' objectives. It also allows an arbitrary ordering of observations, signals, and actions. At each of any number of stages, each agent has three possible activities: observing information, sending signals, and taking actions. He may undertake none, some, or all of these activities at any particular stage. For convenience, we assume that each agent's signals and actions at each stage become known to all other agents at the next stage, though delays are easily accommodated in the model. Information private to an agent may or may not become known to other agents or the central authority later.

The central authority determines the incentive transfers among the agents on the basis of the information it obtains and the agents' actions and signals. Transfers can be made at each stage or only at the conclusion of the process.

It is assumed throughout that all agents are risk neutral and had common prior beliefs before any information was observed. The objective is therefore simply to maximize the expected total payoff to all agents. Once this is done, all points on the Pareto-efficient frontier can be achieved through lump-sum transfers.

1.7 Payment of the Expected Externality – Incentive-based Decentralization

All of our positive results revolve around the extension of the simple principle – most widely discussed in the context of pollution – of internalizing an externality: Pay each agent the total benefit to all other parties of his action (or change in action). This gives him an incentive to maximize total benefit (see Pigou, 1960). In extending this approach, we allow for uncertainty by using appropriate expected values, for the multistage incentive effect of budget balancing by recursion, and for private information by finding conditions under which the resulting transfers, that lead to a Pareto-efficient equilibrium, can be determined from information known to the central authority. Our formulation, like Arrow's, is a game of incomplete information, with a sequential Bayesian Nash equilibrium concept and incentives induced by transfer payments under the assumption of utility linear in income.

Because we employ the concept of expected externalities, we obtain a global equilibrium directly, without differentiation or restriction to one-dimensional or even continuous variables. We allow agents not only to send messages for use in a known collective decision rule but also to take acts affecting other agents and to communicate selectively with other agents in arbitrarily many stages. Our results apply to utilitarian objectives quite generally, not only to utilitarian collective decisions. They apply in other cases as well, but it is not immediately obvious how these compare with other 'responsive' cases. Besides knowing their own tastes, our agents may have all kinds of information that is not necessarily independent. In some situations our conditions might be hard to interpret or verify. Fortunately, under our predecessors' assumptions of independent information, utilitarian objective, and one stage, our mechanism is implementable if each agent's welfare is unaffected by other agents' private information. This is already more general than the usual models of collective decision, and it is by no means our most general model.

1.8 Examples of Efficient Incentives

The expected externality can be employed to engender efficiency in the sale of an item, with the buyer's and seller's reservation prices unknown. When presenting an early version of this paper at Stanford University, Zeckhauser offered to sell Kenneth Arrow a necktie featuring a pattern of extraordinary creativity and colours of great warmth, altogether befitting the intended purchaser. The bargaining mechanism reflected our recommended procedure. The audience helped to define the probability distribution of Arrow's reservation price for the tie. The expectation of the difference, if positive, between his reservation price and the seller's offering price was the expected externality of the seller's offer. With this amount paid by Arrow to the seller, the offering price will be the seller's reservation price, and a sale will always occur when there is any overlap in the bargaining range (see Chatterjee, Pratt and Zeckhauser (1978) for analytic details).

Several further essential elements of our approach will be illustrated in a pollution control situation. Upstream is a firm that discharges wastes into a river. Downstream is a firm that suffers damages r if the wastes are untreated. Upstream can treat the wastes at a cost c and reduce the damages to $r/2$. Thus the payoffs are:

Upstream Action:	*Treat*	*Don't Treat*
Upstream payoff	$-c$	0
Downstream payoff	$-r/2$	$-r$

Only Upstream knows its cost c, and only Downstream knows its sensitivity r. Assume that c is uniformly distributed on $(0, 1)$ and r is uniformly distributed on $(1, 2)$. Both are exogeneous. (For instance, r may vary according to Downstream's production process, this being dictated by external considerations such as conditions in the product markets.)

Example 1 No communication

Suppose first that Upstream must act with no further knowledge of Downstream's sensitivity. The benefit that Upstream conveys to Downstream by treating, relative to not treating as the benchmark, is $r/2$. At the time of its decision, Upstream's expectation of this externality, which we call the expected externality, is 0.75, since r is uniformly distributed on (1, 2). Paying this amount to Upstream if it treats induces it to treat whenever $c<0.75$. This is the desired group-optimal strategy subject to the no-communication conditions. To balance the budget, given that there is no other player or external banker, Downstream must make this payment. This has no incentive effect on Downstream since Downstream neither acts nor signals.

Example 2 Communication

Now suppose that, before Upstream acts, Downstream sends a signal s of its sensitivity. The group optimum is for Downstream to signal honestly $s=r$ and for Upstream to Treat if $c<s/2$. To make this a Nash equilibrium strategy for Upstream, merely pay him the expected (here also actual) externality he conveys, given honest signalling by Downstream. That externality is $s/2$ for Treat and 0 for Don't, the benchmark. Budget balance requires that Downstream make this payment.

Downstream's signal of sensitivity, whenever it influences Upstream to Treat rather than Don't, conveys two different externalities. There is a direct negative externality, Upstream's treatment cost c, and an indirect positive externality, the later incentive payment $s/2$ paid by Downstream to Upstream. Honest signalling can be made a Nash equilibrium strategy for Downstream by paying him the expected value of the sum of these two externalities given appropriate action by Upstream.

We now compute this expected value for each possible s. The sum is $s/2-c$ when Upstream Treats and 0 otherwise. Given s, Upstream should Treat whenever $c<s/2$. Since c is uniformly distributed on (0, 1), the probability of treatment is then $s/2$, the conditional expected value of c given that Upstream does Treat is $s/4$, and the conditional expected value of the sum $s/2-c$ given treatment is $s/2-s/4=s/4$. The unconditional expected value of the sum is the probability of Treat, times the conditional expected value given treatment, $(s/2)\,(s/4)=s^2/8$. This is the required incentive payment to Downstream. Making Upstream pay it

to balance the budget has no incentive effect on Upstream, since Upstream, having no earlier choices, can have no influence on Downstream's signal.

The net transfer from Upstream to Downstream, which makes group-optimal behaviour a (Bayesian) Nash equilibrium strategy for both, is the incentive payment to Downstream, namely $s^2/8$, less the incentive payment to Upstream, which is $s/2$ if he Treats and 0 otherwise. The net transfer is:

Payment from Upstream to Downstream as function of Upstream action and Downstream signal s

Upstream action:	*Treat*	*Don't treat*
	$s^2/8 - s/2$	$s^2/8$

A constant could be added to both entries, perhaps to make participation attractive to both parties, or in pursuit of some distributional goal. Changing the benchmark, for instance to Treat as the base case, also adds a constant or, in more complex problems, a quantity independent of the agents' actions. Group-optimal behaviour remains a Nash equilibrium under all such changes.

Can self-interested agents with private information always be induced to behave in a group-optimal manner through incentive arrangements of this type? Unfortunately not. Two kinds of difficulty are possible. One occurs if one agent's private information directly affects another's payoff. For example, if a polluter knows the expected health effects of its emissions on a particular day, while the recipient who suffers the impact does not know, and no one can monitor it, then efficiency cannot be induced through incentive payments. If the polluter can be paid an incentive only on the basis of what he reports and the action he takes, then with given treatment costs he will always make the same reports and take the same action, regardless of the health effects he actually predicts. The optimum is not achieved. The other kind of difficulty occurs when the unsignalled information of one agent is probabilistically dependent on the unsignalled information of another. Agents may then know more about expected externalities than the central authority does; the authority may therefore be unable to induce group-optimal behaviour. In the absence of these two specific difficulties, expected-externality methods obtain positive results.

1.9 Outline of the Analysis

We move from the simple to the complex. Section 2 considers single-stage situations. Here extracting the funds for one agent's incentive payment from other agents has no incentive effect on the latter. The key analytic question is when the information available to the central authority suffices to determine the expected externalities.

Section 3 shows that incentive-based decentralization can be employed with an arbitrary number of stages of observations, acts, and signals. In multistage environments, requiring one agent to contribute towards another agent's expected-externality payment has an incentive effect on his earlier choices. Fortunately, a conceptually interpretable mechanism is available to compensate and restore incentives for appropriate signals and actions. In our multistage discussion, we do away with the intuitive but unnecessary distinctions between signals and acts in favour of a simpler and more general framework. We show that,

> 'the team optimum can be achieved by a group using transfer mechanisms that rely solely on the observed actions and signals of agents and information monitored by the central authority, if any information observed by an agent that is not monitored by the central authority is irrelevant to all other agents' valuation functions and either signalled or conditionally independent of all unsignalled, unmonitored information possessed by all other agents.'

This strong positive result has surprising implications. For example, even if it is impossible to monitor the information of agents, the team optimum may be achievable if each agent is required to signal fully (honestly or dishonestly) the information he observes.

Many generalizations and applications of our methods are possible. Section 4 presents some of the most salient and some further remarks.

2 INCENTIVES LEADING A GROUP TO A TEAM OPTIMUM – ONE STAGE

2.1 Problem Formulation

We consider one-stage problems first. Since signals affect only later stages, they are superfluous here. Assumptions 1′ and 2′ apply solely to the one-stage situation. They will be replaced later.

Assumption 1′: Agents' observations–
Each agent i ($i = 1, \ldots, n$) observes the value r_i of a random vector $\tilde{r}_i$, his *observation*. The joint distribution of the $\tilde{r}_i$ is common knowledge. (A tilde in our notation indicates a random variable or vector.)

Assumption 2′: Choice of act–
Each agent i must choose one act a_i depending only on his own observation r_i. The set of available acts depends at most on r_i.

Thus a strategy for agent i is a function A_i on the r_i-space with values $A_i(r_i)$ in the a_i-space. We may and do allow randomized strategies without additional notation by introducing if necessary a component of $\tilde{r}_i$ which is continuously distributed independently of all else. If the agents send signals to a central authority which then acts according to a known rule, as in the 'public goods' or 'collective decision' problem (Section 4), the signals may simply be regarded as actions or components of actions and the formulation of this section applies. If agent i has no information or no choice of action, the r_i-space or a_i-space is a single point. A passive agent is relevant if affected by others and of concern to the group or if contributing to budget balance.

Assumption 3: Receipt of direct benefits–
Each agent i receives direct benefits (possibly negative) determined by the observations and actions of all the agents. He values these direct benefits at v_i, which we shall call his *direct return*.

We assume that individuals are risk-neutral in v_i; they will be maximizing under conditions of uncertainty, and will attempt to maximize the expected value of v_i. This objective is embodied in Assumption 6 below. In the present situation, v_i is a function of $(a_1, \ldots, a_n, r_1, \ldots, r_n)$, but this and the following assumptions will apply in the multistage case as well.

Assumption 4: Receipt of transfer–
Each agent i also receives a transfer payment u_i.

The transfer u_i could be thought of in a variety of ways, including penalties, taxes on externalities, or compensation for damages. Our main purpose is to design transfers that will lead to team-optimal behaviour by the agents. Our derivation will separate u_i into an incentive payment s_i intended to influence agent i and a balancing payment t_i which is agent i's contribution to the other agents' incentive payments ($u_i = s_i - t_i$). For the moment, however, we leave the determinants of u_i in abeyance and require only that the transfers balance across all agents.

Assumption 5: Transfers balance–
The sum of all transfer payments must be 0 for every outcome:

$$\sum_i u_i = 0. \tag{1}$$

The foregoing assumptions describe the physical structure of the situation. We next indicate the objectives of the agents and the group. Later we will specify the sense in which these objectives can be met and we will discuss the determination of the probability distributions that arise in the course of the analysis.

Assumption 6: Self-interested agents–
Agent i's objective is to maximize the expectation of his direct return plus transfer, which we shall call his expected *net return*, $\mathrm{E}\{\tilde{v}_i + \tilde{u}_i\}$.

Assumption 7: Group objective–
The group objective is to maximize $\mathrm{E}\{\sum_i \tilde{v}_i + \tilde{u}_i\}$. Given Assumption 5, this reduces to maximizing $\mathrm{E}(\sum_i \tilde{v}_i)$.

2.2 Derivation of Incentives

The incentive mechanism that we propose is based on paying each agent the expected return, conditional on the information available to him, that all other agents receive in consequence of his action. It may be described as 'paying the expected externality'.

Consider the situation from agent i's point of view as he decides upon an action, having observed r_i. Let agent i's expectation of agent j's direct return be

$$s_{ij} = \mathrm{E}\{\tilde{v}_j r_i\}; \tag{2}$$

it is a function of agent i's action a_i and observation r_i and the other agents' strategies. It is determined as follows: Given a_i and A_i, v_j is a function of the other agents' actions and observations. Given their strategies, the other agents' actions are specified functions of their observations. Thus v_j becomes a function of the other agents' observations. The expectation of $\tilde{v}_j$ given r_i is determined by this functional relationship and by the distribution of the other agents' observations, given r_i.

$$\mathrm{E}\{\sum_j \tilde{v}_j | r_i\} = s_{ii} + s_i, \tag{3}$$

where s_{ii} is agent i's expectation of his own return, and where

$$s_i = \sum_{j \neq i} s_{ij} = \mathrm{E}\{\sum_{j \neq \tilde{v}_j} | r_i\} \tag{4}$$

is his expectation of the total return to the other agents. The quantity s_i may be interpreted as the expected externality of agent i's choice of action. Like the s_{ij}, it is a function of a_i, r_i, and the other agents' strategies. If agent i knew the other agents' strategies, then providing him a transfer payment s_i would make his objective coincide with the group objective.

Unfortunately, such transfer payments would not balance (add to zero) across all agents. Suppose, however, that agent j contributes an amount t_{ji} toward s_i, where

$$\sum_j t_{ji} = s_i, \qquad t_{ii} = 0. \tag{5}$$

This balances the transfer payments. Furthermore, agent j's incentives are unaffected as long as t_{ji} is defined in such a way as to be uninfluenced by agent j's choice of action. This holds, for example, for $t_{ji} = s_i/(n-1)$, and indeed whenever t_{ji} is any function of the same arguments as s_i (the strategies used in defining s_i being fixed throughout).

If such transfers are instituted for every agent i, the net transfer to agent i is

$$u_i = s_i - \sum_j t_{ij}. \tag{6}$$

The resulting transfer scheme balances and makes each agent's objective 'agree' with the group objective, that is, coincide when all other agents follow the team-optimal strategy. This implies that a strategy A_i is optimal for agent i if and only if it is optimal for the group, on the assumption that the other agents use the strategies underlying the definition of the transfers. If, therefore, after finding the team optimum, we determine agent i's transfer payment (6) on the assumption that the other agents' strategies are team-optimal, then agent i will have an incentive to employ a team-optimal strategy also. In (6), the term s_i may be interpreted as an expected externality payment to agent i and $\Sigma_j t_{ji}$ as a balancing payment by agent i.

Specifically, the foregoing transfer scheme and its properties are summarized in the following theorem:

Theorem 1: Expected-externality transfers achieve the team optimum–
Take as given Assumptions 1′, 2′, and 3–7. Find a set of strategies A_i^* achieving the team optimum by maximizing the group objective $E\{\Sigma_i \tilde{v}_i\}$. Find the expected externalities s_i based on these strategies. Define any set of balancing payments t_{ij} depending only on r_i and a_i with $\Sigma_i t_{ij} = s_j$ and $t_{jj} = 0$ for all j. Let the net transfer to agent i be $u_i = s_i - \Sigma_j t_{ij}$. Then, as long as each agent i knows or assumes that the other agents will follow the strategies A_j^*, he can optimize for himself by choosing the strategy A_i^*, and the team optimum will be achieved. This transfer scheme therefore makes the team optimum a Pareto-efficient, Bayesian Nash equilibrium. If the team optimum is unique, then each such A_i^* is a unique optimum for agent i, no agent can deviate without penalty, and the equilibrium is strict.

2.3 Implementability of Incentives Based on Expected Externalities

What knowledge is required to compute and pay the transfers just defined? We are assuming throughout that the central authority knows the joint distribution of the $\tilde{r}_i$ shared by the agents, the actions available to the agents, and the agents' direct return functions. These suffice to determine the team optimum, a set of strategies for achieving it, and transfer rules that provide incentives to use these strategies. The actual transfer payments are in general functions of the agents' actions and observations. We assume throughout that all actions become known to all parties. We wish, however, to allow the agents' observations (and their actual direct returns) to be at least partly unobservable by others. In this case, it is possible that the transfers of Theorem 1 cannot be implemented in practice. We seek conditions under which they can be.

Any part of an agent's observation that becomes known to or can be obtained by the central authority, and any quantity that depends only on such information, will be called *public* or *publicly observable*. It is sometimes convenient to express this in another way. Let z_i be the public portion of agent i's observation, that is, z_i is a publicly observable function of r_i such that any other publicly observable function of r_i is a function of z_i. Then a quantity is publicly observable if, and only if, it is a function of the z_i's.

A transfer rule will be called *implementable* if the information needed to determine all payments that it could ever require is publicly observable. This means that it relies on public information only; no matter what acts the agents choose, all transfer payments are functions only of information that can be obtained by the central authority. Under what conditions are expected-externality transfers implementable? If the expected externality s_i is publicly observable, then the balancing payments t_{ji} can be chosen to be publicly observable (for example, $t_{ji}=s_i/(n-1)$). In any discussion of implementability, we shall take such a choice for granted. This reduces the question to the public observability of the expected externalities s_i. In short, condition (B) below is essentially the definition of (A).

(A) Expected-externality transfers are implementable.

(B) $E\{\tilde{v}_j|r_i\}$ is public for all i and j with $j\neq i$, for all actions a_i, when all agents $j\neq i$ follow the team-optimal strategies A_j^*.

To check implementability in any given situation, of course, one could simply calculate the incentives and see if they are publicly observable. However, general conditions for implementability (listed below) are also useful, especially if they provide some insight.

(C) The distribution of $\tilde{v}_j$ given r_i depends only on z_i (the public portion of r_i), for all i and j with $j \neq i$, for all acts a_i, when all agents $j \neq i$ follow the team-optimal strategies A_j^*.

(D) Each agent's direct return is a function of all agents' actions, his own observation, and only the public portions of the other agents' observations. Each agent's conditional distribution of the other agents' observations given his own observation depends only on the public portion of his own observation.

(E) The public portions of all agents' observations are the same, say z. Each agent's direct return is a function of all agents' actions, his own observation, and z. The agents' observations are conditionally independent given z.

(F) Each agent's direct return is a function only of all agents' actions and his own observation. The agents' observations are independent.

Each of these conditions is stronger than those before it but simpler structurally or intuitively. Others along the same lines could easily be given and might prove useful in particular situations, but these are enough to illustrate the possibilities. Examples could readily be constructed satisfying implementability but not (C), satisfying (C) but not (D), and so on. Condition (D) appears likely to hold in practice, however, in a wide variety of situations. It provides the basis for the title of the following summary theorem, though a weaker Condition (C) could be employed, of course.

Theorem 2: Expected-externality transfers are implementable if the private portions of agents' observations are independent and do not affect each other's direct returns–
Posit Assumptions 1′, 2′, and 3–7 as in Theorem 1. Then if any one of the conditions (C) to (F) holds, implementability, (A) and (B), follows. Moreover, each condition is implied by the next.

Before extending our analysis to two-stage and multistage situations, we should remark that our expected externality transfers are adaptable to a variety of normative criteria which in effect would add or subtract an amount from each player based perhaps on their observations, but not on their actions (see Section 4.2). The level of expected-externality payments provides no ethical baseline in and of itself, just as the effluent charges that would be collected taking zero emissions as the base level – a much simpler problem – may not be the fair fee for a polluter to pay for his action.

3 INCENTIVES LEADING TO A GROUP OPTIMUM WITH ARBITRARILY MANY STAGES OF OBSERVATIONS, ACTIONS, AND SIGNALS

We now consider a general situation in which there is an arbitrary (but fixed and known) number of stages in which observations may be made, acts may be taken, and signals may be sent. We index the stages by the number of stages remaining. Thus stage 0 is the last stage, and stage M, say, is the first stage. All finite sequences of observation, action and signal can be included within our formulation. Now, however, in choosing an action or signal at any stage after the first, each agent can take advantage of what he can learn from the other agents' earlier choices and of any additional observation of his own which he may have made in the meantime. Thus one agent's earlier choices may influence another agent's later ones. This introduces more complicated incentive effects than occur in one-stage situations.

Since signals are structurally equivalent to actions, as mentioned earlier, we shall omit signals from the problem formulation in this more general section. This will simplify the notation and the description of our results. The loss of specificity in dealing with signals will be made up by occasional comments. Furthermore, our results are technically more general, not less, because our theorems require only that no agent can improve the group objective by himself, not that all agents maximize jointly. For example, the team optimum with truthful signals about only a part y_i of each agent i's observation r_i may be inferior to a team strategy conveying more information. The greater information might be conveyed by a truthful signal about r_i or even by an untruthful signal appropriately decoded by the recipient. However, such a signal by one agent cannot improve the team outcome unless another agent interprets it correctly and alters his action accordingly. Thus the team optimum with truthful signals about y_i only has the property that no agent can increase the group objective by himself. This suffices for our theorem to show that this constrained team optimum can be achieved by incentives based on the corresponding expected externalities. A global optimum is not required.

3.1 Problem Formulation

To accommodate the multistage structure, only the first two assumptions need to be changed.

Assumption 1: Agents' observations–
Each agent i ($i = 1, \ldots, n$) observes a value r_i^m at each stage m. Stages are numbered from M to 0 according to the number m remaining. The joint distribution of all $\tilde{\mathbf{r}}_i^m$ is common knowledge.

Assumption 2: Agents' decisions–
At each stage m, each agent i must choose an action a_i^m depending only on his own observations through stage m and all agents' actions in all previous stages. The sets of available actions depend at most on the same quantities.

The direct returns v_i, the transfers u_i, and the individual and group objectives satisfy Assumptions 3 to 7 as before, but v_i and u_i are now functions of all actions and observations. Note that v_i represents the total direct benefits of agent i, including any benefits received before the terminal stage.

A strategy for agent i is now a vector of act-choice functions $A_i^M, \ldots, A_i^0$ with the domains and ranges indicated in Assumption 2. The domains imply perfect recall. Randomized strategies are included as before by adjoining independently, continuously distributed components to the r's as needed.

Signals are simply acts or components of acts which have no influence on the direct returns v_i, that is, are superfluous or 'inactive' as arguments of the direct return functions, once the type of signal, for example, dimension and precision, is chosen. (If signalling costs are to be included, the choice of type of signal should be modelled as a separate action component.) Our formulation thus allows for a signal which is a possibly untruthful report of any portion of agent i's observation, say of $y_i^m = Y_i^m(r_i^M, \ldots, r_i^m)$, where Y_i^m is a known function. An important special case has $y_i^m = r_i^m$; that is, all information is available for exchange.

Assumption 2 implies that all other agents receive the same report from agent i, but this is merely for convenience. Our results would apply even if each agent were allowed to send a different signal to each other agent. Each agent's report may go to a central agency which then disseminates some or all of the information to everyone.

3.2 Derivation of Incentives in the Multistage Case

The principles for deriving incentives are fairly straightforward, though the mechanics in any particular context may prove complicated. Earlier actions (including signals) will influence not only subsequent actions in a direct manner, but also the magnitude of subsequent incentive payments. Self-interested agents will take these effects on later incentive payments into account. Earlier incentive payments will have to be structured to compensate for them. At the last stage, each agent's expected externality (computed assuming all other agents' earlier decisions were in accord with the team optimum) provides an appropriate incentive, since nothing follows. Appropriate adjustments to the incentive payments for the next-to-last action can then be computed in the light of the expected effect each agent's choice of action has on the balancing payments he will be required to make in support of the other agents' last period incentives. Continuing in this way we can fold back to the first stage and its appropriate incentives.

To see how this all works out, we first consider the situation from agent i's point of view as he decides upon his terminal action a_i^0. He knows all his own observations $r_i^M, \ldots, r_i^0$ and all previous actions of all agents, $a_1^M, \ldots, a_n^M, \ldots, a_1^1, \ldots, a_n^1$. We call this his *stage-0 information* and denote it by q_i^0. Let agent i's expectation of agent j's direct return, in the light of this information, be

$$s_{ij}^0 = \mathrm{E}\{\tilde{v}_j | q_i^0\}. \tag{7}$$

It is a function of agent i's terminal action a_i^0 and his information q_i^0 (including his earlier acts) and the other agents' strategies. This expectation is determined as follows: Given q_i^0, v_j is a function of the other agents' terminal actions and their observations $r^M, \ldots, r^0$. Given their strategies and q_i^0, their terminal actions are specified functions of their observations. Thus v_j becomes a function of their observations. The expectation of v_j given q_i^0, is determined by this functional relationship and by the distribution of the other agents' observations $r^M, \ldots, r^0$, given q_i^0.

As before, our first step is to give agent i a transfer payment

$$s_i^0 = \textstyle\sum_{j \neq i} s_{ij}^0 = \mathrm{E}\{\sum_{j \neq i} \tilde{v}_j | q_i^0\}. \tag{8}$$

This also is a function of his terminal action and information and the other agents' strategies. Giving agent i the transfer payment s_i^0 makes his objective coincide with the group objective at the time of his terminal decision and, consequently, at the time of his earlier decisions as well. Suppose we balance this payment by transfers t_{ji}^0 from other agents j to i, where $\Sigma_j t^0_{ji} = s^0_i$ with $t^0_{ii} = 0$. As long as t^0_{ji} is a function of the same arguments as s^0_i, it will have no incentive effect on agent j's terminal decision. It will, however, have an incentive effect on agent j's earlier decisions, since these are included in q^0_i. We can offset this incentive effect by a transfer to agent j equal to his expectation of $\tilde{t}^0_{ji}$ at the time of his decision at stage one. The total of these transfer payments to agent j is

$$s^1_j = \mathrm{E}\{\textstyle\sum_i \tilde{t}^0_{ji} | q^1_j\}. \tag{9}$$

We balance the transfers s^1_j by transfers t^1_{ij} from i to j with $\Sigma_i t^1_{ij} = s^1_j$, but this introduces further incentive effects which need to be offset. Continuing similarly, for $m = 0, 1, 2, \ldots, M$ successively, we define s^0_i by (8), let

$$s^m_i = \mathrm{E}\{\textstyle\sum_j \tilde{t}^{m-1}_{ij} | q^m_i\} \text{ for } 1 \leqslant m \leqslant M, \tag{10}$$

and define any transfers t^m_{ij} depending on the same arguments as s^m_j such that

$$\textstyle\sum_i t^m_{ij} = s^m_j \text{ and } t^m_{jj} = 0 \text{ for } 0 \leqslant m \leqslant M. \tag{11}$$

The transfers s^m_i, and hence t^m_{ji}, are functions of agent i's stage-m action a^m_i and information q^m_i, that is, of $a^M_i, \ldots, a^m_i, r^M_i, \ldots, r^m_i$, and all $a^M_j, \ldots, a^{m+1}_j$ for $j \neq i$. In taking an expectation given q^m_i, agent i's actions $a^M_i, \ldots, a^m_i$ are decision variables but probabilities are conditional on agent i's observations $r^M_i, \ldots, r^m_i$ and whatever inferences he can derive from the other agents' previous actions $a^M_j, \ldots, a^{m+1}_j$ on the assumption that they are following the strategies used in defining the transfers. Since t^M_{ij} depends only on agent j's initial information r^M_j and action a^M_j, it is uninfluenced by any choice made by any other agent and hence no further offsetting of incentive effects is needed.

Combining the foregoing transfers gives a transfer schedule that balances and makes each agent's objective agree with the group objective as regards his entire strategy, provided all other agents follow the strategies used in defining the transfer. In other words a strategy is optimal for agent i if, and only if, it is optimal for the group, when the other agents use the strategies underlying the definition of the transfers. Now suppose that a given set of strategies is *agent-by-agent team-optimal*, meaning that each agent's strategy maximizes the group objective if the other agents use the given strategies. Then, and this is the basis for our central result, the transfers defined above in terms of these strategies will make the strategies optimal for each agent, assuming that the other agents are also following them. Thus, through the use of appropriate transfers, we can induce agents to follow any agent-by-agent team-optimal set of strategies.

Probably the most important case of an agent-by-agent team optimum is the over-all team optimum when there are no constraints on the types of signals to be sent. Note also that a team optimum with truthful messages about known functions y_i^m of the agents' observations is agent-by-agent team-optimal and hence covered by our results. Of course the team optimum with signals depending only on y_i^m may be dominated by the team optimum with signals conveying more information. If, however, practical considerations would limit the information exchanged by the group acting as a team to y_i^m, then the relevant comparison is to a team exchanging just this information, and this is the team optimum we achieve.

Our theorem on incentive properties of multistage expected externality transfers is

Theorem 3: Multistage expected-externality transfers can achieve any agent-by-agent team optimum–
Take as given Assumptions 1 to 7. Let the act-choice functions A_i^{m*} ($i=1, \ldots, n; m=M, \ldots, 0$) form an agent-by-agent team-optimal set of strategies. Use these strategies to define expected externalities s_i^m by (8) and (10) and balancing payments t_{ij}^m satisfying (11) successively for $m=0, 1, \ldots, M$. Let the net transfer to agent i be

$$u_i=\sum_{m=0}^{M}(s_i^m-\sum_{j=1}^{n}t_{ij}^m). \tag{12}$$

If the agents other than i use the strategies A_j^{m*} then agent i can optimize for himself by choosing A_i^{m*}. This transfer scheme makes the agent-by-agent team optimum a sequential, Bayesian Nash equilibrium. The equilibrium is strict if each agent's strategy uniquely maximizes the group objective when the other agents use the strategies A_j^{m*}. The equilibrium is Pareto-efficient in any set of vectors of strategies within which the group objective is maximized by the agent-by-agent team-optimal strategies A_i^{m*}.

Proof

Although the discussion leading up to Theorem 3 was presented so that the theorem would follow naturally, the reader may find a proof useful. If all agents except i employ the strategies A_j^{m*}, then whatever strategy agent i employs we have, by (10),

$$\mathrm{E}\{\tilde{s}_i^m - \sum_j \tilde{t}_{ij}^{m-1} | q_i^m\} = 0. \tag{13}$$

It follows that $\mathrm{E}\{\tilde{s}_i^m - \sum_j \tilde{t}_{ij}^{m-1}\} = 0$ and therefore, by (12),

$$\mathrm{E}\{\tilde{v}_i + \tilde{u}_i\} = \mathrm{E}\{\tilde{v}_i + \tilde{s}_i^0 - \sum_j \tilde{t}_{ij}^M\}. \tag{14}$$

From this it follows in turn, similarly, by (8), that

$$\mathrm{E}\{\tilde{v}_i + \tilde{u}_i\} = \mathrm{E}\{\tilde{v}_i + \sum_{j \neq i} \tilde{v}_j\} - \mathrm{E}\{\sum_j \tilde{t}_{ij}^M\}. \tag{15}$$

The last term is a constant, unaffected by agent i's strategy. Therefore the transfer u_i makes agent i's objective coincide with the group objective. The equilibrium result follows. If the equilibrium is not strict, then some agent can deviate without changing $\mathrm{E}\{\tilde{v}_i + \tilde{u}_i\}$ and hence his strategy does not uniquely maximize the group objective. Thus unique agent-wise maximization implies strict equilibrium. The Pareto-efficiency statement is obvious.

3.3 Implementability of Incentives Based on Multistage Expected Externalities

Now that the expected-externality approach to designing incentives has been extended to multistage situations, we again face the question of implementability. We assume as before that the balancing payments t_{ji}^m are chosen to facilitate implementability, for instance, to be fixed fractions of the incentive payments s_i^m. Then the multistage expected-externality transfers are implementable if the relevant conditional expectations of the agents are publicly observable. The condition at stage 0 is

(a^0) $\mathrm{E}[\tilde{v}_k | q_i^0]$ is public for $k \neq i$.

At stage m, $1 \leqslant m \leqslant M$, the condition is

(a^m) $\mathrm{E}[\mathrm{E}\{\ldots \mathrm{E}(\tilde{v}_k | \tilde{q}_{j_0}^0) \ldots | \tilde{q}_{j_{m-1}}^{m-1}\} | q_i^m]$ is public for $k \neq j_0 \neq j_1 \neq \ldots \neq j_{m-1} \neq i$.

(These and later conditions are to be understood as holding for all possible values of all indices and unbound variables, and distributions conditional on one agent's information are to be calculated on the assumption that all other agents follow team-optimal strategies.)

As before, we can check the implementability of incentive payments based on expected externalities when there are many stages by simply calculating the incentives and verifying if they are publicly observable. Again, however, it is also useful to have general conditions for implementability, and it is possible to give some that have intuitive content. They can be expressed in terms of the following conditions. The exact relationships among conditions are somewhat more complicated than before, however, and will be deferred to the statement of the theorem.

(b^0) The conditional distribution of $\tilde{v}_k$ given q_i^0 is public for $k \neq i$.

(b^m) ($m \geqslant 1$). The conditional distribution of $\mathrm{E}\{\ldots \mathrm{E}(\tilde{v}_k|\tilde{q}_{j_0}) \ldots |\tilde{q}^{m-1}_{j_{m-1}}\}$ given q_i^m is public for $k \neq j_0 \neq j_1 \neq \ldots \neq j_{m-1} \neq i$.

(c^0) Agent i's conditional distribution, given his terminal stage information q_i^0, of all other agents' terminal actions, agent j's observations at all stages, and the public portions of all observations of all other agents, is public for $j \neq i$.

(c^m) ($m \geqslant 1$) Agent i's conditional distribution, given his information q_i^m at stage m, of all other agents' actions at stage m and the public portions of agent j's observations through stage $m-1$, is public for $j \neq i$.

(d^0) Agent i's conditional distribution, given his terminal-stage information q_i^0, of all other agents' observations at all stages, is public.

(d^m) ($m \geqslant 1$) Agent i's conditional distribution, given his information q_i^m at stage m, of all other agents' observations through stage m and the public portion of agent j's observation at stage $m-1$, is public for $j \neq i$.

(e) Each agent's direct return is a function of all agents' acts, his own observations, and only the public portions of the other agents' observations.

The following multistage implementability theorem generalizes Theorem 2.

Theorem 4: Implementability of multistage expected externality transfers–
The multistage expected-externality transfers of Theorem 3 are implementable if condition (a^m) above is satisfied for all m, $0 \leqslant m \leqslant M$. For all m, condition (a^m) is implied by (b^m). If (e) holds, then (b^0) is implied by (c^0) and (c^0) by (d^0). For $m \geqslant 1$, if (a^{m-1}) holds, then (b^m) is implied by (c^m) and (c^m) by (d^m). Implementability, therefore, follows if either (a^0) or (b^0) or (c^0,e) or (d^0,e) holds and, for each $m \geqslant 1$, either (a^m) or (b^m) or (c^m) or (d^m) holds. Conditions $(a^m)-(d^m)$ are unaffected if 'is public' is replaced by 'depends on agent i's observations only through their public portions', or by 'is a function of agent i's actions through stage M, all other agents' actions through stage $m+1$, and only the public portions of agent i's observations through stage m'. In conditions $(b^m)-(d^m)$, publicness of the conditional distribution, given q_i^m, of the other variables mentioned, is equivalent to conditional independence between agent i's observations through stage m and the other variables, given the public portions of the former.

The proof will be given at the end of the next subsection.

3.4 Interpretation of the Requirements for Implementability

Condition (a^0) is equivalent in the one-stage case to condition (B) of Section 2, and (b^0) to (C). Conditions (d^0) and (e) together are equivalent to condition (D), which was the basis of the title of Theorem 2. That (d^0), (d^m), and (e) suffice for implementability in the multistage case is the result stated (very roughly) in the Introduction.

The full meaning of conditions (a^0) and (b^0) becomes apparent upon reviewing the functional dependencies as was done after (7). Whatever his choice of actions (and signals) at all stages, agent i can calculate a conditional mean and distribution of $\tilde{v}_j$, given his observations $r_i^M, \ldots, r_i^0$ and the actions (and signals) of the other agents at all stages before the last, on the assumption that the other agents are using the designated team-optimal strategies. Conditions (a^0) and (b^0) say that whatever agent i chooses to do at the last stage, and whatever he and the other agents have done previously, this conditional mean and distribution, respectively, depend on agent i's observations $r_i^M, \ldots, r_i^0$

only through their public portions, and hence can be determined by the central authority as well as by agent i.

To see the meaning of conditions (a^1) and (b^1), suppose that agent j has calculated $E\{\tilde{v}_k|q_i^0\}$ as just described and that agent j is using a team-optimal strategy. $E\{\tilde{v}_k|q_j^0\}$ is, of course, a function of q_j^0, that is, of $r_j^M, \ldots, r_j^0$, and all agents' actions through stage 1. Now consider agent i. As he makes his choice at stage 1, he knows only q_i^1, that is, $r_i^M, \ldots, r_i^1$ and all agents' actions through stage 2, and the action and signal he will choose at stage 1. If the other agents follow the team-optimal strategy, for each action that agent i might choose at stage 1, he can calculate a conditional distribution, given q_i^1, of the other agents' actions at stage 1 and $\tilde{r}_j^M, \ldots, \tilde{r}_j^0$. He can therefore calculate the conditional mean and distribution of $E\{\tilde{v}_k|\tilde{q}_j^0\}$. Conditions ($a^1$) and ($b^1$) require that, whatever action agent i may choose at stage 1, this conditional mean and distribution depend on his observations $r_i^M, \ldots, r_i^1$ only through their public portions.

The following lemmas further clarify the meaning of our implementability conditions and the relationships among them. They also underlie the proof of Theorem 4. Lemma 1 shows that each condition can be stated in several forms that sound quite different but are actually equivalent. Lemma 2 provides the basic method of showing that successive conditions are stronger.

Lemma 1: Equivalent conditions for a conditional distribution to be public–
Let v be a function, possibly vector-valued, of d and x, where d is a vector of agent i's decision variables and $\tilde{x}$ is, from agent i's point of view, a random vector whose distribution depends only on d. Let q be agent i's information and let z be the public portion of q. The following conditions on the distribution of $\tilde{v}$ given q, denoted $D(\tilde{v}|q)$, are equivalent.

(i) $D(\tilde{v}|q)$ is public.
(ii) $D(\tilde{v}|q)$ is a function of z and d only.
(iii) $D(\tilde{v}|q)$ depends on q only through z.
(iv) $\tilde{v}$ and $\tilde{q}$ are conditionally independent given z.

Conditions (i) to (iii) are to be understood as holding for all q, and (i), (iii), and (iv) for all d. Components of $\tilde{v}$ which are functions of z and d can be omitted with no effect on the conditions. In (iii), 'on q' can be replaced by 'on $\bar{q}$' if $\bar{q}$ is a function of q such that z is a function of $\bar{q}$. In (iv), $\tilde{q}$ can be replaced by any function of $\tilde{q}$ which, together with z, determines $\tilde{q}$. Decision variables in q are irrelevant except as parts of d. What portions of v and x are public or private is also irrelevant.

Lemma 2: Relationships among conditions of publicity–
In the situation of Lemma 1,

$$D(\tilde{x}|q) \text{ is public} \Rightarrow D(\tilde{v}|q) \text{ is public} \Rightarrow \mathrm{E}(\tilde{v}|q) \text{ is public.}$$

If $\tilde{x}$ is substituted for $\tilde{v}$ in conditions (i) to (iv), the resulting conditions are equivalent to one another. If $\mathrm{E}(\tilde{v}|q)$ is substituted for $D(\tilde{v}|q)$ in conditions (i) to (iii), the resulting conditions are equivalent to one another.

Proofs

The lemmas are easily proved once the definitions and concepts involved are clearly understood. In Theorem 4, condition (a^0) says that all s^0_{ij} are public, whence the s^0_i are implementable. If we choose, for instance, $t^0_{ij} = s^0_j/(n-1)$, then the t^0_{ij} will also be implementable, and we will have

$$s^1_i = \mathrm{E}\{\textstyle\sum_{j \neq i} \tilde{t}^0_{ij} | q^1_i\} = \frac{1}{n-1} \sum_{j \neq i} \sum_{k \neq j} \mathrm{E}\{\mathrm{E}\{\tilde{v}_k | q^0_j\} | q^1_i\}. \tag{16}$$

These quantities s^1_i are implementable under condition (a^1), whence so are the quantities $t^1_{ij} = s^1_j/(n-1)$. Continuing similarly, we see that (a^m) for all m implies implementability. The rest of Theorem 4 is proved by applying Lemmas 1 and 2 with careful attention to the variables that are relevant.

3.5 The Case of Common Public Information

If all agents' observations have the same public portions z^m, say, at all stages m, they, of course, become known to all agents immediately. In this case, in conditions (c^m) and (d^m), the only public portion of agent j's observations needed is z^{m-1}, and (c^0) becomes

(c_0^0) Agent i's conditional distribution, given his terminal-stage information q_i^0, of all other agents' terminal action and agent j's observations at all stages, is public for $j \neq i$.

An extreme case is that no observation has a public portion, that is, all information is private; then (c^0) simplifies to (c_0^0) and (c^m) and (d^m) simplify to the following conditions:

(c_0^m) ($m \geqslant 1$) Agent i's conditional distribution, given his information q_i^m at stage m, of all other agents' actions at stage m, is public.

(d_0^m) Agent i's conditional distribution, given his information q_i^m at stage m, of all other agents' observations through stage m, is public.

3.6 The Case of Prompt Publicity

In Theorem 4, the public portions of each agent's observations may not become known to the other agents until after all decisions have been made. They are merely required to be known to the central authority at the time of implementing the transfers. Of course, what is known, when, and by which agents, is reflected in the observation variables r_i^m. An extreme situation is *immediate publicity*; all public information becomes known immediately to all agents. This is equivalent to assuming that the public portions of all agents' observations are the same at all stages. This case was discussed briefly above.

Another interesting possibility is one we shall call *prompt publicity*: the public portion of each agent's observation at each stage becomes known to all other agents *promptly*, meaning at the next (or same) stage. Since each agent's actions also become known promptly, this is equivalent to the condition that the public portion of q_i^m is included in q_j^{m-1} for all $m \geqslant 1$ and $j \neq i$. The public portion of q_i^m, which we denote by p_i^m, consists of the public portions of agent i's observations through stage m, all actions through stage $m+1$, and agent i's action at stage m. Another condition equivalent to prompt publicity is that p_i^m is a function of p_j^{m-1} for all $m \geqslant 1$ and $j \neq i$.

From this characterization, by an elementary chain property of conditional expectations, it follows that, under the condition of prompt publicity,

$$\mathrm{E}|\mathrm{E}(\tilde{x}|\tilde{p}_j^{m-1})|p_i^m\} = \mathrm{E}(\tilde{x}|p_i^m) \text{ for all random variables } \tilde{x}. \tag{17}$$

By repetition one obtains

$$\mathrm{E}[\mathrm{E}\{\ldots \mathrm{E}(\tilde{v}_k|\tilde{p}_{j_0}^0)\ldots|\tilde{p}_{j_{m-1}}^{m-1}\}|p_i^m] = \mathrm{E}(\tilde{v}_k|p_i^m). \tag{18}$$

Note also that $\mathrm{E}(\tilde{x}|q_i^m)$ is public if and only if

$$\mathrm{E}(\tilde{x}|q_i^m) = \mathrm{E}(\tilde{x}|p_i^m). \tag{19}$$

Conditions (a^m) and (b^m) therefore simplify in Theorem 4 as follows:

(a_1^0) $\mathrm{E}(\tilde{v}_k|q_i^0) = \mathrm{E}(\tilde{v}_k|p_i^0)$ for $k \neq i$.

(a_1^m) $\mathrm{E}(\mathrm{E}\{\tilde{v}_k|p_j^{m-1}\}|q_i^m) = \mathrm{E}(\tilde{v}_k|p_i^m)$ for $j \neq i$ and $m \neq 1$ or $k \neq j$.

(b_1^m) The distribution of $\mathrm{E}(\tilde{v}_k|\tilde{p}_j^{m-1})$ given q_i^m is public for $j \neq i$ and $m \neq 1$ or $k \neq j$.

Theorem 5: Implementability when publicity is prompt–
Under the condition of prompt publicity, in Theorem 4, condition (a^m) holds for all m if, and only if (a_1^m) holds for all m, and (b^m) holds for all m if, and only if, (b_1^m) holds for all m.

The only simplification in the remaining conditions of Theorem 4 produced by prompt publicity is that (c^0) and (e) could refer to the public portions of other agents' terminal observations only and (c^m) could refer to agent j's observations at stages m and $m-1$ only.

If multistage expected-externality transfers are defined with balancing payments t_{ji}^m which are always specified fractions of the expected externalities s_i^m, then each s_i^m will be a sum of specified fractions of terms of the type appearing in condition (a^m) of Theorem 4. If these terms are all public, then the expression in (a^m) equals the left-hand side of (18). Under the condition of prompt publicity, this equals the right-hand side of (18), and s_i^m and t_{ji}^m are therefore expressible as a weighted sum of terms $\mathrm{E}(\tilde{v}_k|p_i^m)$. We will now illustrate this for several cases of interest. We assume implementability and prompt publicity throughout.

Two agents

$s_i^m = t_j^m = \mathrm{E}(\tilde{v}_k|p_i^m)$ for $i \neq j$, where $k = j$ for m even and $k = i$ for m odd.

Cyclical balancing payments

Each agent pays the previous agent's expected externalities: $s_i^m = t_{i+1}^m = \mathrm{E}(\Sigma_j^* \tilde{v}_j | q_i^m)$ where the sum is over all j except the j for which $(m+j-i)/n$ is an integer and where $i+1$ is replaced by 1 when $i=n$.

Equally shared balancing payments

Each agent's expected externalities are paid in equal shares by all other agents:

$$s_i^m = \mathrm{E}(b_{m-1}\tilde{v}_i + b_m \textstyle\sum_{j\neq i}\tilde{v}_j | q_i^m),\ t_{ji}^m = \frac{1}{n-1} s_i^m \text{ for } j \neq 1, \tag{20}$$

where

$$b_{-1}=0,\ b_0=1,\ b_1=\frac{n-2}{n-1},\ b_2=\left(\frac{n-2}{n-1}\right)^2+\frac{1}{n-1}, \tag{21}$$

$$b_m=\frac{n-2}{n-1}b_{m-1}+\frac{1}{n-1}b_{m-2}=\sum_{k\leqslant m/2}\binom{m-k}{k}(n-2)^{m-2k}(n-1)^{k-m} \text{ for } m\geqslant 1. \tag{22}$$

The definition of equal sharing used here does not lead to equal values of every agent i's total balancing payment $\Sigma_{j,m} t_{ij}^m$, since agent i does not contribute to balancing s_i^m. An alternative definition would have $t_{ij}^m = s_j^m/n$ for all i including $i=j$. The same net transfer as before can be achieved while satisfying this alternative definition by a suitable redefinition of the s_i^m. Since each agent i will take into account that he will pay a fraction $1/n$ of his own s_i^m, and thus net only $s_i^m(n-1)/n$, the s_i^m need merely be increased by the factor $n/(n-1)$. Specifically, with s_i^m defined as before, let

$$S_i^m = \frac{n}{n-1} s_i^m \text{ and } T_{ij}^m = \frac{1}{n} S_j^m \text{ for all } i,j,m. \tag{23}$$

Then

$$S_i^m - \textstyle\sum_j T_{ij}^m = s_i^m - \frac{1}{n-1}\sum_{j\neq i} s_j^m \tag{24}$$

and the net transfers resulting from the S_i^m and T_{ij}^m are the same at each stage as those resulting from the s_i^m and t_{ij}^m. This holds, of course, whether or not publicity is prompt. With prompt publicity, the alternative definition of equal sharing is satisfied by the same formulas as before, (20) to (22), except that every b_m is multiplied by $n/(n-1)$ and $t_{ji}^m = s_i^m/n$ for all i,j including $j=i$.

4 REMARKS, GENERALIZATIONS AND APPLICATIONS

In Sections 1 to 3 we investigated the conditions under which a group can achieve a team optimum through the use of financial incentives. It was possible, of course, to detail only a few sufficient sets of assumptions. Here we sketch some of the most important further generalizations of our results, which relate to the structure of the value function, possibilities for and restrictions on observing and transmitting information, and uncertainty about settling up or the length of the game. Subsections 4.7 and 4.8 address the application of expected-externality methods to some classic problems in collective decision. (See Pratt and Zeckhauser, 1980, for further remarks, in particular about some properties of the equilibrium.) (See equilibrium.)

We begin this section with a perspective on our approach.

4.1 Features and Limitations

The traditional fodder of decentralization discussions has been market processes, public-good provision and other collective decisions, and the allocation of a scarce resource among divisions of a firm. Our analysis begins with the observation that individuals frequently affect one another directly by their actions; no decision by a central authority need be involved. Members of a cartel set production levels, firms and households near a river pollute it and suffer the pollution, workers' efforts influence company profits, and lawyers' care in drawing up contracts affects their clients. The first key element of our analysis is that *agents' actions may directly affect the welfare of other agents.*

In many situations there is more information worth transmitting than individual preferences or production opportunities. A potential polluter may know something about the cost to others of cleaning up his pollutant. Individuals may have a variety of information about an underlying uncertainty of interest to all. They may even observe one another's information. Our second important feature is to allow agents to *possess and signal information about their own, other agents', or a central authority's costs, actions, or information.*

Allowing agents' actions to be guided by previous signals requires an analysis covering at least two stages, with signals in one stage preceding actions in another. Indeed, in reality, when information and signalling guide agents' actions, there are likely to be many rounds of interaction. We capture this central element of the real world in the third significant aspect of our analysis: a *multiple-stage environment* that can accommodate any sequencing within any finite number of stages. If agents could commit themselves to multistage strategies, and if those commitments could be monitored, the multiple stages could be collapsed to one, with incentive payments depending on the agents' strategies. Clearly, however, such commitment and monitoring are usually impossible; thus collapsing is ruled out.[2]

Our multistage setting is reflected in the form of our incentive payments. It also allows us to generalize and provide intuitive meaning to the information structures under which our approach is successful. These can be quite complicated. Informally, having agents signal private information and rewarding them according to their signals enables us to cope with situations in which the central authority cannot observe information that would otherwise be crucial to determining the incentive payments. Table 13.1 identifies the critical features for competitive markets, dominant-strategy mechanisms for demand revelation, and Bayesian collective decision processes in relation to expected-externality methods of incentive-based decentralisation.[3]

Our solution has three primary weaknesses: First, it is not coalition-proof. Here we are in good company. No relatively general mechanism for eliciting honest information from agents, including the competitive market itself, is defensible against coalitions. Secondly, we obtain only a Bayesian Nash equilibrium. But we have already seen that a necessary price of balancing the budget is to give up dominance. Thirdly, we require that it be known how the agents' probabilistic beliefs about each other's information depend on their own information. This is another sacrifice for budget balance. We take mild reassurance that Arrow (1977, 1979) and d'Aspremont and Gérard-Varet (1975, 1979) invoked both this assumption and independence in their major constructive result for a balanced budget.[4]

What is particularly reassuring about our results is that the incentive scheme that can induce agents to co-ordinate actions efficiently and reveal information honestly is motivated by the strong intuitive notion

Table 13.1 Mechanisms that achieve efficient outcomes

A. *Mechanism*	I *Competitive market with contingent contracts*	II *Demand-revealing dominant strategy processes*			III *Bayesian, collective decision*	IV *Incentive-based decentralisation*
B. *References*	Arrow and Debreu (1954) Arrow and Hahn (1971)	Vickrey (1961)	Clarke (1971)	Groves (1973)	d'Aspremont and Gérard-Varet (1975, 1979); Arrow (1977)	Proposed here
C. *Areas of application*	Private decisions under perfect competition	(a) Allocation of standardised commodity in thin market with no technological externalities (b) Sealed-bid auction of indivisible good	Public goods decision	Decisions in decentralised organisations with asymmetric information	Collective decision	Private decisions, collective decisions, or decentralised organisations; technological externalities and asymmetric information permitted
D. *Acts generating externalities taken by*	No one – agents too small to affect market	Buyers and/or sellers, and centre	Centre	Centre	Centre	Agents and centre
E. *Sequence of information receipt, signals and acts*	Arbitrary; discrete, or continuous time collapsed to present through futures markets; markets clear by *tâtonnement*	(a) 1 Agents signal 2 Centre signals price and reward structure 3 Agents act (b) 1 Agents signal 2 Centre allocates and rewards	1 Agents signal 2 Centre decides	1 Agents signal 2 Centre signals reward structure 3 Agents and centre act	1 Agents signal 2 Centre decides	Sequence arbitrary; any finite number of stages of information receipt, signals and acts by agents and by centre
F. *Signal by an agent depends on*	Own preferences, market prices	Own demand or supply schedule	Own demand schedule	Own information and payoff function	Own payoff function	Own information and earlier acts and signals by other agents and centre

Table 13.1

G. *Agent signals information about*	Own demand or supply schedule at the margin	Own demand or supply schedule	Own demand schedule for the public good	Own information and payoff function	Own payoff function	Own payoff function, information shared with some other agents, information relevant to other agents' payoff functions
H. *Act by an agent depends on*	Own preferences, market prices	Own schedule and price and reward structures set by centre	No acts by agents	Own information and payoff function and centre's signal	No acts by agents	Own information and earlier acts and signals by other agents and centre
I. *Permissible information structures*	No unshared information on contingencies on which contracts are based	Only unknown is agent demand or supply	Only unknown is agent demand	Information among agents and centre mutually independent	Agents' information either (a) independent, or (b) in discrete case satisfies conditions for consistency of relevant set of inequalities	Agents' expectations of externalities they generate are known, as when each agent's information is public, signalled or independent of other agents' information, and private portion does not affect another agent's payoff
J. *Incentive transfers defined by*	None needed – voluntary exchange at market prices	Graphical equivalent of agent's addition to others' surplus	Graphical equivalent of marginal cost to others of agent's demand	Agent's contribution to centre's expectation of other agents' profits	(a) integral equal to agent's expectation of others' payoffs minus average of corresponding expectations of other agents (b) existence theorem	Expected externality (including later transfers) generated by action or signal of agent
K. *Properties of solution*	Dominant strategies Balanced budget	Dominant strategies Budget not balanced	Dominant strategies Budget not balanced	Dominant Strategies Budget not balanced	Bayesian Nash equilibrium Balanced budget	Bayesian Nash equilibrium Balanced budget

of paying the *expected externality* that one's signals and/or actions impose on the rest of the group. The externality concept, well established with respect to the direct effects of actions on others' welfare, is less obvious for announcements that influence the actions of the centre or, as in our general setting, influence the later acts and signals of other agents. That the budget can be balanced is also not obvious, but very welcome.

4.2 Generalization of the Value Function

If a function of some or all agents' observations is added to agent *i*'s direct return v_i, it is clear that no choice by any agent will affect this added portion of v_i. Hence this has no incentive effect, and no change in incentive payments is needed. The expected-externality payments will in fact change, but only by functions of the agents' observations. Though such a change does not alter the agents' incentives, it may well affect implementability. Thus it is a real generalization to say that, if the agents' direct return functions v_i differ from the functions $\bar{v}_i$ only by functions of the agents' observations, then the expected externality payments based on the $\bar{v}_i$ will have the same incentive properties for the v_i as those based on the v_i themselves, and will be implementable if, in addition, the $\bar{v}_i$ satisfy the implementability conditions. In short, if implementable incentives exist for some $\bar{v}_i$ differing from the v_i only by functions of the agents' observations, then the same incentives will serve for the v_i.

Another generalization occurs if $\Sigma_i v_i$ is a function only of the agents' observations. Then the group objective is unaffected by the agents' choices, and no incentives are needed. Unfortunately, one cannot combine this possibility with others by a simple process of addition. If $v_i = v_i' + v_i''$ where $\Sigma_i v_i''$ is a function only of the agents' observations, then the group-optimal strategies are the same for v_i as for v_i', but the incentive payments based on v_i' will not serve for v_i because the individual v_i'' may depend on the agents' actions and hence have incentive effects.

These types of generalizations, and any others one might think of, can of course be combined if the problem is completely separable into subproblems, that is, if the agents can be partitioned into subsets and the direct returns of the agents in each subset are determined by the acts and observations of agents in that subset alone. Less trivial types of combinations, and other types of generalization, are a subject for further research.

4.3 Choice of Observations

Our formulation assumed that all agents will make the same observations r_i^m regardless of any decisions by any of the agents. That is, the agents have no choice about the observations they make; they have no choice of experiments. The definition of the expected-externality payments extends immediately to situations in which each agent may choose at each stage among possible quantities to observe; the observations will be revealed to him and perhaps to others at the next stage. The incentive properties of the payments remain the same. It appears that the only change needed in the implementability conditions is that they should hold for all possible choices of observations by the agents, provided the choices are public. If an agent's choice of observation is itself private, the situation is more complicated. We have not yet examined either case in detail.

4.4 Differential Transmission of Information

For convenience and specificity, our formulation requires that all agents be informed about all acts and receive all signals. The derivation of the expected-externality transfers in the multistage case (Section 3) does not require this, however, and in fact is completely general. The conditional expectations (8) and (10) have simply to reflect whatever information agent i actually has at the stage in question. There must, of course, be a process with finitely many stages in which one agent's choices at any stage do not become known to other agents until a later stage, if at all. Implementability in a completely general situation will again require that information observed by an agent but not monitored by the central authority be irrelevant in determining expected externalities, for instance by not affecting any other agent's direct return and meeting an independence condition.

Our formulation can allow for a variety of situations in which there is a choice of how much information to signal and to whom. If there is a cost of transmission to an additional agent, then the team presumably would balance the benefits of better co-ordination against the costs of having an additional receiver. The group can do the same. The easiest way, given our formulation, would be to include the choice of who receives signals as an agent action.

If there is a cost of having the central authority monitor the information needed to determine the transfer payments, then obviously a team can outperform a group by the magnitude of this cost if the team can transmit the information it needs costlessly. This is not really an appropriate comparison. The question we are addressing in this chapter is whether a decentralized incentive mechanism for a group can reproduce the outcome for the team, disregarding any costs of administering that incentive mechanism. The costs of having the central authority monitor the relevant acts, signals, and observations, are transaction costs, playing a role equivalent to the cost of filling out the checks when making transfer payments.

4.5 Example of Efficient Incentives When Actions Convey Information

Information can be conveyed through actions as well as signals. A group can take advantage of this possibility. This has already been reflected in Section 3 in the incorporation of signals into acts and in the conditioning of agent *i*'s stage-*m* probabilities on his stage-*m* information q_i^m. Beyond this, it is even possible for a properly co-ordinated group to gain by 'distorting' its actions to convey information. Our approach can provide incentives supporting a collective strategy of this type provided only that the individual agents' strategies are agent-by-agent optimal for the group.

Let us create a new, slightly more elaborate externality example. The Upstream polluter has traditionally dumped 10 units per period. Pollution remains in the water for one period. The cost to Upstream for dumping an amount $d \leqslant 10$ is $(10-d)^2$.

The Downstream firm now comes on river. Its sensitivity to pollution, s, is unknown; the shared prior probability distribution on s is that it is equally likely to have the value 2 or 20; s is constant from period to period. In each period, Downstream suffers a cost equal to the amount of pollution times its sensitivity. Downstream has a means to reduce its cost. It can decide to clean up the pollution. Cleanup costs 9.2 and removes 50 per cent of the pollution dumped.

In an analogous problem we saw that incentive-based externality payments could achieve the team optimum if Downstream could signal its sensitivity. In this problem, no signals are permitted. Upstream can only draw inference about s from the actions of Downstream. Still the team optimum, where the team is subject to the same communication limitations, is achieved through the use of appropriate incentives.

Let us observe what happens in a two-period world. We start at stage 2 with ten units of pollution in the water. The sequence of actions will now unfold:

Stage 2 – Downstream observes s. It then decides whether or not to undertake cleanup in period 1.
Stage 1 – Upstream decides how much to dump, d.
Stage 0 – Downstream decides whether to clean up in period 2.

With a bit of bookkeeping and a dash of differentiation, we can compute the team optimum:

Stage 2 – Clean up if $s=20$; do not clean up if $s=2$.
Stage 1 – Dump 5 if Downstream did clean up at stage 2. Dump 9.5 if Downstream did not clean up at stage 2.
Stage 0 – Clean up independent of the value of s.

The team-optimal strategy has its interesting aspects. At stage 2, if $s=2$, Downstream does not clean up even though the cost of cleanup, 9.2, is less than the pollution damage avoided, 10. The reason, as we suggested at the outset, is that actions convey information. With signalling not allowed, it is beneficial on net to take an action that yields a lower payoff in and of itself but is more informative. (If Downstream did clean up, Upstream at stage 1 could not distinguish between $s=20$ and $s=2$.) Given that $s=2$, there are two local optima for Upstream's stage 1 dumping decision. The local optimum that assumes cleanup at stage 0 is superior.

If the group is to achieve the team optimum, we must employ the externality incentives for that pair of strategies. Let us start at the end. No incentive is needed at stage 0; Downstream will do whatever is optimal since its action neither conveys information that could inform a future action nor affects the payoff to another party. At stage 1, Upstream 'knows' the value of s from Downstream's action at stage 2. Cleanup implies $s=20$; no cleanup implies $s=2$. Its incentive payment as a function of a dumping decision d is merely the net amount Downstream receives from d. For example, with $s=2$, Downstream, which cleans up at stage 0, receives $-(2d/2+9.2)$: this is the incentive payment to Upstream. Upstream's decision at stage 1 is thus to maximize $-(10-d)^2-2d/2-9.2$. The optimum value of d is thus 9.5. The net payoff to Upstream is -18.45.

A parallel calculation for $s=20$ yields the incentive payment to Upstream at stage 1 of $-(20d/2+9.2)$. When Upstream optimizes, it dumps 5 units; its net payoff is -34.2.

We are now in a position to fold back to stage 2 and to provide appropriate incentives for the Downstream cleanup decision at that stage. It must receive Upstream's net payoff at stage 1, contingent on whether or not there was cleanup. Quite simply, Downstream receives an incentive payment of -34.2 if it cleans up, and of -18.45 if it does not. In response to these incentives, it will choose to clean up when $s=20$, but not when $s=2$. To summarise, the net transfers are:

Payment From Downstream to Upstream

Cleanup at Stage 2	*No Cleanup at Stage 2*
$34.2-(20d/2+9.2)$	$18.45-(2d/2+9.2)$
$=25-10d$	$=9.25-d$

4.6 Discounting and Chance Termination

The analysis in this paper is directed to problems with a fixed, finite number of stages. Casual observation suggests that many real groups function over a considerable period of time, often without a fixed terminal date. We have not been concerned with the mechanics of discounting. If all agents agree on the appropriate discount rate, we need merely date all consequences and transfers and discount them at the agreed-on rate.

If there is chance termination, we believe that all of our results go through with only minor complications so long as no player has unsignalled private information about the likelihood of termination. If settling up is not possible at the time of termination, then the payments conditional on non-termination will have to be accordingly higher, to make the expected payment equal the expected externality.

In some situations we may need agents to take actions that foster termination because on a discounted expected-value basis they can foresee that the total group payoff will be diminishing. We might mistakenly conclude that problems would arise if post-termination settlement was impossible and if individuals could be 100 per cent sure of terminating. Presumably, they would terminate when their individual payoff would start to decline. The way around that problem is to simply pay them a sufficient transfer (that is, the expected externality from continuation divided by the probability of termination if they act optimally) should the game continue. To compensate, some lump-sum amount could be charged to the individual from the start. Thus, all ex ante Pareto-optimal outcomes are achievable even though individuals can assure themselves of a zero-payoff future by terminating the game.

Situations that never terminate present no problem in principle, we believe, so long as there is discounting. Delaying a payment by a further period merely multiplies the magnitude of that payment by one plus the interest rate. Provided settling up is not delayed indefinitely, individuals can be rewarded on a discounted expected-value basis for behaviour that helps the group. Likewise, we foresee no problems if there is uncertainty about the settling-up date or if, as seems likely, there is only partial settlement in any one period. As with credit cards, there may always be some float. Because many real-world situations persist over long periods of time, we believe consideration of situations without foreseeable termination will be of value.

4.7 Bargaining and Public Goods

Usual bargaining processes do not provide adequate incentives for honest revelation. Moreover, they may break down when a mutually beneficial agreement would be possible. Section 1.8 illustrated how expected externality methods can be employed, as in Chatterjee, Pratt and Zeckhauser (1978), to assure sale of an object whenever it would be efficient.

Consider now a public-goods decision. A project costing c is contemplated. Each agent i must declare a value x_i, which the government will assume is the true value to him of the project. The government will undertake the project if and only if $\Sigma_i x_i > c$. Without loss of generality, we may take $c=0$. (Let r_i be agent i's value in excess of c/n, and x_i the value he declares in excess of c/n.) If the $\tilde{r}_i$ are independent, the subsidy defined by Theorem 1 turns out to be

$$s_i = \int_{-x_i}^{\infty} y \, dH_i(y) \tag{25}$$

where H_i is the cumulative distribution function of $\Sigma_{j \neq i} \tilde{r}_j$, the total value to the other agents. The subsidy is a single-humped function of x_i, with maximum at $x_i = 0$, that is, when the agent quotes a value equal to the cost per person. It may be derived as follows. Agent i's direct return is

$$v_i = r_i S(\sum_i x_i) \tag{26}$$

where $S(u) = 1$ if $u > 0$; otherwise $S(u) = 0$. The group optimum clearly occurs when all agents declare $x_i = r_i$. Agent i's expectation of agent j's direct return if the other agents follow the group optimal strategies is ($j = i$ allowed)

$$s_{ij} = \mathrm{E}\{\tilde{r}_j S(x_i + \sum_{j \neq i} \tilde{r}_j) | r_i\}. \tag{27}$$

Thus agent i's expected externality is

$$s_i = \mathrm{E}\{\sum_{j \neq i} \tilde{r}_j S(x_i + \sum_{j \neq i} \tilde{r}_j) | r_i\}, \tag{28}$$

which is s_i as defined above.

It is easy to verify directly that $s_i(x_i)$ provides the asserted incentive. Agent i's subsidy plus expected direct return, if his value is r_i and he announces x_i, is

$$s_i + s_{ii} = \int_{-x_i}^{\infty} (y + r_i) dH_i(y). \tag{29}$$

Since the integrand is negative for $y < -r_i$ and positive for $y > -r_i$, the integral is maximized when the lower limit is $-r_i$, that is, $x_i = r_i$.

We remark that the subsidy s_i differs only by a constant from agent i's expectation of what he would receive under a demand-revealing scheme (see Section 1.2). Under the usual variant of that scheme, agent i must pay $|y|$, where $y = \Sigma_{j \neq i} x_j$, if y and $x_i + y$ have opposite signs (x_i changes the decision). This scheme has the very strong property of making honesty dominant, but does not balance the budget. To see the relation with s_i, observe that if the other agents are honest, then $\tilde{\mathbf{y}}$ has cumulative distribution function H_i and agent i's expected payment is

$$\int_0^{\infty} y dH_i(y) - \int_{-x_i}^{\infty} y dH_i(y) = \int_0^{\infty} y dH_i(y) - s_i. \tag{30}$$

4.8 Application to Collective Decision Problems

The public-goods problem above has been generalized to the choice of level of expenditure, and still further to arbitrary collective decisions with informational decentralization. Even the latter, general problem is still a special case of our model with just one stage.

Specifically, let r_i describe agent i's true preferences and a_i be his report. Let $v_i(a_1, \ldots, a_n; r_i)$ be his value for the collective decision that the central authority will make upon receiving the reports $a_1, \ldots, a_n$. Then, for instance, agent 1's expected externality to agent j is $s_{1j} = E\{v_j(a_1, \tilde{a}_2, \ldots, \tilde{a}_n; \tilde{a}_j)|r_1\}$. Note that this is the expectation of the revealed externality $v_j(a_1, r_2, \ldots, r_n; r_j)$ if all other agents are honest. Again the subsidy $s_i = \Sigma_{j \neq i} s_{ij}$ is agent i's expectation of what he would receive under a demand-revealing scheme. If the $\tilde{a}_i$ are independent, as in Theorem 2(F), (p. 455), each agent's expectation is known to the centre and the subsidies are implementable.

5 CONCLUSION

The goal of this investigation was to determine under what circumstances a group of self-interested agents, who observe private information and send signals that may not be verifiable, and constrained to balance the budget, could do as well as a fully co-operating team with identical communication possibilities. Equivalent performance turns out to be possible in substantially more general circumstances than those heretofore identified. Through a process we call incentive-based decentralization, each agent receives a payment equal to the expected externality conveyed to the group by his actions, including the signals he sends, and contributes to the payments to others to balance the budget. Then self-interested actions support a sequential Bayesian Nash equilibrium that is a group optimum. These results provide a happy complement to earlier methods that make honest revelation a dominant strategy but fail to balance the budget.

For the expected-externality incentive payments defined by our methods to be implementable, it suffices that each element of each agent's information either become public, be signalled by him, or be independent of the information of others; and that his non-public information does not directly affect another agent's value. (For various cases, we give precise sufficient conditions of increasing levels of generality.)

In multistage situations, which have hardly been addressed in the incentive compatibility literature, an agent's payments must take account of an additional factor: the effect his actions and signals have on the contributions he must make – because of budget-balance requirements – towards the incentive payments others receive for their later actions and signals. Fortunately, appropriate payments can be defined, though the computations may be complex, and sequential equilibrium can be maintained. Thus, incentive-based decentralization succeeds in multistage contexts, an important feature for the ultimate practical application of this methodology.

NOTES

1. In a footnote, Arrow related his work to that of d'Aspremont and Gérard-Varet, with which he became familiar only after his own was completed. Here we note that ours relates to both his and theirs in essentially the same way, and that, like Arrow, we learned of our closest ancestry only after producing our offspring, Chatterjee, Pratt, and Zeckhauser (1978), and Pratt and Zeckhauser (1980).
2. Some colleagues, nevertheless, have suggested, sometimes quite insistently, that many stages could be reduced easily to one. Several arguments, any one of which amply suffices to demolish this view, are worth sketching, because they clarify different aspects of the situation and because the view seems so hard to dislodge. First, in the 'normal' (one-stage) form of a multistage problem, an agent's expected externality becomes his ex ante expectation of the externality that his strategy provides to others. This may never become known to the centre even though the expectations needed for our multistage incentives do become known. Thus the normal-form expected-externality incentive may not be implementable when the multistage expected-externality incentive is implementable. Second, even if the normal-form expected-externality incentive is implementable, it will in general be different from the multistage one and might well be less palatable, especially ex post. Third, the multistage mechanism employs expectations conditional on information revealed to or learned by an agent along the way, and exploits the stages so that the incentive effects of budget balancing at each stage are offset at the previous stage. Though its properties could, of course, be verified in normal form, the multistage dynamics provide its motivation and derivation. Could the telescoping formula be discovered within a static framework? No one has done so in the many years since the independent, one-stage case was discovered. Fourth, even if a one-stage reduction of the problem could be found that captured our multistage mechanism as a naturally defined expected-externality mechanism, it seems unlikely to provide a simpler derivation in problems that naturally occur in multiple stages, although it might provide theoretical simplification in the sense of unification. Fifth, the sequential type of equilibrium achieved by our approach in extensive form is in an important and desirable way more restrictive than Bayesian equilibrium in normal form. Indeed, even in the limited one-stage case considered by Arrow, as mentioned earlier, he regarded the difference as significant, and it is far more significant when agents choose acts after receiving messages in one or more stages.
3. As already mentioned, the behaviour we seek to induce need not be fully

efficient, a global group optimum. It suffices that each agent's strategy optimize for the group, given any constraints he and the group are under and given the others' strategies. Furthermore, our incentives make the desired strategy a Bayesian Nash equilibrium for each agent at each stage, not merely initially.

There has been recent interest in how to structure games so that individuals will not drop out as information unfolds. See, for example, Holmstrom and Myerson (1983). In the expected externality formulation, a player's utility may diminish as the game passes through stages. To deter the defection of players, there might be an external enforcer, say the government. Or there might be a bonding mechanism, such as a requirement that each player put on deposit a sum that exceeds the maximum drop in his expected value at any stage in the game.

4. Theorem 6 of d'Aspremont and Gérard-Varet would coincide with our Theorem 2(F) the most special case of our theorem for a single stage, were we to restrict that theorem to situations in which individuals transmit information merely about their own preferences and do not take actions. In the discrete case, d'Aspremont and Gérard-Varet (1979) prove the existence of the required transfers under a weaker condition that unfortunately seems to resist an intuitive interpretation. Arrow's related results are described in subsections 1.3 and 1.7.

REFERENCES

Arrow, K. J. (1951) *Social Choice and Individual Values* (New York: Wiley). 2nd edn, 1963.

Arrow, K. J. (1977). 'The Property Rights Doctrine and Demand Revelation Under Incomplete Information', Discussion Paper 580, November 1977 (Harvard Institute of Economic Research: Harvard University). Published in Michael Boskin (ed.) (1979) *Economics and Human Welfare* (New York: Academic Press) pp. 33–9.

Arrow, K. J. and G. Debreu (1954) 'Existence of Equilibrium for a Competitive Economy', *Econometrica*, 22: 265–90.

Arrow, K. J. and F. Hahn (1971). *General Competitive Analysis* (San Francisco: Holden-Day).

d'Aspremont, C. and L.-A. Gérard-Varet (1975) 'Individual Incentives and Collective Efficiency for an Externality Game with Incomplete Information', CORE Discussion Paper 7519 (Catholic University of Louvain).

d'Aspremont, C. and L.-A. Gérard-Varet (1979) 'Incentives and Incomplete Information', *Journal of Public Economics*, 11: 25–45.

Chatterjee, K., J. W. Pratt and R. Zeckhauser (1978) 'Paying the Expected Externality for a Price Quote Achieves Bargaining Efficiency', *Economics Letters*, 1: 311–13.

Clarke, E. H. (1971) 'Multipart Pricing of Public Goods', *Public Choice*, 11: 17–33.

Green, J. R. and J.-J. Laffont (1979) *Incentives in Public Decision-Making* (Amsterdam: North-Holland).

Groves, T. (1973). 'Incentives in Teams', *Econometrica*, 41: 617–31.

Groves, T. and J. Ledyard (1977) 'Optimal Allocation of Public Goods: A Solution to the "Free Rider" Problem', *Econometrica*, 45: 783–809.

Groves, T. and M. Loeb (1979) 'Incentives in a Divisionalized Firm', *Management Science*, 25: 221–30.

Holmström, B. and R. Myerson (1983) 'Efficient and Durable Decision Rules With Incomplete Information', *Econometrica*, 51: 1799–815.

Hurwicz, L. (1959) 'Optimality and Informational Efficiency in Resource Allocation Processes', in K. J. Arrow, S. Karlin, and P. Suppes (eds.) *Mathematical Methods in the Social Sciences* (1959) (Stanford: Stanford Univ. Press) pp. 27–46.

Hylland, A. (1980). 'Collective Decisions and Individual Incentives: Review of the Literature', Discussion Paper 82D (Kennedy School of Government: Harvard University).

Laffont, J.-J. and E. Maskin (1979) 'A Differential Approach to Expected Utility Maximizing Mechanisms', in J.-J. Laffont (ed.) *Aggregation and Revelation of Preferences* (Amsterdam: North Holland) pp. 289–308.

Loeb, M. (1977) 'Alternative Versions of the Demand-Revealing Process', in T. N. Tideman (ed.), *Public Choice*, 29.

Marschak, J. and R. Radner (1972) *Economic Theory of Teams* (New Haven: Cowles Foundation and Yale University Press).

Pigou, A. C. (1960) *The Economics of Welfare*, 4th edn. (London: Macmillan).

Pratt, J. W. and R. J. Zeckhauser (1980) 'Incentive-based Decentralization: Expected-Externality Payments Induce Efficient Behavior in Groups', Discussion Paper 83D (Kennedy School of Government: Harvard University).

Schultze, C. L. (1977) *The Public Use of Private Interest* (Washington, DC: The Brookings Institution).

Tideman, T. N. (ed.) (1977) 'A Collection of Papers on the "Demand-revealing Procedure",' *Public Choice*, 29.

Tideman, T. N. and G. Tullock (1976). 'A New and Superior Process for Making Social Choices', *Journal of Political Economy*, 84: 1145–59.

Vickrey, W. (1961) 'Counterspeculation, Auctions, and Competitive Sealed Tenders', *Journal of Finance*, 16: 8–37.

14 Arrow and the Theory of Discrimination

Henry Y. Wan Jr.*

1 INTRODUCTION

Many years have passed, since the appearance of Arrow's (1973) study of discrimination – a study that is definitive in two senses:

First, it is the coda for the neoclassical literature on this topic, over the half century bracketed between Edgeworth (1922) and Becker (1971). Discrimination involves the efficiency and equity of an entire economic system, under *laissez-faire* as well as under government legislations. To reach general and conclusive results, there is no alternative to the theory of general equilibrium. As one of the founders of the abstract theory of general equilibrium, Arrow sets a high standard for all theorists. By his personal example, he demonstrates that the insights and perspective of abstract studies are ultimately justified by their services for social concerns. Rigorously and exhaustively, Arrow proves for all ages, that under the usually-made assumptions, those who indulge in discrimination must suffer reduced income in the short run. Additionally, only the least-discriminating firms may survive in the long run. In short, within the competitive system, the 'virtuous' always outcompetes the 'vicious'.

Second, the paper is also a clarion call for action. Always the complete scientist and never an ideologue, Arrow does not allow his appreciation of the power of neoclassical analysis to becloud his sense of realism. He passes his judgement with finality, 'since discrimination

* It is always an inspiring experience to work on themes pioneered by Professor Arrow and to use the methodology he fashioned. In 1970 Simone Clemhout and I had the pleasure of applying the theory of learning-by-doing to the area of infant industry protection, following the trail Arrow blazed. This time, my pleasure is two-fold for I apply an analysis that grew out of his theory of moral hazard to the topic of the economics of discrimination – an area where he made the pivotal contribution. We all wish that in the years to come we shall be able to repeat our fruitful exercises, following Arrow into the realm of many unresolved economic issues.

survives, . . . the model must have . . . limitations'. After pinpointing imperfect information as the fly in the ointment (and incidentally as the wave of the future in economics), Arrow then proceeds with the theory he and Phelps (1972) independently founded – the theory of 'statistical discrimination', the established theory, ever since (see also Aigner and Cain, 1977). This is the theory of the vicious cycle, with two components: (a) the discouraged group of the disadvantaged who would less frequently invest in their own human capital, and (b) the imperfectly-informed employers who perpetuate the expectation that those disadvantaged are less likely qualified to take on responsible functions. It does not rule out the need for government policies that may elevate society from a discriminatory second best to the non-discriminatory first best (see, for example, Lundberg and Startz, 1983). None the less, it is a theory with plenty of victims, but no genuine villain.

It would have been perfect if the above theory explained all there is, within our daily experience. Arrow's own example does not allow us to rest on such complacent thoughts, however. A nagging doubt remains: Despite more than a decade of government efforts – let alone in the absence of them – unequal treatments are meted out to equally qualified persons, based on race, sex and creed, with perfect information about productivity, and unpunished as well as unabated under our competitive system. One might dispute, case by case, the charge of discrimination on the grounds of malice. Or one might entertain the hope that the 'Mill of God' grinds slowly but surely, so that the day of reckoning lies ahead for the miscreant. None the less, following in Arrow's footsteps, we must search for some alternative, but internally consistent, explanations for what we have long suspected. There may be cases where, if the public does not act, there will be discrimination, but never punishment. Such a quest may lead us down novel and untrodden paths, but here again, Arrow (and Hahn, 1971) has set a precedent by exploring various alternative models, including a model of disequilibrium.

Many years have passed. In economic analysis too generations of newly-cast artillery have arrived at the breach. The new equipment *par excellence* within our arsenal pertains to the incentive compatibility constraints. Its lineage traces back to Arrow's (1963) theory of moral hazard (see Radner, 1982, for the 'roots' of the principal-agent model). The question then is: With new tools is the profession ready for new discoveries? The challenge then is: to prove analytically that competitive forces do not right all wrongs and that affirmative legislation is needed to end discrimination. And, is there much promise in our quest?

Our answer is positive but somewhat tentative. An example is provided where employer discrimination can carry on with impunity, under competive conditions. In fact, discrimination can go on in two alternative forms.

The basis of our example is information asymmetry in the principal-agent model, as in Hurwicz and Shapiro (1978), Harris and Townsend (1981), and Foster and Wan (1984a,b). That model is slightly modified in Section 2 and discrimination will take the 'first-to-fire, last-to-hire' form towards the disadvantaged group. Unlike in the statistical theory of discrimination in this model, the employers are always perfectly informed that there is no behavioural difference between the disadvantaged and the privileged groups and the employers who discriminate do not fare any worse in whichever possible way relative to those who do not discriminate.

In Section 3, we vary the previous example to allow for two types of jobs, each producing a particular 'productive service' and the combination of the latter yields the final output. One type of job admits perfect monitoring; the other type is shirking-prone so that superior performance is encouraged with bonus payments that include a 'bribe'. At equilibrium, the former job yields less utility to workers than does the latter, yet the incentive compatibility constraint bars 'arbitrage', since any pay reduction on the latter job is against the employer's interest. Which worker is assigned to what job is in the power of the employer – a power that may be abused to satisfy his taste to discriminate.

Finally, in Section 4, to provide a deeper perspective, we explore the relationship between our model and the conventional model of competitive equilibrium.

2 THE 'BASIC' MODEL AND DISCRIMINATORY EMPLOYMENT

Foster and Wan (1984a) shows that in an economy with M identical firms and L units of homogeneous labour, information asymmetry may cause each firm to hire N units only, leaving $L\text{-}MN$ jobless. While the jobless fare worse than those working, they cannot get hired by wage concessions. This happens because firms, accepting their own inability to monitor, pay voluntarily a bonus to deter shirking. As it is in the interest of the employer to reward more, it is futile for the jobless to offer to be paid less. In our context, any employer who rations coveted jobs among workers with identical productivity, can also discriminate with impunity, on grounds totally irrelevant to production.

The following summary of the gist of the example in Foster and Wan (1984a) helps make our discussion self-contained, and prepares the ground for Section 3:

We assume that the output of a worker depends on the effort and status of that worker and the number of workers in the firm. Specifically, the output is proportional to effort. The worker's status may be t (for tired) or h (for healthy), with the output under h higher than the output under t by a factor $a > 1$, other things being equal. Finally, congestion reduces exponentially the output per worker, as the number of workers increases. The (net) utility of the worker is the utility of reward minus the disutility of work; specifically, it is the reward in output units minus the square of effort. Firms know only the probability of workers' statuses, distributed identically and independently over all workers, but not the status of any particular worker. They know the workers' preferences, not any individual's effort. Workers know their own efforts, and their own statuses just before they decide their own efforts. Unable to deduce exactly the worker's effort, firms reward workers by output. They select the size of their labour force and the (possibly non-linear) reward schedule to maximize their expected profit, which is output minus reward. Since workers have two statuses only, in setting the reward schedule a firm focuses on output and reward targets, for each of the statuses, making sure that workers would neither 'quit' nor 'shirk'. Quitting means zero effort, hence zero output, so that even by paying zero reward, the firm nets zero profit. For prevention, the reward schedule must be sufficiently generous in absolute terms, for each status s. Shirking means the concealing of the true status s, and producing the target output for status $s' \neq s$, so that one may become better off under the reward schedule. This subverts the firm's plan and generally reduces its expected profit. For prevention, the reward schedule must be sufficiently generous, in relative terms, for each true status s, *vis-à-vis* any other $s' \neq s$, corresponding to all (s,s') pairs. These form the individual rationality (*IR*) and self-selection (*SS*) constraints for the target rewards and outputs.

Here, we come to the crux of the matter for Foster and Wan (1984a). Congestion means diminishing returns for employment. Firms hire no more than their equilibrium size of labour force, unless workers make concessions on contract terms. The jobless may be ready to make concessions to modify the equilibrium reward schedule. Yet the schedule is determined by *IR* and *SS* constraints. Concessions violating *IR* will not be made: or else working is worse than quitting. Concessions violating *SS* will not be accepted: such concessions have no way to be enforced, given information asymmetry favouring the worker. Hence, 'involuntary' unemployment may exist in an equilibrium, and the coveted jobs must be rationed among a larger number of equally qualified applicants.

Such a situation is avoidable, in principle, either by a heavy application fee, exacted from the workers, or by permitting negative reward for low outputs. Both work by end-running the *IR* constraint. In reality, the first is financially infeasible for the workers, and the second is legally unenforceable due to the prohibition of human bondage.

We now supply the details of the example. Let $y(s)$, $r(s)$, $z(s)$ and $Z(s)$ be the target-output, target-reward, target-effort and the disutility associated with such effort, for a worker in status $s=t$ or h. Let $Q>0$ (with $L-MQ>0$) be a constant, then, the production function is:

$$y(t)=z\,\exp(-N/Q)$$

$$y(h)=az\,\exp(-N/Q),$$

the utility index for the worker is:

$$\begin{aligned} u &= r-Z \\ &= r-z^2, \end{aligned}$$

the effort requirement per output is:

$$k(s,N)\equiv\begin{cases} \exp(N/Q) & s=t \\ a^{-1}\exp(N/Q) & s=h \end{cases}$$

the worker's utility in fulfilling the status s' target, when the actual status is s, is:

$$u(s',s,N)=r(s')-y^2(s')k^2(s,N),$$

so that the problem for the firm is:

$$\underset{N\geqslant 0}{\text{Max}}\quad \underset{r(s),y(s)}{\text{Max}}\quad \mathrm{E}\{y(s)-r(s)\}=P$$

$$
\text{s.t.}\quad
\begin{array}{lllll}
u(t,t,N) & & & & \geqslant 0 \\
 & u(h,h,N) & & & \geqslant 0 \\
u(t,t,N) & & -u(h,t,N) & & \geqslant 0 \\
 & u(h,h,N) & & -u(t,h,N) & \geqslant 0
\end{array}
\quad
\begin{array}{l} IR \\ \\ SS \end{array}
$$

$$N, y(s), r(s) \geqslant 0$$

where E(·) is the expected value operator.

Alternatively, one can transform the above problem to:

$$
\underset{N \geqslant 0}{\text{Max}} \quad \underset{r(s),\, y(s)}{\text{Max}} \quad \mathrm{E}\{-r(s) + Z^{1/2}(s)/k(s, N)\} \qquad (1)
$$

$$
\text{s.t.} \quad
\begin{pmatrix}
1 & -1 & 0 & 0 \\
0 & 0 & 1 & -1 \\
1 & -1 & -1 & a^2 \\
-1 & a^{-2} & 1 & -1
\end{pmatrix}
\begin{pmatrix}
r(t) \\ Z(t) \\ \mathrm{r}(h) \\ Z(h)
\end{pmatrix}
\geqslant 0
$$

$$N, r(s), Z(s) \geqslant 0.$$

Given N, the above is a concave programming problem with a polyhedral constraint set. Its optimal solution can be shown as:

$$
\begin{aligned}
r(t) &= a^4(1-p)^2\exp(-N/Q)/4(a^2-p)^2 \\
r(h) &= a^2((a^2-p)^2 + (a^2-1)(1-p)^2)\exp(-N/Q)/4(a^2-p)^2 \\
Z(t) &= a^4(1-p)^2\exp(-N/Q)/4(a^2-p)^2 \\
Z(h) &= a^2\exp(-N/Q)/4
\end{aligned}
$$

where p is the probability of any worker being in the status h, and $0<p<1$. The dual vector is: $(N, 0, 0, Np)$. The optimality property may be verified by the saddle-point criterion for the Lagrangian (see Foster and Wan, 1984b).

We can then show that the optimal value of N is Q.

The essence of this exercise is that, at the equilibrium:

(i) Unemployment exists.
(ii) Such unemployment is involuntary, since for the jobless, the expected utility is zero. For those working, it is:

$$u_0 = p[r(h) - Z(h)] = pa^2(a^2-1)(1-p)^2/4(a^2-p)^2\exp(1) > 0.$$

3 THE EXTENDED MODEL AND DISCRIMINATORY ASSIGNMENT

We now turn to the case where between two equally qualified persons, one privileged and one disadvantaged, the latter is not left jobless, but assigned a job yielding a lower level of expected utility than the one assigned to his privileged counterpart. This appears similar to the job segregation phenomenon of Bergman (1971). For such a situation to persist, there must be some barrier against the disadvantaged to take the better job. Thus, it seems this is a case close to our example in the last section. Call the less desirable job X and the better job Y. The same mechanism which prevents the wage structure to fall in Y may resemble what prevails in Section 2.

Seeking insights and not generality at this stage, we shall expand the example in Section 2 in two ways: First, change the nature of the product in Section 2 from final good to intermediate good, and call it Y-good. Secondly, introduce job X to absorb all workers not working on Y-good. Their output will be called X-good. X-good and Y-good are combined to form the universal consumption good, G, by some production function. This is assumed to be a constant returns, Cobb-Douglas form: $G=C\sqrt{XY}$, which is probably as simple as one can get.

We assume that Y is produced in a way similar to the final good in Section 2, with one exception: v, the unit value of Y, is no longer a constant.

Next we assume that the production of X causes no disutility, and depends on neither the worker's status, nor effort; presence alone is what matters. We can select unit for good X, so that the output of a worker is unity. Given the form of the worker's utility function, the utility yielded by job X is equal to the wage rate of job X, which is also the same as the unit value of the service of X. This value will be called w.

We now utilize the property of the specific Cobb-Douglas function, that the total value of X, always equals the total value of Y:

$$wX=vY.$$

or,

$$\begin{aligned} w(L-MQ) &= vMQEy\,(s), \\ &= vMQy_0 \end{aligned} \tag{2}$$

say.

The last equation is derived under the assumption, that like in Section 2, we have that particular type of equilibrium where each of the M firms will hire Q units of labour. In such an equilibrium, X-jobs should yield less utility than Y-jobs. Our intuition indicates this will be the case for large value of L/M. So we test it below.

From Section 2 the expected utility for a worker on a Y-job is:

$$u_0 v \tag{3}$$

The fact that y_0 and u_0 in Section 2 should be replaced by vy_0 and $u_0 V$ in (2) and (3) can be verified by replacing $1/k(s, N)$ with $v/k(s, N)$ in (1) Section 2. Our previous calculation states that the utility for a worker on an X-job is;

$$w = \frac{MQy_0}{L - MQ} v \qquad \text{(by (2))}$$

Hence,

$$w \leqslant u_0 v$$

if, and only if:

$$\frac{Q}{(L/M) - Q} \leqslant \frac{u_0}{y_0}$$

which is equivalent to:

$$L/M \geqslant \frac{1 + (u_0/y_0)}{(u_0/y_0)} Q\text{'}$$

which clearly substantiates our intuition.

In other words, when the supply of labour is abundant relative to the 'means of production' (as represented by the outfit of plant and equipment owned by the firms), and when some jobs (by the information structure) tend to promise higher utility levels for the worker, firms can discriminate with impunity.

The 'technocratic infrastructure' ushered in by the rise of our quintessential market economy seems to generate Y-jobs in various parts of the economy. The monitoring of the effort intensity in mental endeavours is difficult, both in actual and fictional form, (even in 1984!) Consequently, one cannot trust the market mechanism alone to deal with discriminatory job assignments.

4 FINAL REMARKS

We now relate our examples within the context of Arrow and Debreu (1954) in three remarks:

First, the discriminatory equilibria here *are not* the competitive equilibria of the literature. Discrimination takes various forms, two of which are considered in this paper: In one, a job is denied to the disadvantaged, but is open to members of the privileged group, with exactly the same qualifications. In the other, two equally qualified persons hold two jobs which differ in pay and amenities, with the disadvantaged being worse off than the privileged. Both seem to be quite common. The latter case corresponds to the notion that the powerful favours his favourite. The former case is also frequent grist for the journalists' mill: newspapers often highlight the high unemployment rates for the disadvantaged, and such unemployment must be involuntary. Were the choices between working and not working indifferent to the marginal worker, such news would never be newsworthy. Both cases imply that the labour market is not cleared, hence, not in the equilibrium of either Marshall or Walras. However, they are equilibrium positions in a principal–agent model, and, therefore, in a game theoretic model. (Recall that one period principal–agent models are games in two moves, as Radner (1981) noted.)

Secondly, the competitive equilibrium *is* a particular type of market game equilibrium. We now clarify the nature of the noeclassical competitive equilibrium from some new vantage point. Consider the market for the labour service provided by one particular kind of household. For simplicity, assume there is a continuum of such workers, none of them working part time. Moreover, assume that leisure generates no utility, but work generates disutility, the intensity of which varies from job to job. The first implication of these is that the labour supply is always constant. The second implication is that the market co-ordinates labour allocation by a signal of labour scarcity other than a single wage rate.[1] The presence of the compensating wage differential means that workers consider alternative job offers according to the utility levels these jobs respectively promise. Hence, for the derived demand schedule of labour for any firm, employment quantity may be plotted against the expected utility this firm is willing to promise its employee, and not the wage rate, in the more general case. Consider now the contours of the maximum (expected) profit over the first quadrant for (N, r) pairs, where N stands for the size of labour force and r stands for the actual utility promised to the worker. Such contours in the neclassical context are concentric loci of the horseshoe shape, opening at the bottom. This shape means that profit declines when the employment deviates from its optimal value in either direction, but profit always improves if the firm can promise less utility to the worker. Since the market signal is the minimum utility, R, which a firm must promise, the second implication above assures that the firm will promise exactly that utility level, no more and no less. No less because otherwise no employee will be forthcoming; no more because otherwise less profit will be earned. When the disutility of work is not job-specific, the wage serves well as the market signal and we return to the familiar case: competitive firms pay market wages. What is usually not realized is that this result follows two separate rules of not paying more, and not paying less, each with its own different reasoning. The two – as one probably will expect – do not always hold true together as we shall see later. Presently, the above discussion is illustrated with Figure 14.1. The line joining the apex points of all iso-profit loci is the derived demand curve.

Finally, our solution concept in the example of Sections 2 and 3 *may be regarded as* a generalization of the concept of competitive equilibrium.[2] We shall show that it is not always in the interest of the employer to promise the employee a barely adequate utility level to attract him. Under competitive equilibrium, employers always promise only the minimum. In Figure 14.1, the employer's optimal (N,r) pair is always found at the boundary of the feasible set. For our examples, say, the one in Section 3, an interior optimum may arise. But then, a boundary optimum may also happen. To make our point, introduce an additional equality constraint on the employer's programming problem in Section 2:

$$E[r(s) - Z(s)] = r,$$

and define the maximized value of P as $P(N,r)$. It can be shown (see Foster and Wan, 1984b) that for each r, there exists a unique N where $P(N,r)$ is a maximum. The iso-profit contours are nested 'simple closed

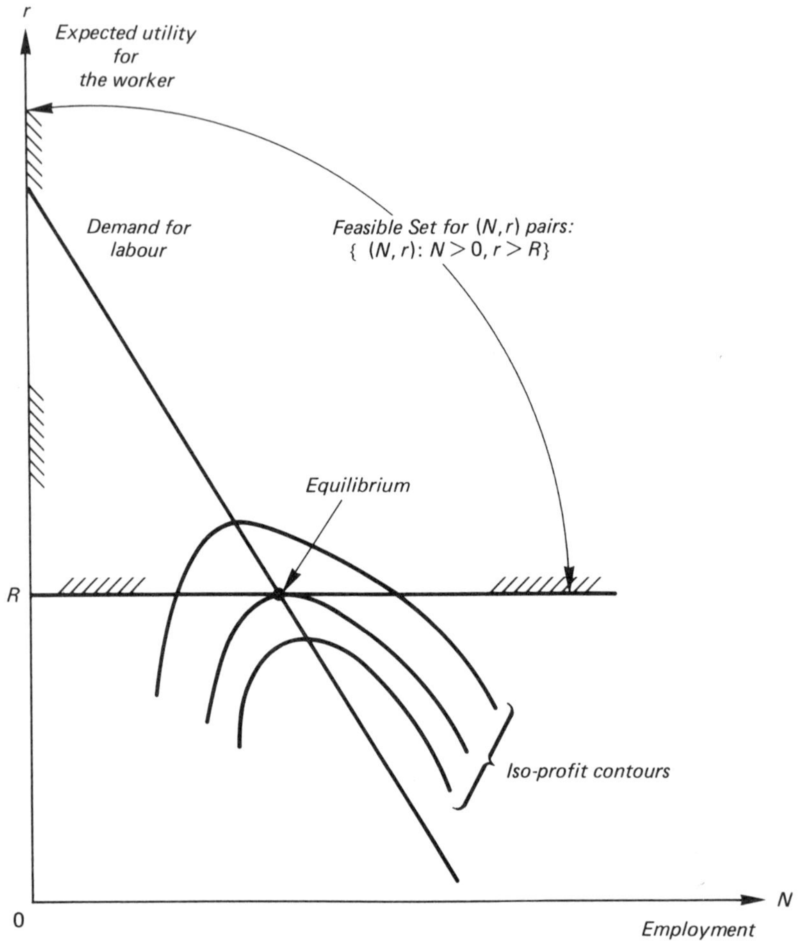

Figure 14.1 Labour market: conventional model of competitive equilibrium

curves', with an unconstrained maximum located at (N_0, r_0), for some $r_0 > 0$, as in Figures 14.2 and 14.3. In the example of Section 2, $R = 0$, showing that the unemployed workers have no alternative. In the example of Section 3, a loose labour market will have $0 < R < r_0$ as in Figure 14.2, and a tight market will have $r_0 \leqslant R$, as in Figure 14.3. The employer has an interior solution in the former, offering the opportunity to discriminate with impunity. He has a boundary solution in Figure 14.3, quite similar to the situation in Figure 14.1, under the

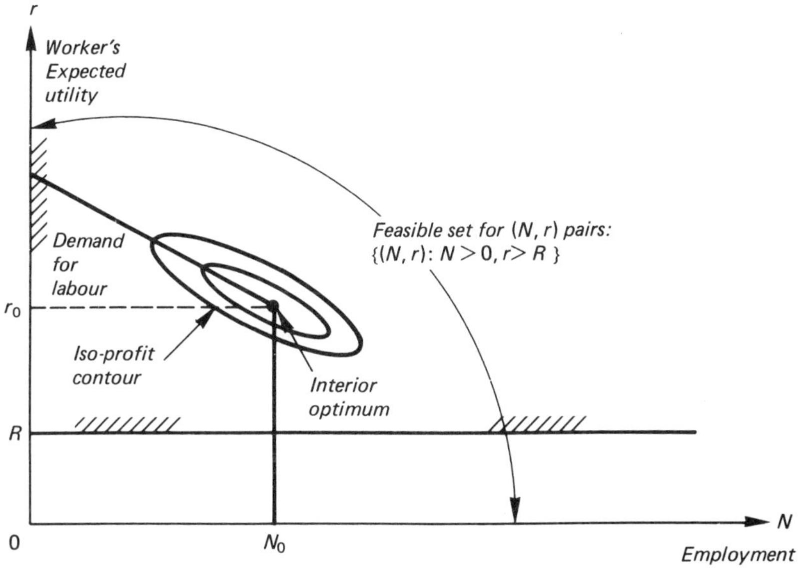

Figure 14.2 An extended model with loose labour market

conventional model of competitive equilibrium. R is the expected utility for workers in the X-sector in Section 3. Here, discrimination is a costly taste.

One should also note that information asymmetry is not the only reason for the employer to be interested in rewarding the employee at more than the market rate. This is so also because of *inter alia* (a) physical reasons; better pay means better health and better working potential, (b) social reasons; a certain wage structure is regarded as conducive to high productivity, for example, the rule-of-thumb restriction:

the foreman's pay/the subordinate's pay $\geqslant 1.2$,

which is gaining credibility among personnel managers (see, for example, Wan, 1973). Each and every such case implies that the wage structure affects productivity, that workers on certain jobs fare better than their peers, and that which one of a large number of equilibria[3] will prevail depends upon the employer's whim. Here lies the source of discrimination that the competitive force cannot redress.

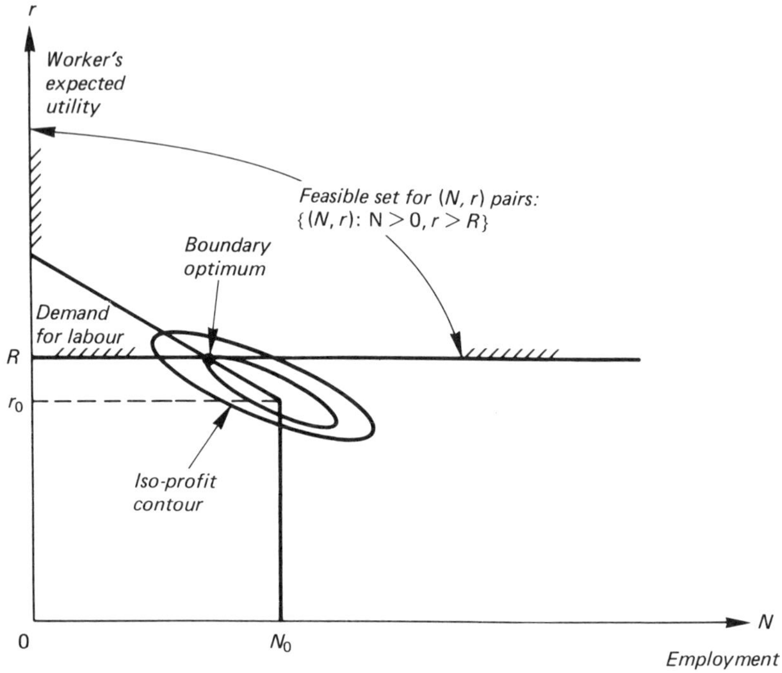

Figure 14.3 An extended model with tight labour market

NOTES

1. An alternative is to give up the concept of an aggregate market demand schedule for labour, which is summed up over the needs of all 'jobs'. Then, one can follow Arrow and Debreu (1954), treating the demands for the same type of labour to fill different jobs, as demands for different types of labour services, and a household may supply some labour for more than one job type. But if we treat the same work at different effort intensities as different labour types, we may have to deal with the added complexities of infinite-dimensional commodity spaces; the effort level can take any non-negative values. Thus, for expository purposes, our approach also has its advantage.
2. As Radner (1982) notes, most of the extant axiomatic theory of competitive equilibrium only deals with exogenous risks, and not endogenous moral hazard like 'shirking' in our model. Prescott and Townsend (1984) is an exception for the linear technology, zero profit case. Since their firms are indifferent about employment size, their contribution cannot be applied for our purpose in Sections 2 and 3 for analyzing discrimination.
3. Each distinguished by which worker fills what job, if any.

REFERENCES

Aigner, D. J. and G. G. Cain (1977) 'Statistical Theories of Discrimination in Labor Markets', *Industrial and Labor Relations Review*, 30: 175–87.

Arrow, K. J. (1973) 'The Theory of Discrimination', in O. Aschenfelter and A. Rees (eds) *Discrimination in Labor Markets* (Princeton: Princeton University Press).

Arrow K. J. (1963) 'Uncertainty and the Welfare Economics of Medical Care', *American Economic Review*, 53: 941–73.

Arrow, K. J. and G. Debreu (1954) 'Existence of an Equilibrium for a Competitive Economy', *Econometrica*, 22: 265–90.

Arrow, K. J. and F. H. Hahn (1971) *General Competitive Analysis* (San Francisco: Holden-Day).

Becker, G. S. (1971) *The Economics of Discrimination* (Chicago: University of Chicago Press).

Bergman, B. G. (1971) 'The Effect on White Incomes of Discrimination in Employment', *Journal of Political Economy*, 79: 194–313.

Edgeworth, F. Y. (1922) 'Equal Pay to Men and Women for Equal Work', *Economic Journal*, 32: 431–57.

Foster, J. E. and H. Y. Wan, Jr. (1984a), 'Involuntary Unemployment as a Principal–Agent Equilibrium', *American Economic Review*, 74: 476–84.

Foster, J. E. and H. Y. Wan, Jr. (1984b) *Competition Restores Efficiency*, mimeo.

Harris, M. and R. M. Townsend (1981) 'Resource Allocation Under Asymmetric Information', *Econometrica*, 49, 33–64.

Hurwicz, L. and L. Shapiro (1978). 'Incentive Structures Maximizing Residual Gain Under Incomplete Information', *Bell Journal of Economics*, 9: 180–91.

Lundberg, S. and R. Startz (1983) 'Private Discrimination and Social Intervention', *American Economic Review*, 73: 340–47.

Phelps, E. S. (1972) 'The Statistical Theory of Racism and Sexism', *American Economic Review*, 62: 659–61.

Prescott, E. C. and R. M. Townsend (1984) 'Pareto Optima and Competitive Equilibria with Adverse Selection and Moral Hazard', *Econometrica*, 52: 21–46.

Radner, R. (1981) 'Monitoring Cooperative Agreements in a Repeated Principal–Agent Relationship', *Econometrica*, 48: 1127–48.

Radner, R. (1982) 'Equilibrium Under Uncertainty' in K. J. Arrow and M. D. Intriligator (eds) *Handbook of Mathematical Economics*, vol. 2 (Amsterdam: North Holland).

Wan, H. Y. Jr. (1973) *A General Theory of Wages, Employment and Human Capital*, Department of Economics Working Paper, no. 51 (Cornell University).

15 Specialization, Search Costs, and the Degree of Resource Utilization

Melvin W. Reder*

I

In most contexts, an economy's rate of output is said to be determined by its resource endowment, technology, tastes, the distribution of resource ownership, and so on. Although most items on such a list occasion no disagreement, there is one prominent exception: to suggest that the degree to which productive resources are utilized materially influences an economy's level of output will immediately provoke a dispute with those who consider that departures from *full utilization* are transitory or even illusory.

This is not to suggest that most economists adhere rigidly either to the assumption of full employment, or to the reverse. Indeed, many of us assume full employment for some problems, and under-employment for others, as seems appropriate to the purpose at hand. But while such analytical flexibility is convenient, it raises a serious question as to the consistency of the models used in micro and macroeconomic theory and in the various branches of applied economics.

To economists such as Kenneth Arrow, who are concerned both with the internal consistency of economic theory and its applicability to real world problems, such a question presents a continuing challenge. As Arrow put it many years ago,

> one of the major scandals of current price theory, is the relation between microeconomics and macroeconomics ... I believe firmly that the mutual adjustment of prices and quantities represented by the neoclassical model is an important aspect of economic reality

* Edward Lazear, Robert Lucas and Kevin Murphy have all found errors in a first draft and suggested important ways to improve the exposition. None of them is in any way responsible for such errors as remain.

worthy of the serious analysis that has been bestowed on it; and certain dramatic historical episodes – most recently the reconversion of the United States from World War II and the postwar European recovery – suggest that an economic mechanism exists which is capable of adaptation to radical shifts in demand and supply conditions. On the other hand, the Great Depression and the problems of developing countries remind us dramatically that something beyond, but including, neoclassical theory is needed.[1]

This chapter does not aspire to end the scandal to which Arrow drew attention. Its less ambitious objective is to characterize the (persisting) scandal more adequately than heretofore, by showing that the equilibrium level of real output varies with the level of effective demand in a model in which (i) all prices are set in Walrasian style auctions; (ii) all transactors are price takers; (iii) equilibrium prices are known to all transactors; (iv) all trades are made at equilibrium prices; (v) there is neither money nor other financial assets; (vi) all individuals know the distribution of search times required to find a trading partner in markets where there is non-zero search cost; (vii) the expected cost of a unit transaction diminishes as the number of transactors in the market increases; and (viii) there are no intertemporal relations among any variables in the model (that is, we are concerned with static equilibria exclusively).

Assumption (i) prevents wage and/or price stickiness from playing any role in the model, (iv) precludes the possibility of behaviour in response to misperceived prices, and (v) precludes money illusion and/or confusion between nominal and real price changes.

One crucial difference between the models presented in this paper and models with 'full Walrasian equilibrium' in every market is that here we assume that, in at least one market, there is positive search cost for transactor partners, although (as in iv) all transactions take place at equilibrium prices. Given our other assumptions, it is necessary to assume non-zero search cost in at least one market for variations in the level of aggregate real output and employment to be possible. However, our results hold even when the wage rate is set by a Walrasian auctioneer and there is zero search cost in the labour market.

There have been many attempts to construct theoretical models that reconciled the seemingly incompatible ideas that (i) resources are scarce and efficiently allocated and (ii) real output and resource utilization would be greater if only effective demand were greater, while resources and technology were unchanged.[2] With few exceptions, if any, previous attempts at reconciliation have posited either wage-price stickiness or departures from competitive equilibrium. The only non-Walrasian features of the models presented here are (i) transaction cost is non-zero in at least one market, though all transactions are (nevertheless) executed at Walrasian equilibrium prices, and (ii) transaction (or search) cost diminishes as the number of transactors in the market increases.

This chapter is a parsimonious reconciliation of one strand of thought in Keynes's *General Theory* with general equilibrium theory. Its message is that in a 'near Walrasian' equilibrium customers may be more or less scarce and that, up to a point, more customers facilitates greater specialization, exchange, and output. To paraphrase Adam Smith, 'The specialization of labour is limited by the cost of using the market'.

Of course, the General Theory has facets other than the one considered here. In particular, it stresses the idea that shortage of customers (deficient aggregate demand) is related to involuntary unemployment. That idea is not well captured by the argument of this paper; however, I doubt that 'involuntary unemployment' can be usefully considered in any equilibrium model.

Recently, James Tobin (1983) remarked,

> (It is, by the way, both puzzling and unfortunate that Keynes, in spite of the Chamberlain-Robinson revolution that was occurring in microeconomics at the same time he was making his macro revolution, chose to challenge orthodoxy on its own microeconomic ground of competitive markets.)

I suggest that one reason for Keynes's 'puzzling' choice was that *inter alia* he wanted to consider the effect of variations in effective demand on output, which effect can occur even in the comparative statics of a model where competition is ubiquitous and all decision makers optimize. (That Keynes may have had other, and possible incompatible, reasons for this choice is not disputed.) The next two sections of this paper attempt to justify the above assertions.

II

In this century, Keynes's *General Theory* has been the leading example of a theory that permits equilibrium at differing levels of resource use and output. As in most other theories that possess (or claim) this characteristic, in the General Theory less than full use of resources is assumed to be reflected in unemployment of labour.[3] To the present day, the principal analytical difficulty of the General Theory has been reconciliation of less than full employment of labour with the maintained hypothesis that individual workers are constrained utility maximizers who treat current prices (including money wage rates) as parameters. That is, if 'less than full employment' is interpreted as implying that 'there are unemployed workers who would accept the same wages as employed workers whose marginal products are no higher than those of the unemployed', how can the unemployed be considered as utility maximizers, that is, why don't the unhired workers bid down the wage rate? Attempts to answer this question have led to a great deal of tortured argument, recently caricatured by Herschel Grossman (1984) as a quest for 'kosher bacon'.

The strategy of this section is to circumvent the problem of reconciling involuntary unemployment of labour with individual optimization by treating the explanation of unemployment as separable from the relation of (aggregate) effective demand to real output and employment. I shall argue that the equilibrium level of resource use can plausibly be made dependent on the level of effective demand for output, even though there is no unemployment.

I begin by constructing an equilibrium model in which attention is focused upon differences among individuals in the cost of locating suppliers of goods and services; call these cost differences, differences in 'search efficiency'. These differences lead to a division of the labour force into employers, employees (wage earners) and self-sufficient (and also self-employed) workers. For simplicity, we exclude self-employed workers who are also not self-sufficient; self-sufficiency is defined as implying absence of interpersonal exchange.

To concentrate upon differences in search efficiency, assume that all individuals have the same utility function, and that this function has two arguments; (i) a vector of v goods and (ii) hours of leisure time. This (common) utility function is assumed strongly separable as between goods and leisure time, and homothetic in goods. Further assume that everyone is risk neutral; and that total utility is increasing and marginal utility decreasing in all arguments. Except for the compensation in goods, individuals derive no utility from using time at any kind of work. Therefore, they are indifferent to a minute used to produce one good and a minute used to produce another; they are also indifferent to the allocation of time among self-sufficiency, working for wages and acting as an employer, if the level of goods consumption is the same.

Assume further that possession of wealth (W) in the form of consumption bundles has a positive marginal utility. (For simplicity, assume that wealth held in any form other than consumption bundles yields no utility.) Still further: assume that (i) no one will save anything unless his current consumption exceeds the income produced in self-sufficiency, but that saving is an increasing function of the level of income in excess of what is attainable in self-sufficiency ((i) implies that only employers save, since the equilibrium income of a wage earner is equal to what he could obtain in self-sufficiency (see below)); (ii) W is stored and is not used in production – that is, its only yield is the utility of possession.

The economy is a barter economy; there is no money. The wage is paid in units of a consumption bundle. Since every individual has the same utility function which is homothetic in goods and all face the same prices of goods, all individuals consume every pair of goods in the same ratio. That is, consumption of goods of any one individual is a scalar multiple of the consumption of any other; the scale factor being real income. Assume that when they are self-sufficient (all) individuals are equally productive, and that in self-sufficiency each individual produces some positive quantity of each good. Then, in self-sufficiency, every individual will produce the same output of every good, and all will obtain the same level of utility.

Still further, assume that every individual has exactly one speciality (identified with a particular good) at which he is more efficient than (most) others, and that all individuals having the same speciality are equally efficient (in the speciality). For convenience, assume that all employers hire exactly one worker and that each employer also works (for himself). Most important, assume that when search cost is zero (for everyone in all markets) there is an unique competitive equilibrium in which a non-zero quantity of each of the v goods is produced by at least one specialized employer-worker pair.

To avoid complications, assume that every individual with the same speciality is endowed with an identical stock of capital goods which are self-renewing in the production process. Since individuals may choose either to be self-sufficient or to specialize, it will prove convenient to imagine each individual's stock of capital as divided into two parts: (i) the part used in self-sufficient production, which is the same for everyone, and (ii) the part used in specialized production which is the same for everyone having the same speciality, but differs across specialities.

Employment relations arise because of differences in search efficiency across individuals. An employer is conceived as paying a worker a wage in units of the consumption bundle, receiving in exchange the worker's output of the particular good he produces. The employer then trades the particular good that he and his employee produce for each of the other goods in the consumption bundle, and assembles consumption bundles with which he pays wages. To accomplish the necessary exchanges, the employer must use valuable time to search for trading partners.

The wage paid cannot be less than the worker's output under self-sufficiency; otherwise the worker would choose to be self-sufficient. For the employer to gain from offering employment, the value of the individual's output must exceed the wage.

The usual explanation of gains from specialization accounts for the difference between the exchange value of a worker's output (in consumption bundles) and what he could produce (also in consumption bundles) under self-sufficiency. But the worker must share the gain from specialization with his employer because it is necessary to compensate him (the employer) for the loss of expected utility that results from using potential leisure time to search for trading partners willing and able to exchange one or another of the various items in the consumption bundle for the worker's (specialized) output.

If a worker were as efficient in searching as his employer, he could do his own searching (that is, be self-employed and sell his own product) without net loss of time or utility. It is only because employers are more efficient at searching (than workers) that they can profitably offer consumption bundles as wages in exchange for specialized output.

To relate search efficiency and gains from specialization to the characteristics of a 'near-Walrasian' equilibrium, assume that all goods (and non-labour services) are traded on competitive markets in each of which the price is set by a Walrasian auctioneer and is public. Also assume that the identity of sellers with available supplies is not publicly known, and must be ascertained by each trader through a search process. As already remarked, individuals are assumed to differ in their endowed capacity to conduct such searches.

Assume further that there are effective institutional rules that prevent trading at non-equilibrium prices, that is, transactions occur at the equilibrium price or not at all. That is, every good is traded only at its Walrasian equilibrium price, and in its (Walrasian) equilibrium quantity; there is no 'false trading'. However, the amount of (potential) leisure time that any individual must sacrifice to accomplish his desired quantity of trades is a random variable (see below), the expectation of which is conditional upon endowed search efficiency, and varies across individuals. (The (common) utility function is strictly separable as between goods and leisure time.) (Obviously, search time is not incorporated in the 'ordinary' Walrasian model.) [4]

The assumption of no false trading is arbitrary and powerful; it operates as an implicit restriction upon the set of price-quantity decisions that is admissible. Such a restriction might even be shown to be equivalent to postulating some particular pattern of price stickiness. However, without *some* assumption about price behaviour during the search process (that is, some assumption about the behaviour of reservation prices) there is no way of considering how variations in search cost affect quantity decisions. All that is claimed for the particular assumption made is that it facilitates exposition.

In contrast with the markets for goods, search in the labour market is assumed to be costless. That is, workers and employers are assumed able to locate one another instantaneously and without effort so that the labour market clears continuously at the equilibrium wage without dissatisfied transactors or sacrificed leisure. This implies that search occurs only in the markets for goods and is performed only by employers.

To characterize the search process further, assume that time is divided into a set of finite periods of equal length, long enough to permit all potential transactions (that is, transactions desired by both parties) to be executed at equilibrium prices. Assume that any transactor may trade with any other (provided the trades are at equilibrium prices), but traders may not publicly disclose either the goods they are offering or the goods they are seeking. Let traders be allowed to give esoteric signals indicative of what they have to offer and for what they wish to trade, and assume that individuals differ in their endowed ability to decipher these signals, with greater ability implying greater *search efficiency*. Search efficiency is measured as the inverse of the expected time required (for a given individual) to exchange an extra unit of good v for its value equivalent in units of the consumption bundle.[5] (The rules about disclosure and signalling are for the purpose of rationalizing a state of affairs in which expected search time is non-zero.) Crucial to our argument is the assumption that the greater is the number of potential trading partners in the market, the greater is search efficiency for every individual.[6] That is, given the trading rules, a greater number of traders reduces the expected time necessary to exchange a given volume of output. Alternatively, for any trader, expected search cost varies inversely with the number of traders in the market, given the quantity of goods he desires to trade. This implies that if an additional employer-trader enters the market he increases (slightly) the expected productivity of any given quantity of search time of all other employer-traders.

To describe further the economy analyzed, postulate that a positive quantity of each of the v goods is produced by enough employers (specialized in its production) to enforce competition. Assume that for each of the v goods there is at least one worker (whose speciality it is) who chooses to remain self-sufficient. On these assumptions, every employee will receive a wage no greater than what he would have earned if he were self-sufficient. Otherwise, his employer would replace him with a self-sufficient worker (of equal capacity) willing to work at a wage equal to his earnings under self-sufficiency. Conversely, any employee would opt for self-sufficiency if his wage fell below his earnings under self-sufficiency.

Under these (highly restrictive) assumptions, all gains from specialization accrue to employers. Every worker receives the same bundle of goods, and attains the same utility level, regardless of the extent to which production is specialized. Employers receive all the gains from specialization as rents of differential search efficiency. The marginal or 'no rent' employer is the one whose profit from employing a worker is just sufficient to compensate him for the loss of expected leisure associated with the search activity necessary to pay the equilibrium wage. Employers who are more efficient (at search activity) than the no-rent employer will earn differential rents.

The strong analogy of this model to the Ricardian rent model is obvious, and intentional. Differences of search efficiency across employers are precisely analogous to differences in fertility across plots of land and their effect on the distribution of rents is similar. It is because of this strong analogy that I have omitted specification of many formal details of the model such as consideration of the conditions for optimization by individuals.[7] However, such details are familiar and largely irrelevant to the purpose at hand.

To develop the important implications of the model let us compare two equilibrium positions: Suppose that there is a uniform increase of search efficiency throughout the economy, with *production technology*, tastes and resource endowments unchanged. That is, suppose that the expected search time needed to obtain consumption bundles for any specified number of workers declines by (say) 10 per cent for every individual in the economy. Call the pre-improvement state, 1, and the post-improvement state, 2. Movement from 1 to 2 will not affect the wage rate nor the utility level of any employee or self-sufficient individual who opts for the same status in both states. Anyone who chooses to be an employer in 1 will also choose to be an employer in 2, and none who would choose to be a non-employer in 2 would choose to be an employer in 1. However, some individuals (one or more depending upon the magnitude of the difference in search efficiency in the two states) who would choose *not* to be an employer in 1 will gain by choosing otherwise in 2.

For example, consider an individual who would have been a 'no-rent employer' in 1. (Such an individual would be one for whom the expected utility gain from employing one worker, as compared with being an employee, was exactly offset by the expected utility loss due to the sacrifice of expected leisure required to market the resulting product.) The effect of increased search efficiency reduces the expected search time such an individual would require to obtain the consumption bundles necessary to pay one employee the equilibrium wage; therefore increasing search efficiency generates an expected gain in his utility. Similarly every inframarginal employer in 1 will gain expected utility from the reduction in expected search time required to obtain the equilibrium consumption bundles.

Thus none of the gains from moving from 1 to 2 accrue to individuals who are workers in 2, that is, they accrue as increased rents of search efficiency to those who are, or become, employers in 2. However, the move creates no losers; those who would be workers in 2 will be indifferent as to which state obtains. In short, movement from 1 to 2 is associated, unambiguously, with an increase in production; it will be a Pareto-improvement.

The essential point is that because of an exogenous increase in search efficiency, some individuals who would choose self-sufficiency in 1 choose to be employer-traders in 2. This switch makes it possible to realize more of the potential gains from specialization in 2 than in 1. Alternatively, in 2 less of the potential gains from specialization are sacrificed to avoid the expected cost of transacting.

In the above discussion, the increase in search efficiency occurs because of an exogenous improvement in search technology. However, it can also arise from an increase in the number of potential trading partners (customers) for any employer-trader while search technology is constant.[8] An increase in the number of potential customers faced by any given trader (prices given) can reasonably be interpreted as an increase in the level of (aggregate) effective demand.

Now let us amend the common utility function so that the level of utility associated with a given increase in the stock of W, leisure time and consumption constant, varies with a random variable, γ, drawn from a known distribution which is given exogenously. Assume that the value of γ is publicly known as soon as it is drawn. In keeping with the previous notation, consider two possible values of γ, 1 and 2, with 2 referring to a state in which every individual derives a higher level of utility from an increase in W than he would have derived in 1, with the consumption (of goods) and leisure time remaining the same.

In 2 some individuals who chose self-sufficiency in state 1 will choose to be employers and savers, thereby increasing the number of traders. As it appears to any individual employer, in 2 there are more customers for his output than in 1; that is, there are more employer-traders seeking to make exchanges. Since this statement holds for every employer, and since (equilibrium) prices are the same at all values of γ, it is reasonable to identify higher values of γ with higher levels of effective demand.

Thus the higher level of effective demand in 2 causes a greater number of employees to be hired, and a correspondingly greater level of aggregate real output (valued at constant prices) to be produced, than in 1. As before, all employers are better off in 2, though wage earners do not share in the gain since in both states the wage equals the earnings of self-sufficiency. This result has a distinctly Keynesian flavour; aggregate output and (wage earning) employment varies directly with the level of effective demand whatever the cause of the variation.

There are many possible interpretations for a variation of γ: one is that γ is a proxy for the locus of the marginal efficiency of investment schedule. On this interpretation, shifts of γ reflect changes in 'animal spirits', in anticipations of future shocks, and so on. But however interpreted, a shift of γ is exogenously caused and, in turn, causes an increase in search efficiency of each employer by increasing the number of his potential customers. In other words, the level of γ determines the number of individuals for whom it is efficient to become employers. It is to be emphasized that the above argument is based on the assumption that all prices and the level of γ are public information. It is further assumed that based on this information each individual accurately infers the number of traders and his own (implied) expected search time.

Thus an exogenous shift of γ causes an increase in the level of aggregate production that causes further increases and so on (multiplier effect). It is assumed that all such multiplier effects are accurately taken into account by individual decision makers. Moreover, it is assumed that for any set of prices and level of γ, there is an unique and stable equilibrium. Equilibrium prices are the same at all levels of γ, but (equilibrium) output and employment increase with the level of γ.

A further characteristic of this model that is of theoretical interest is the implicit role of *liquidity preference*. To speak of liquidity preference in a non-monetary economy, it is very helpful to assign an unique role in transaction to some one good *vis-à-vis* all other goods. In this model, the good performing this role is the 'consumption bundle'. The consumption bundle has the property that it is generally acceptable in payment of wages or in exchange for any other good (every good is a component of the consumption bundle). This general acceptability makes the consumption bundle the only good that can be exchanged for any other, or for labour service, at an equilibrium price with zero transaction cost.[9] (Throughout the paper, transaction cost is synonymous with search cost.)

Assume that in the absence of transaction cost there would be no preference for 'liquidity', or even a meaning for the term. Also let the market value (at equilibrium prices) of the lump-sum payment an employee would require to be indifferent between being paid in his own product, and being paid in consumption bundles, be defined as his liquidity premium.[10] Similarly, at any given level of search efficiency, define the liquidity premium of any individual as the minimal difference between the market value of the output of one worker and the worker's wage that he would demand as a condition of becoming an employer.

Given these definitions, a shift from 1 to 2 may be interpreted as a decline in the liquidity premium of every employer. That is, in this model, an increase in effective demand (from 1 to 2) is equivalent to a decline in every employer's liquidity premium, and is associated with increases both in output and (wage earning) employment.

This interpretation of liquidity preference contrasts sharply with the customary interpretation which treats liquidity preference as a determinant of the demand for cash balances. As our model contains no financial assets (neither cash, debt nor equities), there is no possibility of confusion between the two interpretations. What is offered is a definition of liquidity preference for a non-monetary model.

In this model, the desire for liquidity derives from the desire to avoid the loss of potential leisure time implied by the obligation of employers to pay wages in consumption bundles which entails an obligation to search for customers who offer (other) ingredients of the consumption bundle in exchange. That is, the employment relation involves a commitment to pay consumption bundles to employees (in exchange for specialized output), with the loss of leisure associated with the exchange process as the sole element of employer cost.[11,12]

III

Let us call the model used in the previous section, Model I. A striking feature of that model is that wage earners always find employers at zero expected search cost; this precludes the possibility of unemployment. To consider unemployment, we must reconstruct the model; call the reconstruction Model II.

In Model II all individuals have the same common utility function as in Model I and, as before, have identical capacities for production under self-sufficiency. As in Model I, all individuals have one speciality at which they are more productive than most others, and all individuals with a given speciality are equally productive (at that speciality). Also, as in Model I, the prices of all goods and the wage rate are determined in each period by a Walrasian auction with no trading permitted at non-equilibrium prices.

Unlike Model I, information as to the location of transactors in every good is free so that output is sold without transaction (that is, search) costs. However, information about labour markets is costly. For convenience, assume that job searching is done entirely by workers; employers are passive. Workers are differentially endowed with skill at locating employers; analogous to Model I, greater skill is reflected in a lower expected search time required to find an employer.

Assume that workers optimize by planning to devote a maximum amount of (potential) leisure time per period to job search; this maximum is the same for all, that is, all job seekers search with the same stopping rule.[13] It is assumed that failure to locate an employer within the time allotted to search does not deter individuals from halting search and remaining unemployed for the period. Although individuals are assumed identical with respect to the *maximum* time they allot to job search, they differ with respect to the *expected* time they require to find an employer.[14] Greater endowments of search skill are reflected in lower *expected* amounts of time devoted to search, and correlatively more expected time available for leisure.

We conceive individuals as choosing between self-sufficiency and wage earning, with wage earners bearing the time cost of finding an employer. The expected utility of wage earning depends on the wage paid and the expected time devoted to job search. As in Model I, there is no risk aversion. For the individual at the margin of transfer between wage earning and self-sufficiency is equal to the expected utility of the vector whose elements are the equilibrium wage received (when wage-earning) and the expected loss of potential leisure time on account of job search. Inframarginal workers earn searcher's (differential) rent in addition to the equilibrium wage. Individuals who are relatively inept at job search will choose self-sufficiency.

Whether, in a given period, an individual finds an employer or remains unemployed is a random variable, with the probability of obtaining employment increasing with skill at job search. The penalty for being unemployed is loss of wage income for the period.[15] To permit survival while unemployed, assume that all individuals are equally endowed with stocks of consumption bundles sufficient to defray consumption for 'several' periods. Loss of part of this stock causes loss of utility, but does not alter subsequent choices. To preclude catastrophes, (that is, running out of wealth) assume that (for any given individual) the probability of a 'long run' of bad luck at searching is so low as to be negligible. In each period, unemployment is measured as a dichotomous variable; those who find jobs are employed and job searchers who fail are unemployed, with each unemployed individual counting as one unit of unemployment.

To act as an employer requires no particular skill not possessed in the same degree by all other individuals with the same speciality. Retaining the assumption (from Model I) that in every speciality there is at least one individual who opts for self-sufficiency, it follows that the earnings of an employer must be equal to those of self-sufficiency. In keeping with this characterization of employers and job searchers, we define skill at job search as ability to locate individuals (willing to serve as employers) having the same speciality as that of the searcher.

Given the search technology, institutional rules, and endowed search skills, each individual job seeker has an expected search time. Designate the vector of expected search times for the set of all individuals as Ω, and make Ω depend upon the state of search 'technology'. As in Model I, let 1 and 2 refer to two (different) states; in this case states of search technology, with 2 referring to a superior technology to 1 (that is, every individual has a shorter expected search time in 2 than in 1). Then a shift from 1 to 2 will lead at least one individual to shift from self-sufficiency to employment seeking, thereby causing increases in expected output, expected employment (in specialized production) and creating expected rents of job search for all individuals who had opted for job search in state 1 and, *a fortiori*, in 2.

Now let us examine the comparative static properties of Models I and II.

1. In Model II, as in Model I, the shift from 1 to 2 leads to increases in *expected* values of output, employment, and wages. However, in Model II *realized* values may differ from expected values as determined by the individual probability density functions of time spent at job search; the convolution of the realized values will vary from one drawing to another.

   In Model I, both output and employment are sure numbers but, for employers, realized leisure may differ from expected leisure. Since, in Model I, it is assumed that the labour market always clears, there can be no unemployment. But in Model II, there is both (positive) expected unemployment and a distribution of realized unemployment.
2. In Model II, both expected unemployment and (the distribution of) realized unemployment change with the shift from 1 to 2. However, we cannot predict the direction of the change of expected unemployment because of the following reason: Everyone who was a job seeker in 1 will also be a job seeker in 2, and will have a higher probability of being employed in 2; but in addition some who were self-sufficient in 1 will become job seekers in 2. Because of their inferior search skill, all of these 'status shifters' will have in 2 a higher probability of being unemployed than any of the individuals who had been job seekers in 1. Therefore the change in expected number of unemployed associated with the shift from 1 to 2 will depend upon (i) the relative number of individuals who become job seekers (that is, change employment status) in response to the shift, and (ii) the magnitude of the median difference in the probability of being unemployed in 2 of members of the two groups (that is, those seeking jobs in both 1 and 2, and those seeking jobs only in 2). (ii) depends upon the shape of the density function of expected search time over all individuals. Given the characteristics of this density

function, (i) will vary with the 'size' of the change in job search technology associated with the shift from 1 to 2.

Low relative numbers of status shifters and small changes of search technology lead to dominance of the 'employment-status-invariant' individuals in determining the impact of the shift on expected unemployment, that is, they reduce expected unemployment. The reverse tendencies lead to dominance of 'employment status shifters' which permits – though it does not assure – an increase in expected unemployment.

In a nutshell, the forces considered in Model II allow an exogenous increase in effective demand to increase expected output and expected employment. However, increases in employment do not imply decreases in expected unemployment. This point further illustrates what is shown by Model I; deficient aggregate demand has no direct implications for the behaviour, or even the existence, of unemployment. Unemployment is, of course, an important phenomenon; but its occurrence depends upon the manner in which an economy uses (and accounts for) the time of job seekers while they are engaged in the search process, and not upon the level of effective demand.[16]

IV

For convenience, the discussion in this section is conducted entirely in terms of Model I. Reformulating the analysis in terms of Model II or a more complicated model in which there is non-zero search cost in more than one market would increase the variety of possible outcomes resulting from an exogenous increase in demand, but would not exclude the particular Keynesian case upon which I wish to focus.

The principal result of section II which I propose to develop is that potential output may be sacrificed because the gains of additional specialization are more than offset by the additional costs of transacting (searching for buyers). To recapitulate, at any given level of output, the transaction (or search) cost associated with employing a worker declines as the number of buyers increases. And the number of buyers increases with the level of effective demand, indicated by the (exogenous) level of γ. Therefore, if an increase could somehow be induced, a Pareto-improvement would ensue.

In the simple world of Model I, any increase in γ would cause a (Pareto-improving) increase in output and employment so long as there was a self-sufficient individual who would choose to specialize if transaction costs were zero. The policy problem(s) is to find a way to influence the (allegedly) exogenous γ and, having done so, to set its level high enough to drive transaction level costs to zero.[17]

A *deus ex machina* with the capacity to levy differential lump-sum taxes (payable in consumption bundles) on employers according to their receipts of search rent could act as 'demander of last resort', using the tax proceeds to finance purchases and reimbursing the tax payers with transfers of the consumption bundles purchased. It is easy to show that such a deical act would generate additional output that would accrue as search rent, and would constitute a Pareto-improvement.

But to identify such a *deus* with a hypothetical government, that has whatever characteristics are considered to be essential, is a step that the model can neither justify nor decry. If actions, governmental or otherwise, required to effect an increase in γ were costless, such actions would surely be beneficial in a Model I world. Failing this condition, nothing in the argument of this chapter can be used either to rationalize or to oppose public sector efforts to alter γ.

What this chapter claims to do is to provide a bridge across the chasm between macro and micro theory. It is to be emphasized that this bridge does not require appeal to incompleteness of information of any decision-maker. It is also assumed that all prices and the value of γ (that is, the number of buyers) are public and certain. To avoid possible misinterpretation let me reiterate: Suppose that the value of γ is announced by an Economic Co-ordinator after a (costless) study of everyone's work, search and saving plans. The announced value of γ is assumed to be its true value, and is known as such by everyone.

As already explained, an arbitrary increase in γ will reduce the expected search-transaction cost of every individual, thereby increasing the equilibrium number of employers and specialized workers and the level of aggregate output. This, in turn, will cause a further reduction in everyone's expected search cost and result in further increases in output and employment, as modelled by the Keynesian Multiplier.[18] However, given γ, individuals are assumed correctly to infer the implied expected search time (transaction cost) for every individual and, from this inference and the implied number of individuals who will choose to become employers, to make their own (optimal) specialization decision. Thus, in a manner compatible with rational expectations, an increase in γ will increase total output.

In the real world, errors of calculation and inference are very likely, and may dominate the observed relation of aggregate output (and related variables) to γ. Because of this possibility, it is conceivable that inaccurate – even deliberately inaccurate but authoritative – announcements of γ could increase equilibrium real output. However, the argument of this paper does not consider such possibilities; it is based on the assumption that all decision variables – prices, and expected search costs (as inferred from) γ – are known accurately and with certainty.

In the final analysis, there are two distinct causes for the chasm between micro and macro. The one that has attracted most attention in recent years stems from the implications of incomplete information. But while consideration of these implications has greatly enriched conventional general equilibrium theory, it has presented it with no fundamental challenge.

The second cause, which is stressed here, does present such a challenge. This challenge arises from the Underconsumptionist aspect of the General Theory. The challenge may be expressed in the counter-intuitive proposition that, 'scarcity of resources notwithstanding, Demand may create its own Supply'. Put differently, 'scarcity of customers inhibits use of resource production even though prices (and wages) are in equilibrium and expectations are rational'.

The relative importance of demand deficiency and incomplete information, as explanations of aggregate behaviour is distinct from their relative capacity to fascinate economists. Like Arrow and most other economists of my generation, I consider it plausible to regard the Great Depression of the 1930s, at least in part, as a manifestation of a sharp decline in γ. I would go further to suggest that even in less obvious outliers than the Great Depression, movements of γ have been operative. (I do not know if Arrow would join this last speculation.)

But to regard movements in γ as the whole story, even of the 1930s, would be unacceptable. Intertemporal substitution of investment demand relates low values of γ's in some periods to high values in others, and so on. Often what might appear to be a series of exogenous and uncorrelated shifts of γ might also be interpreted as the interrelated realizations of a structurally invariant stochastic process. To the extent that the latter interpretation was valid, substantial intertemporal variations in levels of resource utilization might be efficient.

To the extent that exogenous and temporally unrelated shifts of γ are considered prime movers of macro variables, the conflict of micro and macro theory will persist. This is because 'suboptimal supply of customers in competitive equilibrium' is a notion repugnant to conventional price theory. Conversely, temporally interdependent variations in resource utilization (for example, equilibrium business cycles, Lucas style) may be quite compatible with a Pareto-efficient economy. In the future, and perhaps even now, the major issue in the struggle of micro and macro will concern the interpretation of temporal variations in the degree of resource use. But that issue is empirical; the sole purpose of this chapter has been to clear away some theoretical confusions that have impeded discourse.

NOTES

1. Arrow (1967) pp. 734–5.
2. The literature on this subject is huge. Good sets of references and discussions may be found in Drazen (1980), Iwai (1981) and Negishi (1979), although these are slightly dated.

   Until I had almost completed the first draft, I imagined that the argument developed here was quite novel. At that point, Robert Lucas drew my attention to an excellent paper by Peter Diamond (1982). While there are many differences in the detailed structure of my models from those in Diamond's paper, to say nothing of differences in exposition and mathematics, a basic idea in both papers is that exogenous differences in the level of aggregate demand for goods will be (inversely) associated with differences in the expected cost (to any individual) of searching for trading partners. This change in search cost alters the quantity supplied by each individual, and of aggregate supply (that is, output and resource use) for the economy.
3. It is not the present purpose to inquire whether and why Keynes paid relatively little attention to unemployment of factors other than labour.
4. The special assumptions of this paragraph can be interpreted in terms of Clower's (1965) distinction between notional and effective demand in the following manner: because of the assumption that all mutually desired exchanges of goods are (eventually) made after some search and at equilibrium prices, notional and effective demands for every good are equalized in each period. The implication of this equalization is that deviations of the actual from expected rates of trading are reflected solely in (oppositely signed) deviations of realized from expected leisure. Because of the assumed separability of leisure and goods, this departure has no effect upon demand for any *good.* I am indebted to Edward Lazear for drawing my attention to this point.
5. For convenience, assume that search efficiency is the same, for any given individual, in all goods.
6. This statement holds strictly only where all traders (that is, employers) have equal quantities to offer. In this model, the condition is satisfied because all employers hire only one worker, have the same utility function, and are differently endowed only with respect to search ef-

ficiency. Differences in search efficiency lead to differences in utility only through differences in expected leisure.

7. In particular, I ignore the problem of (possible) variation in number of hours worked by individuals, *de facto*, every individual is assumed either to work (for wages) zero hours per period or to work some finite number which is the same for everyone and independent of the wage rate. Implicitly, I assume that it is impossible to work part time for wages and part time in self-sufficiency.

   Further, I ignore the problem of determining which individuals will work for wages and which will be self-sufficient. Analogous to the Ricardian differential rent model, the number of individuals in each category is (or can be made to be) determinate, but there is no way of deciding which individuals will choose self-sufficiency and which will choose wage earning.
8. For any individual employer-trader, the number of potential trading partners is the number of all other employer-traders who produce a good or service different from his own. The designation of trading partners as 'customers' is deliberately suggestive, but formally inconsequential. Remember that we are speaking of a barter economy in which the designation of a trading partner as buyer or seller is arbitrary. However, treating trading partners as buyers is intuitively helpful in interpreting an increase in number of trading partners as an increase in effective demand.
9. The assertion concerning zero transaction cost is a (convenient) definition and not a theorem. The consumption bundle, or money, is the most liquid of all assets in that exchanging a unit for a quantity of good v (that is, any other good) involves less expected search time than exchanging a unit of any other good, v^*, for v. But this does not imply that the expected search time (or transaction cost) for exchanging a consumption bundle unit against a quantity of v is zero; it implies only that it is 'minimal'. For convenience, I assume minimal to be zero, but it would not matter if I set minimal equal to some positive constant.
10. To avoid irrelevant complications, I assume that any given individual must be paid either exclusively in consumption bundles, or (exclusively) in his own product.
11. All production functions are assumed to be exact (that is, sure) relations without a stochastic element. Thus, an agreement to accept labour services in exchange for consumption bundles is equivalent to an agreement to accept (specialized) output in exchange for consumption bundles at the equilibrium rate of exchange.
12. To avoid the complications associated with an equilibrium involving both stocks and flows, I have eliminated all stocks from the model and deal only with flows. Nevertheless, this model does incorporate obstacles to transacting, and the associated costs. Because these obstacles exist in the model, it is necessary to account for the resources used to overcome them. This is accomplished by assuming that the employer uses whatever potential leisure time is required to obtain the promised consumption bundles.
13. As used here, the 'stopping rule' refers to the rule that determines the maximum number of search attempts to be made per period, at a

predetermined acceptance price. This is in the same spirit, but literally different from the conventional definition which determines the acceptance price as a function of the search procedure and the realization of previous search attempts.

14. That is, we assume that, through sufficient search, employers are always able to honour their commitments to pay wages on time. Here again, arbitrary but not unfamiliar restrictions must be imposed on the relevant stochastic process to preclude the possibility of default.

    One restriction that would suffice is limiting the distribution of possible times required for complete search of all transactors to no more than the length of one period. An alternative restriction, that would also suffice, is to assume that all individuals recognize the existence of a (small) probability of default on wage contracts, the same for all employers, and to include compensation for the associated risk in the transfer price between self-sufficiency and wage-earning. These, or similar restrictions, are akin to those necessary to exclude the possibilities of being 'stock-out', or in loan default, and so on, in models where assets appear.
15. Individuals who choose to search for an employer are assumed to forgo the opportunity of being self-sufficient during the period in question.
16. I discuss this topic in some detail in 'Disguised Unemployment Revisited: Variations on a Theme of Joan Robinson' (forthcoming).
17. I assume, without argument, that there exists a finite level of γ such that transaction costs will be zero, and that at zero transaction cost every individual will specialize. The question-begging nature of these assumptions should be obvious.
18. An arbitrary small increase in γ, which will drive the level of output correspponding to full specialization (that is, whether Model I is locally stable), depends upon the rate of increase in expected transaction cost across individuals as the number who specialize increases. Arbitrarily, I assume that there is local stability at all points.

REFERENCES

Arrow, K. J. (1967) 'Samuelson Collected', *Journal of Political Economy*, 75: 730–37.

Clower, R. W. (1965) 'The Keynesian Counterrevolution: A Theoretical Appraisal' in F. H. Hahn and F. P. R. Brechling (eds) *The Theory of Interest Rates* (London: Macmillan).

Diamond, P. A. (1982) 'Agregate Demand Management in Search Equilibrium', *Journal of Political Economy*, 90: 881–94.

Drazen, A. (1980) 'Recent Developments in Macroeconomic Disequilibrium Theory', *Econometrica*, 48: 283–306.

Grossman, H. I. (1984) 'Review of Frank Hahn, *Money and Inflation*', *Journal of Political Economy* 92: 337–40.

Iwai, K. (1981) *Disequilibrium Dynamics: A Theoretical Analysis of Inflation and Unemployment* (New Haven and London: Yale University Press).

Lucas, R. E., Jr (1983) 'Expectations and the Neutrality of Money', *Studies in Business Cycle Theory* (Cambridge, Mass,; M.I.T. Press) pp. 66–89.

Negishi, T. (1979) *Microeconomic Foundations of Keynesian Macroeconomics* (Amsterdam, New York and Oxford: North-Holland).

Tobin, J. (1983) 'Okun on Macroeconomic Policy: A Final Comment', *Macroeconomics, Prices, and Quantities* (Washington, DC: The Brookings Institution) p. 299.

16 Information Disclosure and the Economics of Science and Technology

Partha Dasgupta and Paul A. David*

1 ARROW, INFORMATION AND THE UNDERDEVELOPED ECONOMICS OF SCIENCE

Economists understand technology less deeply than some might hope. But they understand the world of technology far better than they do the world of science (see, for example, Rosenberg, 1982, especially chapter 7). Kenneth Arrow's famous 1962 essay, and the literature it inspired, is in good part to blame for this state of affairs. In 'Economic Welfare and the Allocation of Resources for Inventions', Arrow laid the foundations for modern economic analysis of research and development (R&D) activities. On that base, a large, and impressive edifice of research devoted to the economics of technological invention and innovation has since been erected. By absolute as well as comparative standards, the economics of science has remained lamentably underdeveloped. That too is traceable to the 1962 essay.

Of course, we do not attribute to Arrow the profession's concern with the microeconomic processes of technological change. By the

*This essay owes much to the many conversations that each of us has held over the years with Kenneth Arrow. Among these we can pleasurably recall pertinent discussions of economics of information, allocation of resources to the scientific research, and the organization of communities of academic scientists. Although these pages are offered in his honour, and we would ourselves be honoured to have them accepted as an extension of the line of thought represented by his seminal 1962 paper on the allocation of resources for inventions, Arrow himself must not be blamed for the views expressed herein.

A first draft was prepared while Dasgupta was a Visiting Fellow at the Center for Economic Policy Research at Stanford University during the summer of 1984. The present version has benefited from the comments and suggestions made by Bengt Lundvall, R. C. O. Matthews, Roger Noll, Jean-Jacques Salomon, Walter G. Vincenti, and participants in the Technological Innovation Program Workshop in the Department of Economics at Stanford University during Fall Quarter, 1984. Joshua Rosenbloom provided able research assistance.

1950s a rapidly growing number of economists appreciated that technological progress was not exogenous and had as one of its sources the purposive, profit-motivated quest for certain kinds of information on the part of individuals and firms. Yet, prior to Arrow (1962), no writer had so forcefully articulated an information-theoretic approach to the subject of technologically-oriented research and invention; no one had so clearly seen that inasmuch as research and invention are directed to producing *information*, an economic analysis of R&D activities must inevitably rest upon recognition of the peculiar characteristics of information viewed as an economic commodity.

Arrow's essay began by pointing out that the production of information (additions to the stock of technological knowledge) itself is a business that must be conducted under great uncertainties, and, due to moral hazard, many of these risks cannot be efficiently insured. He next observed that the costs of transmitting information typically are very much smaller than the costs of producing it, so that, considered from the supply side, information has the attributes of a public good. Turning then to the demand for information, Arrow pointed out that its use was subject to certain indivisibilities, in the sense that once a certain piece of information had been acquired there was no value added in acquiring it again.[1] An awkward corollary followed: potential purchasers of information could not ascertain its value exactly, since to disclose it would be to convey the information without cost.

Together these properties made information a commodity quite distinct from the goods traded in the sorts of markets which economists normally analyzed. There was a strong presumption that decentralized resource allocation mechanisms which yielded socially desirable outcomes with 'standard commodities' would break down in the case of a commodity having the properties of information. Uninsurable risk, the difficulties of recovering fixed production costs under competitive conditions of information transmission, and, most of all, the difficulties of appropriating the benefits derived by users, all suggested that a perfectly competitive market economy would underinvest in R&D. A rationale was thus suggested for public subsidization of R&D investment on grounds of 'market failure', one that has become the principal intellectual underpinning for such technology policy as the United States currently may be said to have (see Mowery, 1983).

We can see now that the ramifications of this conceptual approach reach well beyond consideration of the category of scientific and engineering information associated with the performance of R&D. Arrow stopped short, however, without explicitly tackling the economics of science. While his discussion of the properties of information was carried through at a high level of generalization, the subject of inventive activity closely circumscribed the application of his framework on that occasion. He did not inquire into the relationship between the allocation of resources in the two lines of human endeavour whose intertwined development has played so crucial a role in the epoch of modern economic growth.

Although an information-theoretic path had been marked by Arrow for others to follow towards a better understanding of the economics of science, as well as of the economics of technology, very few economists actually have ventured to explore it. Unfortunately, in the intervening years the track has become somewhat obscured by an overgrowth of other approaches to the subject.[2]

We shall take up the inquiry on the present occasion just where Arrow left off, by posing the question: Is it useful for economists to distinguish between science and technology? Can a reasonably precise analytical distinction be drawn between the forms of research and invention with which Arrow was preoccupied in 1962, and the information-seeking activities referred to commonly as 'science'?

The question is limited, but it is not an idle one. Behind the façade of semantics, a real difference does exist between these two spheres of human endeavour, one which we believe should be more widely appreciated by those formulating economic policies affecting science and technology. We will argue that to recognize this difference is to better understand why the position of academic science in modern industrial societies is at once exalted and economically so precarious as to require constant public nurturing. Although the contributions of scientists and technologists in the search for knowledge may be perceived to be interdependent and even symbiotic, we shall suggest that science as a social entity today is in danger of being undermined by the technological community's conception of knowledge as a form of productive capital.

The question is also not a new one – at least not to scholars in disciplines outside of economics. We will therefore need to consider (in Section 2) several of the differentiating criteria that have been proposed by historians and sociologists of science and technology. To summarize briefly, there are those who hold that scientific and technological research should be distinguished from one another by the 'technology' of research; for example, by the alleged fact that scientific research is on the whole the riskier of the two. Then there are those who would draw the contrast on the basis of the nature of the commodity produced by the research; for example, by whether or not the addition to knowledge has practical applications. Finally, we take notice of the observation that science and technology are distinguished from one another by differences in the way they treat the information-products; in particular, by the divergence of attitudes, behaviour and institutions relating to the *communication* of research findings (see Section 3 below).

Some of these distinctions, including the principle that Arrow (1962) proposed for separating 'basic' from other research, turn out on closer inspection not to be so useful for our purposes after all. Others come closer to the heart of the matter, in our view, but still leave many loose ends. To tie these up, we will suggest (Section 4) that an economically consequential difference may be discerned between the respective *goals* that the two communities – scientists and technologists – have set for themselves.

Roughly speaking, the scientific community appears concerned with the *stock* of knowledge and is devoted to furthering its growth, whereas the technological community is concerned with the private economic *rents* that can be earned from that stock. Put another way, in the social role of 'scientist', a researcher is expected to view the stock of knowledge as a *public consumption* good, while in the role of 'technologist', he or she regards it as a *private capital* good. As would be expected, each community seeks to inculcate in its members, through training and incentives, those attitudes and mores concerning research procedures and findings that tend to further its particular goals.

One manifestation of this – and the one we shall highlight – is the greater urgency shown by scientists in disseminating newly-acquired information throughout the research community. The same imperative is evidently not shared by technology-researchers, who are free to adopt information strategies ranging from disclosure to total secrecy in regard to their discoveries and inventions. Sociologically astute observers of the two research communities (for example, Salomon, 1973), are quite likely to remark upon this difference. But they have not probed deeply for explanations of the phenomenon. Why should these two cultures – which in the modern world are so similar in other respects, and between which the same individuals are increasingly observed to move with ease – diverge so sharply on the standards for acceptable behaviour in regard to secrecy and disclosure of information?

Our classificatory principle suggests one mode of explanation. It also leads quite directly (in Section 5) to an understanding of the function that priority of discovery has an incentive mechanism in science, and of its relationship to the complex incentive mechanism which the patent system seeks to create in the sphere of technology-research. Having distinguished between science and technology according to their respective objectives, incentive structures, and approved modes of behaviour for participants, we are able to see more clearly (in Section 6) both the areas of compatibility and the worrisome sources of tension that characterize relationships between the two research communities.

Finally, we may remark that the contrast drawn here between science and technology also helps to explain why economists have less trouble turning their attention to the latter, but have generally shied away from studying the allocation of resources for science. Needs and desires for consumption goods are usually treated as data in modern economics. Their origins, and their influence upon the organization and conduct of consumption activities are regarded to be proper subject matter for biology, psychology and sociology, but not for economics.[3] The demand for capital goods, on the other hand, is a *derived* demand and may be more readily disentangled from questions of 'tastes'. When information generated by research is conceived of purely as a capital good, as is the case in the realm of technology, it becomes immediately more amenable to the accepted style of economic analysis. But this has resulted in the underdeveloped condition in which we now find the economic analysis of science.

2 DO SCIENCE AND TECHNOLOGY PRODUCE DIFFERENT KINDS OF KNOWLEDGE?

The word 'science' means 'knowledge' in Latin, but much time has been spent elaborating hierarchies of knowledge in which a place is reserved for 'science' in the uppermost branches. Thus, medieval Western scholars drew a distinction between speculative, theoretical or abstract knowledge; and art, or practical knowledge. Labels were taken from the Greek: the former was referred to as *episteme*, and the latter as *techne*. Countless writers, down to the present day, draw a distinction along just these lines between 'science' and 'technology', regarding science to be occupied with the production of knowledge that is more general and fundamental to understanding the natural order but of less immediate practical applicability.

This perspective can be seen in the assignment made by Price (1967), who identifies knowledge about natural phenomena and activities involved in its discovery as belonging to science; knowledge concerning useful mechanisms and processes he assigns to technology. In Price's taxonomic scheme, science and technology are pursuits that proceed largely independently of one another, and may be distinguished principally by the nature of their respective products. Technology, he suggests, might almost be defined 'as a field where the chief intended product is an object, a manufacture, a process, a chemical . . .', whereas the chief object of science is the production of 'a paper' – a published record of one's discovery (Price, 1967, p. 10).

The same notions, or ones very closely related, surfaced in the distinction that Arrow (1962, p. 618) sought to draw between 'basic research' and other kinds of research, including invention. A 'basic' form of knowledge-generation was defined implicitly as one 'the output of which is only used as an informational input into other inventive activities'. Although science was not explicitly placed in the category of 'basic research' by Arrow, many readers probably found it natural to make that extension. After all, the argument being advanced was that the more 'basic' the character of the research, the more in need it would be of public support. This followed from two propositions:

1. There was inherently greater difficulty in appropriating the value of information produced to serve as an input into further research, compared with appropriating the value of information applicable directly to the production of physical commodities;
2. 'the value of information for use in developing further information is much more conjectural than the value of its use in production and therefore much more likely to be underestimated'. (Arrow, 1962, p. 618).

Upon closer consideration, however, it seems less and less promising to separate research in science from that in technology on the basis of the characteristics of the knowledge generated by these activities, or by their mode of generation. The production of new knowledge and of useful devices and processes move along very similar lines. An outside observer would be hard-pressed to decide whether a research worker was a scientist or a technologist, merely by categorizing the sequence of activities in which he or she was engaged, or examining the results obtained at any given point in the research programme. A working scientist frequently would appear to be producing what in Price's (1967) scheme would have to be counted as technology, in the shape of the specialized equipmemt developed to test hypotheses or to make more accurate measurements. The invention of the bubble chamber and of the electron microscope are two oft-cited illustrations.

A 'device-seeking' technologist, in turn, may generate new empirical findings and explanatory models that would qualify as science in the same classificatory scheme. The discoveries concerning the properties of semiconductors by the Bell Laboratory research group that invented the point contact transistor and the junction transistor, is a well-known case in point (see, for example, Nelson, 1962; Levin, 1982). Examples of this interplay abound in the fields of molecular biology, biochemistry, and solid state physics.

Moreover, observers of the modern science and technology scene have remarked upon the strongly convergent tendencies within the two research disciplines in precisely these regards. Brooks (1967, pp. 38–9) writes that 'the newer technologies, such as nuclear energy, electronics, and computers tend to be more externally oriented than the older technologies. There is more conscious effort to conceptualize technological knowledge'. Correspondingly, Salomon (1973, p. xi) describes the 'specific characteristics of modern scientific research' as the fact that 'it increasingly abolishes any lack of continuity between the generalization stages and the application stages of the process of discovery and invention'. Whatever the historical differences that may have separated the methods of technologists from those of scientists, it would seem that as we look to the future there is more and more reason to treat research, both scientific and technological, as one continuous process of iteration between phases of generalization and application.

Be this as it may, many will still find it hard to relinquish the intuitive and commonly-held idea that science seeks the abstract and general while technology pursues the concrete and particular; that science as a vocation is other-worldly, whereas technology compels its practitioners to be firmly mired in mundane facts. The difficulty in clinging to this outlook does not arise in the drawing up of boundaries and the dividing of the varieties of knowledge along such lines. One can make the distinctions, however approximately. The problem for the economist – indeed for social scientists more broadly – is that one does not know what to *do* with the resulting classification of research disciplines. Thus, to choose an example within the realm of science, chemistry as it is understood today is really atomic physics writ large. That is, chemical laws, such as those of molecular bonding, are based on quantum physics. In an obvious and trivial sense then, physics is more fundamental, more general, than chemistry. Likewise, much of current-day biology, such as molecular biology, is chemistry writ not-so-large. To the extent this is so, chemistry is the more fundamental, the more general. But nothing of moment appears to follow from this. What advantage could be gained in grappling with resource allocation issues by insisting that somewhere within an extended ordering of *this* kind we may locate various technological disciplines?

Nor does it seem much more helpful to differentiate between science and technology on the basis of the degree of uncertainty in the products of research. There is a temptation to view the outcomes of scientific research as being particularly clouded by uncertainties, and to depict technological research as time-consuming, and costly, but more routinized and thus comparatively predictable. One can agree with Arrow (1962) that some significant resource allocation consequences would follow from this distinction. But the empirical premise is not well founded. 'Normal science' – and we are using the term in the sense of Kuhn (1962) – is not expecially risky.[4] To be sure, even in normal science one does not know exactly what one will discover. But this is the case with *all* research. Indeed, it appears to be true even in contract research, where the commodity eventually produced is often different in design and use from the product for which the development contract was drawn up (see, for example, Klein, 1962). Quite aside from the issue of the predictability of the characteristics, or the commercial value of the fruits of R&D programs, the uncertainty of project completion times in industrial research organizations is widely acknowledged.

One further point should be noted, especially in regard to Arrow's (1962) designation of 'basic' research as being intrinsically riskier because the value of information for use as a capital input in developing further information is 'more conjectural'. The main difficulty with this is that it cannot provide an operational basis for ex ante classification of research programmes. As we have pointed out, scientific and technologically-oriented programmes of investigation both entail interaction between phases of generalization and application. It is always possible that the search for information to be used, in a roundabout manner, to yield further information, will be temporarily short-circuited by a discovery that has direct application in commericial production. Likewise, the search for specific, commercializable devices may uncover scientific principles that further the process of discovery. It is certainly conceivable that awards could be made in accordance with the ex post assessments of research programme's results on this scale of 'basic-ness'; as a practical proposition one would expect such awards to closely resemble the prizes offered by scientific and engineering societies. An efficient ex ante incentive scheme intended to subsidize programmes of research which are directed towards producing 'pure' generalizations rather than applications must be harder to design, however; all however; all programmes would find it advantageous to seek support on the grounds that they aimed at laying a foundation for further research. The best one could do would be to ask some independent authority to guess at what an ex post assessment of programme results on the scale of 'basic-ness' would turn out to be, and award support acccordingly.

From the foregoing discussion it should be evident that we do not believe the most useful distinctions to notice between science and technology are the ones most often drawn, namely classifications of research activities according to the intended or realized characteristics of their 'products'. A more promising approach is to be found by focusing, not upon the production of varieties of information, but upon observable differences in the *social ethos* of research, as reflected by researchers' attitudes and actions in regard to the *transmission* of information.

3 INSTITUTIONALIZED DISCLOSURE VERSUS SECRECY

The germ of this alternative classificatory principle certainly is contained, along with the other material we have already sifted, in Price's description of science as having for its chief objective the publication of 'papers', public recordings of discoveries. Price (1967, pp. 10–11), however, did not elaborate upon it much beyond offering the aphoristic observation that scientists 'are highly motivated to publish but not to read', whereas technologists read assiduously but are not motivated to publish. Both the principle of classification, and the source of the suggested difference in researchers' motivation regarding information transmission, deserve to be further developed.

One can only do this by treating research activities and researchers not as atomistic entities, but rather as parts of a larger, *social* construction. For, it is as social constructs that science and technology appear to differ most markedly. Individuals and teams engaging in research based upon 'scientific methods' will spend their time postulating theories, developing models, intended to explain phenomena and predict 'facts' yet to be discovered. When their attention is directed to the natural world, we distinguish them from other generalizers and fact-collectors and affix to them the label of 'natural scientists'. Not all actions in this mode belong to the realm of science. For we conceptualize 'science' as a voluntary collective organization, a community, or club that imposes particular rules upon those who wish to be recognized as participating members.

Some of these rules have to do with acceptable procedures for the statement and testing of theories, and for the form in which predictions are cast. These matters have been much discussed by philosophers and sociologists of science and need not be elaborated here. Instead, we emphasize a crucial additional feature of the 'scientific ethos', which is that scientists act as if they were obligated immediately to disclose all new discoveries and submit them for critical inspection by other members of the community. In other words, the community rules instruct scientists to regard a new theory, or the principles underlying a new piece of equipment, or a newly-observed phenomenon, as a *public good* regardless of the identity of its originator. Thus, in submitting their own findings to their peer group, scientists *qua* scientists surrender their claim to exclusive control of that information. In fact the social criterion is even more stringent: *complete* disclosure is the rule.

In an insightful and important contribution, Jean-Jacques Salomon (1973) argues that it is precisely in this respect that science and technology differ significantly. Scientists hasten to publicize their findings, whereas technologists are more likely to display reticence:

> The channel of science is in principle open, based on criticism by peers, easily and rapidly accessible to all researchers in the specialized literature, while the channel of technology is less available, more subject to the restraints of industrial organization and competition, bound by secrecy or, more simply, by the difficulty of transmitting the subleties of the 'know-how' of processes that depend more on apprenticeship on the job than on the understanding of concepts. (Salomon, 1973, p. 80)

Even when the latter difficulties of transmission have been erased – by the increasing tnedency towards conceptualization and generalization which Brooks (1967) noted in the newly-emerging areas of technological research – the difference in the patterns of institutionally-sanctioned behaviour between the two communities is more than likely to persist.

Let us then draw a sharp distinction between science and technology in regard to the disposition of their respective research findings, and express it in the form of a *social* imperative: if one joins the science club, one's discoveries and inventions must be completely disclosed, whereas in the technology club such findings must not be fully revealed to the rest of the membership. There should be little doubt that this is a caricature, rather than a careful piece of sociology. But a good analytical distinction which points the user in the right direction can afford to be overdrawn. Its defect takes another form: it describes without explaining. For we should by now be asking *why* scientists and technologists persist in displaying such different attitudes towards the disposition of their findings.

4 PUBLIC CONSUMPTION VERSUS PRIVATE CAPITAL

To ask that question is to see almost immediately where an answer can be found. It must lie in the fact that there is a difference in the goals of the social organizations to which they belong. And the only thesis that can explain the phenomena of disclosure and secrecy is that science aims at increasing the stock of knowledge, while the goal of technology is to obtain the private rents that can be earned from this knowledge.[5] Roughly speaking then, science views knowledge as a public consumption good, whereas technology regards it as a private capital good.[6]

The benefits to the scientific community from disclosure are twofold. First, we may note that the existing stock of knowledge is a crucial input in the production of new knowledge. (Among other inputs are the ability and zeal of the investigator!) Disclosure increases the expected span of application in the search for new knowledge. In other words, disclosure raises the social value of new discoveries and inventions by lowering the probability that they will reside with persons and groups who lack the resources required to exploit them. Secondly, disclosure enables peer groups to screen and to evaluate the new finding. The result is a new finding containing a smaller margin of error. The social value to the community of scientists is that scientific users of new discoveries can tolerate a higher degree of risk arising from other sources of incomplete information.

Contrast this with the situation in the community of technologists. If each member is obliged to be concerned with the private rents that can be earned from new discoveries (or new uses of old discoveries – it comes to the same thing), secrecy is precisely what would be practised. It would not matter so much that the discovery has not been screened by fellow-professionals. What matters more is that it proves useful in yielding a privately capturable rent. Disclosure would reduce the private rents to the discoverer because there would then be many people to share the rent with.

But a piece of knowledge can simultaneously be used by any number of people any number of times. Technically speaking it is a public good, that is, there need be no rivalry in its use. It follows that knowledge, once produced, ought to be freely available to all (assuming of course that transmission costs are insignificant).[7] Thus what we are identifying as the common purpose of science is consonant with society's aim. Disclosure in particular is a necessary condition for the effieient use of knowledge. This explains why so much science has throughout been supported by public institutions in centres of learning such as universities.[8] Secrecy and the efficient use of knowledge are inimical.

The difficulty with disclosure, which Arrow (1962) made clear, is that the removal of appropriate 'private' incentives hampers the production of knowledge in a decentralized environment. Society at large may seek to solve this problem by allocating funds for science through public bodies. But what is the guarantee that scientists will not slack? The insititutions of science appear as having been adapted to meet this particular problem at least partially, by nurturing the rule of priority. And somewhere between full disclosure and secrecy there lies another, related incentive mechanism: the institution of patents, which technology often relies upon. In the following section we re-examine these familiar social contrivances.

5 PRIORITY AND PATENTS

The priority rule used by the scientific community to reward its members, serves two purposes at once. First, it establishes a contest for scientific discoveries. Since effort cannot in general be monitored, reward cannot be based upon it. So a scientist is rewarded not for his effort, but for his achievement. An alternative would be a fixed fee, but as one collects the fee whether or not one has produced anything of interest, this dulls the incentive to work hard. Since it is difficult in general to determine how far behind the winner the losers of a scientific race are when discoveries are made, it is not possible to award prizes on rank (Science, unlike tennis tournaments, does not pay the 'runners-up'.) The remaining type of payment scheme that is compatible with individual incentives is the one where the 'winner takes all'. Priority mimics this.[9]

But taken alone, the priority rule places all the risk firmly on the shoulders of the scientist. This cannot be efficient if scientists, like lesser mortals, are risk-averse. So of course scientists must be paid something whether or not they are successful in the races they choose to enter. It is in this light that Arrow's (1962, p. 623) remark, 'the complementarity between teaching and research is, from the point of view of the economy, something of a lucky accident', assumes its full significance.

The second purpose that the rule of priority serves is in eliciting public disclosure of new findings. Priority creates a privately-owned asset – a form of intellectual property – from the very act of relinquishing exclusive possession of the new knowledge. It is truly a remarkable device. In science priority often *is* the prize, for 'moral possession' is thereby awarded to the discoverer even when legal possession is neither possible nor desired by any party (on 'moral possession,' see Medawar, 1982, p. 260). Priority is the basis upon which scientific societies award various tokens of public recognition and it is also the ground for claims to informal recognition of one's accomplishments by one's scientific colleagues. The most prestigious awards are those that are made by scientific bodies possessing the most extensive scope. In particular, the widest possible publication of a research contribution is a prerequisite for claiming the greatest honours that the scientific community can bestow.

We have now at hand an economic rationale for the extraordinary, and otherwise puzzling degree of importance that scientific communities accord to resolving priority disputes among contestants. The rule of priority is a particular form of payment to scientists. It is often a non-pecuniary award. We have noted that it fills two roles, both of which are instrumental in furthering the common purpose of science. It is surely to be expected that scientists, as individuals and as members of collective bodies, will devote great attention to priority disputes.[10]

Compare this form of reward with the one in technology. The rewards of the technologist, *qua* technologist, are linked to the privately appropriated rents from knowledge. The beneficiary of such additions to knowledge – which may or may not have met the test of being additions to scientific knowledge – is presumably willing to pay for them. This creates the possibility of a reward structure that is not linked with priority of discovery. A commercially successful application of a long-accepted scientific principle will typically award the adaptor, not the originator of the theory, even when the adaptor has contributed nothing more than the restatement of the principle in terms that have exposed its commercial relevance.

We have noted that secrecy provides a means of capturing rents from new findings. But secrecy is not completely reliable. Apart from anything else there may be little to prevent rivals from making the same discovery at a later date and sharing the rent. The patent institution of assigning patent protection attempts to remedy this. Patent systems in principle allow people and firms to disclose an addition they have made to the stock of knowledge, without obliging them to share the rents that can be earned from their finding. The system in effect offers a private reward for disclosure and makes the award on the basis of priority of disclosure. The reward itself is tied to the private rents that can be earned from the new knowledge which in turn the patent is intended to help secure. (In contrast, the reward in science may be entirely non-pecuniary.) By connecting the realm of *techne*, through conveyance of a right to exclusive use, with the realm of *episteme*, through the requirement of disclosure, the patent system undertakes to solve the problem of *financing* the pursuit of scientific – that is, publicly-disclosed – knowledge.[11]

The patent system is both interesting and problematic because it represents a conjunction of the distinctive and antithetical mores of science and technology in regard to the treatment of new information. Looking backward it seeks to reward additions to knowledge that are disclosed, and does so on the basis of priority. But to finance the award it looks ahead to a contrived limitation of access to the new knowledge. As a social invention it incorporates the fundamental feature of the reward structure of the scientific community which seeks to create intellectual property from a public good. By leaving the determination of the economic value of that property to the workings of the market, the assignment of patent rights necessarily inhibits the utilization of that public good.

While the patent system itself is a remarkably ingenious social device, economic analysts properly persist in asking whether the social benefits it confers through the encouragement of invention are worth the social costs of creating a private property right whose economic value derives from restricting the use of knowledge which has already been acquired.[12] Moreover, it has been shown that under a wide array of circumstances the device works in a way that elicits too much expenditure of resources in the races among rival research groups to obtain patent-properties which are allocated on the basis of priority (see, for example, Dasgupta and Stiglitz, 1980a, 1980b). The social inefficiency manifests itself in excessive duplication of research effort – leading, on average, to too many of Professor Merton's 'multiples' – or to too fast a pace of advance of the frontiers of knowledge.[13]

More to the immediate point, however, are the imperfections of the patent system which are traceable to the attempt to engage private rent-seeking as a means of eliciting the disclosure of certain kinds of useful knowledge. Here we are laying more stress upon the problem of 'disclosure' than upon the problem of 'utilization' of that which has been disclosed. On the one side, a complete monopoly over the use of the knowledge cannot be conveyed (even for a finite period) by an arrangement which is designed to elicit some significant degree of information disclosure. From the standpoint of the patentor, the instrument appears defective in risking the communication of sufficient information to render alternative, and commercially competitive solutions, less costly to obtain than was the original invention. The original patentee will remain uncompensated for the depreciated value of the patent right in the event of that likelihood being realized.

At some level this failing may be ineluctable, since the mere disclosure that a problem is solvable (that is, that at least one solution has been verified by an independent authority) may serve to channel inventive resources in directions that increase the likelihood that a substitute (or, worse still, a superior solution) will be found. For example, it has been said that research on semiconductors was sufficiently far advanced in many places by the close of 1947 that 'from the mere knowledge that such a thing as a transistor was possible, there were perhaps twenty-five organizations which could have made one' (Braun and MacDonald, 1978, p. 52). The Bell Laboratories group which discovered the point contact transistor in late December of that year, therefore faced a conflict between its perceived need to better understand the transistor for the purposes of filing patent applications, and the interests of the inventors (John Bardeen and William Brattain) in establishing their scientific priority by publishing a paper in the *Physical Review*. Although the first patent application was filed in February 1948, the discovery was kept a close secret within Bell Labs for some seven months, up to the eve of publication of the Bardeen-Brattain paper.[14]

On the other hand, the patent system may permit inventors to advertise in a more credible way their claims to possess useful knowledge, whilst not compelling them fully to divulge it to others. It is a commonplace observation that the research experience leading to a patentable invention generates technical knowledge that is not contained in the patent application itself, but is complementary to it. Such information may be difficult to systematize and costly to transfer to a potential licensee. But when such necessary knowledge can be transmitted readily, the purpose of filing the patent may be less that of seeking to deter imitators than of signalling the availability of trade secrets for sale by the patentor.

A vivid instance of the coupling of patent disclosure with secrecy is contained in Vincenti's (1985) history of the Davis airfoil design. The latter specified the shape of the fore and aft sections of the airplane wing, selected in 1938 for the B-24 bomber built be the Consolidated Aircraft Corporation of San Diego. In 1934 David R. Davis, a lone inventor, had filed a patent ('Fluid Foil') that described a method of generating airfoil sections by using a pair of mathematical equations. The derivation of these equations remained rather mysterious, and the patent itself did not reveal the values of the two constants that would generate an optimum airfoil. On the basis of the superior wind-tunnel performance of a wing model produced in 1937 by the inventor, Consolidated first set one of its engineers to discover the profile by guessing at values for the constants and drawing the corresponding airfoils from the equations of Davis's patent. The Company soon abandoned the attempt as hopeless, and, in February 1938, signed an agreement to pay royalties on a sliding scale if they adopted the Davis airfoil on any Consolidated airplane. In exchange, the inventor supplied the co-ordinates of the airfoil section for the model that had tested so well, and a corresponding pair of parameter values.[15]

The imperfections we have examined in the patent as a device for rewarding disclosures of knowledge are not at all surprising; a stone flung at two birds really ought not be expected to make a clean strike on either.

6 SCIENCE AND TECHNOLOGY – THE PERILOUS BALANCE

The intellectual property that is created once priority has been established derives much of its value from a desire for recognition and esteem. Given the common purpose of science it is clear why, among other things, scientific training is so designed as to arouse this desire in a particularly sharp form. It is true that part of the reward enjoyed by a scientist is the research activity itself. But the pleasure and excitement of conducting research must be comparable in technology since, by our classification, programmes in science and technology can easily entail what from an epistemological perspective is the same course of research.

An alternative source of value of a finding to the discoverer is, as we have noted, the private rent that he can capture from its use through a patent, secrecy and so forth.[16] It would seem then that the value of a scientific reward (through priority) needs to be measured against the prospective economic rents that can be collected by taking one's discovery to the realm of technology. But this would suppose that the investigator, pursuing the method of science, is able freely to decide *after* the discovery whether to disclose it, as in science, or to capture the private rents, as in technology. Such discretion is sometimes open to investigators, but more often organized scientific research projects demand precommitment from their members. If the findings are proprietary and are not to be disclosed publicly, one has a project precommitted to what we have classified as technology. Precommitment to public disclosure is the hallmark of projects organized in the realm of science. An economic basis of choice between alternative commitments on the part of the investigator can be obtained by comparing the expected values of the returns derived under each set of conditions regarding disclosure.

But now consider what would happen if over a period the value of privately appropriable rents from knowledge – or anyhow, certain types of knowledge – increases at a sharp rate. The cost of maintaining the level of resources engaged in science rises as research workers are drawn increasingly to precommit themselves to technology. The economic returns in technology thus affect the state of science. This is hardly surprising and does not need elaboration.

There is, however, a different effect to be considered, one that runs in the opposite direction: from science to technology. The existing pool of knowledge is an essential input in the production of new knowledge. That is why technology draws so heavily upon the infrastructure provided by science. If, to take an extreme example, science were to close down, each enterprise in technology would, roughly speaking, have to rely on its private knowledge pool. This would dampen technological progress enormously, as technological enterprises would then, for the most part, be conducting duplicative research. The public-good-producing aspect of science is, of course, recognized to be of considerable importance to the technological community, which is why, on occasion, one sees groups of technological enterprises spontaneously joining to support activities organized under the rules of science. But the preceding discussion also indicates why this is inadequate and leaves science constantly in need of shoring up. Unless investigators are socially conditioned to be imbued with the scientific spirit, the material rewards offered for participation in technology will draw them away. Science faces a continual struggle to command talent in the face of competition from technology, and the more closely the two research disciplines resemble each other, the more vulnerable science must become.

There is, however, one exceptional feature. Fame and recognition and prizes are not the only possible private returns that one can expect from participation in science. Establishment of priority, which requires disclosure, provides a clear signal about the discoverer's talent, and this typically affects the conditions of a researcher's future employment – including the option of finding employment in technology. A reputation won in science increases the quality of offers the researcher can obtain for entering projects in technology. As a limiting case, entrance into science can be viewed purely as an investment in acquiring the appropriate reputation for subsequent entry into technology.

It follows immediately that in this limiting case – on which we now will concentrate our attention – the attraction that science offers to the eligible researcher is negatively related to (i) the rate of time discount, and (ii) the rate of obsolescence of signals acquired by gaining recognition for achievement in science. If the rate of growth of knowledge is rapid, and if gaining recognition requires some minimum time (for discoveries to be publicized and confirmed and for priority to be ascertained), the risk of obsolescence is high. Other things remaining the same, fewer research workers will be motivated to enter science for the purpose of acquiring a visible signal of their creative capabilities. When the growth rate of scientific knowledge is high, the scientist needs to show not only that he is creative, but also intellectually flexible. In order to demonstrate the latter he has to remain in science and continue to be creative. But this postpones entry into technology!

What this means is that scientific research *programmes* cannot continue to gain cumulative momentum simply by the chance attraction of participants. A programme in its infancy may even display increasing returns to scale, since the risk of obsolescence is then very low. Of course, a more 'progressive' research programme (which, in the sense of Lakatos, 1980, generates more new theories with any given number of participants) can gain adherents because the chance of achieving scientific recognition is higher even though the risk of obsolence is also higher.

The preceding discussion leads us to the somewhat surprising conclusion that science, as a social institution, could be maintained even when no pecuniary prizes are awarded for priority of discovery, and even when people are not motivated by the quest for fame.[17] What it requires is a parallel social organization, called technology, and a capital market for aspiring technologists to borrow from so that they may subsist while making a reputation in science. But we have also noted that if the returns in technology become very high, science is likely to suffer; scientific reputation may be less of an advantage, and individuals' continuing participation in scientific research will be curtailed as they seek to 'cash in' on their past credential-generating investments.

Consider now what happens in science when, for some reason, the rate of entry into it drops. Assuming that people embark on careers in science in the hope of establishing a public record of achievement indicative of their talent (the signal!), the inherently more able will on average acquire their signal sooner and depart for the realism of technology. The only thing that prevents the average level of talent among scientists from falling by this selective exit mechanism is the continuing entry by new cohorts, among whom the talent for research is presumably distributed randomly. When the rate of attraction into science falls, the average talent among scientists also falls. Given the programmes of scientific research, the combined effect of a reduction in the number of participants and a decrease in the average level of talent among them would tend to reduce the flow of new scientific theories. Feed that back into the system we have been describing and the result is depressing. For, if the public knowledge pool becomes stagnant, technology suffers.

We have seen that the science-technology interaction is quasi-stable in the upward direction. If the growth of scientific knowledge rises, the rate of recruitment into science is kept in check as entrants go directly into technology. This implies that while the launching of a new highly-progressive research programme could initiate a science-technology boom, the boom cannot be expected to last even if the programme's potential for generating new theories remained undiminished. But things are alarmingly unstable in the downwards direction. Should the exhaustion of the previously progressive programme of scientific research diminish the flow of new theories, causing a displacement of the system downwards, the whole process appears to slide to some low level equilibrium. Along that dismal path both science and technology appear less and less economically attractive in comparison with other fields of human endeavour until, presumably, enterprises engaged in technology find it worth while to finance research projects committed to public disclosure and so stabilize the system at some much lower level.

The implications of this are serious. It suggests that the growing dependence of modern economic growth upon the science-technology nexus has made the stability of this growth at acceptably high levels a hostage of what we would think are some quite extraneous features of the cultural and political environment. It is the taste for the lifestyle of academic science, the compatibility of research with teaching, and the persistence of public authorities in subsidizing science at a level to which none of the constituents would willingly subscribe, that prevents the collapse of the economic structure erected upon a high level of scientific activity. If the support is removed, the effects in our view would be quite disastrous.

Of course, the spontaneous appearance of a new programme of scientific research could initiate a boom. The point though is that the waiting time between such occurrences will be lengthened if the resources commanded by science are allowed to settle at their low level equilibrium. Modern economic growth under those conditions would continue to be grounded in the exploitation of scientific knowledge, but it would lose the sustained character that has been taken by many to distinguish it fundamentally from the process of economic change in earlier epochs.

NOTES

1. A formal demonstration of the fact that this implies a non-convexity in the value of information under a wide class of circumstances is provided by the first example in Wilson (1975).
2. Why this happened is less than obvious. An explanation is perhaps to be found in the fact that Arrow's 1962 paper was really a pair of essays packaged as one. The first part examined information as a commodity and inquired what economic theory has to say about its production and allocation in a decentralized, free enterprise system. The second part analyzed the effect of market structure upon the incentive to produce a cost-reducing invention, under conditions in which the structure of the market would not affect the inventor's ability to appropriate the benefits. The economics profession took longer to absorb the full implications of the first part of Arrow's essay, so that its second part for a time exercised the greater influence upon the literature – specifically, the literature devoted to studying the relationship of invention and innovation to the structure of markets.

   This was a minor misfortune in itself. The mathematically formalized analysis in the essay's second part succeded in fixing theoretical attention upon the way incentives for R&D investment were affected by the structure of product markets. Without explicitly addressing the suggestion by Schumpeter that an existing monopoly position was an ideal platform for undertaking innovation, Arrow showed that 'preinvention monopoly profits' *per se* constituted a comparative disincentive to invent.

The conclusion Arrow, (1962, p. 622) drew was that 'the only ground for arguing that monopoly may create superior incentives to invent is that appropriability may be greater under monopoly than under competition'. Arrow's restatement of Schumpeter's hypothesis in these terms, stressing the possible appropriability effects of monopoly power, appeared as the natural adjunct to the main message that economists took from the essay as a whole: incomplete appropriability of the benefits of research and invention would result in the provision under a competitive system of a less-than-socially optimal allocation of resources for such activities. The theoretical contribution made in the second part thereby perpetuated the Schumpeterian tradition in which, by and large, the reciprocal influences of R&D performance upon market structure were ignored (see Scherer, 1984, especially pp. 59–65, 170–206, on research in this vein; Dasgupta and Stiglitz, 1980a, 1980b, for treatment of market structure as endogenous). Dasgupta (1985) elaborates further upon these points.

3. We are not defending this treatment, merely stating it as a fact.
4. Witness the fact that university science departments continually produce doctorates in science on an average of five to six years of graduate studies with little by way of variance.
5. We are ignoring important aggregation problems here. Of course, there are different *types* of knowledge. Nothing of importance is lost by our ignoring this issue at this point.
6. By this we do not mean that science is not interested in applications. Nor that it is interested exclusively in knowledge for the sake of knowledge. Scientists regularly investigate phenomena with a view to applications. But science insists on the publicity of knowledge and is ultimately concerned with knowledge and its applications as consumption goods.
7. It does not follow that all ought to be trained to use the knowledge, since training involves costs.
8. That the monastic tradition in the West contributed greatly to the methodology of the 'new science' of the seventeenth century is well known. An important feature was the tradition of reproducing ancient texts and checking their accuracy. This established an association between the open transfer of knowledge and the contents of both ancient and Arabic manuscripts, which were the sources of such theoretical science as the medieval world inherited. One should note that the financial support of the monk-copyists within an institution that was in turn supported by the economic surplus of a rural society required dispersion of the repositories of knowledge. The tradition of open exchange of texts was important in widening the community of scholars and assisting their labours. We would argue that the financial support of the Church was important for the establishment of the rule of disclosure. Other social groups, such as the Sanskrit scholars of classical India, tended to be less generous in sharing their knowledge. These scholars were, generally speaking, obliged to provide for their own support by acquiring pupils and by performing religious rites.
9. We are discussing an intricate matter in a rough and ready way here. There are complicated reward systems that can be devised under the incomplete information we have implicitly postulated in the text. The

problem at hand is one that combines adverse selection (how does one ensure that the right people undertake the research?) with moral hazard (how can one guarantee that the scientists will not slack?) The problem of incentive compatibility has been much discussed in the recent economics literature.

10. Contrast this with the sociopsychological explanation offered by Robert Merton: 'scientific *knowledge* is not the richer or the poorer for having credit given where credit is due: it is the social *institution* of science and individual men of science that would suffer from repeated failures to allocate credit justly' (Merton, 1957, p. 648). On the history of the priority rule see Boorstin (1984, chapter 53). On Merton's 'multiples'; that is, the more or less simultaneous discovery of a phenomenon (or a theorem) by more than one research unit, see Merton (1973).
11. It is not unusual to think of patents as belonging to the realm of *techne*, not least because English and American patent laws, as forerunners of modern patent laws elsewhere, made it impossible to patent a 'fact of nature'. This might suggest that a useful distinction between technology and science is to be found in whether the knowledge is patentable. The problem is that it is not self-evident what is a fact of nature. This was made clear in the recent litigation over the Stanford and the University of California (Berkeley) patents on recombinant DNA.
12. Arrow (1962, p. 617), phrased the problem this way:

    > In a free enterprise economy, inventive activity is supported by using the invention to create property rights; precisely to the extent that it is successful, there is an underutilization of the information. The property right may be in the information itself, through patents and similar legal devices, or in the intangible assets of the firm if the information is retained by the firm and used only to increase its profits.

    For more recent, empirical evaluations, see Taylor and Silberston (1973); Mansfield *et al.* (1982), chapter 7 and references therein.
13. See also Dasgupta and Maskin (1985). We should add that this can be the case in science as well, provided that the reward to the discoverer under the priority rule is tempting enough.
14. J. Bardeen and W. H. Brattain (1948), 'The transistor, a semiconductor triode', *Physical Review*, (15 July) pp. 230–1, acknowledged the help of William Shockley and others at Bell Laboratories. See Braun and MacDonald (1978, pp. 41–51) for this account, much of which draws on personal interviews. Nelson's (1962) account, written closer to the events and more from a Bell Laboratories' viewpoint, dwells upon the creative 'link between science and invention' and glosses over the tensions between them.
15. The B-24 went on to become one of the most successful Second World War bombers; 19 000 of them had been built when production was terminated in 1945 – more than any other bomber designed in history. Vincenti (1985, n. 37), notes that although Davis signed an agreement with the Government in 1943 limiting his royalties on Davis-Wing aircraft bought by the US, after the War he sued the US for additional payments

on their sales of war-surplus B-24s to private buyers. The Court of Claims, ruling in favour of the Government's refusal of these further royalties, declared the original patent to have been invalid because it required experimentation with the values of the constants to be used in the equations. Davis's right to retain the royalties he had previously received, however, does not appear to have been challenged; it seems doubtful that his patent would have been contested had he not sued the US.

16. Patents are a means of obtaining both fame (through public disclosure) and fortune (through monopoly rents), but they are often an unreliable means for the latter, since rivals frequently invent around patents.
17. There is in fact a particular set of circumstances where scientific knowledge, as we have defined it here, is capable of generating economic rents. This is when the knowledge in question is complementary in production with some resource that has been monopolised. The rents derived by owners of mineral resources from scientific advances in geology and organic chemistry are a case in point, where owners of resources will clearly pay for scientific theories. In a well-known article Hirshleifer (1971) recalls that Eli Whitney, the inventor of the cotton gin, died a pauper because of his inability to establish a patent. He then remarks that Whitney could have avoided this fate had he purchased large tracts of land in South Carolina prior to announcing his invention.

REFERENCES

Arrow, K. J. (1962) 'Economic Welfare and the Allocation of Resources for Inventions', in R. R. Nelson (ed.) *The Rate and Direction of Inventive Activity: Economic and Social Factors* (Priceton: Princeton University Press).

Boorstin, D. (1984) *The Discoverers: A History of Man's Search to Know His World and Himself* (New York: Random House).

Braun, E. and S. MacDonald (1978) *Revolution in Miniature: The History and Impact of Semiconductor Electronics* (Cambridge: Cambridge University Press).

Brooks, H. (1967) 'Applied Research: Definitions, Concepts, Themes', in US Congress, House Committee on Science and Astronautics, Subcommittee on Science, Research and Development, *Applied Science and Technological Progress* (Washington, DC: USGPO).

Dasgupta, P. (1985) 'The Theory of Technological Competition', in J. Stiglitz and F. Mathewson (eds) *New Developments in the Theory of Market Structure* (London: Macmillan Press) and (Cambridge, Mass.: MIT Press).

Dasgupta, P. and E. Maskin (1985) 'The Economics of R and D Portfolios' mimeo. (Faculty of Economics, University of Cambridge).

Dasgupta, P. and J. Stiglitz (1980a) 'Industrial Structure and the Nature of Innovative Activity', *Economic Journal*, 90: 266–93.

Dasgupta, P. and J. Stiglitz (1980b) 'Uncertainty, Industrial Structure and the Speed of R and D', *Bell Journal of Economics*, 11: 1–28.

Hirshleifer, J. (1971) 'The Private and Social Value of Information and the Reward for Inventive Activity', *American Economic Review*, 61: 561–74.

Klein, B. H. (1962) 'The Decision Making Problem in Development', in R. R. Nelson (ed.) *The Rate and Direction of Inventive Activity: Economic and Social Factors* (Princeton: Princeton University Press).

Kuhn, T. (1962) *The Structure of Scientific Revolutions* (Chicago: University of Chicago Press).

Lakatos, I. (1980), in J. Worrall and G. Currie (eds) *The Methodology of Scientific Research Programmes: Philosophical Papers*, Vol. 1, (Cambridge: Cambridge University Press).

Levin, R. (1982) 'The Semiconductor Industry', in R. R. Nelson (ed.) *Government and Technical Progress: A Cross-Industry Analysis* (New York: Pergamon Press).

Mansfield, E. *et al.* (1982) *Technology Transfer, Productivity, and Economic Policy* (New York: Norton).

Medawar, S. (1982) *Plato's Republic* (Oxford: Oxford University Press).

Merton, R. K. (1957) 'Priorities in Scientific Discovery', *American Sociological Review*, 22: 635–59.

Merton, R. K. (1973) in N. W. Starer (ed.) *The Sociology of Science: Theoretical and Empirical Investigation* (Chicago: University of Chicago Press).

Mowery, D. (1983) 'Economic Theory and Government Technology Policy', *Policy Sciences*, 16: 27–43.

Nelson, R. R. (1962) 'The Link Between Science and Invention: The Case of the Transistor', in R. R. Nelson (ed.) *The Rate and Direction of Inventive Activity: Economic and Social Factors* (A Conference of the Universities' National Bureau Committee for Economic Research) (Princeton: Princeton University Press) pp. 549–83.

Price, D. J. de S. (1967) 'Research on Research', in D. L. Arm (ed.) *Journeys in Science: Small Steps–Great Strides*, (Albuquerque: University of New Mexico Press).

Rosenberg, N. (1982), *Inside the Black Box: Technology and Economics* (New York: Cambridge University Press) (especially chapter 7–'How Exogenous is Science?').

Salomon, J. -J. (1973) *Science and Politics*, translated by N. Lindsay (London: Macmillan Press).

Scherer, F. M. (1984) *Innovation and Growth: Schumpeterian Perspectives* (Cambridge, Mass.: MIT Press).

Taylor, C. and Z. A. Silberston (1973) *The Economic Impact of the Patent System* (Cambridge: Cambridge University Press).

Vincenti, W. G. (1985) 'The Davis Wing and the Problem of Airfoil Design: Uncertainty and Growth in Engineering Knowledge', unpublished manuscript, Stanford University School of Engineering (Winter).

Wilson, R. (1975) 'Informational Economics of Scale', *Bell Journal of Economics*, 6: 184–95.

PART IV
Decision-making under Uncertainty

17 Von Neumann–Morgenstern Utilities, Risk Taking, and Welfare

John C. Harsanyi*

1 INTRODUCTION

Von Neumann and Morgenstern (1953, p. 28) have made it very clear that their utility theory *disregards* the utility (or the disutility) of the act of *gambling* itself. It seems to me that the utility functions defined by their theory have often been misinterpreted by paying insufficient attention to this fact. The purpose of this paper is to suggest a more adequate interpretation of von Neumann-Morgenstern (vNM) utility functions.

There is now an impressive amount of empirical evidence to show that in their choice behaviour many people violate the rationality axioms of the vNM theory in various ways. But, of course, this must be seen in proper perspective: the other rationality postulates of economic theory, including such fundamental ones as transitivity and extensionality,[1] are likewise commonly violated by experimental subjects (see, for example, Tversky and Kahneman, 1981; Arrow, 1982.)

Yet, these findings do raise two related, but essentially different, questions. One is how far we can rely on the *predictive* validity, or at least the *approximate* predictive validity, of economic models, based on the assumption that people's behaviour will conform to the vNM axioms, and to the other rationality axioms of economic theory. The other question is how much validity these axioms really have even as *normative* rationality requirements.

These are two logically independent questions. For even if a given set of axioms represents very convincing normative rationality requirements, most of us may very well find that we have no spontaneous natural inclination to act in accordance with these axioms. Thus, it is

*I want to express my gratitude to Ken Arrow for all the intellectual stimulation I received from him before I became, while I was, and after I had been his student at Stanford University in 1956–8. I also want to express my thanks to the National Science Foundation for supporting this research through grant SES-8218938 to the Center for Research in Management, University of California, Berkeley.

quite possible that the vNM axioms are perfectly valid rationality postulates for decisions involving risk; yet that natural selection has failed to equip us with an instinctive propensity to conform to these axioms without special effort. After all, our prehuman ancestors and even most of our human ancestors never had to face the problem of how to make a rational choice between two alternatives one or both of which may be rather complicated lotteries; and they presumably suffered no disadvantage in natural selection by being somewhat deficient in this particular skill.

I propose to argue that:

1. Even though the vNM axioms apparently do not have full *predictive* validity about people's actual behaviour, they do have full *normative* validity as rationality requirements under suitable conditions.
2. More specifically, their normative validity is *restricted* to situations where people have compelling prudential and/or moral reasons to take a strictly *outcome-oriented* point of view, that is, to be guided by the utilities and disutilities they assign to the various possible outcomes, which I will call their *outcome utilities*; and to neglect the utilities and disutilities they might derive from the process of gambling itself, which I will call their *process utilities*.
3. Consequently, people's vNM utility functions represent only their utilities for the various possible outcomes and completely exclude their utilities for gambling as such.
4. Yet, this means that the widely accepted assumption that people's vNM utility functions express their *attitudes toward gambling* is true only in a very limited sense. These utility functions express only their *instrumental* attitudes toward gambling, that is, their willingness to gamble as determined by the intensity of their desires to achieve or to avoid various possible outcomes (and as indicated, for example, by the extent to which they have decreasing or increasing marginal utilities for money). But these utility functions do not in any way express people's *intrinsic* attitudes towards gambling, that is, their intrinsic like or dislike for the process of gambling itself.
5. It has often been suggested that vNM utility functions have no place in *welfare economics* and in *ethics* because they merely indicate people's attitudes toward gambling, and these have no genuine moral significance (Arrow, 1951, p. 10; Rawls, 1971, pp. 172, 323). I will argue that this suggestion would be valid only if these vNM utility functions indicated people's *intrinsic* attitudes toward gambling, which is, however, not the case. In actual fact, people's vNM

utility functions are an important piece of information for welfare economics and ethics because they are natural measures for the *intensity* of people's desires, preferences, and wants.

2 THE AXIOMS

I will distinguish between *pure* and *mixed* alternatives. The former do not, whereas the latter do, involve risk or uncertainty. Mixed alternatives will also be called *lotteries*.

$A\rho B$ will mean that A is *non-strictly preferred* to B by the decision-maker under discussion. If both $A\rho B$ and $B\rho A$, then we will say that A and B are *indifferent* or *equivalent*, and I will write $A \sim B$.

Let L be a lottery yielding alternative A_i as outcome (that is, as prize) if event e_i occurs ($i=1, \ldots, n$). Then I will write

$$L=(A_1/e_1; \ldots; A_n/e_n). \tag{1}$$

The events $e_1, \ldots, e_n$ will be called *conditioning events*. It will be assumed that they are mutually exclusive and exhaust all possibilities.[2] If lottery L' can be obtained from lottery L by *permuting* the outcomes and the conditioning events, yet by still associating each possible outcome A_i with the *same* conditioning event e_i as in L, then the two lotteries will be regarded as identical.

Suppose the decision-maker *knows* (or thinks he knows) the objective probabilities $p_1, \ldots, p_n$ associated with the conditioning events $e_1, \ldots, e_n$. Then L will be called a *risky* lottery, and will be written as

$$L=(A_1, p_1; \ldots; A_n, p_n). \tag{2}$$

Of course, these probabilities must satisfy:

$$p_i \geqslant 0 \text{ for } i=1, \ldots, n; \text{ and } \sum_{i=1}^{n} p_i = 1. \tag{3}$$

If a given lottery L concentrates *all* probability weight on *one* particular alternative A_i, then it will be identified with this latter alternative. Accordingly, any pure alternative A_i will be regarded as a (degenerate) lottery.

A lottery will be called an *uncertain* lottery if the objective probabilities associated with some or all conditioning events are *unknown* to the decision-maker (or are simply undefined). As the vNM theory is restricted to choices among risky lotteries, so will be my own discussion in this paper.

Let L be any risky lottery as described by (3). Suppose that a given utility function U has the property that, for any such lottery L, it defines the utility $U(L)$ of this lottery as being equal to its *expected utility*, so that

$$U(L)=\sum_{i=1}^{n} p_i U(A_i). \tag{4}$$

Then, we will say that U has the *expected-utility property*. Any utility function with this property will be called a *von Neumann-Morgenstern utility function*.

As is well known, von Neumann and Morgenstern's original axioms include propositions that essentially restate the axioms of probability theory. Of course, we can greatly simplify their axioms if we omit such propositions and instead treat the results of probability theory as part of our background knowledge that we can freely use in our mathematical proofs. If we are willing to do this, then we need only four axioms:

Axiom 1 (*complete pre-ordering*). Over the set X of all risky lotteries, non-strict preference is a complete pre-ordering (that is, it is a transitive and complete relation).

Axiom 2 (*continuity*). Suppose that $A\rho B\rho C$. Then there exists a probability number p such that

$$B \sim (A,p;\ C,1-p). \tag{5}$$

Axiom 3 (*the sure-thing principle*). Suppose that $A\rho A^*$. Then, for any possible alternative B, and for any possible probability p, if we set

$$L=(A,p;\ B,1-p) \text{ and } L^*=(A^*,p;\ B,1-p), \tag{6}$$

we must have

$$L\rho L^*. \tag{7}$$

Axiom 4 (*probabilistic equivalence*). Suppose that

$$L=(A_1|e_1;\ldots;\ A_n|e_n) \tag{8}$$

and

$$L' = (A_1 | f_1; \ldots ; A_n | f_n); \tag{9}$$

and suppose that the decision maker *knows* that the objective probabilities characterizing the two lotteries satisfy:

$$Prob(e_i) = Prob(f_i) = p_i \text{ for } i = 1, \ldots, n. \tag{10}$$

Then for him or for her,[3] we must have

$$L \sim L'. \tag{11}$$

In other words, two lotteries yielding the same outcomes $A_1, \ldots, A_n$ with the same probabilities $p_1, \ldots, p_n$ are equivalent – even if they generate these probabilities with very *different* physical processes. (Thus, for instance, a one-stage lottery is equivalent to a two-stage lottery if they both yield the same final outcomes with the same final probabilities.) It is easy to verify that we can derive the original vNM axioms from the above four axioms and from the rules of the probability calculus. Consequently we can state:

Theorem. If a given person's choice behaviour is consistent with Axioms 1 to 4, then he or she will possess a vNM utility function.

3 NEED FOR AN OUTCOME-ORIENTED POSITION

Now I propose to consider the normative validity of our four axioms.

To start with Axiom 1 (complete pre-ordering), this is a rather non-controversial rationality axiom used in every branch of economic theory. On the other hand, Axiom 2 (continuity) is not really a rationality axiom at all, but rather is a convenient regularity assumption.

We do need some version of this continuity axiom in order to ensure the existence of a *scalar-valued* vNM utility function. Yet, if we drop this axiom, but retain the remaining three axioms, then we can still prove the existence of a utility indicator possessing the expected-utility property. But, in general, this utility indicator will be *vector-valued*, with two or more lexicographically ordered components (Hausner, 1954).

Thus, the question of how much normative validity the vNM axioms have essentially boils down to the question of how much normative validity our Axioms 3 and 4 possess. To answer this question, for any person who has to choose among alternative lotteries, I propose to distinguish between his *outcome utilities* and his *process utilities*. The former are the (positive, negative, or zero) utilities he assigns to the alternative *outcomes* of the various lotteries; whereas the latter are the (positive, negative, or zero) utilities he assigns to the process of gambling itself and, in particular, to the *psychological experiences* associated with gambling, such as the nervous tension he is likely to feel; the joy, the feeling of success, the self-satisfaction, and possibly the social admiration, he is likely to experience with a favourable outcome; and the sorrow, the regret, the self-reproach, and possibly the social criticism, he is likely to experience with an unfavourable outcome. Note that what I propose to call process utilities were called the *utility* (or disutility) *of gambling* by von Neumann and Morgenstern (1953). I will say that a given person takes a strictly *outcome-oriented* position if in his choice behaviour he is guided entirely by his outcome utilities, without paying any attention to his process utilities. I will argue below (Section 4) that when people are making important decisions, they will often have very compelling reasons, both prudential and ethical, for taking such an outcome-oriented position.

I now submit that both Axioms 3 and 4 are *essential rationality requirements* – but only for people who take such a strictly outcome-oriented position.

In the case of Axiom 4 (probabilistic equivalence) this is rather obvious. If a person is interested only in the final outcomes of his alternative actions, then he must surely be indifferent between lotteries yielding the same possible prizes with the same probabilities, even if the two lotteries use quite different physical processes to produce these probabilities. No doubt, some people do violate this axiom. For instance, they may prefer to bet on the outcomes of their favourite roulette wheel rather than on those of another roulette wheel. Yet, unless they have reasons to think that the two roulette wheels have a different statistical behaviour, such a preference can be regarded only as irrational.

Reflection will show that Axiom 3 (the sure-thing principle) is likewise an essential rationality requirement for any person taking a strictly outcome-oriented attitude. Yet, since this point has been questioned by Allais (1953 and many subsequent papers) and by his followers, I propose to argue this in some detail.

As will be recalled, Axiom 3 asserts that a rational person who has the preference ApA^* must also have the preference LpL^*. That is to say, a person who entertains ApA^* cannot rationally refuse to exchange a participation in lottery L^* for a participation in lottery L. Yet, this follows from the fact that by exchanging L^* for L he will merely exchange a given probability of winning A^* for the same probability of winning A; and this he *cannot rationally refuse* to do because, given his preference ApA^*, he would certainly be *willing to exchange* prize A^* for prize A in case he participated in lottery L^* and happened to win this prize A^*. Rationally, it *cannot make any difference* to him whether he would exchange A^* for A only after winning A^* in lottery L^*, or whether he would exchange the entire lottery L^* for lottery L. (For similar reasoning, see Arrow's brief discussion of the Allais paradox in Arrow, 1983, pp. 9–10.)

On the other hand, for a person who does *not* take a strictly outcome-oriented position, and who does pay attention to the *process utilities* associated with gambling, Axioms 3 and 4 in general will have *no* normative validity. This is quite obvious in the case of Axiom 4 (probabilistic equivalence). Suppose that L is a one-stage lottery, whereas L' is a two-stage lottery yielding the same prizes with the same probabilities as L would do. Then, we cannot reasonably expect that a person who was interested in the process utilities associated with gambling should be indifferent between L and L', as Axiom 4 would require. For L, being a one-stage lottery, will generate only *one* period of nervous tension in waiting for the actual outcome; while L', being a two-stage lottery, will typically generate *two* such periods of nervous tension. Thus, even though L and L' will yield the same *outcome utilities* with the same probabilities, they are very likely to yield very different *process utilities*. People who tend to assign a higher utility to a lottery involving only *one* period of nervous tension than to one involving *two* such periods will rationally prefer L over L'; whereas people whose process utilities are shaped the opposite way will rationally prefer L' over L. (Of course, the psychological experiences associated with L and with L' may differ also in many respects other than the time pattern of nervous tension they generate. These differences may produce further differences in the process utilities generated by these two lotteries.)

Yet, once Axiom 4 loses its normative force, so also does Axiom 3 (the sure-thing principle). I have argued that, for a person disregarding all process utilities, ApA^* must rationally imply LpL^*. But this is no longer true for a person who does pay attention to his process utilities. For example, suppose that A is a lottery ticket while A^* is a pure alternative. Then, lottery L will become a two-stage lottery. Therefore, a person who dislikes two-stage lotteries may very well prefer the one-stage lottery L^* to this two-stage lottery L – even if he does prefer alternative A to the one-stage lottery A^*.

To put it differently, once process utilities are taken into account, the total utility of a one-stage lottery like A may *change* when it is embedded in a two-stage lottery like L, because this may change the process utilities associated with it.

4 PRUDENTIAL AND MORAL REASONS FOR AN OUTCOME-ORIENTED POSITION

It is clear that von Neumann and Morgenstern (1953, p. 28) fully realized that their axioms implicitly assumed that what they called the *utility of gambling*, and what I propose to call *process utilities*, were absent or had only a negligible significance. But they apparently considered this to be merely a provisional simplifying assumption without intrinsic merit, one to be dropped when suitable less restrictive axioms had been devised. Yet, I propose to argue that, under certain conditions, this no-process-utilities assumption does have a clear normative justification. More particularly, when people make really *important decisions*, they will often have compelling reasons, both prudential and moral reasons, to *disregard* their process utilities and to take a strictly outcome-oriented attitude.

Of course, without special reasons to the contrary, a reasonable person will pay attention to *all* utilities associated with his actions, including both his outcome utilities and his process utilities. In fact, when people engage in gambling for *entertainment*, the process utilities they expect to experience may play an essential role. No doubt, recreational gambling is undertaken partly in the hope of winning money; but, in most cases, an enjoyment of the process of gambling itself will also be a major consideration.

On the other hand, in making *very important* risky decisions with very high stakes, many people will feel that as a matter of *prudence* they should make an all-out effort to obtain the best possible *outcomes* – rather than be side-tracked by the psychological experiences and the resulting positive or negative process utilities associated with the process of risk taking itself.[4] Thus, in choosing between different jobs or different investments, we often feel, in retrospect, that we were unreasonably *bold* or were unreasonably *timid*, that is, we made the wrong decision by undue attention to our process utilities. Indeed, if people's decisions are likely to affect also the important interests of *other people* for whose well-being they feel morally responsible, they will also have compelling *moral* reasons to strive for the best possible outcomes, rather than being concerned with their own process utilities. This moral principle applies with particular force to people in leadership positions, such as public officials, business executives, and officials of important social organizations. When they make a risky decision, they are gambling primarily with other people's lives, money, and other vital interests. Surely, their only morally admissible objective will be to achieve the best possible *results* for their constituents, quite independently of whether they personally derive positive or negative utilities from the act of gambling itself.

5 THE ECONOMIC MEANING OF VON NEUMANN–MORGENSTERN UTILITY FUNCTIONS

People's vNM utility functions represent their choice behaviour in situations where they act in conformity with the vNM rationality axioms and, therefore, in situations where they take a strictly *outcome-oriented* position. Consequently, these utility functions can take account only of people's *outcome utilities*, and must completely exclude their *process utilities*, that is, their utility or disutility for the process of gambling itself. Accordingly, the commonly accepted statement that a person's vNM utility function basically expresses his *attitude* toward *risk taking*, that is, toward *gambling*, can be true only in a very limited sense.

Suppose Mr A buys for $10 a lottery ticket giving him a 1/1000 chance of winning $1000, even though the actuarial value of this ticket is of course only $1. There will be two possible explanations for this action of his. One is that it was a purely *instrumental* action. Mr A may really not take any pleasure in gambling at all. But his desire for a sum of $1000 is *very strong* – at least *as compared* with the strength of his desire not to lose the $10.

Instead of talking about the relative strengths (relative intensities) of Mr A's various desires, we could state essentially the same explanation also in terms of the *relative importance* he assigns to his various goals. One of his goals is to win $1000. Another is, of course, not to lose $10. But the *relative importance* he assigns to the first goal is *so high* as compared with the relative importance he assigns to the second that he considers a 1/1000 chance of obtaining his first goal preferable over obtaining his second goal. Mr A's vNM utilities can be regarded essentially as *mathematical measures* for the *relative importance* he assigns to his various goals—or, equivalently, for the *relative intensities* of his various desires, preferences, or wants. In fact, the intuitive argument of the last paragraph can be directly translated into the language of vNM utilities.

Let U denote Mr A's vNM utility function. Then, what his behaviour shows is that

$$U(\$10) \leqslant \frac{1}{1000} U(\$1000),$$

that is, that $U(\$1000)/U(\$10) \geqslant 1000$. This in turn must mean that his utility function must have at least one interval of *increasing marginal utility* for money between \$10 and \$1000.

The other possible explanation for Mr A's behaviour is of course that he takes an *intrinsic pleasure* in gambling. (Obviously, we could also combine these two explanations in various ways.) Note that the second explanation would make essential use of Mr. A's process utilities. Clearly, if we want an explanation that can be stated in terms of his vNM utility function, then we must rely solely on the first explanation.

More generally, in talking about a person's attitude toward risk taking, we must distinguish between his *instrumental attitude* and his *intrinsic attitude* toward risk. The former is his attitude toward risk as far as it is determined by his outcome utilities; whereas the latter is his attitude toward risk as far as it is *not* determined by his outcome utilities, but rather is determined by his process utilities, that is, by his *intrinsic pleasure or displeasure* in the process of gambling itself. Given the fact that a person's vNM utility function reflects only his outcome utilities, it cannot possibly tell us anything about his *intrinsic attitude* toward risk; it can only tell us about his *instrumental attitude* toward risk taking.

Therefore, it seems to me that it is rather *misleading* to describe vNM utility functions as being primarily expressions of people's attitude toward risk taking or gambling. First of all, they do not in any way express people's *intrinsic attitude* toward gambling, that is, their intrinsic like or dislike for gambling. To be sure, they do express their purely *instrumental willingness* to gamble. In fact, we always estimate a person's vNM utility function by observing his instrumental attitude toward gambling as indicated by his choices between a pure alternative and a lottery, or between two different lotteries. But his vNM utility function does much more than *express* his instrumental attitude toward gambling: it also *explains* this attitude. Thus, in our example, Mr. A's vNM utility function not only *expresses* the fact that he is willing to pay \$10 for a 1/1000 chance of winning \$1000. It also *explains* this willingness of his by the high value of the utility ratio $U(\$1000)/U(\$10)$, indicating the relative *intensities* of his desires for \$1000 and for \$10 or, equivalently, the relative *importance* to him of these two amounts of money.

6 COMPLEMENTARITY, SUBSTITUTION, AND VON NEUMANN–MORGENSTERN UTILITIES

Von Neumann and Morgenstern have introduced what we now call vNM utility functions as analytical tools in the theory of risk taking. But once these utility functions are available to us, they can be used for many other purposes as well. One way they can be used is for providing *much simpler definitions* than the customary Hicks-Allen definitions for complementarity and substitution relationships between commodities (Hicks, 1939).

Let U be a person's vNM utility function, and let A and B be two commodities. It is natural to say that A and B will be *complements* for him if

$$U(A\&B) > U(A) + U(B), \tag{12}$$

where $U(A)$ and $U(B)$ are the *separate* utilities he obtains by consuming only A or only B, whereas $U(A\&B)$ is the *joint utility* of the two commodities if he can consume the two together. Likewise, A and B will be *substitutes* if

$$U(A\&B) < U(A) + U(B), \tag{13}$$

and they will be *independent* commodities if in (12) and (13) we can replace the inequality signs by an equality sign. These definitions will permit us to go one small step further in *explaining* people's instrumental attitudes toward risk taking. As is well known, any person, who conforms to the vNM axioms and, therefore, has a well-defined vNM utility function, will be more willing to take risks the more concave (or the less convex) his vNM utility function for money is in the relevant range. In other words, he will be more willing to take risks the more his vNM utility function shows *increasing*, rather than *decreasing*, marginal utility for money.

It is commonly assumed that, in most people's vNM utility functions for money, intervals of decreasing marginal utility predominate; whereas intervals of increasing marginal utility are less frequent and are of limited length. In terms of (12) and (13), the explanation may be that, as most economists would agree, most commodities are *substitutes* (typically rather weak substitutes) for each other. Complementarity is a much rarer occurrence. Yet, ranges of increasing marginal utility are likely to arise where important *complementarity* relations hold among the commodities consumed by the relevant individual.

Note that, from this point of view, *indivisibilities* must be considered to be special cases of complementarity; they are based on the fact that the various components of a commodity unit can be regarded as complementary goods, whose joint utility often greatly exceeds the sum of their separate utilities.

For example, even a person who takes no intrinsic pleasure in gambling may buy a lottery ticket at a price far in excess of its actuarial value if he badly needs a car but has no money to buy it: he can reasonably invest a small amount of money, the loss of which would not matter too much to him, in order to obtain at least a small chance of winning enough money to buy a car. (For a similar use of cardinal utilities in defining substitution and complementarity, see Hagen, 1984.)

7 CONCLUSION: VON NEUMANN–MORGENSTERN UTILITY FUNCTIONS IN WELFARE ECONOMICS AND IN ETHICS

It has been claimed that vNM utility functions have no legitimate use in welfare economics and in ethics because they merely express people's attitudes toward gambling, which are morally irrelevant (Arrow, 1951, p. 10; Rawls, 1971, pp. 172, 323). In contrast, I have argued that a person's vNM utility function does not express his *intrinsic attitude* toward gambling at all, in the sense of expressing his personal like or dislike for gambling as such. It expresses only his *instrumental attitude* toward gambling, that is, his willingness or unwillingness to gamble for the sake of the prizes he may win. In fact, it does more than *express* this latter attitude; it also *explains* it in terms of the relative importance this person assigns to his alternative goals or, equivalently, in terms of the relative *intensities* of his various desires, preferences, and wants.

Accordingly, a person's vNM utility function is an important piece of information for welfare economics and ethics because it provides a direct measure for the intensity of his desires for alternative benefits. Indeed, if *interpersonal comparisons* between different people's vNM utilities are permitted, then we can compare also the intensity of *different people's* desires for various benefits by means of their vNM utility functions. Yet, this is surely not morally irrelevant information. If two otherwise equally qualified people compete for university admission, it will not be irrelevant information that one of them has been so keen on obtaining higher education that he has risked his life by illegally crossing a well-guarded border in order to obtain such education, whereas the other would never take such risks.[5]

To sum up, the statement that von Neumann–Morgenstern utility functions are indicators of people's attitudes toward gambling is in need of careful qualifications; and when the proper qualifications are added, then the usual objections to using these utility functions in welfare economics and in ethics lose their logical foundation.[6]

NOTES

1. Following Arrow (1982), by extensionality I mean the assumption that people's choice behaviour will not depend on how the alternatives available are described to them, as long as the different descriptions are logically equivalent. Thus, it should not matter whether a given glass is described to them as being 'half full' or as being 'half empty'. In actual fact, the description used often *does* make a lot of difference.
2. For simplicity, I will restrict my discussion to lotteries with a finite number of possible outcomes.
3. For stylistic reasons, in what follows I will sometimes omit the female pronoun in phrases like this.
4. To disregard one's process utilities amounts to disregarding some of one's *first-order* preferences on the basis of one's *second-order* preferences.
5. I am assuming that as we have no reasons to think that the value the two individuals place on life differs greatly, the differences between their attitudes are based on differences in the value they assign to education.
6. I have tried to show in earlier papers (Harsanyi, 1953, 1955) how vNM utility functions can be used in welfare economics and ethics. I have also tried to show that these utility functions must enter *linearly* into any admissible social welfare function.

REFERENCES

Allais, M. (1953) 'Le Comportement de l'Homme Rationel devant le Risque: Critique des Postulats et Axioms de l'Ecole Americaine', *Econometrica*, 21: 503–46.

Arrow, K. J. (1951) *Social Choice and Individual Values* (New York: Wiley).

Arrow, K. J. (1982) 'Risk Perception in Psychology and Economics', *Economic Inquiry*, 20: 1–9.

Arrow, K. J. (1983) 'Behaviour Under Uncertainty and Its Implications for Policy', *Technical Report no. 399* (Center for Research on Organizational Efficiency: Stanford University).

Hagen, O. (1984) 'Neo-Cardinalism', to appear in Hagen, O. and F. Wenstrop (eds) *Progress in Utility and Risk Theory* (forthcoming).

Harsanyi, J. C. (1953) 'Cardinal Utility in Welfare Economics and in the Theory of Risk Taking', *Journal of Political Economy* 61: 434–5 (reprinted in Harsanyi, 1976).

Harsanyi, J. C. (1955) 'Cardinal Welfare, Individualistic Ethics, and Interpersonal Comparisons of Utility', *Journal of Political Economy* 63: 309–21 (reprinted in Harsanyi, 1976).

Harsanyi, J. C. (1976) *Essays on Ethics, Social Behavior, and Scientific Explanation* (Dordrecht, Holland: Reidel).

Hausner, M. (1954) 'Multidimensional Utilities', in R. M. Thrall *et al.* (eds) *Decision Processes* (New York: Wiley) pp. 167–80.

Hicks, J. R. (1939) *Value and Capital* (London: Oxford University Press).

von Neumann, J. and O. Morgenstern (1953). *Theory of Games and Economic Behavior* (Princeton: Princeton University Press).

Rawls, J. (1971) *A Theory of Justice* (Cambridge, Mass.: Harvard University Press).

Tversky, A. and D. Kahneman (1981) 'The Framing of Decisions and the Psychology of Choice', *Science*, 211: 453–8.

18 Arrow–Bayes Equilibria: A New Theory of Price Forecasting

Horace W. Brock

INTRODUCTION

'It's Back to the Doghouse for Economists – Their Predictions are Turning out to be Wrong'. Thus begins a report in the 4 February, 1985 issue of *U.S. News and World Report*. This, and many other articles, bespeak serious difficulties besetting the economics profession at the time of writing. For better or worse, economists are expected to make forecasts, and we are judged by the 'correctness' of our forecasts.

There are essentially two kinds of forecasts: macroeconomic, and microeconomic. While much publicity attaches to forecasts of macroeconomic variables such as GNP and inflation, it is microeconomic forecasting – price forecasting in particular – that arguably matters most to decision-makers in the private sector. Extensive resources are dedicated to answering such questions as:

> What will 3-month Treasury bills yield in 6 months? Where are gold prices headed? How likely is it that the price of oil will fall below US \$25 per barrel? When will copper prices rise and once again exceed the marginal cost of US production? How volatile will the US dollar be over the next year, and how much should we pay to hedge our position?

Decision-makers have every reason to be concerned about the quality of answers economists can presently give to these and related questions. But the criticisms that are voiced are generally misplaced. For example, an inability to 'call' prices in an inherently uncertain world should no more indict economics than physics should be indicted for the inability of physicists to predict the path of a scrap of paper falling from a desktop.

The true problem lies in the kind of knowledge generated by most price forecasting models, as well as in the way it is used. As for the kind of information that is used, consider that most price forecasting models are quasi-reduced form models 'estimated' with historical data. They do not embody future-oriented expert knowledge of the kind required for rational forward planning. Worse, forecasts are usually deterministic in nature, with the mean of some distribution serving as the 'forecast'. Yet decision theory instructs us in the importance of determining at least the second moment of the forecast variable if we are to make rational decisions under conditions of uncertainty and risk aversion.

The present chapter is offered as an antidote to this state of affairs in the theory and practice of price forecasting. I shall sketch a somewhat novel approach based jointly upon Kenneth Arrow's 'economics of uncertainty' and Bayesian decision theory. The framework presented addresses the normative question: How *should* we forecast prices under conditions of uncertainty, assuming we wish to use a forecast for purposes of rational forward planning?

Section 1 discusses some implications of Bayesian decision theory for price forecasts that are 'rational' in the sense that they abet rational decision-making. To anticipate, I propose that primary emphasis be placed upon determining the likelihood of future states of the world rather than upon estimating regression coefficients. I also argue that since experts seems to think most naturally in terms of structural (as opposed to reduced form) models, these should often be used in preference to quasi-reduced form models.

Section 2 draws on Kenneth Arrow's model of contingent markets. The notion of a price forecasting model in 'stochastic structural form' is introduced and is used to characterize an 'Arrow–Bayes' price forecast. This model amounts to a conceptual generalization and restatement of familiar structural form models sometimes used in price forecasting (for example, Friedman and Roley, 1977). The event space in this model is a set of alternative supply and demand schedules parametrized by alternative states of the world. Once probabilities have been determined for these events, the probabilities of prices can be determined endogenously. The probabilistic or 'contingent' prices that result are called Arrow–Bayes prices.

Section 3 contrasts the new model with a rather general version of econometric price forecasting models: Bayesian structural models of the kind used by Brainard and Smith (1976) in their estimation of flow-of-funds equations in financial markets. One interesting difference between the Arrow–Bayes model, as we have implemented it, and traditional econometric models lies in a linearity assumption of most econometric models: the price elasticity coefficients of supply and demand are assumed to be independent of the future state of the world. Relaxing this assumption can yield a very different and interestting price distribution.

Section 4 discusses a strategy for estimating an Arrow-Bayes model via construction of an *Expert-System* as prescribed in the new field of artificial intelligence. When estimated within this framework, the variance of the Arrow–Bayes price forecast can be interpreted as the generalized degree of confidence of all those experts—including 'history' – underlying the Expert-System. Finally, Section 5 presents some insights I have gathered from constructing Arrow-Bayes forecasting models of the US credit market, the dollar market, the world gold market, and the world copper market. These models are shown to be helpful in explaining the high volatility of prices observed in certain markets. The appendix to this chapter contains a personal note on the origins of the proposed theory, and on the contribution of Kenneth Arrow to my research in price forecasting, as well as to my interest in economic science.

This chapter is the first of several papers dedicated to the problem of price forecasting in an uncertain environment. Accordingly, its purpose is to provide an overview of the problems and prospects as I now see them. Unsolved technical and conceptual problems remain, and I hope the present chapter will stimulate others to deepen and extend the new model.

To make the essay accessible to a broad readership, the exposition is primarily geometric. Partly for this reason, classical supply and demand schedules, rather than production and consumption sets, are depicted.

Domain of Application of the New Theory

Here, at the outset, it should be helpful to note the kinds of decision problems that occasioned the development of the Arrow-Bayes theory.

Investment Management in Turbulent Markets

The volatility of financial markets in recent years has largely transformed investment management into 'interest rate risk management'. This development has been facilitated by a host of new techniques and instruments (for example, options, futures, and swaps) that make insurance more available and less expensive than ever before. But new and difficult questions must be answered: 'Given the cost of hedging, is it rational for me to hedge? And if so, how much should I hedge?'

The answers to such questions hinge upon the investor's risk attitude, as well as upon the price risks involved, that is, the *probabilities* of future security yields, exchange rates, or whatever. Yet in practice, these risks are never assessed and quantified, except at the trivial level of documenting recent market 'volatility'.[1]

Resource Planning

Corporations undertaking major investments in natural resources face extraordinary price risk. To begin with, it can take six or seven years to bring a mine into production. Yet for periods longer than twenty months out, forward markets do not exist for all practical purposes. In the absence of insurance, long-run commodity price forecasts thus play a critical role in Go/No Go decisions. Work we have done in this area suggests that top management is highly frustrated with the kind of price forecasting currently available to help them analyse such decisions – unbelievable point forecasts as opposed to thoughtfully derived distributions.

General Strategic Planning

In appraising most strategic decisions, top management's primary uncertainty centres on the bottom line, that is, on 'profit risk'. But profit risk is often 'price risk' in disguise. To see this, simply expand profit as:

$$\begin{aligned}\text{PROFIT} &= \text{REVENUE} - \text{COST}\\ &= [\tilde{\mathbf{p}}_o \times \mathbf{q}_o] - [\tilde{\mathbf{p}}_i \times \mathbf{q}_i]\end{aligned}$$

where the tilde represents a random variable; where **p** denotes a price vector, **q** a quantity vector, the subscript *o* denotes output, and the subscript *i* denotes input. Uncertainty about profit is thus seen to factor entirely into uncertainty about price, assuming that the quantity vectors are regarded as 'acts', not uncertain outcomes. (Of course, this is a special case in which uncertainty about the production process has been suppressed.)

1 BAYESIAN DECISION THEORY AND 'RATIONAL' PRICE FORECASTING

By Bayesian decision theory we mean expected utility theory coupled with the Bayesian or 'subjectivist' approach to probability theory. This theory implies several normative guidelines for sound price forecasting. In the present section, we suggest criteria concerning the information on which a price forecast should be based. Then in Section 2, we show how to transform this knowledge into a price forecast proper.

1.1 Price Uncertainty as 'Future State' Uncertainty

When we say the decision-maker is uncertain about future price, exactly what do we mean? He knows that the future price will be determined by the state of the world that eventually obtains. Then 'uncertainty means not knowing which state will in fact hold' (Arrow, 1972, p. 226). And in Bayesian decision theory, such uncertain knowledge as the decision-maker has about the future is captured by his subjective probability distribution on alternative future states of the world. Assessment of his (prior) probability distribution over some set of Bayesian regression weights is no substitute for this state-of-the-world knowledge. Nor is the mean and variance of a classical regression distribution. More will be said about this in Section 3 where we contrast the regression framework with the Arrow-Bayes framework.

1.2 Knowledge as Future-Oriented Expertise

In Bayesian decision theory, the subjective probabilities with which a decision-maker represents his knowledge about future states of the world have a particular interpretation: they will represent his own 'betting odds' on future states. In practice, he is likely to feel unqualified to specify his own betting odds and will often delegate this task to an expert in whom he has confidence, that is, he will search and pay for the best expertise available. He will then adopt his expert's subjective probabilities as his own for the purpose of the decision to be made.

Now in a business setting, those strategic decisions that percolate to top levels of management typically require expertise about a future that little resembles the past. Just consider the following examples from our own research:

> What will the ongoing deregulation of world capital markets imply for credit flows and US interest rates? Or, what are the implications for copper supply (and hence for price) of the political situation in Chile and in Zaire? Or, what will the rise of black labor unions do to the costs and output of South African gold, and hence to the future price of gold?

Convincing answers to such questions are not generally provided by historical time series methods. In our view, this is one reason why the views of economists are often by-passed at the highest levels of many organisations. For economists are as comfortable with time series methods as they are uncomfortable with 'speculating' in the absence of 'hard data'. The expertise of other, more future-oriented, experts is thus sought in practice, and the unique synthesizing skills of the economist are not utilized. This situation can and should change. But economic pedagogy must change first (see Epilogue).

1.3 Inference about the Likelihood of Future States via Probabilistic Expansion and Bayes's Theorem

When encoding expert information about future states of the world, great care must be taken to obtain meaningful and logically consistent intelligence. Two operations that prove indispensable to this end are probability expansion and Bayes's theorem (Howard, 1970, gives a discussion of both). Expansion simply permits the unconditional distribution of a variable to be obtained in terms of a family of underlying conditional distributions. Expansion is useful because experts almost always think in terms of conditional statements, whereas analysis often requires unconditional distributions.

Bayes's theorem is useful, not only for incorporating sample information into prior information, that is, for 'learning', but also for information inversion. By the latter, we mean passage from a conditional probability assessment with which an expert is comfortable into the inverse distribution that may be required for analytical purposes. (This operation is called 'tree flipping' in the field of decision analysis.) In sum, a decision-maker should draw on expansion and on Bayes's Theorem when synthesizing his knowledge about future states. Yet these tools are rarely used in practice.

1.4 Structural versus Reduced Form Intelligence

Experts asked about future price movements will typically factor their knowledge into assertions about events affecting supply, as distinct from events affecting demand. For example, a capital markets expert might discuss future interest rate levels in terms of Fed policy (supply of credit), the deficit (demand), and foreign capital flows (currently supply).

To the extent this is true, structural form models should be used in preference to quasi-reduced form models. For they will better accommodate expert opinion (for example, Friedman and Roley, 1977; Smith and Anabtawi, 1985). These ideas will be developed at greater length in subsequent sections of this chapter.

1.5 'Riskiness' as Degree of Confidence

The variance of the decision-maker's forecast provides a first-order measure of the 'riskiness' of the future as he sees it. Now in a Bayesian context, riskiness will have a particular forward-looking interpretation. It will denote his (or his expert's) degree of confidence in the forecast. As represented by this variance, riskiness will not generally coincide with any measure of the past variability of the variable in question.

For an example of the distinction here between forward-looking and historical risk assessment, suppose it were November 1979 and you have been asked to assess interest rate risk for the 1980–81 period. Fed Chairman Paul Volcker has just announced his celebrated change in monetary policy. How would you proceed to characterize uncertainty? You would find little solace in measures of recent market volatility, much less in the standard error of a forecast generated by some historically estimated quasi-reduced form model. The Arrow-Bayes model was formulated with precisely this kind of problem in mind.

1.6 Summary

I have suggested that Bayesian decision theory places normative constraints on the informational domain of price forecasting. First, 'states of the world' are taken to be the primitive events of central interest. This idea is taken from probability theory. Events such as the 'true value' of regression weights are ancillary. Secondly, Bayesian decision theory places significant constraints upon the way we obtain, interpret, and process intelligence about future states of the world. Finally, particular care must be taken in characterizing and interpreting 'risk'.

2 ARROW-BAYES PRICE EQUILIBRIA

Having discussed 'knowledge' in terms of inference about future states of the world, we shall now construct a map that transforms a decision-maker's knowledge into a probabilistic price forecast. The basic idea is very simple. A separate supply function and demand function is associated with each state of the world. These are the contingent supply and demand functions that will 'exist' and characterize producer/consumer behaviour *if* the underlying state eventuates.

The probability of each supply/demand function is simply that of the state of the world that labels it. Given these probabilities, it is possible to solve the contingent market system for a vector of contingent prices and their probabilities. This constitutes the desired price forecast.

As the pioneering work of Kenneth Arrow (1953) is central to our research, we shall begin by reviewing such price forecasting as is implicit in his 1953 model of contingent markets. First we need some notation.

2.1 Notation

For the sake of convenience, brackets $\{\cdot\}$ will not denote 'the set of . . .' but rather 'the subjective probability distribution of . . .' Thus let x denote any random variable. Then $\{x\}$ will denote the decision-maker's (or expert's) subjective probability distribution over x; and $\{x|y\}$ denotes the conditional distribution of x given y.

S denotes a finite set of states of the world, with component element $s \in S$. This set is the union of two (not necessarily disjoint) subsets:

> S_d and S_s, where S_d denotes the components of S relevant to the future behaviour of consumers ('demanders'), and S_s the components of S relevant to producers ('suppliers'). We shall call S_d the *demand-states*, and S_s the *supply-states*.

j indexes the demand-states, of which there are J; and k indexes the supply-states, of which there are K. If we wish to refer to the jth demand-state, we write s_{dj}, and we write s_{sk} for the kth supply-state.

$\{s\}_i$ denotes the ith market participant's subjective probability distribution over the set S of future states of the world. We should think of this distribution as the *joint* distribution over the set of demand-states and supply-states.

$\{s_d\}_i$ and $\{s_s\}_i$ denote respectively the marginal distributions over the sets of demand and supply-states. These distributions are naturally assumed consistent with the joint distribution $\{s\}_i$.

p denotes the price of the commodity whose price we are forecasting. Strictly speaking, we should write p_t where t represents the time horizon for the forecast, but we shall suppress the subscript t and restrict ourselves to some assumed future point in time;

$\{p\}_i$ denotes the ith market participant's subjective probability distribution over future price. This distribution will be either exogenously given or endogenously determined, depending upon context.

q_{sk} denotes quantity supplied in supply-state k, and q_{dj} denotes the quantity demanded in demand-state j.

F_s denotes a set of K supply schedules, with representative element $f_{sk} \in F_s$ corresponding to supply-state k. There is one such schedule for each supply-state. In each schedule, quantity supplied is assumed to be a function only of price. That is, $q_{sk} = f_{sk}(p)$.

F_d denotes a set of J demand schedules, with representative element $f_{dj} \in F_d$ corresponding to demand-state j. There is one such schedule for each demand-state. As with supply, $q_{dj} = f_{dj}(p)$.

$\{f_s\}_i$ denotes i's subjective probability distribution over the components of the set F_s, and likewise $\{f_d\}_i$ denotes the distribution over the components of F_d. The probability assigned to a given schedule is assumed to be the probability of the state of the world labelling it.

2.2 Price Forecasting in Arrow's Original Model

Arrow's 1953 model is not concerned with price forecasting. Its aim is to characterize an optimal allocation of resources under conditions of uncertainty and risk aversion. None the less, it will be helpful to review the manner in which price forecasting enters his framework.

In the model, commodities as we ordinarily think of them become 'contingent commodities' in the sense that they are contingent upon (and labelled by) alternative future states of the world. Thus 'Nebraska wheat in 1987 under conditions of a drought' is one commodity, whereas 'Nebraska wheat in 1987 given no drought' is another.

The participants in the model know and can 'take as given' the equilibrium prices (and quantities) in all these markets, an equilibrium we can denote as p^*. But if the equilibrium is known, how does forecasting enter the model? It enters by assuming that each participant i is uncertain about which state of the world will hold, and is assumed to possess a subjective probability distribution $\{s\}_i$ expressing his betting odds on alternative future states. Note that the domain of the forecast is the set of future states, not the set of future prices.

But Arrow labels each price by the state of the world in which it will be an actual equilibrium price. Thus the ith participant's state forecast $\{s\}_i$ is essentially the same as his price forecast $\{p^*\}_i$:

$$\{p^*\}_i = \{s\}_i \tag{1}$$

For our purposes this is important because it permits Arrow to abstract from the real world difficulty of passing from probabilities of future states of the world to a probabilistic price forecast – a problem that in practice amounts to a complex transformation-of-variables problem (see below).[2]

The real world departs in many ways from Arrow's deliberately idealized model. For one thing, there exists no explicit future market equilibrium p^* that investors can take as given. Moreover, the price forecasting problem cannot be suppressed: market participants must compute on their own their probabilities of future prices. But how?

2.3 Models in Stochastic Structural Form

Let us henceforth put ourselves in the shoes of the ith market participant, and drop the subscript *i*. Assume that this participant is an investor who is contemplating a significant investment in some commodity, and who is highly uncertain about the future price of that commodity. For concreteness, let the commodity in question be credit, and let the price at issue be future short-term interest rates.

How can the investor arrive at a price forecast that is rational in the Bayesian sense of representing his (or his experts') betting odds on future states of the world? To begin with, his knowledge about the future $\{s\}$ will typically be partitioned into information about future supply (for example, the savings rate, international capital flows, Fed policy, and so on) and information about future demand (the deficit, state and local borrowing, consumer credit demand, and so on), that is, the information $\{s_s\}$ and $\{s_d\}$.

It thus makes sense to construct a *structural* model embodying explicit supply and demand functions. But more is required, for the challenge is to create a structural model that generates a price forecast unambiguously linked to the particular knowledge the investor has – knowledge about future states of the world. This can be achieved by means of a model in stochastic structural form.

Figure 18.1 schematizes this model in a simple case where there are four states of the world: s_{dL}, s_{dH}, s_{sL}, and s_{sH} with respective probabilities .5, .5, .4, .6. These states indicate respectively a 'low-credit-demand' state of the world, a 'high-credit-demand' state, and *mutatis mutandis* for supply. For example, s_{dL} could represent a low (for example, $50 billion) fiscal deficit, and s_{sH} could represent a high savings rate of, say 6.5 per cent.

Associated with the two pairs of states of the world are two demand schedules and two supply schedules: f_{dL}, f_{dH}, f_{sL}, and f_{sH}. The probability of each supply schedule and demand schedule is that of the associated state of the world. These probabilities appear as decimal numbers located on the four schedules in the diagram. There are four price/quantity equilibria. Under the tentative and unnecessary assumption that the probability distributions $\{f_d\}$ and $\{f_s\}$ are stochastically independent, the probability of any one price equilibrium is simply the *product* of the probabilities of the pair of supply and demand schedules intersecting at that point. Thus the probability of a 7 per cent T-bill rate is:

$$(.6) \times (.5) = (.30).$$

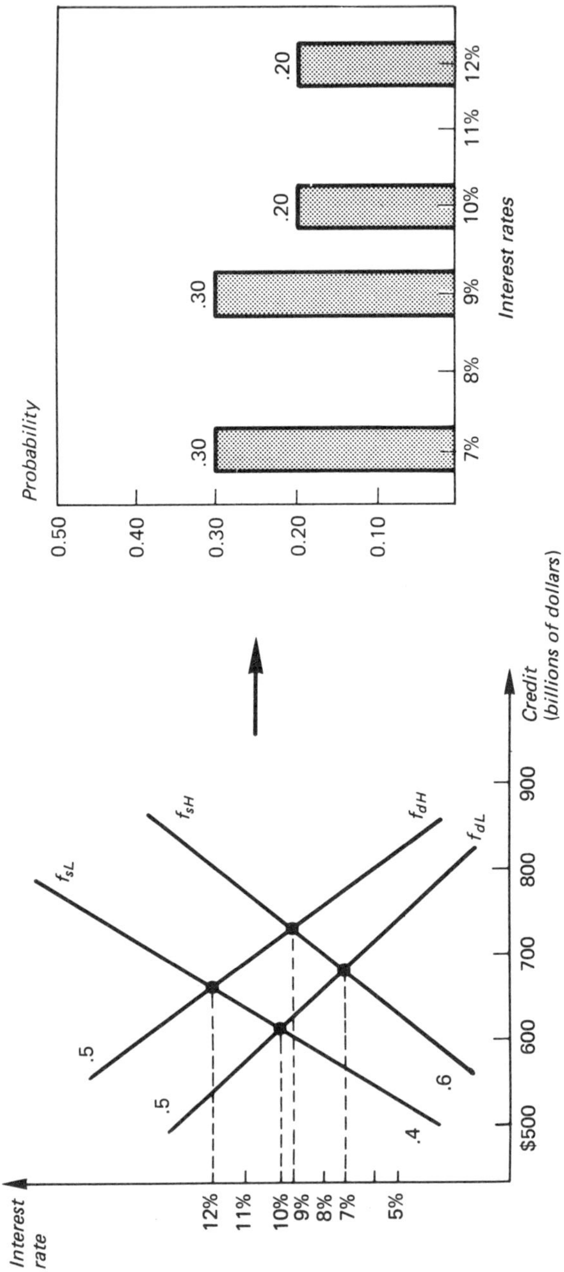

Figure 18.1 1985 US credit market

The resulting interest rate forecast is indicated in the histogram. Let us summarize matters more formally, and introduce two definitions:

Definition 1: A model in *stochastic structural form* consists of a specification of K supply-states and K associated supply schedules f_{sk}; of J demand-states with J associated demand schedules f_{dj}; and of a joint (subjective) probability distribution $\{s\}$ over the set S of future states of the world. This distribution implies two marginal distributions $\{s_d\}$ and $\{s_s\}$ over the demand-states and supply-states.

The probability of any supply (demand) schedule is assumed to be that of the supply (demand) state associated with it, that is, $\{f_d\}=\{s_d\}$ and $\{f_s\}=\{s_s\}$.

The system of $K+J$ supply-demand relations is assumed to determine $K\times J=M$ non-negative stochastic price/quantity equilibria.

Definition 2: The prices determined by a model in *stochastic structural form* will be called *Arrow-Bayes prices* provided that the information embedded in the model's probability distributions satisfies the Bayesian *desiderata* set forth in Section 1 above.

Several points about this framework should be noted.

Contingent Commodities and Their Dual Interpretation

Depending upon the context and the purpose of analysis, the stochastic structural model can be given either of two interpretations. First, it can be viewed as characterizing the differing supply/demand relations associated with each of M 'contingent' commodities. Under this interpretation, one contingent commodity is different from another contingent commodity, even though each may share a common generic label (for example, 'credit' or 'copper').

Alternatively, the model can be interpreted as a familiar structural form model of a single non-contingent market – but a structural form model that has been probabilistically disaggregated. Under this interpretation, a commodity (for example, credit or copper) is one and the same regardless of the state of the world in which its equilibrium price and quantity are determined.

In a forthcoming paper I shall argue that the former interpretation is more general and useful. This is especially true when we wish to make 'intra-commodity differentiations' on the basis of product quality, resource purity, consumer perception, and so on. Moreover, the degree to which one commodity is a substitute or complement for another will depend on the state of the world. An Arrow-Bayes framework would seem necessary if price forecasting is to reflect this situation.

The Demand/Supply Schedules

We have assumed that sufficient expertise is available to associate a well-defined demand (supply) schedule with each demand-state (supply-state). This assumption would be realistic if the states of the world are defined in very rich detail. In implementations, the most that is possible is a mapping of each state into some 'most likely' price-quantity schedule. A method for estimating the required state-to-schedule maps is discussed in Section 4.

The Probability Distributions

We have assumed that the probabilities of the demand and supply schedules are those of the states of the world associated with them, that is,

$$\{f_d\} = \{s_d\} \text{ and } \{f_s\} = \{s_s\} \qquad (2)$$

No such condition arises in Arrow's model where there is a direct identification of each state of the world with its associated (and known) price equilibrium, and where there is no need for probability distributions over the supply and demand schedules *per se*.

The Fundamental Transformation of Variables

In Arrow's model, there is no need to solve for the probability of price, as (1) makes clear. In the present model, the objective is to do just that. Thus we may write:

$$\{p\} = T[\{f_d\}, \{f_s\}] \qquad (3)$$

indicating that $\{p\}$ is derived from the random variables $\{f_d\}$ and $\{f_s\}$. T should be thought of as a probabilistic version of the law of supply and demand. Figure 18.1 offers a geometric representation of T in the special case of stochastic independence.

While Figure 18.1 exploits stochastic independence, the map T is perfectly general in this regard. Figure 18.2 schematizes the general situation. Here the state vector consists of three components, the events x_1, x_2, and x_3. It is assumed that the variable x_1 is the *only* source of stochastic dependence between the supply and demand schedules. This is indicated by the use of solid lines at the x_1-node of the event tree.

To arrive at an Arrow-Bayes forecast, we first determine two *conditional* distributions $\{p|x_1\}$, one for each of the two values of the variable x_1 sketched in the tree. These two conditional price forecasts are obtained by applying the procedure of Figure 18.1 separately within the two bracketed regions of the event trees – regions denoted in dotted lines. Due to their conditioning on a specific value of x_1, the supply and demand schedules *within* each grid are stochastically independent, so this procedure is valid. We then determine the desired unconditional price distribution $\{p\}$ by simple expansion of the conditional distributions $\{p|x_1\}$ over the distribution $\{x_1\}$.

In a study of the long-run price of copper (Brock, 1983), the role of x_1 was played by a variable called 'growth of free world industrial production between 1982–1987'. We were able to partition the other state variables x_i ($i=2, \ldots, 31$) into disjoint demand-state and supply-state groupings that were roughly independent of one another.

Probabilistic Comparative Statics

The model in stochastic structural form resembles a probabilistic version of comparative statics. This becomes clear by recalling Samuelson's (1967, p. 7) emphasis on shifts in the functional relations that describe a market:

> It is important that our analysis be developed in such terms that we are aided in determining how our variables change qualitatively or quantitatively with changes in explicit data. Thus, we introduce explicitly into our system certain data in the form of parameters [here 'states of the world'], which in changing cause shifts in our *functional* relations. (Parenthetical remark and emphasis added.)

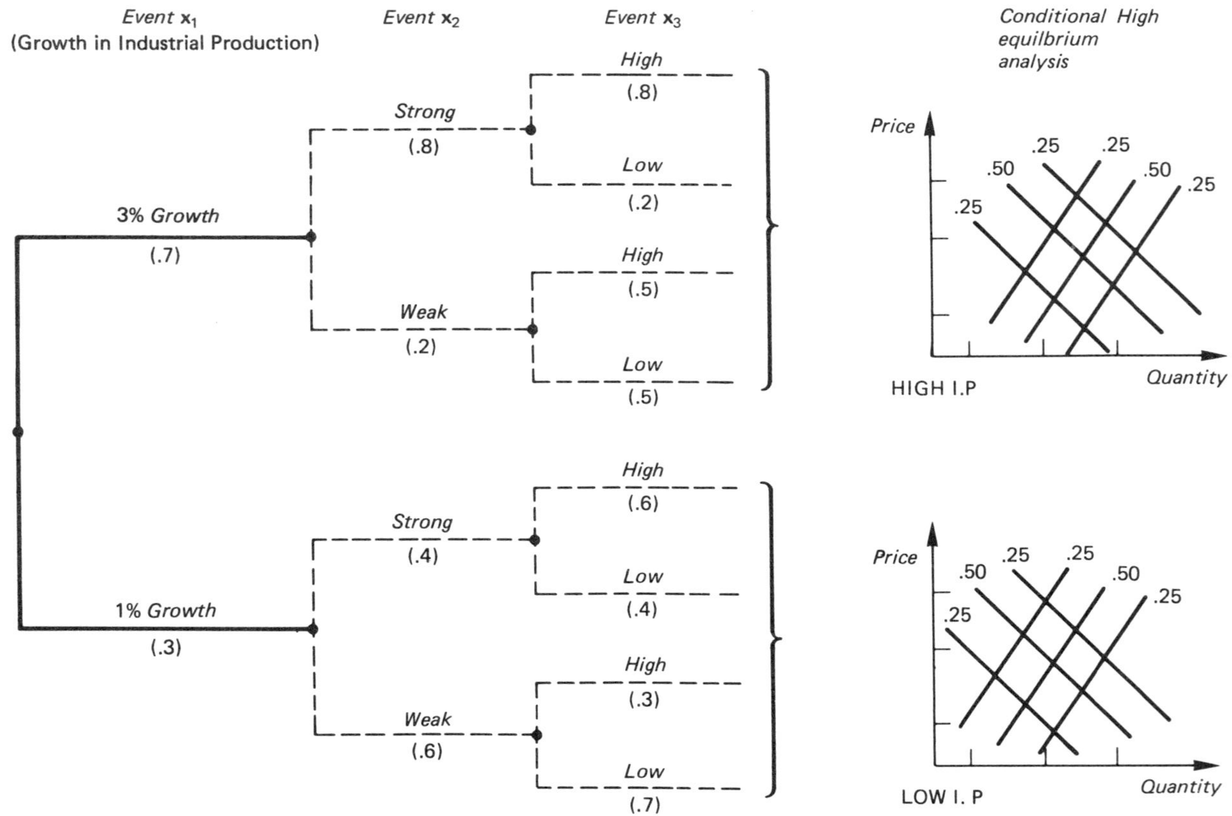

Figure 18.2 The case of dependence

3 COMPARISON WITH TRADITIONAL ECONOMETRIC MODELS

To a trained economist, quantitative price forecasting is synonomous with specifying and estimating some variant of the general linear model, whether an auto-regressive model, a quasi-reduced form model, or a structural form model. The estimation strategies used can be either classical or Bayesian. How does the Arrow-Bayes model compare with these forecasting models?[3]

In this section, we sketch an answer to this question by comparing the Arrow-Bayes model with the most comparable econometric model: a Bayesian econometric price forecasting model in structural form. Two considerations make this Bayesian model most comparable to the Arrow-Bayes model. First, it is a structural form model. Secondly, it permits expert judgement to be included in the form of prior distributions over the parameter space. For a rare example of such a model, see Brainard and Smith (1976) who use Bayesian methods with informative priors to estimate flow-of-funds equations (see also Smith, 1981).

3.1 A Bayesian Structural Model

A Bayesian structural model for price forecasting consists of a pair of supply and demand equations

$$q_d = a_o + a_1 p + a_2 x_2 + a_3 x_3 + \ldots e_d \tag{4A}$$

$$q_s = b_o + b_1 p + b_2 x_2 + b_3 x_3 \ldots e_s \tag{4B}$$

where q_d and q_s are the dependent variables (quantity demanded and supplied); where p denotes the price of the commodity in question; where the vectors **a** and **b** are random vectors of regression weights; where e_d and e_s are the error terms (Bayesian 'process variance') of the demand and supply equations; and where **x** and **y** are vectors of the independent variables. Forecast values for these independent variables must be given exogenously.

Note: For purposes of comparison with the Arrow-Bayes model, the components of **x** will be identified with a subset of the set S_d of demand-state variables; and **y** will be identified with a subset of the set S_s of supply-state variables.

Suppose the system (4) has already been estimated via Bayesian regression, and that the regression weights and error terms possess posterior probability distributions. How can we then use (4) to arrive at a price forecast?

3.2 Solving For a Price Forecast

The most natural way to solve for a forecast is to render the relations (4) deterministic. This can be done by plugging in forecast values of the independent variables **x** and **y**, and by plugging in the (posterior) means of all random variables. This will yield two equations in two unknowns, interpretable as two Bayesian regression lines. We can then solve for the desired price-quantity equilibrium (p^*, q^*). But this equilibrium tells us nothing *per se* about the *probability* of future price. It will be of limited help in rational decision-making under uncertainty.

Then how do we obtain a probabilistic price forecast in this framework? Were we dealing with a classical non-Bayesian model, we could solve for this analytically, assuming certain highly restrictive statistical assumptions could be made. To do so, we would pass from the model estimated in structural form to its reduced form. In doing so, we could solve for the variance-covariance matrix of the two endogenous variables: price and quantity. One element of this matrix will be the desired variance of forecast price. Goldberger *et al.* (1961) offer a thorough analysis of this problem in a macroeconomic simultaneous equations setting (but not in a supply/demand setting).

But in the case of Bayesian structural models, we have been unable to find equivalent analytical expressions, and numerical methods would doubtless have to be used. None the less, we can sketch the situation geometrically, and doing so will abet a comparison of (4) with the Arrow-Bayes model.

For each price p within some price interval, determine the conditional posterior distributions $\{q_d|p\}$ and $\{q_s|p\}$ from the right-hand side of each equation. Then take fractiles of each of these distributions, for example, quartiles, and for *every* price, plot them as in Figure 18.3. Analytical expressions for these fractiles in the case of single-equation Bayesian regression models are given in Pratt, Raiffa, and Schlaifer (1965, Section 24.4.6).

This scheme induces a probabilistic partition of the price-quantity space, as does the stochastic structural model. But the two schemes

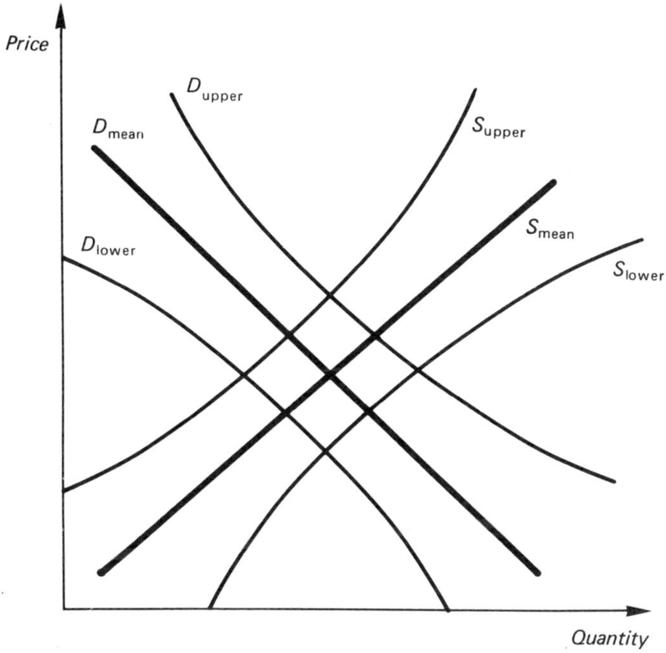

Figure 18.3 A Bayesian (or classical) regression framework

are different. In particular, the curves appearing in Figure 18.3 cannot be interpreted as demand/supply schedules contingent upon specific states of the world. They are merely quartile demarcations. More importantly, the schemes imply different price forecasts. The price forecast implied by the Bayesian regression model will typically give rise to a normal (or nearly normal) price distribution. Figure 18.3, along with a modicum of geometric intuition, suggests why. Analytically, this forecast is given by the mean and variance of the reduced form solution of price p. Let us denote this price forecast by $\{p\}_r$ where the subscript denotes 'regression'.

3.3 Comparing the Forecasts $\{p\}_r$ and $\{p\}$

A comparison of the two underlying models is required to compare their forccasts. We shall undertake the comparison in two steps. First, we shall note some of the essential differences between the two models that arise in practice. This will prepare us for the second step where we lay out the formal relationship between the models. The Arrow-Bayes model is seen to have a more general structure than the Bayesian regression model. In particular, it is inherently non-linear. Additionally, its informational structure is very different. Of course, this added generality might be deemed irrelevant were the model too general to be estimated. In Section 4 we sketch an estimation strategy that shows this not to be the case.

Non-linearity

In applications we have made of the Arrow-Bayes framework, an interesting non-linearity crops up. Using the notation of (4), this is:

$$a_1 = g(\mathbf{x}) \text{ and } b_1 = h(\mathbf{y}), \tag{5}$$

that is, the slope of the supply and demand schedules tends to vary with the state of the world, as in Figure 18.1, where the non-parallel demand (supply) schedules emphasise this situation. As an example of this non-linearity, we have found that in the household and business sectors of the US credit market, the price sensitivity of credit demand is notably less in a state of 'optimism' about the future than in a state of 'pessimism' (CRED-INTEL system, 1984, volume 2). As another example, changes in the tax laws regarding depreciation schedules and the deductibility of interest expense alter the price sensitivity. In the latter cases, the alternative states of the world at issue tend to be discrete and small in number. For example, 'The odds are 70/30 that Congress will repeal the provision', a two-state case.

Figure 18.4 suggests the possible implications of such non-linearity for a probabilistic price forecast. The model is a simple one with four states of the world. The implications of non-linearity for the resulting price forecast – especially its variance – are dramatic.

Naturally, non-linearities of the form of (5) could be incorporated in econometric regression models by including appropriate product terms, but in practice they rarely have been. In contrast to this, the very structure of the Arrow-Bayes model (see Section 5) *facilitates* the incorporation of such phenomena in a natural manner. For it requires a separate supply (demand) function to be associated with every state of the world.

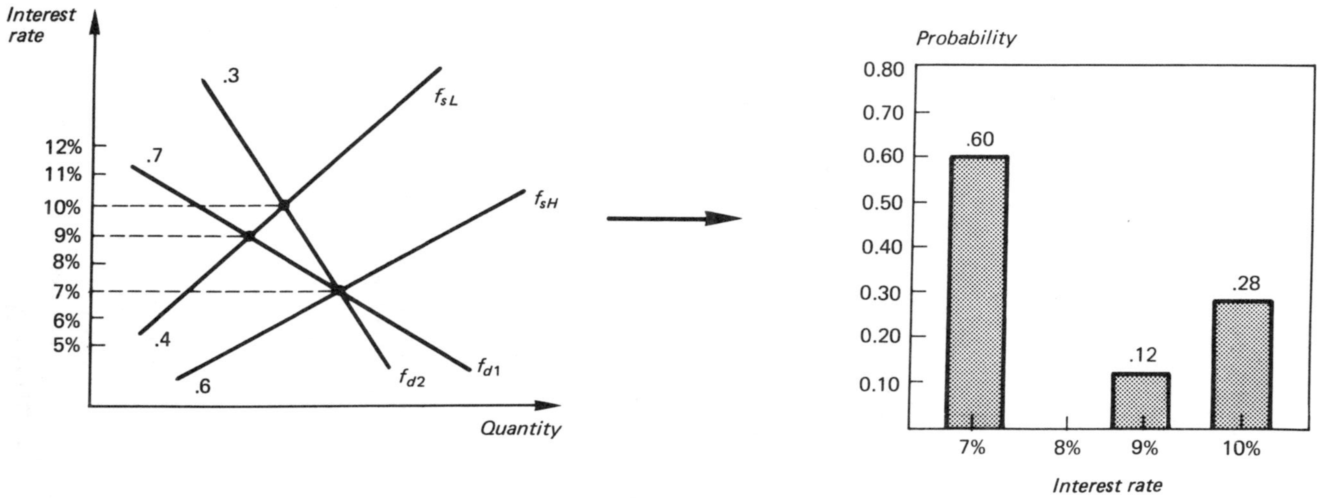

Figure 18.4 Example of state-dependent price sensitivities

State-Versus-Weight Knowledge

In the Arrow-Bayes model, the decision-maker's uncertain knowledge about price $\{p\}$ derives from uncertainty about the future state of the world represented by the distribution $\{s\}$. Moreover, knowledge about future price is *directly* linked to knowledge about future states by means of the derived distributions $\{f_d\}$ and $\{f_s\}$ (recall equations (2) and (3)). Because of this linkage, the decision-maker's 'betting odds' on future price will directly reflect his betting odds on future states of the world. This seems desirable from an espistemological standpoint, as we pointed out in Section 1.

In the Bayesian regression model (4), as in the classical regression model, uncertainty about the future state of the world is almost always suppressed: the forecast values of **x** and **y** are deterministic. Thus, $\{p\}_r$ cannot be said to embody any state-of-the-world uncertainty at all! Such uncertainty as it does incorporate pertains to the regression coefficients and the error term. This situation does seem to put the horse before the cart. There is no clear answer to the question: 'On what am I betting when I use the entity $\{p\}_r$ to represent my betting odds on future price?'

A simple generalization of the regression model can go part way towards remedying this situation (for example, Brock, 1981, Appendix). We simply substitute probability distributions $\{\mathbf{x}\}$ and $\{\mathbf{y}\}$ for the deterministic entities **x** and **y** appearing in (4). Terms such as a_3x_3 and b_3y_3 now represent product distributions of the random variables involved. As a result of this substitution, the quartiles of Figure 18.3 will become more spread out, reflecting the greater uncertainty in the posterior distribtuions $\{q_d|p\}$ and $\{q_s|p\}$. The result will be a generalized price distribution $\{p\}_r'$ with a variance greater than that implicit in (4). But even this forecast is problematic. For $\{p\}_r'$ reflects a scrambling together of future state uncertainty, regression weight uncertainty, and error term uncertainty. How is regression weight uncertainty related to future state uncertainty?

Regression Weights and 'Suppressed' State Variables

At the most fundamental level, there exists a relationship between regression weights, on the one hand, and 'suppressed' state variables, on the other. Consider the assessment of a prior distribution $\{b_1\}$ on the price parameter in the supply schedule (4B). Let the domain of the distribution be the interval (0.75, 1.25). It is our experience that when assessing his betting odds on these events, an expert will be able to articulate the 'conditions' – namely the states of the world – under which he will expect a high sensitivity of, say, 1.2, as well as the conditions under which he would expect a low sensitivity of, say, 0.8. But these particular states are not usually identified, much less included, as independent variables in the regression.

Assessing a distribution on the regression weights can thus be interpreted as a proxy for assessing distributions on these suppressed state variables. The former exercise might be unnecessary were more attention paid to the latter. And the resulting probabilistic price forecast might have a clearer interpretation. Our comments are not intended to downplay the role of sensitivity weights at an appropriate level of analysis, whether in a linear or non-linear context. We are merely trying to clarify the proper domain of probability assessment – so that we end up with 'betting odds' on future price that are rooted in something meaningful, and that can be used with confidence in rational decision-making.

3.4 Formal Comparison of the Two Models

We now show how the Bayesian regression model can be interpreted as a linear approximation of the more general Arrow-Bayes model.

Recall that an Arrow-Bayes model in stochastic structural form consists of sets of demand and supply functions – with one demand function for each demand-state, and one supply function for each supply-state. We can write:

$$q_{dj}=f_{dj}(p) \qquad \text{for all } j \tag{6A}$$

$$q_{sk}=f_{sk}(p) \qquad \text{for all } k \tag{6B}$$

where the subscript *dj* denotes demand-state *j* and *sk* denotes supply-state *k*. Under suitable assumptions, this system of equations (6) gives us $J\times K=M$ price-quantity equilibria, one for each contingent market. We can mathematically restate (6) in the form:

$$q_d=f_d(p,s_d) \tag{7A}$$

$$q_s=f_d(p,s_s) \tag{7B}$$

Here we have conflated the contingent market (6) into a single market described by one pair of equations. (7) can be viewed as a *structural form* representation of our *stochastic structural* model (6). At a purely formal level, (6) and (7) are equivalent and imply the same price forecast $\{p\}$. For in both (6) and (7), quantity demanded (supplied) is a function of price and of the state of the world.

But at an analytical and conceptual level, there are important differences between the two models. Most notably, it is straightforward to estimate and to solve (6) for a probabilistic price forecast. Why is this true? To begin with, (6) consists of a set of $K+J$ functions that are very *simple* in form. Each such function (for example, f_{dj} and f_{sk}) is a monotonic function of one and only one variable: price Estimating these 'contingent' price-quantity relations is quite easy. The trade-off for this ease is, of course, the large *number* of relations that must be estimated. This and related estimation issues will be discussed in Section 4.

Matters are also simplified by the straightforward stochastic structure of (6). In this regard, recall equation (2). Finally, analytical determination of the price forecast is fairly straightforward. Each price-quantity equilibrium is determined by the single pair of simple equations (for example, the pair f_{dj} and f_{sk}) that characterize the equilibrium; and its probability is determined by relations (2) and (3). Recall Figures 18.1 and 18.2 which sketch the solution process geometrically.

In contrast to all this, f_d and f_s in (7) will necessarily be extremely difficult both to specify and to estimate. For by construction, the information contained in these two single relations must replicate everything contained in the extensive state-dependent system (6). As an additional complication, derivation of a price forecast from (7) – once estimated – will require passage from the structural to the reduced form of the model. This transition may well prove analytically intractable. It is difficulties such as these that have caused general structural form models such as (7) to be replaced with linear approximations estimated via regression analysis.

Two strong assumptions are required to transform (7) into a (Bayesian) regression model. First, a linearity assumption of some kind must be imposed on f_d and f_s. The distortion to the resulting price forecast due to one linearity requirement was discussed in connection with Figure 18.4. Secondly, we must represent our expert knowledge about the future not in terms of distributions on the sets of future supply-states S_s and demand-states S_d, but rather via forecast values (possibly probabilistic) for **x** and **y,** as well as via posterior distributions on the entities **a, b,** e_d, and e_s. We have already discussed some of the epistemological difficulties posed by a regression strategy that places its primary emphasis on 'weights'.

Introducing these two assumptions yields a structural form Bayesian regression model similar to (4):

$$q_d = {}_L f_d(p, \mathbf{x}, e_d) \tag{8A}$$

$$q_d = {}_L f_d(p, \mathbf{y}, e_s) \tag{8B}$$

The subscript L here denotes the assumed linearity of the functions. The probabilistic price forecast $\{p\}_r$ is implicit in this structural form model, one that we have discussed in the context of Figure 18.3.

Equation (8) is clearly a special case of the Arrow-Bayes model (6), and it would be surprising if the two models were to yield comparable probabilistic price forecasts in practice. In the following section, we discuss the problem of estimating an Arrow-Bayes model.

4 IMPLEMENTATION AND ESTIMATION VIA AN EXPERT-SYSTEM

The estimation strategy outlined in this section was developed in analyses of the US credit market, and of the world gold and copper markets. Our efforts have centred on integrating Bayesian inference and the notion of an Expert-System as advanced in the field of artificial intelligence (Winston, 1984).

4.1 An Arrow-Bayes Event Tree

Figure 18.5 is an 'event tree' of US Treasury borrowing for the year 1985. This Figure is taken from an analysis of the US credit market currently being implemented (CRED-INTEL System, 1984). The US Treasury is one of four borrowing sectors analyzed. Let us denote it as the jth sector. Five supply sectors are also analyzed. When the sectoral results are aggregated, it is possible to determine the desired interest rate forecast $\{p\}$.

The nodes in the tree represent a subset of the set S_d of demand states. They are the four components of a 19-component demand-

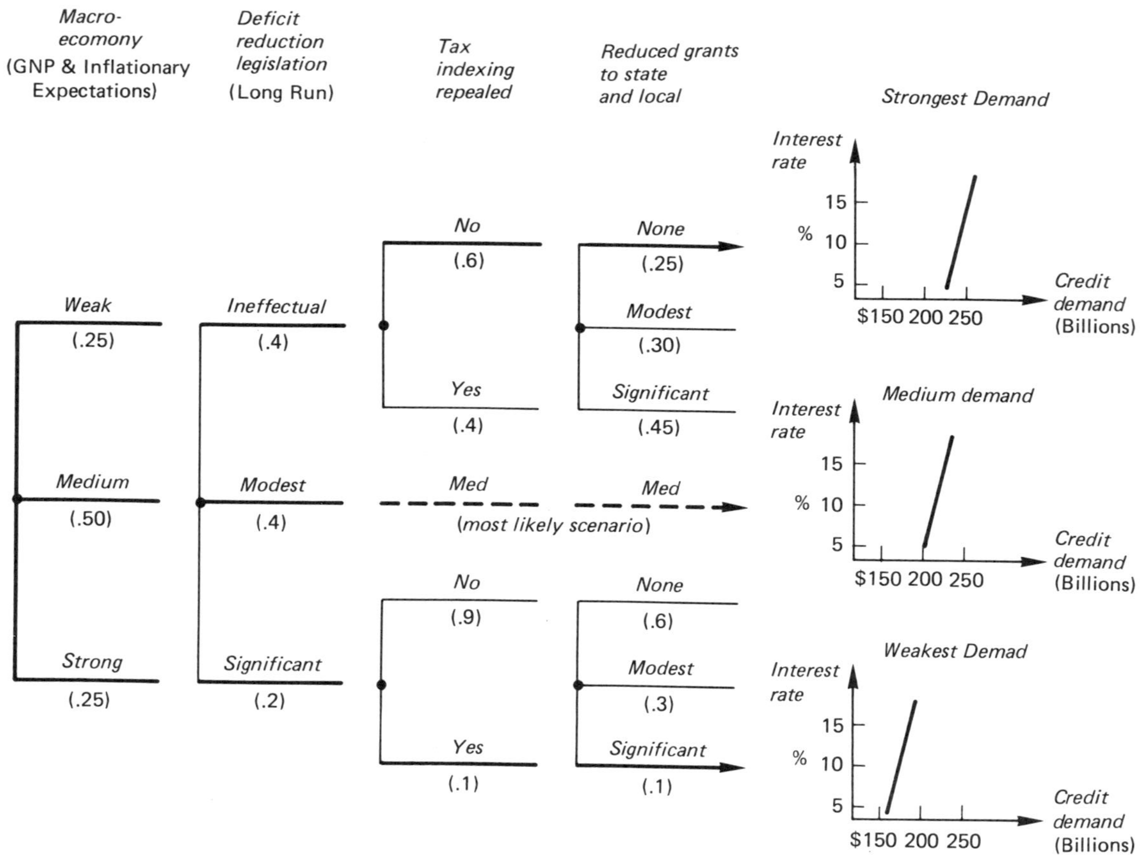

Figure 18.5 Net Treasury borrowing in 1985

state vector that helped us forecast Treasury borrowing under a particular set of circumstances deemed relevant in November 1984. (The 'Macro' node is in fact a conflation of three other nodes). A numerical value is associated with each branch of every node, but lack of space prevents our showing these.[4]

As stipulated in Section 2, a demand schedule is associated with each and every scenario. Three of these are shown at the far right of the Figure. These correspond to the top-most path through the tree, namely the scenario of greatest borrowing; the bottom-most path, that is, the scenario of minimal borrowing; and the middle or 'most likely' scenario of events.

As required by condition (2), the probability of each demand schedule will be the probability of the associated demand-state. In the present case, this probability is simply the product of the probabilities of the branches defining the demand-state.

The peculiar slope of the demand schedules has a simple explanation: Treasury borrowing is an increasing function of interest rates since higher rates increase the interest expense on the debt, *ceteris paribus*.

4.2 The Expert-System

The data appearing in this tree and in the other event trees derive from an *N+1 Person Expert-System*: *N* living experts, and 'History'. The expertise of living people is accessed via the modes of Bayesian inference discussed in Section 1. History must be accessed by the familiar methods of statistical inference.

A distinction can be made between two kinds of information needed in estimating the system:

Type A Data: Assessment of the conditional probability distributions for each component of the state vector (that is, for each node in the tree);

Type B Data: Specification of a price–quantity schedule for each state of the world.

Typically, there will be one expert responsible for assessing the probabilities of each component of the state vector. There will also be one expert responsible for specifying the state-dependent demand (supply) schedules in each demand (supply) sector. As this latter type of expertise may be unfamiliar to the reader, let us sketch what is required.

Estimation of the Price–Quantity Schedules: Let the jth expert in the Expert-System be charged with identifying the schedules of demand sector j, for example, the demand schedules of Treasury borrowing. How in practice might he generate an entire schedule? A simple interpolation procedure is helpful. We taken three price points p_i corresponding to some 'high', 'medium', and 'low' prices. The requirements on expert j can then be represented by the mappings:

$$E_j : s_{dj} \times p_i \rightarrow q_{dji} \qquad i = 1,2,3; \text{ all } S_{dj} \in S_d \tag{9}$$

Thus for a given state s_{dj}, he is required to associate a scalar ('quantity demanded by the Treasury') with each of three prices p_i. A demand schedule is then created by linear interpolation between the resulting q_{dji}.

It is important to note that the Type B expert charged with estimating E_j need know nothing about the probabilities of the demand states, for example, about the likelihood of serious deficit reduction. This is a Type *A* assessment, and the Type *B* assessments are always *conditional* upon a given state of the world.

The strategy for garnering intelligence is thus one of divide and conquer so as to obtain experts' knowledge in as pure (conditional) a form as possible. Synthesis of diverse expertise is then possible via the Bayesian operations of expansion and of Bayes's theorem (Section 1).

4.3 Other Considerations Bearing on Implementation

Use of Regression Analysis: An expert will often use quantitative models of various sorts to help him carry out the operation E_j. One model he can use is regression analysis, either classical or Bayesian. He will use this either as a starting point in his analysis, or else as his final model (in which case E_j essentially *is* a regression equation). It is interesting that in our research, very few experts have opted to use regression results – even when available and familiar to them. The reason for this reluctance is usually the belief that regression results are too biased by 'history' in a world that has changed.

Note the generality of the system: regression analyses *can* be used where appropriate. None the less, the resulting price distribution will be an Arrow-Bayes distribution $\{p\}$ and not the problematic distribution $\{p\}_r$ discussed in Section 3. The structure of the Expert-System assures this.

Approximation Methods: The curse of dimensionality looms large in exercises of this kind. For in any given supply or demand sector there are apt to be anywhere from 20 to several hundred states. Approximation methods ('curve-clustering' procedures) are being developed to facilitate estimation. The objective here is for invariance of the price forecast $\{p\}$ under approximation.

Sectoral Aggregation: Aggregation of the sectoral stochastic demand curves into aggregate stochastic demand curves is required, as is aggregation on the supply side. In this process, stochastic dependence between the various demand (supply) sectors must be dealt with as it arises.

Determination of the Arrow-Bayes Forecast $\{p\}$: Once stochastic aggregate supply and demand schedules have been obtained, the desired forecast $\{p\}$ is derived analytically by solving a model in stochastic structural form as in Section 2.

VAR $\{p\}$ *as a Generalized Degree of Confidence:* Since the price forecast $\{p\}$ incorporates the betting odds of $N+1$ experts, the decision-maker using $\{p\}$ should interpret VAR$\{p\}$ as a generalised (or 'multi-expert') degree of confidence. VAR$\{p\}$ cannot be construed as any single person's betting odds.

The Expert-System versus 'Consensus' and Delphi Methods: The proposed approach is fundamentally different from approaches that arrive at a conclusion by 'averaging out' differences of opinion among experts. Here, the decision-maker is assumed able to identify one expert (or possibly a team of experts) for each node of the event tree, as well as for each set of sectoral price-quantity relationships. Such 'synthesis' as is embedded in $\{p\}$ is due to the laws of probability theory and to the transformation wrought by the stochastic law of supply and demand (3).

Flexibility: Perhaps the most important aspect of the construction of a system such as CRED-INTEL is that, once constructed, little additional data is needed to solve the system under different conditions. Suppose conditions change, and new information is received about, say, two or three state variables. Posterior distributions can be determined for these state variables, and a revised price forecast $\{p\}'$ can be determined without contacting most, if any, of the $N+1$ experts.

This situation should be contrasted with the fundamentally different approach of, say, the 'Blue Chip Indicators' in synthesizing expert opinion. In this and related schemes for polling experts, no effort is made to obtain experts' views about the *functional* relationships underlying a given price forecast. Hence it is necessary to survey all parties involved whenever conditions change.

5 EXPLAINING AND FORECASTING PRICE VOLATILITY: COPPER AND CURRENCIES

As Arrow (1982) and others have observed, investors (and decision-makers generally) tend to underestimate market risk. We shall now draw on recent analyses of the copper market and the US dollar spot market to argue that the Arrow-Bayes framework can help decision-makers do a better job in capturing the true magnitude of the price risk they confront. At the same time, the framework can help to explain the great volatility of these two markets – volatility that has caused consternation if not outright bewilderment during the past few years.

5.1 Copper Price Variability

Two things have been remarkable about the price of copper in the past four years: the average price level – the lowest (in real terms) since the 1930s, and the volatility of prices. Explaining the low average price is straightforward. The reason lies in stagnant demand and in high levels of government subsidized production by certain Third World nations, notably Zaïre, Peru, Chile, and Zambia. But what accounts for the volatility of copper prices? The situation here is much trickier, and industry experts have not been able to offer any fundamental explanation of observed price volatility.

The Arrow-Bayes framework not only helps explain observed price variability, *ex post*, but also incorporates this 'true risk' in the forecast

$\{p\}$ it generates *ex ante*. To see this, it will suffice to give a future-oriented and a past-oriented interpretation to Figure 18.6, an Arrow-Bayes characterization of the 1987 copper market undertaken in 1983 (Brock, 1983).[5]

The aggregate supply curve represents the sum of (i) Third World production, (ii) other Free World production, and (iii) recycled scrap. The peculiar '*S*'-shape of this schedule reflects an important political phenomenon. In those Third World nations that currently produce about 40 per cent of aggregate Free World output, the short to intermediate term supply curve is backward-sloping between the prices of about 50 cents and 70 cents a pound – the actual price interval in the past several years. Within this range, political considerations oblige the Third World nations mentioned above to *increase* their production as prices fall (for example, by mining higher grade ores). They must do so to maintain revenues as well as foreign exchange earnings.

Consider now the *S*-shaped aggregate supply curves that result from this situation. Clearly, any shift in such a schedule will give rise to a much greater change in price than would a corresponding shift of some standard, positively-sloped supply curve. This should be clear geometrically. The implications of this can be interpreted in two ways. *Ex post*, it becomes apparent why small random shifts in the supply and demand schedules translate into wide price fluctuations. *Ex ante* from a forecasting vantage point, use of an Arrow-Bayes model yielded a copper price forecast $\{p\}$ with a large variance descriptive of this 'true' risk.

Compare this analysis to that of classical econometric modelling. History's sample of copper prices is weighted by prices that were much higher and more stable than they have been in the past few years. Econometric estimates of the copper supply schedule reflect positive slopes comparable to the slope in the $0.70-$1.25 price range of Figure 18.6. As a result, such models have yielded problematic price forecasts that overstated the price and understated the risk of the market – to the extent that risk was assessed at all. The result has been disenchantment with 'economics' on the part of mining executives.

5.2 Asymmetric Price Risk

The asymmetry between the 'downside' price risk and the 'upside'

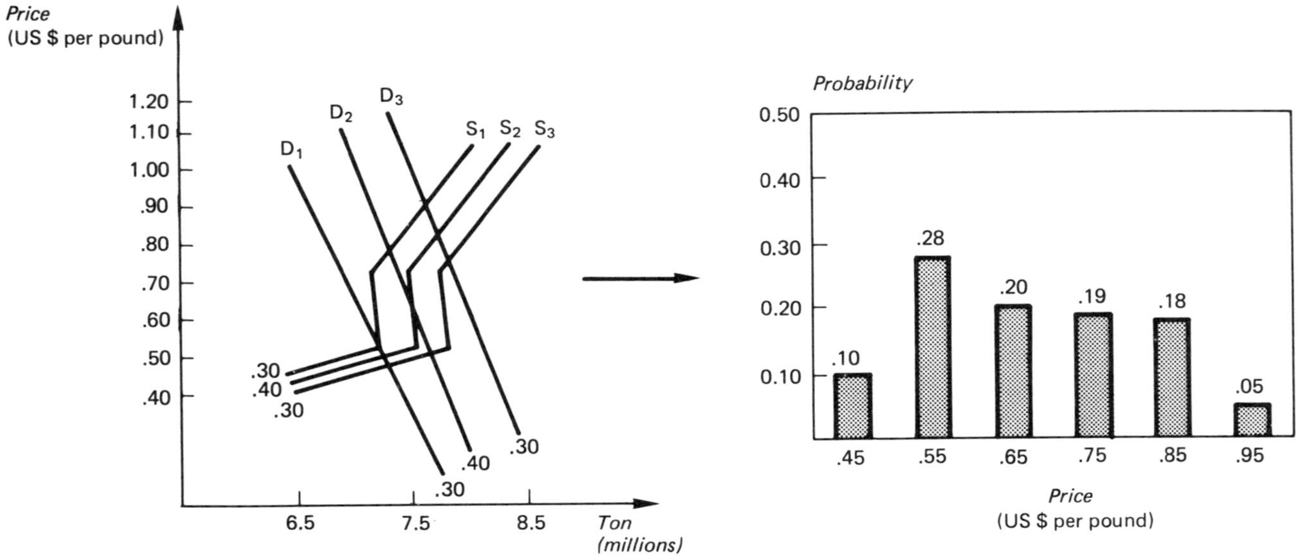

Figure 18.6 The 1987 world copper market

price risk shown in the copper price histogram is particularly notable. The asymmetry largely stems from the S-shaped supply schedule. Now risk-averse mining executives are particularly concerned with the *bottom* half of the price distribution. The exact shape of this 'lower tail' significantly affects the certain equivalent value of their prospective investments.

The Arrow-Bayes model can generate and can explain this non-normality, whereas alternative estimation procedures tend not to do so. Indeed, most quasi-reduced form models *assume* a normally distributed error term.

5.3 Dollar Volatility in the Spot Market

It is customary to ascribe the high volatility of spot market currency prices to the fluctuating demand for currency by foreign investors with mercurial asset demand functions, coupled with the 'overshoot' phenomenon (for example, Dornbusch, 1980). The modes of inference used in these investigations are typically quasi-reduced form models estimated with historical data.

Figure 18.7 suggests an alternative, yet complementary, explanation for this volatility in the context of the US dollar. The inelastic dollar supply schedules reflect the observed 'stickiness' of trade deficits in the short and intermediate term – a stickiness that holds for moderate changes in currency values. (Recall that it is the nation's current account deficit that 'supplies' dollars to the spot market – dollars that foreign investors will demand at some equilibrium dollar price.)

The probabilistic shifts in the dollar supply schedule reflect possible future changes in the US merchandise deficit due to differential economic growth rates among nations. For example, the US trade deficit would decrease if its economy slows and/or the rest-of-the-world's economy accelerates. The probabilistic demand schedules reflect uncertainty about the future asset preferences of foreign investors for dollar-denominated financial assets. The underlying uncertainty here pertains to the expected relative returns from holding dollar assets, as well as to the direction of speculative 'rolls' in the market.

Ex ante, the large (Arrow-Bayes) price risk shown in the figure reflects the inelasticity of supply in the spot market, as well as uncertainty about the future location of the supply and demand schedules (see CRED-INTEL System, 1984, number 2). Under an *ex*

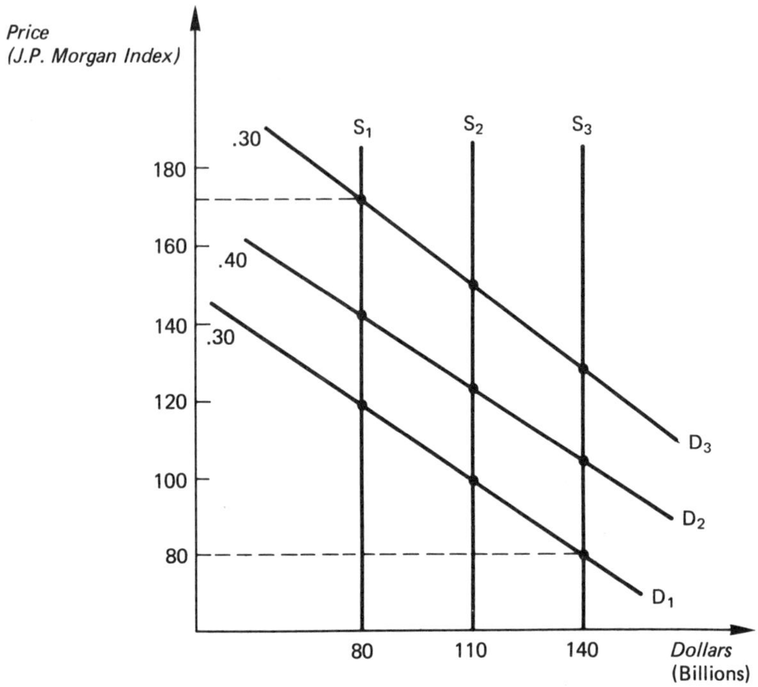

Figure 18.7 The 1985 US dollar spot market

post interpretation, that is, ignoring the probabilities, the figure helps explain the dollar price volatility we observe and bemoan.

CONCLUDING REMARKS: EPILOGUE ON PEDAGOGY

Two principal arguments have been set forth in this chapter. First, a commitment to rational decision-making imposes restrictions on the kind of price forecast that a decision-maker should use. Secondly, there exists a model that is consistent with Bayesian rationality criteria, namely the Arrow-Bayes model. This model generalizes the classical linear model, and overcomes certain limitations of the latter that arise in a forecasting context.

Should a student be interested in using the proposed framework to assess price risk, he will need a pedagogy different from that currently available in most economics programmes. First, he must become comfortable working with future-oriented data that is often very 'soft'. In particular, he must learn how to conduct interviews with a wide range of people in diverse circumstances.

Secondly, his economics curriculum must place more emphasis on applied probabilistic inference, and less on classical statistical methodology. Such a curriculum would help decision-makers do what they are usually paid to do: take future-oriented, calculated risks. And after all, that is what business – indeed life – is all about.

ACKNOWLEDGEMENT AND PERSONAL NOTE

My primary debt in this work is to Kenneth Arrow whom I first met in 1970 when I was completing Harvard Business School. My keen interest in the role of uncertainty in strategic planning had led me to study decision theory and game theory. Ken Arrow encouraged me to do work in mathematics, and told me about a Master's Degree programme in applied mathematics offered at Harvard. I completed this course the following year and then went on to Princeton. My dissertation was a theory of distributive justice based on the valuation theory of *n*-Person games. Ken's ongoing constructive criticism of my ideas helped me bring this effort to fruition (for example, Brock, 1979).

In 1977, while working at SRI International, I led a National Science Foundation Project to review the large-scale energy planning models developed since the 1973 OPEC crisis (Brock and Nesbitt, 1977, 1979). Ken again gave generously of his time in assisting my team with problems of interpretation. The scope of this project permitted me to discern difficulties with existing price-forecasting models. I was particularly struck by the absence of and need for structural form models that could meaningfully explain past and prospective oil price changes. I was also impressed by the need to introduce uncertainty into the analysis – but was not satisfied by the treatment of uncertainty in decision analysis. Here, 'price risk' is encoded directly without any use of structural supply and demand analysis.

In 1980, the Executive Committee of the Anglo American/de Beers Group commissioned the consulting firm I had just founded to analyze the prospective world gold market of the late 1980s (Brock, 1981). It was during this project that the Arrow-Bayes framework came into being. The need for a model in 'stochastic structural form' became clear in light of (1) the irrelevance of historical gold market data, (2) the need for a structural form model, and (3) management's request that we model the economic and political uncertainties involved. During this and subsequent projects, Ken Arrow once again gave of his time and helped straighten out my thinking as it developed. My debt of gratitude here also extends to Harry F. Oppenheimer, a particularly far-sighted business leader who appreciated the need for a new approach to market analysis.

Ken brought the work of Jacques Drèze to my attention. Indeed I am grateful to Professor Drèze for explaining to me the relationship to my present effort of his and his colleagues' earlier work on modelling the stochastic demand for electricity (Drèze, 1964). Ben Friedman, Gary Smith, Vance Roley and John Cochrane have been invaluable in helping me structure my firm's CRED-INTEL system, an ongoing Arrow-Bayes analysis of the US credit market. Finally, John Harsanyi has taught me to think about the problem of characterizing subjective probability distributions in terms of symmetry considerations, both in game theory and in price theory.

Clearly, I bear sole responsibility for all errors extant in the present work.

NOTES

1. In the field of interest rate forecasting, 'passive' portfolio managers sidestep forecasting and as a matter of philosophy accept the 'market's own forecast'. But assuming these investors are risk averse, and assuming they wish to make rational investment decisions, then they must make an interest rate forecast: for while the market offers them a kind of mean, it does not give them the *variance* needed for rational decision-making under uncertainty. An Arrow-Bayes model generates both mean and variance endogenously.

For a sophisticated discussion of interest rate risk assessment by conventional techniques, see Meltzer and Mascaro (1983). In their model, which is not a forecasting model, interest rate risk is interpreted as the historical variability of the unanticipated growth in monetary aggregates. In contrast to this, interest rate risk in the CRED-INTEL forecasting system (1984) is characterized in terms of some 40 future-oriented uncertainties – one of which is unanticipated growth in the monetary aggregates.

2. In the second version of Arrow's model, financial institutions serve as a substitute for missing contingent claims markets assumed to exist in his first model. When this is the case, there is an asymmetry between the forecasting activities of consumers and producers. In the Appendix to his paper, Arrow notes that the managers of firms should base their production decisions on a set of quasi-objective price probabilities r_s endogenously determined by the

market: remarkably, r_s is the price of a security that pays $1.00 in state *s*, and pays nothing otherwise. Notwithstanding this, owners of firms will have their own subjective forecasts that will not in general coincide with r_s.

3. Economists attempting to explain the past usually employ reduced form models. For forecasting the future, use of a reduced form model is problematic for reasons of *how* experts think and know what they know (recall Section 1, and see Sections 3 and 4). Additionally, if for some reason a reduced form model is required, it can be derived from a structural model. See Friedman and Roley (1977) for a convincing statement of the benefits of such an approach. The result will be a model that is richer and more significant from an epistemological standpoint.

4. The demand-state/supply-state variables appearing in the tree are not necessarily the most 'important' variables in the sense of having the greatest explanatory power or 'forecasting power'. Rather they will be those highly uncertain variables possessing a high expected 'value of information'. Important variables whose future values are predictable (for example, the population of the US in 1988) will enter into the analysis via a deterministic model of some sort. No Bayesian expert assessments of these factors will be called for.

5. The stochastic equilibrium analysis of Figure 18.6 is conditional upon a 2 per cent Free World growth rate in industrial production between the 1982–7 period. The desired unconditional distribution $\{p\}$ would, of course, result from expansion over this variable that gives rise to stochastic dependence between the supply and demand schedules (recall Figure 18.2). We have not shown this due to lack of space.

REFERENCES

Arrow, K. J. (1953) 'Le role des Valeurs Boursières pour la Repartition la Meilleure des Risques', *Econometrie: Colloques Internationaux du Centre National de la Recherche Scientifique*, 11.

Arrow, K. J. (1972) 'General Economic Equilibrium: Purpose, Analytic Techniques, Collective Choice', *Nobel Memorial Lecture*, The Nobel Foundation.

Arrow, K. J. (1982) 'Risk and Perception in Psychology and Economics', *Economic Inquiry*, 20.

Brainard, W. and G. Smith (1976) 'The Value of *A Priori* Information in Estimating a Financial Model', *The Journal of Finance*, 31(5).

Brock, H. W. (1979) 'A Game Theoretic Account of Social Justice', *Theory and Decision*, 11.

Brock, H. W. (1981) 'The Future World Price of Gold', *Optima*, 30(2).

Brock, H. W. (1983) 'The Future World Price of Copper', Strategic Economic Decisions Research Report, May 1982 (revised in October 1983).

Brock, H. W. (1985) 'Making Money While Managing Risk', *Trusts and Estates*.

Brock, H. W. and D. M. Nesbitt (1977) *Large Scale Energy Planning Models: A Methodological Analysis*, Stanford Research Institute Report, Prepared for the National Science Foundation, Contract No C-915, May 1977.

Brock, H. W. and D. M. Nesbitt (1979) 'General Equilibrium, Duality Theory, and the "Translog",' *Economie Appliquée*, 32.

CRED-INTEL System (1984) *Strategic Economic Decisions*, vols 1–6.

Dornbush, R. (1980) 'Exchange Rate Economics: Where Do We Stand?' *Brookings Papers*, 1980: I.

Drèze, J. H. (1964) 'Some Postwar Contributions of French Economists to Theory and Public Policy', *American Economic Review*, 54(4).

Friedman, B. M. and V. V. Roley (1977) 'Structural Models of Interest Rate Determination and Portfolio Behavior in the Corporate and Government Bond Markets', *American Statistical Association: Proceedings of the Business and Economics Statistics Section.*

Goldberger, A. S., A. L. Nagar and H. S. Odeh (1961) 'The Covariance Matrices of Reduced-Form Coefficients and of Forecasts for a Structural Econometric Model', *Econometrica*, 29(4).

Howard, R. H. (1970) 'Decision Analysis: Perspectives on Inference, Decision, and Experimentation', *Proceedings of the IEEE*, 58(5).

Meltzer, A. and A. Mascaro (1983) 'Long and Short Term Interest Rates in a Risky World', *Journal of Monetary Economics*, 12.

Pratt, J. W., H. Raiffa and R. Schlaifer (1965) *Introduction To Statistical Decision Theory* (New York: McGraw-Hill).

Samuelson, P. A. (1967) *Foundations of Economic Analysis* (New York: Atheneum).

Smith, G. (1981) 'The Systematic Specification of a Full Prior Covariance Matrix for Asset Demand Equations', *The Quarterly Journal of Economics.*

Smith, G. and I. Anabtawi (1985) 'The Credit Market Approach to Financial Markets', paper submitted for publication, 1985.

Winston, P. H. (1984) *Artificial Intelligence* 2nd edn (Reading: Addison Wesley).

19 Rational Learning and Rational Expectations

Margaret Bray and David M. Kreps*

1 INTRODUCTION

Much recent work in the economics of information has stemmed from the observation that demand functions, and therefore prices, reflect agents' private information. Given an adequate understanding of the relationship between private information and equilibrium prices, it is possible to infer some or all of the private information. It seems natural to suppose, therefore, that agents will endeavour to use the information contained in equilibrium prices.

The current fashion in microeconomic theory is to tailor these ideas into the concept of a rational expectations equilibrium. (Grossman, 1981, gives a survey of applications.) In equilibrium there is a functional relationship between private signals and equilibrium prices that establishes a statistical relationship between payoff-relevant variables and equilibrium prices. If an agent knew both the statistical relationship and the equilibrium price, the agent would use Bayes's rule to compute a posterior assessment on the payoff-relevant variables and use this posterior to formulate demand. In a rational expectations equilibrium it is supposed that every agent *knows* the correct statistical relationship, and markets clear at equilibrium prices when the information contained in equilibrium prices is taken into account by each agent.

As is well known, this concept of equilibrium poses certain problems. Equilibria need not always exist (see Green, 1977; Kreps, 1977),

*Conversations with Kenneth Arrow, Adam Brandenburger, and Paul Milgrom were very helpful. This research was supported in part by National Science Foundation Grant SES80-06407 to the Graduate School of Business, Stanford University, by the Office of Naval Research Contract N00014-77-C-0518 to Yale University, and by the Graduate School of Business, Stanford University.

It is a pleasure for us to be able to participate in honouring Kenneth J. Arrow. This essay specifically concerns a topic on which he has written. But more generally, the general topic area – the dynamics of equilibrium through time and under uncertainty – is one for which he is chiefly responsible. His work has always been both model and inspiration for us, and it is with gratitude that we dedicate this essay to him.

although in many cases they exist generically (Radner, 1979; Allen, 1981; Jordan, 1982a) or when the right sort of noise exists (Anderson and Sonnenschein, 1982). The question of implementation of these equilibria is complex; if agents need to know the equilibrium price before they can formulate their demand, how is the equilibrium price determined? If the mechanism employed is to have each agent submit a demand correspondence, difficulties may arise (Beja, 1976). Some iterative mechanisms have been studied (Kobayashi, 1977; Jordan, 1982c), but they seem unrealistic. Realistic mechanisms do not give rational expectations equilibria, even in the perfectly competitive case (Dubey, Geanakoplos and Shubik, 1983).

In this paper we shall ignore these difficulties to concentrate on another. The supposition in a rational expectations equilibrium is that agents all know the correct statistical relationship between payoff-relevant variables and prices. How do they come to have this knowledge? One possibility, in the spirit of Radner's (1972) equilibria of plans, prices and price expectations, is that all agents are very good analysts who understand their environment and can work out the equilibrium functional relationship between information and prices, and so infer the correct statistical relationship between payoff-relevant variables and prices. This is incredible on two grounds: first, agents must have very detailed knowledge of their environment (utility functions of their fellows and such) and they must possess an extraordinary level of analytic ability. Early proponents of the concept have offered another explanation: Imagine that the underlying uncertainty in this economy is stationary. Then, over time, agents will learn the true relationship between payoff-relevant variables and prices. At the very least, if they supposed a relationship other than one given by a rational expectations equilibrium, in time they would learn the error of their ways.

It does seem reasonable that only a rational expectations equilibrium could persist as a stationary relationship in a stationary environment. But it does not follow that agents will ever figure out the correct stationary relationship; it is at least not obvious that a stationary relationship will ever emerge. There are substantial difficulties in supposing that agents will learn what is going on: Agents, as they learn, will modify their demand and thus will change the equilibrium relationship. Even if the underlying environment is stationary, if agents are learning there is every reason to suppose that the relationship between prices and payoff-relevant variables will *not* be stationary. So we come back to the question: Will agents learn the correct relationship – will the economy settle down into a stationary rational expectations equilibrium?

Two rather different types of models have been used to study this question. The first type, which we call 'irrational learning models', imposes exogenously the way in which agents learn. The analyst assumes that agents use some reasonable learning procedure, perhaps the sort of learning procedure that is taught in econometrics courses, and then the analyst shows whether convergence to a stationary and correct model ensues. Radner (1982) and Bray (1982, proposition 4) both suppose that agents are hard to convince, but once convinced their conviction is (nearly) total: Agents suppose a stationary relationship holds, and they observe what happens for a very long time *without changing their beliefs*. Thus throughout this period there is a stationary relationship between prices and payoff-relevant variables. If the agents' initial beliefs are confirmed (in the long run) by what they see, nothing happens, but if the stationary relationship that emerges is different from what they initially supposed, they simultaneously adopt for their models what they have observed. (It is supposed that they hold on to their initial beliefs 'long enough' so that when they 'update', they update to the stationary relationship that ensues from their initial beliefs.) Of course, when they change their beliefs, they may change the equilibrium relationship, but they hold on to their new model long enough to learn the stationary relationship that it engenders, then they update to this stationary relationship, and so forth. The question is whether this sequence of stationary relationships, each one being the equilibrium relationship that ensues if agents believe that the previous relationship is correct, will converge to some relationship that does hold when agents employ it as their model.

Blume and Easley (1982) study an economy where agents maintain the belief throughout that one of a finite number of stationary models is correct. Each time agents get a new observation, they reassess their subjective probability distribution on which model is correct. Of course, because agents are changing their beliefs, the truth is that *none* of their models is correct – the true relationship between prices and states of nature is non-stationary.

Bray (1982, proposition 5) and Bray and Savin (1984) look at an economy where the true rational expectations equilibrium has as price a linear function of the private information, something that the agents do in fact know at the outset. But, it is supposed, agents do not know the coefficients of this linear function; their response is to engage in ordinary least-squares (OLS) estimation, to try to learn this coefficient, where at any point in time they use their best estimate to-date to formulate their demand. Of course, this use of OLS is correct if their environment is stationary, which it is not: as their best estimate to-date changes, so does the current equilibrium relationship.

In each of these papers it is found that convergence to the correct stationary rational expectations equilibrium is possible. Roughly put, this will happen if the effect of the learning process on the equilibrium from one date to the next is small; if, for example, only a small fraction of the agents are learning. But Radner (1982) and Bray (1982, proposition 4) can produce examples of cycles and divergence, Bray (1982, section 5) can (probably) produce divergence, and Blume and Easley (1982) have a whole menagerie as possibilities: cycles can exist, beliefs can diverge, and there can even be convergence of beliefs to an incorrect model. That is, it is possible that a stationary relationship emerges that is *not* the one that agents suppose is emerging.

The second type of model used to study the question of learning is a 'rational learning model'. In such a model, agents' uncertainty about the correct relationship between prices and payoff-relevant variables stems from their uncertainty about the values of certain parameters of the economy. If we specify how agents learn – how they update their assessments about these parameters – and how they formulate demand at each date given their beliefs, then a relationship emerges between payoff-relevant variables and equilibrium prices. This relationship is usually non-stationary. Note that the price at date t will depend not only on current signals; it will depend on previously encountered signals, because those signals have influenced what agents have (so far) learned and, therefore, their current demand. A rational learning model is one where at each date t agents *know* this correct relationship between prices and payoff-relevant variables up to the value of the unknown parameters, in the sense that their demand at each date maximizes their expected utility, conditional on all the information that is contained in previous and current equilibrium prices (and their private signals). This is at least as demanding in terms of the analytic ability of agents as the original story in which agents calculate the rational expectations equilibrium. Indeed, we have done nothing more than generate a *grander* rational expectations equilibrium that allows for subjective uncertainty about variables treated as known parameters in standard models. Starting with the way in which agents learn, we generate actual equilibrium relationships, and we then close the system by insisting that the learning process is in accord with the actual equilibrium relationships. The question of how agents learn *about* the equilibrium relationship is moot. They *know* what the relationship is – what we really have is a model of rational learning of the (unknown) parameters *within* a rational expectations equilibrium.

A number of authors (Arrow and Green, 1973; Blume and Easley, 1981; Lewis, 1981; Frydman, 1982; and especially Townsend, 1978 and 1983) have studied particular simple cases of such rational learning models, and they have always found convergence to the correct stationary relationship. Because they have studied very simple and special examples, it is not clear that this result will generalize. In this chapter we argue that the result does generalize, at least in so far as one is interested in convergence of beliefs: If learning is rational, then agents' beliefs will converge with probability one. And beliefs will *not* converge to some incorrect conclusion. But if one is after the stronger result that the economy settles down into some stationary rational expectations equilibrium (assuming the underlying stationarity required if there is to be any hope of this result), then one should be hopeful but not cocksure: The convergence of beliefs gives a powerful lever for obtaining the stronger result, but there are potential pitfalls (arising primarily from the possibility of multiple equilibria) that we, at least, do not know how to avoid in any generality.

The reader should be forewarned that the conclusions that beliefs converge, and that they do not converge to something incorrect, are trivial once the right mathematical weapon is identified: the martingale convergence theorem. This result is quite general; it does not rely on the particular context of rational expectations equilibrium, but is true about any model of Bayesian learning (hence it applies as well to Nash equilibria of games, multi-armed bandit problems, and so on). Indeed, it is surprising that this result, which applies to any model of rational, sequential learning and which can have powerful consequences, is so little used by economists. (It is certainly well known by probabilists and statisticians.) Also, beyond working out another particular example, we have very little to say concerning going beyond the convergence-of-beliefs result; we can point out the pitfalls, but we have little (or nothing) positive to add.

We begin in Section 2 by presenting a rational learning model for the economy studied by Bray (1982). In the context of this economy, we show that there is a unique equilibrium with rational learning and rational expectations, in which agents' beliefs converge, prices settle down and agents (eventually) learn the true value of the parameter(s) about which they were initially uncertain.

With this as prototype, we proceed to examine the pieces of the argument, to see how (and to what extent) the pieces might generalize. Section 3 concerns the very general result that beliefs will (nearly) always converge in a rational learning model, and the limit of beliefs cannot be incorrect. As noted above, this has nothing particular to do with the subject of rational expectations – these are statements about any model in which an agent updates beliefs rationally in light of increasingly finer information.

Sections 4 and 5 discuss the adaptation of the general results of section 3 to the context of rational expectations equilibria. In section 4 we sketch a fairly general formulation of rational expectations equilibria for economies with a sequence of markets – all that is done is to meld together the usual notion of a rational expectations equilibrium with Radner's (1972) equilibrium of plans, prices and price expectations. We then specialize to contexts in which one might hope to derive convergence through time to a stationary rational expectations equilibrium; that is, economies that are stationary up to some (partially unknown) parameters. We discuss how multiplicity of equilibria can make life miserable for anyone who seeks positive results, and how (if one can somehow avoid the problems of multiple equilibria) 'smoothness' assumptions can be used to derive convergence of equilibrium prices and allocations to some stationary rational expectations equilibrium. Finally, we discuss examples that show how it will generally be difficult to say to what stationary equilibrium one will converge, if one indeed does converge at all.

Concluding remarks and discussion are given in Section 6. As noted above, our results deal not with the question of learning about a rational expectations equilibrium but rather with that of learning within a rational expectations equilibrium. It is not a question of agents who lack computational power, but agents who are great at computing equilibria and who lack critical information about their environment. Since we have titled the paper 'Rational Learning and Rational Expectations', it might seem that we identify *rational learning* with *learning within*. Can one speak of rational learning *about* a rational expectations equilibrium? We will contend in Section 6 that, according to the standards of *rationality* that are commonplace in economic theory, this would reduce to learning *within*. However this should be seen as a negative statement about the current standards: We conclude in the end that while the models investigated here set a benchmark of extreme rationality, the best work to be done on this subject will be in models where learning is a bit more realistic and a bit (or even a lot) less rational.

2 RATIONAL LEARNING: AN EXAMPLE

Consider an economy with two agents, one informed and the other uninformed.[1] At each date $t=0,1,2,\ldots$, each agent is endowed with one unit of a one period risky asset yielding a random gross return r_t at date $t+1/2$. There is also a safe asset traded at date t; it is in zero net supply, and its price at date t and its (certain) gross return at date $t+1/2$ are both normalized to unity. Agent n (for $n=I$ for informed and $n=U$ for uninformed) has a von Neumann-Morgenstern utility function

$$-e^{-(x_t^n r_t + y_t^n)/\theta^n}$$

where x_t^n and y_t^n are the agent's holdings (from date t to $t+1/2$) of the risky and the safe assets, respectively, and where θ^n is agent n's coefficient of risk tolerance. Returns from the assets are not storable – realized at date $t+1/2$, they must be consumed immediately. To preserve analytical tractibility, we will not worry about negative consumption or physical feasibility. The only constraint imposed on agents is the budget constraint: If p_t is the price of the risky asset at date t (recalling that the safe asset is numeraire), then the budget constraint for agent n is

$$x_t^n p_t + y_t^n = p_t.$$

Both agents observe last period's return on the risky asset, r_{t-1}, prior to date t trading. In addition, the informed agent observes an unbiased predictor ρ_t of r_t. We assume that $\{\rho_t\}$ is an i.i.d. sequence of normal random variables, and that $r_t=\rho_t+\varepsilon_t$, where $\{\varepsilon_t\}$ is also a sequence of i.i.d. normal random variables and where the full collection of random variables $\{\rho_t,\varepsilon_t;t=0,1,\ldots\}$ is independent. The error terms ε_t have zero means and variances σ^2.

If all the agents knew ρ_t at date t, they would have no reason to attempt to draw inferences about ρ_t from the price. If the price were p, agent n would demand $(\theta^n/\sigma^2)(\rho_t - p)$, and thus the equilibrium price would be

$$p = \rho_t - \frac{2\sigma^2}{\theta^I + \theta^U}.$$

Of course, agent U does not know ρ_t. But if the equilibrium price (as a function of ρ_t, σ^2, θ^I *and* θ^U) is given by $p = \rho_t - 2\sigma^2(\theta^I + \theta U)$, and if *agent U knows that this is so*, then agent U can discern from the equilibrium price the value of ρ_t, demand $(\theta^n/\sigma^2)(\rho_t - p)$, and (thus) establish $p = \rho_t - 2\sigma^2/(\theta^I + \theta^U)$ as the equilibrium price. This, then, is a *rational expectations equilibrium.* Note: this requires that agent U know the formula $p = \rho_t - 2\sigma^2/(\theta^I + \theta^U)$. The question is: How does agent U come to know that this formula gives equilibrium prices?[2]

If agent U knows the values of σ^2, θ^I and θ^U, then agent U (assuming that he is very good at economic analysis) can compute this as the equilibrium. (In this example this is the unique rational expectations equilibrium, so no ambiguity can ensue.) But suppose that at the outset agent U does not know the value of θ^I. To be precise, suppose agent U's prior assessment (at date $t = 0$) as to the value of θ^I is given by a distribution function F_0 on some subinterval $[a,b]$ of $(0,\infty)$. Assume that F_0 has a continuous density on $[a,b]$, and that θ^I is independent of $\{\rho_t, \varepsilon_t\}$. Assume also that agent U knows the values of σ^2 and (of course) θ^U.

Roughly speaking, if agent U sees a high equilibrium price for the asset at date zero, he can now attribute it to either of two factors: It could be due to a high value of ρ_t that would, *ceteris paribus*, increase I's demand. Or it could be due to a high value of θ^I; I's demand increases the more risk-tolerant he is. At date zero, U must weigh these two factors to discern what information is contained in the equilibrium price; then, later in period 0, agent U learns the value of r_0. Suppose that the equilibrium price p_0 was high, but r_0 was low. Then agent U will conclude that the high value of p_0 was *more* likely to be due to high θ^I than to high ρ_0. Agent U updates his assessment of θ^I accordingly – let F_1 be the distribution function of his new assessment – and the process continues. It is important to note two things: First, if $F_1 \neq F_0$, then (presumably) the equilibrium price at date 1 (as a function of θ^I and ρ_1) will be different from the price at date 0 (as a function of θ^I and ρ_0), because agent U's new assessment will (presumably) change his demand at every price p. Secondly, the distribution function F_1 is a *random* function; it depends on the actual realizations of θ^I, ρ_0 and ε_0.

Agent U's behaviour at any date t is composed of two parts. First, given F_t, what inferences about ρ_t (and thus r_t) does U draw from the equilibrium price, and how does this affect his demand? Secondly, given realizations of the equilibrium price and (later) r_t, how does U update to get F_{t+1}? Once we know the answers to these questions, we can describe the (possibly random) evolution of the economy. (In this simple example, we can and do assume that agent I's demand at date t is given by $(\theta^I/\sigma^2)(\rho_t - p)$. Even if agent I is initially unaware of θ^U, its value is irrelevant to him; he learns ρ_t and so has no reason to look for any further information in equilibrium prices. In more general models we would have to be concerned with the same two parts of agent I's behaviour: his demand and his learning process.)

For example, following Bray (1982) and Bray and Savin (1984), we might make the following suppositions: Agent U is a good enough economist to realize that in the stationary equilibrium ρ_t is a stationary and linear function of p_t, $\rho_t = a + bp_t$. In the rational expectations equilibrium, this is, of course, correct; the coefficients are $a = 2\sigma^2/(\theta^I + \theta^U)$ and $b = 1$. The problem is that the uninformed agent does not know the coefficients. This agent also cannot observe ρ_t but can observe $r_t = \rho_t + \varepsilon_t$. The agent estimates the coefficient by OLS regression of r on p. Let a_{t-1} and b_{t-1} be the estimates obtained using observations $\{p_1, r_1, \ldots, p_{t-1}, r_{t-1}\}$. Agent U's demand at time t is based on the hypothesis that $\rho_t = a_{t-1} + b_{t-1}p_t$, and the next estimate is obtained by updating in OLS fashion given p_t and r_t.

With these assumptions, the actual equilibrium price function at date t is the solution of

$$\theta^U \frac{(a_{t-1} + b_{t-1}p_t - p_t)}{\sigma^2} + \theta^I \frac{(\rho_t - p_t)}{\sigma^2} = 2. \tag{1}$$

Note that agent U is misapplying his knowledge of econometrics; he does OLS correctly, but his model of the economy is misspecified. He supposes that $\rho_t = a + bp_t$, where a and b do not change with time. But, in fact, the solution to (1) is

$$\rho_t = \frac{\sigma^2}{\theta^I}\left(2 - \frac{\theta^U a_{t-1}}{\sigma^2}\right) + \frac{\sigma^2}{\theta^I}\left(\frac{\theta^I + \theta^U}{\sigma^2} - \frac{\theta^U}{\sigma^2} b_{t-1}\right) p_t.$$

The coefficients do change with time.

In general, if we specify a 'learning and discerning (thus demand)' model for agent U, we will get out *actual* equilibrium price functions for each date. The price at date t, p_t, will be some function

$$p_t(\rho_t;F_0,\theta^I,\rho_0,\rho_1,\ldots,\rho_{t-1},\varepsilon_0,\ldots,\varepsilon_{t-1}).$$

(If U's current assessment F_t of θ^I is sufficient for $(F_0,\rho_0,\ldots,\rho_{t-1},\varepsilon_0,\ldots,\varepsilon_{t-1})$ in terms of all subsequent behaviour, then we can abbreviate this as $p_t(\rho_t;F_t;\theta^I)$. We are treating θ^U and σ^2 as parametric in these functions.) We shall ignore questions of existence and uniqueness of equilibria that arise here; we carry on assuming that an equilibrium exists and that a selection has been made if there is more than one equilibrium.[3]

Agent U's econometric model would be correctly specified if he based all his inferences on these being the equilibrium price functions; if his demand at date t, as a function of equilibrium price p_t and past data $p_0,\ldots,p_{t-1}$ and $r_0,\ldots,r_{t-1}$, is based on his conditional assessment of ρ_t (and hence r_t) given these data, and if he updates his assessment of θ^I, given the realizations of p_t and r_t in Bayesian fashion using a correctly specified likelihood function and the function p_t. We shall say that we have a *rational expectations learning model* when behaviour so determined by a sequence of functions $\{p_t\}$ leads to those functions as equilibrium prices for the economy. (If this is too vague, the reader should consult the general formulation in Section 4).

Does a *rational expectations learning model* exist for our economy? Yes, one does, and it is unique. We now show how to construct it recursively. Assume that at date t, based on all data received so far, agent U's assessment of θ^I is given by the distribution function F_t on $[a,b]$ that has continuous density function f_t. (As we said earlier: U's initial assessment is that θ^I is independent of $\{(\rho_t,\varepsilon_t)\}$. Thus his assessment at date t is that θ^I is independent of $\{\rho_s,\varepsilon_s);s\geqslant t\}$.)

Recall that demand by the informed agent, as a function of the price p, the information ρ_t, and θ^I, is

$$X^I(p,\rho_t,\theta^I)=\theta^I(\rho_t-p)/\sigma^2. \tag{2}$$

In equilibrium, $X^I+X^U=2$, so the uninformed agent can infer X^I from his own equilibrium holding X^U.[4] Equation (2) can be used to compute ρ_t as a function of θ^I and the other, known, variables (σ^2, X^I and p):

$$\rho_t=(\sigma^2X^I/\theta^I)+p. \tag{3}$$

The uninformed agent's current assessment of θ^I, together with his prior on ρ_t, thus yields a posterior on r_t (which will not be normal in general). This yields a demand function for the uninformed agent that is downward sloping and depends only on p, as follows:

Fix some p in (3) for the moment, and let X^I vary. As X^I increases, the uninformed agent's assessment over ρ_t and thus over r_t shifts (stochastically) upward. At any price p, this increases the desirability of the risky good for the uninformed agent: We can compute the uninformed agent's demand given the equilibrium data X_I and p, obtaining a schedule $x^U(p,X^I)$ that is increasing in X^I (and that depends, implicitly, on the density f_t). An equilibrium condition is that $X^I+x^U(p,X^I)=2$, and since x^U increases with X^I, for each p there is a *unique* X^I satisfying this equation. Calling this value $x^I(p)$, we have the demand of the uninformed agent, as a function of p alone, as $X^U(p)=2-x^I(p)$. Differentiating $x^I(p)+x^U(p,x^I(p))=2$ yields

$$\frac{dx^I}{dp}=-\frac{\partial x^U}{\partial p}/(1+\frac{\partial x^U}{\partial x^I})>0,$$

and, since $dx^I/dp=-dX^U/dp$, $X^U(p)$ is downward sloping. Recalling that $X^I(p,\rho_t,\theta^I)$ is a decreasing function of p, this implies that there is a unique and well-defined equilibrium price p_t solving

$$X^I(p,\rho_t,\theta^I)+X^U(p)=2. \tag{4}$$

This price p_t depends upon θ^I, ρ_t, and the density function f_t. In order to specify the entire equilibrium, we must finally specify how this density f_t evolves through time. Suppose that the agent, after learning r_{t-1} at time t, has an assessment given by f_t and then acts as above. At time $t+1$ he has three new pieces of data: p_t – the equilibrium price last period; x_t^U – his allocation; and r_t. As $X_t^I=2-X_t^U$, he can infer X_t^I. From (3), the likelihood of observing p_t, X_t^U and r_t given θ^I, is the likelihood that $\rho_t=(\sigma^2(2-X_t^U)/\theta^I)+p_t$ given r_t, which, as $r_t=\rho_t+\varepsilon_t$ and (ρ_t,ε_t) is normal, is the normal density function $g(\cdot|r_t)$ of ρ_t, given r_t. Thus using Bayes's rule, the revised posterior assessment for θ^I is:

$$P(\theta^I\leqslant z|p_t,r_t) = \frac{\int_a^z f_t(\theta)g\,(\,(\sigma^2(2-x^U(p_t)\,)/\theta)+p_t|r_t)d\theta}{\int_a^b f_t(\theta)g(\,(\sigma^2(2-x^U(p_t)\,)/\theta)+p_t|r_t)d\theta}. \tag{5}$$

Note that as the uninformed agent begins with a prior over θ^I that has a density function on the interval $[a,b]$, (5) ensures that the posterior will also be of this form. As we assume that agent U begins with such a prior, all subsequent posterior distributions will have this form.

It is worth noting that while we have not computed the equilibrium prices, we could, in principle, do so. (All that would be needed is a large computer budget and, almost certainly, a good graduate student.) The major difficulty is in computing $x^U(p,X^I)$ – since the uninformed agent's posterior assessment for r_t is not normal, finding his optimal net trade is quite difficult. If this can be done efficiently, then solving numerically $x^I(p)+x^U(p,x^I(p))=2$ to get $X^U(p)$, and then (4) and (5), will not be difficult. But closed form solutions are out of the question.

If F_t did not have a continuous density function we would still obtain a unique equilibrium price $p(\rho_t;\theta^I,F_t)$. Of course, in this case F_{t+1} would not necessarily have a continuous density. But there will be an equilibrium price. And this price changes continuously in F_t:

Lemma 1. Consider the function $p{:}R\times[a,b]\times M[a,b]\rightarrow R$ constructed above (where R is the real line and $M[a,b]$ is the space of Borel measures on $[a,b]$). The function $F\rightarrow p(\cdot,\cdot,F)$ is continuous in the weak topology on $M[a,b]$ to the topology on $R^{R\times[a,b]}$ given by uniform convergence on all compact subsets of the domain.

This is a matter of epsilons and deltas, and it is left to the reader.

Now that we know that a rational learning model exists, what can be said about its evolution? Although we cannot write down the equilibrium prices, we can derive a fairly strong result:

Proposition 1. For the rational learning model derived above, F_t converges weakly to a point mass at θ^I, and thus prices at date t, $p(\rho_t;\theta^I,F_t)$, converge to $\rho_t-2\sigma^2/(\theta^U+\theta^I)$, with probability one.

That is, agent U eventually learns the true value of θ^I, and the equilibrium prices (and allocations) settle down to those of the 'stationary rational expectations equilibrium'.

The proof of this is best taken in steps:

Step 1A: For Λ any measurable set in $[a,b]$, the sequence of random variables $\{F_t(\Lambda)\}$ (meaning the probability assessed by agent U at date t that $\theta^I\in\Lambda$) converges to some random variable F_Λ with probability one.

This is the crucial step, and the easiest one as well, once the proper mathematical tool is applied. In any model of Bayesian learning,

$E[F_{t+1}(\Lambda)|\text{information available at date } t] = F_t(\Lambda)$.

In words, the average probability assessed at date $t+1$ that an event occurs, averaged according to date t data, is simply the probability assessed (on the basis of that data) at date t. Thus the sequence of random variables $\{F_t(\Lambda)\}$ forms a martingale. The martingale is obviously bounded (between zero and one), and so the martingale convergence theorem implies that $F_t(\Lambda)$ will converge to some number with probability one (see Doob, 1953; or Chung, 1974).[5]

Step 1B: With probability one, the (random) distribution functions will converge weakly to *some* limiting (random) distribution function F_∞. Moreover, this F_∞ will be a regular version of the conditional probability of θ^I that U will make based on *all* the information he obtains.

This is a strengthening of Step 1A, extending the convergence from sequences of numbers $\{F_t(\Lambda)\}$ to the sequence of distribution functions $\{F_t\}$. It involves a bit of tedious analysis, but nothing more than that – the statement in a general setting is given in Section 3 as Proposition 3.

Step 2: The price function at date t, $p(\cdot,\cdot,F_t)$, converges (with probability one) to $p(\cdot,\cdot,F_\infty)$ in the topologies of Lemma 1.

This is a simple corollary of Lemma 1 and Step 1B.

Step 3: The joint distribution of the random variables r_t and $p(\rho_t;\theta^I,F_\infty)$, for the true value of θ^I, is eventually 'known' to agent U with probability one.

To be precise, this distribution function is measurable with respect to all the information that U receives. This is a simple application of Step 2 and the law of large numbers, either weak or strong. For any real numbers r and p, if agent U simply keeps a running average of the number of times that $r_t \leqslant r$ and $p_t = p(\rho_t;\theta^I,F_\infty) < p$, then this will (with probability one) converge to the probability that any $r_t \leqslant r$ and $p(\rho_t;\theta^I,F_\infty) \leqslant p$, because $\{\rho_t,\varepsilon_t)\}$ forms an i.i.d. sequence. (To be more precise, this will be true for pairs (r,p) that are continuity points of the joint distribution function, and those values are distribution determining.)

Step 4: For any distribution function F, the joint distribution of $(r_t,p(\rho_t;\theta^I,F))$ as a function of θ^I is one-to-one in θ^I. Thus the true value of θ^I is measurable (with probability one) with respect to all the information collected by agent U. And thus, since F_∞ is a regular version of U's conditional assessment of θ^I, conditional on all the information he collects, F_∞ will be a point mass at θ^I. (And, therefore, by Lemma 1, equilibrium prices will approach the 'stationary rational equilibrium prices'; that is, $p(\rho_t;\theta^I,F_\infty)=\rho_t-2\sigma^2/(\theta^I+\theta^U)$.)

Only the first part of this requires any elaboration, and even this part is simple: Holding F constant, X^U is unaffected by changes in θ^I, while X^I is increasing in θ^I, so for each possible value of r_t the distribution of the corresponding $p(\rho_t;\theta^I,F)$ is strictly increasing in θ^I.

3 RATIONAL LEARNING MODELS AND CONVERGENCE OF BELIEFS

The proof of proposition 1 can be thought of as comprising the following parts: (a) definition of a rational learning model; (b) the demonstration that, in this context, there is a rational learning model and it is unique, with the *only* thing linking the past with the date t spot market equilibrium being the uninformed agent's posterior assessment of θ^I, given information received through date $t-1$; (c) convergence of beliefs in a rational learning model (Steps 1A and 1B); (d) going from convergence of beliefs to the statement that prices settle down into a stationary relationship, and thus that agents will all 'learn' that relationship (Lemma 1, plus Step 2, and then Step 3); and (e) Step 4 – the assertion that this relationship reveals the unknown parameters.

What mathematical magic there is here comes in step (c). In this section we provide in a very general context the mechanics that give us (c). It is unnecessary in doing so to mention anything pertaining to the economy or to rational expectations; we simply consider a probability space, an agent with some prior probability assessment over that space, and a sequence of increasingly finer information that this agent receives. *Rational learning* is defined as Bayesian learning; computation of conditional probabilities. In subsequent sections we will then apply these general ideas to rational expectations equilibria.

Consider a measure space (Ω, G) and a probability measure P on the space. Think of P as the prior probability assessment of some agent over the space. Through some process or other, this agent receives information about the state of the world as time passes: Time is indexed by $t=1,2, \ldots,$ and we write $\{H_t; t=1,2,\ldots\}$ for the filtration of information received by this agent; that is, each H_t is a sub-sigma field of G, giving those events that the agent is able to perceive at date t. It is assumed that the H_t are non-decreasing; our agent doesn't forget things once learned. Let H_∞ denote the collection of all things this agent ever learns; that is, $H_\infty = \vee_t H_t$.

Fix any event A from G. We assume that, at date t, our agent assesses probability $P(A|H_t)$ that A will occur. Of course, this conditional probability is a random variable depending in general on what information the agent has received up to time t; what observations he has made; and so on. The point is that these random variables will, with probability one, converge to some limit belief, and this limit will not be 'incorrect'.

Proposition 2. For any event A, the limit (in t) of $P(A|H_t)$ almost surely exists and is equal to $P(A|H_\infty)$. Moreover, there is probability zero that the agent will in the limit assess probability zero to A when A is true, and there is probability zero that the agent will assess probability one to A when A is false. (In other words, $P(A \cap \{\omega : P(A/H_\infty)=0\})=0$, and $P(A^C \cap \{\omega : P(A/H_\infty)=1\})=0$.)

For some people, this proposition is quite incredible; for others it seems obvious. Let us first state the case for it being obvious. As one learns more and more, one refines one's assessments of the probability of the event A. There is certainly meaning in the term 'one's limit assessment', this being the assessment that one would make given *all* the information that one will ever receive. The convergence part of the proposition, then, simply asserts that as one gets more and more of all the information one will ever get, one's assessments will converge to that limit assessment. Thinking in terms of a finite partition generating G, the convergence is obvious; for each ω there is some cell of H_∞ containing ω, and for all (large enough) t this cell will be in H_t. Thus, once this large enough t is reached, the conditional probability of A stays constant. For infinite partitions underlying the sigma-field G, convergence is less obvious, but with the finite case for intuition, convergence is hardly surprising.

But a case can also be made that the extension to general G is, if not surprising, at least non-trivial. We cannot (even in the finite case) dispense with the qualification that convergence occurs almost surely only. Consider, for example, watching a bent coin being flipped over and over, with H_t the information embodied in the first t flips of the coin. If one's prior assessment is that the coin flips are exchangeable, then one will assess probability one that some long-run proportion of flips will be heads; call this the *bias* of the coin. Let Λ be the event: the bias of the coin is 50 per cent or less. (Suppose the prior probability of Λ is between zero and one.) Now there are strings of heads and tails that will lead to the conditional assessments of Λ to vary endlessly between (nearly) zero and one; strings where there are many heads (which will drive the conditional probability of Λ towards zero); followed by many more tails (which will drive the conditional probability of Λ towards one); followed by many, many more heads, and so on. (But, guaranteed by the proposition, the set of all such strings has prior probability zero.) The infinite G case is distinguished from the finite G case, not in the qualification that convergence occurs only a.s. – that qualification is required for both – rather, the difference is that in the infinite case there may be no finite time t at which one is aware that an event of prior probability zero has occurred; in the finite case the agent will know in finite time that something 'unusual' has happened.

Does this qualification make the proposition less than obvious? We think so, but this is surely a question of the power of one's intuition and/or imagination. In any event, the proof of convergence is quite easy once a (non-trivial) result is enlisted, namely the martingale convergence theorem. For the sequence $\{(P(\Lambda|H_t),H_t);t=0,1,\ldots,\infty\}$ forms a bounded, closed martingale, and the result follows immediately (see Chung, 1974, Theorem 9.4.6). And the second part of the proposition is equally easy:

$$\int_{\{P(\Lambda|H_\infty)=0\}} P(\Lambda|H_\infty)=\int_{\{P(\Lambda|H_\infty)=0\}} 1_\Lambda$$

by the definition of conditional probability. The left hand side is zero, and the right hand side is $P(\Lambda\bigcap\{\omega:P(\Lambda/H_\infty)=0\})$. The converse to this is similarly proved.

This proposition concerns the evolution of the conditional probability of a single set Λ – at the cost of a technical assumption, we can consider the evolution of the agent's entire posterior. Suppose that Ω is a complete and separable metric space and that (Ω,G) is a Borel space. Then for each t (including $t=\infty$) we can fix regular versions of conditional probability $P(\cdot|H_t)$.

Proposition 3. Given the assumptions above, $P(\cdot|H_t)$ converges weakly (in t) to $P(\cdot|H_\infty)$, $P-$a.s.

The proof is straightforward analysis, and details are omitted.

4 RATIONAL LEARNING WITHIN A RATIONAL EXPECTATIONS EQUILIBRIUM

We now specialize the very general results of Section 3 to the context of rational learning within a rational expectations equilibrium for an economy with a sequence of markets. As a first step, we sketch the definition of a rational expectations equilibrium for such an economy.

We fix I agents, indexed $i=1,2,\ldots,I$, and a (possibly terminating) sequence of dates $t=0,1,\ldots$ There is an underlying measure space (Ω,G) of states of the world and, for each agent i, a prior probability assessment P^i on (Ω,G). (These probability assessments could be identical, but they needn't be.) Agent i is endowed with a filtration of *private information* $\{G^i_t;t=0,1,\ldots\}$. This is meant to include all exogenously available information, including that which is available publicly. We write G_t for $\vee^I_{i=1}G^i_t$ – the sum of all information in the economy at date t.

In this economy there is a sequence of markets of all varieties: spot, futures, security, etc. Assume that there are N commodites, indexed $n=1,\ldots,N$, that are eaten at each date, and M other 'assets' that are traded at each date. Relative prices at any date, then, are random variables with range the simplex in R^{N+M}_+ – we use p_t to denote the (random) price at date t.

From 'equilibrium economic activity', agents learn things beyond what is encoded in their private information. For concreteness, we will assume that agents learn (only) from equilibrium relative prices. Given random vectors $\{p_t;t=0,1,\ldots\}$, write H^i_t for the sigmafield generated by G^i_t and $\{p_0,\ldots,p_t\}$. (We sometimes will write $H^i_t(p_0,\ldots,p_t)$ or $H^i_t(p)$ to show the dependence of these sigma-fields on the random vectors p_0 through p_t.)

Finally, agent i has preferences over consumption streams, a feasible consumption set, and (given prices) budget constraints. For concreteness we will assume that preferences are additively separable over time and states; more precisely, agent i seeks to maximize the expectation of $\sum^\infty_{t=0}u^i_t(x^i_t,\varphi^i_t)$, where x^i_t is a random vector with range R^N_+ and φ^i_t is some G^i_t – measurable random element.

In the spirit of Radner (1972), a rational expectations equilibrium of plans, prices and price expectations for this economy would be a sequence of prices $\{p_t;t=0,1,\ldots\}$, where p_t is measurable with respect to G_t, and sequences of net trades, one for each agent i, $\{y_t^i;t=0,1,\ldots\}$, where y_t^i is H_t^i measurable, such that markets clear for all dates and all states (with probability one – say with respect to the measure $\Sigma_i P^i/I$), and each agent's net trade maximizes his expected utility subject to budget constraints, consumption feasibility constraints, and the constraint that net trades must be adapted to $\{H_t^i\}$. The terms 'markets clear', 'budget constraints', and 'consumption feasibility constraints' are made precise in the usual way (and are of no real concern to us here). From the point of view of *rational expectations*, the important constraint is that of measurability; agent's net trades at date t must be measurable with respect to their information, including the equilibrium level of prices.

The reader will note that this general definition can be made more general at little cost. We have assumed that private information is given exogenously; we could make endogenous private decisions by agents on how much private information to gather, or we could add markets for information. We have assumed that the same markets are open at each date and in each contingency, but we could easily have markets that are open only in certain dates and/or contingencies. We have assumed a particular functional form for agents preferences, but this is unnecessary. And we have assumed that agents learn only from equilibrium prices (in addition to what they learn from their private information), but we could have them learn from other equilibrium variables or, as in Jordan (1982c), even from out-of-equilibrium variables. Indeed, as we have posed things, each agent's private information is supplemented only by relative prices, and not by some absolute level of prices. It would make no difference to our development if one modified things so that prices were not constrained to lie in the simplex but instead in R_+^{N+M}, so that the absolute price level might be informative. (But we would still wish to insist on p_t being G_t measurable; without the addition of some third party, such as the government, it is hard to imagine that equilibrium prices could reflect more information than all agents put together possess.)

As this is just the obvious melding of the single-date rational expectations equilibrium that is common to the literature and Radner's equilibrium of plans, prices and price expectations, the usual issues of existence and implementation arise (and are ignored here). Instead, we are concerned with rational learning within this environment. As things have been set up, there is little more to be said. For any event A from Ω, Proposition 2 applies. If Ω happens to satisfy the assumptions of Proposition 3, then it applies. Since it may happen that the assumptions of Proposition 3 are not met for all of Ω, note that Proposition 3 can be applied as follows: Suppose that we have a finite dimensional random vector θ defined on (Ω,F). Think of θ as the values of some finite number of parameters of the economy in question (for example, the levels of risk aversion of some of the participants of the economy). Denote by F^i_t the distribution function of agent i's (conditional) assessment for θ given the information H^i_t received up to date t. Then Proposition 3 is trivially applied to give the conclusion that these distribution functions converge weakly (P^i-a.s.) to some F^i_∞, which is the c.d.f. of the agent's conditional assessment for θ given all the information the agent ever receives.

5 CONVERGENCE TO A STATIONARY RATIONAL EXPECTATIONS EQUILIBRIUM

In the example of Section 2 we obtained more than convergence of beliefs; we found that equilibrium prices and allocations settled down into a stationary rational expectations equilibrium. We shall argue in this section that in general, this further step is rather more problematic.

Of course, to obtain a further result of this sort, it is necessary for the economy to possess some underlying stationarity. So we begin by specializing the formulation of Section 4.

We suppose first that Ω has the form $\Theta \times \Phi_0 \times \Phi_0 \times$ ... The reader should think of Θ as being the state space for some (random) parameters of the economy (in Section 2, the risk aversion coefficients of the agents), and Φ_t as the state space for uncertainty specific to period t (in the example, this would include the values of r_t and ρ_t). In fact we will assume that there are random elements $\theta,\varphi_0,\varphi_1$, and so on, that define Ω in the usual way; that the sigma-field F is generated by the cylinder sets of these random elements, and agents assess that the sequence $\{\theta_t\}$ is i.i.d. conditional on the value of θ. Finally, Θ will be assumed to satisfy the assumptions of Proposition 3, so that the proposition can be applied to the agents' posterior assessments concerning the value of θ.

We next assume that preferences are stationary. It is easiest to do this by assuming that agent i's utility function is of the form $\Sigma_{t=0}^{\infty} \propto^t u^i\,(x^i_t,\omega,\varphi_t)$for some $\propto < 1$.

And, finally, we need to assume that the savings opportunities afforded agents are stationary. We did a bit of this already when we assumed that the number of asset markets does not change through time. Now we must label assets in such a way (and assume that they can be labelled in such a way) that the 'rights' conferred by the asset bearing a particular label depend on (at most) the value of θ and the current value of φ_t. This could get rather tricky, insofar as assets may be long-lived, and hence what they are worth at some subsequent date may be endogenous. We could get around this by assuming that all assets are commodity futures. But even then we will have problems; insofar as wealth can be transferred between periods, the distribution of wealth at any date becomes relevant to the future evolution of the economy. That is, we will need to take as a state variable in our economy the distribution of wealth, and we cannot expect that prices will settle down to something independent of wealth levels. We avoided this in the example by having no wealth transfers whatsoever between dates; the only thing that linked the economy at one date with the next were the beliefs carried forward from the past. (*Caveat emptor*, this is not quite correct, see below.) For the sake of discussion, let us make this assumption – there are only commodity spot markets. And endowments at date t depend only on θ and φ_t.

Now we are able to initiate analysis. Assume there is a rational expectations equilibrium for this economy. (This is, we stress, a non-trivial assumption.) Then the previous results ensure that agents' beliefs concerning the value of θ approach some limit (with probability one); the entire posterior distributions approach some weak limit distribution. Suppose, as in the example of Section 2, we know (i) for every set of beliefs by agents concerning the value of θ and for every value of φ, there is a *unique* spot market equilibrium for the economy;[6] and suppose that (ii) this spot market equilibrium is continuous in the beliefs concerning θ; then we would certainly be able to conclude that the economy will settle down as time passes. And if we also know that (iii) the information communicated by spot prices concerning θ is continuous in equilibrium prices (hence in the beliefs concerning θ with which agents begin the period), then we would know that the economy is settling down to a stationary rational expectations equilibrium. In our example we could show (i) and (ii), and (iii) was moot because, in the limit, there was no information left to learn concerning θ. But what hopes are there for these conditions in general?

In general there can be little hope for (i); for general economies, one will sometimes find multiple equilibria, and when there are multiple equilibria in the spot market economies, very bad things can happen in our sequence economies. One sort of problem that can arise is evident even in cases when there are no parameters to learn (where there is a single possible value for θ). Suppose that in this case, the (now single) spot market economy admits multiple equilibria. In the sequence economy, we have as equilibria any sequence chosen from the spot market equilibrium set. We could have one equilibrium for a while, a second for longer, and then back to the first, and so on. We could have the selection of any spot equilibrium at date $t+1$ depend on the outcome of some publicly available random variable from date t or any prior date (and in either time homogeneous or inhomogeneous manner). In other words, although there is no physical link between periods, they can now be linked by more than the posterior assessments concerning θ. Proving that the spot market equilibria settle down is clearly out of the question, unless we are willing to somehow restrict which sequence economy equilibria we will consider. Similar things apply when there is some non-trivial learning going on.

But with non-trivial learning, things can be worse still: Suppose we have a situation where θ can take on one of two values, and this is revealed at the outset to some (informed) traders but not to others (the uninformed). Suppose, as well, that the informed observe at the outset some payoff-irrelevant, continuum random variable, that the uninformed do not see. If the spot market economies have multiple equilibria (and here we are being a bit loose, since in the spot markets what is an equilibrium depends on what the uninformed learn from equilibrium prices, hence from the sequence economy equilibrium), then we could have the informed select among the multiple equilibria according to the value of the random variable. (This is not uncompetitive behaviour; if there are a continua of informed agents, each one will do this if all others do it.) This selection is random from the point of view of the uninformed, and hence it changes what the uninformed learn from the equilibrium prices; *changing the randomization changes non-trivially how much the uninformed have figured out at any finite date.*

And still worse is possible: One might hope, at least, that such random selections among the spot equilibria would not affect the limiting beliefs of the uninformed; in the end they learn the same things. But this is false. We can construct examples in which the sequence economy has multiple equilibria; in one the uninformed learn with probability one the true value of θ, while in others they learn nothing at all.

Details of the construction are not especially illuminating and will be omitted, but the basic idea is relatively straightforward. Imagine an economy as above; a two good exchange economy with one type of informed and one type of uninformed agents. The informed agent learns, at the outset, the value of a parameter θ that takes one of two values and that determines the indifference curves of the two types. (A noxious feature of this example is that the uninformed agents do not learn this parameter – in a sense, they do not learn their period-by-period felicity as time goes on. This can be dispensed with, at the cost of complicating and blurring the intuition of the construction.) The uninformed agents begin with some prior knowledge over the value of this parameter.

In each period the uninformed trade with the informed. The endowment of the uninformed agents is fixed, so we can trace out the offer curve of the uninformed, *under the assumption that they do not learn anything about the value of θ from equilibrium prices*. There is further uncertainty in this economy, pertaining to the endowment and preferences of the informed. This changes with time and is parameterized by a random variable φ_t. The sequence $\{\varphi_t\}$ is i.i.d. and independent of θ. The informed agents learn, period by period, the value of φ_t, while the uninformed do not.

If θ takes on its first value, then for each φ_t there are two spot market equilibrium prices p_1 and p_3, assuming the uninformed learns nothing but acts according to the offer curve described above. (Dependence on φ_t is suppressed, but it is implicit.) If θ takes on its second value, there is for each φ_t a single spot market equilibrium price p_2. Suppose it just so happens that, ranging over the values of φ_t, the distribution function of p_2 is some convex combination of the distribution functions of p_1 and p_3. Then, assuming that the informed all have access to a payoff-relevant continuum random variable at the outset (which is not revealed to the uninformed) they could use this to select 'randomly' between the p_1 and p_3 spot equilibria (if θ takes on its first value), so that the observations (of equilibrium prices, period-by-period) by the uninformed tells them nothing about the value of θ. This gives us a completely non-revealing rational expectations equilibrium for the sequence economy.

On the other hand, if the informed agents always select one of the two spot market equilibria for the first value of θ (and we assume that, say, $p_1 > p_3$ for each φ_t), then arguments similar to those in Section 2 can be used to show that the uninformed must learn θ eventually.

(The reader may object that this equilibrium is very non-generic; it hinges critically on the fact that the distribution of p_2 is a convex combination of those of p_1 and p_3. Note in this regard that it would be sufficient that the distribution of p_2 be a φ_t dependent mixture of those of p_1 and p_3. That is, we can have the mixing probability (if θ takes on its first value) depend period-by-period on the value of φ_t. The ability to create such a mixture is robust in the Whitney C^1 topology on the three distribution functions, if those distributions are continuously differentiable and have non-zero derivatives everywhere. Of course, the non-zero derivation condition is not very palatable, since relative prices near 1 and 0 seem unlikely. We do not know if this condition can be dispensed with. And the reader may not like to restrict perturbations in the economy to topologies so strong that the resulting perturbations in the distribution functions of prices are continuous in the Whitney C^1 topology. Still, this sort of example can be made 'robust' in at least some sense.)

Since we are concerned with non-stationary limit behaviour, we now add a final embellishment. Suppose that we have the informed agents randomize between the two equilibria (if θ takes one its first value), using the results of that randomization for the first two periods, then they re-randomize, using the results of that for the next four periods, and then they randomize again, using that result for eight periods, and so forth. As a function of the underlying values of φ_t, the economy will certainly not settle down.

Multiple spot market equilibria, then, will prove rather troublesome if general results are sought. And uniqueness of equilibrium in general may be hard to come by. Gross substitute assumptions are hard to justify when prices communicate information; Admati (1985), for example, shows that, in a multi-asset rational expectations equilibrium, demand for one asset can behave perversely in the price of a second, even in an otherwise very 'regular' economy. (To be fair, it should also be noted that, for the economies Admati considers, there is a single equilibrium among a 'reasonable' class.) In any event, we have no general results along these lines to offer.

For (ii) and (iii), however, there may be greater reason to be sanguine *if* one can first deduce that the spot market equilibria are unique. It seems intuitive that equilibrium should not change drastically with small changes in underlying distributions. Of course, this intuition is not vindicated in general in the context of rational expectations equilibria; an immediate corollary to Radner (1979) is that one can always find economies 'near by' any given economy (in terms of the distribution of underlying random variables, with distance measured by the Prohorov metric of weak convergence) where there are fully revealing rational expectations equilibria. But, as many authors have argued, this simply points out a weakness in the mathematical formalism; small changes in prices ought not to convey so much information.

In the example of Section 2, we obtained continuity by assuming that there was exogenous noise in each period sufficient to make very strong inferences impossible. Whatever price is seen, it is consistent with any value of the parameters of the economy. We were aided in this regard by the simple form of demand; the informed needn't make any inferences, and then the inferences of the uninformed can be tackled directly. It ought to be possible to derive similar results in general; to, say, assume that there is full dimensional supply noise (say, in net demand from a sector that supplies/demands completely inelastically), and then to derive that equilibrium prices, in accommodating for this exogenous supply, must be similarly noisy.

But even if we assume that spot market equilibrium is unique, we are incapable of providing a general result of this sort. All we can do is to point out a course that (very directly) leads to success: Modify the definition of rational expectations equilibrium to be as in Anderson and Sonnenschein (1982). There it is assumed that (a) there is 'sufficiently rich' supply noise and (b) agents, in drawing inferences from prices, use 'smoothed' versions of the actual distributions. From (b), agents will draw similar inferences from two prices that are close together. This is the (conceptually) crucial assumption; prices that are close do not convey radically different information. Assumption (a) is given because, in the authors' analysis, one only has upper hemi-continuity of the equilibrium correspondence, hence small changes in models could lead to drastic changes in equilibrium. Hence (a) should be less important here; in so far as one has pinned hopes on finding environments in which the spot market equilibria are unique, upper hemi-continuity becomes continuity – and that continuity is just what is needed for (ii) and (iii).

Suppose that we could show that (i), (ii) and (iii) all hold, so that the economy does indeed settle down. What can be said about the position to which it does settle down? In the example of Section 2 we showed that the uninformed agents learned the true value of θ with certainty. There are two parts to this, neither of which can be expected to generalize. First, what is learned depends (a.s.) only on the value of θ and not on the particular $\{\varphi_t\}$. Standard examples concerning the two-armed bandit problem show that this is not so, even in single person settings; 'bad' draws early on can lead one to take actions that stop the flow of additional information, while good draws early on keep the agent experimenting, eventually learning the true value of the parameter. (If the reader is unhappy about the discrete nature of the two-armed bandit problem, it should be noted that models with a continuum of actions, such as in Grossman, Kihlstrom and Mirman, 1977, can be constructed that give this sort of result.) The second part is that the value of θ is revealed completely. Any example that disproves the generality of the first part (necessarily) works to disprove the generality of this as well. But the model of Section 2 is easily modified to give another (counter)example: Imagine in the economy of Section 2 that the uninformed agents are uncertain about both the risk tolerance of the informed and about the amount of residual variance there is in the asset return, given the signal to the informed. Imagine also that the uninformed do not see those signals, but only the actual asset returns. Then whatever they observe, they can never discern between two pairs of values for θ^I and σ^2 that lie on the same ray through the origin. (Along such rays the demand of the informed is constant, given their observations.)

In sum, moving beyond the very general convergence of beliefs result is apt to take special arguments tailored to special cases. One shouldn't be surprised if an equilibrium for a particular model is given in which things do settle down, since beliefs must do so. But, owing especially to the possibility of multiple spot market (hence grand) equilibria, looking for a general results is apt to be hard.

6 CONCLUDING REMARKS

We have titled this paper 'Rational Learning and Rational Expectations'. And then we have throughout made the distinction between learning *within* and learning *about* an equilibrium, saying that we are concerned with learning *within*. Implicitly, then, we have identified *rational learning* with *learning within*. Need this be so? Can one make sense of *rational learning about* in some sense other than as formally equivalent to *rational learning within?*

We take as the *sine qua non* of rational learning that agents are Savage-rational, employing Bayesian inference through time. Bayesian inference about a parameter θ, given data $\{x_t\}$, requires a prior distribution on θ and a conditional distribution of $\{x_t\}$, given θ. Taken together, these yield a joint distribution on θ and $\{x_t\}$; our theorems that the posterior on θ converges refers to almost sure convergence with respect to this joint distribution, held subjectively by the agent who is learning. In *any* model of individual rational learning that we can imagine, this sort of model would be used by each individual, albeit with a highly abstract space of parameters θ.

But convergence with respect to the agent's subjective beliefs does not finish the story, because the agent's subjective beliefs could be wrong on two counts: the parameter θ may lie outside the support of the prior (or, said differently, the 'true' θ may lie outside the set of states of the world on which convergence is attained); or the conditional distribution function may be misspecified. We might instead be interested in applying the convergence theorem to objective, exogenously given, probabilities. And if the convergence theorem is to be used in this fashion, then the agent's subjective beliefs, taking into account his ignorance of θ, must have the same support as the objectively given distribution.

This is far from a trivial requirement because, in many economic models, the conditional distribution of $\{x_t\}$, given θ, will depend on how agents learn about θ; that is, on the prior and the conditional distribution held by all agents. It seems to us that this requirement is that agents must be in a grand rational expectations equilibrium, taking into account their ignorance of θ. Our example and others (Townsend, 1978; Brandenburger, 1984) show that such a grand rational expecations equilibrium may exist, although there are no general existence results and (as we have argued) there is every reason to expect difficulties. And these equilibria, when they exist, will not be simple objects; in particular, even if, in the simple rational expectations equilibrium where agents know θ, the conditional distribution of $\{x_t\}$, given θ, is i.i.d., in the grand rational expectations equilibrium learning about θ makes the relationship non-stationary and non-independent.

The models of Bray (1982), Bray and Savin (1984), and Blume and Easley (1982), can all be interpreted as models of Bayesian inference, based on the incorrect assumption that the conditional distribution of $\{x_t\}$, given θ, is i.i.d. In these papers the posteriors may converge to the 'truth' about θ. But for other parameterizations, convergence needn't be to a 'correct conclusion'; there may be divergence, and there may be cycles, all with respect to an exogenously-given objective probability distribution. Our theorems *do* apply to these models; the agents who are learning attach (subjectively) probability one to convergence to something 'true'. If the objective distribution does rule, their surprise at what happens might cause them to rethink their learning procedure (which could mean rethinking their model of the world), but there is no apparatus that we know that would allow us to pursue this point.

Bayesian learning *per se* doesn't get one much, at least if one wishes then to measure results using the probability distribution of some 'objective reality'. Insisting that the learning is based on correctly specified priors and conditional distributions brings us back to learning within a grand rational expectations equilibrium. It guarantees convergence of posteriors on parameter values, but merely pushes one stage back the question how agents learn about the rational expectations equilibrium.

Perhaps the most accurate statement that we can make is that our analysis also applies to *learning about* equilibria when (i) the learning is rational (Bayesian) on the individual level and (ii) agents' models are consistent (and consistent with reality). This need not and should not be read as an assertion that only models that satisfy such stringent requirements are interesting. In fact, we are of the opinion that such models are of less interest than those that have in place some level of individual irrationality or some level of inconsistency or both. It seems incredible indeed that agents are so rational and consistent. The models analyzed here provide a benchmark, but we strongly believe that this is a sterile benchmark and that there is much more to be learned by studying models that are somewhat less sterile. A failing of economic theory in general has been that it has proved remarkably resistant to movements away from models with full rationality and consistency; here, perhaps, is an area where there has been a bit of progress, and the promise of a good deal more.

NOTES

1. The economy to be described is a minor variation on the model of Grossman and Stiglitz (1980). To justify the price-taking assumption that we subsequently make, the reader may wish to think instead of two continua of agents, one of each type. In this case there are qualifications that must be made about priors being common knowledge, and so on.
2. Another question which we do not investigate here is: How can agent U know this period's equilibrium price *prior* to submitting his demand function? Clearly, the possibility of U extracting and using information from equilibrium prices depends on the way in which those prices are formed. We assert here that the equilibrium above can be sustained by a specific price setting mechanism; namely, the mechanism in which each agent submits a demand correspondence and equilibrium prices and allocations are computed by finding a fixed point. Note that with this mechanism, agent U submits the demand correspondence $x^U(p)=2\theta^U/(\theta^U+\theta^I)$; his demand is insensitive to the equilibrium price. It is agent I's demand function that is downward sloping and that determines the equilibrium price. This 'submit a demand correspondence' mechanism often does implement a rational expectations equilibrium, but in some cases it will fail, see Beja (1976). Note also that other mechanisms will give other equilibria, in which U cannot extract so much information, see Dubey, Geanakoplos and Shubik (1983).
3. *Caveat emptor*, there is more to this remark than meets the eye (see Section 5).
4. We should be careful here. We are looking for an equilibrium in which the

equilibrium allocation to U is a function of past data and the current equilibrium price. If we allowed allocations which were optimal given the information contained in those allocations and *where that information could exceed the amount of information in equilibrium prices* (and other privately-held information), then we can, under mild conditions, always get the full communication equilibrium as an informational equilibrium. On this point, see Jordan (1982b). We do *not* wish to find such equilibrium, so the reader should audit our construction to ensure that, at the end, X^u is measurable with respect to past and current prices and the other things that U observes.

5. Note that it is not Bayesian learning *per se* that drives this result but the equality of today's assessment and tomorrow's expected assessment. If one is interested in learning models that are not necessarily Bayesian rational but that still satisfy this equality, then the proposition goes through without difficulty.
6. This would tell us that the grand rational expectations equilibrium is unique, and that it can be constructed iteratively as in Section 2.

REFERENCES

Admati, A. R. (1985) 'A Noisy Rational Expectations Equilibrium for Multi-Asset Securities Markets', *Econometrica*, 53: 629–58.

Allen, B. (1981) 'Generic Existence of Completely Revealing Equilibria for Economies with Uncertainty When Prices Convey Information', *Econometrica*, 49: 1173–99.

Anderson, R. M. and H. Sonnenschein (1982) 'On the Existence of Rational Expectations Equilibrium', *Journal of Economic Theory*, 26: 261–78.

Arrow, K. J. and J. R. Green (1973) 'Notes on Expectations Equilibria in Bayesian Settings', Working Paper no. 33 (Stanford: IMSSS).

Beja, A. (1976) 'The Limited Infomation Efficiency of Market Processes', Research Program in Finance Working Paper no. 43 (Berkeley: University of California).

Blume, L. E. and D. Easley (1981) 'Rational Expectations Equilibrium and the Efficient Market Hypothesis', mimeo. (Cornell University).

Blume, L. E. and D. Easley (1982) 'Learning to be Rational', *Journal of Economic Theory*, 26: 340–51.

Brandenburger, A. (1984) 'Rational Expectations as Bayesian Equilibrium', mimeo. (Cambridge University).

Bray, M. M. (1982) 'Learning, Estimation, and the Stability of Rational Expectations', *Journal of Economic Theory*, 26: 318–39.

Bray, M. M. and N. E. Savin (1984) 'Rational Expectations Equilibria, Learning and Model Specification', Economic Theory Discussion Paper no. 79 (Cambridge University).

Chung, K. L. (1974) *A Course in Probability Theory*, 2nd edn (New York: Academic Press).

Doob, J. L. (1953) *Stochastic Processes* (New York: Wiley).

Dubey, P., J. Geanakoplos and M. Shubik (1983). 'Revelation of Information in Strategic Market Games: A Critique of Rational Expectations', Cowles Foundation Discussion Paper no. 634 (Yale University).

Frydman, R. (1982) 'Towards an Understanding of Market Processes, Individual Expectations, Market Behaviour and Convergence of Rational Expectations Equilibrium', *American Economic Review*, 72: 652–68.

Green, J. R. (1977) 'The Non-existence of Information Equilibria', *Review of Economic Studies*, 44: 451–63.

Grossman, S. J. (1981) 'An Introduction to the Theory of Rational Expectations Under Asymmetric Information', *Review of Economic Studies*, 48: 541–60.

Grossman, S. J., R. E. Kihlstrom and L. J. Mirman (1977), 'A Bayesian Approach to the Production of Information and Learning by Doing', *Review of Economic Studies*, 44: 533–47.

Grossman, S, J. and J. E. Stiglitz (1980) 'On the Impossibility of Informationally Efficient Markets', *American Economic Review*, 70: 393–408.

Jordan, J. S. (1982a) 'The Generic Existence of Rational Expectations Equilibrium in the Higher Dimensional Case', *Journal of Economic Theory*, 26: 224–43.

Jordan, J. S. (1982b) 'Admissible Market Data Structures: A Complete Characterization', *Journal of Economic Theory*, 28: 19–31.

Jordan, J. S. (1982c) 'A Dynamic Model of Expectations Equilibrium', *Journal of Economic Theory*, 28: 235–54.

Kobayashi, T. (1977) 'A Convergence Theorem on Rational Expectations Equilibrium with Price Information', Working Paper no. 79 (Stanford: IMSSS).

Kreps, D. (1977) 'A Note on Fulfilled Expectations Equilibria', *Journal of Economic Theory*, 14: 32–43.

Lewis, G. (1981) 'The Philips Curve and Bayesian Learning', *Journal of Economic Theory*, 24: 240–69.

Radner, R. (1972) 'Existence of Equilibrium of Plans, Prices and Price Expectations in a Sequence of Markets', *Econometrica*, 40: 289–303.

Radner, R. (1979) 'Rational Expectations Equilibrium – Generic Existence and the Information Revealed by Prices', *Econometrica*, 47: 655–78.

Radner, R. (1982) 'Equilibrium Under Uncertainty', in K. J. Arrow and M. D. Intriligator (eds) *Handbook of Mathematical Economis* vol. 2 (Amsterdam: North-Holland).

Townsend, R. M. (1978) 'Market Anticipations, Rational Expectations and Bayesian Analysis', *International Economic Review*, 19: 481–94.

Townsend, R. M. (1983) 'Forecasting the Forecasts of Others', *Journal of Political Economy*, 91: 546–88.

20 Aspects of Investor Behaviour Under Risk

Benjamin M. Friedman and V. Vance Roley*

A greatly enhanced understanding of the nature of economic uncertainty, and with it substantial insight into economic behaviour in circumstances under which uncertainty is central to necessary decisions, stand as one of Kenneth Arrow's most significant contributions. His classic lectures on *Aspects of the Theory of Risk-Bearing* clarified key elements of the theory of choice under uncertainty, formalized crucial aspects of risk-averse behaviour, and explored the implications of the relevant theory for such important economic activities as resource allocation and insurance. These lectures, together with many of Arrow's other papers on risk and uncertainty, have provided a foundation that is now standard in monetary and financial economics.

The object of this chapter is to analyze several aspects of the asset demands characterizing investors' portfolio behaviour under risk. Section 1 derives asset demand functions exhibiting wealth homogeneity and linearity in expected asset returns – two convenient properties that are often simply assumed, especially in the monetary economics literature. The main result here is that, among the numerous familiar sets of specific assumptions sufficient to derive mean-variance portfolio behaviour from the more general theory of expected utility maximization, the assumptions of constant relative risk aversion and joint normally distributed asset return assessments are also jointly sufficient to derive asset demands with these properties, as close approximations, either in continuous time or in discrete time if the time unit is small.

Section 2, however, provides empirical evidence that contradicts the plausibility of these assumptions – and, for that matter, a variety of others as well. In particular, a standard feature of asset demands,

* The authors are grateful to the late John Lintner for many helpful conversations that importantly influenced this research, as well as to the National Science Foundation and the Alfred P. Sloan Foundation for research support.

also often simply assumed in applied research, is that the responses of these demands to expected asset returns are symmetric. The evidence summarized here, based on the observed portfolio behaviour of both institutional and individual investors in the US, casts doubt on the hypothesis of symmetry and therefore also casts doubt on the set of more fundamental assumptions that imply symmetry in this sense.

Section 3 considers another aspect of investors' portfolio behaviour implied by a familiar group of utility functions. It is well known that the quadratic utility function implies a wealth satiation level, or 'bliss point'. The analysis here shows that a number of other familiar utility functions similarly exhibit wealth satiation when investors' behaviour is restricted only by the distribution of asset returns. This property imposes still another important caveat in applications to the study of investors' behaviour based on such functions.

Section 4 briefly summarizes the chapter's principal conclusions.

1 THE DERIVATION OF LINEAR HOMOGENEOUS ASSET DEMAND FUNCTIONS

The asset demand functions used for both analytical and empirical research, especially in the monetary economics literature, are often assumed to exhibit the two convenient properties of wealth homogeneity and linearity in expected asset returns.[1] The convenience afforded by the tractability of the linear form is apparent enough, and the wealth homogeneity property in particular is often especially important in empirical applications to aggregate data.[2] Despite the frequent use of such return-linear and wealth-homogeneous asset demand functions, however, there exists (to the authors' knowledge) no readily available source setting forth sufficient conditions for the derivation, from underlying principles of expected utility maximization, of asset demands simultaneously exhibiting both of these properties.[3]

The purpose of this section is to show that, among the numerous familiar sets of specific assumptions sufficient to derive mean-variance portfolio behaviour from more general expected utility maximization in continuous time, the assumptions of (a) constant relative risk aversion and (b) joint normally distributed asset return assessments are also jointly sufficient to derive, as approximations, asset demand functions with the two desirable (and frequently simply assumed) properties of wealth homogeneity and linearity in expected returns.

Constant relative risk aversion and joint normally distributed asset return assessments are also sufficient to yield such asset demands as approximations in discrete time if the time unit is small.[4]

1.1 Analysis in Continuous Time

To begin with expected utility maximization, the investor's objective as of time t, given initial wealth W_t, is

$$\max_{\boldsymbol{a}_t} E[U(\tilde{W}_{t+dt})] \tag{1}$$

subject to

$$\boldsymbol{a}_t'\mathbf{1} = 1, \tag{2}$$

where $E(\cdot)$ is the expectation operator, $U(W_\tau)$ is utility as a function of wealth, and $\boldsymbol{a}_t$ is a vector expressing the portfolio allocations in proportional form

$$\boldsymbol{a}_t \equiv \frac{1}{W_t} \cdot \mathbf{A}_t \tag{3}$$

for vector $\mathbf{A}_t$ of asset holdings.

Assumption (a) noted above is that $U(W_\tau)$ is any power (or logarithmic) function such that the coefficient of relative risk aversion

$$\rho \equiv -W_\tau \cdot \frac{U''(W_\tau)}{U'(W_\tau)} \tag{4}$$

is constant.[5] Assumption (b) is that the investor perceives asset returns $\tilde{r}_{i\tau}$, $i=1,\ldots,n$, to be generated as Wiener processes with respective means $r_{i\tau}^e$, standard deviations $\sigma_{i\tau}$ and correlations $\varphi_{ij\tau}$, where the tilde sign indicates a random variable, and the time subscript generalizes the investor's assessments to permit variation over time. Given the assumption of Weiner processes for the asset yields, $\tilde{W}_{t+dt}$ is in turn generated by

$$\tilde{W}_{t+dt} = W_t \cdot \sum_i^n a_{it}(1 + r_{it}^e dt + \sigma_{it}\tilde{z}_{it}\sqrt{dt}) \tag{5}$$

where $\tilde{z}_i$ is the unit normal random variable corresponding to each yield $\tilde{r}_i$.

Expanding $U(\tilde{W}_{t+dt})$ about W_t, for dt sufficiently small, and then taking the expectation yields a representation of the maximand in the form

$$E[U(\tilde{W}_{t+dt})] = \sum_{k=0}^{\infty} \frac{1}{k!} \cdot U^{(k)}(W_t) \cdot E[\tilde{W}_{t+dt} - W_t]^k \tag{6}$$

where the notation $U^{(k)}(\cdot)$ indicates the kth derivative of $U(\cdot)$. Substituting from (5) and omitting terms of higher than second order in dt yields

$$E[U(\tilde{W}_{t+dt})] = U(W_t) + U'(W_t) \cdot W_t \cdot \boldsymbol{a}_t' \mathbf{r}_t^e dt + \frac{1}{2} U''(W_t) \cdot W_t^2 \cdot \boldsymbol{a}_t' \Omega_t \boldsymbol{a}_t dt \tag{7}$$

where Ω_t is a variance-covariance matrix consisting of elements $\sigma_{it}\sigma_{jt}\varphi_{ijt}$. Forming the Lagrangean for the maximization of (7) subject to (2), differentiating with respect to $\boldsymbol{a}_t$, and equating the derivative to zero, yields the first-order condition for the solution of (1) as

$$\boldsymbol{a}_t^* = B_t \mathbf{r}_t^e + \pi_t \tag{8}$$

where the asterisk indicates an optimum. If there is no risk-free asset (because of price inflation, for example), B_t and π_t have the form[6]

$$B_t = -\frac{1}{\rho} [\Omega_t^{-1} - (\mathbf{1}'\Omega_*^{-1}\mathbf{1})^{-1} \Omega_t^{-1} \mathbf{1}\mathbf{1}' \Omega_t^{-1} \tag{9}$$

$$\pi_t = (\mathbf{1}'\Omega_t^{-1}\mathbf{1})^{-1} \Omega_t^{-1} \mathbf{1}. \tag{10}$$

Alternatively, in the presence of a risk-free asset Ω_t is singular, so that it is necessary to partition the system of demands. The resulting solution, in which $\hat{\boldsymbol{a}}_t$,$\hat{\mathbf{r}}_t^e$ and $\hat{\Omega}_t$ refer to the risky assets only, is

$$\hat{\boldsymbol{a}}_t^* = \hat{B}_t \hat{\mathbf{r}}_t^e \tag{8'}$$

where

$$\hat{B}_t = -\frac{1}{\rho} \hat{\Omega}_t^{-1} \tag{9'}$$

and the optimum portfolio share for the risk-free asset is just $(1-\hat{a}_t^{*\prime}\mathbf{1})$.[7]

It is apparent by inspection that the optimum portfolio allocations in both (8) and (8′) exhibit the two properties of wealth homogeneity and linearity in expected returns. Moreover, since Ω_t (or $\hat{\Omega}_t$) is a variance-covariance matrix, the Jacobian B_t (or $\hat{B}_t$) indicates symmetrical asset substitutions associated with cross-yield effects.

1.2 Analysis in Discrete Time

In the discrete-time analog to the model developed above, the investor's single-period objective as of time t, given initial wealth W_t, is

$$\max_{\boldsymbol{a}_t} E[U(\tilde{W}_{t+1})] \tag{11}$$

where

$$\tilde{W}_{t+1} = W_t \cdot \boldsymbol{\alpha}_t'(\mathbf{1}+\tilde{\mathbf{r}}_t) \tag{12}$$

and assessments of $\tilde{\mathbf{r}}_t$ (that is, asset returns between time t and time $t+1$) are distributed as

$$\tilde{\mathbf{r}}_t \sim N(\mathbf{r}_t^e, \Omega_t). \tag{13}$$

Expanding $U(\tilde{W}_{t+1})$ about $E(\tilde{W}_{t+1})$ and then taking the expectation yields a representation of the maximand in the form

$$E[U(\tilde{W}_{t+1})] = \sum_{k=0}^{\infty} \frac{1}{k!} \cdot U^{(k)}[E(\tilde{W}_{t+1})] \cdot \{E[\tilde{W}_{t+1} - E(\tilde{W}_{t+1})]^k\}. \tag{14}$$

It follows from the moment generating function of the normal distribution that the term within brackets in (14) has value

$$E[\tilde{W}_{t+1} - E(\tilde{W}_{t+1})]^k = \frac{k!}{2^{(k/2)}(k/2)!}[\mathrm{var}(\tilde{W}_{t+1})]^{(k/2)} \tag{15}$$

for k an even integer and

$$E[\tilde{W}_{t+1} - E(\tilde{W}_{t+1})]^k = 0 \tag{16}$$

for k an odd integer. Hence (14) simplifies to

$$E[U(\tilde{W}_{t+1})]=\sum_{m=0}^{\infty}\frac{1}{2^m m!}\cdot U^{(2m)}[E(\tilde{W}_{t+1})]\cdot[\mathrm{var}(\tilde{W}_{t+1})]^m. \tag{17}$$

Substituting from (12) and omitting terms of higher than second order yields

$$E[U(\tilde{W}_{t+1})]=U[E(\tilde{W}_{t+1})]+\frac{1}{2}U''[E(\tilde{W}_{t+1})]\cdot W_t^2\cdot \boldsymbol{\alpha}_t'\Omega_t\boldsymbol{\alpha}_t. \tag{18}$$

Forming the Lagrangean for the maximization of (18) subject to (2), differentiating with respect to $\boldsymbol{\alpha}_t$, equating the derivative to zero, and again omitting terms of higher than second order yields the first-order condition for the solution of (11) if there is no risk-free asset as

$$\boldsymbol{\alpha}_t^* = B_t\mathbf{r}_t^e + \boldsymbol{\pi}_t \tag{8}$$

once again, where now

$$B_t=\left\{\frac{-U'[E(\tilde{W}_{t+1})]}{W_t\cdot U''[E(\tilde{W}_{t+1})]}\right\}\cdot[\Omega_t^{-1}-(\mathbf{1}'\Omega_t^{-1}\mathbf{1})^{-1}\Omega_t^{-1}\mathbf{1}\mathbf{1}'\Omega_t^{-1}] \tag{19}$$

and $\boldsymbol{\pi}_t$ is again as in (10). Alternatively, in the presence of a risk-free asset the resulting solution is again (for $\hat{\boldsymbol{\alpha}}$, $\hat{B}_t$ and $\hat{\mathbf{r}}_t^e$ as defined above)

$$\hat{\boldsymbol{\alpha}}_t^* = \hat{B}_t\hat{\mathbf{r}}_t^e \tag{8'}$$

where

$$\hat{B}_t=\left\{\frac{-U'[E(\tilde{W}_{t+1})]}{W_t\cdot U''[E(\tilde{W}_{t+1})]}\right\}\ \Omega_t^{-1} \tag{19'}$$

and the optimum portfolio share for the risk-free asset is again just $(1-\hat{\boldsymbol{\alpha}}_t^{*\prime}\mathbf{1})$. If the time unit is sufficiently small to render W_t a good approximation to $E(\tilde{W}_{t+1})$ for purposes of the underlying expansion, then the scalar term within brackets in (19) and (19′) reduces to the constant coefficient of relative risk aversion, and the discrete-time model yields the same linear homogenous asset demand functions developed above.

1.3 Isomorphic Assumptions

Other combinations of assumptions, if they are isomorphic to constant relative risk aversion and joint normally distributed asset return assessments, also yield asset demand functions exhibiting both wealth homogeneity and linearity in expected returns, either exactly or as an approximation. For example, the negative exponential utility function, with coefficient of absolute risk aversion inversely dependent on initial wealth, yields results equivalent to those derived above.[8] Alternatively, the logarithmic utility function, in conjunction with the assumption of joint lognormally distributed returns, yields asset demand functions that are homogeneous in wealth and log-linear in expected returns, in either continuous or discrete time; but in this case yet a further (apparently reasonable) approximation is necessary, because a linear combination of lognormally distributed returns is not itself distributed lognormally.[9]

2 EVIDENCE ON THE SYMMETRY HYPOTHESIS[10]

Imposition of symmetry restrictions on coefficients describing responses to expected asset returns is a frequent practice in the empirical estimation of systems of asset demands. Wholly apart from the theoretical considerations laid out in Section 1, a typical motive for imposing symmetry in such applied research is simply to reduce the number of independent coefficients to be estimated. In large systems of asset demands, the corresponding gain in degrees of freedom is substantial. As is true in the standard consumer demand paradigm, however, the coefficient matrix applicable to the vector of expected asset returns consists of a combination of symmetric Slutsky substitution effects and (in general) asymmetric Slutsky wealth effects.[11]

The analysis in Section 1 shows that in some specific cases the relevant wealth terms do exhibit symmetry. The linear homogeneous asset demands derived in Section 1 under constant relative risk aversion and joint normal asset return distributions provide a clear example. More generally, in terms of expected utility functions that reduce to exact mean-variance preference orderings, the symmetry restriction *per se* has corresponding behavioural implications. In particular, when such a mean-variance expected utility function has wealth as its argument, symmetry implies that investors exhibit constant *absolute* risk aversion.[12] When the argument is instead the portfolio rate of return, with wealth homogeneity as in Section 1, symmetry implies constant *relative* risk aversion if the time unit is sufficiently small to render W_t a good approximation to $E(\tilde{W}_{t+1})$. In both cases the symmetry restriction implies that the Slutsky expected wealth (or portfolio rate of return) effects are identically equal to zero, leaving only a symmetric substitution matrix. By contrast, the symmetry property does not follow from (for example) the quadratic utility function, a form frequently encountered in the applied literature.

The symmetry property is therefore an empirically testable restriction. It does not necessarily hold for any reasonable but arbitrarily chosen form of expected utility maximizing behaviour. Hence evidence indicating whether investors' behaviour does or does not exhibit symmetry provides potentially useful information.

2.1 Evidence from Institutional Investors

Evidence based on the demands for two maturity classes of US Treasury securities by institutional investors in the United States suggests that these investors' portfolio behaviour does not exhibit symmetric responses to movements of asset returns. Table 20.1 summarizes this evidence for six major categories of institutional investors in the US markets, including life insurance companies, other insurance companies, mutual savings banks, savings and loan associations, private pension funds, and state and local government retirement funds. The equations summarised in the Table are estimated using quarterly Federal Reserve data (seasonally adjusted) for 1960–75. The data disaggregate the total financial asset holdings of each investor group into asset classes such as corporate bonds, US Treasury securities, equities, commercial paper, mortgages, and currency and demand deposits. The data further disaggregate each group's holding of US Treasury securities into four weighted maturity classes. The evidence in the Table focuses on each of the six investor groups' demands for two distinct classes of Treasury securities: those with maturities ranging from about $1\frac{1}{2}$ to 5 years (S), and those with maturities over 10 years (L).[13]

As is typical in empirical models of financial asset demands, the specific form of asset demand functions estimated here rests on the assumption that transaction costs preclude complete portfolio adjustment to desired asset holdings within one calendar quarter. The specific form of adjustment model used to describe this aspect of short-run

Table 20.1 Estimated institutional asset demand responses

Investor category	Asset	Unconstrained estimates $\beta_{\cdot S}$	$\beta_{\cdot L}$	$\bar{R}^2$	SE	DW	Constrained estimates $\beta_{\cdot S}$	$\beta_{\cdot L}$	$\bar{R}^2$	SE	DW
Life Insurance Companies	S	.0270	−.0190	.81	21	2.18	.0215		.80	22	2.14
		(5.6)	(−4.6)				(5.1)				
	L	−.0025	.0165	.92	39	2.32	−.0174	.0174	.88	48	2.32
		(−0.3)	(2.0)				(−5.2)	(5.2)			
Other Insurance Companies	S	.1102	−.0637	.67	52	1.76	.0827		.67	52	1.72
		(3.8)	(−2.6)				(3.7)				
	L	−.0091	.0128	.71	52	1.81	−.0363	.0363	.68	54	1.84
		(−0.4)	(0.6)				(−1.9)	(1.9)			
Mutual Savings Banks	S	.1005	.0313	.52	57	2.01	.0782		.49	59	1.74
		(4.2)	(0.8)				(3.9)				
	L	.0406	−.0151	.64	25	2.40	−.0035	.0035	.62	25	2.19
		(2.4)	(−1.4)				(−0.4)	(0.4)			
Savings and Loan Associations	S	.0134	.0269	.76	46	1.99	−.0029		.69	52	2.25
		(0.9)	(1.4)				(−0.4)				
	L	.0063	.0079	.81	38	2.12	.0029	.0076	.77	41	2.05
		(0.5)	(0.8)				(0.4)	(0.7)			
Private Pension Funds	S	.0044	.0500	.57	161	1.64	.0660		.57	162	1.77
		(0.1)	(1.2)				(2.5)				
	L	.0263	−.0239	.67	52	2.20	−.0115	.0115	.65	53	2.13
		(2.0)	(1.8)				(−1.1)	(1.1)			
State-Local Retirement Funds	S	−.0071	.0294	.36	26	2.15	.0074		.32	26	1.59
		(−0.9)	(2.4)				(1.1)				
	L	−.0796	.1498	.61	112	2.07	−.0074	.0074	.47	130	2.22
		(−2.6)	(3.8)				(−1.1)	(1.1)			

portfolio behaviour is the multivariate optimal marginal adjustment model

$$\Delta \mathbf{A}_t = \theta(\mathbf{A}_t^* - \mathbf{A}_{t-1}) + \boldsymbol{\alpha}_t^* \cdot \Delta W_t \tag{20}$$

where $\mathbf{A}_t^*$ is the vector of equilibrium asset holdings corresponding to $\boldsymbol{\alpha}_t^* \cdot W_t$ for $\boldsymbol{\alpha}^*$ defined as in (8), and θ is a matrix of adjustment coefficients with column sums identically equal to an arbitrary scalar.[14] Substituting for $\mathbf{A}^*$ and $\boldsymbol{\alpha}^*$ from (3) and (8) yields

$$\Delta \mathbf{A}_t = \theta B \mathbf{r}_t^e \cdot W_t + \theta \boldsymbol{\pi} \cdot W_t - \theta \mathbf{A}_{t-1} + \boldsymbol{\pi} \cdot \Delta W_t + B \mathbf{r}_t^e \cdot \Delta W_t. \tag{21}$$

For each of the six investor groups, only two asset demands are subjected to the symmetry test in the estimated equations.[15] In the data used here, however, investors' asset holdings are disaggregated into a minimum of nine categories, and selected yields on these other assets appear in the estimated demand equations. As a whole, therefore, the set of parameters in the estimated demand equations is under-identified either with or without the symmetry constraint. The subset of parameters relevant to the symmetry test is identified, however. Specifically, the null hypothesis corresponds to $\beta_{SL} = \beta_{LS}$ and $\Sigma_j \beta_{ij} = 0$ $(i = S, L)$, for $\{\beta_{ij}\} = B$.[16] Moreover, because only this subset of the estimated parameters is identified, the system of equations may be estimated without using a non-linear estimation technique.

The asset return series used in the symmetry test reported in Table 20.1 are the Federal Reserve yield series on '3-to-5-year' (r_S^e) and 'long-term' (r_L^e) US Treasury securities. Hence for this test simple observed yields are taken as proxies for expected rates of return.[17] The cross-equation symmetry restriction involves the coefficients on the $r_S^e \cdot \Delta W$ and $r_L^e \cdot \Delta W$ terms in (21). Coefficients on $r_j^e \cdot \Delta W$ terms specified with these yields along with other yields are then used to form the within-equation row-sum constraints also implied by symmetry.

Table 20.1 shows the results of applying full-information instrumental variables estimation to (21). Although the undersized sample problem precludes such alternatives as full-information maximum likelihood or three-stage least squares, a full-information technique is nevertheless required to allow for contemporaneous error covariances in tests involving the two separate asset demands by each investor category.[18]

The left-hand side of Table 20.1 reports summary statistics and estimated β_{ij} coefficients for the 12 asset demand equations (two for each of the six investor categories).[19] The estimated own-yield responses exhibit theoretically correct positive values in 9 of the 12 cases, and the majority of these positive responses are statistically significant at the .05 level.

The estimated coefficient matrix is inconsistent with symmetry, however. The right-hand side of Table 20.1 reports the corresponding constrained symmetric estimates. For five of the six investor categories, the null hypothesis of symmetry can be rejected at the .05 level.[20] For the sixth category (savings and loan associations), symmetry can be rejected at the .10 level. As a whole, therefore, the results indicate that the observed portfolio behaviour of US institutional investors does not exhibit symmetry, and hence does not conform to the type of risk aversion implied by symmetry.

2.2 Evidence from Individual Investors

Evidence from the portfolio behaviour of US households also casts doubt on the assumption of symmetric responses of asset demands to expected asset returns, although less strongly so than in the case of institutional investors. Table 20.2 presents summary results, based on analogous quarterly data for 1960–80, for the estimation of the US household sector's aggregate demands for three broad classes of financial assets that differ from one another according to the risks associated with holding them: Short-term debt (S) includes all assets bearing real returns that are risky, over a single year or calendar quarter, only because of uncertainty about inflation. Long-term debt (L) is risky because of uncertainty not only about inflation but also about changes in asset prices directly reflecting changes in market interest rates. Equity (E) is risky because of uncertainty about inflation and about changes in stock prices.

The pre-tax nominal return associated with the short-term debt category here is a weighted average of zero (for money), the Federal Reserve average rate on time and saving deposits (for other deposits bearing regulated yields), and the four-to-six month prime commercial paper rate (for all other instruments maturing in one year or less), weighted in each quarter according to the composition of the US household sector's aggregate portfolio. The pre-tax nominal return on long-term debt is the Moody's Baa corporate bond yield plus the fitted value (from a simple univariate auotregressive process) of annualized percentage capital gains or losses approximated by applying the

Table 20.2 Estimated household asset demand responses

Unconstrained estimates						
Asset	$\beta_{\cdot S}$	$\beta_{\cdot L}$	$\beta_{\cdot E}$	$\bar{R}^2$	*SE*	*DW*
S	−.0192 (−1.7)	.00283 (1.3)	.00575 (2.7)	.78	11.71	1.53
L	.00201 (0.6)	−.000231 (−0.3)	−.00117 (−1.8)	.16	10.41	1.49
E	.0172 (2.2)	−.00260 (−1.8)	−.00458 (−3.0)	.25	3.43	1.81

Constrained symmetric estimates						
Asset	$\beta_{\cdot S}$	$\beta_{\cdot L}$	$\beta_{\cdot E}$	$\bar{R}^2$	*SE*	*DW*
S	−.0135 (−2.5)			.78	11.74	1.52
L	.00266 (2.0)	−.000299 (−0.8)		.16	10.42	1.48
E	.0108 (2.6)	−.00237 (−2.4)	−.00847 (−2.7)	.18	3.58	1.73

standard consol formula to changes in the Baa yield.[21] For equity the pre-tax nominal return is the dividend-price yield on the Standard and Poor's 500 index plus the fitted value (from an analogous autoregressive process) of annualized percentage capital gains or losses on that index.[22] For each asset, the return used for $\mathbf{r}^e$ in (8) is the corresponding after-tax real return, calculated by applying the household sector's average effective marginal tax rates in each year for interest, dividends and capital gains to the respective components of the pre-tax nominal returns, and then subtracting the annualized percentage change in the consumer price index.[23]

Because there is substantial evidence that individual investors do not fully rebalance their portfolios within a time span as short as one quarter-year, it is again appropriate not to estimate (8) directly but to embed it within some model of portfolio adjustment out of equilibrium. The most familiar such model in the asset demand literature is the multivariate partial adjustment form

$$\Delta \mathbf{A}_t = \theta(\mathbf{A}_t^* - \mathbf{A}_{t-1}) \tag{22}$$

where $\mathbf{A}^*$ is the vector of equilibrium asset holdings as before, and θ is now a matrix of adjustment coefficients with columns satisfying 'adding up' constraints analogous to those applying to B. Substituting for $\mathbf{A}^*$ from (3) and (8) yields

$$\Delta\mathbf{A}_t = \theta B\mathbf{r}_t^e \cdot W_t + \theta\boldsymbol{\pi}\cdot W_t - \theta\mathbf{A}_{t-1}. \tag{23}$$

Table 20.2 shows the results (B estimates and summary statistics only) of applying non-linear maximum likelihood estimation to (23), using data for $\mathbf{r}^e$ as described above and Federal Reserve data on actual household sector asset holdings for $\mathbf{A}$ (and hence W).[24] These data are constructed for each of the three assets by decrementing backward from the reported 1980 year-end value using the corresponding seasonally adjusted quarterly flows.[25] In addition, for equities (the only one of the three assets for which the asset stock data are at market value), quarterly valuation changes are included without seasonal adjustment. The data for W include the three financial assets only, in part to avoid inadequacies in the available data describing holdings of, and returns on, non-financial assets, and in part simply to limit the scope of the analysis. The data for W also omit the household sector's outstanding liabilities, since the great bulk of household borrowing is tied to the ownership of non-financial assets.[26]

Because each term in (23) has the dimension of nominal dollars, care is necessary to avoid spurious correlations due to common time trends. For purposes of estimation, therefore, the data for $\mathbf{A}$ (and hence W) are rendered in real per capita values, using the consumer price index and the total US population series. In addition, both $\Delta\mathbf{A}_t$ and W_t exclude the current period's capital gains or losses (although the vector of lagged asset stocks $\mathbf{A}_{t-1}$ reflects the previous periods' gains and losses), so that the estimated form focuses strictly on the household sector's aggregate net purchases or sales of each asset associated with the sector's net saving. Defining the asset flows in this way is equivalent to assuming that investors do not respond within the quarter to that quarter's changes in their holdings due to changing market valuations, but do respond to market valuations as of the beginning of each quarter.

The upper panel of Table 20.2 reports summary statistics and estimated β_{ij} values for each of the three asset demand equations, estimated in this way with no further constraints.[27] These β_{ij} estimates clearly bear little apparent relation to any asset demand response matrix that makes sense in theoretical terms, however, in that all three estimated on-diagonal 'own' responses are negative. More to the point here, despite the absence of any contradiction in signs among the three pairs of off-diagonal responses, the data are inconsistent with symmetry. The lower panel of the table reports analogous summary statistics and estimated β_{ij} values for the same three equations estimated by exploiting the non-linear maximum likelihood procedure to impose the set of three constraints that here comprise symmetry. The value of the test statistic for these three restrictions is $\chi^2(3) = 8.0$, which warrants rejecting the restrictions at the .05 level.

Because the after-tax real returns on all three classes of financial assets were serially correlated during the 1960–80 sample, the unconditional variation of the observed returns used for $\mathbf{r}^e$ in the estimation of these results presumably overstates the uncertainty that investors actually associated with their expectations of asset returns, over each coming calendar quarter, throughout this period.[28] An alternative (and presumably superior) way of conducting such an analysis, therefore, is to construct some representation of investors' perceptions of these asset returns and risks that takes more careful account of what information investors did or did not have at any particular time.

As of the beginning of each calendar quarter, investors presumably know the stated interest rates on short-term debt instruments, the current prices and the coupon rates on long-term debt instruments, the current prices and (approximately) the dividends on equities, and the relevant tax rates. The three uncertain elements that they must forecast in order to form expectations for the coming quarter of the after-tax real returns on the three broad classes of assets considered here are, therefore, inflation, the capital gain or loss on long-term debt, and the capital gain or loss on equity.

Table 20.3 presents an alternative set of results based on a procedure that infers investors' risk perceptions by representing investors as forming expectations of these three uncertain return elements, at each point in time, by estimating a linear vector autoregression model giving the best linear projection of these elements from past values. In other words, at the beginning of each period investors estimate the three-variable vector autoregression using all then-available data (through the immediately preceding period), and then use the estimated model to project inflation and the respective capital gains on long-term debt and equity for the period immediately ahead. After that period elapses, investors incorporate into the sample the new observation on the three random variables, re-estimate the vector autoregression, and use the updated model to project the relevant unknowns for the subsequent period.

This inherently backward-looking forecast procedure enjoys the advantages and suffers the shortcomings of expecting the immediate future to be like the immediate past, so that the degree of success achieved by the resulting one-period-ahead forecasts naturally varies according to the extent of the serial correlation in the series being forecast. The first-order serial correlation coefficients of the realizations of the three random variables (again based on quarterly movements during 1960–80) are .90 for price inflation, .44 for long-term debt capital gains, and .31 for equity capital gains. The simple correlation coefficients between the realizations and the corresponding forecasts derived from this continual updating procedure are .88 for inflation, .42 for long-term debt capital gains, and .23 for equity capital gains.[29] The simple correlation coefficients between the realizations of after-tax real returns and the corresponding forecasts are .83 for short-term debt, .51 for long-term debt, and .30 for equity.

Table 20.3 Household asset demand responses estimated from forecasted returns

Unconstrained estimates						
Asset	$\beta_{\cdot S}$	$\beta_{\cdot L}$	$\beta_{\cdot E}$	$\bar{R}^2$	*SE*	*DW*
S	.00923	−.0000482	.00190	.79	11.49	1.66
	(0.6)	(−0.0)	(1.1)			
L	−.00515	.0000231	−.000338	.19	10.24	1.61
	(−0.9)	(0.0)	(−0.5)			
E	.00408	.0000251	−.00157	.16	3.68	1.68
	(−0.4)	(0.0)	(−1.4)			

Constrained symmetric estimates						
Asset	$\beta_{\cdot S}$	$\beta_{\cdot L}$	$\beta_{\cdot E}$	$\bar{R}^2$	*SE*	*DW*
S	−.00255			.80	11.36	1.65
	(−2.5)					
L	.000645	−.000294		.20	10.17	1.58
	(1.8)	(−1.2)				
E	.00191	−.000351	−.00156	.17	3.66	1.69
	(2.8)	(−1.4)	(−3.3)			

Table 20.3 reports estimation results, analogous to those shown in Table 20.2, for the same system of three asset demands estimated using these continually updated return forecasts for $\mathbf{r}^e$. Here too, the results are hardly satisfactory in theoretical terms. The unconstrained esti-

mates, shown in the top panel of the table, still indicate a negative estimated response of the demand for equity to the estimated return on equity. More to the point here, two of the three pairs of off-diagonal estimated responses have opposite signs.

The lower panel of Table 20.3 reports the corresponding results for the same estimation subject to the further constraint that matrix *B* be symmetric. Although imposition of the symmetry restriction is not strictly inconsistent with the data in a statistical sense (the test statistic value is $\chi^2(3)=2.65$), the constrained estimates are even less plausible than their unconstrained counterparts. Here the estimated responses of all three asset demands to their respective 'own' expected returns are negative, as they were in Table 20.2. Moreover, all three asset pairs are now not substitutes but complements. Although asset complementarity is plausible enough in general, in this context there is nothing in the unconditional variance-covariance structure of the three assets' returns, or in the conditional variance-covariance structure that results from the continually updated forecast procedure, to suggest complementarity among any of these three asset pairs.

For individual as well as institutional investors, therefore, the available evidence suggests that asset demands exhibiting symmetry do not describe the observed portfolio behaviour. Given the connection between symmetric asset demands and the specific assumptions underlying the maximization of expected utility, these results therefore cast doubt on the validity of standard assumptions often used – either explicitly or implicitly – to characterize the behaviour of risk averse investors.

3 THE 'BLISS POINT' PROBLEM

In both theoretical and empirical analyses of investor behaviour under risk, specific utility functions are frequently assumed to represent investors' preferences. The most analytically tractable, and therefore most widely used, utility functions are those that reduce to preference orderings over the mean and variance of wealth (or portfolio rate of return) under uncertainty. Because quadratic utility reduces in a straightforward manner to such a mean-variance function for all probability distributions of end-of-period wealth, it in particular is often applied to represent investors' utility.[30] The existence of a 'bliss' (or wealth satiation) point in quadratic utility is widely acknowledged. In this case utility has a finite maximum with a corresponding satiation level of end-of-period wealth.

The possible existence of a different bliss point has also been shown in mean-variance models. A sufficient condition for this other bliss point to exist is that a riskless asset is not available and indifference curves are convex in variance-mean space.[31] The untenable implication of this second bliss point is that a satiation level of *beginning*-of-period wealth exists. In other words, there exist levels of initial wealth such that an investor maximizes utility by disposing of some of his wealth before selecting his portfolio.

The existence and implications of initial wealth satiation have been frequently misinterpreted. In particular, initial wealth satiation is usually interpreted as being the same as end-of-period wealth satiation in quadratic utility.[32] These bliss points are in fact distinct, however. Indeed, in the quadratic utility case, initial wealth satiation occurs at a lower level of expected utility than end-of-period wealth satiation. Hence those researchers who have placed importance on restricting the range of application of quadratic utility because of end-of-period wealth satiation should logically have restricted its application still further because of initial wealth satiation. Moreover, initial wealth satiation limits the usefulness not only of quadratic utility but also of many other common mean-variance utility functions.

Two specific examples serve both to show the existence of initial wealth satiation and to examine its consequences.[33] These examples involve quadratic utility and negative exponential utility with joint normally distributed asset returns. Before considering these two cases, however, it is useful to define initial wealth satiation in more precise terms. Initial wealth satiation is attained at initial wealth W_t^* if all levels of initial wealth $W_t < W_t^*$ yield lower mean-variance utility, and if, given $W_t > W_t^*$, an investor will maximize utility by disposing of an amount of initial wealth equal to $W_t - W_t^*$. In other words, at sufficiently high levels of initial wealth, marginal mean-variance utility is negative with respect to increments of initial wealth. The implication of this bliss point is therefore highly untenable, in that it is inconsistent with a generally accepted norm of rational behaviour.

3.1 Quadratic Utility

Perhaps the most interesting example of initial wealth satiation involves quadratic utility

$$U(\tilde{W}_{t+1}) = \tilde{W}_{t+1} - b \cdot \tilde{W}_{t+1}^2 \qquad (24)$$

where b is a positive scalar. While this utility function has been severely criticized for displaying increasing absolute risk aversion, it nevertheless is the only von Neumann-Morgenstern utility function that reduces to an exact mean-variance preference ordering for all probability distributions of end-of-period wealth.[34] The quadratic utility function also possesses a global maximum at

$$\tilde{W}^*_{t+1} = \frac{1}{2b} \tag{25}$$

thereby implying the existence of a satiation level of end-of-period wealth.

Expected quadratic utility immediately follows from (24) and may be written as

$$E[U(\tilde{W}_{t+1})] = E(\tilde{W}_{t+1}) - b \cdot E(\tilde{W}_{t+1})^2 - b \cdot \text{var}(\tilde{W}_{t+1}). \tag{26}$$

In selecting an optimal portfolio, an investor maximizes (26) subject to the constraint

$$\mathbf{A}_t'\mathbf{1} = W_t. \tag{27}$$

Equivalently, in the case considered here in which no risk-free asset exists, the optimal portfolio is the one that maximizes expected utility subject to the efficiency locus

$$\text{var}(\tilde{W}_{t+1}) = \frac{W_t^2(\mathbf{r}_t^{e\prime}\Omega_t^{-1}\mathbf{r}_t^e) - 2W_t(\mathbf{r}_t^{e\prime}\Omega_t^{-1}\mathbf{1}) \cdot E(\tilde{W}_{t+1}) + (\mathbf{1}'\Omega_t^{-1}\mathbf{1}) \cdot E(\tilde{W}_{t+1})^2}{(\mathbf{1}'\Omega_t^{-1}\mathbf{1}) \cdot (\mathbf{r}_t^{e\prime}\Omega_t^{e\prime}\Omega_t^{-1}\mathbf{r}_t^e) - (\mathbf{r}_t^{e\prime}\Omega_t^{-1}\mathbf{1})^2} \tag{28}$$

which is a parabola in variance-mean space dependent on the level of initial wealth and on the parameters of the joint probability distribution of asset returns.[35] Figure 20.1 displays an efficiency locus $c[W_t^*]$ with initial wealth equal to W_t^*. The well-known result that investors with convex indifference curves will always select efficient portfolios is readily apparent from the parabolic curvature of the efficiency locus. With quadratic utility, maximum mean-variance utility is obtained at $[E(\tilde{W}_{t+1})^*, \text{var}(\tilde{W}_{t-1})^*]$, with expected utility U^2, as illustrated in the figure.

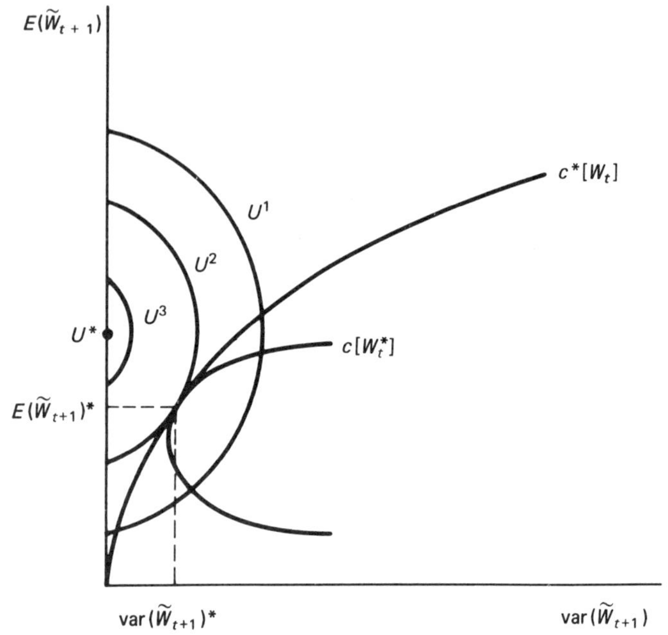

Figure 20.1 Quadratic utility

To find the conditions that lead to initial wealth satiation, the level of invested wealth is then varied to form a family of efficiency loci representing sets of feasible portfolios. The boundary of the set of all possible portfolios, denoted as $c^*[W_t]$ in Figure 20.1, is given by the envelope of the efficiency loci, expressed as[36]

$$\mathrm{var}(\tilde{W}_{t+1}) = E(\tilde{W}_{t+1})^2 \cdot (\mathbf{r}_t^{e'} \Omega_t^{e-1} \mathbf{r}_t^{e})^{-1}. \tag{29}$$

Each point on this boundary corresponds to a unique level of invested wealth.

To demonstrate that expected quadratic utility has a point of initial wealth satiation, a finite solution to the maximization of (26), subject to (29), must be found. The first- and second-order conditions associated with this problem are

$$1 - 2b \cdot (1 + (\mathbf{r}_t^{e'} \Omega_t^{-1} \mathbf{r}_t^{e})^{-1}) \cdot E(\tilde{W}_{t+1}) = 0 \tag{30}$$

$$-2b \cdot (1 + (\mathbf{r}_t^{e'} \Omega_t^{-1} \mathbf{r}_t^{e})^{-1}) < 0. \tag{31}$$

These conditions are jointly satisfied for the unique level of invested wealth

$$W_t^* = (1/2b)\cdot\mathbf{1}'(\Omega_t + \mathbf{r}_t^e\mathbf{r}_t^{e\prime})\mathbf{r}_t^e. \tag{32}$$

Consequently, a satiation level of initial wealth exists at W_t^*, and all initial wealth above this level will be divested.

Figure 20.1 illustrates the existence of initial wealth satiation in the quadratic utility case. The maximum possible level of expected utility is

$$U^* = \frac{1}{4b} \tag{33}$$

which occurs at the centre of the set of concentric indifference curves. The level of expected utility associated with initial wealth W_t^* is

$$U^{**} = (\mathbf{r}_t^{e\prime}\Omega_t^{-1}\mathbf{r}_t^e)\cdot[4b\cdot(1+\mathbf{r}_t^{e\prime}\Omega_t^{-1}\mathbf{r}_t^e)]^{-1} \tag{34}$$

which is always less than that of of the unconstrained maximum ($U^* > U^{**}$). It is therefore *initial* wealth satiation, not end-of-period wealth satiation, that effectively places the upper limit on the level of expected quadratic utility. Moreover, restrictions insuring $\tilde{W}_{t+1} < \tilde{W}_{t+1}^*$ do not necessarily preclude $W_t > W_t^*$. Initial wealth must instead be restricted to be less than W_t^* in order to circumvent the effective bliss point problem in the quadratic utility model.

3.2 Negative Exponential Utility with Joint Normally Distributed Asset Returns

An expected utility model that also enjoys widespread use is derived from the combined assumption of negative exponential utility

$$U(\tilde{W}_{t+1}) = -\exp(-b\cdot\tilde{W}_{t+1}) \tag{35}$$

and joint normally distributed asset returns. One of the attractive features of this specification is that absolute risk aversion is non-decreasing. This model also exhibits increasing relative risk aversion.[37]

The expected utility model consistent with these assumptions can be shown to be maximized when the form

$$U[E(\tilde{W}_{t+1}),\ \mathrm{var}(\tilde{W}_{t+1})] = E(\tilde{W}_{t+1}) - (b/2)\cdot\ \mathrm{var}(\tilde{W}_{t+1}) \tag{36}$$

is maximized. To obtain the satiation level of initial wealth, expected utility (36) may be maximized with respect to $\mathbf{A}_t$, subject to (29), with the constrained optimum yielding first- and second-order conditions

$$1 - b\cdot(\mathbf{r}_t^{e\prime}\Omega_t^{-1}\mathbf{r}_t^e)^{-1}\cdot E(\tilde{W}_{t+1}) = 0 \tag{37}$$

$$-b\cdot(\mathbf{r}_t^{e\prime}\Omega_t^{-1}\mathbf{r}_t^e) < 0. \tag{38}$$

These conditions are satisfied for the unique level of initial wealth

$$W_t^* = (1/b)\cdot(\mathbf{1}'\Omega_t^{-1}\mathbf{r}_t^e). \tag{39}$$

Figure 20.2 illustrates the initial wealth satiation point inherent in this expected utility model. The envelope of the efficiency loci and indifference curves are labelled as in Figure 20.1. This further example

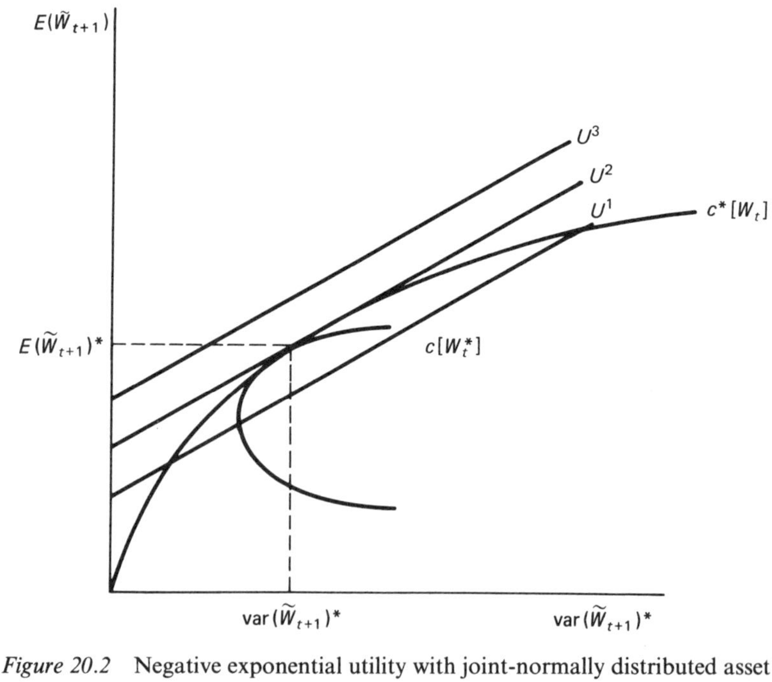

Figure 20.2 Negative exponential utility with joint-normally distributed asset returns

serves to highlight the important fact that initial wealth satiation is an issue completely unrelated to whether the utility function possesses an unconstrained maximum, since $U(\tilde{W}_{t+1})$ in (35) is monotonically increasing in $\tilde{W}_{t+1}$.

These results suggest that other mean-variance utility models with convex indifference curves in variance-mean space are also consistent with initial wealth satiation. Analogous satiation points also occur when utility is specified over portfolio rate of return instead of end-of-period wealth. Initial wealth satiation does not, however, occur either when the utility function is logarithmic with lognormally distributed end-of-period wealth, or when mean-variance utility is viewed as an arbitrarily close approximation to expected utility with constant relative risk aversion.[38] The presence of initial wealth satiation points in many common mean-variance utility functions does nevertheless limit the usefulness of these specific models.

4 SUMMARY AND CONCLUSIONS

Following the lead of Kenneth Arrow's significant contribution to the theory of behaviour under uncertainty, the development of the theory of portfolio behaviour has led to a greater understanding of the combined effects of uncertainty and risk aversion on many aspects of individual and institutional financial behaviour. The focus of this paper is on aspects of this theory involving the properties of investors' asset demands including in particular specific characteristics of asset demands that in the consideration of equilibrium asset returns in the monetary economics literature are often simply assumed, and in the financial literature are often ignored altogether.

The three sections of this paper support three related conclusions: First, asset demands with the familiar properties of wealth homogeneity and linearity in expected returns follow as close approximations from expected utility maximizing behaviour under the assumptions of constant relative risk aversion and joint normally distributed asset returns. Secondly, although such asset demands exhibit a symmetric coefficient matrix with respect to the relevant vector of expected asset returns, symmetry is not a general property, and the available empirical evidence warrants rejecting it for both institutional and individual investors in the US. Finally, in a manner analogous to the finite maximum exhibited by quadratic utility, a broad class of mean-variance utility functions also exhibits a form of wealth satiation that necessarily restricts its range of applicability.

NOTES

1. Brainard and Tobin (1968) and the voluminous work following their lead provide numerous examples in both abstract and empirical work.
2. Friedman (1956) and De Leeuw (1965) in particular provide useful discussions of the importance of the homogeneity property. For an alternative view, however, see Goldfeld (1966, 1969).
3. Cass and Stiglitz (1970) show that constant relative risk aversion implies wealth homogeneity (and vice versa), but they did not consider the form of dependence on expected returns in this context. A large literature has investigated the conditions under which, in the presence of a risk-free asset, the ex post *demands* for risky assets that emerge from the market clearing process are linear in expected returns and linear homogeneous with respect to the total amount invested in risky assets only; see, for example, Sharpe (1964), Lintner (1965), Hakansson (1970), Cass and Stiglitz (1970) and Merton (1971). Nevertheless, these results do not apply to the ex ante *demand relations* that are usually the focus of analysis in the monetary economics literature, as exemplified by Tobin (1958). Moreover, these results do not carry over in general to cases in which there is no risk-free asset; and even when there is a risk-free asset the homogeneity is not with respect to total wealth (as is usually assumed in the monetary economics literature) and does not apply to the demand for the risk-free asset.
4. The rationale for mean-variance analysis provided by Samuelson (1970) and Tsiang (1972) suggests that mean-variance analysis *per se* is only an approximation that depends on (among other factors) a small time unit.
5. Friend and Blume (1975), who proceeded along the lines followed here (as did Ross, 1975), offered empirical evidence supporting the assumption of constant relative risk aversion. See also, more recently, Friend and Hasbrouck (1982).
6. Matrix B is singular, of course, so that the asset demand system (8), in conjunction with a given vector of asset supplies, will be capable of determining all relative yields and all absolute yields but one. See Brainard and Tobin (1968) and Smith (1975) for discussions of empirical implementation of such asset demand systems in the specific context of this singularity.
7. In the case including a risk-free asset, vector $\hat{\mathbf{r}}_t^e$ expresses the mean risky returns in excess of the risk-free return. See Roley (1977) for a detailed treatment of the distinctions based on the presence or absence of a risk-free asset.
8. For given initial wealth, this assumption is equivalent to expressing utility as a function of portfolio rate of return, with constant absolute risk aversion; see Melton (1975).
9. See Lintner (1975) for a comprehensive treatment of portfolio behaviour based on the logarithmic utility function.
10. This section is based on Roley (1983) and Friedman (1984, 1985); see these papers for future details about the data and estimation procedures used.
11. Others have recognised the similarity between systems of demand equations derived from consumer and portfolio theories; see, for example, Royama and Hamada (1967) and Bierwag and Grove (1968).

12. With a mean-variance expected utility function, $U[E(\tilde{W}_{t+1}), \text{var}(\tilde{W}_{t+1})]$, a necessary and sufficient condition for a symmetric coefficient matrix on expected asset returns is $\partial^2U/\partial E^2 = \partial^2U/\partial E\partial\text{var} = 0$. This condition in turn implies constant absolute risk aversion.
13. The weighted maturity class data are defined in terms of four 'definite' areas and three 'borderline' areas. The definite areas corresponding to the two maturity classes examined here are 2 to 4 years and over 12 years to maturity. Securities with maturities in the borderline areas – in this case securities with 1 to 2 years and 8 to 12 years to maturity – are allocated to the definite classifications according to a weighting scheme.
14. The basic notion behind the optimal marginal adjustment model is that investors can allocate new investable flows ΔW_t less expensively than they can reallocate assets already in their portfolios, and that such flows will be allocated according to desired asset proportions; see Friedman (1977).
15. The estimated model corresponds to that reported in Roley (1981). Additional asset demands are included in expanded versions of the model; see Roley (1982).
16. The *columns* of *B* must sum to zero regardless of whether the *B* matrix is symmetric. The *rows* of *B* are required to sum to zero only when symmetry is imposed.
17. Alternative measures of expected returns are considered below in the context of symmetry tests based on household sector portfolio behaviour.
18. The technique used is a modified version of a technique suggested by Fair and Parke (1980). Under this procedure, the covariances of the errors between equations in an individual investor category are in general non-zero, but the error covariances between equations of different categories are constrained to equal zero.
19. The standard errors reported in the table are in millions of dollars.
20. The statistic presented by Gallant and Jorgenson (1979) is used to test the symmetry restriction. Under the null hypothesis, this test statistic is asymptotically distributed as χ^2 with three degrees of freedom.
21. The equation is

$$\underset{}{cg_{Lt}} = \underset{(-1.2)}{-1.63} + \underset{(5.0)}{0.567}\, cg_{L,t-1} \underset{(-2.8)}{-0.366}\, cg_{L,t-2}$$

$$\underset{(2.9)}{+0.387}\, cg_{L,t-3} \underset{(-0.0)}{-.000615}\, cg_{L,t-4}$$

$$\bar{R}^2 = .28 \qquad SE = 11.25 \qquad DW = 1.99$$

where the standard error is in per cent per annum.

22. The equation is

$$cg_{Et} = \underset{(2.1)}{5.85} + \underset{(3.5)}{0.393}\, cg_{E,t-1} \underset{(-2.2)}{-0.268}\, cg_{E,t-2}$$

$$\underset{(-0.0)}{-0.00331}\, cg_{E,t-3} \underset{(0.1)}{+0.017}\, cg_{t-4}$$

$$\bar{R}^2 = .12 \qquad SE = 23.18 \qquad DW = 2.00$$

where the standard error is again in per cent per annum.

23. The marginal tax rates applied to interest and dividends are values estimated by Estrella and Fuhrer (1983), on the basis of Internal Revenue Service data, to reflect the marginal tax bracket of the average recipient of these two respective kinds of income in each year. The marginal tax rate applied to capital gains is an analogous estimate, including allowances for deferral and loss offset features, due to Feldstein *et al.* (1983). Preliminary experimentation with the respective price deflators for gross national product and personal consumption expenditures indicated that the results presented below are not very sensitive to the choice of a specific inflation measure.
24. The non-linear maximum likelihood procedure facilitates not only the direct estimation of asymptotic *t*-statistics on the elements of *B* but also the imposition of constraints as discussed below.
25. The purpose of this procedure is to generate series of seasonally adjusted end-of-quarter asset stocks without any gaps or inconsistencies due to splicing of data series. (The Federal Reserve System does not construct such series.)
26. Out of $1494 billion of household sector liabilities outstanding at year-end 1980, $971 billion consisted of mortgage debt and $385 billion of installment and other consumer credit.
27. The standard errors reported here have the dimension of thousands of constant 1967 dollars per capita.
28. The simple first-order serial correlation coefficients are .86 for short-term debt, .51 for long-term debt, and .33 for equity.
29. In comparing these 'fit' correlations to the corresponding serial correlations, it is helpful to recall that investors did not know the 1960–80 serial correlation properties of these variables until after this period had ended. The forecasting procedure applied here uses only information that investors had at the time they needed to make each quarter's forecast.
30. In fact, Borch (1969) proved that the quadratic utility function is the only von Neumann-Morgenstern (1944) utility function that induces mean-variance preferences for all probability distributions of end-of-period wealth.
31. Bierwag and Grove (1966) demonstrated that convexity of the indifference curves is a sufficient condition. Jones and Roley (1981) generalized this result and showed that some utility functions with concave mean-variance indifference curves also have bliss points.
32. Borch (1969) and Hakansson (1972), for example, interpreted the result of Bierwag and Grove (1966) as implying that indifference curves in standard deviation-mean space are concentric circles with the point of highest utility represented by a single point at the centre. This bliss point corresponds to *end*-of-period wealth satiation in quadratic utility. Bierwag and Grove (1966), however, did not examine the case in which indifference curves in standard deviation-mean space have this representation. Instead, they assumed convex indifference curves in variance-mean space, and showed that this assumption implies a preference ordering in asset space represented by concentric circles. The centre of these circles represents the point of *initial* wealth satiation.
33. See Jones and Roley (1981) for a more general analysis.

34. See Arrow (1965) for a discussion of the adverse risk aversion properties of quadratic utility.
35. For convenience, here and throughout the remainder of Section 3 **r** indicates gross returns, rather than net returns as above. Following Markowitz (1952), the efficiency locus may be derived from the problem

$$\underset{\mathbf{A}_t}{\text{minimize}}\ \mathbf{A}_t'\Omega_t\mathbf{A}_t \text{ subject to } \mathbf{A}_t'\mathbf{r}_t^e = E(\tilde{W}_{t+1}) \text{ and } \mathbf{A}_t'\mathbf{1} = W_t.$$

36. The envelope of the efficiency loci may be derived from the problem

$$\underset{\mathbf{A}_t}{\text{minimize}}\ \mathbf{A}_t'\Omega_t\mathbf{A}_t \text{ subject to } \mathbf{A}_t'\mathbf{r}_t^e = E(\tilde{W}_{t+1}) \text{ and } \mathbf{A}_t'\mathbf{1} = W_t.$$

37. Arrow (1965) argued, on both theoretical and empirical grounds, that relative risk aversion is an increasing function of wealth.
38. This latter result is due to Jones (1979). The additional cases mentioned here are examined by Roley (1977) and Jones and Roley (1981).

REFERENCES

Arrow, K. J. (1965) *Aspects of the Theory of Risk-Bearing* (Helsinki: The Yrjö Jahnsson Foundation).

Bierwag, G. O. and M. A. Grove (1966) 'Indifference Curves in Asset Analysis', *Economic Journal*, 76: 337–43.

Bierwag, G. O. and M. A. Grove (1968) 'Slutsky Equations for Assets'. *Journal of Political Economy*, 76: 114–27.

Borch, K. (1969) 'A Note on Uncertainty and Indifference Curves'. *Review of Economic Studies*, 36: 1–4.

Brainard, W. C. and J. Tobin (1968) 'Pitfalls in Financial Model-Building', *American Economic Review*, 57: 99–122.

Cass, D. and J. E. Stiglitz (1970) 'The Structure of Investor Preferences and Asset Returns, and Separability in Portfolio Allocation: A Contribution to the Pure Theory of Mutual Funds', *Journal of Economic Theory*, 2: 122–60.

De Leeuw, F. (1965) 'A Model of Financial Behavior', in Duesenberry *et al.* (eds) *The Brookings Quarterly Econometric Model of the United States* (Chicago: Rand McNally).

Estrella, A. and J. Fuhrer (1983) 'Average Effective Marginal Tax Rates on Interest and Dividend Income in the United States, 1960–1979', mimeo. National Bureau of Economic Research.

Fair, R. C. and W. R. Parke (1980) 'Full-Information Estimates of a Nonlinear Macroeconometric Model'. *Journal of Econometrics*, 13: 269–91.

Feldstein, M., J. Poterba and L. Dicks-Mireaux (1983) 'The Effective Tax Rate and the Pretax Rate of Return'. *Journal of Public Economics*, 21: 129–53.

Friedman, B. M. (1977) 'Financial Flow Variables in the Short-Run Determination of Long-Term Interest Rates'. *Journal of Political Economy*, 85: 661–89.

Friedman, B. M. (1984) 'Crowding Out or Crowding In? Evidence on Debt-Equity Substitutability', mimeo. National Bureau of Economic Research.

Friedman, B. M. (1985) 'The Substitutability of Debt and Equity Securities', in Friedman (ed.) *Corporate Capital Structures in the United States* (Chicago: University of Chicago Press).

Friedman, M. (1956) 'The Quantity Theory of Money: A Restatement', in Friedman (ed.) *Studies in the Quantity Theory of Money* (Chicago: University of Chicago Press).

Friend, I. and M. E. Blume (1975) 'The Demand for Risky Assets', *American Economic Review*, 65: 900–22.

Friend, I. and J. Hasbrouck (1982). 'Effect of Inflation on the Profitability and Valuation of U.S. Corporations', in Sarnat and Szego (eds) *Savings, Investment and Capital Markets in an Inflationary Economy* (Cambridge, Mass.: Ballinger).

Gallant, A. R. and D. W. Jorgenson (1979) 'Statistical Inference for a System of Simultaneous, Non-Linear, Implicit Equations in the Context of Instrumental Variable Estimation'. *Journal of Econometrics*, 11: 275–302.

Goldfeld, S. M. (1966) *Commercial Bank Behavior and Economic Activity* (Amsterdam: North Holland).

Goldfeld, S. M. (1969) 'An Extension of the Monetary Sector', in Duesenberry *et al.* (eds) *The Brookings Model: Some Further Results* (Chicago: Rand McNally).

Hakansson, N. H. (1970) 'Optimal Investment and Consumption Strategies Under Risk for a Class of Utility Functions'. *Econometrica*, 38: 587–607.

Hakansson, N. H. (1972) 'Mean-Variance Analysis in a Finite World'. *Journal of Financial and Quantitative Analysis*, 7: 1873–80.

Jones, D. S. (1979) *A Structural Econometric Model of the United States Equity Market*, PhD dissertation (Harvard University).

Jones, D. S. and V. V. Roley (1981) 'Bliss Points in Mean-Variance Portfolio Models', mimeo. (National Bureau of Economic Research).

Lintner, J. (1965). 'The Valuation of Risky Assets and the Selection of Risky Investments in Stock Portfolios and Capital Budgets'. *Review of Economics and Statistics*, 47: 13–37.

Lintner, J. (1975) 'The Lognormality of Security Returns, Portfolio Selection and Market Equilibrium', mimeo (Harvard University).

Markowitz, H. (1952) 'Portfolio Selection'. *Journal of Finance*, 7: 77–91.

Melton, W. C. (1975) *Simultaneous Restricted Estimation of a New Model of Commercial Bank Portfolio Behavior: Estimates for Swedish Commercial Banks*, PhD dissertation (Harvard University).

Merton, R. C. (1971) 'Optimum Consumption and Portfolio Rules in a Continuous-Time Model'. *Journal of Economic Theory*, 3: 373–413.

Neumann, J. von, and O. Morgenstern (1944) *Theory of Games and Economic Behavior* (New York: Wiley).

Roley, V. (1977) *A Structural Model of the U.S. Government Securities Market*, PhD dissertation (Harvard University).

Roley, V. V. (1981) 'The Determinants of the Treasury Security Yield Curve'. *Journal of Finance*, 36: 1103–26.

Roley, V. V. (1982) 'The Effect of Federal Debt-Management Policy on

Corporate Bond and Equity Yields'. *Quarterly Journal of Economics*, 97: 645–67.

Roley, V. V. (1983). 'Symmetry Restrictions in a System of Financial Asset Demands: Theoretical and Empirical Results'. *Review of Economics and Statistics*, 65: 124–30.

Ross, S. A. (1975) 'Uncertainty and the Heterogeneous Capital Good Model', *Review of Economic Studies*, 42: 133–46.

Royama, S. and K. Hamada (1967) 'Substitution and Complementarity in the Choice of Risky Assets'. In: Hester and Tobin (eds) *Risk Aversion and Portfolio Choice* (New York: Wiley).

Samuelson, P. A. (1970) 'The Fundamental Approximation Theorem of Portfolio Analysis in Terms of Means, Variances, and Higher Moments', *Review of Economic Studies*, 37: 537–42.

Sharpe, W. F. (1964) 'Capital Asset Prices: A Theory of Market Equilibrium Under Conditions of Risk', *Journal of Finance*, 19: 425–42.

Smith, G. (1975) 'Pitfalls in Financial Model Building: A Clarification', *American Economic Review*, 65: 510–16.

Tobin, J. (1958) 'Liquidity Preference as Behavior Towards Risk', *Review of Economic Studies*, 25: 65–86.

Tsiang, S. C. (1972) 'The Rationale of the Mean-Standard Deviation Analysis, Skewness Preference, and the Demand for Money', *American Economic Review*, 62: 354–71.

21 Oligopolistic Uncertainty and Optimal Bidding in Government Procurement: A Subjective Probability Approach

Robert E. Kuenne

Kenneth Arrow's early and continuing interest in the economics of risk and uncertainty and his contributions to the literature it inspired were pivotal in the developments that have characterised the field in the last 20 years. A re-reading of the *Essays in the Theory of Risk Bearing* – some of which date back a quarter century or more – confirms in detail the impressions they created at first reading. In them Arrow moves effortlessly between the rigour of mathematical analysis and the brilliantly intuitive and conjectural.

At the core of his interest is the desire to integrate risk and uncertainty into the theory of general equilibrium, with the implied need to create universal futures markets or other institutions for risk-shifting. The seminal question emerges from his analysis: why has the market economy failed to provide these opportunities for the risk-averse? The search for answers leads Arrow into imaginative and insightful discussion of moral hazard, the economics of health care, the role of and demand for information, the conceptual foundations of insurance, and the nature of research and development activities. The contributions in these fields are characterized by an ease of brilliance: effortless movement from insight to insight at a pace that exhausts the reader. As a concrete example, Essay 5 – 'Insurance, Risk and Resource Allocation' – must surely rank among the most insightful ten pages in economic literature.

One of Arrow's pioneering contributions to the field was the acceptance of subjective probability as a valid and primitive conceptual basis for the analysis of choice under uncertainty. The notion that agents' attitudes toward uncertain events are shaped by intuitive and experiential feelings of obscure origin and with little prospect of successful explanation is still a difficult one to accept for some economists. The attitude that unless one can derive the probability density function ruling over an outcome space from the objective evidence of the phenomena one does not have the basis for a fruitful analysis is still apparent in such fields as the theory of bidding.

Despite the fact that the early interest of Arrow in the economics of uncertainty arose from a concern with government procurement contracting (notably cost-plus contracts as a means of shifting risk to the government at some cost in moral hazard), the theory of bidding was one of the few topics in the theory of decision-making under uncertainty that escaped his scrutiny. The present paper does not arrogate itself to an assertion of lineal descent from Arrow's seminal work, but it does attempt to work within frameworks that are clearly indicated by that work to analyze oligopolistic bidding strategies using subjective probability as the core concept. It acknowledges, therefore, its debt to Arrow in pointing to untravelled routes into difficult territory for exploratory excursions.

1 BIDDING IN A COMPETITIVE MARKET STRUCTURE

Modern optimal bidding theory reveals two distinct sources. The earlier strand of research interest originated in operations research, and was given initial form in the seminal work of Friedman (1956). Indeed, that term is peculiarly appropriate because the article was abstracted from Friedman's dissertation, which earned him the first PhD degree awarded in the field of operations research. That work, and subsequent work by operations research specialists quite naturally focused upon the strategic decision-making of the firm, largely abstracting from the interdependence of rival bidders' expectations (see, for example, Kortanek, Soden, and Sodaro (1973) and Attanasi and Johnson (1975, 1977)). It did, however, incorporate the economic theoretic work of Arrow (1971) and Pratt (1964) in preferences under risk – notably risk aversion.

The second stream of contributions was originated by economists, with pioneering work by Vickrey (1961) and the development of games with incomplete information by Harsanyi (1967–68). It shifts the emphasis to the game-theoretic interdependence of bidders, employing the notion of a Nash non-co-operative equilibrium among their expectations of rivals' behaviour. Impressive work in the development of these competitive auction behaviour theories has been contributed by Wilson (1967, 1969, 1977, 1978); Engelbrecht-Wiggins (1980); Harris and Ravio (1981); Holt (1980); McCall (1970); Baron (1972); Milgrom (1981); Milgrom and Weber (1982); and Kuhlman and Johnson (1983).

Paradoxically, the adoption of a game-theoretic orientation leads to an impersonality and state of ignorance about rivals' costs and opportunities that are inappropriate in many oligopolistic bidding contexts. Although they may vary somewhat among authors, the following assumptions about competititve bidding environments in a procurement contract auction[1] are characteristic of the literature:

1. Each bidder knows the value of the contract to himself (equal to his opportunity cost or reservation price) but he is ignorant about his rivals' valuations and reservation prices in the small – that is, rival by rival.[2]

2. The reservation prices for all firms are independently-drawn realizations from a sample space under the regime of the same probability density function.

3. All bidders have symmetric preferences and information concerning rival bidders, and hence it is assumed (in order to obtain a Nash equilibrium) that all bidders will determine a bid from a common bidding function with opportunity cost the argument.

4. The bidder's specific bid will be affected by his expectation of the lowest bid of his rivals as a body, derivable by order statistics from 2 and 3.

In major government procurement contracts, as well as in many other auction contexts, these assumptions do not permit an adequate analytical description of the rivalry among bidders. Rivals may be few in the oligopolistic sense, with rather accurate knowledge of their competitors' opportunity costs, attitudes toward risk, management styles, desires to establish a continuing relation with the contractor, normal profit margins, and so forth. In no sense can the reservation prices – which may depart from strict opportunity costs in these circumstances – be treated as independent drawings from a common probability density function. Moreover, the relevance of a Nash equilibrium for expected bids is questionable, given the limited scope for conjectural variation reasoning, the once-for-all and secret nature of the bidding, and the rival-specific bidding functions forthcoming in oligopolistic bidding structures.

This chapter seeks to model oligopolistic bidding in sealed tenders for government contracts in manners that approach more closely the practices, states of knowledge and strategic thinking of oligopolists. That implies a return to the interests of earlier researchers when oligopoly was featured rather than anonymous competition. It incorporates knowledge and belief held by the bidder as subjective probabilistic 'hunches' about rivals' bids that can be approximated by families of familiar probability functions. And, lastly, it attempts to derive some policy implications for government in designing its contracting requirements and conventions.

2 THE FIRM'S BIDDING DECISION

We assume that a government purchasing agent requests bids from producers for delivery of q units of product over a specified time period. It is further assumed that the firm has alternative private sector markets for the product and that its industry is oligopolistic. For the time period in question the firm's capacity to produce the good sets an upper bound of k units, all of which could be sold in the private sector market at positive profit levels. How would the profit-maximizing firm decide whether to bid on the contract, and if it does decide to bid, how does it determine the size of that bid in its state of imperfect but existent knowledge of its rivals' cost, profit, market share, and management profiles?

Rival 1 – whose bidding decisions we analyze – has expectations about its private sector sales potential in the form of a family of conditional probability density functions

$$h(p|w), \qquad 0 < w \leqslant k, \tag{1}$$

which state, for each hypothetical sales level w, the subjective expectations about prices p at which it could be sold. We will not be more specific about these functions except to say that they are expected to be unimodal, strongly peaked, and with small variances, given rival 1's extensive experience in its primary market.

More important for our immediate interests is the stochastic structure of rival 1's decision-making in the bidding procedure. Central to our modelling of that process are four assumptions:

1. Given its acquaintance with the demand and cost structure of the industry, and perhaps formal or informal maximum bid signals from the government, firm 1 formulates a lower bound L and upper bound U, within which it is certain the successful bid will lie.

2. For each of its perceived rival bidders, firm 1's expectations of the bidder's circumstances can be expressed as probabilities the bid will be a given price or less. Rival 1 can formulate several such defining probabilities for given bid levels for each of its perceived rivals.

3. For each of rival 1's competitors, the defining probabilities can be used by firm 1 to approximate its subjective expectations with a cumulative density function of simple form over the domain $b_j \in [L, \infty]$, where $b_j, j \neq 1$, are the bids of rivals j. For convenience, we may normalize the bids with the transformation,

$$x = \frac{b_j - L}{U - L}, \qquad (2)$$

   and define the cumulative functions over $x \in [0, \infty]$.

4. A preference function for choices under risk can be calculated for rival 1, and its bid will be determined by its desire to maximize the expected utility of profits. For purposes of simplicity, these preferences will be taken to be approximately risk-neutral, given the 'normal' income levels anticipated under the contract, so that they are linear in profits.

Because we are interested in modelling oligopolistic decision-making in an operational manner that approximates the capabilities and habits of the actual decision-makers, attention is called to an important feature of (2). It is not supposed that rival 1 constructs or is in command of a probability distribution over rival j's bids, specifying the 'probability' of any particular bid. Rather, the much more realistic assertion is that rival 1 can specify hunches about several critical values: the most likely (modal) bid, the value below which rival 1 is 95 per cent certain that rival j will bid, the likelihood of rival j bidding rival 1's estimate of his opportunity cost or less, and so forth. After fitting a cumulative density function to this subjective information, the underlying rival's probability density function can be *derived* from the operational information, but it is not presumed to have a meaningful pre-existence in the active decision process of the decision-maker.[3]

Consider, now, rival 1's appraisal of rival *j*'s decision process. In the framework assumed in (2) a cumulative probability density function, $G_j(x)$, is determinable, where $x=(b-L)/(U-L), x\in[0,\infty]$. Although x is unbounded, firm 1 expects that $G_j(x)$ can be approximated by a Weibull cumulative density function,

$$G_j(x)=1-e^{-(x/a_j)^{c_j}}, \qquad 0\leqslant x\leqslant\infty, \tag{3}$$

where a_j is a scale parameter and c_j a shape parameter.

The Weibull is adopted because it is a flexible two-parameter distribution with convenient mathematical properties. With (say) $G_j(.995)=.995$, one degree of freedom in fitting $G_j(x)$ is used. If firm 1 can specify its guess as to firm *j*'s most likely bid, it may be used as the mode,

$$\text{Mode}=\begin{cases} a_j(1-\frac{1}{c_j})^{1/c_j}, & c_j>1 \\ 0, & c_j\leqslant 1, \end{cases} \tag{4}$$

in firm *j*'s underlying estimated *bidding density function*,

$$g_j(x)\equiv G_j'(x)=\frac{c_j}{a_j^{c_j}}x^{c_j-1}e^{-(x/a_j))^{c_j}}. \tag{5}$$

This function is a Weibull distribution yielding the *implied* probabilities of firm *j* bidding in the small interval about x.

When $c_j=1$, the Weibull is the negative exponential function, and when $c_j=2$ it is the Rayleigh distribution. Note that the mode is non-zero for $c_j>1$. Given the inverse of the cumulative function,

$$G_j(x)^{-1}=a_j\left(ln\frac{1}{1-\alpha}\right)^{1/c_j}, \tag{6}$$

where α is a specified probability, and either a second point that can be put in (6), or the mode in (4), the values for a_j and c_j can be solved for.

The flexibility of the Weibull is illustrated in Table 21.1, where the values of $G_j(x)$ are recorded for a wide range of c_j, a_j, and implied modes. This flexibility, its two-parameter nature, and its ease of mathematical manipulation make the Weibull an ideal distribution for the approximation of firm 1's subjective notions of its rivals' behaviour.

Table 21.1 Values of the cumulative Weibull distribution for a variety of parameter and modal values

				$[c_j, a_j]$			
x	[2,0.43]	[3,0.57]	[4,0.66]	[5,0.71]	[10,0.84]	[15,0.89]	[20,0.92]
.10	.05	.01	—	—	—	—	—
.25	.29	.08	.02	.01	—	—	—
.50	.74	.49	.28	.16	.01	—	—
.75	.95	.90	.81	.73	.28	.07	.02
.85	.98	.96	.94	.91	.68	.39	.19
.95	.99	.99	.99	.99	.97	.93	.85
Mode	.30	.50	.61	.68	.83	.89	.92

The probability firm 1's normalized bid x will win over rival j's bid is

$$f_j(x) = 1 - G_j(x) = e^{-(x/a_j)^{c_j}}, \tag{7}$$

and the probability x will win the contract, when firm 1 considers each rival in similar fashion, is

$$f(x) = \prod_j f_j(x) = \prod_j (1 - G_j(x)) = e^{-\Sigma_j (x/a_j)^{c_j}}. \tag{8}$$

It is noted that for all $c_j > 0$, and realistic $0 < a_j \leqslant 1$, $f(x)$ is continuous, negatively sloped, with second-order derivatives.

For simplicity we will assume that variable costs, v, per unit of firm 1's product are constant. Further, we assume that the increasingly burdensome costs of doing business with the federal government are capable of being monetized by the firm, and may be approximated by m dollars per unit of q. Among such costs are the legal costs of coping with voluminous contracts and of submitting to potential litigation for violations of Equal Opportunity Employment, Affirmative Action, Minority Business, Small Business, and so on, statutes; the costs of submitting to specified cost escalation indices that do not accurately track market costs; the costs of being unable to allocate to the government on a fractional basis in periods of shortage; the costs of being unable to invoke *force majeure* in times of raw material unavailability; the burdens of testing and retesting the product to assure its conformance to government specifications; and so forth.[4]

The expected profit of the firm in its total operations may be written as a function of its actual bid, b_1, on the contract, and its normalized value x_1:

$$E(\pi_1)=f(x_1)\{q(b_1-v-m)+(k-q)\,(\textstyle\int_0^\infty p\cdot h(p|k-q)dp-v)\}+ \\ (1-f(x_1)\,)\{k(E(p|k)-v)|, \tag{9}$$

where $E(p|k-q)$ and $E(p|k)$ are the expected prices obtained from sales of $k-q$ and k units respectively on the private market. Expected total profits are the sum of (1), the probability of winning the contract times the contract's net revenue and net revenue from the sale of remaining output in the private market and (2), the probability of losing the contract times the expected net revenue from sale of capacity output in the private market. More compactly,

$$E(\pi)=f(x)[q(x\cdot(U-L)+L-v-m)]+f(x)\,[E(\bar{\pi}_{k-q})- \\ E(\bar{\pi}_k)]+E(\bar{\pi}_k), \tag{10}$$

where $E(\bar{\pi}_{k-q})$ and $E(\bar{\pi}_k)$ are expected profits in the private market from the sale of $k-q$ and k units respectively.

Then, first order conditions for a maximum are

$$\frac{dE(\pi)}{dx}=f(x)\cdot q\cdot(U-L)+f'(x)\,[q\cdot(x\cdot(U-L)+L-v-m)]+ \\ f'(x)\,[\Delta E(\bar{\pi})]=0. \tag{11}$$

From (11),

$$x^0=r^0-(\frac{L-v-m}{U-L})-\frac{\Delta E(\bar{\pi})}{q\cdot(U-L)}, \tag{12}$$

where $r^0=f(x^0)/-f'(x^0)$. A necessary and sufficient condition that $E(\pi)$ be strictly concave is that $f'(x)<-.5f''(x)r$. Since $f'(x)<0$, a sufficient condition for strict concavity is $f''(x)\leqslant 0$, but it cannot be expected to be met in some relevant domains of $f(x)$. Hence, the quantitative relationships for specific forms of $f(x)$ must be evaluated. For the

Weibull formulation, $f''>0$ in its upper domain, but strict concavity will hold for all $x>0$.

Note that (12) is on a normalized per unit of q basis, and that multiplication of both sides by the normalizing factor $(U-L)$ converts to dollars per unit of q. Indeed, condition (12) is more readily interpretable after conversion to

$$b^0 = v + m - \frac{\Delta E(\bar{\pi})}{q} + r^0(U-L) \tag{13}$$

$$= v + m - \frac{\Delta E(\bar{\pi})}{q} + s^0 \tag{14}$$

$$= o + s^0.$$

The optimal bid price per unit of q by firm 1 will be (1), unit variable and contracting cost (2), less the net gain or plus the net loss in private market profit per unit of contract quantity because $k-q$ units instead of k are sold, plus (3), s^0, or an *oligopoly bidding surplus* per unit of q. We will term (1)+(2) the opportunity cost of a unit of q, or o.

In an oligopolistic bidding context there may exist in the typical bidder's tender a positive rent over and above any oligopoly surpluses that are present in $\Delta E(\bar{\pi})$ *(and therefore* o*).* Its source lies wholly in the uncertainty that inheres in a bidding rivalry in which the market structure does not lead bidders to expect rivals to bid opportunity cost. Consider (13):

$$b^0 - o = s^0 = r^0(U-L) \tag{15}$$

$$= \frac{f(x^0)}{-f'(x^0)}(U-L) = \frac{f(x^0)dx}{-f'(x^0)dx}(U-L).$$

The first order condition may be written

$$q(b^0 - o)\,(-f'(x^0)dx = q{\cdot}f(x^0)dx(U-L). \tag{16}$$

At the maximum, a slight rise in $b, db=(U-L)dx$, the probability of losing the contract rises by $(-f'(x)db)/(U-L)$, the marginal risk of loss. The left-hand side of (16), therefore, is the marginal expected loss with a rise in b. The right-hand side is the marginal expected gain from the rise. Hence, (16) states the requirement that b be set at the level that equates marginal expected loss to marginal expected gain from small changes in b. Thus, *s is the marginal expected benefit per unit of contract sales per unit of marginal risk.*

For convenience, henceforth we will use normalized bids x and r, which is s per unit of normalized bid. It is a summary index of firm 1's perceived information about its opportunity cost advantages or disadvantages relative to rivals, the aggressiveness of rival managements, and these managements' capabilities of perceiving similar situations and attitudes of their rivals.[5]

The existence of r (and s) is not recognized in competitive bidding theory as summarized in Section 1. Consider, for example, the competitive bid derivation of firm 1's tender as depicted in Figure 21.1. We graph $r(x)$ on the vertical axis as a function of x on the horizontal axis. The function $r(x)=f(x)/-f'(x)$ is drawn as quite large in the early phases since for very low bids firm 1 views $f(x)$ as close to 1 and $-f'(x)$ as close to zero. If all firms were viewed as having the same opportunity costs, then $r(x)$ would be near-infinite over the domain $x \in [0,x_0]$, with x_0 the normalized bid transformation of the common opportunity cost. At x_0 in this identical cost case $r(x)$ would fall discontinuously to the horizontal axis and then coincide with it in the interval $x \in [x_0,1]$, on which domain $f(x)=0$.

The normalized unit surplus function, $h(x)=x-[(v+m-L-\Delta E(\bar{\pi})/q)/(U-L)$, depicting the excess above costs any bid is in normalized units, is positively sloped at a unitary value and intersects the horizontal axis at normalized opportunity cost. In the identical cost case this would be at x_0, and firm 1 (and all firms) would find the intersection of $r(x)$ and $h(x)$ at x_0, with $r=0$.

Figure 21.1 may also be used to depict the monopoly bid. In the interval $x \in [0,1[$, r is 'infinitely' large, then drops discontinuously to 0 at $x=1$. The $h(x)$ function 'intersects' $r(x)$ in this discontinuity and determines the optimal bid at $x^0=1$.

Figure 21.2, by contrast, depicts the more realistic oligopolistic decision process. The bid x_c is now firm 1's (normalized) opportunity cost, and $r(x)$ is depicted as negatively sloped. The optimal (normalized) bid, x^0, occurs where $h(x^0)=r(x^0)$, with $r^0>0$. From the definition of $r(x)$,

$$\frac{dr(x)}{dx}=\frac{f(x)\cdot f''(x)}{(f'(x))^2}-1=r\frac{f''(x)}{-f'(x)}-1. \tag{17}$$

In interpreting this expression it is useful to recall that $f''(x)$ is the

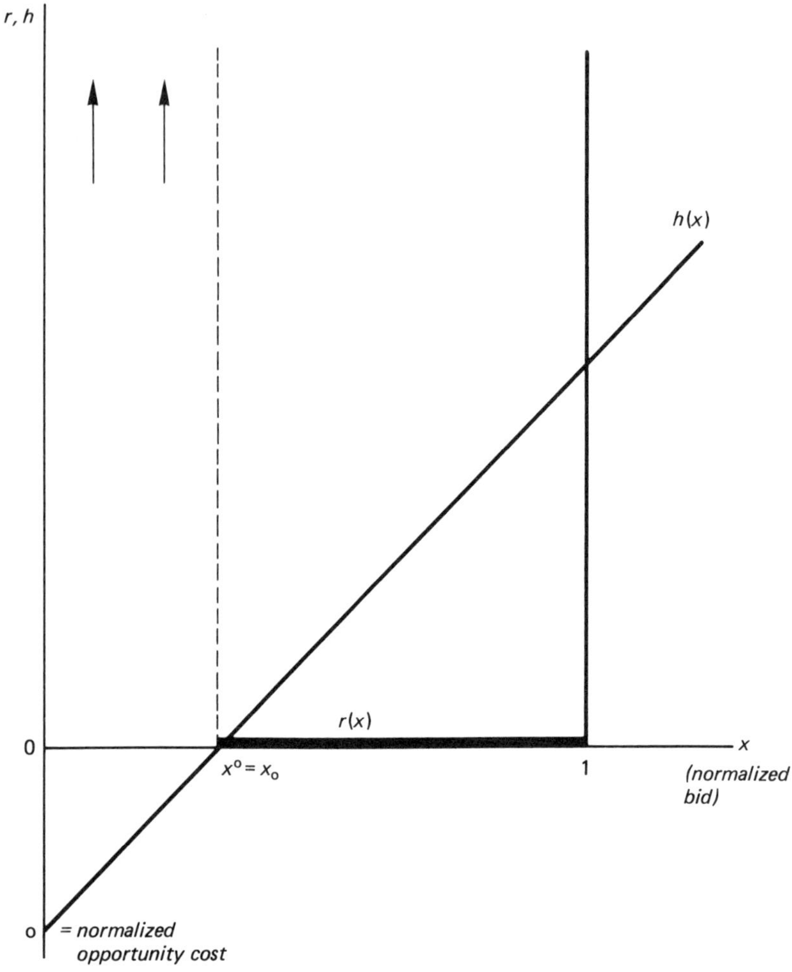

Figure 21.1 The firm's optimal bid in an identical cost industry

(negative of the) slope of $-f'(x)$. The function $f(x)$ will typically be concave in its lower domain and convex in its upper domain, so that $-f'(x)$ will rise to a modal value (where $f''(x)=0$) and fall from that value.

From (17), in the concave portion of $f(x)$, where $-f'(x)$ is rising, $dr/dx<0$. Where $f(x)$ is convex, it is possible for $dr/dx \geqslant 0$. From (17),

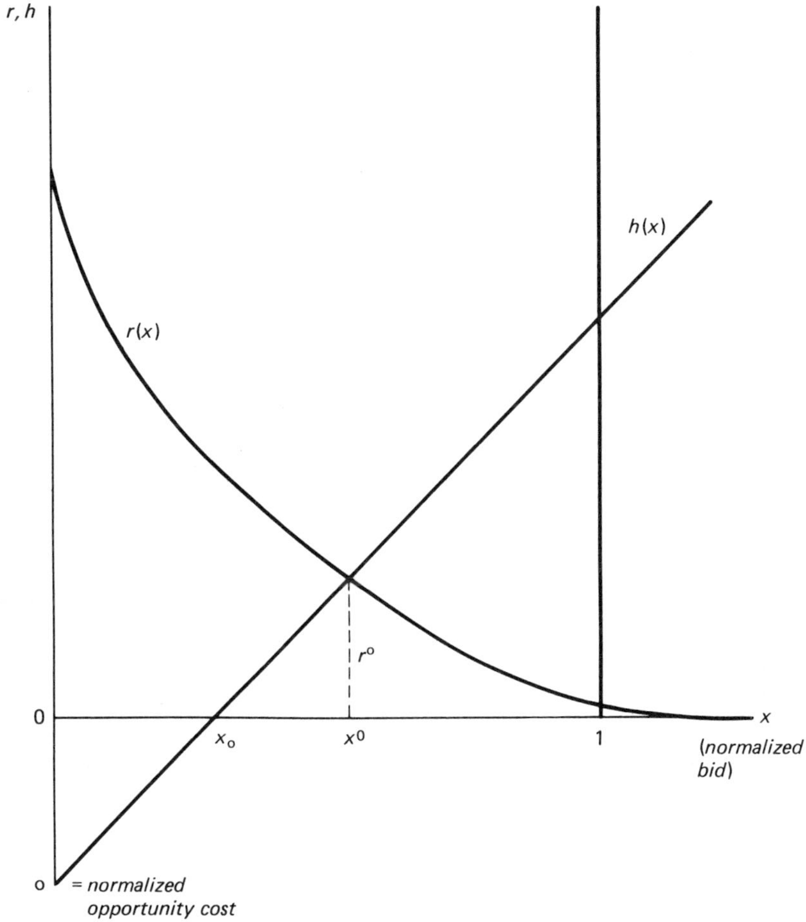

Figure 21.2 The oligopolistic firm's optimal bid

$$\frac{dr(x)}{dx} \geqslant 0 \rightarrow \frac{f''(x)}{-f'(x)} \geqslant \frac{-f'(x)}{f(x)}. \tag{18}$$

That is, when the percentage fall in $-f'(x)$ is greater than or equal to the percentage fall in $f(x)$ as x rises, (18) will hold.

Consider, now, the Weibull approximations to the firms' perceived $f_j(x)$ functions. From (8), for firm 1,

$$r(x)=[\sum_j \frac{c_j}{a_j^{c_j}} x^{c_j-1}]^{-1}, \tag{19}$$

and, suppressing identifying firm subscripts to reduce clutter,

$$\frac{dr(x)}{dx}=-r^2[\sum_j \frac{c(c-1)}{a^c} x^{c-2}], \tag{20}$$

A sufficient condition for $dr(x)/dx=0$ is that all $c_j=1$, in which case all $G_j(x)$ (see (3)) are the cumulative negative exponential function. From (8), then, $-f'(x)$ will be a negative exponential density function. The characteristic of such functions is that the equality of (18) holds, and $r(x)$ is a horizontal linear function. Of course, in this case, $f(x)$ is strictly convex on $x \in [0, \infty]$.

However, from (20) where all $c_j>1$, $dr(x)/dx<0$ as drawn in Figure 21.2. Also,

$$\frac{d^2r(x)}{dx^2}=\frac{2(r'(x))^2}{r}-r^2\{\sum_j \frac{c(c-1)(c-2)}{a^c} x^{c-3}\}, \tag{21}$$

where r is the initial value of $r(x)$ and j-subscripts have been suppressed. When $1<c_j \leqslant 2$, all j, $r(x)$ will be convex as drawn. When all $c_j>2$, $r(x)$ can be shown to be convex as well.

As a last example, suppose $-f'(x)$ is a normal density function, and $\bar{x}$ is in terms of standard deviation units. Then

$$\frac{dr(\bar{x})}{d\bar{x}}=\bar{x}r-1, \tag{22}$$

and $\bar{x}r$ reaches a maximum of .978 for $\bar{x}=+3.27$, well beyond the value where $f(\bar{x})$ attains .99. The function $r(x)$, therefore, is everywhere negatively sloped.

3 PARAMETRIC DISPLACEMENT ANALYSES

To understand better the nature of the firm's decision-making, and as a prelude to the analysis of appropriate policy actions by government procurement officials to reduce r in bidders' tenders, it will be useful to analyze the impact of changes in a_j and c_j upon $r(x)$. Recall that these are the *perceptions* by firm 1 of the parameters of the probability density functions of firms j underlying firm 1's confidence-of-winning function $f(x)$.

3.1 Displacement of a Scale Parameter, a_k

Consider rival k's probability density function over x as given in (5) and as derived from firm 1's perceptions, with mode defined in (4) and

$$\text{Mean} = a_k \Gamma\left(\frac{c_k+1}{c_k}\right) \tag{23}$$

$$\text{Variance} = a_k^2\left\{\Gamma\left(\frac{c_k+2}{c_k}\right) - \left(\Gamma\left(\frac{c_k+1}{c_k}\right)\right)^2\right\}.$$

The role of a_k is clear: when it is increased the mode and mean rise proportionately and the variance as the square of the factor of change. A rise in a_k 'shifts' the distribution to the right, increasing the variance as a consequence of the enlarged scaling unit.

If firm 1 believes that firm k's level of confidence has risen generally or that its management has become somewhat less concerned to win the contract, perhaps because of increased demand in the private market, this may be depicted as a rise in a_k. If for every normalised bid x the probability that firm k will bid no more than x falls, the change may be interpreted as a rise in a_k, at least in relevant domains of x.

From (8),

$$\dot{f}'_{a_k} = \frac{df(x)/da_k}{f(x)} = \frac{c_k}{a_k}\left(\frac{x}{a_k}\right)^{c_k} > 0. \tag{24}$$

The perceived rise in a_k (and firm k's confidence) increases firm 1's expectations of winning with a bid x. Also,

$$-\dot{f}'|_{a_k} = \frac{d(-f'(x)/da_k)}{-f'(x)} = \frac{c_k x^{c_k-1} r}{a_k^{c_k+1}}(x - c_k r) \tag{25}$$

$$= \dot{f}'|_{a_k} - \frac{c_k^2 x^{c_k-1} r}{a_k^{c_k+1}}$$

which is ambiguous as to sign. But

$$\dot{r}\big|_{a_k}=\frac{dr(x)/da_k}{r(x)}=\frac{c_k^2 x^{c_k-1}}{a_k^{c_k+1}}r=\dot{f}\big|_{a_k}-(-\dot{f}\big|_{a_k})>0. \tag{26}$$

Hence, if $(-\dot{f}\big|_{a_k})$ is positive it will be smaller in absolute size than $\dot{f}\big|_{a_k}$. A rise in a_k may increase the probability that dx will lose a bid for firm 1, but it will be swamped by the rise in firm 1's probability of winning with bid x. A rise in any or all a_j's in firm 1's field of perception will shift its $r(x)$ function upward in Figure 21.2 and lead to a rise in its bid and its bidding surplus.

This proposition underscores an interesting aspect of the oligopolistic bidding context. Every oligopolistic bidder determines its own probability of winning the contract *indirectly* by formulating expectations of its rivals' attitudes and opportunities. Subject to the constraint of its opportunity cost and judgment of L and U, each rival formulates a bid as a composite reflection of others' perceived potential actions. Government contracting policies will impact a rival, therefore, not directly, but via their imagined impacts upon competitors. It is the anomaly of oligopolistic bidding in this probabilistic context that such *direct* reactions cannot occur, for there are no functions defining each firm's probability density functions over bids. Such functions have only a shadow existence in the expectations of rivals, since even that existence derives from the cumulative density functions subjectively perceived by those rivals.

3.2 Displacement of the shape parameter, c_k

The shape parameter, c_k, in a Weibull distribution permits the study of the impact of perceived changes in the variance of a rival's density function by firm 1 rather well isolated from changes in the expected value of the function. Table 21.2 reveals the behaviour of the expected value, the mode, and the variance of the $g_j(x)$ Weibull functions as c_j varies within relevant ranges with a_j constant.

Note from Table 21.1 that the domain of c_j that seems most relevant for realistic choices of U and L is between 10 and 20. Over this domain the expected values and modes of the $g_j(x)$ maintain a rather constant absolute relationship and rise moderately in value as c_j rises with a_j constant. Most notable, however, is the fall in variance that occurs over the interval. It is not possible to dissociate changes in c_j from changes in

Table 21.2 Values of expected value, mode, and variance of Weibull probability density functions for relevant c_j values

$c_j=$	2	4	10	15	20
Expected Value	$.8862a_j$	$.9064a_j$	$.9514a_j$	$.9687a_j$	$.9735a_j$
Mode	$.71a_j$	$.93a_j$	$.99a_j$	$.99a_j$	$.99a_j$
Variance	$.2146a_j^2$	$.0647a_j^2$	$.0131a_j^2$	$.0103a_j^2$	$.0036a_j^2$

central tendency; however, the largest impact of changes in c_j with a_j constant is upon the variance of the distribution.

What does a rise in rival 1's perception of a single competitor's c_k do to its bid, when expected value does not change much but the variance contracts greatly about a somewhat larger mode? From (19)

$$\dot{r}\big|_{c_k} = \frac{dr(x)/dc_k}{r(x)} = \frac{-rx^{c_k-1}}{a_k^{c_k}}(1 + c_k[lnx - lna_{kk}]). \tag{27}$$

The $r(x)$ function of Figure 21.2 'pivots' at $x_p = a_k e^{-c_k-1}$ with *ceteris paribus* changes in c_k.[6] To the left of this value $(x < x_p)$, the new $r(x)$ function lies above the old, so that if $h(x)$ intersects $r(x)$ in this region the bid and oligopoly surplus will rise. But for $x > x_p$ the new function will lie below the old, and x^0 and $r(x^0)$ will fall. From Table 21.1, for $c_k \in [10,20]$ a_k will range between .84 and .92, yielding values for x_p between .76 and .88. In most instances bids must be expected to occur above such levels, and, therefore, bids and surpluses to fall with a rise in any c_k.

Hence, even though a rise in c_k raises firm 1's expectation of the modal bid of firm k, and would be expected to raise firm 1's bid, the decrease in the variance of firm k's bidding density function overcomes this tendency for realistic bid values. The fall in the risk of losing with the bid enhancement is not large enough to outweigh the expected fall in $f(x)$:

$$\dot{f}\big|_{c_k} = \frac{df(x)/dc_k}{f(x)} = -\left(\frac{x}{c_k}\right)^{c_k}[lnx - lna_k], \tag{28}$$

so that for $x > a_k$, $f(x)$ falls.

It follows that decreases in the variance of firms' expectations of rivals' bidding density functions should reduce bids and the associated surplus if such firms receive accurate information about the maximum bid the government is willing to consider. Formally or informally this should be communicated to all potential bidders. Also, the publication of past winning and losing bids by the bidders may have this effect, for example, of reducing variance. In mature oligopolies, where rivals have had the opportunity to experience each others' bids and pricing policies over long periods, the variances of expected bidder density functions should be smaller than in newer industries, and hence should yield bids closer to opportunity costs with smaller oligopoly surpluses.

3.3 The Expected Value of Information

Suppose firm 1 were able to purchase information on rival k's bidding intentions. How would it value the information?

If the nature of the intelligence were simply whether or not firm k would bid, the answer is straightforward. If firm 1 has no additional information, its subjective view of firm k's intentions are included in $f(x)$ and optimal bid x^0 and unit surplus r^0 are as determined in (12) and on Figure 21.2. If firm 1 knew that firm k would bid, then its own bid is unaltered at x^0 and *ex post facto* the information is of no value. If firm 1 learns that firm k will not bid, then the $r(x)$ function of Figure 21.2 shifts upward, and the optimal bid rises to x^* with $r(x^*)=r^*$. *Ex post facto* the value of the information is $r^* - r^0$ (per unit of contract sales).

Firm 1's willingness to pay – given the risk neutrality we have assumed throughout – is the convex combination of the payoff if firm k bids times the probability of its bidding and the payoff of knowing firm k will not bid times the probability of that, or

$$\text{EVI (expected value of information)} = p\cdot 0 + (1-p)(r^* - r^0), \quad (29)$$

where p is the perceived probability of firm k's bidding. If, *ex ante facto*, the best guess must be based on $g_k(x)$, then

$$\text{EVI} = \int_0^1 g(x)\cdot 0\,dx + \int_1^\infty g(x)(r^* - r^0)\,dx. \quad (30)$$

For the Weibull formulation

$$\text{EVI} = e^{-\bar{a}_k^{c_k}}(r^* - r^{*0}). \quad (31)$$

This value may be termed the *exclusionary component* of the value of information, determined by the reduction in uncertainty the elimination of a bidder causes, as registered in other bidders' oligopoly surpluses and the perceived probability the rival will exclude himself.

Suppose, now, the information offered is x_k, rival k's bid. Let us assume that the cost of bidding for rival 1 is zero. The potential elimination of uncertainty by the exclusion of $g_k(x)$ from $f(x)$ will shift $r(x)$ upward to $r^*(x)$ as in the exclusionary component. However, this potential knowledge also will truncate $f(x)$ at x_k, rival k's potentially knowable bid, and $f(x)=0$ for $x>x_k$.

Let x^* and $r^*=r^*(x^*)$ be the bid and expected oligopoly rent that would occur in the exclusionary component. The truncation effect must now be included as a *participating component* of the value of information. If $x_k<o$, firm 1's opportunity cost, firm 1 will leave the bidding and the value of the information will be zero. If $o\leqslant x_k<x^*$, then firm 1 must alter its bid to (slightly under) x_k, and the expected value of the information to firm 1 is $r(x_k)$. If $x_k>x^*$, firm 1's bid will be x^*, and the value of the information will be r^*-r^0.

In deciding whether to purchase the information, firm 1 must apply some probabilities that x_k lies within each of these regions, and, for the region $o\leqslant x_k<x^*$, probabilities for each potential bid. If its best available information is that encapsulated in $g_k(x)$, then EVI (the expected value of information) is

$$\text{EVI}=\int_0^o g_k(x)\cdot 0dx+\int_o^{x^*} g_k(x)r^*(x_k)dx+\int_{x^*}^{\infty} g_k(x)\,(r^*-r^0)dx$$

$$=\int_o^{x^*} g_k(x)r^*(x_k)dx+\int_{x^*}^{\infty} g_k(x)\,(r^*-r^0)dx. \tag{32}$$

In the Weibull formulation,

$$\text{EVI}=\int_0^{x^*}\left(\begin{matrix}\dfrac{k_k}{a^{ck}}\left(\dfrac{x}{a_k}\right)^{ck-1}e^{-(x/a_k)^{ck}}\\[2ex] \Omega_{j\neq k}\dfrac{c_j}{a^{cj}}\left(\dfrac{x}{a_j}\right)^{cj-1}\end{matrix}\right)dx+e^{-(x^*/a_k)^{ck}(r^*-r^0)} \tag{33}$$

which yields meagre results in this general form. If firm 1 has n rivals with $a_j=a$, $c_j=c$, for all j, and $c=2$, then (33) simplifies to

$$\text{EVI}=\frac{a}{2(n-1)}\,(e^{-(o/a)^2}-e^{-(x^*/a)^2}+e^{-(x^*/a)^2}(r^*-r^0). \tag{34}$$

4 CONCLUSION

More than two decades ago, Arrow wrote:

> With some inaccuracy, descriptions of uncertain consequences can be classified into two major categories, those which use exclusively the language of probability distributions and those which call for some other principle, either to replace or to supplement. The difference in viewpoints is related, though not perfectly, to the dispute between those who interpret probability as a measure of degree of belief (e.g., I. Fisher or Lord Keynes . . .) and those who regard probability as a measure (objective) of relative frequency . . . The latter concept clearly cannot encompass certain types of ignorance. (Arrow, 1971, pp. 8–9).

He goes on to point out that if an event is to happen only once, the degree of belief interpretation is the only one acceptable.

I have argued in this paper that to move bidding theory into an oligopolistic context requires the acceptance of cumulative subjective probability functions as primitive constructs, much as consumer preferences are accepted as data in conventional theory. Bidding theory at the hands of economists suffers the same fate as general equilibrium analysis: a flight to the comforting confines of competitive analysis and its deceptive, faceless universals.

But buried deep within the Arrovian canon, suitably parenthesized and written by Arrow, the future co-author (with Hahn) of *General Competitive Analysis* and decades before the first light awakened some of us, is another significant insight of relevance to this last criticism:

> In my judgment, this will be an increasingly common situation in economic theory; broad general theorems of the kind we admire can usually only be found under undesirably restrictive conditions. What theory can imply in a broad range of cases is a computing algorithm. To test theory, then, we need econometric evidence or at least well-informed quantitative judgments as inputs into the computing process. (Arrow, 1971).

This observation is peculiarly relevant to oligopoly analysis, whose distinctive feature is its *sui generis* essence. In this paper I have urged a step in the direction of moving the analysis of oligopolistic bidding toward operational frameworks by experimenting with flexible and manipulable probability functions that require a few obtainable observations. For some time I have believed that the measurement of power structures in oligopolistic industries is essential to the analysis of their pricing decisions. Indirectly, in oligopolistic bidding theory, that is also central to the determination of bids and their component rents, via subjective probability.

NOTES

1. We deal with a sealed bid procurement contract tender which awards the contract to the lowest bidder at its price, provided it is at or below the reservation price of the buyer. This is a *first-price* or *discriminatory* auction with a buyer reservation price.
2. Alternatively, the value of the contract to all bidders is assumed to be identical and known to all as such.
3. Compare Arrow's consumer: 'the consumer cannot seriously be expected to write down in any explicit way his maximand. Rather the process of optimization consists of a series of comparisons among alternative ways of spending marginal dollars; the utility function is revealed to the consumer in the process'. (Arrow, 1971, p. 229).

   Insufficient attention has been devoted to deriving underlying objective functions that are being optimized unconsciously by an economic agent following intuitive rules of conduct.
4. These costs and their inspired reluctance on the part of firms to bid on government contracts in periods of strong private economy demand or material shortages are well known to government contracting personnel. A recent experience was in the petroleum shortage of 1979, when government purchasers of jet fuel confronted reluctant bidders with patriotic appeals and threats of invoking the Defense Production Act.
5. Kortanek, Soden, and Sodera (1973) term a similar term a 'competitive advantage fee'. As indicated in the discussion, this does not adequately convey its origin in oligopoly structure, its perceptual basis, nor its functioning as an economic rent.

   Another interpretation of r is that it is the 'force of survival', akin to the 'forces of mortality' in reliability theory, in that in the neighbourhood of a bid it measures the 'cover' firm 1 has in raising its bid slightly.
6. To a good approximation for values of c_k between 10 and 20, the mode of $g_k(x)$ approximates $a_k e^{-c_k^{\Gamma-2}}$. Hence,

   $$x_p \approx \text{Mode}\ (exp[-c_k^{-1}(1-c_k^{-1})])$$

   and, in the domain of c_k cited x_p will lie below the mode of the underlying density function for rival k.

REFERENCES

Arrow, K. J. (1971) *Essays in the Theory of Risk-Bearing* (Chicago: Markham).

Attanasi, E. D. and S. R. Johnson (1975) 'Expectations, Market Structure, and Sequential Bid Pricing', *Southern Economic Journal*, 42: 18–32.

Attanasi, E. D. and S. R. Johnson (1977) 'Sequential Bidding Models: A Decision Theoretic Approach', *Industrial Organization Review*, 14: 234–45.

Baron, D. P. (1972). 'Incentive Contracts and Competitive Bidding', *American Economic Review*, 62: 384–94.

Engelbrecht-Wiggins, R. (1980) 'Auctions and Bidding Models: A Survey', *Management Science*, 25: 1272–7.

Friedman, L. (1956) 'A Comparative Bidding Strategy', *Operations Research*, 4: 104–12.

Harris, M. and A. Ravio (1981) 'Allocation Mechanisms and the Design of Auctions', *Econometrica*, 49: 1477–99.

Harsanyi, J. C. (1967–1968) 'Games With Incomplete Information Played by "Bayesian" Players', *Management Science*, 14: 159–82; 15: 320–334, 486–502.

Holt, C. A. Jr. (1980) 'Competitive Bidding for Contracts Under Alternative Auction Procedures', *Journal of Political Economy*, 88: 433–45.

Kortanek, K. O., J. V. Soden and D. Sodaro (1973) 'Profit Analysis and Sequential Bid Price Models', *Management Science*, 20: 396–417.

Kuhlman, J. M. and S. R. Johnson (1983) 'The Number of Competitors and Bid Prices', *Southern Economic Journal*, 50: 213–20.

Milgrom, P. R. (1981) 'Rational Expectations, Information Acquisition, and Competitive Bidding', *Econometrica*, 49: 921–44.

Milgrom, P. R. and R. J. Weber (1982) 'A Theory of Auctions and Competitive Bidding', *Econometrica*, 50: 1089–1122.

Pratt, J. W. (1964) 'Risk Aversion in the Small and in the Large', *Econometrica*, 32: 122–36.

Vickrey, W. (1961) 'Counterspeculation, Auctions, and Competitive Sealed Tenders', *Journal of Finance*, 16: 8–37.

Wilson, R. (1967) 'Competititve Bidding With Asymmetrical Information', *Management Science*, 13: A816–A820.

Wilson, R. (1969) 'Competitive Bidding With Disparate Information', *Management Science* 15: 446–8.

Wilson, R. (1977) 'A Bidding Model of Perfect Competition', *Review of Economic Studies*, 4: 511–18.

Wilson, R. (1979) 'Auctions of Shares', *Quarterly Journal of Economics*, 93: 675–98.

22 Taking Pure Theory to Data: Arrow's Seminal Contribution

Robert M. Townsend*

It is sometimes thought that the Arrow-Debreu model is a strange if not dubious starting point for empirical work. This short note honouring Arrow's (1953) seminal contribution takes the opposite point of view. It argues that the Arrow-Debreu model is rich in empirical implications, both directly, on its own, and indirectly, as the fountainhead of contributions that seek to explain otherwise anomalous observations.

To review briefly, one of the key insights of Arrow (1953) and Debreu (1959) was that the standard general equilibrium model could be easily modified to incorporate uncertainty. Essentially, one need only expand the commodity space by indexing all commodities to states of nature, publicly observed realizations of the random components of the model. Further, standard theorems on the existence and characterization of Pareto-optimal allocations and on the existence and optimatlity of competitive equilibria, of Arrow, Debreu, McKenzie and others, follow naturally in this framework. This insight, then, gave birth to two complementary contributions. The first is an incredibly powerful analytic method. The second is a systematic way of ordering observations. I shall take up each of these in turn.

The analytic method is so powerful that it is now standard in much of the profession. In teaching students of economics about the possibilities of risk sharing, for example, it is common to present them with an Edgeworth box diagram with two state-contingent commodities. One then emphasizes that a Pareto-optimal allocation has the property, following Hicks, and barring exceptional cases, that marginal rates of substitution across these two commodities should be equated. More generally, this kind of state-space analysis underlies the subsequent contributions of Wilson (1968) and others in the determination of

*As will have become evident, Arrow's work has had a deep influence on my own research. In fact, a more personal interpretation of this chapter is that it documents that influence, hence the frequent references to my own work.

Pareto-optimal risk-sharing arrangements, *vis à vis* concave programming problems. One might also go further in such set-ups, allowing representative individuals to buy and sell in competitive markets contingent claims on consumptions, taking (market-clearing) prices as given. Indeed, following Arrow (1953), securities are naturally viewed as bundles of such contingent claims. Then, with non-trivial production possibilities, earlier Modigliani-Miller invariance results on the value of the firm follow immediately. The point, again, is that the state-space approach is a useful way to conduct analysis in economic models.

The second, complementary contribution of the Arrow (1953)–Debreu (1959) model, and more to the point of this chapter, is that it is rich in empirical implications. Since this point may be in contention, some elaboration on the method of economic science seems necessary. The view adopted here is essentially that exposited by Lucas (1980), that a model is an experimental laboratory. We, the modellers or experimenters, specify the endowments, preferences, and technology available to agents of the model, the subjects of the experiment, as it were, and then we attempt to predict how the agents will behave. A fundamental tenet for single-agent models is that the single agent will attempt to do as well as possible for himself under the specified endowments, preferences, and technology, much like Robinson Crusoe.

Multi-agent models, as Lucas notes, are more complicated, requiring in addition some specified form of interaction or some premise as to the outcome of this interaction. For example, we might suppose with Lucas that the outcome is necessarily the one that would be achieved in competitive markets, or, alternatively, that the outcome be in the core, or, more weakly, that the outcome be Pareto-optimal. But the point is that, in conjunction with the maximization hypothesis, any such premise delivers (in principle) a well-defined mapping from endowments, preferences, and technology into actions and allocation. It is thus that a theory can have empirical content.

It is in this way, then, that the possibility of exchanging contingent claims on consumption is transformed from a theoretical and analytically powerful insight into a definite, fundamental prediction about what we should see happening in actual economies. In particular, the theory predicts that, except for what would seem to be very special cases, rather strong alignments of preferences and endowments, there will definitely be some sharing of exogenous risk, some agreement to smooth consumption across individuals relative to autarky. In the Edgeworth-box economy described earlier, for example, assuming common beliefs and no shocks to preferences, each of the two individuals would share some (variable) fraction of the social pie, the sum of their endowments. Since versions of this should be true more generally, beyond the confines of the two-agent economy, one might predict that risk-sharing arrangements would be pervasive in actual economies. Further, if one is willing to take a stand on individual preferences, perhaps up to specified parameters, then it seems that the theory can be fitted to actual data, that is, to series on individual and aggregate consumption. This idea has been forwarded by José Scheinkman (1984) and a student at Chicago, Paulo Leme (1984).

It is in conjunction with the supposed operation of competitive markets, however, that contingent claims theory has been found wanting empirically. As Arrow (1953) noted in his original contribution, we do not seem to see individuals trading claims on consumption, claims that are indexed by all possible states of the world. And so, on the face of it, the theory just fathered was in immediate jeopardy. But Arrow (1953) went on to point out that not all these contingent commodities would be needed, that with spot markets it would be enough for individuals to trade securities at an initial date; securities denominated in nominal terms and promising nominal payoffs contingent on the state of nature. Since we do observe the existence of such securities, it is certainly not obvious that the theory is invalid. In fact, as Arrow and others have pointed out, it is enough that returns on a given set of securities span the space of all possible returns. For example, as Townsend (1978) has shown, even the non-contingent claims on commodities associated with forward commodity markets can have the spanning property under rather general circumstances. It is thus that the theory proves useful in ordering observations and, ultimately, in providing a framework for policy analysis.

Still, all in all, the idea persists that securities and commodity markets are incomplete. Perhaps one reason for this is that the theory only makes predictions about what would happen if states of the world were publicly observable, whereas, as Radner (1968) and others have emphasised, in actual economies, private information would seem to be pervasive. Indeed, if contracts in such economies were limited to publicly observed states, as Radner suggests, the attainable consumption set of individuals would be more limited than what might be suggested *a priori* by the results of the spanning literature. For example, in Townsend (1979) and Baiman and Demski (1980), costly verification of privately-observed states can make formal contracts quite limited, relative to the possibilities suggested by nature. The point, then, is that we begin to see here the productive role of the Arrow (1953) contribution not only in ordering observations but also in guiding us to better theory.

In fact, the incorporation of private information into the Arrow-Debreu general equilibrium model has led again to two complementary contributions, one analytic and the other tied to ordering observations. Again, these will be discussed in turn.

Many of the earlier efforts of contract theory and game theory which incorporated private information were brought together, made formal, and forwarded in the papers of Harris and Townsend (1981) and Myerson (1979, 1982) on resource allocation mechanisms, following in the spirit of the earlier work of Hurwicz (1972). In these papers, the indexation insight of Arrow and Debreu was applied rather ruthlessly, so that, in the end, commodities could still be tied (potentially) to states of the world, even though the states were privately observed. The key result that allowed this outcome is termed the 'revelation principle'; that without loss of generality certain incentive compatibility constraints can be imposed, so that individuals with private information are given an incentive to announce their information truthfully. The result, then, for a given economic model is a programming problem and access (potentially) to the same set of powerful analytic methods mentioned earlier. Further, as argued by Myerson (1979) and Prescott and Townsend (1984a, 1984b), for example, these programming problems can be made concave by the use of lotteries, again, an important analytic advantage. In any event, these programming methods underlie the analysis of the principal-agent paradigm, for example, and much recent work. Of course, in drawing a distinction between risk sharing and incentives, these papers give us a useful way to think about the world.

Regarding the ordering of observations directly, it seems fair to say that the incorporation of private information into the Arrow-Debreu general equilibrium paradigm has had some rather unexpected consequences. First, the theory predicts that in many circumstances the incentive compatibility constraints should preclude trade, consistent with earlier results, but that in other circumstances the indexation of commodities to private information should be non-trivial, with active exchange contingent on privately-announced outcomes, followed by stringent prohibitions on further exchange. Secondly, and again, the theory predicts the use of lotteries in some circumstances, allowing beneficial trade that would otherwise be precluded. And thirdly, in conjunction with the competitive market hypothesis, the theory, as extended by Prescott and Townsend (1984a, 1984b), predicts a trade in commodities that seems to have no analogue in actual markets.

One is reminded then of scepticism regarding the usefulness of the original Arrow contribution. In fact, however, as Prescott and Townsend have argued, several of these strong predictions may find support in actual observations. In particular, a trade in commodities tied to individual announcements of privately-observed shocks can take the form of trade in contracts with options, options effected entirely by the individual at his own discretion, without verification of claimed events. Indeed, futures contracts have such options, as detailed examination reveals; delivery, for example, is sometimes made contingent on circumstances that only the shipper might know. And on reflection it seems that many labour contracts have similar options. The use of lotteries, however, remains problematical, but Prescott and Townsend do argue that queues and first-come-first-served allocation devices may induce the requisite artificial risk predicted by the theory. The point, again, is that the theory predicts the use of options and lotteries as mutually beneficial arrangements. These are indeed the arrangements that maximizing, self-interested agents would come to in worlds with uncertainty and private information. Thus, we should either find these arrangements in actual situations or search for elements missing from the theory. Either way, one hopes to make some progress.

There remains, of course, a variety of observations and institutions that cannot be explained with the Arrow-Debreu paradigm, even with the incorporation of private information. Perhaps the most prominent of these is the use of currency and written financial instruments. In fact, here we might part company with Arrow (1953) somewhat and note that his security arrangements were imposed exogenously; there is nothing in his theory that predicts the use over time of nominally denominated securities, as opposed to direct initial trade in contingent commodities themselves. Indeed, 'money' in this sense is inessential in the Arrow-Debreu paradigm, as such diverse authors as Brunner and Meltzer (1971), Cass and Shell (1983), Clower (1971), Hahn (1973), and Wallace (1980) have pointed out.

But the point of this note is that it is a virtue of the Arrow-Debreu paradigm that it delivers such strong implications patently inconsistent with the facts. In using it we are forced to seek additional key elements beyond uncertainty and private information, elements such as limited commitment and limited communication as in Townsend (1980), and Townsend (1985), respectively. Indeed, it is in drawing a distinction among these elements that we force analytic advances. In turn, as our thinking is made more precise, we are better able to confront observations. In short, far from being devoid of empirical content, the Arrow-Debreu model illustrates economic science at its best.

REFERENCES

Arrow, K. J. (1953) 'Le Role des Valeurs Boursières pour la Repartition la Meilleure des Risques', *Econometrie: Colloques Internationaux du Centre National de la Recherche Scientifique*, 47–8.

Baiman, S. and J. Demski (1980) 'Economically Optimal Performance Evaluation and Control Systems', *Journal of Accounting Research*, Supplement: 184–220.

Brunner, K. and A. Meltzer (1971) 'The Uses of Money: Money in the Theory of an Exchange Economy', *American Economic Review*, 61: 784–805.

Cass, D. and K. Shell (1983) 'Do Sunspots Matter?', *Journal of Political Economy*, 91.

Clower, R. W. (1971) 'Theoretical Foundations of Monetary Policy', in G. Clayton, J. C. Gilbert and R. Sedwick (eds) *Monetary Theory and Policy in the 1970's* (Oxford: Oxford University Press).

Debreu, G. (1959) *Theory of Value* (New Haven: Yale UP).

Hahn, F. H. (1973) 'On the Foundations of Monetary Theory', in M. Parkin and A. R. Nobay (eds) *Essays in Modern Economics* (New York: Harper & Row).

Harris, M. and R. M. Townsend (1981) 'Resource Allocation under Asymmetric Information', *Econometrica*, 49: 33–69.

Hurwicz, L. (1972) 'On Informationally Decentralized Systems', in C. B. McGuire and R. Radner (eds) *Decision and Organization* (Amsterdam: North Holland).

Leme, P. (1984) 'Integration of International Capital Markets', manuscript (University of Chicago).

Lucas, R. (1980) 'Methods and Problems in Business Cycle Theory', *Journal of Money, Credit and Banking*, 12.

Myerson, R. (1979) 'Incentive Compatibility and the Bargaining Problem', *Econometrica*, 47.

Myerson, R. (1982) 'Optimal Coordination Mechanisms in Generalized Principal-Agent Problems', *Journal of Mathematical Economics*, 10: 67–81.

Prescott, E. C. and R. M. Townsend (1984a) 'Pareto Optima and Competitive Equilibria with Adverse Selection and Moral Hazard', *Econometrica*, 52: 21–46.

Prescott, E. C. and R. M. Townsend (1984b) 'General Competitive Analysis in an Economy with Private Information', *International Economic Review*, 25: 1–20.

Radner, R. (1968). 'Competitive Equilibrium under Uncertainty', *Econometrica*, 36: 31–58.

Scheinkman, J. (1984) 'General Equilibrium Models of Economic Fluctuations: A Survey of Theory', manuscript (Univ. of Chicago).

Townsend, R. M. (1978) 'On the Optimality of Forward Markets', *American Economic Review*, 68: 54–66.
Townsend, R. M. (1979) 'Optimal Contracts and Competitive Markets with Costly State Verification', *Journal of Economic Theory*, 21: 265–93.
Townsend, R. M. (1980) 'Models of Money with Spatially Separated Agents', in J. H. Kareken and N. Wallace (eds) *Models of Monetary Economies* (Federal Reserve Bank of Minneapolis).
Townsend, R. M. (1985) 'Economic Organization with Limited Communication', manuscript (Univ. of Chicago).
Wallace, N. (1980) 'The Overlapping Generations Model of Fiat Money', in J. H. Kareken and N. Wallace (eds) *Models of Monetary Economies* (Federal Reserve Bank of Minneapolis) pp. 49–78.
Wilson, R. (1968) 'The Theory of Syndicates', *Econometrica*, 36: 119–32.

PART V
Arrow's Reflections on the Essays

23 Reflections on the Essays

Kenneth J. Arrow

That my work has helped to motivate such a large number of excellent studies, queries, and even criticisms is a source of considerable satisfaction. A full set of comments would occupy more space than would be appropriate to the occasion. I will confine myself to scattered thoughts stimulated by reading the papers that deal with impersonal scholarly issues. The reader of the essays that deal with me more personally should, I think, be spared the refraction imposed by any comments I might make.

I follow the grouping of chapters in the book.

Negishi (Chapter 10) offers a small but important history of examples of non-existence of equilibrium going back to W. T. Thornton in 1869. Thornton, as is well known, had a great influence on John Stuart Mill in one of his last essays. The examples are, of course, all characterized by discontinuous demand curves; as is well known, continuous demand and supply curves, with Walras's law, must inevitably lead to the existence of equilibrium. Negishi has an interesting wrinkle: he points out that exchange out of equilibrium can frequently converge to a determinate conclusion which nevertheless is not an equilibrium in the strict sense.

Wilson (Chapter 11) embarks seriously on the problem of characterizing in true game theoretic terms the operations of markets with many buyers and many sellers. Valuations are private information as is usually assumed in Walrasian markets. He characterizes very elegantly at least one equilibrium of this process in time. It does have the property that for large numbers the limit of this process is indeed the Walrasian equilibrium, although the transactions typically take place at non-equilibrium prices. It provides a much finer structure for the analysis of disequilibrium than the old fashioned ideas of stability, discussed at the time of Walras and even earlier, and systematized by Samuelson.

Roberts (Chapter 12) has taken a great step in embedding a very simple imperfectly competitive situation into a general equilibrium model. The firms are Bertrand competitors in the sense that they choose prices and wages, but recognition of interactions leads to a game theoretic analysis. There are some elements of Keynesian macroeconomic interdependence, though they assume novel forms. Among other conclusions, his work reinforces the idea that when the assumption of perfect competition is dropped very specific institutional differences may have large consequences for the working of the model.

Pratt and Zeckhauser (Chapter 13) deal with what is widely recognized as a basic situation; one where co-ordinated effort is valuable, but different agents have different interests and different information. Their argument is based on the Bayes-Nash approach. The problem is to design a game whose outcomes are the same as those of a fully optimal team with the same information limitations. They show that the proper rewards are the expected externalities calculated as if the actions were in fact optimal and determine under what conditions such expected-externality transfer payments are in fact implemented.

Wan's paper (Chapter 14) concentrates strictly speaking on a situation where jobs, or at least some jobs, are not capable of direct and full monitoring. As a result wage systems are designed to penalize shirking. Thus we can have unemployment or, more generally, situations in which identical workers do not end up in identical jobs. Because of the multiplicity of equilibria there is room for discrimination along any particular group lines without cost to the employer. It should be noted, however, that this model does not create a definite incentive for discrimination as such, but merely holds that any discriminatory tastes on the part of the employer can be met at zero cost. Even that is correct only if the numbers of the individuals in the groups are within certain limits.

Reder (Chapter 15) comes to grips with the basic contradiction between microeconomics and macroeconomics. In a competitive general equilibrium model, there is no meaning to variations in effective demand, whereas to most of us, including Reder and myself, it appears obvious that effective demand varies over time and that the variations are intimately linked with the degree to which economic resources are utilized. Reder introduces one departure from standard assumptions, that search is costly, so that some individuals will at some point refrain from search. He adds that search is less costly the greater the number of transactors in the economy. Many of the characteristics of the Keynesian economy, even analogues of liquidity preference, appear in the model. I would suggest one variation of the hypothesis that search costs decrease as economic activity increases, namely that it is the departure from equilibrium (full employment) that makes search and coordination so difficult. Put slightly differently, it is the variation from some expected norm rather than the absolute level of transactions, that governs search costs. This view is particularly consistent with the long-standing empirical evidence that resource allocation is less efficient in recessions, even beyond the sheer wastage of resources. Empirically fitted production functions have consistently shown negative residuals in recessions, a generalization of which Okun's law is a pithy expression. Neoclassical theory certainly implies that disequilibrium is inefficient, though we need a version that does not imply that disequilibrium never exists.

Dasgupta and David (Chapter 16) address the distinction between science and technology as seen by economists. They argue that the essential difference is that between public and private goods and that the reward systems are adapted functionally to this distinction. Even technology, however, has potential public-goods aspects, and, therefore, a special reward system is needed. Thus, rewards are based on priority for scientists and on patents for technologists. There are more general applications of these insights. The incentive compatibility literature needs to learn the lesson of the priority system; rewards to overcome shirking and free rider problems need not be monetary in nature; society is more ingenious than the market. The authors conclude with a further analysis that also has wider import. Science may serve as a way of supplying signals about personal quality to technology. The effect of this system on the performance of science is ambiguous; it increases the incentive to enter the field but also that to leave it at a later point. More generally, any system by which one activity, with its own values, is also used as a screening device for other purposes (higher education and business careers, for example) is liable to have unexpected repercussions, good or bad.

Harsanyi (Chapter 12) defends the proposition that the von Neumann axioms characterize rational behaviour under uncertainty when the economic agent may be regarded as 'outcome-oriented', that is, there are no utilities attached to the process by which the outcome is generated. (Process utilities might attach to the excitement of gambling, suspense, hope, fear, and so forth; of course, the substitution axiom could hardly be valid then!) He then infers that von Neumann utilities attach to the outcomes as such and therefore can be regarded as measures of intensity of preference. This conclusion is needed if these utilities are to be used as welfare information in the presence of choice under uncertainty.

Brock (Chapter 18) shows how the Bayesian analysis in terms of states of nature can be used to estimate distributions of future prices. He correctly holds that in behaviour under uncertainty (for example, investment) single-valued expectations are insufficient. Further, economic analysis makes prices derivative from more fundamental supply and demand factors. Hence, a true Bayesian distribution of future prices must be a transformation of the joint probability distribution of these basic factors. This programme puts more emphasis on expert judgment than on either classical or Bayesian regression methods.

Bray and Kreps (Chapter 19) have made a fundamental contribution to the meaning of rational expectations equilibrium, specifically, the issue how individuals come to learn the relevant distributions. Consider the most favourable situation for achievement of equilibrium, that in which in effect the same underlying situation is observed over and over. Since, however, behaviour is influenced by expectations and expectations by past observations, the data are not drawn from repetitions of the same experiment. Each individual agent has to recognize that other individuals are also learning. They point to a fundamental tool, the martingale convergence theorem; as applied to the process of successive Bayesian updatings, which certainly constitute a bounded martingale, the theorem implies that the updatings converge (almost surely) along any one history. They show that in some simple cases, some further assumptions (especially, uniqueness of spot equilibria for almost all parameter values and sets of beliefs) will indeed ensure convergence to the true distributions. But these assumptions are certainly not valid in general, and learning the true distributions is not a general phenomenon.

Friedman and Roley (Chapter 20) combine theoretical and empirical analyses of portfolio selection to test for suitability functions of income. I find it especially surprising that initial wealth satiation, empirically unlikely, is implied by some very reasonable-appearing models. The need for more thorough screening is made clear.

Kuenne (Chapter 21) takes up an oligopolistic bidding model. His approach is novel in moving away from the game-theoretic considerations that have been dominant since the time of Cournot. Instead, the presence of competitors is registered in subjective probability distributions over their behaviour (their bids, in this case). This approach makes expectations of others a central primitive in the system and cuts out the conundrums of mutual learning that Bray and Kreps study, at the expense of creating a weaker theory, in the sense of one with a greater number of primitive concepts.

Townsend (Chapter 22) takes a viewpoint I would agree with about the theory of contingent securities and indeed about economic theory generally. The implications have to be drawn strongly, regardless of superficial empirical verisimilitude. Partly this methodology motivates a search for unexpected and not easily visible exemplifications of the theory; partly, it motivates a search for explanations for the divergence between theory and observation.

Index*

*See also index to *Arrow and the Foundations of the Theory of Economic Policy*.